READINGS IN
Public Sector Economics

EDITED BY

D0223866

Samuel H. Baker
COLLEGE OF WILLIAM AND MARY

Catherine S. Elliott
NEW COLLEGE OF THE
UNIVERSITY OF SOUTH FLORIDA

D.C. HEATH AND COMPANY
Lexington, Massachusetts   Toronto

Photo: Ed Malitsky

Copyright © 1990 by D. C. Heath and Company.

All rights reserved. No part of this publication may be reproduced or transmitted in
any form or by any means, electronic or mechanical, including photocopy,
recording, or any information storage or retrieval system, without permission in
writing from the publisher.

Published simultaneously in Canada.

Printed in the United States of America.

International Standard Book Number: 0-669-18027-0

Library of Congress Catalog Card Number: 89-84052

10 9 8 7 6 5 4 3 2 1

Preface

We see at least two objectives in using *Readings in Public Sector Economics* to supplement public sector economics texts: to present policy issues, allowing students an opportunity to apply the theory discussed in class, and to show students how material is developed in the literature by having them read some of the classics, as well as current contributions. To fulfill these goals, we have attempted to bring together thought-provoking policy pieces, good examples of economic argument, and well-done surveys. The purpose of this volume is to make the widest possible array of such work accessible to undergraduate students at a challenging, yet manageable, technical level.

This volume is the outgrowth of our experience in teaching public sector economics. Each year, while using library reserve reading lists and, more recently, copying services, we would ask publishers if a current readings book was available, and each year the answer would be no. Thus, this project began. Because of the large literature in public sector economics, we were forced to choose from among many outstanding contributions in order to limit the readings to a manageable number. Fortunately, we were able to reprint a large number of selections that provide a broad range of topics as well as ideological balance.

To use this book, individual instructors and students can choose those readings most suitable to their interests. We have not tied the readings to any one textbook, but have maintained a wide scope to go with the many well-written textbooks in the field. We also chose readings that could be used in courses on public policy as well as public finance, and thus, in graduate as well as undergraduate programs. Selections can be understood without a high level of mathematical sophistication. In addition, the anthology can serve as a main text by itself. The volume's introduction and the questions and summaries that guide the student through each reading were written with this purpose in mind.

Readings in Public Sector Economics has benefited from the suggestions of colleagues at numerous universities and from the reactions of the students who class-tested the readings. Such advice and feedback proved crucial. We invite more of it, for we harbor hopes that future editions will continue to track new developments and policy issues, thus further serving this lively field.

We are indebted to a number of people for their help. This project could not have been completed without James Miller and Laurie Johnson of D. C. Heath, and Karen Dolan, Lee Blumberg, Christine Flint, John Aris, and Stewart Harvey. A number of reviewers contributed useful criticism and suggestions, for which we are most grateful: George Break (University of California, Berkeley), Gary Crakes (Southern Connecticut State College), Roger L. Faith (Arizona State University), Roger H. Goldberg (Ohio Northern University), Dilip Mookherjee (Stanford University), and John L. Solow (University of Iowa). Finally, we are grateful to the publishers and authors who kindly allowed us to reprint these articles.

S. H. B.
C. S. E.

Contents

General Introduction

Public sector economics examines both how democratic governments make finance and expenditure choices, and how their decisions influence the economy and thus the welfare of its members. Thirty years ago, the readings in this book would have focused on sources of government revenues, and the volume would have been entitled *Readings in Public Finance.* With government expenditures in western developed nations now ranging between 30 and 70 percent of Gross National Product, public sector economics has been one of the fastest growing and exciting areas in microeconomics. The current title, *Readings in Public Sector Economics,* reflects the significant broadening of the field in recent years.

Changes in public sector economics reflect not only expansion into new research areas but also the more recent analyses of traditional topics such as public goods and externalities. The expansion in the field is most evident when one compares the table of contents of Richard Musgrave's classic text (*The Theory of Public Finance,* 1959) with those of texts published in the last few years. Both Musgrave and more recent books contain chapters on budget determination through voting, taxation, and public debt. But new texts also contain chapters on externalities and public policy, the behavior of government bureaucracies, benefit-cost analysis, and various expenditure programs such as Social Security and assistance to the poor. One topic receiving less emphasis now is macroeconomic theory, although macroeconomic implications of policy still appear in discussions of government finance through taxation and public debt.

A number of fine textbooks have been written on public sector economics, providing an expanded scope that accommodates the recent developments in the field. However, many authors, like good politicians, position their textbooks ideologically (and methodologically) to appeal to the median taste of their constituency (instructors, students, and other readers). This may maximize sales, but the resulting homogeneity is not representative of the actual research arena of economics books and journals, where the theories and philosophies of public sector economics originate, clash, and develop. Editors of a readings book, on the other hand, are less constrained than authors of a textbook.

Supplementary readings are indispensable for appreciating the field's diversity and achieving a broad, thorough understanding of its issues. While this volume attempts to provide an overall balance of views, each individual reading does not take a middle of the road stance. Readers thus have the opportunity to judge for themselves the shades of gray—the areas of controversy. This collection should serve as a useful supplement to textbooks, helping students to build and weigh arguments, to identify the strengths and weaknesses of opposing viewpoints, and ultimately to draw their own conclusions.

Public sector economists base most of their analyses on the concepts of economic efficiency, economic inefficiency, and distributional welfare. While every textbook includes a discussion of efficiency criteria and equity considerations, not every reader of this volume will be using a textbook. Thus, the following straightforward numerical example introduces these principles of public sector analysis.

Economic Efficiency versus Economic Inefficiency

The criterion of economic efficiency is easy to grasp and, seemingly, easy to apply. Once it is explained, almost everyone intuitively feels that it is a worthwhile and beneficial goal for a society to pursue. Simply put, arrangements are said to be efficient if the only possible way to make any one person in the economy better off is to make someone else worse off. Contrast this state of affairs with an economy that is operating inefficiently. Someone could be better off *without anyone else having to suffer*: a "free lunch." What could be a more reasonable goal than to institute all policy changes that would benefit society in this way? It seems that both politicians and their constituents would find themselves in the unusual position of agreement on this question.

Actual examples of inefficiencies that can be corrected easily without hurting anyone are not easy to find, because usually common sense already has led to the efficient arrangement. Consider the gain that results from traffic regulation on streets. Assume that initially roads are completely unregulated, with vehicles moving in opposite directions on either side of the road. Drivers operate slowly to make certain they have enough time to dodge vehicles coming from the other direction, particularly when they are going around sharp turns and over hills. On flat, open roads, on the other hand, drivers can travel faster by using, for example, turn signals to indicate a desire to pass approaching vehicles on one side or the other.

Despite drivers' reducing their speed at blind spots in the road, and signaling on the flat stretches, head-on collisions occur often, injuring travelers and damaging vehicles. Therefore, a traffic regulation that requires all vehicles to travel on the right side (or left side) of the road represents a nondetrimental move to an economically efficient arrangement: Such coordination should make all drivers better off, without making any driver worse off.

Once an economy is operating efficiently, however, hard choices must be made if any additional changes are desired. It becomes no longer possible to improve the welfare of one group without imposing a cost on another group, i.e., there are no more free lunches. Although economists would certainly vote in favor of any policy that benefits society at no one else's expense, their personal beliefs and preferences would have to come into play for them to choose between different, yet equally efficient, economic policies.

Any two randomly chosen voters are likely to disagree over who should receive the benefits and who should bear the costs of two different, but equally efficient, distributions of market resources. In the example above, a policy that requires individuals to drive on the right side of the road, coupled with a regulation that steering wheels be placed on the left, could be equally as efficient as left-side driving and right-side steering. However, drivers will disagree on which policy is more efficient, depending upon the type of car they currently own or prefer to drive, and who is made responsible for the cost of the policy.

Economic efficiency and inefficiency are linked to the Pareto criterion for judging when government can and cannot act strictly in the public interest. When a public policy makes any individual worse off, it has not been in the interest of every member of the public and therefore does not meet the Pareto criterion. On the other hand, if no one has been harmed by the policy, the Pareto criterion has been met, and the change is said to reflect a Pareto improvement.

By definition, it is impossible to institute a Pareto improvement if the economy is operating efficiently. It follows, then, that if the Pareto criterion has been met by a policy change, the original state of affairs must have been economically inefficient. However, a Pareto improvement does not necessarily guarantee efficiency, because the criterion does not require the economy to have reached the goal of economic efficiency. In addition, even if public policy achieved an efficient state, one could not conclude that the Pareto criterion had been met at each step of the way.

A Numerical Illustration

Economists often use a method of judging economic efficiency that is analogous to a private business achieving the greatest possible profits. If all benefits and costs of a public policy can be quantified, then economic efficiency is equivalent to maximizing total social benefits (benefits to all members of a community) net of total social costs (costs to all members of a community). This difference is termed *net social benefits* and is sometimes referred to as society's surplus, i.e., the extra benefits, above cost, enjoyed by the members of an economy at any given time. As before, adoption of a policy based on this

Table 1   Benefits and Costs of Alternative Fire Stations ($1,000s)

Both		South-End Station				North-End Station			
Q	TSC	TB_s	TB_n	TSB	NSB	TB_s	TB_n	TSB	NSB
1	400	450	170	620	220	116	340	456	56
2	500	550	200	750	250	140	420	560	60**
3	600	645	225	870	270	160	496	656	56
4	700	735	245	980	280*	176	568	744	44
5	800	818	257	1075	275	186	634	820	20

*Designates maximum NSB for south-end station.
**Designates maximum NSB for north-end station.

criterion of economic efficiency constitutes a Pareto improvement only if those who gain compensate those who lose, so that no one is worse off.

Consider a city that has the task of determining how to allocate $1.2 million earmarked for residential fire protection services. These services may be provided on the town's affluent south end, or on its poorer north end, or on both ends by splitting the services in some way. Fire protection services consist of fire engines and the accompanying labor, building, land, and water.

In Table 1, the annual total social cost (TSC) to the community of operating and financing a fire station on either end of town is assumed to be the same, rising as the number of fire engines (Q) increases. Residents have a certain maximum willingness to pay for any given level of Q, determined by, among other things, the amount an increase in Q lowers both the insurance rates and psychic costs associated with the threat of fire. The combined maximum willingness to pay of all south-enders is given by TB_s, and of all north-enders, by TB_n. Note that residents of one end of town benefit when the firehouse is built on the other end of town, but not as much as when the firehouse is on their end of town.

The total social benefit (TSB) schedules in Table 1 give the combined benefits to south- and north-end residents for different levels of Q at the two fire station locations. The difference between TSB and TSC is then the social surplus, or net social benefits, enjoyed by the entire community for any given level of fire protection.

The economically efficient choice maximizes net social benefits (NSB), which is the excess of TSB over TSC. Given the figures in Table 1, this will be accomplished by providing unequal levels of fire protection on both ends of town. Because the two NSB columns represent all net social benefits from each station for each level of Q, the efficient solution is found by (1) determining where the sum of south-end NSB plus north-end NSB is maximized, and at the same time (2) making certain that the budget constraint is satisfied. Given the budget of $1.2 million, net social benefits are maximized when $700,000 is spent on four engines in the south end and $500,000 is spent on two engines in the north end. The two maximum levels of NSB are designated with single and double asterisks in Table 1 ($280,000 and $60,000). Thus, a total expenditure of $1,200,000 provides maximum net social benefits of $340,000.

Equity

Economic analysis helps to identify efficient policies as well as the distributional consequences of these policies, but it cannot judge the overall desirability of the resulting redistribution of benefits among members of the community. Whether or not an efficient policy is fair or equitable is a separate issue which must be decided through a political process that includes voters, elected officials, and relevant government agencies. It is more difficult to analyze equity than efficiency, because equity means different things to different people. Understandably, the subject of distributional justice is an unsettled area of public sector economics.

A policy choice made on the basis of a criterion of fairness could require the same number of fire engines on both ends of the city. Given the budget of $1.2 million and the cost data in Table 1, the community could afford three fire engines per station. Net social benefits would then equal $326,000, resulting in a loss in social surplus of $14,000. Because net social benefits are less than those resulting from the solution of four fire engines in the south and two in the north, this arrangement is economically inefficient.

The members of this community still may decide to place three fire engines at each station. However, if this solution is adopted, it is important to realize that it would have to be made on different grounds than those of economic efficiency. Proponents of this policy would have to argue that the gain in equity more than makes up for the loss of $14,000 in net social benefits.

These alternative solutions can also serve to illustrate the difference between the efficiency criterion and the Pareto criterion. If a change from an allocation of three engines on each side of town to the unequal but economically efficient policy were simply made by edict, the resulting policy change would *not* meet the Pareto criterion. Although net social benefits would rise, the efficient system would not be instituted without causing harm to some residents. North-end residents lose in total benefits, while south-end residents gain.

Using the values from Table 1 again, the north-end residents benefit an additional $20,000 when the fourth fire engine is placed in the south, but they lose $76,000 in total benefits, because only two engines are left in the north station. In contrast, the south-enders are more than willing to give up the $20,000 they lose when the number of engines in the north end decreases from three to two—they gain $90,000 in benefits from the additional fire services in the south end.

The south-enders gain net benefits of $70,000; the north-enders lose net benefits of $56,000. Therefore, the $14,000 gain in net social benefits would not reflect a Pareto improvement. Only if the south-enders were persuaded to compensate the north-enders in some way for the loss of $56,000 could the new solution be said to meet the Pareto criterion.

This example illustrates a subtle, yet controversial, paradox surrounding the use of the efficiency criterion. Because of the promise of maximum net social benefits, many are persuaded that society should work toward the goal of economic efficiency. In addition, allusions to the possibility of accomplishing that goal by fulfilling the Pareto criterion makes economic efficiency seem even more attractive. Unfortunately, satisfaction of the efficiency criterion does not imply satisfaction of the Pareto criterion. As in the fire engine example, changes from an inefficient solution to an efficient solution will not necessarily be a Pareto improvement.

The Arrangement of This Book

The readings in this book are arranged in six sections, corresponding to six major areas of research in public sector economics. Each section is introduced, and each article is preceded by a brief discussion of the issues and a list of questions to guide the reader through the selection. Most of the technical terms used by the authors are defined in the articles themselves. The volume concludes with suggestions for further reading, arranged by section.

Perspectives on Economics and the Public Sector

The first five selections set the stage for the discussion of particular topics in the field of public sector economics. Economic analysis is an invaluable tool in the formulation, evaluation, and understanding of public policy. Recent developments in public sector economics focus on the behavior of voters, politicians, and bureaucrats, while earlier work concentrated on the response of private market participants to government tax and expenditure policies. These developments are viewed as useful for understanding the working of the public sector even by political scientists, who today use many of the analytical techniques developed by economists.

SELECTION 1

ALEC CAIRNCROSS
Economics in Theory and Practice

Alec Cairncross presented this invited (Richard T. Ely) lecture at the 1984 annual meeting of the American Economics Association. Cairncross examines the problems in putting economic theory into practice. For theory to be a useful guide to policy, it must distinguish correctly between relevant and irrlevant detail, present policy recommendations convincingly, and blend economic and noneconomic considerations. The latter include organizational, political, and institutional settings.

QUESTIONS TO GUIDE THE READING

1. What advantage do economists have over noneconomists in making public policy recommendations?
2. Why may economists be likely to overlook the influence of organizations on economic activity?
3. Why have economists found it difficult to apply theory to practical problems?

> *Do you not know, my son, with how little wisdom the world is governed?*
>
> OXENSTIERNA

Let's face it. Whatever economics was in the past, it is now virtually an industry. It stretches from the building of new models by the theorists to the supply of advice, forecasts, proposals, and programs by the practitioners, and caters mainly for a market of policymakers in business and government. In the economics business, market forces work feebly, particularly at the level of theory. The competitive process derives little benefit from price adjustments, and suppliers are often remote from the market and unaware of market pressures. But the usual phenomena of growth and development are all at work: investment, economies of scale, and the interaction between technical innovation and market expansion. Some of our colleagues confine their activities to production while others occupy themselves with the busi-

Alec Cairncross "Economics in Theory and Practice," *American Economic Review* 75 (May 1985), 1–14. Reprinted by permission of the author.

Sir Alec Cairncross is Professor of Economics at St. Peters College, University of Oxford.

ness of packaging and marketing. Division of labor has made rapid progress, both horizontally and vertically. On the one hand, we have specialists in different branches of economics: macroeconomics, industrial economics, transport economics, health economics, international economics, mathematical economics, etc., etc. On the other hand, we have a lengthening chain of intermediaries between the priestly who live in clouds of theory and the lay brethren in Washington, Whitehall, and elsewhere, who do battle in the corridors of power. Where so many labor, their efforts merit scrutiny as yet another branch of economics.

I do not propose today to embark on so ambitious a task as an exposition of the economics of economics. Having spent half my working life in a succession of government departments and international bodies, I thought it best to set myself a more modest task and draw on my own experience as an intermediary in the market for economic advice. I propose to limit myself to an examination of the links between theory and practice, between the theorists who seek to trap the inner secrets of the economy in their models and the practitioners who live in a world of action where time is precious, understanding is limited, nothing is certain, and noneconomic considerations are always important and often decisive.

Action can take two forms. It may go no further than policy recommendations, or it may consist in taking policy decisions. When I speak of practitioners I shall normally have in mind those who busy themselves with what the policy should be, whether professional economists or not, rather than those who take the final decisions on policy. But I may on occasion feel obliged to refer to the difficulties of the decision taker in making use of economic advice as opposed to those of his economic advisers in formulating it.

When one looks around, theory and practice are often far apart. In many countries there is even a physical separation: the theorists remain in their universities, the practitioners in their departments of government, with little contact between the two. And since ideas circulate most freely through personal contact, the physical segregation carries with it an intellectual segregation. The thinking of advisers on policy proceeds largely in isolation from the thinking of the academics. Even in countries where there is some circulation between universities and government, and some mixing of one set of economists with the other, there is a strong tendency for the thinking of each to stay within its own orbit, the insiders pursuing lines of thought independently of contributions from outside, and vice versa.

It is hardly surprising that there should be some divorce between theory and practice when their starting points are so different. As in medicine, engineering and other human activities, one can ask either: "what is the truth of the matter?" or: "what ought I to do?" according as one's interest is in theory or practice. An economist entering a business concern or a government department, unless consigned to the outer darkness of a research section, finds himself in an atmosphere where action takes precedence over intellectual speculation. The question at issue for the practitioner is always:

"what is to be done?" That is a question which the pure theorist may decline to answer because he feels that he has no special competence to do so. He may share the view of Nassau Senior that "the conclusions of the economist, whatever their generally and truth, do not authorize him in adding a single syllable of advice."[1] But it is not a question that can be evaded; and presumably a training in economics is of some help in answering it.

How much help does theory provide? Sometimes the honest answer is "very little." It may elucidate, but certainly does not resolve, controversial issues of economic policy. An obvious example is the controversy in Britain in the early 1970s over the desirability of joining the Common Market, with half the academic economists signing a letter in favor, and the other half signing a letter against. Or one can point to the conflict of view between those who put their faith in monetary policy and those who regard it as a broken reed, or between the advocates and opponents of floating rates of exchange, or between those in favor of and those against a statutory incomes policy. Even when the theorists are in agreement, the issue of policy remains undecided. There is widespread agreement that in theory an expenditure tax is preferable to an income tax. But so far as I am aware, the Finance Ministries of the world have remained unmoved. There has been no rush to change over to an expenditure tax and the only countries which did, India and Sri Lanka, gave up the experiment almost at once.

The limitations of economic theory were brought home to me when I was asked to organize a course of instruction for senior administrators who had come to Washington for six months to learn as much as possible about the kind of economic policies their countries ought to pursue. They did not want to study economic theory as such, and had indeed no time in which to master it, but were interested in the practical upshot of economic thinking and speculation about economic development. They asked quite simple questions—some of them with a familiar ring—such as: "can inflation assist or does it retard economic development? How much can one safely borrow abroad? What tax system is most likely to favor economic development?" I found, as you might expect, that economic theory was indispensable for analyzing their problems, but that it very rarely allowed one to arrive at policy conclusions with any confidence.

Later I encountered a similar group who had come to study investment appraisal and had become well versed in the theory of discounted cash flow. But investment appraisal involves a lot more than economic theory. I asked the group what rate of interest they would use on their return home. There was a long pause until one bold spirit suggested "Bank Rate." Nobody contradicted him. Nobody had other suggestions to offer.

An earlier occasion on which I asked myself to what use I would be able to put my knowledge of economic theory was when I joined the British War Cabinet Secretariat in 1940. There could be no doubt of the profound influence on policy in wartime of a comparatively small group of professional economists. And yet I never saw much use made of the more refined and esoteric parts of economic theory. I concluded, as my colleague, the late

Ely Devons put it, that "in so far as economic theory is useful in enabling us to understand the real world and in helping us to take decisions on policy, it is the simple, most elementary and, in some ways, the most obvious propositions that matter" (1961, pp. 13–14). But, as he was careful to add, before the simple propositions become part of normal processes of thinking and cease to be "kept in a separate compartment labeled 'economic theory'," familiarity with the subject needs to advance well beyond the elementary level (pp. 25–26). Lionel Robbins said much the same when he argued that

> . . . the most useful economic principles, when stated in their most general form, seem often mere banalities, almost an anti-climax after the formidable controversies amid which they have emerged. Yet experience seems to show that, without systematic training in the application of such platitudes, the most acute minds are liable to go astray.[2]

I found that two or three rather elementary economic concepts, which I had assumed would be familiar to everyone, were often not at all well understood by noneconomists but were of particular value in policy formulation. Among these concepts I should include as of first-rate importance the idea of the interaction of supply, demand, and price; the concept of opportunity cost; and the marginal theory of value. Later, I concluded that it was even more important to be able to think of market forces operating within an economic *system,* and to recognize the coordinating function of the price mechanism. Many other elementary concepts, particularly at the macro level, were equally fundamental, but these examples are enough for purposes of illustration.

Noneconomists have rarely sorted out in their mind how supply and demand operate on market prices and have no instinctive appreciation of the virtues—indeed the indispensability—of the price mechanism. On the contrary, their bias is almost always towards an organizational or political approach to economic problems. They like fixed prices because they seem to inject an element of stability and predictability. During and after World War II, when something became scarce the immediate reaction of business men or bureaucrats was nearly always in favor of control and rationing without any thought for the contribution that *some* rise in price might make to relieving or ending the shortage. The pricing of coal, for example, at the time of the nationalization of the industry in Britain in 1947, paid not the slightest regard to the chronic shortage of fuel and the danger that that shortage would arrest industrial recovery, as in the end it did. The pricing of foreign exchange, in much the same way, was divorced from market pressures and continued to be regarded by ministers as a moral or organizational issue: they believed that planning and control could do all that devaluation of the currency could do.

Of course, economists may fall into the opposite error and think that market forces, left to themselves, will always do the trick. At the end of World War II, when practically every country except the United States was running a balance of payments deficit, there were those who regarded the dollar shortage as an invention of governments that were determined to prolong the shortage by overvaluing their currencies. How far rates might have to fall and what the consequences of such a fall might be were matters rarely explored. In the early postwar years, with demobilization in progress and production well below capacity, it was not at all self-evident that a general realignment of currencies and a consequential revamping of the price structure would do much to restore balance of payments equilibrium, however necessary it might prove later on. On the contrary, there was good reason to take direct action to limit imports, encourage exports, develop alternative sources of supply and restrict the export of capital, that is, to make use of planning rather than prices.

Similarly, at the outbreak of war the necessary reallocation of manpower cannot easily be brought about by market forces alone. It might be possible in theory to work through variations in the funds at the disposal of different departments and agencies, but if the government means to impose its priorities on the market it will achieve quicker and more predictable results by direct methods. Where a major upheaval is required, market forces operate slowly and blindly.

Opportunity cost is another concept that does not come naturally to the noneconomist. Few people have given thought to the inner meaning of "cost," or habitually decide on a course of action on the basis of the alternatives that might be adopted. Yet in my experience the concept is indispensable in policy analysis and lends itself to very wide applications. This is equally true of the idea of the margin: the average man thinks of averages rather than increments and often goes off on the wrong tack for this reason, particularly in relation to pricing and investment decisions.

Both concepts, however, need careful handling. Marginal theory is usually taught in terms of a single margin when in fact there are a great many. No businessman thinks of output and prices as his only variables, and even when he does, has to consider the repercussions of changing either of them over a whole series of time horizons. With opportunity cost there is a similar danger of neglecting the full range of possibilities. Lord Kaldor has recently used the concept to justify keeping open high-cost coal mines under conditions of heavy unemployment. But the logical conclusion of his line of argument is that so long as there is substantial unemployment, no firm should ever be allowed to close down and no one should ever be sacked, since it is better to have some output than none. The alternatives compared have to have regard to the full consequences, not just the immediate ones.

When I read the literature on shadow prices I have a rather similar reaction that the idea of opportunity cost can be carried too far. The notional prices corresponding to the opportunity cost of capital, labor, or foreign exchange may be enforceable on the limited sector of the economy under the government's control; but that introduces distortions between the controlled and uncontrolled sectors, which may thwart the government's intentions. Besides, the enforcement of shadow prices that diverge widely from market prices is far from easy, even within the controlled sector. Subordinate authorities are apt to take little notice of a hypothetical test rate of discount in deciding on their investment program and do their sums on the basis of the rate they have to pay on borrowed money, diluted by any subsidies from the central government. To make a shadow rate take effect throughout the public sector, the central government is unlikely to get very far by directives unsupported by offers of capital at the shadow rate.

The biggest single advantage that economists have is their way of thinking. It comes naturally to them to think in terms of alternatives and to trace the implications of alternative lines of action within the logical framework of an economic system. They are alive to the interaction of economic forces within that system and hence to the full economic impact of policy decisions. They are not at a loss, like Prime Minister Attlee, to understand how it is that when activity is so brisk at home there should be so much trouble with the balance of payments. They do not need to be persuaded like Lord Radcliffe—perhaps the most outstanding lawyer of his day—that an enquiry into the working of the monetary system may involve a study of the working of the capital market (though I must admit that there are professional economists who even now seem to share Lord Radcliffe's view).

The importance of an adequate framework of thought was strikingly illustrated in the controversy over central economic planning after World War II. Administrators and politicians alike tended to overlook the role of the price mechanism in their enthusiasm for planning. Two of the most outstanding figures of the period, Sir Oliver Franks and Sir Stafford Cripps—one a top administrator and later Ambassador in Washington, the other a memorable Labour Chancellor of the Exchequer—published expositions of the case for central planning without any hint that there are always powerful forces at work to close any gap between supplies and requirements and that it may be well to pay regard to these forces.[3] Few administrators or politicians, unless trained in economics, perceive that there can be no question of relying exclusively on government planning, or alternatively on the price mechanism, and that the real problem is always how to combine the two.

It can happen, as in wartime, that the price mechanism plays only a minor part because the government's priorities must take precedence over those of individual consumers; and in the wake of such circumstances the role of prices may be overlooked. It can also happen that economists are so mesmerized by the price mechanism that they limit their vision to the study of market forces when the phenomena of government planning merit equal attention. Just as administrators may fail to understand the workings of the price mechanism, so economists are apt to disregard organizational influences on economic activity. What goes on *inside* the firm, *inside* the government department, *inside* the Cabinet, is often left on one side. Yet it cannot make sense to pursue the study of market failure and undertake no systematic analysis of the weaknesses of alternative agencies of coordination.

To the four elementary economic concepts I have just discussed—supply and demand, opportunity costs, the margin and the economic system—

I could add some familiar maxims such as "Bygones are forever bygones," or "There is no such thing as a free lunch." These, too, are very helpful in coping with muddled thinking in high places. They form a small but indispensable part of the economists' stock-in-trade. Where the full range of tools is most likely to be brought into play is in economic forecasting. Here indeed the practitioner has to keep in close touch with current theory. The relationship between theory and practice in economic forecasting raises many interesting questions, since those who prepare the forecasts and are perhaps best equipped to judge the risk of error may have little contact with those who use them and run their risks on the basis of the forecasts. But economic forecasting is much too large a subject for me to do more than touch on.

I turn instead to examine some of the reasons why economists find difficulty in bringing their theoretical apparatus to bear on practical problems. As Jacob Viner, who had plenty of experience, emphasized years ago, "the list of handicaps of the economic theorist as a participant in public policy . . . is discouragingly long" (1958, p. 109). Some of these handicaps arise from the practical difficulties that attend the use of economic theory in trying to work out an appropriate policy; others relate to the presentation of the policy so that it carries conviction and obtains support; others again derive from the need to marry economic with noneconomic considerations in making a policy acceptable. Let me take these in turn.

I. Limitations of Economic Theory

Economic theory is fundamentally an exploration of models and conceptual relationships couched in hypothetical terms and necessarily abstracts from many features of the real world. Without abstraction and simplification it would not be possible to begin thinking about economic problems. There is no option but to leave out what may seem to some people highly important. As Wicksell pointed out, it is not to be expected that economic theory should attach significance to the features of the real world according to their prominence in the eyes of the layman since "it is not the purpose of science to describe the obvious in elaborate terms" (1934, p. 19). But abstraction can be carried too far. The theorist may follow paths that lead him further and further from the real world and expose him to the danger of what one economist has called "theoretic blight" (E. R. Walker, 1943, p. 57). He may be tempted to select problems that lend themselves to sophisticated technical analysis rather than on grounds of practical importance; and become lost in admiration of the conceptual schemes he has developed without regard to the unrealistic premises on which they are constructed. He may also make the common mistake of getting things the wrong way round; or leave out what really does matter or can only be left out provisionally. He may then be deceived into thinking that he understands how things work when in fact the model is misconceived. Theory, as someone once put it, can be "an organized way of going wrong with confidence." To be a useful guide it has to separate correctly what is adventitious from what is truly significant.

Economic policy, on the other hand, has to deal with practical problems and specific situations. While it is possible to develop a branch of economics bearing on these problems and situations and call it applied economics, such a branch is still part of economic theory. It still consists of a set of logically consistent propositions and abstracts from many of the circumstances that may in practice govern the policy pursued. What is to be done is never a simple corollary of theoretical conclusions.

The need for care in drawing conclusions from theory was brought home to me in Berlin in the winter of 1945–46 when I took part in a discussion between Sir Paul Chambers (later Chairman of I.C.I.) and General William H. Draper (then Economic Adviser to General Clay). Sir Paul, challenged as to the accuracy with which he had been able to forecast budgetary revenue as Director of Statistics and Intelligence in the Inland Revenue, gave us a short exposition of the theory of probability. "If you toss a penny and it comes down tails ten times in succession," he said, "that doesn't affect the probability that it will come down heads next time. The chances remain fifty-fifty." "Shall we test that?" said General Draper, producing a penny. "Will you call?" Ten times Sir Paul called heads and each time the penny came down tails. Before tossing it again, General Draper revealed that the exercise of a little sleight of hand might be affecting the behavior of the penny. It is always necessary to enquire whether the assumptions of theory are valid in the case at hand before applying it; and if the facts do not conform to theoretical expectations it may be the facts that need looking into, not the theory.

Whatever the limitations of economic theory, it is very powerful stuff, more powerful the more general it comes. We certainly cannot dispense with it in trying to understand any economic system. If we enter a maze we need a thread to guide us in it and the purpose of theory is to furnish that guide. On the other hand, we cannot hope to get very far with theory alone and there are serious dangers in moving from the world of theory to the real world without regard to the difference between the two. One danger is that the theory may be obsolete. It isn't just the practical man who may become the slave of some defunct economist. Even professional economists, deeply immersed in their everyday duties in some government department, have to live on an intellectual capital that is rapidly depreciating and need an opportunity of rebuilding it in an academic environment. There may also be times when the boot is on the other foot and it is the practitioner who is alive to truths disregarded in current theory. Theory may suffer from a distortion of emphasis or a quirk of intellectual fashion that throws into prominence the wrong variables, the wrong problems or the wrong formulations of them; attention may then be diverted from the things with which theory should be occupying itself. When that happens, economic theory must be accounted not just irrelevant, but bad: for the primary purpose of theory is to assist us in posing questions, and if we are moved to ask the wrong questions theory has failed us.

The most serious problem for the practitioner is that the theorists differ, even on technical economic issues. There is no agreement on how the economy works—on what governs the level of output or employment or prices. Where the disagreements go so deep as they do nowadays it is difficult to speak with authority on technical economic issues. I need not dwell on the problems this creates in advising on policy.

And yet there are times when I wonder whether the disagreements between economic theorists, even now, go so deep as their solidarity when confronted with the heresies which so often shape the policies of governments. To take an extreme case, we may debate whether the money supply is too great or too small: but what of governments—and there have been some—that try to do away with money altogether or come to power, like the Social Credit party, preaching that there is never enough? Or, to come nearer home, what of the comment made to me on the Radcliffe Committee by the President of the National Union of Mineworkers, one of Arthur Scargill's predecessors: "You fellows seem to worry about what the rate of interest should do. But my members don't see why there should be a rate of interest at all." Or, still on the subject of interest rates, what are we to make of Chancellors of the Exchequer who exclaim like Hugh Dalton: "You can't allow higher interest rates while resisting higher wage rates." It can sometimes be easier to reach agreement between economists on what should be done than on matters of theory.

A further difficulty facing the practitioner relates not to theory but to economic information. Economic theory has always to be mixed with a large dollop of fact before prescriptions for action can be framed; but the facts are usually obscure, disputed, seen through different eyes against a different experience of life and stretching far beyond the limited economic context within which the economist seeks to analyze them.

The theorist moreover is in control of his starting point, since he is free to make his own assumptions; but the practitioner is never quite sure where he is. As Lord Roberthall, who was Economic Adviser to the British government for fourteen years, used to say: "it's very hard to forecast where you are now." Indeed, you don't even know where you *were*. The official statisticians are busy rewriting history from the word "go"; and they don't stop. When I look back at the British balance of payments deficits in the three years after World War II, for example, I find that the figures for the current account first published added up to £1245 m., were revised by 1953 to show a total of £740 m., and continued to be revised over the next thirty years until they dwindled to £585 m. Instead of working out at exactly the level assumed in the Washington Loan Negotiations in 1945, the cumulative deficit is now put at less than half and British capital exports over the period are consequently estimated at a total higher than was thought at the time by $2\frac{1}{2}$ b., that is, by two-thirds of what was borrowed from the United States. Another example is the way in which the U.K. monthly index of industrial production in 1964 was completely flat in the nine months up to September— a General Election was due in October—but was revised over the next two years so that it was sloping steeply upwards in official publications in 1966 and then was further revised until now it is flat again, as in 1964.

I cite these changes, which could easily be multiplied, to show that if the future is uncertain, so also is the past. I have often been intrigued to see how patiently economists apply themselves to explaining what, if later information is to be trusted, never occurred and how figures of assorted reliability are given equal treatment by those who do not live among them. The practitioner, recognizing the uncertainty of the information at his disposal, can have only a limited grasp of what is going on. He has to make the best of incomplete, inconsistent, and changeable data, relying on human judgment to derive a plausible, self-consistent picture of the existing situation. He is quite likely to find, as I have found, that the best way to reconcile the data is to begin by making a forecast of the future as a way of deciding on the underlying trends and then work backwards to a consequential interpretation of the present. The judgment he makes—as in the examples I have cited—may be crucial to the choice of policy. If for instance, you think the economy is stuck, you opt for policies very different from those appropriate to a rip-roaring expansion.

A further difficulty is that the economy never works in quite the same way for very long. You may feel confident that you can explain how it worked in the recent past and set your conclusions down in equations with all the coefficients, lags, etc., carefully estimated. But, as Keynes put it, human behavior is not "homogeneous through time."[4] Whether you realize it or not, you are always working with relationships that are obsolescent without knowing just how obsolescent they are. One day you can count on people spending more when prices go up; then you find them spending less. One day the unemployment figures go up when the vacancy figures come down; then they both go up together. It is always necessary to be on the look out for some departure from normal patterns and pay attention to straws in the wind. They may reveal, earlier than any statistics, new forces at work or a strengthening of existing forces. Analysis of these forces has to be coupled with a good eye for straws.

Then there is the limitation imposed by the need to be specific: in particular, to deal in specific magnitudes and at specific points in time. Many of the more important generalizations in economics make no reference to magnitudes or time. They may be of assistance to a government that wants to know in which direction it should be operating; but they do not, in their general form, offer much help to a government wanting to know how far to go.

For example, it may be possible on general grounds to indicate that the government should be thinking in terms of increasing taxation. But the question that has operational significance is, how much should the increase be? This requires immersion in a mass of statistical detail and the working out of far more definite views of the functioning of the economy than found their way into the traditional textbooks in economics some years ago.

Then there is the content of the tax package. What *taxes* should be increased? What effect will the increases have? What other action, if any, should accompany the increases in tax or be contemplated for introduction later?

Another set of issues relates to timing. When should the government act? When will it be possible to judge whether the action has been effective? Is it likely to be necessary to take further action later?

It takes time to become aware of changes in the situation, to size up the strength of the forces at work, to prepare the appropriate response. One cannot wait for certainty, but it is also a mistake to act prematurely when the diagnosis may prove to be quite wrong. Delay may be inescapable. After the devaluation of sterling in November 1967, there was a great burst of consumer spending and a clamor for early action to restrain it. The right time to act was of course in November, but when that opportunity was missed it was not easy, for technical reasons, to redeem the error by imposing additional taxation in the weeks immediately before Christmas. In January it seemed better to put all possible effort into a battle for lower government expenditure and by the end of the month the budget was already in sight only a few weeks away. So although the need for action was not in dispute, it was four months before a suitable package of measures could be introduced.

Another source of difficulty is that many of the questions on which advice is sought from economists have very little to do with conventional economics. Cabinet ministers, I found, don't ask the questions you are ready to answer. They want to know how people will react, both to events and to their policies. Will there be a strike or won't there? Will the rate of exchange weaken or strengthen? Will it be possible to get backing for this or that line of policy?

I concluded that attitudes were just as important as prices and that economic policy had to embrace efforts to change attitudes, not just efforts to make better use of market forces. Just as economic events and policies may have their biggest impact outside the functioning of the economy—as world depression could clear the way for Hitler—similarly the most effective levers of economic policy sometimes bypass the market by operating on confidence and opinion, expectations and attitudes. In the same way as economists so often neglect goodwill in discussions of industrial economics, so they tend to neglect the prestige, credit, standing, authority—call it what you will—of governments and the ways in which morale and endeavor are affected by factors other than pay.

II. Presentational Difficulties

Let me turn next to presentation. This raises problems at two levels, that of the theorist and that of the practitioner.

Theorists may confine themselves to the business of producing theories without much regard to the market for them. But in applying economics in practice, it is impossible to overlook the importance of the consumer. This is obviously true in the short-run sense that one has to have regard to the chances that any attention will be paid to suggested lines of action by those who have it in their power to act on them. It is true also, in a much wider sense: that those parts of economic theory that do not supply useful answers tend to receive little attention in business or government, while those that purport to throw light on practical problems, and point in the direction of specific ways of dealing with them, command respect and interest.

Practitioners face a rather different problem of presentation. Governments are almost as much concerned about what to say and how to say it as about what to do. Indeed, what they say may have more effect on the markets than what they do. They may be given credit for cutting public expenditure by simply announcing that that is their intention even when, as in the first four years of Mrs. Thatcher, it continues to increase. Similarly they may be given credit for mastering inflation when all they have done is to contribute to an international depression that brings down import prices. The public reacts to the declared aims of government as presented in speeches, often without close enquiry into the success with which these aims are pursued. This being so, economists can neither ignore how policies are presented nor how market opinion may narrow the scope for government action. Against the extra leverage that skillful presentation of policy may provide must be set the danger that the government may become the prisoner of market opinion, forced to conform to the role assigned to it by that opinion, and so transmuting into rational expectations what would otherwise have no rational foundation.

The issue of presentation is obviously highly important when any major change of policy takes place. If, for example, a more restrictive policy is proposed involving higher taxes, the Minister of Finance needs to see the case presented in persuasive terms so that the government, in turn, can be persuaded and the new policy defended in public debate. There is always a question of how the higher taxes can be presented with the minimum damage to the credit and authority of the government and its capacity to carry through the rest of its program. What is to be said and how is it to be said? The handling and presentation of the decision is part of the decision itself and cannot be dismissed as irrelevant to it. It is partly because this is so that it becomes difficult to find a use for those parts of economic theory that are not easily translated into simple language.

Taxation provides many illustrations of the problem of presentation. I can remember Chief Festus of Nigeria recounting how he had to withdraw a tax on cosmetics because, as he explained, holding up a large, pudgy hand, "I burnt my fingers." In Britain the Selective Employment Tax introduced in 1965 was withdrawn six years later, in part at least because the refined economic logic by which it was justified did not make sense to the general public. Or take corporation tax. Economists might agree that there is no strong case in theory to have a corporation tax at all. But a proposal to abolish the tax would certainly be laughed out of court by politicians and would be unintelligible to the general public.

In stressing presentation and acceptability, I should not want to be interpreted as defending mere sycophancy and time-serving, automatic approval of any act of policy that is likely to gain popular approval and command a Parliamentary majority. Neither Parliament nor the public has any prerogative of wisdom in economic affairs, whatever democratic theory may imply, and the test of sound policy can never be made on acceptability alone. On the contrary, the economist is wise to be on his guard, as Marshall emphasized, when his views are popular and all men speak well of him (cited by Pigou, 1925, p. 89). He owes it to his profession to speak up for what he thinks right, to denounce policies that he thinks mistaken and to try to persuade those in power of the dangers they run if his advice is neglected. But if he wishes to be heard, he has to learn when to keep his peace and when to press his point. There are times when policies have to be ruled out because the political leadership required for their adoption simply does not exist; and when indeed the policies that seem right to the economist in his study might provoke adverse reactions, of which he has taken little or no account, but would make nonsense of the policies. There are other times when new ideas could fill a political vacuum, and what was previously unacceptable can be taken down from the shelf and put on sale.

In practice, political choices are rarely a matter of good and bad, black and white. They usually turn on a balance of considerations among which economic factors are not decisive. I don't know what undergraduates make of the questions they are asked to decide in three-quarters of an hour in final examinations. But if they have difficulty in coming to firm conclusions they are in good company. One can make a case—and generally quite a respectable case—for a variety of economic policies at any point in time and argument is unlikely to destroy every case but one and leave the surviving case as indisputably "right." Economists do notoriously disagree. So what they have to square with their conscience is usually not failure to demonstrate the error of some politician's ways but failure to offer the right degree of resistance, to do battle with the right degree of conviction, to use what Lord Roberthall once designated "the right tone of voice." Like the lawyer, the economist comes to see the case that can be made for and against, and loses the campaigning spirit with which he set out. He has to be forever pointing out that things are not quite so simple as politicians suppose, forever dwelling on the hidden snags. Policies cease to be right or wrong, but just better or worse, and often only marginally so. The occupational disease that he has to fight is not time serving but atrophy of conviction and the sense of commitment.

III. Noneconomic Factors in Economic Policy

I come next to the implications of the obvious fact that the policies of governments are by definition a political matter. If you are considering what governments should do, you can hardly avoid taking account of what sort of government you have, and how much government you want. It makes quite a difference whether you have been brought up to regard the government as Santa Claus, Stalin, or a dog fight. One government may be benevolent, another dictatorial, a third incapable of making up its mind. All of them have the failings of their human components, ministerial and bureaucratic.

Governments are political animals, moved by political considerations. They have to ask themselves what they *can* do and this may rule out many otherwise attractive lines of action. There are commitments by which they are bound—to other governments, to particular interests, to the party supporting them in office. They hesitate to fly in the face of prevalent attitudes and opinions. They are more conscious of immediate pressures and short-term considerations that of what is desirable in the long run and usually prefer to put off the evil day. Even when they are anxious to do the "right" thing, as a surprising number are, or when they give priority to long-term objectives over short, they tend to do so with an obstinacy fatal to their hopes: either because they lack understanding of the appropriate sticking-points, or because they hesitate to give ground for fear of unsettling opinion and losing the support they need. One of the most difficult problems in policymaking is to know how far to persist and when to bend. Overcommitment can be worse than opportunism.

In any event, the economist has to recognize that policy does not take shape in a vacuum but within a machine that has several well-defined organizational characteristics with which he would do well to become acquainted. Government is not a simple optimizing activity that can be reduced to a second differential in a mathematical equation. It is more likely to be a collection of bald-headed and somewhat bewildered men sitting round a table, harassed and short of time, full of doubts and dogmatism, with all the strengths and failings of successful politicians. Such men may survive for a long time without any policy at all except in the form of a series of specific responses to matters forced on their attention and calling for immediate decision.

If, therefore, the economist wants to influence policy and asks where policy is formed, the answer may be either anywhere or nowhere. It is not unknown for political theorists studying a government department to come to the conclusion that no intelligible answer can be given to the question: "who forms policy?" A succession of battles on a succession of issues may rage within or between departments, involving different groups at different times, and there may be no consistency in the outcome of their debates except what is imposed in ignorance by some later historian. Or decisions may be taken low down in the hierarchy by someone who is unaware that he has taken any decision at all (such as the decision to do nothing); and although the matter may be fought out at increasingly exalted levels until it reaches the Cabinet, ministers may have no option but to accept the inevitable, even if so little disposed to recognize their own impotence that they go through the charade of further debate and carefully minuted decision. It is one of the curiosities of government how frequently what is plainly due to the force of events is attributed to free and deliberate choice.

This is not to say that policy itself is a hallucination and not worth bothering about. What governments do can hardly be discussed in such a ludicrous fashion. The point is rather that one has to understand the scope for policy, the times at which it may be influenced, and the pressures that gov-

ern it. Similarly, one has to have some awareness of the bureaucratic atmosphere within which economic problems arise and have to be tackled. That
atmosphere is somewhat different from the comparative calm of university
life. Many years ago I described how "the various divisions in many government departments (were) loosely geared together, uncertain of the limits
of their responsibilities, losing and gaining staff almost every week, themselves dissolving from time to time into new divisions or subdivisions, and
facing an avalanche of fresh problems on which to advise, fresh cases to
decide, and fresh policies to apply."

No doubt that exaggerates a little; but it brings out some of the features
of life with Leviathan that an academic economist might overlook. These
features condition the way in which economic theory impinges on policy and
limit in particular the chances of drawing on highly complex bits of theory.

Allowance has to be made next for the political setting: the need, if one
is in business, to guess what the government will do next, or, if one is in a
government department, what is likely to prove feasible and acceptable to a
government wishing to stay in office. A wise decision on what should be
done cannot be based on economic reasoning or models that pay no regard
to the distribution of political power, the frame of mind of the public, or the
political ambitions and anxieties of the party in office.

Suppose, for example, that one thinks, like one of my distinguished
Cambridge colleagues, that the economic situation calls for the use of import
restrictions. One may begin by setting out the economic arguments. Then
one has to reflect on the political situation. If on January 1, 1973, Britain
has just joined the European Economic Community, one has to ask whether
it makes sense to urge ministers *a week later* to introduce import restrictions
that will fall heavily on imports from Common Market countries. If in June
1975 a referendum is to be held on continued membership of the Community
and the Cabinet is split down the middle on the issue, one has again to ask
if it makes sense to press the Chancellor, just ahead of the referendum, to
budget in April for import restrictions, especially if the identical remedy was
appropriate two years earlier in very different circumstances. If the advice
is accepted and an international row brings on a run on the pound, how is
the Chancellor to explain to the IMF that he acted in the interests of greater
stability in the exchange rate, and how is he to put it to his continental colleagues—most of them struggling with heavier unemployment than Britain—
that he felt compelled by the intolerable level of unemployment to set aside
his treaty obligations.

It is not only the organizational and political setting that is important.
Economic problems have also to be seen in their institutional setting. It is
(or should be) impossible to discuss monetary policy without regard to the
kind of banking system and methods of credit control in operation, just as it
is or should be impossible to discuss wage theory without regard to the way
in which wage bargains are struck and bringing in various kinds of legislation
affecting bargaining power (for example, in relation to minimum wages, the
powers and practices of trade unions and employers' associations, redundancy, labor mobility, and so on).

Frank Knight in his latter days used to agonize over the futility of being an economist. He doubted whether society would ever take advantage of anything he had to contribute to the solution of its problems. Others like Max Planck have turned away from economics because of its appalling complexity. Others again have given up in despair of arriving at finality: they are repelled by the inconclusiveness of the subject—what Wicksell called "the permanent state of war" (1958, p. 52) between diametrically opposed views neither of which is ever vanquished or disappears from the field as would happen with the natural sciences. There is no received body of doctrine— only a "technique of thinking."

In spite of what I have said about the limitations of economic theory as a guide to policy, the contribution it can make seems to me none the less invaluable. Any doubts on that score are soon quelled by life among noneconomists in positions of power. Moreover, the very inconclusiveness of economics has its value as a preparation for the world of affairs where the same inconclusiveness rules. In government and business there is rarely a conclusive answer; instead there is an equally enduring "state of war." The evidence on which an answer might be reached, even on matters of fact, tends also to be inconclusive since there is rarely any finality in the statistical data that purport to summarize the facts. It is necessary to decide between alternatives in the light of uncertain and often contradictory evidence. The decision, it is true, rarely turns exclusively on economic considerations. But it is a great advantage to be able to assess the force of these considerations, just as it is also a great advantage to be able to test the data with the kind of insight into the underlying relationships at work that economic theory engenders.

In the application of economics to practical problems, that kind of insight needs to be reinforced by imagination and accurate observation. Imagination is kindled by good theory but is powerless or mischievous if fed with inadequate or inaccurate information. In the social sciences there is no substitute for getting the facts right, and observation ranks at least as high as logic. Most theoreticians tend to treat far too lightly the difficulty of obtaining and presenting the information necessary to a sound decision. If you want to understand how the economy works, you need to have an eye for the information that matters; and since the unexpected keeps happening you need very up-to-date information. An economist like Keynes may owe his reputation to his originality as a theorist; but in my judgment he stands out from the other economists of his time at least as much for his flair in picking on significant statistics, often from relatively obscure sources before anybody else, and piecing them together by conjectural arithmetic to reveal a danger not then fully appreciated. Other economists of the first rank commonly have a similar power to startle with unfamiliar figures that give a new perspective to events.

Those who have done their homework thoroughly, and have mastered every scrap of information likely to be of assistance will be of little use, however, without the imagination to conceive of alternative policies and visualize the reasons why they may not work as expected. They may fail to make use of available information because they do not appreciate its relevance and overlook or misconstrue important relationships. For example, price control is obviously not enough by itself to remove the danger of inflation in wartime. But it required considerable imagination in World War II to invent three new devices for that purpose: postwar credits (an acceptable form of forced saving); points rationing (the circulation of a new currency to be used exclusively for the purchase of rationed goods); and subsidies to stabilize the prices of key commodities, making up a kind of iron ration. All these were expedients, not intended to last indefinitely, but they did contribute to a general stabilization of incomes and prices.

IV. Conclusions

It has been part of my theme that economics has more to offer by way of analysis than prescription. So it is hardly surprising that I should have few proposals for improving the state of affairs I have described. I have three rather modest suggestions.

The first can be put in a word: circulate. The practitioners need to mix with the theorists and vice versa. More than that—the practitioners need to be given a chance to catch up with theoretical developments by release from time to time from their duties. They should be offered sabbatical leave, or enabled to attend conferences or at the very least given time to read the journals. They also need encouragement and opportunities to make their own contributions to current theoretical controversy. Conversely, the academics need a modicum of experience of policy formulation. A spell in government or business can do wonders in changing the outlook of a theorist on the best way of spending his time, on the choice of problems to study, and on the limits within which action can be taken. In some countries, however, including my own, it has become more difficult to move in and out of government. Twenty years ago a remarkably high proportion of top British economists had had experience of service in government. Today there is very little circulation. That seems to me a step in the wrong direction.

Secondly I think we need to revalue and upgrade the work of intermediaries between the profession and the public. Financial journalism, for example, is an increasingly demanding skill and has become both more sophisticated and professional and more influential since the war. The press also carries articles by professional economists, and a number of specialized publications reprint (or commission) articles by them that help to illuminate current issues. But the mass media are largely untouched by this trend. It may be that nothing can be done about this. But there does seem to me great scope for those economists who have a gift for conveying the thinking of the profession, with all its doubts and dissensions, to the man in the street.

Finally, don't let us be overwhelmed by our disagreements: we have also plenty to agree about. As I have tried to show, it is often the most elementary propositions in economics, on which we all agree, that matter for practical purposes. Similarly, we should not underrate the value of the habits of mind

that are nourished by economic analysis, even if they yield no common program of action. Where we continue to disagree, let us try to understand and
narrow our differences, remembering always that we have a duty to our
fellow citizens to offer them the best advice we can.

NOTES

1. Quoted by John Jewkes (1953, p. 29).
2. Quoted from an official wartime memorandum in my *Essays in Economic Management* (1971, p. 203).
3. Sir Oliver Franks (1947); Sir Stafford Cripps's exposition appeared anony-
   mously in the *Economic Survey for 1947* (Cmd 7046).
4. Keynes to Harrod, Collected Writings (1973, pp. 296–97), quoted by Bernard
   Corry (1978, pp. 5–6).

REFERENCES

Cairncross, Alec, *Essays in Economic Management,* London: George Allen and Unwin, 1971.

Corry, Bernard, "Keynes in the History of Economic Thought," in *Keynes and Laissez-Faire,* London: Macmillan, 1978.

Devons, Ely, "Applied Economics—the Application of What?," in *Essays in Economics,* London: George Allen and Unwin, 1961.

Franks, Sir Oliver, *Central Planning and Control in War and Peace,* London: London School of Economics, 1947.

Jewkes, John, "The Economist and Public Policy," *Lloyds Bank Review,* April 1953,
28, 18–32.

Keynes, John Maynard, *The General Theory and After: Part II, Defence and Development,* Collected Writings, Vol. XIV, London: Macmillan, 1973.

Pigou, A. C., *Memorials of Alfred Marshall,* London: Macmillan, 1925.

U.K. Treasury, *Economic Survey for 1947,* London: HMSO, 1947.

Viner, Jacob, *The Long View and the Short,* Glencoe: Free Press, 1958.

Walker, E. R., *From Economic Theory to Economic Policy,* Chicago: Chicago University Press, 1943.

Wicksell, Knut, *Lectures on Political Economy,* Vol. I, London: George Routledge
and Sons, 1934.

————, *Selected Papers on Economic Theory,* London: George Allen and Unwin,
1958.

KENNETH J. ARROW

Social Responsibility and Economic Efficiency

Kenneth Arrow points out that profit-maximizing behavior by firms may produce socially inefficient results when firms do not bear all the social cost of production (as in the case of pollution) or when sellers have more information about products than buyers (as with regard to safety). He discusses alternative institutional arrangements that can be utilized to promote socially efficient behavior.

QUESTIONS TO GUIDE THE READING

1. What is the case for firms maximizing profits?
2. What socially undesirable effects can result from profit maximization?
3. Why does Arrow believe that the remedy of legal liability is imperfect as an institution promoting the social responsibility of firms?
4. Why are some ethical codes unlikely to be viable in promoting social responsibility? Under what circumstances are ethical codes most useful?

This paper makes some observations on the widespread notion that the individual has some responsibility to others in the conduct of his economic affairs. It is held that there are a number of circumstances under which the economic agent should forgo profit or other benefits to himself in order to achieve some social goal, especially to avoid a disservice to other individuals. For the purpose of keeping the discussion within bounds, I shall confine my attention to the obligations that might be imposed on business firms. Under what circumstances is it reasonable to expect a business firm to refrain from maximizing its profits because it will hurt others by doing so? What institutions can we expect to serve the function not merely of limiting profits but of limiting them in just those ways that will avoid harm to others? Is it reasonable to expect that ethical codes will arise or be created? My

Kenneth J. Arrow, "Social Responsibility and Economic Efficiency," *Public Policy 21* (Summer 1973), 303–17. Reprinted by permission of the author.

Kenneth J. Arrow is Joan Kenney Professor of Economics and Professor of Operations Research at Stanford University. He received a Nobel Prize in Economics in 1972.

purpose in discussing these questions is not so much to achieve definitive answers as to analyze the kinds of consideration that enter into discussing them.

First of all, it may be well to review what possible ways there are by which the economic activity of one firm may affect other members of the economy. A substantial list comes to mind; a few illustrations will serve. A firm affects others by competing with them in the product markets and in the factor markets, in the buying of labor, buying of other goods for its use, and in the selling of its products. It pays wages to others. It buys goods from others. It sets prices to its customers, and so enters into an economic relation with them. The firm typically sets working conditions, including—of greatest importance—conditions that affect the health and possibility for accident within the plant. We are reminded in recent years that the firm, as well as the private individual, is a contributor to pollution. Pollution has a direct effect on the welfare of other members of the economy. Less mentioned, but of the same type, are the effects of economic activity on congestion. Bringing a new plant into an already crowded area is bound to create costs, disservices, and disutilities to others in the area if by nothing else than by crowding the streets and the sidewalks and imposing additional burdens on the public facilities of the area. Indeed, although congestion has not been discussed as much as has pollution, it may have greater economic impact and probably even greater health costs. Certainly the number of automobile deaths arising from accidents far exceeds the health hazards arising from automobile pollution. The firm affects others through determining the quality of its products, and again, among the many aspects of product quality we may especially single out the qualities of the product with respect to its pollution-creating ability, as in the case of automobiles, and with respect to its safety, the hazards it poses to its user. The question of social responsibility takes very different forms with regard to the different items on this varied list. It is not a uniform characteristic at all.

Let us first consider the case against social responsibility: the assumption that the firms should aim simply to maximize their profits. One strand of that argument is empirical rather than ethical or normative. It simply states that firms *will* maximize their profits. The impulse to gain, it is argued, is very strong and the incentives for selfish behavior are so great that any kind of control is likely to be utterly ineffectual. This argument has some force but is by no means conclusive. Any mechanism for enforcing or urging social responsibility upon firms must of course reckon with a profit motive, with a desire to evade whatever response of controls are imposed. But it does not mean that we cannot expect any degree of responsibility at all.

One finds a rather different argument, frequently stated by some economists. It will probably strike the noneconomist as rather strange, at least at first hearing. The assertion is that firms *ought* to maximize profits; not merely do they like to do so but there is practically a social obligation to do so. Let me briefly sketch the argument:

Firms buy the goods and services they need for production. What they

buy they pay for and therefore they are paying for whatever costs they impose upon others. What they receive in payment by selling their goods, they
receive because the purchaser considers it worthwhile. This is a world of
voluntary contracts; nobody *has* to buy the goods. If he chooses to buy it,
it must be that he is getting a benefit measured by the price he pays. Hence,
it is argued, profit really represents the net contribution that the firm makes
to the social good, and the profits should therefore be made as large as possible. When firms compete with each other, in selling their goods or in buying labor or other services, they may have to lower their selling prices in
order to get more of the market for themselves or raise their wages; in either
case the benefits which the firm is deriving are in some respects shared with
the population at large. The forces of competition prevent the firms from
engrossing too large a share of the social benefit. For example, if a firm tries
to reduce the quality of its goods, it will sooner or later have to lower the
price which it charges because the purchaser will no longer find it worthwhile to pay the high price. Hence, the consumers will gain from price reduction at the same time as they are losing through quality deterioration. On
detailed analysis it appears the firm will find it privately profitable to reduce
quality under these circumstances only if, in fact, quality reduction is a net
social benefit, that is, if the saving in cost is worth more to the consumer
than the quality reduction. Now, as far as it goes this argument is sound.
The problem is that it may not go far enough.

Under the proper assumptions profit maximization is indeed efficient in
the sense that it can achieve as high a level of satisfaction as possible for any
one consumer without reducing the levels of satisfaction of other consumers
or using more resources than society is endowed with. But the limits of the
argument must be stressed. I want to mention two well-known points in
passing without making them the principal focus of discussion. First of all,
the argument assumes that the forces of competition are sufficiently vigorous. But there is no social justification for profit maximization by monopolies. This is an important and well-known qualification. Second, the distribution of income that results from unrestrained profit maximization is very
unequal. The competitive maximizing economy is indeed efficient—this
shows up in high average incomes—but the high average is accompanied by
widespread poverty on the one hand and vast riches, at least for a few, on
the other. To many of us this is a very undesirable consequence.

Profit maximization has yet another effect on society. It tends to point
away from the expression of altruistic motives. Altruistic motives are motives whose gratification is just as legitimate as selfish motives, and the
expression of those motives is something we probably wish to encourage. A
profit-maximizing, self-centered form of economic behavior does not provide any room for the expression of such motives.

If the three problems above were set aside, many of the ways by which
firms affect others should not be tampered with. Making profits by competition is, if anything, to be encouraged rather than discouraged. Wage and
price bargains between the firm and uncoerced workers and customers rep-

resent mutually beneficial exchanges. There is, therefore, no reason within the framework of the discussion to interfere with them. But these examples far from exhaust the list of interactions with which we started. The social desirability of profit maximization does not extend to all the interactions on the list. There are two categories of effects where the arguments for profit maximization break down: The first is illustrated by pollution or congestion. Here it is no longer true (and this is the key to these issues) that the firm in fact does pay for the harm it imposes on others. When it takes a person's time and uses it at work, the firm is paying for this, and therefore the trans- action can be regarded as a beneficial exchange from the point of view of both parties. We have no similar mechanism by which the pollution which a firm imposes upon its neighborhood is paid for. Therefore the firm will have a tendency to pollute more than is desirable. That is, the benefit to it or to its customers from the expanded activity is really not as great, or may not be as great, as the cost it is imposing upon the neighborhood. But since it does not pay that cost, there is no profit incentive to refrain.

The same argument applies to traffic congestion when no change is made for the addition of cars or trucks on the highway. It makes everybody less comfortable. It delays others and increases the probability of accidents; in short, it imposes a cost upon a large number of members of the society, a cost which is not paid for by the imposer of the cost, at least not in full. The person congesting is also congested, but the costs he is imposing on others are much greater than those he suffers himself. Therefore there will be a tendency to over-utilize those goods for which no price is charged, particu- larly scarce highway space.

There are many other examples of this kind, but these two will serve to illustrate the point in question: some effort must be made to alter the profit- maximizing behavior of firms in those cases where it is imposing costs on others which are not easily compensated through an appropriate set of prices.

The second category of effects where profit maximization is not socially desirable is that in which there are quality effects about which the firm knows more than the buyer. In my examples I will cite primarily the case of quality in the product sold, but actually very much the same considerations apply to the quality of working conditions. The firm is frequently in a better position to know the consequences (the health hazards, for example) in- volved in working conditions than the worker is, and the considerations I am about to discuss in the case of sale of goods have a direct parallel in the analysis of working conditions in the relation of a firm to its workers. Let me illustrate by considering the sale of a used car. (Similar considerations apply to the sale of new cars.) A used car has potential defects and typically the seller knows more about the defects than the buyer. The buyer is not in a position to distinguish among used cars, and therefore he will be willing to pay the same amount for two used cars of differing quality because he can- not tell the difference between them. As a result, there is an inefficiency in the sale of used cars. If somehow or other the cars were distinguished as to their quality, there would be some buyers who would prefer a cheaper car with more defects because they intend to use it very little or they only want it for a short period, while others will want a better car at a higher price. In fact, however, the two kinds of car are sold indiscriminately to the two groups of buyers at the same price, so that we can argue that there is a distinct loss of consumer satisfaction imposed by the failure to convey information that is available to the seller. The buyers are not necessarily being cheated. They may be, but the problem of inefficiency would remain if they weren't. One can imagine a situation where, from past experience, buyers of used cars are aware that cars that look alike may turn out to be quite different. Without knowing whether a particular car is good or bad, they do know that there are good and bad cars, and of course their willingness to pay for the cars is influenced accordingly. The main loser from a monetary viewpoint may not be the customer, but rather the seller of the good car. The buyer will pay a price which is only appropriate to a lottery that gives him a good car or a bad car with varying probabilities, and therefore the seller of the good car gets less than the value of the car. The seller of the bad car is, of course, the beneficiary. Clearly then, if one could arrange to transmit the truth from the sellers to the buyers, the efficiency of the market would be greatly improved. The used-car illustration is an example of a very general phenomenon.

Consider now any newly produced complex product, such as a new automobile. The seller is bound to know considerably more about its properties than all but a very few of its buyers. In order to develop the car, the producer has had to perform tests of one kind or another. He knows the outcome of the tests. Failure to reveal this knowledge works against the efficiency of satisfying consumers' tastes. The argument of course applies to any aspect of the quality of a product, durability or the ability to perform under trying circumstances or differing climatic conditions. Perhaps we are most concerned about the safety features of the automobile. The risks involved in the use of automobiles are not trivial, and the kind of withholding of safety information which has been revealed to exist in a number of cases certainly cannot be defended as a socially useful implication of profit maximization. The classical efficiency arguments for profit maximization do not apply here, and it is wrong to obfuscate the issue by invoking them.

Perhaps even more dramatic, though on a smaller scale, are the repeated examples of misleading information about the risks and use of prescription drugs and other chemicals. These again manifest the same point. Profit maximization can lead to consequences which are clearly socially injurious. This is the case if the buyers are on the average deceived—if, for example, they have higher expectations than are in fact warranted. They are also injured when on the average they are not deceived but merely uncertain, although here the argument is more subtle. One consequence may be the excessively limited use of some new drugs, for example. If the users of the drugs become fully aware of the risks involved but are not able to assess the risk with respect to any particular drug, the result may be an indiscriminate rejection of new treatments which is rational from the point of view of the user; this, in the long run, may be just as serious an error as the opposite.

Defenders of unrestricted profit maximization usually assume that the consumer is well informed or at least that he becomes so by his own experience, in repeated purchases, or by information about what has happened to other people like him. This argument is empirically shaky; even the ability of individuals to analyze the effects of their own past purchases may be limited, particularly with respect to complicated mechanisms. But there are two further defects. The risks, including death, may be so great that even one misleading experience is bad enough, and the opportunity to learn from repeated trials is not of much use. Also, in a world where the products are continually changing, the possibility of learning from experience is greatly reduced. Automobile companies are continually introducing new models which at least purport to differ from what they were in the past, though doubtless the change is more external than internal. New drugs are being introduced all the time; the fact that one has had bad experiences with one drug may provide very little information about the next one.

Thus there are two types of situation in which the simple rule of maximizing profits is socially inefficient: the case in which costs are not paid for, as in pollution, and the case in which the seller has considerably more knowledge about his product than the buyer, particularly with regard to safety. In these situations it is clearly desirable to have some idea of social responsibility, that is, to experience an obligation, whether ethical, moral, or legal. Now we cannot expect such an obligation to be created out of thin air. To be meaningful, any obligation of this kind, any feeling or rule of behavior has to be embodied in some definite social institution. I use that term broadly: a legal code is a social institution in a sense. Exhortation to do good must be made specific in some external form, a steady reminder and perhaps enforcer of desirable values. Part of the need is simply for factual information as a guide to individual behavior. A firm may need to be told what is right and what is wrong when in fact it is polluting, or which safety requirements are reasonable and which are too extreme or too costly to be worth consideration. Institutionalization of the social responsibility of firms also serves another very important function. It provides some assurance to any one firm that the firms with which it is in competition will also accept the same responsibility. If a firm has some code imposed from the outside, there is some expectation that other firms will obey it too and therefore there is some assurance that it need not fear any excessive cost to its good behavior.

Let me then turn to some alternative kinds of institutions that can be considered as embodying the possible social responsibilities of firms. First, we have legal regulation, as in the case of pollution where laws are passed about the kind of burning that may take place, and about setting maximum standards for emissions. A second category is that of taxes. Economists, with good reason, like to preach taxation as opposed to regulation. The movement to tax polluting emissions is getting under way and there is a fairly widely backed proposal in Congress to tax sulfur dioxide emissions

from industrial smokestacks. That is an example of the second kind of institutionalization of social responsibility. The responsibility is made very clear:
the violator pays for violations.

A third very old remedy or institution is that of legal liability—the liability of the civil law. One can be sued for damages. Such cases apparently
go back to the Middle Ages. Regulation also extends back very far. There
was an ordinance in London about the year 1300 prohibiting the burning of
coal, because of the smoke nuisance.

The fourth class of institutions is represented by ethical codes. Restraint
is achieved not by appealing to each individual's conscience but rather by
having some generally understood definition of appropriate behavior. Let
me discuss the advantatges and disadvantages of these four institutions.

In regard to the first two, regulation and taxes, I shall be rather brief
because these are the more familiar. We can have regulations governing pollution. We can also regulate product safety. We may even have standards to
insure quality in dimensions other than safety. The chief drawback of direct
regulation is associated with the fact that it is hard to make regulations flexible enough to meet a wide variety of situations and yet simple enough to be
enforceable. In addition, there is a slowness in response to new situations.
For example, if a new chemical, such as a pesticide, comes on the market
and after a period of time is recognized as a danger, it requires a long and
complicated process to get this awareness translated into legal action. One
problem is that legislative time is a very scarce factor; a proposal to examine
the problems involved in some pesticide may at any given time be competing
with totally different considerations for the attention of the legislature or
regulatory body. In short, there is considerable rigidity in most regulatory
structures. For certain purposes it is clear that regulation is best but it is
equally clear that it is not useful as a universal device. In the case of taxes
on the effects, rather than on the causes, there is a little more built-in flexibility. To combat pollution, taxation is probably the most appropriate device;
a tax is imposed on the emission by the plant, whether in water or in air.
Now this means the plant is free to find its own way of minimizing the tax
burden. It is not told it must do one thing, such as raising smokestacks to a
certain height. It is free to try to find the cheapest way of meeting the pollution problem. It may well decide that the profitability situation is such that
it will continue to pollute and sell the product presumably at a somewhat
higher price. This decision is not necessarily bad; it implies that the product
is in fact much desired and it provides an automatic test of the market to see
whether it is worth polluting or not, because in effect the consumer is ultimately paying for the pollution he induces. However, it is difficult to see
how this method, useful though it is in the case of pollution, would have any
relevance to safety, to see how one could frame a tax which would make
very much sense. Taxation appears to be a rather blunt instrument for controlling product safety.

Legal liability can be and has been applied; i.e., courts have allowed
damages in cases arising out of pollution or out of injury or death due to

unsafe products. The nature of the law in this area is still evolving; under our system this means that it is being developed by a sequence of court decisions. Just exactly what the company or its officers have to know before they can be regarded as liable for damages due to unsafe products is not yet clear. No doubt it would certainly be held even today that if officers of a company were aware that a product had a significant probability of a dangerous defect and they sold it anyway without saying so, and if the defect occurred, legal liability would be clear. But it is frequently hard to establish such knowledge. No doubt if society wants to use the route of legal liability as a way of imposing social responsibility, then it can change the principles on which the decision is based. For example, one might throw the burden of proof on the company, so that in the case of any new product they have to run tests to show positively that it is safe. Their failure to make such tests would be an indication of their liability. One could imagine changes of this kind which would bring the law more into line with what is desirable. But there are some intrinsic defects in the liability route which, in my opinion, make it unsuitable in its present form as a serious method of achieving social control or of imposing responsibility on profit-making firms. First, litigation is costly. In many cases there are social wrongs or social inefficiencies which are quite significant in the aggregate and are perceived by a large number of people, each of whom bears a small part of the cost. This is characteristic of pollution and may be the case with certain kinds of quality standards. It really does not pay any particular person to sue, and if a few people do sue it does not really do the company much harm.

Another problem is that the notion of liability in law is really too simple a concept. Legal liability tends to be an all-or-none proposition. Consider a product such as plastic bags. They are perfectly all right for storing clothes or food but there is a risk that small children will misuse them, with serious consequences. One would hardly want to say that there is any legal liability ascribable to the plastic-bag makers, for even the safest product can be misused. On the other hand, one might argue that a product that can be misused ought to be somewhat discouraged and perhaps some small degree of responsibility should be imposed, particularly if no adequate warning is issued. The law does not permit any such distinctions. Thus, in an automobile case, one party or the other must be found wrong, even though in fact a crash may clearly be due to the fact that both drivers were behaving erratically, and it would be reasonable to have some splitting of responsibility. At present, with some minor exceptions, the law does not permit this, and I suppose it would confuse legal proceedings irreparably to start introducing partial causation. Economists are accustomed to the idea that almost nothing happens without the cooperation of a number of factors, and we have large bodies of doctrine devoted to imputing in some appropriate way the consequences of an action to all of its causes. It is for these reasons that this kind of crude liability doctrine seems to be unsuitable in many cases.

A number of other problems with litigation could be mentioned. Consider very high-risk situations that involve a very low probability of death or other serious adverse consequence, as in the case of drugs, or possible radiation from nuclear power plants. The insurance companies are willing to insure because the probability is low. But once insurance is introduced the incentive to refrain from incurring the risk is dulled. If you are insured against a loss you have less of an incentive to prevent it. In the field of automobile liability, it has become clear that the whole system of liability has to a very great extent broken down. The result is a widespread movement toward no-fault insurance, which in effect means people are compensated for their losses but no attempt is made to charge damages to the persons responsible. Responsibility is left undecided.

Finally, litigation does not seem suitable for continuing problems. Pollution will be reduced but not eliminated; indeed it is essentially impossible to eliminate it. There remain continuous steady damages to individuals. These should still be charged to firms in order to prevent them from polluting more. But enforcement by continuous court action is a very expensive way of handling a repetitious situation. It is silly to keep on going to court to establish the same set of facts over and over again. For these reasons taxes which have the same incentive effects are superior.

Let me turn to the fourth possibility, ethical codes. This may seem to be a strange possibility for an economist to raise. But when there is a wide difference in knowledge between the two sides of the market, recognized ethical codes can be, as has already been suggested, a great contribution to economic efficiency. Actually we do have examples of this in our everyday lives, but in very limited areas. The case of medical ethics is the most striking. By its very nature there is a very large difference in knowledge between the buyer and the seller. One is, in fact, buying precisely the service of someone with much more knowledge than you have. To make this relationship a viable one, ethical codes have grown up over the centuries, both to avoid the possibility of exploitation by the physician and to assure the buyer of medical services that he is not being exploited. I am not suggesting that these are universally obeyed, but there is a strong presumption that the doctor is going to perform to a large extent with your welfare in mind. Unnecessary medical expenses or other abuses are perceived as violations of ethics. There is a powerful ethical background against which we make this judgment. Behavior that we would regard as highly reprehensible in a physician is judged less harshly when found among businessmen. The medical profession is typical of professions in general. All professions involve a situation in which knowledge is unequal on two sides of the market by the very definition of the profession, and therefore there have grown up ethical principles that afford some protection to the client. Notice there is a mutual benefit in this. The fact is that if you had sufficient distrust of a doctor's services, you wouldn't buy them. Therefore the physician wants an ethical code to act as assurance to the buyer, and he certainly wants his competitors to obey this same code, partly because any violation may put him at a disadvantage but more especially because the violation will reflect on him, since the buyer of the medical services may not be able to distinguish one doctor from another.

A close look reveals that a great deal of economic life depends for its viability on a certain limited degree of ethical commitment. Purely selfish behavior of individuals is really incompatible with any kind of settled economic life. There is almost invariably some element of trust and confidence. Much business is done on the basis of verbal assurance. It would be too elaborate to try to get written commitments on every possible point. Every contract depends for its observance on a mass of unspecified conditions which suggest that the performance will be carried out in good faith without insistence on sticking literally to its wording. To put the matter in its simplest form, in almost every economic transaction, in any exchange of goods for money, somebody gives up his valuable asset before he gets the other's; either the goods are given before the money or the money is given before the goods. Moreover there is a general confidence that there won't be any violation of the implicit agreement. Another example in daily life of this kind of ethics is the observance of queue discipline. People line up; there are people who try to break in ahead of you, but there is an ethic which holds that this is bad. It is clearly an ethic which is in everybody's interest to preserve; one waits at the end of the line this time, and one is protected against somebody's coming in ahead of him.

In the context of product safety, efficiency would be greatly enhanced by accepted ethical rules. Sometimes it may be enough to have an ethical compulsion to reveal all the information available and let the buyer choose. This is not necessarily always the best. It can be argued that under some circumstances setting minimum safety standards and simply not putting out products that do not meet them would be desirable and should be felt by the businessman to be an obligation.

Now I've said that ethical codes are desirable. It doesn't follow from that that they will come about. An ethical code is useful only if it is widely accepted. Its implications for specific behavior must be moderately clear, and above all it must be clearly perceived that the acceptance of these ethical obligations by everybody does involve mutual gain. Ethical codes that lack the latter property are unlikely to be viable. How do such codes develop? They may develop as a consensus out of lengthy public discussion of obligations, discussion which will take place in legislatures, lecture halls, business journals, and other public forums. The codes are communicated by the very process of coming to an agreement. A more formal alternative would be to have some highly prestigious group discuss ethical codes for safety standards. In either case to become and to remain a part of the economic environment, the codes have to be accepted by the significant operating institutions and transmitted from one generation of executives to the next through standard operating procedures, through education in business schools, and through indoctrination of one kind or another. If we seriously expect such codes to develop and to be maintained, we might ask how the agreements develop and above all, how the codes remain stable. After all, an ethical code, however much it may be in the interest of all, is, as we remarked earlier, not in the interest of any one firm. The code may be of value to the running of the system as a whole, it may be of value to all firms if all firms maintain it, and yet it will be to the advantage of any one firm to cheat—in fact the more so, the more other firms are sticking to it. But there are some reasons for thinking that ethical codes can develop and be stable. These codes will not develop completely without institutional support. That is to say, there will be need for focal organizations, such as government agencies, trade associations, and consumer defense groups, or all combined to make the codes explicit, to iterate their doctrine and to make their presence felt. Given that help, I think the emergence of ethical codes on matters such as safety at least, is possible. One positive factor here is something that is a negative factor in other contexts, namely that our economic organization is to such a large extent composed of large firms. The corporation is no longer a single individual; it is a social organization with internal social ties and internal pressures for acceptability and esteem. The individual members of the corporation are not only parts of the corporation but also members of a larger society whose esteem is desired. Power in a large corporation is necessarily diffused; not many individuals in such organizations feel so thoroughly identified with the corporation that other kinds of social pressures become irrelevant. Furthermore, in a large, complex firm where many people have to participate in any decision, there are likely to be some who are motivated to call attention to violations of the code. This kind of check has been conspicuous in government in recent years. The Pentagon Papers are an outstanding illustration of the fact that within the organization there are those who recognize moral guilt and take occasion to blow the whistle. I expect the same sort of behavior to occur in any large organization when there are well-defined ethical rules whose violation can be observed.

One can still ask if the codes are likely to be stable. Since it may well be possible and profitable for a minority to cheat, will it not be true that the whole system may break down? In fact, however, some of the pressures work in the other direction. It is clearly in the interest of those who are obeying the codes to enforce them, to call attention to violations, to use the ethical and social pressures of the society at large against their less scrupulous rivals. At the same time the value of maintaining the system may well be apparent to all, and no doubt ways will be found to use the assurance of quality generated by the system as a positive asset in attracting consumers and workers.

One must not expect miraculous transformations in human behavior. Ethical codes, if they are to be viable, should be limited in their scope. They are not a universal substitute for the weapons mentioned earlier, the institutions, taxes, regulations, and legal remedies. Further, we should expect the codes to apply only in situations where the firm has superior knowledge of the situation. I would not want the firm to act in accordance with some ethical principles in regard to matters of which it has little knowledge. For example, with quality standards which consumers can observe, it may not be desirable that the firm decide for itself, at least on ethical grounds, because it is depriving the consumer of the freedom of choice between high-quality, high-cost and low-quality, low-cost products. It is in areas where someone is typically misinformed or imperfectly informed that ethical codes can contribute to economic efficiency.

NOTES

Note: This is a revised version of the Carl Snyder Memorial Lecture delivered at the University of California, Santa Barbara, April 1972.

SELECTION 3

JAMES M. BUCHANAN
Public Finance and Public Choice

Recent developments in public finance provide a fuller
understanding of the public sector by adding to tax incidence
theory analyses of both the expenditure side of the government's
budget and the public decision making process. James Buchanan
summarizes late nineteenth century developments in the European
theory of public finance and the related post-World War II
evolution of modern public finance. The scope of modern public
finance encompasses a number of new dimensions, including
analyses of voting, constitutions, and the supply of public goods.

QUESTIONS TO GUIDE THE READING

1. Why did Wicksell warn economists not to offer advice as if a benevolent dictator were listening?
2. What nineteenth-century developments in the European theory of public finance were ignored in pre-World War II English language discussions of taxation?
3. What impact did the works of Duncan Black and Kenneth Arrow have on the research of modern economists?
4. How does the change in public finance brought about by the addition of public choice analysis raise new questions about a government program such as Social Security?

"Public finance," as a quasi-independent subdiscipline in the American academic setting, has been substantially transformed in the thirty years after the ending of World War II, although heritages of the earlier tradition remain, and notably as these affect practical political discussion. From its relatively minor role as one among many fields of applied microeconomic theory—akin to industrial organization, agricultural economics, or labor economics—public finance emerged to become "public economics," which, at least conceptually, is on all fours with "private economics," or, more familiarly, the economics of the private sector. If relative weights are as-

James M. Buchanan, "Public Finance and Public Choice," *National Tax Journal 28* (December
1975), 383–94.

James M. Buchanan is Harris University Distinguished Professor of Economics and General
Director of The Center for Study of Public Choice at George Mason University. He received a
Nobel Prize in Economics in 1986.

signed in accordance with relative shares in GNP, "public economics" promises, for better or for worse, to grow still more important in decades ahead.

My purpose in this survey paper is to discuss this transformation of
"public finance" from a public choice perspective, one that reflects my own
methodological presuppositions. I shall not include reference to the "theory
of fiscal policy," which bloomed brightly in the early post-Keynesian environment only to fade somewhat in the face of political realities. The macroeconomic policy emphasis derived from Keynes is a causal element in the
relative growth of the governmental sector and, as such, one source for the
increasing attention to "public economics." But there is no direct relationship between this emphasis and the fundamental paradigm shift that is the
primary subject of my treatment in this paper.

Post-Marshallian Public Finance

I can commence by describing the content of "public finance" in post-Marshallian economics, as limited to English-language discourse. Positive analysis was restricted almost exclusively to theories of tax shifting and incidence. And, indeed, as Marshall himself explicitly recognized,[1] the theory
of tax shifting becomes almost the ideal instrument for applying the principles of competitive price theory. Comparative statics offered a plausible predictive framework for analyzing tax alternatives. Within limits, and for certain simple forms, the economist could confidently predict the effects of a
tax on the behavior of persons and firms in the private economy, and,
through this, on the aggregate effects on such variables as relative prices,
outputs, profits, and industry structure in particular sectors. For this strictly
positive analysis, which could also yield empirically refutable propositions,
the economist had no reason to inquire about the political purpose of taxation, no reason to introduce external evaluation of alternative tax instruments.[2] This subarea of public finance, which is essentially applied price
theory, has continued to be developed through more sophisticated technical
analysis which has now moved beyond the Marshallian partial-equilibrium
framework to general-equilibrium settings, including extensions to open
economies. No basic paradigm shift has occurred here, but this subarea has
necessarily been relegated to a relatively less important role in the larger
theory of "public economics" which has emerged.

Alongside this post-Marshallian positive theory of taxation, there existed what I may label as the post-Pigovian normative "theory" of taxation.
This unfortunate and somewhat confused discussion stemmed vaguely from
the utilitarian philosophical tradition and had as its purpose the derivation
of normative "principles" for taxation. The most sophisticated of these, developed most fully by Pigou,[3] was that of "equi-marginal sacrifice," which
was based on a simplistic application of the calculus in a context of assumed
interpersonal utility comparability. This normative discussion was much less
rigorous intellectually than the positive analysis of tax incidence, and, indeed, the normative treatment of taxation among English-language econo-

mists was almost a half-century out of phase from the more sophisticated discussion on the European continent. The normative "principles" of taxation that were seriously discussed may seem bizarre when viewed in a modern post-Wicksellian or public-choice paradigm. But these "principles" assume continuing practical importance as soon as we recognize that observed institutions of taxation find their intellectual origins in these norms, which also, to a large extent, inform modern political criticisms of tax structures, along with continuing calls for tax reform. For example, the most vocal modern advocates for reform, notably Joseph Pechman and Stanley Surrey, base their arguments on presupposed norms for the distribution of tax shares, norms which are derived independently.

There are two related, but quite distinct, gaps in the normative public finance of the post-Marshallian, post-Pigovian tradition. There is, first, the long-continued, and methodologically inadmissable, neglect of the expenditure side of the fiscal account. The necessary interdependence between the two sides of the public-sector budget must be incorporated into any analysis, even if the purpose is to lay down ideal standards drawn from some external scale of evaluation. Secondly, there is the neglect or oversight of the collective decision structure itself. The shift in paradigm which has occurred involves the incorporation of both these elements.

The European Theory of the Public Economy

Following the central contributions of the early 1870s, the economic theory of markets assumed a unified structure. The simultaneous operation of productive input and final product markets accomplished evaluative allocative, and distributive functions. The European attempts to extend this aesthetically satisfying logic structure to "explain" the operation of a public as well as a private sector now seem to represent predicted increments in scientific progress. The puzzle in intellectual history does not concern these efforts; the puzzle lies in the long-continued failure of English-language economists to make comparable extensions of their basic framework or to acknowledge an interest in the continental efforts.

As early as the 1880s, Mazzola, Pantaleoni, Sax, and De Viti De Marco made rudimentary efforts to analyze the public economy within an exchange framework. Sax and Mazzola discussed the demand side of public goods by identifying collective as distinct from private wants. Pantaleoni extended the marginal calculus to apply to the legislator who makes choices for both sides of the budget. De Viti De Marco explicitly constructed a model in which the consumers and the suppliers-producers of public goods make up the same community of persons.[4]

The most sophisticated contribution was made by Knut Wicksell in 1896.[5] He explicitly identified the fundamental methodological error in the then-orthodox approach, and he combined positive criticism with normative suggestions for reform. Wicksell recognized the necessity of bridging the two sides of the fiscal account, and he noted the indeterminacy of any proposed normative principles that were limited to tax-side considerations. More importantly, Wicksell admonished economists for their failure to recognize the elementary fact that collective or public-sector decisions emerge from a political process rather than from the mind of some benevolent despot. His suggestions for reform were concentrated on the institutional structure for fiscal decision-making, on the institutions of "public choice." The unanimity rule was presented as the normative benchmark for efficiency in public-sector decisions, and a clear distinction was made between those situations where genuine gains-from-trade might emerge and those which involve zero-sum transfers. Despite the essentially normative setting for Wicksell's reform suggestions, the groundwork was laid for subsequent positive analysis of political decision structures.

Subsequent to these early contributions, work was carried forward, notably in Sweden and in Italy. Erik Lindahl's attempt to examine more closely the relationship between standard efficiency norms and the political bargaining process offered a halfway house between Wicksell's seminal effort and modern analyses of public finance in democratic process.[6] Lindahl's proposed solution, the set of so-called Lindahl tax-prices, or Lindahl equilibrium, has come to occupy the attention of several sophisticated analysts who have attempted to extend the modern theory of general competitive equilibrium to include the public sector.[7]

The Italian tradition, following the early work by Pantaleoni and De Viti De Marco, was characterized by an emphasis on the necessary political assumptions required for either a positive or normative theory of the public economy. The Italians devoted much more attention to the implications of nondemocratic political structures for the emergence and viability of fiscal institutions, on both the tax and the expenditure sides, than did their continental counterparts. These aspects, in particular, become helpful in the analysis of the supply institutions of the public economy, an analysis that remains in its formative stages. Apart from these substantive contributions, Barone and Einaudi, in particular, were sharply critical of the naive utilitarian framework of the English-language normative discussion of tax principles.

The Transitional Setting

The substantial transformation in American public finance did not spring full blown from some rediscovery of the European theory of the public economy, although it might legitimately be claimed that this theory, appropriately modernized, was sufficiently complete to have allowed for this as an alternative intellectual scenario. The transformation emerged slowly and in bits and pieces, influenced by several sources other than the strict analysis of the continental scholars. Precedence in presenting the central ideas of what he called the "voluntary exchange" theory of the public economy belongs to R. A. Musgrave who, in his first paper, offered a highly critical evaluation.[8] However, Musgrave's analysis was not such as to attract independent and complementary attention to the body of work discussed. And Howard Bowen, in his original and much-neglected 1943 paper, showed no signs of having been influenced by the European analysis.[9] Bowen's paper combined two elements that were to be more fully developed later as separate strands of analysis, the theory of demand for public goods and the theory of voting. Although flawed by minor analytical errors, Bowen's paper was perhaps neglected because it was too much in advance of the analytical mind-set of its time. My own efforts, in my first substantive paper in 1949, one that was also largely neglected, were concentrated in a methodological critique of the post-Pigovian normative framework. In this, I was influenced almost exclusively by a fortuitous discovery of Wicksell's basic work.[10]

Developments of note came rapidly during the 1950s and 1960s. These may be discussed initially in terms of their independent emergence, with little or no direct interconnection one with another and with the corpus of public finance theory. In what follows, I shall discuss briefly four lines of inquiry or analysis: (1) the theory of demand for public goods; (2) the theory of voting; (3) the theory of constitutions; and (4) the theory of supply of public goods. In each of these, I shall attempt to distinguish positive and normative elements of analysis. After these strands are separately examined, I shall try to integrate these as they relate to modern public finance theory. Finally, I shall use a single example to demonstrate how the modern public-choice paradigm in public finance differs from the post-Marshallian, post-Pigovian paradigm which, although conceptually flawed, continues to inform some policy discussion.

The Theory of Demand for Public Goods

As previously noted, there were two gaping holes in the pre-World War II normative analysis of taxation, a neglect of the expenditure side of the fisc and a neglect of the collective decision process. Modern public finance theory incorporates both of these elements, but they remain conceptually distinct and they were, to an extent, independently developed. An internally consistent set of principles for efficiency in the public economy may be elaborated with no attention to the political decision process. This was the framework for Paul A. Samuelson's seminal paper in 1954,[11] in which he laid down the necessary marginal conditions for allocative efficiency in the provision of public or collective goods to a defined community of persons. Samuelson extended the accepted norms of theoretical welfare economics from the private to the public sector of the economy, using individual evaluations as the building blocks. Perhaps his primary contribution lay in his rigorous definition of a "collective consumption" good, embodying both complete nonexclusion and complete efficiency from joint consumption, the two acknowledged attributes of "publicness." Early criticisms of the polarity features of Samuelson's classification were, in my view, misplaced because this initial step seemed essential before the further elaboration of taxonomic detail could take place.

The Samuelson mathematical formulation of the conditions for public sector efficiency did not contain a comparable normative theory of the distribution of tax shares. Income-effect feedbacks of tax-shares on individual evaluations of collective-consumption goods were incorporated in the analysis, but the tax-share distribution itself was arbitrarily selected by resort to a social welfare function. This normative construction is quite different from that which is required for the definition of the allocative conditions for efficiency. Within Samuelson's conceptual framework, resort to the social welfare function for tax-share distribution was an implication of his unwillingness to close the model in a manner analogous to the exchange process of the private sector. He did not conceive the fiscal process as one of "exchange," even at the level of abstraction that the formal statement of the necessary marginal conditions for efficiency required.

Nonetheless, the Samuelson analysis can readily be interpreted positively, which necessarily implies an exchange framework. In this case, the necessary marginal conditions for allocative efficiency become conditions that must be satisfied for an equilibrium solution to the complex "trades" that the political or collective choice process embody. One such solution is the Lindahl equilibrium, which meets the basic Samuelson requirements, although it is arbitrarily restricted in its distribution of tax shares inframarginally. The more general Wicksellian approach makes no attempt to specify particulars of an equilibrium. Instead this approach concentrates on the institutions for "trading," and implicitly defines efficiency to be present when all gains-from-trade are exhausted. In a setting of zero transactions costs, including bargaining costs, unanimous agreement will be possible on both marginal tax-share distribution and on the quantity of public goods to be purchased, although the position of agreement will not be unique and its characteristics will depend strictly on the path of adjustment.[12]

The Theory of Voting

The Wicksellian paradigm for fiscal exchange, ideally operative under a decision rule of unanimity without prior constraints on tax-share distribution, places the "public economy," methodologically, on all fours with the "private economy." The importance of this Wicksellian benchmark or starting point for the developments that have followed cannot be overestimated. But the world is not characterized by zero transactions costs, and these loom especially large when many persons must agree on single outcomes. The two-party dimensionality of private-goods training, especially as constrained by the presence of numerous alternatives on both sides of exchange, allows the costs of reaching agreement to be minimized, and, because of this, to be largely neglected in analysis. No such neglect is possible for the complex trading process that politics embodies. Necessary departures from the idealized models become much more apparent, and enter analysis even at the level of institutional design. Wicksell himself recognized, in his discussion of qualified majorities, that the ideal political constitution could not embody a strict unanimity rule, even for the legislative assembly. And, of course, historical experience in democratic politics includes a wide variety of voting and decision rules-institutions, only a few of which approximate the unanimity-rule benchmark.

Once the ideal is abandoned, as necessary for the operation of political decision structures in accordance with more inclusive efficiency norms, what rules for collective choice should be chosen? Before this question can be addressed at all, there must be positive analysis of alternative voting rules and institutions. From a current vantage point, in 1975, it seems almost incredible that American public-finance economists completely ignored analysis of voting rules prior to World War II, even though they must have recognized that fiscal outcomes were related directly to the political structure. Aside from the paper by Bowen, noted above, there was no discussion of voting rules prior to the seminal contributions of Duncan Black and Kenneth Arrow, in the late 1940s and 1950s.[13]

Black's earlier efforts had been strictly within the post-Marshallian tradition of incidence analysis.[14] His reading of the Italian works was an acknowledged source of his shift of emphasis to an analysis of voting rules. Black's major work was largely confined to an analysis of majority rule as a means of reaching decisions in collectivities. In his analysis, which included the discovery of precursory work by Borda, Condorcet, and most notably, Lewis Carroll, Black noted the possibility of the majority cycle, but his emphasis was placed on the workability of majority rule rather than the reverse. This emphasis led him to examine restrictions on preference domains that might produce unique majority solutions. He discovered that if all individual preferences could be arrayed over alternatives so as to appear as single-peaked, the majority-rule outcome will always be that which meets the preferences of the median voter in the group. This median-voter construction was to emerge as an important tool in the public-choice theory of the 1960s, and especially in public-finance applications. Single-peakedness in preferences becomes a plausible assumption for many fiscal decision variables.

Kenneth Arrow's work exerted far more influence on economic theory generally than did the closely related work of Duncan Black. However, the specific effects on public-finance theory are less direct. Arrow placed his analysis squarely in the social welfare function discussion that had emerged from theoretical welfare economics, and he demonstrated that there existed no collective decision rule for amalgamating individual preference orderings into a consistent social or collective ordering. This rigorous generalization of the cyclical-majority phenomenon, along with Arrow's emphasis on the impossibility of generating a social ordering meeting plausible criteria, had the effect of putting the analysis of collective decision rules directly on the research agenda of modern economists. Faced with results that they did not welcome, and with their somewhat naive political presuppositions exposed, economists were slowly forced to acknowledge that social welfare functions do not exist. Only two alternatives remained open. They might become public-choice analysts and examine the operation of alternative decision rules, no one of which is ideal. Or, they might revert to the normative post-Pigovian stance which requires the explicit introduction of private and personal value standards that bear little or no relationship to the decision-determining institutions of the real world.

The Theory of Constitutions (Voting Rules)

Once positive analysis of the operation of alternative voting rules was placed on the agenda, along with the Wicksellian recognition that no nonunanimity rule could guarantee efficiency in the narrow sense, the way was open for the development of a theory of constitutions, based on an analysis of the choice among a set of less-than-ideal institutions for generating collective outcomes. This was the setting for *The Calculus of Consent,* which I jointly authored with Gordon Tullock, and which was published in 1962.[15] This work carried forward the analysis of alternative decision rules, with emphasis on the political external diseconomies inherent in any less-than-unanimity rule and on the prospects for vote trading as a means of mitigating the results of differential preference intensities. Our central purpose was, however, that of analyzing the choice among collective decision rules, and of deriving criteria for "optimality" at this constitutional level. Our procedure was to shift backwards, to the level of choice among rules, the Wicksellian unanimity or general consensus criterion. The transactions costs barrier to general agreement may be fully acknowledged at the stage of reaching collective decision on specific fiscal (tax and spending) variables. But this need not imply that persons cannot agree generally on the rules or institutions under which subsequent decisions will be made, whether these be majority rule or otherwise. To the extent that individuals' future preference positions are uncertain and unpredictable under subsequent operation of the rules to be chosen, they may be led to agree on the basis of general criteria that are unrelated to economic position.[16]

Our analysis was positive in the conceptual sense, and we made few suggestions for institutional reform. Nonetheless, our discussion was admittedly informed by a vision or model of constitutional process that embodied individualistic norms. This vision was, in its turn, used to "explain" features of existing political structures, features which might, with comparable methodological legitimacy, be "explained" with alternative normative models. Our analysis of constitutions was not sufficiently complete to allow us to discriminate among widely varying explanations for the emergence and existence of observed political institutions.

The Theory of Supply of Public Goods

This gap in our analysis of the choice among constitutional rules stemmed, in part, from our neglect of the supply side of the public-goods exchange process. The theory of demand for public goods, the theory of voting, and the theory of voting rules—each of these lines of inquiry initially embodied the implicit assumption that individual demands for public goods, once these could be articulated and combined through some collective-choice process, would be efficiently and automatically met. It was as if the alternatives for public choice were assumed to be available independently from some external source; there was no problem concerning the behavior of the suppliers or producers. Governments are, however, staffed by persons who make up only a subset of the community, and any full analysis of fiscal exchange must allow for differences between the behavior of persons in producing-supplying roles and in consuming-demanding roles.

Precursors of supply-side analysis can, of course, be found in the Italian theory of public finance in the nondemocratic or monopolistic state. Models of this political structure were developed in some detail, models in which some ruling group or class collects taxes from the masses who are ruled and utilizes the proceeds to its own maximum advantage. But attention was also paid to the feedback or reaction effects on the behavior of those who were exploited. At the turn of this century, Puviani developed the interesting and still-relevant concept of "fiscal illusion," which he applied to both the tax and the spending side of the fiscal account.[17] However, aside from my own summary of some of these elements, which I did not sufficiently stress, there was no direct linkage between the monopolistic-state analysis of the Italians and the emergence of the modern theory of public-goods supply.

American scholars have operated within a continuing presupposition that their own political institutions remain basically democratic. Even within this structure, however, the demanders and the suppliers of public services must occupy differing economic roles, and the interests of the two groups need not coincide. The seminal American contribution toward the ultimate development of a theory of public-goods supply was made by Anthony Downs. In his book, *An Economic Theory of Democracy,* published in 1957, Downs presented a model of political party competition analogous to the competition among firms in an industry, with vote-maximization serving as the analogue to profit maximization.[18] The predictive power of Downs's model was sharply criticized by William Riker, who introduced a game-theoretic framework to suggest that political parties, even when treated as monolithic decision-taking entities, will seek to organize winning coalitions of minimal size rather than to maximize vote totals.[19] For purposes of this survey, however, the central contribution of these efforts lay not in the explanatory potential of the models themselves but rather in the fundamentally different setting offered for viewing the activities of governments. Once governments came to be viewed as collectivities of persons who were themselves maximizers—whether these persons be party organizers, political representatives, elected officials, judges, or bureaucrats—the emerging paradigm involving the passively efficient supply response to public-goods demanders was dramatically changed in course.

The Downs-Riker models of interparty competition, which have been carried forward and elaborated in more sophisticated forms by other scholars, were paralleled by the development of a theory of bureaucratic behavior, both at the level of the individual member of the hierarchy and that of the agency or bureau itself. Gordon Tullock introduced the maximizing bureaucrat, who responds to his own career incentives like everyone else, and analyzed the implications of this behavioral model for the control problem faced by those at the top of the hierarchy.[20] Even on the extreme assumption that the agency head desires to meet the demands for public goods efficiently, Tullock's analysis suggests that this objective could not be met in organizations requiring personal services.[21]

William Niskanen boldly challenged the orthodox conception of bureaucracy by modeling separate bureaus as budget-maximizing units.[22] The implication of his polar model is that bureaus, acting as monopoly suppliers of public services, and possessing an ability to control the elected political leaders through a complex and interested committee structure in the legislature, fully drain off the potential taxpayers' surplus that might be possible from public-goods provision. Once again, it is not the particular predictive power of Niskanen's analysis that is relevant for our purposes; what is relevant is the contrasting setting within which the operations of agencies and bureaus may be examined.

The theory of public-goods supply has not been fully developed, and efforts to integrate this theory, as it exists, with the theory of demand, including the theory of voting and voting rules, have only commenced.[23]

The Expanded Domain for Positive Analysis

In the four preceding sections of this paper, I have briefly summarized four main lines of inquiry or analysis that have combined to form the still-emerging subdiscipline of "public choice."[24] My purpose has not been that of describing the substantive content of these separate but closely related bodies of analysis; this would have required further treatment of the specific modern contributions in each area.[25] My purpose has been the more restricted one of sketching with a broad brush the separated strands of public choice theory in order to suggest how these have combined to effect the transformation in public finance theory during the decades after World War II.

Methodologically, the central element in this transformation is the dramatic expansion in the scope or domain for positive economic analysis. The subject matter of public finance has shifted outward; the economist now has before him many more questions than his counterpart faced a half-century ago. This expansion in the set of opportunities for applying the economists' tools, both conceptual and empirical, may be discussed in terms of specific categories.

1. *The Effects of Alternative Fiscal Institutions, Existing and Potential, on the Behavior of Persons and Groups in the Private Economy.* As I have noted earlier, this is the only domain for positive economic analysis in post-Marshallian public finance. The results of the public-choice transformation have been to remove this still-important avenue for investigation from its place of exclusive dominance and to put it alongside other significant and

equally legitimate applications of economic theory. This does not, of course, suggest that the theory of shifting and incidence, with expenditures added to taxes, has been reduced in absolute importance. The hard questions in incidence theory have not all been resolved, and these will, and should, continue to command the attention of economists.

2. *The Effects of Alternative Fiscal Institutions, Existing and Potential, on the Behavior of Persons and Groups in the Public Economy, in Public Choice*. In a relative sense, however, traditional incidence theory must be reduced in significance because other questions beckon. If the effects of a designated fiscal institution, say a specific excise tax, on the behavior of persons in private markets may be analyzed, what is to deter the intellectually curious and competent economist from examining the effects of this tax on the behavior of persons in "public markets"? If persons pay for public goods through such a tax, might they not be predicted to "purchase" differing quantities than they would do under alternative taxing schemes? Once such questions are raised, the need for answers along with the opportunities for research seem self-evident. An implicit assumption of invariance in fiscal choice over widely divergent institutional structures will simply not stand up to scrutiny.

The whole set of questions raised here stem from the "publicness" of the goods as these are demanded and consumed and as these are supplied through political or governmental institutions. Individuals do not pay "prices" for partitionable units of these goods. They pay "taxes," which are coercively imposed upon them through a political process, and this coercion is, in turn, made necessary by the "free rider" motivation inherent in general collective action. Few persons will voluntarily pay taxes if they expect to receive the benefits of generally available public goods. But what quantity will persons, when they act collectively in public-choice capacities—as voters, actual or potential, as members of pressure groups, as elected politicians, as government employees—choose to provide and to finance? This choice depends on the bridge that is constructed between the benefits or spending side of the account and the costs or taxing side. Differing fiscal institutions influence the weighing of accounts. What are the implications for budgetary size if taxes are spread more generally than benefits? And vice versa? Quite apart from the "true" distribution of tax shares and benefit shares, the "perceived" distribution matters. Fiscal perception becomes an important and relevant area for positive analysis. By necessity, "fiscal psychology" merges with fiscal economics. The research potential for positive analysis seems almost unlimited, and relatively little has been done.[26]

3. *The Effects of Alternative Political or Collective-Choice Institutions, Existing or Potential, on the Behavior of Persons and Groups in the Public Economy, in Public Choice*. A closely related, but somewhat different agenda for positive analysis and one that is more central to what might be called "public-choice theory," as such, involves the choice-making institutions themselves, as these may be predicted to generate fiscal outcomes. This is the public-finance application of the theory of voting, summarized above.

What budget characteristics can be predicted to emerge under simple majority rule? What differences in size and composition might emerge when general-fund budgeting is compared with separate-purpose budgeting, with earmarked tax revenues? What differences in the willingness to issue public debt can be predicted when the effective voting franchise is expanded from local property owners to all members of the local electorate? What will be the comparative levels of public outlay on, say, education, when these services are provided through a set of monopoly school districts and through the market response to educational vouchers provided directly to families? What are the effects of school-district consolidation on budget size? What are the effects of franchising bureaucrats on the level and growth of public spending?

These are only a few of the questions that have been, and are being, asked by those who approach public finance from the general public-choice paradigm. As these sample questions suggest, the domain for positive analysis here includes institutional analysis at a level where explanatory hypotheses are derived deductively from extract models, and also at a level where these hypotheses are tested empirically.[27]

4. *Analysis of the Behavior of Persons and Groups in the Collective Constitutional Choice among Fiscal Institutions.* This area for positive analysis is the direct public-finance application of the theory of constitutions, previously summarized. As they may be historically observed, certain fiscal institutions take on quasi-permanent or constitutional characteristics. For example, basic changes in the tax code are discussed as if these are expected to endure over a sequence of periods. Neither taxes nor spending programs are chosen carte blanche at the onset of each budgetary period. Indeed one of the primary difficulties in reducing the explosive rate of increase in federal outlays in the 1970s is alleged to be the high proportion of uncontrollable spending in the budget. Once the quasi-permanence of institutions is recognized, the analysis of fiscal choices is modified. Differing criteria for choice must be invoked, criteria which may be less directly identified with self-interest of persons and groups. The models which are designed to derive hypotheses become different in this context.

I shall not attempt to suggest research opportunities that exist in this extension of positive analysis, one that is perhaps less fully developed than the others. My point of emphasis in this listing is to indicate that at least three areas of actual and potential positive analysis now exist over and beyond the severely limited post-Marshallian field of shifting and incidence.

The Modified Domain for Normative Discussion

The domain for positive analysis in public finance has been greatly expanded. But what about the domain for normative discourse? So long as the economist proffers his advice as if some benevolent despot is listening to him, he may be much more willing to devote his efforts to persuasion based ultimately on his own personal, private scale of values, even if the argument is couched in quasi-philosophical terms. Despite Wicksell's clearly stated admonitions in 1896, this remains the setting for much of the normative discourse in public finance, even in 1975. If the public-choice paradigm is accepted, however, the assumption of the benevolent despot cannot accompany normative advice, even at the subconscious level. The economist must recognize that collective outcomes emerge from a complex political process in which there are many participants. Almost by necessity, he will be less willing to devote time and effort to persuasion here, even though his own personal convictions about ideal outcomes may be equally as strong as in the despotic paradigm. It should come as no surprise, therefore, that modern public finance is less characterized by normative advice concerning the "best tax" program and more concerned about predicting the effects of alternatives.

The public-choice paradigm does, however, allow for a parallel expansion in the normative realm of discourse. Once it is recognized that fiscal decisions emerge from a complex collective choice process, the economist may concentrate his normative advice on "improvements" in the process itself. He may, for example, say that direct taxation is preferred to indirect taxation, not because direct taxation is likely to be more or less progressive, but simply because direct taxation leads to a more rational choice calculus among voters and their representatives than indirect taxation. Similarly, he may suggest that withholding, as an institution, tends to reduce the rationality of the choice process because it tends to make the taxpayer somewhat less conscious of his costs. These are admittedly normative suggestions that emerge from a paradigm of the political world, one that embodies the democratic-individualistic standard that persons should get what they want so long as each person counts for one. This seems a more secure normative base than that which lays down criteria for choosing among separate persons and groups, in which one man must somehow count for more than another. These comments may, however, reflect my own personal normative biases and I shall not pursue them further in this survey.[28]

An Example: The Provision and Financing of Social Security

I shall conclude this paper by a brief discussion of a single example, one that is of current importance. I shall demonstrate that the transformation in public finance produced by the public-choice paradigm allows different and additional questions to be asked. In the process, policy discussion must be improved, independently of this or that economist's preferred set of norms.

Consider, first, the application of the post-Marshallian theory of shifting and incidence, along with the post-Pigovian norms for taxation. The social security system is financed by payroll taxes, and the shifting and incidence of these, both the employees' and the employers' shares, are proper subjects for inquiry. These taxes are, when viewed in isolation, "regressive," and this characteristic leads the post-Pigovian to denounce it on normative grounds.

Strictly speaking, this is all that public finance might have contributed to the policy discussion in the methodological mind-set prior to World War II. Straightforward extension of analysis to the other side of the budget, quite apart from the public-choice extension, would have allowed positive analysis of the effects of public pension commitments on the rate of private saving in the economy.[29] Similarly, the effects of the public pensions on retirement behavior might be analyzed. The normative strictures arising from the regressivity of the payroll tax might also have been tempered somewhat by the extension of simple incidence analysis to the benefits side, where progressive elements are significant.

The public-choice paradigm draws direct attention to the bridge between the tax and the spending side of the account. As quoted earlier, this bridge is influenced by perception, and even within the confines of payroll-tax analysis, the effects of the structural features on voter-politician attitudes become important. In the first place, the public-choice analyst would note the earmarking features of the financing; payroll taxes are earmarked for the social security trust fund account. This fact, in itself, strongly suggests that these taxes are viewed differently from other general-fund revenue sources. Secondly, the public-choice theorist would suggest that the withholding feature of the employee share makes payroll taxes less influential on behavior than orthodox incidence analysis might imply. More importantly, he would suggest that the employers' share of payroll taxes, even if ultimately paid by the workers, may not directly influence the attitude of workers. The suppliers of pensions, the authorities of the social security administration, may have been privately quite rational in their early arguments for making this employee-employer tax separation.

The public-choice theorist would try to predict the effects of a proposed shift of the financing of social security, in whole or in part, from earmarked payroll taxes to the sources of general-fund financing, notably to personal and corporate income taxation. Rudimentary analysis would suggest that the direct linkage between tax and benefit sides would be severed by such a change, and that both sets of institutions would be subjected to wholly different political criteria. Could pensions be kept related to earnings (and contributions) under such a change? Could a means test for benefits be avoided? Even if the existing structure does not reflect the operation of genuine "insurance" principles, taxpayer-voters, and their political representatives, may acquiesce in its continuance so long as the intergeneration transfer process which the system seems to embody is plausibly acceptable. Young workers who enter the system may not worry when they are told that the present value of tax obligations exceeds manyfold the present value of future pension benefits provided that they continue to expect that future legislatures will insure a reasonable rate of return on their total contributions. Such continuing support may depend, however, on maintaining the separation of the system from the government's general fiscal account and also on insuring that severe limits are imposed on departures from earnings-related benefits.

The public-choice economist, to the extent that he is willing to make suggestions for reform, seems more likely to suggest institutional adjustments designed to insure against the "political bankruptcy" of the system than he is to suggest that the payroll taxes be made more progressive. Whether the discussion takes the form of positive analysis or normative statement, the public-choice economist looks on the fiscal process as a complex exchange, which must involve two sides of the account simultaneously. Those who pay the ultimate costs of public goods need not, of course, be identical with those who enjoy the ultimate benefits. But, in democracies, the intersection between these two sets must be large, especially when the budgets are considered in composite totals and over a sequence of time periods. Regardless of political structure, the proportion of the community's membership that shares in genuine "fiscal surplus" is related inversely to the size and coercive power of the government's police force.

NOTES

Note: I am indebted to my colleague Gordon Tullock for helpful comments.

1. ". . . there is scarcely any economic principle which cannot be aptly illustrated by a discussion of the shifting of the effects of some tax. . . ." Alfred Marshall, *Principles of Economics,* 8th Ed. (London: Macmillan, 1930), p. 413.

2. Beginning attempts were made to extend an analogous positive analysis to the expenditure side of the fiscal ledger (see for example, Earl Rolph, "A theory of Excise Subsidies," *American Economic Review,* 42, September 1952, 515–27). But, as noted, the predominant emphasis was, and remains, on taxation.

3. A. C. Pigou, *A Study in Public Finance* (London: Macmillan, 1928).

4. For a brief summary discussion of the early continental contributions, see Richard A. Musgrave, *The Theory of Public Finance* (New York: McGraw Hill, 1959), pages 68–80. For a more extended discussion which is, however, concentrated largely on the Italian contributions, see my, *Fiscal Theory and Political Economy* (Chapel Hill: University of North Carolina Press, 1960), pages 24–74. For translations of most of the important contributions here, see *Classics in the Theory of Public Finance,* ed. by R. A. Musgrave and A. T. Peacock (London: Macmillan, 1958).

5. Knut Wicksell, *Finanztheoretische Untersuchungen* (Jena: Gustav Fischer, 1896). Major portions of this are translated and included in *Classics in the Theory of Public Finance, op. cit.*

6. Erik Lindahl, *Die Gerechtigkeit der Besteuerung* (Lund, 1919). A central portion of this has been translated and is included in *Classics in the Theory of Public Finance, op. cit.*

7. See, for example, Duncan Foley, "Lindahl's Solution and the Core of an Economy With Public Goods," *Econometrica,* 38 (January 1970), 66–72; T. Bergstrom, "A Scandinavian Consensus Solution for Efficient Income Distribution Among Nonmalevolent Consumers," *Journal of Economic Theory,* 4 (December 1970), 383–98; D. J. Roberts, "The Lindahl Solution for Economies With Public Goods," *Journal of Public Economics,* 3 (February 1974), 23–42.

8. H. A. Musgrave, "The Voluntary Exchange Theory of Public Economy," *Quarterly Journal of Economics,* 53 (February 1938), 213–37.

9. Howard R. Bowen, "The Interpretation of Voting in the Allocation of Resources," *Quarterly Journal of Economics,* 58 (November 1943), 27–48.

10. See my "The Pure Theory of Government Finance: A Suggested Approach," *Journal of Political Economy,* LVII (December 1949), 496–505, reprinted in my *Fiscal Theory and Political Economy, op. cit.,* pp. 8–23.

    I may add here an autobiographical note concerning this discovery that will be familiar to my students and former colleagues but which may deserve wider dissemination. In the summer of 1948, having finished my dissertation and fresh from having passed the German-language requirement, I spent some weeks wandering about the stacks in Harper Memorial Library at the University of Chicago. By chance, I picked up Wicksell's *Finanztheoretische Untersuchungen,* a book that had never been assigned or even so much as mentioned in my graduate courses, and, as I later ascertained, one of the very few copies in the United States. Quite literally, this book was responsible directly for the paradigm shift that I experienced.

11. Paul A. Samuelson, "The Pure Theory of Public Expenditure," *Review of Economics and Statistics,* XXXVI (November 1954), 387–89.

12. My book, *The Demand and Supply of Public Goods* (Chicago: Rand McNally, 1968), develops public-goods theory in the Wicksellian framework. The book's title is somewhat misleading; the analysis is almost exclusively devoted to the demand side; the supply side is neglected.

13. Their first papers appeared in 1948 and 1950, respectively. See, Duncan Black, "On the Rationale of Group Decision Making," *Journal of Political Economy,* LVI (February 1948), 23–34; Kenneth Arrow, "A Difficulty in the Concept of Social Welfare," *Journal of Political Economy,* LVIII (August 1950), 328–46.

    These were followed by their full-length works. See Kenneth J. Arrow, *Social Choice and Individual Values* (New York: Wiley, 1951); Duncan Black, *The Theory of Committees and Elections* (Cambridge: Cambridge University Press, 1958).

14. Duncan Black, *The Incidence of Income Taxes* (London: Macmillan, 1939).

15. James M. Buchanan and Gordon Tullock, *The Calculus of Consent* (Ann Arbor: University of Michigan Press, 1962).

16. The setting for our analysis has an obvious affinity to that which is used by John Rawls in his derivation of the principles of justice, a setting that has been made familiar since the publication of Rawls's treatise [John Rawls, *A Theory of Justice* (Cambridge: Harvard University Press, 1971)]. Although our approach was independently developed, Rawls had employed the "veil of ignorance" in earlier papers in the 1950s. Other scholars have used essentially similar devices as a means of moving from the individual's short-term interest to which may be called, in one sense, the "public interest."

17. For a summary discussion of Puviani's contribution, along with a treatment of fiscal illusion more generally, see my, *Public Finance in Democratic Process* (Chapel Hill: University of North Carolina Press, 1967), Chapter 10. An English translation of Puviani's basic work will be published in 1976, under the supervision of my colleague, Charles Goetz.

18. Anthony Downs, *An Economic Theory of Democracy* (New York: Harper, 1957).

19. William H. Riker, *The Theory of Political Coalitions* (New Haven: Yale University Press, 1962).

20. Gordon Tullock, *The Politics of Bureaucracy* (Washington: Public Affairs Press, 1965).

21. Tullock's analysis of the bureaucrat represents perhaps the closest that public-choice analysis comes to a parallel, but quite different, development in modern economic theory, that which has been called the theory of property rights. The latter work of Alchian, McKean, Demsetz, Pejovich, and others, has been concentrated on predicting the effects of differing reward-penalty structures, as defined in terms of rights to property, on individual behavior. For a summary, see, Eirik Furubotn and Svetozar Pejovich, "Property Rights and Economic Theory: A Survey of Recent Literature," *Journal of Economic Literature*, X (December 1972), 1137–1162.

22. William Niskanen, *Bureaucracy and Representative Government* (Chicago: Aldine, 1971).

23. Two introductory attempts should be noted: Albert Breton, *The Economic Theory of Representative Government* (Chicago: Aldine, 1974); and Randall Bartlett, *Economic Foundations of Political Power* (New York: Free Press, 1973).

24. Because of space limits, I have not included a fifth line of analysis, that of locational public choice, or "voting with the feet," which has exerted a significant influence on public finance theory, especially as applied to local governments and to the interrelations among levels of government. The seminal paper which stimulated much of this analysis was that by Charles Tiebout, "The Pure Theory of Local Expenditure," *Journal of Political Economy*, LXIV (October 1956), 416–24.

25. For a more extensive survey paper which does have this as its objective, see, Dennis Mueller, "Public Choice: A Survey," *Journal of Economic Literature* (forthcoming).

26. My own book, *Public Finance in Democratic Process* (1967), *op. cit.*, is largely a call for such research, along with a summary of some initial efforts, and the provision of a suggested research agenda.

27. Some of the early applications are contained in the separate studies included in the volume, *Theory of Public Choice*, edited by James M. Buchanan and Robert Tollison (Ann Arbor: University of Michigan Press, 1972). For a textbook in public economics that consistently employs a fiscal choice paradigm, see Richard E. Wagner, *The Public Economy* (Chicago: Markham, 1973).

28. My methodological views are developed in several of my books, some of which have been noted. In my most recent book, I try to examine some of the problems that emerge in trying to define "an individual," including the preliminary distribution of rights. See, my, *The Limits of Liberty: Between Anarchy and Leviathan* (Chicago: University of Chicago Press, 1975).

29. Cf. Martin Feldstein, "Social Security, Induced Retirement, and Aggregate Capital Accumulation," *Journal of Political Economy*, 82 (September/October, 1974), 905–26.

KARL BRUNNER AND WILLIAM H. MECKLING

The Perception of Man and the Conception of Government

These authors contrast different models of human nature utilized in the social sciences, focusing particularly on a sociological model and on "resourceful, evaluating, maximizing man" (REMM). They argue that the debate over the appropriate role of government, while often explained as arising from differing ideological views, can be attributed to these two alternative models. These models produce divergent assessments of the functioning of market and political organizations.

QUESTIONS TO GUIDE THE READING

1. Why would REMM behave altruistically?
2. Why is "sociological man" neither resourceful nor evaluating?
3. How do the REMM and sociological models of human nature differ in their explanations of criminal behavior?
4. How do the authors relate the sociological model to socialist doctrine?

1. Introduction

The long-run tendency toward expansion of government that has dominated social developments in the Western democracies for many years is attracting increasing attention from an array of social science scholars in search of a systematic explanation. This paper is an attempt to contribute a small fragment to that discussion. It addresses the rationale underlying conflicting views about the role, range and function of government. Alternative intellectual approaches to the "limits of government" appear to us to be critically influenced by the models of man employed by the various discussants.[1] The set of characteristics with which man is endowed in the development of social science theory inevitably controls the body of theory that is forthcom-

Karl Brunner and William H. Meckling, *Journal of Money, Credit, and Banking* 9 (February 1977), 70–85, is reprinted by permission. © 1977 by the Ohio State University Press. All rights reserved.

Karl Brunner is Fred H. Gowen Professor of Economics and Director of the Bradley Policy Research Center at the University of Rochester. **William H. Meckling** is Dean Emeritus of the William E. Simon Graduate School of Business Administration, University of Rochester.

ing. What is less frequently recognized is the impact that views about the nature of man have on the evaluation of political and market institutions.[2]

2. Alternative Conceptions of Man in the Social Sciences

While the various social sciences address many of the same or at least widely overlapping phenomena, the division of labor among the various disciplines—political science, sociology, economics, anthropology, psychology—is difficult to rationalize. To some extent it is an accident of history. Economics deals primarily with the economic organization and man's behavior in that context. Political science, on the other hand, examines man's political organization. "Sociologists concern themselves mostly with the social effects of cultural heritage, mores, customs, ethnic background, taboos, value systems, and social classes in modern societies. . . . Psychology embraces an almost endless array of more or less disjointed topics. . . ." [5] Organizational or social psychology offers a more focused connection with the central concern of social sciences, since it looks at man's behavior in specified organizational contexts (e.g., the business firm).

The various disciplines have also tended to establish claims to specified subject areas. Crime "belongs" to sociology, markets and exchange to economics, government and political institutions to political science and primitive tribes to anthropology. Recent developments have somewhat blurred and eroded these classifications. Many economists, for example, have begun to write and research subjects traditionally assigned to political science, sociology, psychology, and even anthropology. For our discussion here, it will be useful to distinguish intellectual endeavors directed toward understanding social institutions and processes on the basis of the perceptions of man employed in those efforts. Four different models of man can be distinguished: A. REMM—Resourceful, Evaluating, Maximizing Man—the model of man developed in economics; B. The "sociological" model of man; C. the "political" model of man; and D. the "psychological" model of man.

These labels express the relative dominance of the ideas in the various fields, but the use of the models by various social scientists is not confined to the fields from which the labels are taken. For example, the political or sociological models of man are often encountered in the literature produced or arguments developed by economists, while at the same time, sociologists and political scientists sometimes use REMM as the basis of their research and analysis. The following summary of the characteristics of each of these models of man is largely based on [5].

A. REMM—Resourceful, Evaluating, Maximizing Man

The codification of the characteristics of man as a unit of analysis in economics is the product of at least two hundred years of research. While intensive attention to the formal codification can and has occasionally side-tracked attention from the underlying substance, this substance can be summarized in terms of three crucial strands.

1. Man is an evaluator. He is not indifferent. He cares about the world around him. He differentiates, sorts, and orders[3] states of the world, and in this ordering he reduces all entities encountered to a commensurable dimension. Things valued positively are preferred in larger magnitudes. Moreover, the evaluation depends on the context. Any given increment of a positively valued object suffers a lower evaluation as the total available to the individual rises. Man is willing to trade off in all dimensions. He is always willing to forfeit some quantity of any given valued item for a quantity of some alternative item that he values more highly. His evaluations tend to be transitive, expressing a consistency in his value system.

2. Maximizing man recognizes that all resources are limited, including his own time. Whatever his resources, man attempts to achieve the best position he can under the constraints facing him. This optimization occurs on the basis of less than perfect information, and it recognizes that decision making itself involves costs.

3. The resourceful aspect of man is analytically the most troublesome to handle. Resourcefulness emerges whenever man is confronted with new and unfamiliar opportunities, or when man searches for ways to modify the constraints and opportunities. Coping, groping, and learning all express man's resourcefulness and form an essential aspect of his systematic behavior.

The REMM model does not describe man as a brainy, but heartless calculating machine. Charitable behavior, love of family, compassions, can be consistently subsumed. Man appears as a search organism, responding systematically to incentives and stimuli. These are systematically associated with institutional arrangements surrounding man. Market and nonmarket institutions can be analyzed in terms of the incentives structures they generate. In contrast with the other models, the REMM model explains man's behavior as a consequence of interaction between the *individual's* value system and constraints or opportunities. This formulation is usually supplemented with the assumption that the variability of the constraining conditions dominates the variability of the preference system.[4] Changes in behavior are thus dominantly attributed to variations in opportunities and not to variations in values.[5]

The basic ideas of the REMM model were introduced more than two hundred years ago by Mandeville, Ferguson, and Adam Smith. The idea of REMM was an essential building block in the analysis that led them to conclude that a social equilibrium results as an unintended by-product of the interaction of self-seeking men.

B. The Sociological Model of Man

"Sociological man is conformist and conventional. His behavior is a product of his cultural environment; the taboos, customs, mores, traditions, etc., of the society in which he is born and raised. . . . If behavior is determined by acculturation, then choice, or purpose, or conscious adaptation are meaningless. . . . Sociological man is not an *evaluator,* any more than ants, bees and termites are evaluators." [5]

Cultural conditions and historical forces certainly affect human behavior, but the sociological and the REMM model differ in their treatment of this effect. In the REMM model acculturation conditions the constraints and the preferences of the individual in his coping, groping, and interested behavior. In contrast, the sociological model asserts that individual behavior is directly determined by social factors and cultural conditions. Man is neither resourceful nor an evaluator, he is a conformist enslaved by conventions.

Structuralist interpretations of sociology reveal some basic properties of the model. Members of a society are essentially viewed as role players. Society determines an array of social positions that determine roles assumed by members of society with specific role obligations. Social anticipations concerning the performance of specific role obligations are supplemented with appropriate sanctions to assure adequate performance. The interaction between social positions, role anticipations, and sanctions determines individual behavior. There is no room for adaptive creativity, or for evaluating responses to incentives. The sociological model attributes a crucial significance to the exogenous existence of social values and social norms. These values and norms establish the social order independently of individuals.

The sociological view of man is particularly prominent in Marxian writings. Lukasz stresses the role of "social totality" as an entity above and beyond all individuals and their interaction. This view is repeated by Adorno, who maintains that all social phenomena, including the individual, depend on the social totality. Others argue that a reduction of social phenomena to the behavior of men, i.e., the explanation of social phenomena in terms of individual behavior, is basically false and inadmissible. These scholars insist that individual behavior be traced to a social whole. Society determines individual behavior, not the other way around.[6]

The impact that the use of alternative models of man has upon the analysis of social phenomena and attitudes toward such phenomena is nowhere more apparent than in matters concerning crime. Those who start with a sociological view of man regard criminal activity as a reflection of the social environment. The sociological model fosters the view that society creates crime; that crime is the unavoidable consequence of particular types of social order exogenously imposed on individuals. This view denies that the range and frequency of criminal activities depends on opportunities. Actions designed to modify relative opportunities (i.e., changes in expected costs and gains of criminal activities) are useless given the sociological interpre-

tation of crime. Punishment itself is also useless. Crime can be brought under control only by changes in the social environment. Conviction of criminals can only be justified as a means of social rehabilitation. If conviction
and deprivation of liberty palpably fail to rehabilitate, the rationale for conviction disappears. In one of the more extreme modern variants, the sociological model transforms criminals into more or less conscious political ac-
tivists responding to a brutalizing social environment.

While the REMM model does not deny the role of social institutions, it
directs attention to other factors. In particular, it directs attention to the
individual's resourceful adjustment to relative opportunities—to the conditions shaping expected gains and costs associated with criminal and alternative activities. It suggests examination of the legal system, and how its
operation lowers or raises the probabilities of conviction and of various degrees of punishment. It also leads to the study of the incentives shaping the
behavior of policemen, judges, and prosecutors functioning in the legal system.[7] It is hardly surprising that the policy conclusions drawn from the two
alternative conceptions differ so radically.

C. Political Man

Political man is an evaluator and maximizer, but he evaluates and maximizes
on behalf of the public interest, rather than his own. Political man predom-
inates in public policy discussions, where goodwill or public interest guides
the behavior of politicians, legislators, and functionaries in the bureaucracy.
An increasing number of economists and political scientists have turned
their attention in the past ten years to developing a better body of theory
explaining the results produced by the political sector. Many of these attempts abandon the public interest theory and admit a measure of self-seeking behavior. Legislators are assumed to maximize their chances of reelection, or incumbent parties to maximize the proportion of votes cast in their
favor. While these formulations approximate the REMM model, they are not
identical to individual welfare maximization. Moreover, the public interest
theory of political behavior continues to be widely employed by social scientists though in a subtle implicit manner. Thus, one of the favorite pastimes
of economists is searching for circumstances (externalities, public goods,
moral hazards) in which markets are nonoptimal. Once such circumstances
are found, it is customary to jump immediately to the conclusion that government should intervene.[8] Government is the deus ex machina that can be
relied upon to remove negative external effects and produce positive external effects. Moreover, normative statements involving optimization of social
aggregates (optimal rate of inflation, optimal budgeting, optimal consumption and capital accumulation, etc.) are converted into positive statements
about the world by suitable conjunction with a public interest theory. Much
of the so-called theory of economic policy only makes sense in the context
of a public interest theory.[9]

D. Psychological Man

Psychological man differs both from sociological man and REMM because his evaluations are incommensurable. His valuations are structured in a hierarchy. His needs are absolute. He will not trade off some of one source of value, e.g., physical hunger for another, e.g., security, until the former is completely satisfied. The psychological model of man produces an array of ad hoc motivational explanations with little systematic analytic coherence. Moreover, these motivational explanations are usually incompatible with evaluating trade-offs and with the notion of resourceful search to adjust relative opportunities. This sketch of psychological man is included for the sake of completeness, but will not be used in the subsequent discussion.

3. The Role of the Perception of Man for the Conception of Society and Government

In the following three sections we attempt to clarify the role played by the conception of man in social and political discussions. Socialist doctrine and the liberal doctrine respectively offer excellent vehicles for this purpose. In the last section the problem of corruption provides a specific example showing how the sociological and REMM models yield fundamentally different evaluations of governmental institutions.

A. Socialist Doctrine

1. The Ideal Socialist State.   The vision of the ideal socialist state has an important influence in contemporary society. It conditions the views of the intellectual establishment in Western societies in many and often very subtle ways. The socialist argument opens with a moral condemnation of the capitalist system. Market economies are inherently evil. They destroy man and prevent the development of his human faculties. Capitalist societies are suffused with commercial values that dominate human relations. These values obstruct the evolution of finer values. Men become the tools of corporate interests; and corporations are compelled by their place in the social totality to pursue dehumanizing behavior.

This perception of economies organized on the basis of markets, private property and voluntary exchanges is juxtaposed to the socialist vision of a New Society. This New Society is egalitarian and assembles men in a communal fraternity. It opens avenues for man's perfectability and the realization of his full human faculties. The prehistory of man in capitalism will be ended with the advent of the socialist state, and the true history of true man will emerge. The vision emphasizes the change in man's attitudes and nature that unavoidably occurs in the new society replacing the old capitalist system. The socialist argument looks to a society with men "acting according to finer motives than accumulation, to better values than manipulation, and evolving an ethic beyond the appetite of self" (attributed to Irwin Howe in

[6]). An authentic socialism introduces a cooperative fraternity and equality without the individual competition so pernicious to finer human values.

2. Sociological Man in the Socialist Vision.   Although this general theme has many variations, the essence of the argument is clear. The sociological model of man plays a crucial role in this socialist argument. The evil and injustice of capitalism are built into the social order. Men ensnared and enmeshed in the system are shaped by the social pressures of this totality. They cannot avoid behaving according to a pattern imposed by society. They are compelled to pursue roles determined by the social positions they have been allotted. The uselessness of efforts to patch up the market system is a natural consequence of this view.

In a curious way, the sociological model attributes self-seeking behavior to men in commercialized societies. Self-seeking, of course, really means economic man in the narrowest and meanest sense. But more than that, such behavior is not a matter of conscious choice on the part of individuals, nor a part of man's nature given the fact of scarcity. Self-seeking behavior is imposed by the social totality. Man is self-seeking in the same sense that ants and termites are self-seeking, but his self-seeking behavior is not genetic nor purposeful. It is culturally determined, in particular, by the existence of markets, private property, and exchange.

In centering attention on the "Produktiansverhaltsuisse," the pattern of ownership in nonhuman resources, self-seeking behavior is equated with the profit motive and the predominance of commercial values. The theologian Niebuhr exemplifies this position with his admonition that self-interest is the cause of injustice and conflict. He argues that "the power residing in economic ownership cannot be made responsible" and, therefore, "must be destroyed." Self-seeking behavior and irresponsible control over resources will only disappear with a change in the social order, and the sociological model of man assures us that a new society will generate a new life-style, liberating man from the bonds of self-seeking behavior. Neither vision nor argument expresses any doubt that the restructuring of society with the abolition of private property will create a man with a new moral vision.

The apparent perfectability and malleability of man's basic nature, which is inherent in all socialist arguments, follows directly from the sociological model. In the Marxian versions, this result is linked with the materialist interpretation of history. Marx's interpretation of history depends crucially on the class struggle, which is nothing more than the reduction of individual behavior to the social totality. The social totality as an entity sui generis exhibits an Eigengesetzlichkeit, i.e., is subject to its own laws, independent of interacting individual behavior. This Eigengesetzlichkeit is expressed by the laws of motion of history, which move the social process to its eschatological fulfillment. Sociological man is a crucial ingredient. He is a necessary condition to the social Eigengesetzlichkeit. With the individualist approach properly exorcised, an explanation of the social totality can only occur in terms of an Eigengesetzlichker process, subject to its own and independent laws of historical motion. Moreover, these laws imply that all specifically social laws are relativized to a phase in history characterized by the prevailing social order. This relativization of social laws assures an opportunity for alterations in the behavior of an essentially malleable man.[10]

3. Socialist Doctrine and the Emergence of Social Order.   Beginning with the work of the Scottish philosophers, economic analysis has demonstrated that social order (equilibrium) emerges from interaction among REMMs in the marketplace. Market conditions confront each individual as an objective reality, but the same market conditions are also the net result of individuals' actions. The usefulness of the notion that equilibrium emerges from the interaction among individuals is, of course, not limited to the marketplace, but extends to a wide variety of organizational structures, e.g., the political organization.

It is important to recognize the unintended character of this social equilibrium. The social order does not emerge from intentional individual behavior directed to *that* purpose. This unintentional consequence, so clearly formulated by Adam Smith, was either uncomprehended, overlooked, or rejected in the sociological literature of the nineteenth century. Since in every individual's personal experience consequences seemed to be associated with directed, intentional behavior, the idea that social order would emerge from the interaction of REMMs without direction was ignored or rejected. It follows that society, social order, and institutions are the "total alien, objective reality outside and beyond all individuals." Every individual encounters society as an external force imposed on his activity and life experience. This psychological impression was the basis of the social determinism more or less explicit in the sociological model. These impressions, combined with an implicit argument that consequences and intentions must be correlated suggested the thesis that social phenomena and the social totality are ontological entities beyond individual volition, and "cannot be reduced to individual behavior."[11]

4. The Socialist Doctrine and Ideology.   The socialist vision and the socialist critique of capitalism are never accompanied by a description of the institutional arrangements that will prevail, much less a searching examination of the impact those institutional arrangements would have. The REMM model has led to the construction of a coherent body of theory relating individual behavior to specific institutional contexts. It has (testable) implications for behavior not only in the context of markets, but in the context of nonmarket organizations as well. It implies, for example (in contrast to the suggestion emanating from the sociological model as it is applied in the socialist argument), that there exists no society and no social order without individual competition. Such competition occurs in very different forms determined by the incentives fostered by the prevailing institutions. In the presence of scarcity, human wants conflict. An understanding of this fundamental fact directs our attention to the crucial question: How is this conflict resolved? Markets and private ownership represent one set of institutions that resolve this conflict; nonmarket institutions represent another. What is the nature of the competition generated by alternative institutional settings? The REMM model explicitly directs our attention to a range of questions that cannot be addressed in the context of the socialist argument because of the fundamental nature of the sociological model of man. The fact that every individual's goals conflict with the goals of others is swept aside with vague allusions to fraternity and community.

The pervasive neglect of institutional arrangements and incentive structures implicitly fostered by the sociological model separates the socialist vision from all sense of reality. This autonomy of the vision should alert us to its significance as a marketing technique in the sale of socialism as a way of life. Brunner has emphasized on another occasion [2] that man is the metaphysical animal. For millennia, man has manifested a pervasive and persistent demand for sweeping, all-embracing orientations. The viability of these orientations depends on a felicitous mixture of factual references, emotively satisfying valuations, and vast inherently unassessable speculations. The orientations offered to Western societies by Christian vision and theology have been gradually decaying over the past few centuries, and in this century, have faded to a pale shadow. But man demands a vision, and socialism has thus found a receptive market.

The socialist argument as developed and cultivated by the new clerics (i.e., the intelligentsia) provides the necessary theology by combining factual references and valuational speculation in a viable new mixture. But this implies that it is useless to expect adherence to relevant cognitive standards in the socialist argument, or to insist that the vision be disciplined by systematic reflection on persistent patterns of human nature operating under specifiable alternative institutions. Such cognitive requests miss the politico-religious purpose of the socialist argument.[12]

B. The Liberal Argument

Though the socialist argument is more prominent in Europe than in the United States, it is also very influential in intellectual and political circles here. It is, however, what we might call the *liberal vision* that dominates the intellectual establishment in the United States. The very diffusion of the liberal position makes it difficult to summarize its content. We have therefore chosen a specific example, Okun [8], as a basis for our discussion. Okun's standing as a professional economist assures us that we should find the liberal argument presented with as much skill and balance as can reasonably be expected.

1. The Liberal View.   The liberal argument is cautiously reserved and somewhat suspicious of markets, or, more generally, of the role of voluntary exchange as a means of social coordination and organization. It recognizes that markets and exchange contribute to the efficient use of resources. It even concedes that efficiency results from REMMs interacting in the right (perfectly competitive) environment. But there is also substantial distrust of market institutions. They create inequalities, foster the appreciation of dollar values, and endanger the viability of noncommercial values: "The imperialism of the market's valuation accounts for its contribution, and for its threat to other institutions. It can destroy every other value in sight." The tyranny of the dollar "would sweep away all other values . . ." [8].

The "admissible" range available for market operations must be limited, moreover, by deliberate political action: "the basic transgression of the market place on equal rights must be curbed by specific detailed rules on what money should not buy" [8, p. 31]. Political processes and institutions are necessary to balance the social effect of market mechanisms and market institutions. The apprehension concerning the "one-dimensional human values" resulting from market processes are not matched by similar apprehension concerning the political process. "The good sense of public officials and professional codes of ethics" [8, p. 26] can be expected to protect the working of political institutions. There are allusions to some problems associated with political institutions and political control, but these concerns are vague and muted. The relative size of the government sector or the range of government activities does not threaten individual liberty or the range of individual choices. Private ownership of resources does not involve "the same kind of basic liberty as freedom of speech or universal suffrage" [8, p. 38]. Moreover, "the issue of government versus private ownership of industry has little to do with freedom, but much to do with efficiency" [8, p. 61].

This view of government is in large measure a result of the central role of egalitarian objectives in the liberal vision. The liberal economist recognizes constraints encountered in the realization of the vision. Efficiency is lowered and material welfare sacrificed. Government's central function is to make the liberal vision a reality at as small a sacrifice in material welfare as possible.

2. Liberal Doctrine and Sociological Man.   Okun's book shows clearly the intrusion of both the sociological and political models of man in the liberal argument. These models of man appear in the discussion simultaneously with REMM. Such eclectic combination of contradictory cognitive building blocks is characteristic of the liberal argument. The obvious contradictions are removed by suitably partitioning the argument. REMM is confined to market processes; political man operates in the nonprofit environment, i.e., in government; and sociological man emerges in the discussion of broad social issues. This partitioning reflects the influence of the central theme in the sociological model—that the social environment determines man's lifestyle and individual values. Individuals enmeshed in market processes are socially compelled to pursue dollar values at the cost of other values. Individuals embedded in the political process, i.e., politicians and bureaucrats, behave as political man. They act in the public interest, meaning in accord with whatever the particular expositor would like.

Okun's contraposition of commercial values and other values provides a classic illustration of the application of the sociological model. The normative appeal of the argument is enhanced by identifying REMM with dollar signs, i.e., with the pursuit of commercial values, even though REMM behavior is perfectly consistent with the list of ultimate values (family, marriage, friendship, love, etc.) that Okun himself extols.

The influence of the sociological model can also be found in the discussion of political rights. Business and wealth endanger these rights and produce counterfeit votes, whereas the political manipulation exercised by labor unions and other special interest groups are no cause for concern. The dangers to noncommercial values (such as family, companionship, friendship, and love) arise from self-interested behavior in markets, but there is no danger that REMM behavior in the political arena might stifle the cultivation of higher values.

Okun's vision of the good society parallels the socialist vision in its failure to specify what institutional structures will be invoked, or provide any analysis of their impact. We are told that "equality of income would give added recognition to the moral worth of every citizen, to the mutual respect of citizens for one another and the equivalent value of membership in the society for all" [8, p. 47]. Hardly anyone would use this language to describe the effect of *any* of the income transfer programs we now have in the United States. Surely the opposite would be more accurate. Welfare must be one of the major sources of alienation—alienation of the recipients from the welfare bureaucracy, alienation of the welfare bureaucracy from the taxpayer, and alienation of the taxpayer from the recipients. The REMM model suggests that egalitarian patterns will have to be coercively imposed, and it is hard to see how such coercion can be used with the felicitous results so lyrically proclaimed by Okun. He finesses this problem with sociological man. When the vision is realized we will all happily accede to equality *of outcome*. Acculturation will make it so.

The sociological model is also reflected in the tendency to lend organizations, particularly society, human qualities, i.e., to treat them as if they were individuals choosing and acting on the basis of their own objective function. Thus, we read, "society does not try to ration the exercise of rights" [8, p. 7]. "Society refuses to turn itself into a giant vending machine that delivers anything and everything in return for the proper number of counts" [p. 13]. "Society decides it will not let old people starve" [p. 19]. "It explains why the political process rather than the market place must judge the legitimacy of some preferences" [p. 78]. References to "the need for collective action or choices" whenever the "market fails in one respect or another" [8, p. 99] provide another example. The terminology "collective action or choice" obscures the fact that only individuals can act or choose.

What is different about different choice situations is not that some are collective and some individual. What is different is the institutional framework through which the choices are exercised. The "collective choice" terminology injects a Rousseauesque flavor with the correct overtones of goodwill and public interest. In a similar vein, we note that the "Consumer Protection Agency . . . is one worthwhile step to strengthen the public's power" [8, p. 29]. We are left to determine who that public is.

One of the most interesting facets of Okun's analysis is that he apparently understands the agency problem—the problem a principal has in getting an agent to maximize the principal's welfare—but he never realizes that this problem exists in government. Thus, he points out that "managers . . . have interests and objectives of their own, quite distinct from the profitability of their firm" [8, p. 42]. On the other hand, we are asked to believe that bureaucrats, legislators, the judiciary, etc., do not *"have interests and objectives of their own,"* or at least will not have such interests and objectives when the vision is realized. (This is discussed in [4].)

3. Liberal Doctrine and Political Man.   Okun's book skillfully demonstrates the usefulness of the sociological model as a sales technique in the political market. "Society," treated as an entity with human characteristics, appears as a guardian of the ethical principle. The discussion is sprinkled with normative admonitions—"rights granted by society ought not to be traded," [8, p. 25] or men "ought not to spend money for the purpose of influencing votes," [p. 78] or "the legitimacy of individual preferences ought to be judged by society," [p. 31] or lastly, that society should judge the admissible range of voluntary exchange.

Government's role as ethical guardian means that the political model of man takes on crucial significance. Because of political man we can safely expect the results emanating from the political process to coincide with society's (Okun's?) goals. The political model eliminates the danger that the actual performance of politicians and bureaucrats responding as REMMs to specific institutional incentives will violate the ethical principles expressed by society. Okun's faith in political man is unswerving. We are assured that "closing a bad escape valve (via the market) may be an efficient way of promoting the development of better ones through the political process" [8, p. 21]. We are also told that "absurdly low paid or risky jobs should be kept out of the market place." No concern is exhibited that the institutions replacing or controlling the market might introduce incentives that convert the initial intention into radically different results.

The public interest theory of government service appears with remarkable explicitness in the view advanced that "the safeguards against special pleading" or the pressures and temptations resulting from lobbying activities "must lie in the good sense (and informed skepticism) of the public official and in stronger professional codes of ethics . . ." [8, p. 26]. Because they are political men, officials will adhere to moral codes in spite of the incentives created by the new institutions.

4. The Liberal Vision and Freedom.   Perhaps the most important issue raised by the liberal argument bears on the relation between individual freedom and the role of government. The liberal argument generally denies any threat to individual freedom from an expanding government sector and the persistent replacement of market mechanisms with political institutions or processes. Okun asserts that the relation between collective and private ownership "has little to do with freedom, but much to do with efficiency" [8, p. 61]. The institution of private ownership can therefore only be justified in terms of efficiency [8, pp. 37–8]. It is furthermore suggested that the "misuse of powers by the government sector" occurs independently of the relative size of the government sector and its budget [8, p. 39]. The sociological model of man encourages this posture. Social dangers can only lurk in activities suffused with "dollar values." Whatever dangers exist in institutions that control nonowned resources or regulate private activities are easily exorcised with professional codes of ethics. The public interest theory of government behavior, of course, reenforces this view. With freedom dismissed as an issue, the private sector can be justified only on efficiency grounds, and the case for an expanding government sector follows more easily. Again, the issue is of crucial significance in marketing the liberal vision.

Okun's discussion of property rights and freedom comes down to a denial that private ownership has any relationship to freedom. He concludes that discussion with the statement: "Yet some people argue the case for private ownership of such items as though it were the same kind of basic liberty as freedom of speech or universal suffrage." That statement makes the error so commonly made by those who employ sociological and political man, namely, confusing normative and positive propositions. As a positive matter, the right to property, the right to free speech, and suffrage, are on all fours. In each case, the law simply provides that the police powers of the state will be used to ensure with high probability that an individual will be permitted to engage in certain behavior—voting, speaking, selling, or what have you. What Okun is really trying to persuade his readers to accept is the proposition that these various rights do not occupy the same moral grounds—that property rights, the right to own a house or car, for example, should not be valued as highly as the right to vote or the right to speak out. If he had put his proposition in those terms, he would have encountered a much less sympathetic audience. The implicit normative nature of his argument is less damaging to his views than his outright denial that rights in property are freedoms. Carried to its logical conclusion, his argument implies that we would all be equally free if there were *no* private rights in *any* property, e.g., if *all* property were held in the name of the state. He is led to this conclusion by an argument perfectly analagous to the following. If a law is passed denying Okun the right to reply to these comments, we cannot tell whether that increases or decreases the range of human freedom. His freedom (right) to speak out has been decreased, but our freedom (right) not to have his comments appear has been increased—ergo, freedom of speech, per se, is not a value that we must be concerned about.

C. The Case of Corruption

The problem of so-called corporate corruption has attracted much attention in recent months. This problem offers a useful vehicle for contrasting the results of an analysis of a social problem using REMM, and an analysis of that same problem using the sociological and political models of man. We are not here concerned with the question of whether or not the corrupt behavior is immoral. What we are concerned with is explanations for the phenomena. Unless we understand the institutional factors that foster the corruption, policy measures are likely to do more harm than good. Moral indignation, unaided by substantive analysis, usually produces measures extending the conditions favoring corruption or curtailing individual freedom of action without solving the underlying problem.[13]

Ranking members of the intellectual establishment have recently presented their views in two articles published in the *Wall Street Journal* [9, 7]. Arthur Schlesinger, Jr. contrasts a "self-policing" public (i.e., government) sector with a private sector apparently suffering under pervasive habits of corrupt behavior. Corruption in Schlesinger's judgment shows a clear case of delinquency on the part of business. The basic responsibility lies with the business sector. The low moral level of businessmen affects the government sector. Corrupt behavior by officials results from the influence of bad guys, i.e., the businessmen. All this means, of course, a "crisis in legitimacy of business." Schlesinger states moreover that "if business cannot clean its own house, the government will clean the house of business." He concludes with a warning that business must show a greater "capacity for collective self-discipline."

Ralph Nader and Mark Green argue that corrupt activities are criminal and should be subject to serious punishment. They also suggest that corrupt business behavior is the crux of the problem. Government corruption is a consequence of business corruption. A solution of the problem can be found, according to Nader and Green, with severe penalties imposed on businessmen and more extensive regulation of business by government.

Once again we see the influence of the sociological model of man combined with the public interest view of government service. Profit seeking is at the heart of the corruption. The involvement of government officials in these corrupt transactions is a "fall from grace," but is not inherent in the role government is being asked to play. To protect itself and the public, the government sector must extend its role and powers even further.[14]

A radically different interpretation of the phenomenon and very different policy conclusions emerge from an application of the REMM model. The REMM model directs attention to the large array of government agencies with arbitrary powers to interpret mandates and regulations. Shifting interpretations, procedures, and criteria can and do involve for "the clientele of the agencies" large capital gains and losses. Thus, controls and regulations offer an opportunity to the controllers and regulators to accept (or extract) payments of money or favors in exchange for favorable treatment.

Transactions involving purchase or acquisition of resources (including appointments of staff) or sales and disposal of resources (sale of land, supply of various licenses, etc.) also offer opportunities for government officials to engage in corrupt exchanges. The expectation of corruption associated with sales and disposal (e.g., licenses) are enhanced to the extent that the item supplied is officially priced below its market value.

A recent review of nationalized banking in India provides an excellent example of the kind of analysis of the corruption phenomenon the REMM model produces.

> Because profit criteria are, as a matter of policy, no longer being stringently applied to many of the banks' operations, opportunities for corruption also have increased and the chances of detection diminished. Once loans are made on the basis of social and political rather than commercial criteria these can easily be juggled to the mutual profit of the recipient and the bank official. . . . It is perhaps not surprising that the most popular Marathi play currently being performed in Bombay (*Kashi Kai Wat Chuklan?* or *How come you lost your way in this poor neighbourhood?*) deals with the problem of bank corruption in India!
>
> Even before nationalization there was, admittedly, a problem of fraud and senior bank officials were sometimes known to use bank funds to buttress their own private businesses. However, there were strong independent checks on them provided by the auditors, the government inspectors and the law courts. Since nationalization these groups are not radically separate bodies acting as a constraint on the banks from outside; rather they are all part of a shapeless inter-related government bureaucracy. Furthermore, there is no clear owner who loses by these depredations and who might be expected to combat them vigorously since his self-interest demanded it. Since nationalization, fraud has become democratic in the sense that far more people have an opportunity to participate in it and the new fraud-enfranchised groups have not been slow to exploit these opportunities. [5, pp. 1205–6]

The existence of potential gains from corruption does not by itself imply that the potential will be exploited. The extent to which corruption occurs will also depend upon the costs confronted by government officials, and those costs will be a function of the probability of detection as well as of the size of the penalties assessed if detected. As the article on corruption in the Indian banking system suggests, there are some analytical reasons for suspecting that the costs a government servant can *expect* to suffer as a result of corruption are lower than what his business counterpart can expect, probably because detection costs are higher in government. This is not inconsistent with the fact that most of the corruption that has been brought to light has taken the form of payments to government officials rather than payments to executives in other private firms.

Neither the inadequate analysis nor the sketchy evidence we present here on the corruption problem is intended to be definitive. We are simply trying to emphasize that the REMM model generates one framework within which to consider such questions, while the sociological and/or political models may yield an entirely different framework within which to consider those questions.

Concluding Remarks

The conflict between those who believe that human welfare can be improved only by enlarging the role of government and those who believe the opposite has occupied center stage in the social sciences for many years. Differences of view in that debate are often attributed to different ideological commitments. What appears to be ideological, however, often turns out to be substantive. One of the most important substantive issues that lies at the bottom of differences about the role of government is the perception of man used in analysis of social questions. In the social sciences two radically different models of man have come to be used: REMM and sociological man. Political man has been introduced as a special case derivable from the sociological model. REMM and sociological man yield substantially different analyses of the operation of political and market organizations, and have very different policy implications. Much of the conflict about government can thus be reduced to the conflict between alternative models of man.

These models contain propositions about man and his behavior that are in principle assessable. This assessability pushes questions of value, ideology, and social norms another step backward in resolving the disputes over the role of government. The dispute contains a cognitive core that we propose to emphasize in the marketplace for ideas.

NOTES

Note: This paper was presented by Karl Brunner at Ohio State University on April 30, 1976, in recognition of Everett D. Reese's contributions to the university. The paper has been influenced by many discussions with Allan H. Meltzer and Michael Jensen. We also gratefully acknowledge valuable comments offered by William Dewald on a first draft.

1. Normative views about the role of government are also conditioned by the conception of justice employed. An enquiry into the impact of alternative views of justice on political and social ideas is postponed to another occasion.

2. Professional articulators usually explain the dispute between advocates of severely limited government and the proponents of large and not clearly limited government in terms of different ideological commitments. This is a rather shallow and unrevealing answer. It is easily understandable, however, in terms of the characteristics of the "market for words" conditioning the intelligentsia's behavior. Of course, ideological dimensions enter all our intellectual endeavors. The occurrence of these ideological components does not justify per se the re-

jection of any hypothesis or theory. Whatever the ideological influences at work, the informative value of a hypothesis can only be judged by appropriate cognitive procedures.

3. It is often argued by the intelligentsia that "men are not concerned and do not care." What they really mean is that many men do not care as much, comparatively, for the things the intelligentsia is concerned about. Men differentiate and sort; and different men sort differently.

4. This assumption has been useful for explanations of many phenomena. It does not preclude an examination of conditions shaping preferences. The historical or cultural conditioning of preferences does not change the crucial propositions of the REMM model. Even changes in preferences are subject to REMM behavior.

5. The emphasis on variations in values is frequently quite confused; two senses of the changes in values are, in much of the social science literature, not adequately distinguished. One sense means changes in the preference system and the other means changes in location of the state point within a fixed preference field. The latter occurs, of course, as a result of changing opportunities.

6. A detailed analysis of the sociological conception can be found in Vanberg [12]. Vanberg's excellent study also covers the individualistic approach developed by Georg C. Homans. A survey prepared by Hans Georg Monissen for the Third Interlaken Seminar on Analysis and Ideology indicates, however, that variations on the sociological model dominate the thinking and work of German academic sociologists. Vanberg also notes the tension between the sweeping and essentially programmatic meta-discussions elaborating in general terms the sociological model and the ad hoc individualism emerging in allusions to concrete problems or situations. A similar point was made by Meckling in [5]. But these allusions are not subsumed under a coherent framework. They occur as loose, disconnected fragments violating the essential thrust of the programmatic orientation.

   The reader may also find useful information bearing on the thesis developed in the text in Tenbruck [10].

7. The reader may find an interesting description of the issue in [11]. Economists, using a REMM model, increasingly contributed to the analysis of criminal or illegitimate activities. The work of Gary Becker should of course be mentioned foremost in this respect.

8. One of the unhappy results of this practice is the enormous talent and effort regularly devoted to unearthing some new set of circumstances under which markets are nonoptimal. If a fraction of that energy were devoted to understanding political processes, the social sciences would be in a far better position than they are to say some useful things in the policy arena.

9. The reader should consider as an example the discussion of the relation between number of targets and number of instruments and the applications made over the range of policy problems, or the more recent analysis on controllability.

10. It is noteworthy that an endless literature invoking the laws of motion and producing mountains of discussions, meta-discussion and $(meta)^n$-discussions never formulated such laws. We obtain vague classificatory sequential allusions in a descriptive ex post facto mood.

11. The continuing prevalence of these views is nowhere more evident than in dis-

cussions of national economic planning. Thus, a recent advertisement, endorsed by Nobel Prize winner Wassily Leontieff, which advocated national planning, said: "No reliable mechanism in the modern economy relates needs to available manpower, plant and materials . . . the most striking fact about the way we organize our economic life is that we leave so much to chance. We give little thought to the direction in which we would like to go."

12. The development of Protestant theology within the last hundred years offers interesting examples bearing on the general argument in the text. Bartley [1] said, "The Protestant liberals considered revolution in human motivation to be the chief political need of their time." Liberal theology argued that motives of helpfulness and goodwill must replace the motive for private gain, selfless behavior should replace self-seeking behavior. Bartley continues: "The vague liberal assumption about man's dignity; and their Kantian belief that the obligation to do one's duty was a universal human experience, led many of them to feel that such a change of attitude was possible on a large scale. Few of them were definite about just what kind of social institutions would accompany that change. But they agreed that in principle social and economic institutions existed which would be compatible with the ethic of the Sermon (on the Mount). Human motivation and social justice could, in principle, be reconciled. . . ." [1, p. 34/35] Bartley effectively describes the substitution of religious commitment for an assessable empirical analysis of behavior under alternative institutional arrangements. The socialist theology continues thus a well-established tradition.

13. A peculiar immorality of professional moralizing can be observed at this point: They refuse a moral commitment to recognize the proper conditions for effective action.

14. It is noteworthy and typical for arguments influenced by the sociological-political model that corporate criminality is viewed somewhat differently than street criminality. Both criminals are the product of their social environment, but corporate criminality results from the evil greed of corporate profit motives, whereas street criminality results from socially deprived, disadvantaged and brutalizing conditions. The street criminal deserves compassion and understanding, whereas the corporate criminal deserves harsh injunctions and penalties. This attitude is clearly reflected in Nader and Green's piece. It is also remarkable that some legal procedures affecting Swedes accused of tax law violations are much harsher than Swedes accused of street criminality.

REFERENCES

1. Bartley, William Warren, III. *The Retreat to Commitment*. New York, 1962.

2. Brunner, Karl. "Knowledge, Values and the Choice of Economic Organizations." *Kyklos* (1970).

3. Davies, Christie. "The Shady Side of Nationalization in India." *The Banker*, 124 (1974).

4. Jensen, Michael C., and William H. Meckling. "Theory of the Firm: Managerial Behavior, Agency Costs and Ownership Structure." *Journal of Financial Economics*, 3 (October 1976), 305–59.

5. Meckling, William H. "Values and the Choice of the Model of the Individual in the Social Sciences." Paper presented at the Second Interlaken Seminar on

Analysis and Ideology, 1975. *Schweizerische Zeitschrift für Volkswirtschaft und Statistik* (Fall 1976).

6. Miller, Stephen. "The Poverty of Socialist Thought." *Commentary* (August 1976).

7. Nader, Ralph, and Mark Green. "What to Do about Corporate Corruption." *Wall Street Journal,* March 12, 1976.

8. Okun, Arthur M. *Equality and Efficiency: The Big Trade-off.* Washington, D.C.: Brookings Institution, 1975.

9. Schlesinger, Arthur, Jr. "Government, Business and Morality." *Wall Street Journal,* March 12, 1976.

10. Tenbruck, Friedrich H. "Zur Deutschen Rezeption der Rollentheorie." *Kölner Zeitschrift für Sozialpsychologie* (1961).

11. Tullock, Gordon, and Richard B. McKenzie. *The New World of Economics: Explorations into the Human Experience.* Homewood, Ill.: Irwin, 1975.

12. Vanberg, Viktor. *Die Zwei Soziologien.* Tubingen, 1975.

STEVEN KELMAN
"Public Choice" and Public Spirit

Are our public officials really driven solely by self-interest? Steven Kelman criticizes models of political behavior that assume people act only in their own self-interest. He argues that despite self-interest serving as a strong force in human behavior, there are aspects of public life that call forth public spirit. He emphasizes, in a vein similar to Kenneth Arrow (Selection 2), that ethical standards are crucial in defining acceptable and unacceptable public behavior. Furthermore, cynical descriptions of government behavior threaten to undermine public spirit.

QUESTIONS TO GUIDE THE READING

1. According to the author, what public policies are not primarily motivated by self-interest?
2. What support does Kelman cite for the view that some public policy is motivated by self-interest?
3. What motivations lead people into public service?
4. How do you think a better understanding of the role of self-interest in political behavior can lead to improved public policy?

James Buchanan has been awarded the 1986 Nobel Prize in Economics. In one sense, the prize is richly deserved. Buchanan has pioneered a new way of thinking about the political process that now comes naturally to academic economists and has made important converts among political scientists. Among his pupils and disciples in government he can count Senator Phil Gramm and Office of Management and Budget director James C. Miller III. In another sense, though, the award is a sad event. It features economists themselves applauding efforts to extend the reach of economic analysis far beyond the area where it is useful—in the analysis of the economy—into areas where the marketplace paradigm is inapposite and pernicious.

Steven Kelman, "Public Choice and Public Spirit," *The Public Interest* 36 (Spring 1987), 80–94. This material is adapted from *Making Public Policy* (Basic Books, 1987). © 1987 by National Affairs, Inc. Reprinted with permission of the author.

Steven Kelman is Professor of Public Policy at the Kennedy School of Government, Harvard University.

Some economists, such as Gary Becker of the University of Chicago (who may himself be up for a Nobel Prize soon), have specialized in escapades such as the economic analysis of romantic love. Others, like Buchanan and his followers, have specialized in economic analysis of the operation of the political process, an approach known within academia as "public choice." These efforts have one thing in common: They all start with the assumption that there is no difference between economic man and romantic man or political man. People act everywhere as they do in the marketplace. They are out only for themselves, and typically in relatively gross, money-seeking ways like the "pigs at the trough" David Stockman once talked about. Do you want to understand why government officials behave the ways they do? All you need to know is that they are trying to maximize the budgets of their agencies. Do you want to understand what drives politicians? All you need to know is that they want to be reelected. Do you want to understand legislation? Just see it as a sale of the coercive power of government to the highest bidder, like a cattle auction.

My own view is that this account of the operation of the political process is a terrible caricature of reality. It ignores the ability of ideas to defeat interests, and the role that public spirit plays in motivating the behavior of participants in the political process. (By "public spirit," a somewhat old-fashioned term that I consciously choose to use, I mean behavior motivated by the desire to choose good public policy.)

The "public choice" argument is far worse than simply descriptively inaccurate. Achieving good public policy, I believe, requires the presence of a significant public spirit in the veins of the body politic. Furthermore, one of the roles of government, separate from any specific substantive policies it produces, is to provide people with a forum where they may display a concern that they want to show for others. In addition, if the political process functions as it should, the process will serve as a school that helps mold character. For all these things to happen, a norm of public spiritedness in political action—a view that people should not simply be selfish in their political behavior—is crucial. The public choice school is part of the assault on that norm.

The Self-Interest View

The view that political behavior is dominated by self-interest has come to achieve prevalence in academic discussions through the extension of the assumptions of microeconomic theory into the analysis of the political process. Beginning with the assumption that people's choices are motivated by self-interested maximization (the effort to get as much as one can of the things one wants for oneself), economics has, in the centuries since Adam Smith, developed a remarkable body of theoretical propositions about the production and exchange of goods in the marketplace. These propositions have been powerful enough and (not unimportantly for scholars) often counterintuitive enough to earn economics the title of "queen of the social sciences"—and to generate a powerful urge among economists to apply the tools of economics to the analysis of institutions outside the marketplace. Thus "public choice" was born.

These efforts emerged with the publication in 1957 of *An Economic Theory of Democracy* by Anthony Downs and of *The Calculus of Consent* by James Buchanan and Gordon Tullock in 1962. Downs began his account with what he called "the self-interest axiom," that is, the view that political behavior is "directed primarily toward selfish ends." Following this general axiom, politicians, Downs assumed,

> act solely in order to attain the income, prestige, and power which come from being in office. . . . [They] never seek office as a means of carrying out particular policies; their only goal is to reap the rewards of holding office per se. They treat policies purely as a means to the attainment of their private ends.

Buchanan and Tullock began with the same behavioral assumptions as Downs. "The average individual," they wrote, "acts on the basis of the same overall value scale when he participates in a market activity and in political activity."

Common to all public choice writing is the important conclusion that, while pursuit of self-interest in the marketplace maximizes social welfare, pursuit of self-interest in the political process creates catastrophe. Different public-choice scholars have reached this common conclusion in different ways. Buchanan and Tullock, in *The Calculus of Consent,* argue that problems arise from simple majority rule, where the majority often gangs up on the minority to steal its property.

Another strand within public choice theory has emphasized the baleful effect of interest groups. The Chicago economist George Stigler argued that the propensity to organize will increase the greater the benefit each member has at stake and the smaller the size of the group. Producer interests, for example, which are often rather small in size and in a position to capture enormous benefits from government, will generally be better organized than consumer interests, since the number of consumers is enormous and the loss per consumer resulting from government policies aiding producers is generally tiny. A benefit of one hundred thousand dollars a year to a producer, if divided among one hundred thousand consumers, will cost each consumer only a dollar. The specific interest will thus win out in the political process over the general interest, even though it may be smaller in numbers.

The force of Stigler's argument applies to the influence of special interests, compared with the more diffuse interests of citizens or consumers. For earlier political science critics of pluralism, "special interests" generally meant the wealthy. The public choice analysis, emphasizing the benefits and costs of organization rather than the sociological status of the rich or the poor, sees the danger of special interests winning out over the public at large in many contexts, and not only when the special interests are wealthy. Special interests may include auto workers winning restrictions on foreign cars or even rifle enthusiasts winning relaxation of gun control. In all these cases, though, the political process will tend to produce inefficient subsidies for the organized at the expense of individually small (but cumulatively large) costs to the unorganized. In the jargon this is often called "rent-seeking" behavior.

Public choice scholars have also applied the self-interest assumption to the behavior of bureaucrats working for government, with similarly grim results. In his book *Bureaucracy and Representative Government,* William Niskanen saw bureaucrats as "budget maximizers." Niskanen argued that bureaucrats are in a good position to obtain large budgets. They are monopoly suppliers of public services that people want, and they have much more information than their legislative overseers about how much it really costs to supply those services. This allows them to claim they need a larger budget than they in fact do. The result of all this is that "all bureaus are too large." Buchanan and Tullock, in separate writings, have followed a somewhat different tack regarding bureaucrats and the size of government. Government grows, writes Tullock, "to a very large extent because the factor suppliers"—that is, people who work for the government—"are permitted to vote." They are a constituency for larger government and will inevitably elect politicians supporting a government that is larger than the median non-bureaucrat citizen would want.

Our "Single-Minded" Congressmen?

The public choice approach to the study of the political process began to migrate in a serious way from economics into political science during the 1970s with the publication of two of the most widely praised and influential political science books of the decade, *Congress: The Electoral Connection* by David Mayhew and *Congress: Keystone of the Washington Establishment* by Morris Fiorina.

Mayhew began with the view that members of Congress are "single-minded seekers of reelection." In a world where the connection between the behavior of individual congressmen and final legislative results is difficult to pin down, and where voters generally have little information about the behavior of their representatives, the single-minded concern with reelection produces two kinds of behaviors. One is what Mayhew called "credit claiming," which he defined as "acting so as to generate a belief" among voters that "one is personally responsible for causing the government" to do something voters like. A second is what Mayhew called "position taking," which he defined as "the public enunciation of a judgmental statement" on issues voters care about.

Both these behaviors have negative consequences for the results of the political process. First, it is easier to take credit for obtaining particularized benefits for one's district, such as a new federal building, since the claim that a congressman is responsible for, say, beating back inflation lacks plausibility. Second, congressmen suffer little disadvantage electorally if what legislation constituents want fails to pass, as long as the member is clearly identified in public with its support. This produces a government that is not necessarily too big or too small, but ill-proportioned. There is too much particularized legislation and too few laws dealing with general problems. Meanwhile, congressmen themselves are windbags, making impassioned statements in order to demonstrate to constituents that they "care" about issues important to them, while displaying an utter lack of interest in actually accomplishing anything.

Fiorina's book presented a portrait of politicians that is even more devastating, if that is possible. Central to Fiorina's argument was the view that congressmen can turn unhappiness with government programs to their own advantage by servicing the problems constituents have with the bureaucracy. Members of Congress have increased their ability to get reelected, Fiorina argued, by voting new government programs that created bureaucratic nightmares—and then helping constituents deal with those problems! Fiorina's analysis, unlike Mayhew's, does produce a government that is too large, for an activist government is required to generate the complaints from constituents that congressmen can then deal with and use for reelection advantage.

It is interesting to note the progression of brazenness that occurs from *The Calculus of Consent* in 1962 to *Congress: Keystone of the Washington Establishment* in 1977. Buchanan and Tullock, in their first book together, adopted a tone that was almost apologetic about their use of the self-interest assumption for the political process. Certainly, they regarded themselves as idiosyncratic; earlier theorists, they noted, had generally assumed that the average political participant "seeks not to maximize his own utility, but to find the 'public interest' or 'common good.'" This tone of humbleness, however, disappeared in later works. In an article published in 1979, Gordon Tullock noted that "the traditional view of government has always been that it sought something called 'the public interest'" but that, "with public choice, all of this has changed." (Tullock adds, with a bit of contempt, that "the public interest point of view still informs many statements by public figures and the more old-fashioned students of politics.") By the time Fiorina writes, what might have once been seen as conspiratorial speculation had become scholarship that is not only respectable but highly acclaimed. Times, and academic fashions, have changed.

In arguing for the extension of the self-interest assumption from the marketplace to political behavior, James Buchanan notes that otherwise

> man must be assumed to shift his psychological and moral gears when he moves from the realm of organized market activity to that of organized political activity. . . . [One must demonstrate that there is] something in the nature of market organization, as such, that brings out the selfish motives in man, and something in the political organization, as such, which in turn suppresses these motives and brings out the more "noble" ones. . . .

This is exactly what an alternate view of the wellsprings of political behavior maintains: There are features of public life that make it an appropriate forum for public spirit. In this alternate view, self-interest does not by any means disappear from political life—it is a far too powerful motivating force in human behavior for that. But public spirit has a pride of place that translates into an important role in the political process.

Public Spirit and Political Behavior

The best test of the importance of public spirit in the political process is the ability of ideas to overcome interests in determining political outcomes. If self-interested behavior, whether of popular majorities or of interest groups, would have dictated one kind of outcome, and general ideas about good public policy another, then the extent to which political choices reflect the ideas rather than the interests will constitute a strong test of the importance of public spirit.

Does self-interest in fact turn out to dominate the political process? It is no trick to come up with countless specific examples of situations where political choices have been crucially determined by participants furthering quite narrow selfish interests. Everyone has a favorite story of the highway that got built because a powerful member of Congress wanted it in his district or of a tax loophole an interest group sneaked through with few in Congress knowing anything about it. Certainly there is no lack of straightforward self-interested behavior in the political process.

As a general rule, however, the more important a policy is, the less important self-interest is in determining the policies we get. Self-interest helps explain the location of a new federal building in Missoula. When all is said and done, however, it does little to help us understand the major policy upheavals of the past decades.

How could a self-interest account of the political process explain, except through the grossest of contortions, the vast increases in spending for the poor that occurred in the 1960s and early 1970s? The poor were not an electoral majority, nor were they well organized into interest groups. (Public choice theorists sometimes point to the power of interest groups representing providers of services to the poor. The hypothesis that an invincible lobby of social workers overwhelmed a defenseless political system is, to put it diplomatically, idiosyncratic.) What about the growth of health, safety, and environmental regulation during the late 1960s and early 1970s? These programs were adopted against the wishes of well-organized producers. They were intended for the benefit of poorly organized consumers and environmentalists. (Much of the organization of environmentalists into interest groups *followed* environmental legislation, rather than preceded it.)

In addition, biases in the political process that public choice advocates believe produce a bloated government can hardly explain the *growth* of government in the 1960s and 1970s unless one can successfully argue that the level of bias increased during the period when the growth took place. Otherwise, the bias should have already produced larger government in the earlier period. Furthermore, the big increases in government spending since the 1950s have not been in grants to localities, which provide particularistic constituency benefits for members of Congress, but in various general transfer programs that do not allow members to demonstrate that they have gotten something special for their districts.

The self-interest model of politics does equally poorly in accounting for rollbacks in government programs during the late 1970s and 1980s. In the late 1970s, the greatest victories for industry deregulation were won in exactly those industries, such as trucking and airlines, where well-organized producers benefited from regulation and the consumers who would benefit from deregulation were largely unorganized. By contrast, little occurred in areas such as environmental policy where well-organized producers supported deregulation. In other words, the pattern of deregulation was exactly the *opposite* of that predicted by the self-interest model.

It is, furthermore, hard to see any one-to-one correspondence between the economic difficulties the country faced during the 1970s and the program of reduced government intervention adopted to deal with these problems. Economic difficulties in the 1930s had produced a growth in the role of government in managing the economy, not a rollback. Economic distress itself neither made government grow nor shrink. What made it grow or shrink was the force of ideas linking the problems everyone perceived with solutions that government could adopt. Furthermore, well-entrenched interest groups fought to retain each government program President Reagan sought to cut. Often only the diffuse interest of taxpayers in general stood on the other side. And, of course, President Reagan's success with tax reform is the latest example of the ability of ideas to overcome even the most entrenched of special interests.

The story of government growth in the 1960s and of its limitation in the 1980s, then, are both stories of the power of ideas. They powerfully reinforce the message that ideas have consequences and that persuasiveness is the most underrated political resource.

Between Cynicism and Pollyanism

The self-interest theories not only have a difficult time explaining most of what has been important in American politics over the past twenty years, they also give, at best, an incomplete feel for the process itself.

To be sure, the naive observer expecting public-spirited deliberation unsullied by parochial perspectives and even by some dirty trickery would hardly be prepared for Washington. But neither would the hard-boiled, street-wise cynic or his public-choice counterpart in academia. The self-interest view has no sense for the importance of being able to make a good argument, of having the facts on one's side, of being able to present an appealing public vision, or of having a reputation for seriousness and commitment. Yet all this clearly appears in descriptions of the process by close observers. For example, two journalists spent significant time following Senators Edmund Muskie and John Culver in the late 1970s, each to observe what the life of a senator was like. What is especially significant about their accounts is that journalists normally are inclined to expect sleaziness from politicians, and yet both these accounts found mostly substance. (Bernard Ashball, who wrote the book on Muskie, was apparently surprised enough by what he saw to title his book *The Senate Nobody Knows*.) Both volumes are filled with accounts of senators, mostly in committee settings and hence on issues about which they are knowledgeable, seriously debating the merits of proposed legislation. The accounts of committee markup sessions (where committee members craft actual legislative language) on Clean Air Act amendments, which take up much of Ashball's account, include surprisingly sophisticated arguments about philosophical and practical questions involved in the design of environmental policy.

The books both emphasize how important the ability to make a credible and convincing argument is for congressmen. "Real power" in the Senate, Muskie is quoted as saying, "comes from doing your work and knowing what you're taking about. . . . The most important thing in the Senate is credibility." Along similar lines, a group of freshmen congressmen, discussing their experiences for political scientists in the book *Congress Off the Record,* "made frequent allusions to the importance of knowledge and expertise" in determining "who wielded real power in committee and in the House."

The view that self-interest is key to understanding how the political process works is also belied by the influence of the media. On superficial examination, the influence of the media might be seen as consistent with the view that people in government are out only for adulation or reelection, since the way one is treated in the media certainly has an impact on attaining either goal. It is necessary to remember, however, that what generates good (or bad) attention in the media are generally actions where one either has sought to do the right thing or instead acted selfishly. If neither people in government themselves nor the voters who select elected officials thought that it was important to try to do the right thing in politics, media brickbats would be a matter of indifference to their intended victims. Sticks and stones could break their bones but names would never hurt them. The great influence of the media suggests, however, that failure to show public spirit indeed *can* hurt these people, in their own eyes and in those of others.

The Pocketbook and the Ballot Box

Moving now from the level of the system as a whole to the behavior of individual citizens and government professionals, how important is self-interest and how important is public spirit in describing their actions? The classic view in the early empirical voting studies of the 1950s was that the voting behavior of individual citizens was mostly guided by self-interest. This view was developed in works appearing in the 1970s on the link between economic conditions and election results. With the modern techniques of social science, these studies confirmed something most politicians already knew intuitively, namely, that incumbents do well in times of economic prosperity and poorly during times of economic distress.

In what has probably been the most interesting body of empirical political science research done in the last decade, extensive evidence has now been uncovered that questions this view. The connection between economic conditions and overall electoral results is indeed a very clear one. What scholars have now done is to move from the aggregate level of *overall* economic conditions and *overall* electoral results to the level of *individual* economic conditions and *individual* voting decisions. When they do so, the results are surprising. If voters vote their personal pocketbooks, one would expect those who have themselves become better off to favor the incumbents. Those not personally sharing in the prosperity would not be expected to display such a tendency. Likewise, in times of economic distress one would expect the individual victims of bad times to punish the incumbents. However, a series of tests by the political scientists Donald Kinder and Roderick Kiewiet, using individual-level survey data, has devastatingly shattered this hypothesis. Respondents' answers to a question about whether their personal financial situation has improved, worsened, or stayed the same over the previous year show essentially *no* connection to changes in voting behavior. By contrast, though, there are substantial correlations between a voters' view of economic conditions in society *as a whole* and the individual's voting behavior. This relationship holds even when one controls the effects of a personal economic situation on the ability to judge the overall economic condition. The observed connection at the aggregate level between the economy and the electoral success of incumbents results not from self-interested rewards or punishments from voters who have personally done well or poorly. The connection comes instead from judgments by voters about whether the economy *as a whole* is doing well, independent of how the voter is doing *personally*.

A conceptually similar body of research has been conducted by the political scientist David Sears and his colleagues at UCLA who have investigated how personal self-interest in a political issue accounts for attitudes on the issue. Thus, for example, these scholars have examined the extent to which attitudes towards the war in Vietnam were influenced by whether one had family or close friends fighting there. The findings are dramatic. Regarding attitudes on Vietnam, having a relative or close friend actually fighting in Vietnam had far less effect on views of what American policy should be than the respondent's self-anchoring on a liberal-conservative scale or his attitudes toward communism. Likewise, in another study, liberal or conservative ideology did a considerably better job predicting a respondent's views on government national health insurance or guaranteed jobs programs than whether the respondent himself was covered by health insurance or had recently been unemployed. In other words, conservatives who themselves had no health insurance protection were less likely to favor national health insurance than liberals who had coverage of their own. As part of a study on business and American foreign policy, the political scientists Bruce Russett and Elizabeth Hanson did a survey of the attitudes of corporate executives on foreign policy issues. They found that respondents' views on domestic liberal-conservative issues such as civil rights did a far better job predicting their foreign policy views than whether their company had lots of defense contracts or investments overseas.

One possible response to these data would be to suggest that politics is not crucially important for most people and that, therefore, it's easy to display public spirit in one's political attitudes because it doesn't cost much. On issues that really are important to people, including political issues, one might, according to their view, expect self-interest to hold sway.

I don't think this argument is incorrect, but I do think it is somewhat off the point. Certainly the evidence is overwhelming that most people are far less than obsessively interested in politics. Significant numbers of citizens have weakly held opinions, or no opinions at all, on many political issues. The point is not that people are saints, willing to sacrifice all for the sake of others. Having political opinions based on general views about the best public policies may indeed often be a low-cost form of altruism (although the cost in taxes may not be insignificant at least in the case where such views lead to government programs that cost money). Nor are most people philosophers or professional policy analysts. Views can be based on general conceptions of right and wrong without being particularly sophisticated. Nonetheless, in a world of many political issues and of an overall modest level of interest in politics, one can expect to find a strong reservoir of political input based on general ideas of what policy would be right. Such input is likely to be an important factor in the process.

I also agree that in situations where people have substantial personal interests at stake, interests that can be perceived fairly clearly and directly, and where some clear government policy will affect those interests, the role of self-interest in the political behavior of individuals is likely to increase. Interests groups such as the Synthetic Organic Chemicals Manufacturing Association, the National Association of Dredging Contractors, the Society of American Travel Writers, or the National Association of Scissors and Shears Manufacturers, which are everywhere in Washington, would hardly seem to have been brought into existence by public spirit. Their behavior can be held in check by public-spirited norms in the system, which affect the way interest groups present their demands and the nature of the demands they can make on the political system. Certainly, the political behavior of many interest groups constitutes the most important exception to the argument that public spirit is important in accounting for the viewpoints that citizens take in the political process.

Why Public Servants Serve

Turning to the behavior of professional participants in government—elected officials, officials of government agencies, judges—a number of comments are in order. These people receive rewards and bear costs far more significant than those of individual citizens casually participating in politics. For example, politicians get their names in the newspapers and on television. They may frequently be the objects of deference and adulation. And all those who possess formal political authority experience some of the feeling of power that comes from the ability to establish public policies with the force of law. But politicians also work very long hours, much of it on the road away from their families, for salaries that are relatively low for work with the responsibilities and time demands their jobs make.

What are the distinctive advantages that might draw people to government? It is hard to see the lust for power, in a general sense, as a *distinctive* advantage of a career in government. Business leaders, within their own firms, doubtless exercise greater power, with fewer checks, than do participants in the political process of a democratic society. "The search for the jugular of power," notes the Yale political scientist Robert Lane, "may very likely lead to the world of finance, journalism, or industry instead of politics." This does not mean that the power-hungry will avoid politics, only that there is no reason to expect that a particularly disproportionate number of such people will participate.

There are two motivations that are, I think, relatively distinctive to government. One (much more so for elected officials than for civil servants or even political appointees) is the desire for attention and adulation. Anyone who has dealt with politicians knows how important media attention can be to them. A second motivation is the desire to participate in the formulation of good public policy. People who go into politics for this reason may be seen as "seeking power," but of a special sort—influence over public choices.

The sparse literature on the topic of why people go into careers in government is not very enlightening, both because of the problems of relying on the self-reports of respondents and because of a tendency on the part of many authors to psychoanalyze their subjects. But the literature does at least suggest that public spirit is an important reason many people go into politics. The largest group in Duke political scientist James David Barber's sample of Connecticut legislators fits into the category he calls "lawmakers"—those who derive satisfaction from producing good legislation. The reasons top federal appointed officials give for going into government heavily emphasize the unique vantage point government service gives for making the world a better place. In a 1984 survey of senior civil service managers in the federal government, respondents were asked, "To what extent are the following reasons to continue working for the government?" Only 18 percent said that their salary was a strong reason for staying (or more of a reason to stay than leave), and only 10 percent said that about their promotional opportunities. Seventy-six percent, however, responded that the "opportunity to have an impact on public affairs" was a reason to stay. A study by Edward Lawler III, a professor of management, comparing the importance of pay for different kinds of managers concluded that "managers in industrial organizations place the most importance on pay; people who work in government agencies place less emphasis on pay; and people who work in hospitals and social service organizations place the least emphasis on pay." The political scientists Dean Mann and Jameson Doig report that recruiters trying to persuade people to take jobs as assistant secretaries, many of whom would be serving at considerable financial sacrifice, make heavy use of arguments about serving one's country. Likewise, they report that the ability to influence policy in the direction of one's policy views was a strong reason why candidates offered these positions accepted them.

Vocational guidance tests provide some interesting insights here. These help young people determine what careers might be appropriate for them through a battery of questions that test their interests and inclinations. The most widely used test does not include "politician" as a possible occupation, but it does include "public administrator." The cluster of occupations in which public administration is included, based on similar responses to the battery of questions, also includes the occupations of rehabilitation counselor, YMCA general secretary, social worker, and minister.

Also, it is worthwhile to note that the desire for adulation and attention does not necessarily work against public spirit, and, in fact, it often works in the same direction. Certainly, people driven by their self-interest are not likely to get far in the estimation of others, who have no particular reason to value the self-interest of another person. Indeed, the type of person who seeks the admiration of others to an unusual degree is one who is unusually likely to realize that others are important.

Nurturing Public Spirit

Clearly, government has become, for many, an appropriate forum to display their concerns for others. Why? That political decisions involve the community as a whole—and often future generations as well—encourages people to think about others when taking a stand. This is in contrast to personal decisions involving mainly oneself, which encourage people to think mainly of themselves when making them. Furthermore, political choices in a democratic society do not only involve others, they also require the consent and participation of others in order to get made in the first place. This requirement for cooperation reminds people of the need to involve others if they want to achieve their goals. Also, the requirement for the consent of others means that political argument inevitably must be formulated in terms broader than that of the self-interest of the individual or the group making the claim, since there is no reason for others to support a claim simply based on my self-interest. Even when making a claim that asks for something one personally wants (such as, say, a poor person demanding increased welfare payments or a journalist demanding freedom from censorship), the claims must be formulated in terms of general ethical arguments.

It is hard, however, to imagine that public spirit could be sustained simply by an accidental agglomeration of individual decisions to regard public spirit as the appropriate motivation for political action. Crucial to any ability to maintain public spirit is the continuing existence of a social norm that declares it appropriate for people to try to do the right thing in public behavior and inappropriate for them simply to seek to advance their personal interests.

Norms are crucial. They can also be fragile. Cynical descriptive conclusions about behavior in government threaten to undermine the norm prescribing public spirit. The cynicism of journalists—and even the writings of professors—can decrease public spirit simply by describing what they claim to be its absence. Cynics are therefore in the business of making prophecies that threaten to become self-fulfilling. If the norm of public spirit dies, our society would look bleaker and our lives as individuals would be more impoverished. That is the tragedy of "public choice."

Economics of Externalities

The common definition of *externality* is "the quality or state of being outside." Economists use the term externality to refer to an effect that takes place outside the mutual voluntary exchange of the market system. A firm polluting a river with a fish-killing chemical imposes a negative externality on fishermen, whose incomes are reduced. A family renovating the exterior of its home bestows positive externalities on neighbors, whose properties appreciate in value as a result. The major characteristic of an externality is the unenforceability of compensation for damages done or services rendered.

The selections in this section address two questions: Under what conditions will the private market system fail to produce efficient outcomes in the presence of externalities? What public policies should be utilized to deal with such deficiencies? Such inquiries take on ideological overtones. 'Conservative' opponents of government intervention in the market argue that such policies are unnecessary when private incentives eliminate the inefficiencies arising from the presence of externalities and inappropriate when government-imposed solutions create greater inefficiency than private arrangements. 'Liberal' advocates of public sector involvement contend that private sector solutions are rare and that corrective action by the government results in more efficient solutions than no action. The middle ground, as these readings demonstrate, is that the appropriateness of a government policy addressing externalities depends on the particular circumstances of each case.

SELECTION 6

LARRY E. RUFF

The Economic Common Sense of Pollution

Larry Ruff's paper states a major theme of this section. In properly functioning markets, private parties must pay for the resources they use, and they use an additional unit of a resource only if their benefits exceed their costs. However, there may be no payment for using the environment—for pouring pollutants into water resources, for allowing fumes to escape into the atmosphere, and so on. In such cases, the environment is a free good, littered with wastes even when private benefits are much smaller than the external costs inflicted on others.

QUESTIONS TO GUIDE THE READING

1. A government could prohibit or regulate environmental abuses by decree. What are the advantages of having the government "price pollution," i.e., place the environment within the normal operation of the market system?
2. Would it be desirable to eradicate all pollution?

We are going to make very little real progress in solving the problem of pollution until we recognize it for what, primarily, it is: an economic problem, which must be understood in economic terms. Of course, there are *noneconomic* aspects of pollution, as there are with all economic problems, but all too often, such secondary matters dominate discussion. Engineers, for example, are certain that pollution will vanish once they find the magic gadget or power source. Politicians keep trying to find the right kind of bureaucracy; and bureaucrats maintain an unending search for the correct set of rules and regulations. Those who are above such vulgar pursuits pin their hopes on a moral regeneration or social revolution, apparently in the belief that saints and socialists have no garbage to dispose of. But as important as technology, politics, law, and ethics are to the pollution question, all such approaches are bound to have disappointing results, for they ignore the primary fact that pollution is an economic problem.

Before developing an economic analysis of pollution, however, it is necessary to dispose of some popular myths.

Larry Ruff, "The Economic Common Sense of Pollution," *The Public Interest* 19 (Spring 1970), 69–85. © 1970 by National Affairs, Inc. Reprinted with permission of the author.

Larry E. Ruff is an economist at the Washington office of Putman, Hayes, and Bartlett.

First, pollution is not new. Spanish explorers landing in the sixteenth century noted that smoke from Indian campfires hung in the air of the Los Angeles basin, trapped by what is now called the inversion layer. Before the first century B.C., the drinking waters of Rome were becoming polluted.

Second, most pollution is not due to affluence, despite the current popularity of this notion. In India, the pollution runs in the streets, and advice against drinking the water in exotic lands is often well taken. Nor can pollution be blamed on the self-seeking activities of greedy capitalists. Once-beautiful rivers and lakes which are now open sewers and cesspools can be found in the Soviet Union as well as in the United States, and some of the world's dirtiest air hangs over cities in Eastern Europe, which are neither capitalist nor affluent. In many ways, indeed, it is much more difficult to do anything about pollution in noncapitalist societies. In the Soviet Union, there is no way for the public to become outraged or to exert any pressure, and the polluters and the courts there work for the same people, who often decide that clean air and water, like good clothing, are low on their list of social priorities.

In fact, it seems probable that affluence, technology, and slow-moving, inefficient democracy will turn out to be the cure more than the cause of pollution. After all, only an affluent, technological society can afford such luxuries as moon trips, three-day weekends, and clean water, although even our society may not be able to afford them all; and only in a democracy can the people hope to have any real influence on the choice among such alternatives.

What *is* new about pollution is what might be called the *problem* of pollution. Many unpleasant phenomena—poverty, genetic defects, hurricanes—have existed forever without being considered problems; they are, or were, considered to be facts of life, like gravity and death, and a mature person simply adjusted to them. Such phenomena become problems only when it begins to appear that something can and should be done about them. It is evident that pollution had advanced to the problem stage. Now the question is what can and should be done?

Most discussions of the pollution problem begin with some startling facts: Did you know that 15,000 tons of filth are dumped into the air of Los Angeles County every day? But by themselves, such facts are meaningless, if only because there is no way to know whether 15,000 tons is a lot or a little. It is much more important for clear thinking about the pollution problem to understand a few economic concepts than to learn a lot of sensational-sounding numbers. . . .

Estimating the Costs of Pollution

Both in theory and practice, the most difficult part of an economic approach to pollution is the measurement of the cost and benefits of its abatement. Only a small fraction of the costs of pollution can be estimated straightforwardly. If, for example, smog reduces the life of automobile tires by 10 per cent, one component of the cost of smog is 10 per cent of tire expenditures. It has been estimated that, in a moderately polluted area of New York City, filthy air imposes extra costs for painting, washing, laundry, etc., of $200 per person per year. Such costs must be included in any calculation of the benefits of pollution abatement, and yet they are only a part of the relevant costs—and often a small part. Accordingly it rarely is possible to justify a measure like river pollution control solely on the basis of costs to individuals or firms of treating water because it usually is cheaper to process only the water that is actually used for industrial or municipal purposes, and to ignore the river itself.

The costs of pollution that cannot be measured so easily are often called "intangible" or "noneconomic," although neither term is particularly appropriate. Many of these costs are as tangible as burning eyes or a dead fish, and all such costs are relevant to a valid economic analysis. Let us therefore call these costs "nonpecuniary."

The only real difference between nonpecuniary costs and the other kind lies in the difficulty of estimating them. If pollution in Los Angeles harbor is reducing marine life, this imposes costs on society. The cost of reducing commercial fishing could be estimated directly: it would be the fixed cost of converting men and equipment from fishing to an alternative occupation, plus the difference between what they earned in fishing and what they earn in the new occupation, plus the loss to consumers who must eat chicken instead of fish. But there are other, less straightforward costs: the loss of recreation opportunities for children and sportsfishermen and of research facilities for marine biologists, etc. Such costs are obviously difficult to measure and may be very large indeed; but just as surely as they are not zero, so too are they not infinite. Those who call for immediate action and damn the cost, merely because the spiney starfish and furry crab populations are shrinking, are putting an infinite marginal value on these creatures. This strikes a disinterested observer as an overestimate.

The above comments may seem crass and insensitive to those who, like one angry letter-writer to the Los Angeles *Times,* want to ask: "If conservation is not for its own sake, then what in the world *is* it for?" Well, what *is* the purpose of pollution control? Is it for its own sake? Of course not. If we answer that it is to make the air and water clean and quiet, then the question arises: what is the purpose of clean air and water? If the answer is, to please the nature gods, then it must be conceded that all pollution must cease immediately because the cost of angering the gods is presumably infinite. But if the answer is that the purpose of clean air and water is to further human enjoyment of life on this planet, then we are faced with the economists' basic question: given the limited alternatives that a niggardly nature allows, how can we best further human enjoyment of life? And the answer is, by making intelligent marginal decisions on the basis of costs and benefits. Pollution control is for lots of things: breathing comfortably, enjoying mountains, swimming in water, for health, beauty, and the general delectation. But so are many other things, like good food and wine, comfortable housing and fast transportation. The question is not which of these desirable things we should have, but rather what combination is most desirable. To determine such a combination, we must know the rate at which individuals are willing to substitute more of one desirable thing for less of another desirable thing. Prices are one way of determining those rates.

But if we cannot directly observe market prices for many of the costs of pollution, we must find another way to proceed. One possibility is to infer the costs from other prices, just as we infer the value of an ocean view from real estate prices. In principle, one could estimate the value people put on clean air and beaches by observing how much more they are willing to pay for property in nonpolluted areas. Such information could be obtained; but there is little of it available at present.

Another possible way of estimating the costs of pollution is to ask people how much they would be willing to pay to have pollution reduced. A resident of Pasadena might be willing to pay $100 a year to have smog reduced 10 or 20 per cent. In Barstow, where the marginal cost of smog is much less, a resident might not pay $10 a year to have smog reduced 10 per cent. If we knew how much it was worth to everybody, we could add up these amounts and obtain an estimate of the cost of a marginal amount of pollution. The difficulty, of course, is that there is no way of guaranteeing truthful responses. Your response to the question, how much is pollution costing *you,* obviously will depend on what you think will be done with this information. If you think you will be compensated for these costs, you will make a generous estimate; if you think that you will be charged for the control in proportion to these costs, you will make a small estimate.

In such cases it becomes very important how the questions are asked. For example, the voters could be asked a question of the form: Would you like to see pollution reduced x per cent if the result is a y per cent increase in the cost of living? Presumably a set of questions of this form could be used to estimate the costs of pollution, including the so-called "unmeasurable" costs. But great care must be taken in formulating the questions. For one thing, if the voters will benefit differentially from the activity, the questions should be asked in a way which reflects this fact. If, for example, the issue is cleaning up a river, residents near the river will be willing to pay more for the cleanup and should have a means of expressing this. Ultimately, some such political procedure probably will be necessary, at least until our more direct measurement techniques are greatly improved.

Let us assume that, somehow, we have made an estimate of the social cost function for pollution, including the marginal cost associated with various pollution levels. We now need an estimate of the benefits of pollution—or, if you prefer, of the costs of pollution abatement. So we set the Pollution Control Board (PCB) to work on this task.

The PCB has a staff of engineers and technicians, and they begin working on the obvious question: for each pollution source, how much would it cost to reduce pollution by 10 per cent, 20 per cent, and so on. If the PCB has some economists, they will know that the cost of reducing total pollution by 10 per cent is *not* the total cost of reducing each pollution source by 10 per cent. Rather, they will use the equimarginal principle and find the pattern of control such that an additional dollar spent on control of any pollution source yields the same reduction. This will minimize the cost of achieving any given level of abatement. In this way the PCB can generate a "cost of abatement" function, and the corresponding marginal cost function.

While this procedure seems straightforward enough, the practical difficulties are tremendous. The amount of information needed by the PCB is staggering; to do this job right, the PCB would have to know as much about each plant as the operators of the plant themselves. The cost of gathering these data is obviously prohibitive, and, since marginal principles apply to data collection too, the PCB would have to stop short of complete information, trading off the resulting loss in efficient control against the cost of better information. Of course, just as fast as the PCB obtained the data, a technological change would make it obsolete.

The PCB would have to face a further complication. It would not be correct simply to determine how to control existing pollution sources given their existing locations and production methods. Although this is almost certainly what the PCB would do, the resulting cost functions will overstate the true social cost of control. Muzzling existing plants is only one method of control. Plants can move, or switch to a new process, or even to a new product. Consumers can switch to a less-polluting substitute. There are any number of alternatives, and the poor PCB engineers can never know them all. This could lead to some costly mistakes. For example, the PCB may correctly conclude that the cost of installing effective dust control at the cement plant is very high and hence may allow the pollution to continue, when the best solution is for the cement plant to switch to brick production while a plant in the desert switches from brick to cement. The PCB can never have all this information and therefore is doomed to inefficiency, sometimes an inefficiency of large proportions.

Once cost and benefit functions are known, the PCB should choose a level of abatement that maximizes net gain. This occurs where the marginal cost of further abatement just equals the marginal benefit. If, for example, we could reduce pollution damages by $2 million at a cost of $1 million, we should obviously impose that $1 million cost. But if the damage reduction is only $0.5 million, we should not and in fact should reduce control efforts.

This principle is obvious enough but is often overlooked. One author, for example, has written that the national cost of air pollution is $11 billion a year but that we are spending less than $50 million a year on control; he infers from this that "we could justify a tremendous strengthening of control efforts on purely economic grounds." That *sounds* reasonable, if all you care about are sounds. But what is the logical content of the statement? Does it imply we should spend $11 billion on control just to make things even? Suppose we were spending $11 billion on control and thereby succeeded in reducing pollution costs to $50 million. Would this imply we were spending too *much* on control? Of course not. We must compare the *marginal* decrease in pollution costs to the *marginal* increase in abatement costs.

Difficult Decisions

Once the optimal pollution level is determined, all that is necessary is for the PCB to enforce the pattern of controls which it has determined to be optimal. (Of course, this pattern will not really be the best one, because the PCB will not have all the information it should have.) But now a new problem arises: how should the controls be enforced?

The most direct and widely used method is in many ways the least efficient: direct regulation. The PCB can decide what each polluter must do to reduce pollution and then simply require that action under penalty of law. But this approach has many shortcomings. The polluters have little incentive to install the required devices or to keep them operating properly. Constant inspection is therefore necessary. Once the polluter has complied with the letter of the law, he has no incentive to find better methods of pollution reduction. Direct control of this sort has a long history of inadequacy; the necessary bureaucracies rarely manifest much vigor, imagination, or devotion to the public interest. Still, in some situations there may be no alternative.

A slightly better method of control is for the PCB to set an acceptable level of pollution for each source and let the polluters find the cheapest means of achieving this level. This reduces the amount of information the PCB needs, but not by much. The setting of the acceptable levels becomes a matter for negotiation, political pull, or even graft. As new plants are built and new control methods invented, the limits should be changed; but if they are, the incentive to find new designs and new techniques is reduced.

A third possibility is to subsidize the reduction of pollution, either by subsidizing control equipment or by paying for the reduction of pollution below standard levels. This alternative has all the problems of the above methods, plus the classic shortcoming which plagues agricultural subsidies: the old joke about getting into the not-growing-cotton business is not always so funny.

The PCB will also have to face the related problem of deciding *who* is going to pay the costs of abatement. Ultimately, this is a question of equity or fairness which economics cannot answer; but economics can suggest ways of achieving equity without causing inefficiency. In general, the economist will say: if you think polluter A is deserving of more income at polluter B's expense, then by all means give A some of B's income; but do *not* try to help A by allowing him to pollute freely. For example, suppose A and B each operate plants which produce identical amounts of pollution. Because of different technologies, however, A can reduce his pollution 10 per cent for $100, while B can reduce his pollution 10 per cent for $1,000. Suppose your goal is to reduce total pollution 5 per cent. Surely it is obvious that the best (most efficient) way to do this is for A to reduce his pollution 10 per cent while B does nothing. But suppose B is rich and A is poor. Then many would demand that B reduce his pollution 10 per cent while A does nothing because B has a greater "ability to pay." Well, perhaps B does have greater ability to pay, and perhaps it is "fairer" that he pay the costs of pollution control; but if so, B should pay the $100 necessary to reduce A's pollution. To force B to reduce his own pollution 10 per cent is equivalent to taxing B $1,000 and then blowing the $1,000 on an extremely inefficient pollution control method. Put this way, it is obviously a stupid thing to do; but put in terms of B's greater ability to pay, it will get considerable support though it is no less stupid. The more efficient alternative is not always available, in which case it may be acceptable to use the inefficient method. Still, it should not be the responsibility of the pollution authorities to change the distribution of welfare in society; this is the responsibility of higher authorities. The PCB should concentrate on achieving economic efficiency without being grossly unfair in its allocation of costs.

Clearly, the PCB has a big job which it will never be able to handle with any degree of efficiency. Some sort of self-regulating system, like a market, is needed, which will automatically adapt to changes in conditions, provide incentives for development and adoption of improved control methods, reduce the amount of information the PCB must gather and the amount of detailed control it must exercise, and so on. This, by any standard, is a tall order.

Putting a Price on Pollution

And yet there is a very simple way to accomplish all this. *Put a price on pollution.* A price-based control mechanism would differ from an ordinary market transaction system only in that the PCB would set the prices, instead of their being set by demand-supply forces, and that the state would force payment. Under such a system, anyone could emit any amount of pollution so long as he pays the price which the PCB sets to approximate the marginal social cost of pollution. Under this circumstance, private decisions based on self-interest are efficient. If pollution consists of many components, each with its own social cost, there should be different prices for each component. Thus, extremely dangerous materials must have an extremely high price, perhaps stated in terms of "years in jail" rather than "dollars," although a sufficiently high dollar price is essentially the same thing. In principle, the prices should vary with geographical location, season of the year, direction of the wind, and even day of the week, although the cost of too many variations may preclude such fine distinctions.

Once the prices are set, polluters can adjust to them any way they choose. Because they act on self-interest they will reduce their pollution by every means possible up to the point where further reduction would cost more than the price. Because all face the same price for the same type of pollution, the marginal cost of abatement is the same everywhere. If there are economies of scale in pollution control, as in some types of liquid waste treatment, plants can cooperate in establishing joint treatment facilities. In fact, some enterprising individual could buy these wastes from various plants (at negative prices—i.e., they would get paid for carting them off), treat them, and then sell them at a higher price, making a profit in the process. (After all, this is what rubbish removal firms do now.) If economies of scale are so substantial that the provider of such a service becomes a monopolist, then the PCB can operate the facilities itself.

Obviously, such a scheme does not eliminate the need for the PCB. The board must measure the output of pollution from all sources, collect the fees, and so on. But it does not need to know anything about any plant except its total emission of pollution. It does not control, negotiate, threaten, or grant favors. It does not destroy incentive because development of new control methods will reduce pollution payments.

As a test of this price system of control, let us consider how well it would work when applied to automobile pollution, a problem for which direct control is usually considered the only feasible approach. If the price system can work here, it can work anywhere.

Suppose, then, that a price is put on the emissions of automobiles. Obviously, continuous metering of such emissions is impossible. But it should be easy to determine the average output of pollution for cars of different makes, models, and years, having different types of control devices and using different types of fuel. Through graduated registration fees and fuel taxes, each car owner would be assessed roughly the social cost of his car's pollution, adjusted for whatever control devices he has chosen to install and for his driving habits. If the cost of installing a device, driving a different car, or finding alternative means of transportation is less than the price he must pay to continue his pollution, he will presumably take the necessary steps. But each individual remains free to find the best adjustment to his particular situation. It would be remarkable if everyone decided to install the same devices which some states currently require; and yet that is the effective assumption of such requirements.

Even in the difficult case of auto pollution, the price system has a number of advantages. Why should a person living in the Mojave desert, where pollution has little social cost, take the same pains to reduce air pollution as a person living in Pasadena? Present California law, for example, makes no distinction between such areas; the price system would. And what incentive is there for auto manufacturers to design a less polluting engine? The law says only that they must install a certain device in every car. If GM develops a more efficient engine, the law will eventually be changed to require this engine on all cars, raising costs and reducing sales. But will such development take place? No collusion is needed for manufacturers to decide unanimously that it would be foolish to devote funds to such development. But with a pollution fee paid by the consumer, there is a real advantage for any firm to be first with a better engine, and even a collusive agreement wouldn't last long in the face of such an incentive. The same is true of fuel manufacturers, who now have no real incentive to look for better fuels. Perhaps most important of all, the present situation provides no real way of determining whether it is cheaper to reduce pollution by muzzling cars or industrial plants. The experts say that most smog comes from cars; but *even if true, this does not imply that it is more efficient to control autos rather than other pollution sources*. How can we decide which is more efficient without mountains of information? The answer is, by making drivers and plants pay the same price for the same pollution, and letting self-interest do the job.

In situations where pollution outputs can be measured more or less directly (unlike the automobile pollution case), the price system is clearly superior to direct control. A study of possible control methods in the Delaware estuary, for example, estimated that, compared to a direct control scheme requiring each polluter to reduce his pollution by a fixed percentage, an effluent charge which would achieve the same level of pollution abatement would be only half as costly—a saving of about $150 million. Such a price system would also provide incentive for further improvements, a simple method of handling new plants, and revenue for the control authority.

In general, the price system allocates costs in a manner which is at least superficially fair: those who produce and consume goods which cause pollution, pay the costs. But the superior efficiency in control and apparent fairness are not the only advantages of the price mechanism. Equally important is the case with which it can be put into operation. It is not necessary to have detailed information about all the techniques of pollution reduction, or estimates of all costs and benefits. Nor is it necessary to determine whom to blame or who should pay. All that is needed is a mechanism for estimating, if only roughly at first, the pollution output of all polluters, together with a means of collecting fees. Then we can simply pick a price—any price—for each category of pollution, and we are in business. The initial price should be chosen on the basis of some estimate of its effects but need not be the optimal one. If the resulting reduction in pollution is not "enough," the price can be raised until there is sufficient reduction. A change in technology, number of plants, or whatever, can be accommodated by a change in the price, even without detailed knowledge of all the technological and economic data. Further, once the idea is explained, the price system is much more likely to be politically acceptable than some method of direct control. Paying for a service, such as garbage disposal, is a well-established tradition, and is much less objectionable than having a bureaucrat nosing around and giving arbitrary orders. When businessmen, consumers, and politicians understand the alternatives, the price system will seem very attractive indeed.

Who Sets the Prices?

An important part of this method of control obviously is the mechanism that sets and changes the pollution price. Ideally, the PCB could choose this price on the basis of an estimate of the benefits and costs involved, in effect imitating the impersonal workings of ordinary market forces. But because many of the costs and benefits cannot be measured, a less "objective," more political procedure is needed. This political procedure could take the form of a referendum, in which the PCB would present to the voters alternative schedules of pollution prices, together with the estimated effects of each. There would be a massive propaganda campaign waged by the interested parties, of course. Slogans such as "Vote NO on 12 and Save Your Job," or "Proposition 12 Means Higher Prices," might be overstatements but would contain some truth, as the individual voter would realize when he considered the suggested increase in gasoline taxes and auto registration fees. But the other side, in true American fashion, would respond by overstating *their* case: "Smog Kills, Yes on 12," or "Stop *Them* From Ruining *Your* Water." It would be up to the PCB to inform the public about the true effects of the alternatives; but ultimately, the voters would make the decision.

It is fashionable in intellectual circles to object to such democratic procedures on the ground that the uncultured masses will not make correct decisions. If this view is based on the fact that the technical and economic arguments are likely to be too complex to be decided by direct referendum, it is certainly a reasonable position; one obvious solution is to set up an elective or appointive board to make the detailed decisions, with the expert board members being ultimately responsible to the voters. But often there is another aspect to the antidemocratic position—a feeling that it is impossible to convince the people of the desirability of some social policy, not because the issues are too complex but purely because their values are "different" and inferior. To put it bluntly: many ardent foes of pollution are not so certain that popular opinion is really behind them, and they therefore prefer a more bureaucratic and less political solution.

The question of who should make decisions for whom, or whose desires should count in a society, is essentially a noneconomic question that an economist cannot answer with authority, whatever his personal views on the matter. The political structures outlined here, when combined with the economic suggestions, can lead to a reasonably efficient solution of the pollution problem in a society where the tastes and values of all men are given some consideration. In such a society, when any nonrepresentative group is in a position to impose its particular evaluation of the costs and benefits, an inefficient situation will result. The swimmer or tidepool enthusiast who wants Los Angeles Harbor converted into a crystal-clear swimming pool, at the expense of all the workers, consumers, and businessmen who use the harbor for commerce and industry, is indistinguishable from the stockholder in Union Oil who wants maximum output from offshore wells, at the expense of everyone in the Santa Barbara area. Both are urging an inefficient use of society's resources; both are trying to get others to subsidize their particular thing—a perfectly normal, if not especially noble, endeavor.

If the democratic principle upon which the above political suggestions are based is rejected, the economist cannot object. He will still suggest the price system as a tool for controlling pollution. With any method of decision—whether popular vote, representative democracy, consultation with the nature gods, or a dictate of the intellectual elite—the price system can simplify, control, and reduce the amount of information needed for decisions. It provides an efficient, comprehensive, easily understood, adaptable, and reasonably fair way of handling the problem. It is ultimately the only way the problem will be solved. Arbitrary, piecemeal, stop-and-go programs of direct control have not and will not accomplish the job.

Some Objections Aren't an Answer

There are some objections that can be raised against the price system as a tool of pollution policy. Most are either illogical or apply with much greater force to any other method of control.

For example, one could object that what has been suggested here ignores the difficulties caused by fragmented political jurisdictions; but this is true for any method of control. The relevant question is: what method of control makes interjurisdictional cooperation easier and more likely? And the answer is: a price system, for several reasons. First, it is probably easier to get agreement on a simple schedule of pollution prices than on a complex set of detailed regulations. Second, a uniform price schedule would make it more difficult for any member of the "cooperative" group to attract industry from the other areas by promising a more lenient attitude toward pollution. Third, and most important, a price system generates revenues for the control board, which can be distributed to the various political entities. While the allocation of these revenues would involve some vigorous discussion, any alternative methods of control would require the various governments to raise taxes to pay the costs, a much less appealing prospect; in fact, there would be a danger that the pollution prices might be considered a device to generate revenue rather than to reduce pollution, which could lead to an overly clean, inefficient situation.

Another objection is that the Pollution Control Board might be captured by those it is supposed to control. This danger can be countered by having the board members subject to election or by having the pollution prices set by referendum. With any other control method, the danger of the captive regulator is much greater. A uniform price is easy for the public to understand, unlike obscure technical arguments about boiler temperatures and the costs of electrostatic collectors versus low-sulfur oil from Indonesia; if pollution is too high, the public can demand higher prices, pure and simple. And the price is the same for all plants, with no excuses. With direct control, acceptable pollution levels are negotiated with each plant separately and in private, with approved delays and special permits and other nonsense. The opportunities for using political influence and simple graft are clearly much larger with direct control.

A different type of objection occasionally has been raised against the price system, based essentially on the fear that it will solve the problem. Pollution, after all, is a hot issue with which to assault The Establishment,

Capitalism, Human Nature, and Them; any attempt to remove the issue by some minor change in institutions, well within The System, must be resisted by The Movement. From some points of view, of course, this is a perfectly valid objection. But one is hopeful that there still exists a majority more concerned with finding solutions than with creating issues.

There are other objections which could be raised and answered in a similar way. But the strongest argument for the price system is not found in idle speculation but in the real world, and in particular, in Germany. The Rhine River in Germany is a dirty stream, recently made notorious when an insecticide spilled into the river and killed millions of fish. One tributary of the Rhine, a river called the Ruhr, is the sewer for one of the world's most concentrated industrial areas. The Ruhr River valley contains 40 per cent of German industry, including 80 per cent of coal, iron, steel and heavy chemical capacity. The Ruhr is a small river, with a low flow of less than half the flow on the Potomac near Washington. The volume of wastes is extremely large—actually exceeding the flow of the river itself in the dry season! *Yet people and fish swim in the Ruhr River.*

This amazing situation is the result of over forty years of control of the Ruhr and its tributaries by a hierarchy of regional authorities. These authorities have as their goal the maintenance of the quality of the water in the area at minimum cost, and they have explicitly applied the equimarginal principle to accomplish this. Water quality is formally defined in a technological rather than an economic way; the objective is to "not fill the fish." Laboratory tests are conducted to determine what levels of various types of pollution are lethal to fish, and from these figures an index is constructed which measures the "amount of pollution" from each source in terms of its fish-killing capacity. This index is different for each source, because of differences in amount and composition of the waste, and geographical locale. Although this physical index is not really a very precise measure of the real economic *cost* of the waste, it has the advantage of being easily measured and widely understood. Attempts are made on an *ad hoc* basis to correct the index if necessary—if, for example, a non-lethal pollutant gives fish an unpleasant taste.

Once the index of pollution is constructed, a price is put on the pollution, and each source is free to adjust its operation any way it chooses. Geographical variation in prices, together with some direct advice from the authorities, encourage new plants to locate where pollution is less damaging. For example, one tributary of the Ruhr has been converted to an open sewer; it has been lined with concrete and landscaped, but otherwise no attempt is made to reduce pollution in the river itself. A treatment plant at the mouth of the river processes all these wastes at low cost. Therefore, the price of pollution on this river is set low. This arrangement, by the way, is a rational, if perhaps unconscious, recognition of marginal principles. The loss caused by destruction of *one* tributary is rather small, if the nearby rivers are maintained, while the benefit from having this inexpensive means of waste disposal is very large. However, if *another* river were lost, the cost would be higher and the benefits lower; one open sewer may be the optimal number.

The revenues from the pollution charges are used by the authorities to measure pollution, conduct tests and research, operate dams to regulate stream flow, and operate waste treatment facilities where economies of scale make this desirable. These facilities are located at the mouths of some tributaries, and at several dams in the Ruhr. If the authorities find pollution levels are getting too high, they simply raise the price, which causes polluters to try to reduce their wastes, and provides increased revenues to use on further treatment. Local governments influence the authorities, which helps to maintain recreation values, at least in certain stretches of the river.

This classic example of water management is obviously not exactly the price system method discussed earlier. There is considerable direct control, and the pollution authorities take a very active role. Price regulation is not used as much as it could be; for example, no attempt is made to vary the price over the season, even though high flow on the Ruhr is more than ten times larger than low flow. If the price of pollution were reduced during high flow periods, plants would have an incentive to regulate their production and/or store their wastes for release during periods when the river can more easily handle them. The difficulty of continuously monitoring wastes means this is not done; as automatic, continuous measurement techniques improve and are made less expensive, the use of variable prices will increase. Though this system is not entirely regulated by the price mechanism, prices are used more here than anywhere else, and the system is much more successful than any other.[1] So, both in theory and in practice, the price system is attractive, and ultimately must be the solution to pollution problems.

NOTES

1. For a more complete discussion of the Ruhr Valley system, see Allen V. Knesse, *The Economics of Regional Water Quality Management* (Baltimore, Md.: Johns Hopkins Press, 1964).

SELECTION 7

WILLIAM TUCKER
Marketing Pollution

William Tucker points out that a government agency could
determine the maximum desirable amount of a particular pollutant
in the environment and then simply sell rights to polluters
permitting them to generate certain amounts of pollution. U.S.
policy dealing with stationary source air pollution has been moving
in this direction. In 1979 the EPA adopted an emission banking
procedure under which a pollution source can receive (under
certain circumstances) a credit for reducing emissions by amounts
exceeding required levels. This credit is deposited in an emissions
bank for later use by that source or for sale to another source.

QUESTIONS TO GUIDE THE READING

1. Why did the United States initially choose environmental laws
   based on the command and control by centralized bureaucracy
   rather than price incentives?
2. What advantages do "marketable pollution rights" have over
   pollution taxes?
3. Do you think pollution permits would be a practical way to
   control pollution emissions from automobiles?

. . . The concept of externalities was first developed in the 1920s by the
English economist A. C. Pigou in *The Economics of Welfare* and explored
much more thoroughly in the early 1950s by Harvard economist Paul Samuelson (winning him the Nobel prize). The basic idea is that the market,
although it achieves optimal levels of production with the resources at hand,
leaves certain other things untended. Pigou and Samuelson cited wide disparities in wealth as an example and called for a partial redistribution of
income.

Pollution, then, is another market externality. We can all go about our
daily business, with the market determining the optimal production of
goods, and still end up with dirty air and polluted waters—even though almost everyone might recognize that this is not what he would have intended

William Tucker, "Marketing Pollution," *Harper's* 262 (May 1981), 31–8. Copyright © 1981 by
Harper's Magazine. All rights reserved. Reprinted from the May issue by special permission.

William Tucker is a New York Correspondent for the *American Spectator*.

personally. The reason is that the market has not put a price on polluting. The best things in life are free, and that includes air and water. Swimming and breathing usually don't cost anything, but neither does throwing away garbage. Since dumping pollution into the environment costs nothing, everybody does it, even though he may wish that he and everyone else would stop doing it. Clean air and water have not been recognized by the market as limited resources that can only absorb so much junk before they start spitting it back—exactly what had started happening by the early 1960s. The solution is to put a price on the use of these limited resources and stop classifying them as "free." Protection of air and water have to be brought into the market system. Very early on, then, the problem was properly diagnosed.

All this might have been successful were it not for a countervailing tendency in the environmental movement, which eventually proved superior. This was the impulse to portray environmental concerns as sacred. In their desire to make an impact on the American consciousness, environmentalists spurned the notion that they were merely another constituency trying to bring sense and order to the way society functioned. On the contrary, in their view their concerns transcended all others. Human survival itself, not simply a commonly perceived public good, was the issue. Mankind was overrunning the ecosystem and turning it into a hotdog stand. By the year 2100, the world would be wall-to-wall people. The new science of ecology showed that every human activity tipped the world closer to doomsday. Computer printouts at MIT proved we had but a few more years to go. Adopting as their motto the lines from the old missionary hymn, "Though every prospect pleases, and only man is vile," environmentalists set out to scrub the universe clean of every last trace of human habitation. A "degraded environment," according to the Sierra Club, was an environment in which human activity had made a mark. "Zero pollution" became the objective, in statute as well as rhetoric. With a question that symbolized the sanctity of their concerns, far above the rough-and-tumble of ordinary politics, environmentalists asked: "How can you put a price on clean air?"

The Cost of Clean Air

But that was exactly the problem. The dilemma we faced was just that: how *do* you put a price on clean air—or at least on the act of fouling it while disposing of society's wastes? Yet in their reluctance to perceive their concern as one of mere economics, environmentalists rejected this approach. It failed to match the religiosity of their cause. Instead, they supported a highly centralized, bureaucratic system based on difficult goals, detailed regulatory prescriptions, and awe-inspiring penalties for noncompliance. Policy would be set in the environmental bureaucracies in Washington and orders sent out to the populace. Market controls, offering the same results through a highly decentralized decision-making system, were not deemed worthy of the task.

The decision to create a bureaucratic system was not automatic. Few people today recall how close we came to a system of environmental laws *not* based on the "command-and-control" module of a centralized bureaucracy. As early as 1969, Senator William Proxmire was proposing legislation that would have put a set of "effluent charges" on sources of water pollution. The aim was to make it cheaper for people to clean up than to go on polluting indiscriminately. The system had been tried in Cincinnati in the 1950s and worked quite well. As late as 1972 a bill for a national tax on airborne sulfur emissions passed the House but was defeated in the Senate.

In the end, the bureaucratic model prevailed. There were several reasons for this. First, Congress still felt more comfortable with the old New Deal model of setting up a powerful federal agency to dictate policy from Washington. Second, market mechanisms had not been widely used up till then, and there was no genuine confidence that they would work. And third, environmental groups themselves felt far more comfortable with the bureaucratic model. The virtue of centralized decision-making, as far as lobbying groups are concerned, is that it exaggerates their powers. Most environmental groups now have elaborate headquarters in Washington, and many run their entire operations within sight of the Capitol. Whereas market-oriented systems would spread decision-making across the country, bureaucratic systems concentrate it in Washington, where the decisions can be easily influenced. Small groups of federal officials or Congressional staff members can be identified, isolated, and influenced by a mere phone call.

The general consensus was that decisions would be made in the halls of the bureaucracy and filter down to the local level. The result is the mess we have today.

The way the Clean Air Act of 1970 affected industry has more or less passed into legend. It is not that it did not produce results. Air pollution has declined in many areas, and has increased in only a few. The real question is the costs that were incurred in the process.

Bureaucratic systems, after all, are not by definition incompetent when specific things have to be done. They are often very efficient. German National Socialism built magnificent roads and designed a "people's car," the Volkswagen, to run on them. Egypt built the pyramids, and the Soviet Union has accumulated armaments with ruthless efficiency. The question is the sacrifices that have to be made in other sectors of the economy in order to achieve these ends; they are often great. This is important to remember as Congress considers the renewal of the Clean Air Act this year. It is not the goal of making clean air a valued good that should be questioned, but the means of getting there.

The Clean Air Act set up 247 regional air-pollution districts around the country. These airshed districts were put under the jurisdiction of the state governments, or interstate agencies where they crossed state lines. The act established federal standards for six pollutants: free hydrocarbons; sulfur dioxide; nitrogen oxides; particulate matter; carbon monoxide; and ozone (nitrogen oxides and ozone are the principal elements of smog). The standards were determined at the federal level, with 1977 set as the target date for compliance. The means of meeting these standards were to be decided by the state governments, subject to federal approval, through the so-called state implementation plans. Pollution sources were divided into two categories, stationary and mobile. The stationary sources were factories, utility plants, municipal incinerators, apartment-house heating units, and so forth. Mobile sources were cars and other vehicles. Since cars are sold everywhere, the federal government tackled the job of getting the manufacturers to reduce their emissions. The state governments were given the task of dealing with stationary sources.

Right from the beginning a clear pattern of state activities emerged. It usually went something like this. The state environmental agency surveyed a pollution district and identified the major stationary sources. They were, say, an oil-burning utility plant, two steel plants using coal for their energy, and a large stone quarry that kicked up significant amounts of dust. The utility company had probably been burning coal ten years before, but had been forced to switch to low-sulfur foreign oil by an earlier state initiative during the 1960s. (On the Atlantic coast, for example, the use of coal fell from 70 percent of all utility fuels—11 million tons—in 1964 to only 15 percent—5.9 million tons—in 1973, solely as the result of state initiatives. It was during this period that much of our dependence on foreign oil was created.)

So the problem the state faced was one of devising a plan that would meet federal standards while being perceived as fair and equitable by all who would have to spend money to cut down on their pollution.

The first thing the state had to do was go out and hire a lot of new environmental experts, whom the makeshift programs that had been set up in the colleges and universities were rapidly churning out. Environmental studies was a growth field during the 1960s. These recruits would go to work studying the pollution levels, the wind patterns, the technologies, the economics of each industry, and the general chances of getting them to cooperate. Then they would draw up a plan that would identify what *each and every industry in the district would have to do to control emissions at each and every smokestack*. Say, for example, it was decided that in order to meet the federal standards, pollution would have to be lowered by one quarter. To be fair, the state would decide, let us say, that every industry would have to reduce its emissions by one quarter. This would be announced as the "state implementation plan." It would go to Washington, where the EPA, after reviewing all the data, would accept or reject it. Once it was accepted, the state would announce the plan to the industries. Then the fun would begin.

Inevitably, the plan would be perceived as unfair by all the participants. The utility would argue, for example, that it had already cut most of its important emissions in half by switching from coal to oil. Asking for another 25 percent reduction would be unfair. Steel company No. 1 would point out that it operated two small plants that together produced about as much pollution as steel company No. 2's one big plant. But the state implementation plan would require it to put pollution-control equipment on both its smokestacks. It would therefore be paying twice as much as steel company No. 2, which was unfair. Steel company No. 2, meanwhile, was announcing that it was the largest employer in the district, and any talk about making it spend more than minimal amounts on pollution control might cause it to think seriously about closing the plant.

At the same time, all three steam generators would argue that it was really the quarry that was generating most of the dust affecting visibility in the region. If the state would only concentrate on that source, there would be no need to bother with the boilers. The quarry, on the other hand, had already hired its own expert, a recent graduate with a B.A. in environmental sciences, who pointed out that it was the potentially harmful sulfates and nitrous oxides from the fuel-burning plants that were the real health hazard. Before long, all the industries were busy hiring the second generation of environmental experts that were now being turned out of the graduate schools even faster. In addition, each firm now had a Special Counsel on Environmental Quality (part of its new Division of Environmental Improvement), and soon all were arguing their cases in court.

Sen. Daniel Patrick Moynihan has remarked that organizations that fight each other usually end up resembling each other. So it has been with the environmental clean-up effort. Every side now has its own experts ready to testify that all the other experts are wrong. There are so many people in California writing environmental impact statements that they have formed their own professional association, with a membership of 600. Yet the effects on the environment have not always been commensurate with the effort. Some people seriously question whether *any* of the improvements in air quality over the past ten years can be directly attributed to the Clean Air Act, or whether it represents merely a combination of the 1960s' switch from coal to oil and a generally declining economy. In many of the country's air-pollution districts, air quality steadily deteriorated for several years after the Clean Air Act, while industry and regulators spent their time fighting out the details in court.

Nor can industry be regarded as simply recalcitrant. The major problem with the Clean Air Act is that it lays the burden of costs *only on the people who make the effort to clean up*. (The large fines were intended mainly as a threat, and are rarely imposed.) *No one has yet put a price on using clean air as a dumping ground*. The only standards for deciding who cleans up and who doesn't are the necessarily arbitrary decisions arrived at by the state environmental agencies. Each industry, therefore, has every incentive to spend years in litigation trying to prove that it is someone else's pollution that is at fault.

The Market in Pollution

Another problem has been the haphazard, almost fatuous, record that the EPA has built up in another extremely important area, the so-called new-source performance standards. At the very start of pollution legislation,

Congress made a fateful distinction between existing sources of pollution and new sources that might be built in the future. Existing sources were to be handled through the state implementation programs. But new sources would be regulated by the EPA, which was instructed to require that the "best available technology" be employed on new pollution sources.

This policy has had an extraordinary effect. It has actively discouraged the construction of new capacity, due to the expense of installing new plant and equipment. In the end, it is probably cheaper for a company to limp along with its old equipment, fending off the EPA in court and pleading poverty, rather than undertake the enormous expenditure of installing the "best available technology." Old plants may be patched up or granted temporary exemptions (there have been a lot of those). But the high cost of a new plant is unavoidable.

What is worse, in areas that are not in compliance with federal standards, many state agencies will allow *no* new construction. Thus in Van Nuys, California, for example, a General Motors auto plant being turned over from large to small cars has been stalled for over a year, because it will constitute a "new source" of pollution.

The effort has been particularly soured by the way the EPA eventually decided to exercise its authority. In a forthcoming book,[1] Yale law professor and public-policy critic Bruce A. Ackerman describes at length the extraordinarily irresponsible fashion in which the EPA arrived at its 1978 decision, which said that all new coal-burning utility plants will have to be outfitted with expensive sulfur-scrubbing equipment *whether or not it is needed to comply with the federal pollution standards*. Ackerman notes that tens of billions of dollars will be spent on the effort, *even though the resulting emissions may not be as clean as they would otherwise have been*.

This extraordinarily wasteful policy is the result of an improbable temporary alliance between the leading environmental groups (the Sierra Club and the Natural Resources Defense Council) and the eastern coal-mining companies (represented in Washington by the United Mine Workers). Together, in 1976, they pressured an obscure Congressional committee to write sulfur-emission standards that could not be met by burning even low-sulfur coal. The coal miners were afraid that without the strict standards, utilities in the Midwest and Ohio Valley would turn away from eastern coal, which is higher in sulfur, and start importing more coal from the West. The environmentalists, of course, were happy to seize on any opportunity to make tougher standards law, regardless of the consequences. Then, when the EPA was facing its 1978 decision on what was the best available technology for enforcing this strict standard, the environmentalists and coal miners once again teamed up to pressure the EPA into choosing mandatory scrubbing.

The results are going to be rather absurd. Billions of dollars will be spent in the western part of the country on sulfur-scrubbers that will have little to clean from low-sulfur coal. At the same time, sulfur-scrubbing is a technology with its own serious consequences. It requires large amounts of water and produces enormous quantities of a hazardous, sulfurous sludge that is itself a serious disposal problem. An entire valley in western Pennsylvania is now being filled with the sulfurous wastes that have accumulated from running one sulfur-scrubbing utility plant for only three years. When the EPA was faced with this problem, it included in its mandate a technology called "dry-scrubbing," which has never been tried anywhere on a large scale, and which only came to the agency's attention a few weeks before its final decision.

As a final irony, sulfur-scrubbers actually require the presence of fair amounts of sulfur in the coal in order to work properly. Many utilities that already have access to low-sulfur coal are going to have to *add* sulfur to their coal supplies in order to keep the scrubbers operating. This is the "best available technology" we have been able to produce.

What can Congress do this year to make the Clean Air Act more workable, without throwing away all the legitimate desires for a better environment that it represents? For many years, economists have been designing what are called "market mechanisms" that can achieve the same results or better through optimally efficient methods. Allan Kneese, of Resources for the Future, one of the oldest and wisest of the environmental groups, has been the principle architect of many of these ideas.

Perhaps the most commonly suggested method—and one that I hope Congress does *not* decide to adopt—is the pollution tax. The idea is that the EPA or state agencies would place a tax on each ton of sulfur oxides or other pollutants emitted into the atmosphere. This would make it profitable for polluters to clean up some of their emissions, until the point came where it would be cheaper to pay the tax. No one has ever thought that air-pollution emissions could be reduced to zero—although the Federal Clean Water Act of 1972 has mandated zero emissions of sewage into the nation's water by 1985, and the EPA is still laboring to meet the deadline.

The emissions tax would do several things that are not done by the present system. First, it would reward partial and incremental improvements. At present, cleaning is an all-or-nothing game. There are no rewards for accomplishing anything besides compliance with the standards, and no incentives for going beyond them. The system would impose immediate penalities for noncompliance, but would reward any and all efforts at improvement. There would be no advantages in court delays. Theoretically, if the agency set the tax at the proper level, the desired clean-up could be achieved in the most efficient way possible.

Unfortunately, a pollution tax would create almost as many problems as it would solve. The difficulty is in deciding where to set the tax. In the end, this would probably involve just as much exhaustive analysis and preplanning by government agencies as does the present system. If the tax were set too high, the clean-up would proceed beyond what was practical or economical. If it were too low, industries wouldn't clean up enough. Resolving this problem would involve the usual bevy of environmental experts, computer printouts, and possibly court challenges as well.

A far more straightforward plan, and one I personally think would be the best, is the "marketable-rights" system originally proposed by Senator Proxmire in the 1960s. In this system, the state agency would determine beforehand how much of each pollutant it was willing to allow in a given airshed. Then it would simply *sell* the rights to generate this pollution on an open market. Industries would have to compete against each other for the right to create this pollution. Inevitably they would bid up these rights-to-pollute to their marginal level—that is, the price at which it is cheaper for every individual to clean up his remaining emissions rather than pay more for the right to pollute. The task of cleaning up the total pollution for the entire airshed would be automatically distributed among the polluters in the most economical way.

The beauty of this system is that all the bureaucrats in the federal and state agencies who are spending countless thousands of hours deciding who should clean up what, when, and where could simply pack their bags and go home. All the decisions would be made where they belong—by the people who are going to bear the costs of deciding how to clean up. Each industry would have a maximum incentive for finding the most efficient way to re- duce its pollution. Innovation would be at a premium because it would make the task easier, whereas under the current system, industries are actively *discouraged* from finding ways to clean up. Once they find them, they will probably have to apply them, no matter what the cost. The EPA can always lower the standards to match the new technology. Nor, under Proxmire's system, would there be any point in going to court. Since the decisions are made by the market, there is nothing to argue.

There is one other extremely attractive aspect of the marketable-rights system. It is that the public could be involved in the process, through a method by which people understand the price of the improvements they are requesting. Currently, when people want cleaner air, the standard practice is to lobby the legislators, start a mailing campaign, or organize a mass movement. Politicians and bureaucrats are pressured into tightening up the emissions standards, and everyone goes home happy. No one takes the least thought as to what it is all going to cost, even though he will eventually pay the bill in higher consumer prices.

But with the marketable-rights system, the possibility exists that the public, either through municipal bodies or environmental groups, can organ- ize itself to *buy* back some of the rights to pollute and "retire" them, thus eliminating more pollution from the atmosphere. This way, the public will be able to improve the air but will understand exactly how much it is costing. People can select it as a clear consumer choice rather than as a hidden tax extracted through higher manufacturing prices, as is done now. Such a sys- tem would also adapt itself readily to technological improvement. As better ways are found to clean up pollution, the marginal price of pollution rights will decline. This will make it easier for people to buy them back, which will in turn encourage more technological improvement, since the public's de- mand for still cleaner air will keep the marginal price up. The EPA would not have to worry about continually changing standards, and industry would not be harassed by unpredictability. The market would assure orderly progress.

The Bubble Concept

Oddly enough, one of the major constituents for this kind of reform has become the EPA itself. Around 1978, a general perception set in around the agency that it had "too many lawyers and not enough economists" (even the lawyers seem to have agreed with this assessment). Over the past few years, the EPA has made giant strides in developing the marketable-rights system on an experimental scale.

In 1979, for example, the EPA introduced the "bubble" concept, which is essentially a marketable-rights system applied to a single plant. The EPA places an imaginary bubble over a factory and considers that all the emissions are coming out of one smokestack. The industry is then left with the decision of how to bring the total emissions within certain prescribed limits. The day the plan was announced, the Du Pont chemical company said it would enable the company to reduce its clean-up costs from $136 million to $55 million.

Since then, the bubble concept has been gaining an enthusiastic following among industry and regulators alike. The Minnesota Mining and Manufacturing Company was able to make production-line changes at a Pennsylvania plant that produced fewer emissions of free hydrocarbons than the EPA had required at $3 million less than originally estimated. The Armco Steel Company in Middletown, Ohio, has planted grass and trees and started a plantwide bus system in order to cut down on dust and nitrogen oxides. The plan is regarded as successful.

Bubble concepts have even gone statewide. A plan is now being developed where a hundred New Jersey chemical companies will be able to combine their hydrocarbon emissions in order to bring them within standards in the cheapest possible way. The EPA is also setting up experimental brokerage houses in Louisville, San Francisco, and Seattle where companies can buy and sell their pollution rights on a citywide basis. Surprisingly, the major problem has been that, like novice Monopoly players, businesses have been reluctant to sell their rights under *any* circumstances, even when they are polluting under their limits. The reason is that they are still afraid the EPA will arbitrarily tighten up standards at some future date, at which point they will have to buy their rights back at exorbitant prices. A nationwide plan guaranteeing that governments could not tighten up existing regulations, except by buying back pollution rights on the open market, would solve this problem and stimulate a brisk trade on the pollution exchanges.

So, strangely enough, the reforms that Congress may be seeking are already operating in the experimental stage at the EPA. So far the agency has been reluctant to go to Capitol Hill with a request for still another change in its approach. Yet the time may have come to broach the subject. The almost perfect coalescence of the EPA's perceptions of the need for decentralized decisions, and the market philosophy of the new administration, offers a reform opportunity that may not come again.

NOTES

1. Bruce A. Ackerman and William T. Hassler, *Clean Coal/Dirty Air,* Yale University Press, 1981.

SELECTION 8

GARRETT HARDIN

The Tragedy of the Commons

Garrett Hardin, a biologist, provides a classic statement of the problem of depletion of common property resources and applies his analysis to overpopulation in particular. Common property ownership occurs when potential users of a resource have unrestricted access because no one person owns the common asset. Examples of assets that can be commonly owned include air, water, and fish. As the demand on such resources increases, common property ownership becomes less attractive than arrangements that exclude access.

QUESTIONS TO GUIDE THE READING

1. How does the "tragedy of the commons" develop?
2. What public policy steps can be taken to avoid this tragedy?
3. Do you agree with Hardin that the "freedom to breed is intolerable"? Under what conditions could Hardin be right?
4. How can you explain that in the American West during the 1800s buffalo were hunted practically to extinction, yet the cattle population increased as more cattle were consumed?

At the end of a thoughtful article on the future of nuclear war, Wiesner and York [1] concluded that: "Both sides in the arms race are . . . confronted by the dilemma of steadily increasing military power and steadily decreasing national security. *It is our considered professional judgment that this dilemma has no technical solution.* If the great powers continue to look for solutions in the area of science and technology only, the result will be to worsen the situation."

I would like to focus your attention not on the subject of the article (national security in a nuclear world) but on the kind of conclusion they reached, namely that there is no technical solution to the problem. An implicit and almost universal assumption of discussions published in profes-

Garrett Hardin, "The Tragedy of the Commons," *Science 162* (December 13, 1968), 1243–48. Copyright 1968 by the American Association for the Advancement of Science. Reprinted by permission of the author and *Science* magazine.

Garrett Hardin is Professor Emeritus, Department of Biology and Human Ecology, at the University of California, Santa Barbara.

sional and semipopular scientific journals is that the problem under discussion has a technical solution. A technical solution may be defined as one that requires a change only in the techniques of the natural sciences, demanding little or nothing in the way of change in human values or ideas of morality.

In our day (though not in earlier times) technical solutions are always welcome. Because of previous failures in prophecy, it takes courage to assert that a desired technical solution is not possible. Wiesner and York exhibited this courage; publishing in a science journal, they insisted that the solution to the problem was not to be found in the natural sciences. They cautiously qualified their statement with the phrase, "It is our considered professional judgment. . . ." Whether they were right or not is not the concern of the present article. Rather, the concern here is with the important concept of a class of human problems which can be called "no technical solution problems," and, more specifically, with the identification and discussion of one of these.

It is easy to show that the class is not a null class. Recall the game of tick-tack-toe. Consider the problem, "How can I win the game of tick-tack-toe?" It is well known that I cannot, if I assume (in keeping with the conventions of game theory) that my opponent understands the game perfectly. Put another way, there is no "technical solution" to the problem. I can win only by giving a radical meaning to the word "win." I can hit my opponent over the head; or I can drug him; or I can falsify the records. Every way in which I "win" involves, in some sense, an abandonment of the game, as we intuitively understand it. (I can also, of course, openly abandon the game—refuse to play it. This is what most adults do.)

The class of "No technical solution problems" has members. My thesis is that the "population problem," as conventionally conceived, is a member of this class. How it is conventionally conceived needs some comment. It is fair to say that most people who anguish over the population problem are trying to find a way to avoid the evils of overpopulation without relinquishing any of the privileges they now enjoy. They think that farming the seas or developing new strains of wheat will solve the problem—technologically. I try to show here that the solution they seek cannot be found. The population problem cannot be solved in a technical way, any more than can the problem of winning the game of tick-tack-toe.

What Shall We Maximize?

Population, as Malthus said, naturally tends to grow "geometrically," or, as we would now say, exponentially. In a finite world this means that the per capita share of the world's goods must steadily decrease. Is ours a finite world?

A fair defense can be put forward for the view that the world is infinite; or that we do not know that it is not. But, in terms of the practical problems that we must face in the next few generations with the foreseeable technology, it is clear that we will greatly increase human misery if we do not, during the immediate future, assume that the world available to the terrestrial human population is finite. "Space" is no escape [2].

A finite world can support only a finite population; therefore, population growth must eventually equal zero. (The case of perpetual wide fluctuations above and below zero is a trivial variant that need not be discussed.) When this condition is met, what will be the situation of mankind? Specifically, can Bentham's goal of "the greatest good for the greatest number" be realized?

No—for two reasons, each sufficient by itself. The first is a theoretical one. It is not mathematically possible to maximize for two (or more) variables at the same time. This was clearly stated by von Neumann and Morgenstern [3], but the principle is implicit in the theory of partial differential equations, dating back at least to D'Alembert (1717–1783).

The second reason springs directly from biological facts. To live, any organism must have a source of energy (for example, food). This energy is utilized for two purposes: mere maintenance and work. For man, maintenance of life requires about 1600 kilocalories a day ("maintenance calories"). Anything that he does over and above merely staying alive will be defined as work, and is supported by "work calories" which he takes in. Work calories are used not only for what we call work in common speech; they are also required for all forms of enjoyment, from swimming and automobile racing to playing music and writing poetry. If our goal is to maximize population it is obvious that we must do: We must make the work calories per person approach as close to zero as possible. No gourmet meals, no vacations, no sports, no music, no literature, no art. . . . I think that everyone will grant, without argument or proof, that maximizing population does not maximize goods. Bentham's goal is impossible.

In reaching this conclusion I have made the usual assumption that it is the acquisition of energy that is the problem. The appearance of atomic energy has led some to question this assumption. However, given an infinite source of energy, population growth still produces an inescapable problem. The problem of the acquisition of energy is replaced by the problem of its dissipation, as J. H. Fremlin has so wittily shown [4]. The arithmetic signs in the analysis are, as it were, reversed; but Bentham's goal is still unobtainable.

The optimum population is, then, less than the maximum. The difficulty of defining the optimum is enormous; so far as I know, no one has seriously tackled this problem. Reaching an acceptable and stable solution will surely require more than one generation of hard analytical work—and much persuasion.

We want the maximum good per person; but what is good? To one person it is wilderness, to another it is ski lodges for thousands. To one it is estuaries to nourish ducks for hunters to shoot; to another it is factory land. Comparing one good with another is, we usually say, impossible because goods are incommensurable. Incommensurables cannot be compared.

Theoretically this may be true; but in real life incommensurables *are* commensurable. Only a criterion of judgment and a system of weighting are needed. In nature the criterion is survival. Is it better for a species to be small and hideable, or large and powerful? Natural selection commensurates the incommensurables. The compromise achieved depends on a natural weighting of the values of the variables.

Man must imitate this process. There is no doubt that in fact he already does, but unconsciously. It is when the hidden decisions are made explicit that the arguments begin. The problem for the years ahead is to work out an acceptable theory of weighting. Synergistic effects, nonlinear variation, and difficulties in discounting the future make the intellectual problem difficult, but not (in principle) insoluble.

Has any cultural group solved this practical problem at the present time, even on an intuitive level? One simple fact proves that none has: there is no prosperous population in the world today that has, and has had for some time, a growth rate of zero. Any people that has intuitively identified its optimum point will soon reach it, after which its growth rate becomes and remains zero.

Of course, a positive growth rate might be taken as evidence that a population is below its optimum. However, by any reasonable standards, the most rapidly growing populations on earth today are (in general) the most miserable. This association (which need not be invariable) casts doubt on the optimistic assumption that the positive growth rate of a population is evidence that it has yet to reach its optimum.

We can make little progress in working toward optimum population size until we explicitly exorcize the spirit of Adam Smith in the field of practical demography. In economic affairs, *The Wealth of Nations* (1776) popularized the "invisible hand," the idea that an individual who "intends only his own gain," is, as it were, "led by an invisible hand to promote . . . the public interest" [5]. Adam Smith did not assert that this was invariably true, and perhaps neither did any of his followers. But he contributed to a dominant tendency of thought that has ever since interfered with positive action based on rational analysis, namely, the tendency to assume that decisions reached individually will, in fact, be the best decisions for an entire society. If this assumption is correct it justifies the continuance of our present policy of laissez-faire in reproduction. If it is correct we can assume that men will control their individual fecundity so as to produce the optimum population. If the assumption is not correct, we need to reexamine our individual freedoms to see which ones are defensible.

Tragedy of Freedom in a Commons

The rebuttal to the invisible hand in population control is to be found in a scenario first sketched in a little-known pamphlet [6] in 1833 by a mathematical amateur named William Forster Lloyd (1794–1852). We may well call it "the tragedy of the commons," using the word "tragedy" as the philosopher Whitehead used it [7]: "The essence of dramatic tragedy is not unhappiness. It resides in the solemnity of the remorseless working of things." He then goes on to say "This inevitableness of destiny can only be illustrated in terms of human life by incidents which in fact involve unhappiness. For it is only by them that the futility of escape can be made evident in the drama."

The tragedy of the commons develops in this way. Picture a pasture open to all. It is to be expected that each herdsman will try to keep as many cattle as possible on the commons. Such an arrangement may work reasonably satisfactorily for centuries because tribal wars, poaching, and disease keep the numbers of both man and beast well below the carrying capacity of the land. Finally, however, comes the day of reckoning, that is, the day when the long-desired goal of social stability becomes a reality. At this point, the inherent logic of the commons remorselessly generates tragedy.

As a rational being, each herdsman seeks to maximize his gain. Explicitly or implicitly, more or less consciously, he asks, "What is the utility *to me* of adding one more animal to my herd?" This utility has one negative and one positive component.

1. The positive component is a function of the increment of one animal. Since the herdsman receives all the proceeds from the sale of the additional animal, the positive utility is nearly $+1$.
2. The negative component is a function of the additional overgrazing created by one more animal. Since, however, the effects of overgrazing are shared by all the herdsmen, the negative utility for any particular decision-making herdsman is only a fraction of -1.

Adding together the component partial utilities, the rational herdsman concludes that the only sensible course for him to pursue is to add another animal to his herd. And another; and another. . . . But this is the conclusion reached by each and every rational herdsman sharing a commons. Therein is the tragedy. Each man is locked into a system that compels him to increase his herd without limit—in a world that is limited. Ruin is the destination toward which all men rush, each pursuing his own best interest in a society that believes in the freedom of the commons. Freedom in a commons brings ruin to all.

Some would say that this is a platitude. Would that it were! In a sense, it was learned thousands of years ago, but natural selection favors the forces of psychological denial [8]. The individual benefits as an individual from his ability to deny the truth even though society as a whole, of which he is a part, suffers. Education can counteract the natural tendency to do the wrong thing, but the inexorable succession of generations requires that the basis of this knowledge be constantly refreshed.

A simple incident that occurred a few years ago in Leominster, Massachusetts, shows how perishable the knowledge is. During the Christmas shopping season the parking meters downtown were covered with plastic bags that bore tags reading: "Do not open until after Christmas. Free parking courtesy of the mayor and city council." In other words, facing the prospect of an increased demand for already scarce space, the city fathers reinstituted the system of the commons. (Cynically, we suspect that they gained more votes than they lost by this retrogressive act.)

In an approximate way, the logic of the commons has been understood for a long time, perhaps since the discovery of agriculture or the invention of private property in real estate. But it is understood mostly only in special cases which are not sufficiently generalized. Even at this late date, cattle-men leasing national land on the western ranges demonstrate no more than an ambivalent understanding, in constantly pressuring federal authorities to increase the head count to the point where overgrazing produces erosion and weed-dominance. Likewise, the oceans of the world continue to suffer from the survival of the philosophy of the commons. Maritime nations still re-spond automatically to the shibboleth of the "freedom of the seas." Profess-ing to believe in the "inexhaustible resources of the oceans," they bring species after species of fish and whales closer to extinction [9].

The National Parks present another instance of the working out of the tragedy of the commons. At present, they are open to all, without limit. The parks themselves are limited in extent—there is only one Yosemite Valley—whereas population seems to grow without limit. The values that visitors seek in the parks are steadily eroded. Plainly, we must soon cease to treat the parks as commons or they will be of no value to anyone.

What shall we do? We have several options. We might sell them off as private property. We might keep them as public property, but allocate the right to enter them. The allocation might be on the basis of wealth, by the use of an auction system. It might be on the basis of merit, as defined by some agreed-upon standards. It might be by lottery. Or it might be on a first-come, first-served basis, administered to long queues. These, I think, are all the reasonable possibilities. They are all objectionable. But we must choose—or acquiesce in the destruction of the commons that we call our National Parks.

Pollution

In a reverse way, the tragedy of the commons reappears in problems of pol-lution. Here it is not a question of taking something out of the commons, but of putting something in—sewage, or chemical, radioactive, and heat wastes into water; noxious and dangerous fumes into the air; and distracting and unpleasant advertising signs into the line of sight. The calculations of utility are much the same as before. The rational man finds that his share of the cost of the wastes he discharges into the commons is less than the cost of purifying his wastes before releasing them. Since this is true for everyone, we are locked into a system of "fouling our own nest," so long as we behave only as independent, rational, free-enterprisers.

The tragedy of the commons as a food basket is averted by private property, or something formally like it. But the air and waters surrounding us cannot readily be fenced, and so the tragedy of the commons as a cesspool must be prevented by different means, by coercive laws or taxing devices that make it cheaper for the polluter to treat his pollutants than to discharge them untreated. We have not progressed as far with the solution of this problem as we have with the first. Indeed, our particular concept of private property, which deters us from exhausting the positive resources of the earth, favors pollution. The owner of a factory on the bank of a stream—whose property extends to the middle of the stream—often has difficulty seeing why it is not his natural right to muddy the waters flowing past his door. The law, always behind the times, requires elaborate stitching and fitting to adapt it to this newly perceived aspect of the commons.

The pollution problem is a consequence of population. It did not much matter how a lonely American frontiersman disposed of his waste. "Flowing water purifies itself every 10 miles," my grandfather used to say, and the myth was near enough to the truth when he was a boy, for there were not too many people. But as population became denser, the natural chemical and biological recycling processes became overloaded, calling for a redefinition of property rights.

How to Legislate Temperance?

Analysis of the pollution problem as a function of population density uncovers a not generally recognized principle of morality, namely: *the morality of an act is a function of the state of the system at the time it is performed* [10]. Using the commons as a cesspool does not harm the general public under frontier conditions, because there is no public; the same behavior in a metropolis is unbearable. A hundred and fifty years ago a plainsman could kill an American bison, cut out only the tongue for his dinner, and discard the rest of the animal. He was not in any important sense being wasteful. Today, with only a few thousand bison left, we would be appalled at such behavior.

In passing, it is worth noting that the morality of an act cannot be determined from a photograph. One does not know whether a man killing an elephant or setting fire to the grassland is harming others until one knows the total system in which his act appears. "One picture is worth a thousand words," said an ancient Chinese; but it may take 10,000 words to validate it. It is as tempting to ecologists as it is to reformers in general to try to persuade others by way of the photographic shortcut. But the essense of an argument cannot be photographed: it must be presented rationally—in words.

That morality is system-sensitive escaped the attention of most codifiers of ethics in the past. "Thou shalt not . . . ." is the form of traditional ethical directives which make no allowance for particular circumstances. The laws of our society follow the pattern of ancient ethics, and therefore are poorly suited to governing a complex, crowded, changeable world. Our epicyclic solution is to augment statutory law with administrative law. Since it is practically impossible to spell out all the conditions under which it is safe to burn trash in the back yard or to run an automobile without smog-control, by law we delegate the details to bureaus. The result is administrative law, which is rightly feared for an ancient reason—*Quis custodiet ipsos custodes?*—"Who shall watch the watchers themselves?" John Adams said that we must have "a government of laws and not men." Bureau administrators, trying to evaluate the mortality of acts in the total system, are singularly liable to corruption, producing a government by men, not laws.

Prohibition is easy to legislate (though not necessarily to enforce); but how do we legislate temperance? Experience indicates that it can be accomplished best through the mediation of administrative law. We limit possibilities unnecessarily if we suppose that the sentiment of *Quis custodiet* denies us the use of administrative law. We should rather retain the phrase as a perpetual reminder of fearful dangers we cannot avoid. The great challenge facing us now is to invent the corrective feedbacks that are needed to keep custodians honest. We must find ways to legitimate the needed authority of both the custodians and the corrective feedbacks.

Freedom to Breed Is Intolerable

The tragedy of the commons is involved in population problems in another way. In a world governed solely by the principle of "dog eat dog"—if indeed there ever was such a world—how many children a family had would not be a matter of public concern. Parents who bred too exuberantly would leave fewer descendants, not more, because they would be unable to care adequately for their children. David Lack and others have found that such a negative feedback demonstrably controls the fecundity of birds [11]. But men are not birds, and have not acted like them for millenniums, at least.

If each human family were dependent only on its own resources; *if* the children of improvident parents starved to death; *if*, thus, overbreeding brought its own "punishment" to the germ line—*then* there would be no public interest in controlling the breeding of families. But our society is deeply committed to the welfare state [12], and hence is confronted with another aspect of the tragedy of the commons.

In a welfare state, how shall we deal with the family, the religion, the race, or the class (or indeed any distinguishable and cohesive group) that adopts overbreeding as a policy to secure its own aggrandizement [13]? To couple the concept of freedom to breed with the belief that everyone born has an equal right to the commons is to lock the world into a tragic course of action.

Unfortunately this is just the course of action that is being pursued by the United Nations. In late 1967, some 30 nations agreed to the following [14]:

> The Universal Declaration of Human Rights describes the family as
> the natural and fundamental unit of society. It follows that any

choice and decision with regard to the size of the family must irrev-
ocably rest with the family itself, and cannot be made by anyone
else.

It is painful to have to deny categorically the validity of this right; denying it, one feels as uncomfortable as a resident of Salem, Massachusetts,
who denied the reality of witches in the 17th century. At the present time,
in liberal quarters, something like a taboo acts to inhibit criticism of the
United Nations. There is a feeling that the United Nations is "our last and
best hope," that we shouldn't find fault with it; we shouldn't play into the
hands of the archconservatives. However, let us not forget what Robert
Louis Stevenson said: "The truth that is suppressed by friends is the readiest
weapon of the enemy." If we love the truth we must openly deny the validity
of the Universal Declaration of Human Rights, even though it is promoted
by the United Nations. We should also join with Kingsley Davis [15] in attempting to get Planned Parenthood-World Population to see the error of its
ways in embracing the same tragic ideal.

Conscience Is Self-Eliminating

It is a mistake to think that we can control the breeding of mankind in the
long run by an appeal to conscience. Charles Galton Darwin made this point
when he spoke on the centennial of the publication of his grandfather's great
book. The argument is straightforward and Darwinian.

People vary. Confronted with appeals to limit breeding, some people
will undoubtedly respond to the plea more than others. Those who have
more children will produce a larger fraction of the next generation than those
with more susceptible consciences. The difference will be accentuated, generation by generation.

In C. G. Darwin's words: "It may well be that it would take hundreds
of generations for the progenitive instinct to develop in this way, but if it
should do so, nature would have taken her revenge, and the variety *Homo
contracipiens* would become extinct and would be replaced by the variety
Homo progenitivus" [16].

The argument assumes that conscience or the desire for children (no
matter which) is hereditary—but hereditary only in the most general formal
sense. The result will be the same whether the attitude is transmitted
through germ cells, or exosomatically, to use A. J. Lotka's term. (If one
denies the latter possibility as well as the former, then what's the point of
education?) The argument has here been stated in the context of the population problem, but it applies equally well to any instance in which society
appeals to an individual exploiting a commons to restrain himself for the
general good—by means of his conscience. To make such an appeal is to set
up a selective system that works toward the elimination of conscience from
the race.

Pathogenic Effects of Conscience

The long-term disadvantage of an appeal to conscience should be enough to condemn it; but has serious short-term disadvantages as well. If we ask a man who is exploiting a commons to disist "in the name of conscience," what are we saying to him? What does he hear?—not only at the moment but also in the wee small hours of the night when, half asleep, he remembers not merely the words we used but also the nonverbal communication cues we gave him unawares? Sooner or later, consciously or subconsciously, he senses that he has received two communications, and that they are contradictory: (1) (intended communication) "If you don't do as we ask, we will openly condemn you for not acting like a responsible citizen"; (2) (the unintended communication) "If you *do* behave as we ask, we will secretly condemn you for a simpleton who can be shamed into standing aside while the rest of us exploit the commons."

Everyman then is caught in what Bateson has called a "double bind." Bateson and his co-workers have made a plausible case for viewing the double bind as an important causative factor in the genesis of schizophrenia [17]. The double bind may not always be so damaging, but it always endangers the mental health of anyone to whom it is applied. "A bad conscience," said Nietzsche, "is a kind of illness."

To conjure up a conscience in others is tempting to anyone who wishes to extend his control beyond the legal limits. Leaders at the highest level succumb to this temptation. Has any President during the past generation failed to call on labor unions to moderate voluntarily their demands for higher wages, or to steel companies to honor voluntary guidelines on prices? I can recall none. The rhetoric used on such occasions is designed to produce feelings of guilt in noncooperators.

For centuries it was assumed without proof that guilt was a valuable, perhaps even an indispensable, ingredient of the civilized life. Now, in this post-Freudian world, we doubt it.

Paul Goodman speaks from the modern point of view when he says: "No good has ever come from feeling guilty, neither intelligence, policy, nor compassion. The guilty do not pay attention to the object but only to themselves, and not even to their own interests, which might make sense, but to their anxieties" [18].

One does not have to be a professional psychiatrist to see the consequences of anxiety. We in the Western world are just emerging from a dreadful two-centuries-long Dark Ages of Eros that was sustained partly by prohibition laws, but perhaps more effectively by the anxiety-generating mechanisms of education. Alex Comfort has told the story well in *The Anxiety Makers* [19]; it is not a pretty one.

Since proof is difficult, we may even concede that the results of anxiety may sometimes, from certain points of view, be desirable. The larger question we should ask is whether, as a matter of policy, we should ever encourage the use of a technique the tendency (if not the intention) of which is psychologically pathogenic. We hear much talk these days of responsible parenthood; the coupled words are incorporated into the titles of some organizations devoted to birth control. Some people have proposed massive propaganda campaigns to instill responsibility into the nation's (or the world's) breeders. But what is the meaning of the word responsibility in this context? Is it not merely a synonym for the word conscience? When we use the word responsibility in the absence of substantial sanctions are we not trying to browbeat a free man is a commons into acting against his own interest? Responsibility is a verbal counterfeit for a substantial *quid pro quo*. It is an attempt to get something for nothing.

If the word responsibility is to be used at all, I suggest that it be in the sense Charles Frankel uses it [20]. "Responsibility," says this philosopher, "is the product of definite social arrangements." Notice that Frankel calls for social arrangements—not propaganda.

Mutual Coercion Mutually Agreed Upon

The social arrangements that produce responsibility are arrangements that create coercion, of some sort. Consider bank-robbing. The man who takes money from a bank acts as if the bank were a commons. How do we prevent such action? Certainly not by trying to control his behavior solely by a verbal appeal to his sense of responsibility. Rather than rely on propaganda we follow Frankel's lead and insist that a bank is not a commons; we seek the definite social arrangements that will keep it from becoming a commons. That we thereby infringe on the freedom of would-be robbers we neither deny nor regret.

The morality of bank-robbing is particularly easy to understand because we accept complete prohibition of this activity. We are willing to say "Thou shalt not rob banks," without providing for exceptions. But temperance also can be created by coercion. Taxing is a good coercive device. To keep downtown shoppers temperate in their use of parking space we introduce parking meters for short periods, and traffic fines for longer ones. We need not actually forbid a citizen to park as long as he wants to; we need merely make it increasingly expensive for him to do so. Not prohibition, but carefully biased options are what we offer him. A Madison Avenue man might call this persuasion; I prefer the greater candor of the word coercion.

Coercion is a dirty word to most liberals now, but it need not forever be so. As with the four-letter words, its dirtiness can be cleansed away by exposure to the light, by saying it over and over without apology or embarrassment. To many, the word coercion implies arbitrary decisions of distant and irresponsible bureaucrats; but this is not a necessary part of its meaning. The only kind of coercion I recommend is mutual coercion, mutually agreed upon by the majority of the people affected.

To say that we mutually agree to coercion is not to say that we are required to enjoy it, or even to pretend we enjoy it. Who enjoys taxes? We all grumble about them. But we accept compulsory taxes because we recognize that voluntary taxes would favor the conscienceless. We institute and (grumblingly) support taxes and other coercive devices to escape the horror of the commons.

An alternative to the commons need not be perfectly just to be preferable. With real estate and other material goods, the alternative we have chosen is the institution of private property coupled with legal inheritance. Is this system perfectly just? As a genetically trained biologist I deny that it is. It seems to me that, if there are to be differences in individual inheritance, legal possession should be perfectly correlated with biological inheritance—that those who are biologically more fit to be the custodians of property and power should legally inherit more. But genetic recombination continually makes a mockery of the doctrine of "like father, like son" implicit in our laws of legal inheritance. An idiot can inherit millions, and a trust fund can keep his estate intact. We must admit that our legal system of private property plus inheritance is unjust—but we put up with it because we are not convinced, at the moment, that anyone has invented a better system. The alternative of the commons is too horrifying to contemplate. Injustice is preferable to total ruin.

It is one of the peculiarities of the warfare between reform and the status quo that it is thoughtlessly governed by a double standard. Whenever a reform measure is proposed it is often defeated when its opponents triumphantly discover a flaw in it. As Kingsley Davis has pointed out [21], worshippers of the status quo sometimes imply that no reform is possible without unanimous agreement, an implication contrary to historical fact. As nearly as I can make out, automatic rejection of proposed reforms is based on one of two unconscious assumptions: (i) that the status quo is perfect; or (ii) that the choice we face is between reform and no action; if the proposed reform is imperfect, we presumably should take no action at all, while we wait for a perfect proposal.

But we can never do nothing. That which we have done for thousands of years is also action. It also produces evils. Once we are aware that the status quo is action, we can then compare its discoverable advantages and disadvantages with the predicted advantages and disadvantages of the proposed reform, discounting as best we can for our lack of experience. On the basis of such a comparison, we can make a rational decision which will not involve the unworkable assumption that only perfect systems are tolerable. . . .

NOTES

Note: This article is based on a presidential address presented before the meeting of the Pacific Division of the American Association for the Advancement of Science at Utah State University, Logan, 25 June 1968.

REFERENCES

1. J. B. Wiesner and H. F. York, *Sci. Amer.* 211 (No. 4), 27 (1964).

2. G. Hardin, *J. Hered.* 50, 68 (1959); S. von Hoernor, *Science* 137, 18 (1962).

3. J. von Neumann and O. Morgenstern, *Theory of Games and Economic Behavior* (Princeton Univ. Press, Princeton, N.J., 1947), p. 11.

4. J. H. Fremlin, *New Sci.,* No. 415 (1964), p. 285.

5. A. Smith, *The Wealth of Nations* (Modern Library, New York, 1937), p. 423.

6. W. F. Lloyd, *Two Lectures on the Checks to Population* (Oxford Univ. Press, Oxford, England, 1833), reprinted (in part) in *Population, Evolution, and Birth Control,* G. Hardin, Ed. (Freeman, San Francisco, 1964), p. 37.

7. A. N. Whitehead, *Science and the Modern World* (Mentor, New York, 1948), p. 17.

8. G. Hardin, Ed. *Population, Evolution, and Birth Control* (Freeman, San Francisco, 1964), p. 56.

9. S. McVay, *Sci. Amer.* 216 (No. 8), 13 (1966).

10. J. Fletcher, *Situation Ethics* (Westminster, Philadelphia, 1966).

11. D. Lack, *The Natural Regulation of Animal Numbers* (Clarendon Press, Oxford, 1954).

12. H. Girvetz, *From Wealth to Welfare* (Stanford Univ. Press, Stanford, Calif., 1950).

13. G. Hardin, *Perspec. Biol. Med.* 6, 366 (1963).

14. U. Thant, *Int. Planned Parenthood News,* No. 168 (February 1968), p. 3.

15. K. Davis, *Science* 158, 730 (1967).

16. S. Tax, Ed., *Evolution after Darwin* (Univ. of Chicago Press, Chicago, 1960), vol. 2, p. 469.

17. G. Bateson, D. D. Jackson, J. Haley, J. Weakland, *Behav. Sci.* 1, 251 (1956).

18. P. Goodman, *New York Rev. Books* 10(8), 22 (23 May 1968).

19. A. Comfort, *The Anxiety Makers* (Nelson, London, 1967).

20. C. Frankel, *The Case for Modern Man* (Harper, New York, 1955), p. 203.

21. J. D. Roslansky, *Genetics and the Future of Man* (Appleton-Century-Crofts, New York, 1966), p. 177.

SELECTION 9

RONALD H. COASE
The Problem of Social Cost

Ronald Coase examines arrangements that can lead to an optimal
allocation of resources when externalities exist. He emphasizes that
the responsibility for damages resulting from externalities is
reciprocal in nature. What has become known as the Coase
theorem is his result that when externalities are present, resource
misallocation will not occur if the involved parties can bargain to
their mutual benefit at no cost. Negotiation leads to an
arrangement, either the polluting party compensating the "victim"
or the potential victim bribing the potential polluter to forgo partly
or completely the harmful acts.

QUESTIONS TO GUIDE THE READING

1. In the arithmetic example involving wandering cattle, why is it
   useful in demonstrating the Coase theorem to consider the
   "crop loss per additional steer" as a marginal bribe schedule
   offered by the wheat farmer to the cattle rancher?
2. Under what conditions would the parties involved in an
   externality be unable to prevent resource misallocation by
   bargaining to their mutual advantage?
3. What is the importance of transactions costs in determining the
   correct public policy for treating an externality?

I. The Problem to Be Examined

This paper is concerned with those actions of business firms which have
harmful effects on others. The standard example is that of a factory the
smoke from which has harmful effects on those occupying neighbouring
properties. The economic analysis of such a situation has usually proceeded
in terms of a divergence between the private and social product of the factory, in which economists have largely followed the treatment of Pigou in
The Economics of Welfare. The conclusion to which this kind of analysis
seems to have led most economists is that it would be desirable to make
the owner of the factory liable for the damage caused to those injured by the

Ronald Coase, "The Problem of Social Cost," *Journal of Law and Economics 3* (October 1960),
   1–44. Reprinted by permission of the author and The University of Chicago.

Ronald H. Coase is Clifton R. Musser Professor Emeritus of Economics at the University of
Chicago.

smoke, or alternatively, to place a tax on the factory owner varying with the amount of smoke produced and equivalent in money terms to the damage it would cause, or finally, to exclude the factory from residential districts (and presumably from other areas in which the emission of smoke would have harmful effects on others). It is my contention that the suggested courses of action are inappropriate, in that they lead to results which are not necessarily, or even usually, desirable.

II. The Reciprocal Nature of the Problem

The traditional approach has tended to obscure the nature of the choice that has to be made. The question is commonly thought of as one in which A inflicts harm on B and what has to be decided is: how should we restrain A? But this is wrong. We are dealing with a problem of a reciprocal nature. To avoid the harm to B would inflict harm on A. The real question that has to be decided is: should A be allowed to harm B or should B be allowed to harm A? The problem is to avoid the more serious harm. I instanced in my previous article[1] the case of a confectioner the noise and vibrations from whose machinery disturbed a doctor in his work. To avoid harming the doctor would inflict harm on the confectioner. The problem posed by this case was essentially whether it was worth while, as a result of restricting the methods of production which would be used by the confectioner, to secure more doctoring at the cost of a reduced supply of confectionery products. Another example is afforded by the problem of straying cattle which destroy crops on neighbouring land. If it is inevitable that some cattle will stray, an increase in the supply of meat can only be obtained at the expense of a decrease in the supply of crops. The nature of the choice is clear: meat or crops. What answer should be given is, of course, not clear unless we know the value of what is obtained as well as the value of what is sacrificed to obtain it. To give another example, Professor George J. Stigler instances the contamination of a stream.[2] If we assume that the harmful effect of the pollution is that it kills the fish, the question to be decided is: is the value of the fish lost greater or less than the value of the product which the contamination of the stream makes possible? It goes almost without saying that this problem has to be looked at in total *and* at the margin.

III. The Pricing System with Liability for Damage

I propose to start my analysis by examining a case in which most economists would presumably agree that the problem would be solved in a completely satisfactory manner: when the damaging business has to pay for all damage caused *and* the pricing system works smoothly (strictly this means that the operation of a pricing system is without cost).

   A good example of the problem under discussion is afforded by the case of straying cattle which destroy crops growing on neighbouring land. Let us suppose that a farmer and cattle-raiser are operating on neighbouring prop-

erties. Let us further suppose that, without any fencing between the properties, an increase in the size of the cattle-raiser's herd increases the total
damage to the farmer's crops. What happens to the marginal damage as the
size of the herd increases is another matter. This depends on whether the
cattle tend to follow one another or to roam side by side, on whether they
tend to be more or less restless as the size of the herd increases and on other
similar factors. For my immediate purpose, it is immaterial what assumption
is made about marginal damage as the size of the herd increases.

To simplify the argument, I propose to use an arithmetical example. I
shall assume that the annual cost of fencing the farmer's property is $9 and
that the price of the crop is $1 per ton. Also, I assume that the relation
between the number of cattle in the herd and the annual crop loss is as follows:

Number in Herd (steers)	Annual Crop Loss (tons)	Crop Loss per Additional Steer (tons)
1	1	1
2	3	2
3	6	3
4	10	4

Given that the cattle-raiser is liable for the damage caused, the additional annual cost imposed on the cattle-raiser if he increased his herd from,
say, 2 to 3 steers in $3 and in deciding on the size of the herd, he will take
this into account along with his other costs. That is, he will not increase the
size of the herd unless the value of the additional meat produced (assuming
that the cattle-raiser slaughters the cattle) is greater than the additional costs
that this will entail, including the value of the additional crops destroyed. Of
course, if, by the employment of dogs, herdsmen, aeroplanes, mobile radio
and other means, the amount of damage can be reduced, these means will
be adopted when their cost is less than the value of the crop which they
prevent being lost. Given that the annual cost of fencing is $9, the cattle-
raiser who wished to have a herd with 4 steers or more would pay for fencing
to be erected and maintained, assuming that other means of attaining the
same end would not do so more cheaply. When the fence is erected, the
marginal cost due to the liability for damage becomes zero, except to
the extent that an increase in the size of the herd necessitates a stronger and
therefore more expensive fence because more steers are liable to lean against
it at the same time. But, of course, it may be cheaper for the cattle-raiser
not to fence and to pay for the damaged crops, as in my arithmetical example, with 3 or fewer steers.

It might be thought that the fact that the cattle-raiser would pay for all
crops damaged would lead the farmer to increase his planting if a cattle-

raiser came to occupy the neighbouring property. But this is not so. If the crop was previously sold in conditions of perfect competition, marginal cost was equal to price for the amount of planting undertaken and any expansion would have reduced the profits of the farmer. In the new situation, the existence of crop damage would mean that the farmer would sell less on the open market but his receipts for a given production would remain the same, since the cattle-raiser would pay the market price for any crop damaged. Of course, if cattle-raising commonly involved the destruction of crops, the coming into existence of a cattle-raising industry might raise the price of the crops involved and farmers would then extend their planting. But I wish to confine my attention to the individual farmer.

I have said that the occupation of a neighbouring property by a cattle-raiser would not cause the amount of production, or perhaps more exactly the amount of planting, by the farmer to increase. In fact, if the cattle-raising has any effect, it will be to decrease the amount of planting. The reason for this is that, for any given tract of land, if the value of the crop damaged is so great that the receipts from the sale of the undamaged crop are less than the total costs of cultivating that tract of land, it will be profitable for the farmer and the cattle-raiser to make a bargain whereby that tract of land is left uncultivated. This can be made clear by means of an arithmetical example. Assume initially that the value of the crop obtained from cultivating a given tract of land is $12 and that the cost incurred in cultivating this tract of land is $10, the net gain from cultivating the land being $2. I assume for purposes of simplicity that the farmer owns the land. Now assume that the cattle-raiser starts operations on the neighbouring property and that the value of the crops damaged is $1. In this case $11 is obtained by the farmer from sale on the market and $1 is obtained from the cattle-raiser for damage suffered and the net gain remains $2. Now suppose that the cattle-raiser finds it profitable to increase the size of his herd, even though the amount of damage rises to $3; which means that the value of the additional meat production is greater than the additional costs, including the additional $2 payment for damage. But the total payment for damage is now $3. The net gain to the farmer from cultivating the land is still $2. The cattle-raiser would be better off if the farmer would agree not to cultivate his land for any payment less than $3. The farmer would be agreeable to not cultivating the land for any payment greater than $2. There is clearly room for a mutually satisfactory bargain which would lead to the abandonment of cultivation.[3] But the same argument applies not only to the whole tract cultivated by the farmer but also to any subdivision of it. Suppose, for example, that the cattle have a well-defined route, say, to a brook or to a shady area. In these circumstances, the amount of damage to the crop along the route may well be great and if so, it could be that the farmer and the cattle-raiser would find it profitable to make a bargain whereby the farmer would agree not to cultivate this strip of land.

But this raises a further possibility. Suppose that there is such a well-defined route. Suppose further that the value of the crop that would be obtained by cultivating this strip of land is $10 but that the cost of cultivation is $11. In the absence of the cattle-raiser, the land would not be cultivated. However, given the presence of the cattle-raiser, it could well be that if the strip was cultivated, the whole crop would be destroyed by the cattle. In which case, the cattle-raiser would be forced to pay $10 to the farmer. It is true that the farmer would lose $1. But the cattle-raiser would lose $10. Clearly this is a situation which is not likely to last indefinitely since neither party would want this to happen. The aim of the farmer would be to induce the cattle-raiser to make a payment in return for an agreement to leave this land uncultivated. The farmer would not be able to obtain a payment greater than the cost of fencing off this piece of land nor so high as to lead the cattle-raiser to abandon the use of the neighbouring property. What payment would in fact be made would depend on the shrewdness of the farmer and the cattle-raiser as bargainers. But as the payment would not be so high as to cause the cattle-raiser to abandon this location and as it would not vary with the size of the herd, such an agreement would not affect the allocation of resources but would merely alter the distribution of income and wealth as between the cattle-raiser and the farmer.

I think it is clear that if the cattle-raiser is liable for damage caused and the pricing system works smoothly, the reduction in the value of production elsewhere will be taken into account in computing the additional cost involved in increasing the size of the herd. This cost will be weighed against the value of the additional meat production and, given perfect competition in the cattle industry, the allocation of resources in cattle-raising will be optimal. What needs to be emphasized is that the fall in the value of production elsewhere which would be taken into account in the costs of the cattle-raiser may well be less than the damage which the cattle would cause to the crops in the ordinary course of events. This is because it is possible, as a result of market transactions, to discontinue cultivation of the land. This is desirable in all cases in which the damage that the cattle would cause, and for which the cattle-raiser would be willing to pay, exceeds the amount which the farmer would pay for use of the land. In conditions of perfect competition, the amount which the farmer would pay for the use of the land is equal to the difference between the value of the total production when the factors are employed on this land and the value of the additional product yielded in their next best use (which would be what the farmer would have to pay for the factors). If damage exceeds the amount the farmer would pay for the use of the land, the value of the additional product of the factors employed elsewhere would exceed the value of the total product in this use after damage is taken into account. It follows that it would be desirable to abandon cultivation of the land and to release the factors employed for production elsewhere. A procedure which merely provided for payment for damage to the crop caused by the cattle but which did not allow for the possibility of cultivation being discontinued would result in too small an employment of factors of production in cattle-raising and too large an employment of factors in cultivation of the crop. But given the possibility of market transactions, a situation in which damage to crops exceeded the rent of the land would not endure. Whether the cattle-raiser pays the farmer to leave the land uncultivated or himself rents the land by paying the land-owner an amount slightly greater than the farmer would pay (if the farmer was himself renting the land), the final result would be the same and would maximize the value of production. Even when the farmer is induced to plant crops which it would not be profitable to cultivate for sale on the market, this will be a purely short-term phenomenon and may be expected to lead to an agreement under which the planting will cease. The cattle-raiser will remain in that location and the marginal cost of meat production will be the same as before, thus having no long-run effect on the allocation of resources.

IV. The Pricing System with No Liability for Damage

I now turn to the case in which, although the pricing system is assumed to work smoothly (that is, costlessly), the damaging business is not liable for any of the damage which it causes. This business does not have to make a payment to those damaged by its actions. I propose to show that the allocation of resources will be the same in this case as it was when the damaging business was liable for damage caused. As I showed in the previous case that the allocation of resources was optimal, it will not be necessary to repeat this part of the argument.

I return to the case of the farmer and the cattle-raiser. The farmer would suffer increased damage to his crop as the size of the herd increased. Suppose that the size of the cattle-raiser's herd is 3 steers (and that this is the size of the herd that would be maintained if crop damage was not taken into account). Then the farmer would be willing to pay up to $3 if the cattle-raiser would reduce his herd to 2 steers, up to $5 if the herd were reduced to 1 steer and would pay up to $6 if cattle-raising was abandoned. The cattle-raiser would therefore receive $3 from the farmer if he kept 2 steers instead of 3. This $3 foregone is therefore part of the cost incurred in keeping the third steer. Whether the $3 is a payment which the cattle-raiser has to make if he adds the third steer to his herd (which it would be if the cattle-raiser was liable to the farmer for damage caused to the crop) or whether it is a sum of money which he would have received if he did not keep a third steer (which it would be if the cattle-raiser was not liable to the farmer for damage caused to the crop) does not affect the final result. In both cases $3 is part of the cost of adding a third steer, to be included along with the other costs. If the increase in the value of production in cattle-raising through increasing the size of the herd from 2 to 3 is greater than the additional costs that have to be incurred (including the $3 damage to crops), the size of the herd will be increased. Otherwise, it will not. The size of the herd will be the same whether the cattle-raiser is liable for damage caused to the crop or not.

It may be argued that the assumed starting point—a herd of 3 steers—was arbitrary. And this is true. But the farmer would not wish to pay to avoid crop damage which the cattle-raiser would not be able to cause. For example, the maximum annual payment which the farmer could be induced to pay could not exceed $9, the annual cost of fencing. And the farmer would only be willing to pay this sum if it did not reduce his earnings to a level that would cause him to abandon cultivation of this particular tract of land. Furthermore, the farmer would only be willing to pay this amount if he believed that, in the absence of any payment by him, the size of the herd maintained by the cattle-raiser would be 4 or more steers. Let us assume that this is the case. Then the farmer would be willing to pay up to $3 if the cattle-raiser would reduce his herd to 3 steers, up to $6 if the herd were reduced to 2 steers, up to $8 if one steer only were kept and up to $9 if cattle-raising were abandoned. It will be noticed that the change in the starting point has not altered the amount which would accrue to the cattle-raiser if he reduced the size of his herd by any given amount. It is still true that the cattle-raiser could receive an additional $3 from the farmer if he agreed to reduce his herd from 3 steers to 2 and that the $3 represents the value of the crop that would be destroyed by adding the third steer to the herd. Although a different belief on the part of the farmer (whether justified or not) about the size of the herd that the cattle-raiser would maintain in the absence of payments from him may affect the total payment he can be induced to pay, it is not true that this different belief would have any effect on the size of the herd that the cattle-raiser will actually keep. This will be the same as it would be if the cattle-raiser had to pay for damage caused by his cattle, since a receipt foregone of a given amount is the equivalent of a payment of the same amount.

It might be thought that it would pay the cattle-raiser to increase his herd above the size that he would wish to maintain once a bargain had been made, in order to induce the farmer to make a larger total payment. And this may be true. It is similar in nature to the action of the farmer (when the cattle-raiser was liable for damage) in cultivating land on which, as a result of an agreement with the cattle-raiser, planting would subsequently be abandoned (including land which would not be cultivated at all in the absence of cattle-raising). But such manoeuvres are preliminaries to an agreement and do not affect the long-run equilibrium position, which is the same whether or not the cattle-raiser is held responsible for the crop damage brought about by his cattle.

It is necessary to know whether the damaging business is liable or not for damage caused since without the establishment of this initial delimitation of rights there can be no market transactions to transfer and recombine them. But the ultimate result (which maximizes the value of production) is independent of the legal position if the pricing system is assumed to work without cost. . . .

VI. The Cost of Market Transactions Taken into Account

The argument has proceeded up to this point on the assumption (explicit in Sections III and IV . . .) that there were no costs involved in carrying out market transactions. This is, of course, a very unrealistic assumption. In order to carry out a market transaction it is necessary to discover who it is that one wishes to deal with, to inform people that one wishes to deal and on what terms, to conduct negotiations leading up to a bargain, to draw up the contract, to undertake the inspection needed to make sure that the terms of the contract are being observed and so on. These operations are often extremely costly, sufficiently costly at any rate to prevent many transactions that would be carried out in a world in which the pricing system worked without cost.

In earlier sections, when dealing with the problem of the rearrangement of legal rights through the market, it was argued that such a rearrangement would be made through the market whenever this would lead to an increase in the value of production. But this assumed costless market transactions. Once the costs of carrying out market transactions are taken into account it is clear that such a rearrangement of rights will only be undertaken when the increase in the value of production consequent upon the rearrangement is greater than the costs which would be involved in bringing it about. When it is less, the granting of an injunction (or the knowledge that it would be granted) or the liability to pay damages may result in an activity being discontinued (or may prevent its being started) which would be undertaken if market transactions were costless. In these conditions the initial delimitation of legal rights does have an effect on the efficiency with which the economic system operates. One arrangement of rights may bring about a greater value of production than any other. But unless this is the arrangement of rights established by the legal system, the costs of reaching the same result by altering and combining rights through the market may be so great that this optimal arrangement of rights, and the greater value of production which it would bring, may never be achieved. The part played by economic considerations in the process of delimiting legal rights will be discussed in the next section. In this section, I will take the initial delimitation of rights and the costs of carrying out market transactions as given.

It is clear that an alternative form of economic organization which could achieve the same result at less cost than would be incurred by using the market would enable the value of production to be raised. As I explained many years ago, the firm represents such an alternative to organising production through market transactions.[4] Within the firm individual bargains between the various cooperating factors of production are eliminated and for a market transaction is substituted an administrative decision. The rearrangement of production then takes place without the need for bargains between the owners of the factors of production. A landowner who has control of a large tract of land may devote his land to various uses taking into account the effect that the interrelations of the various activities will have on the net return of the land, thus rendering unnecessary bargains between those undertaking the various activities. Owners of a large building or of several adjoining properties in a given area may act in much the same way. In effect, using our earlier terminology, the firm would acquire the legal rights of all the parties and the rearrangement of activities would not follow on a rearrangement of rights by contract, but as a result of an administrative decision as to how the rights should be used.

It does not, of course, follow that the administrative costs of organising a transaction through a firm are inevitably less than the costs of the market transactions which are superseded. But where contracts are peculiarly difficult to draw up and an attempt to describe what the parties have agreed to do or not to do (e.g., the amount and kind of a smell or noise that they may make or will not make) would necessitate a lengthy and highly involved document, and, where, as is probable, a long-term contract would be desirable,[5] it would be hardly surprising if the emergence of a firm or the extension of the activities of an existing firm was not the solution adopted on many occasions to deal with the problem of harmful effects. This solution would be adopted whenever the administrative costs of the firm were less than the costs of the market transactions that it supersedes and the gains which would result from the rearrangement of activities greater than the firm's costs of organising them. I do not need to examine in great detail the character of this solution since I have explained what is involved in my earlier article.

But the firm is not the only possible answer to this problem. The administrative costs of organising transactions within the firm may also be high, and particularly so when many diverse activities are brought within the control of a single organisation. In the standard case of a smoke nuisance, which may affect a vast number of people engaged in a wide variety of activities, the administrative costs might well be so high as to make any attempt to deal with the problem within the confines of a single firm impossible. An alternative solution is direct government regulation. Instead of instituting a legal system of rights which can be modified by transactions on the market, the government may impose regulations which state what people must or must not do and which have to be obeyed. Thus, the government (by statute or perhaps more likely through an administrative agency) may, to deal with the problem of smoke nuisance, decree that certain methods of production should or should not be used (e.g., that smoke preventing devices should be installed or that coal or oil should not be burned) or may confine certain types of business to certain districts (zoning regulations).

The government is, in a sense, a superfirm (but of a very special kind) since it is able to influence the use of factors of production by administrative decision. But the ordinary firm is subject to checks in its operations because of the competition of other firms, which might administer the same activities at lower cost and also because there is always the alternative of market transactions as against organisation within the firm if the administrative costs become too great. The government is able, if it wishes, to avoid the market altogether, which a firm can never do. The firm has to make market agreements with the owners of the factors of production that it uses. Just as the government can conscript or seize property, so it can decree that factors of production should only be used in such-and-such a way. Such authoritarian methods save a lot of trouble (for those doing the organising). Furthermore, the government has at its disposal the police and the other law enforcement agencies to make sure that its regulations are carried out.

It is clear that the government has powers which might enable it to get some things done at a lower cost than could a private organisation (or at any rate one without special governmental powers). But the governmental administrative machine is not itself costless. It can, in fact, on occasion be extremely costly. Furthermore, there is no reason to suppose that the restrictive and zoning regulations, made by a fallible administration subject to political pressures and operating without any competitive check, will necessarily always be those which increase the efficiency with which the economic system operates. Furthermore, such general regulations which must apply to a wide variety of cases will be enforced in some cases in which they are clearly inappropriate. From these considerations it follows that direct governmental regulation will not necessarily give better results than leaving the problem to be solved by the market or the firm. But equally there is no reason why, on occasion, such governmental administrative regulation should not lead to an improvement in economic efficiency. This would seem particularly likely when, as is normally the case with the smoke nuisance, a large number of people are involved and in which therefore the costs of handling the problem through the market or the firm may be high.

There is, of course, a further alternative which is to do nothing about the problem at all. And given that the costs involved in solving the problem by regulations issued by the governmental administrative machine will often be heavy (particularly if the costs are interpreted to include all the consequences which follow from the government engaging in this kind of activity), it will no doubt be commonly the case that the gain which would come from regulating the actions which give rise to the harmful effects will be less than the costs involved in government regulation.

The discussion of the problem of harmful effects in this section (when the costs of market transactions are taken into account) is extremely inadequate. But at least it has made clear that the problem is one of choosing the appropriate social arrangement for dealing with the harmful effects. All solutions have costs and there is no reason to suppose that government regulation is called for simply because the problem is not well handled by the market or the firm. Satisfactory views on policy can only come from a patient study of how, in practice, the market, firms and governments handle the problem of harmful effects. Economists need to study the work of the broker in bringing parties together, the effectiveness of restrictive covenants, the problems of the large-scale real-estate development company, the operation of government zoning and other regulating activities. It is my belief that economists, and policy-makers generally, have tended to overestimate the advantages which come from governmental regulation. But this belief, even if justified, does not do more than suggest that government regulation should be curtailed. It does not tell us where the boundary line should be drawn. This, it seems to me, has to come from a detailed investigation of the actual results of handling the problem in different ways. But it would be unfortunate if this investigation were undertaken with the aid of a faulty economic analysis. The aim of this article is to indicate what the economic approach to the problem should be. . . .

IX. The Pigovian Tradition

It is strange that a doctrine as faulty as that developed by Pigou should have been so influential, although part of its success has probably been due to the lack of clarity in the exposition. Not being clear, it was never clearly wrong. Curiously enough, this obscurity in the source has not prevented the emergence of a fairly well-defined oral tradition. What economists think they learn from Pigou, and what they tell their students, which I term the Pigovian tradition, is reasonably clear. I propose to show the inadequacy of this Pigovian tradition by demonstrating that both the analysis and the policy conclusions which it supports are incorrect.

I do not propose to justify my view as to the prevailing opinion by copious references to the literature. I do this partly because the treatment in the literature is usually so fragmentary, often involving little more than a reference to Pigou plus some explanatory comment, that detailed examination would be inappropriate. But the main reason for this lack of reference is that the doctrine, although based on Pigou, must have been largely the product of an oral tradition. Certainly economists with whom I have discussed these problems have shown a unanimity of opinion which is quite remarkable considering the meagre treatment accorded this subject in the literature. No doubt there are some economists who do not share the usual view but they must represent a small minority of the profession.

The approach to the problems under discussion is through an examination of the value of physical production. The private product is the value of the additional product resulting from a particular activity of a business. The social product equals the private product minus the fall in the value of production elsewhere for which no compensation is paid by the business. Thus, if 10 units of a factor (and no other factors) are used by a business to make a certain product with a value of $105; and the owner of this factor is not compensated for their use, which he is unable to prevent; and these 10 units of the factor would yield products in their best alternative use worth $100; then, the social product is $105 minus $100 or $5. If the business now pays for one unit of the factor and its price equals the value of its marginal product, then the social product rises to $15. If two units are paid for, the social product rises to $25 and so on until it reaches $105 when all units of the factor are paid for. It is not difficult to see why economists have so readily accepted this rather odd procedure. The analysis focusses on the individual business decision and since the use of certain resources is not allowed for in costs, receipts are reduced by the same amount. But, of course, this means that the value of the social product has no social significance whatsoever. It seems to me preferable to use the opportunity cost concept and to approach these problems by comparing the value of the product yielded by factors in alternative uses or by alternative arrangements. The main advantage of a pricing system is that it leads to the employment of factors in places where the value of the product yielded is greatest and does so at less cost than alternative systems (I leave aside that a pricing system also eases the problem of the redistribution of income). But if through some God-given natural harmony factors flowed to the places where the value of the product yielded was greatest without any use of the pricing system and consequently there was no compensation, I would find it a source of surprise rather than a cause for dismay.

The definition of the social product is queer but this does not mean that the conclusions for policy drawn from the analysis are necessarily wrong. However, there are bound to be dangers in an approach which diverts attention from the basic issues and there can be little doubt that it has been responsible for some of the errors in current doctrine. The belief that it is desirable that the business which causes harmful effects should be forced to compensate those who suffer damage . . . is undoubtedly the result of not comparing the total product obtainable with alternative social arrangements.

The same fault is to be found in proposals for solving the problem of harmful effects by the use of taxes or bounties. Pigou lays considerable stress on this solution although he is, as usual, lacking in detail and qualified in his support.[6] Modern economists tend to think exclusively in terms of taxes and in a very precise way. The tax should be equal to the damage done and should therefore vary with the amount of the harmful effect. As it is not proposed that the proceeds of the tax should be paid to those suffering the damage, this solution is not the same as that which would force a business to pay compensation to those damaged by its actions, although economists generally do not seem to have noticed this and tend to treat the two solutions as being identical.

Assume that a factory which emits smoke is set up in a district previously free from smoke pollution, causing damage valued at $100 per annum. Assume that the taxation solution is adopted and that the factory-owner is taxed $100 per annum as long as the factory emits the smoke. Assume further that a smoke-preventing device costing $90 per annum to run is available. In these circumstances, the smoke-preventing device would be installed. Damage of $100 would have been avoided at an expenditure of $90 and the factory-owner would be better off by $10 per annum. Yet the position achieved may not be optimal. Suppose that those who suffer the damage could avoid it by moving to other locations or by taking various precautions which would cost them, or be equivalent to a loss in income of, $40 per annum. Then there would be a gain in the value of production of $50 if the factory continued to emit its smoke and those now in the district moved elsewhere or made other adjustments to avoid the damage. If the factory owner is to be made to pay a tax equal to the damage caused, it would clearly be desirable to institute a double tax system and to make residents of the district pay an amount equal to the additional cost incurred by the factory owner (or the consumers of his products) in order to avoid the damage. In these conditions, people would not stay in the district or would take other measures to prevent the damage from occurring, when the costs of doing so were less than the costs that would be incurred by the producer to reduce the damage (the producer's object, of course, being not so much to reduce the damage as to reduce the tax payments). A tax system which was confined to a tax on the producer for damage caused would tend to lead to unduly high costs being incurred for the prevention of damage. Of course this could be avoided if it were possible to base the tax, not on the damage caused, but on the fall in the value of production (in its widest sense) resulting from the emission of smoke. But to do so would require a detailed knowledge of individual preferences and I am unable to imagine how the data needed for such a taxation system could be assembled. Indeed, the proposal to solve the smoke-pollution and similar problems by the use of taxes bristles with difficulties: the problem of calculation, the difference between average and marginal damage, the interrelations between the damage suffered on different properties, etc. But it is unnecessary to examine these problems here. It is enough for my purpose to show that, even if the tax is exactly adjusted to equal the damage that would be done to neighbouring properties as a result of the emission of each additional puff of smoke, the tax would not necessarily bring about optimal conditions. An increase in the number of people living or of business operating in the vicinity of the smoke-emitting factory will increase the amount of harm produced by a given emission of smoke. The tax that would be imposed would therefore increase with an increase in the number of those in the vicinity. This will tend to lead to a decrease in the value of production of the factors employed by the factory, either because a reduction in production due to the tax will result in factors being used elsewhere in ways which are less valuable, or because factors will be diverted to produce means for reducing the amount of smoke emitted. But people deciding to establish themselves in the vicinity of the factory will not take into account this fall in the value of production which results from their presence. This failure to take into account costs imposed on others is comparable to the action of a factory-owner in not taking into account the harm resulting from his emission of smoke. Without the tax, there may be too much smoke and too few people in the vicinity of the factory; but with the tax there may be too little smoke and too many people in the vicinity of the factory. There is no reason to suppose that one of these results is necessarily preferable.

I need not devote much space to discussing the similar error involved in the suggestion that smoke producing factories should, by means of zoning regulations, be removed from the districts in which the smoke causes harmful effects. When the change in the location of the factory results in a reduction in production, this obviously needs to be taken into account and weighed against the harm which would result from the factory remaining in that location. The aim of such regulation should not be to eliminate smoke pollution but rather to secure the optimum amount of smoke pollution, this being the amount which will maximize the value of production.

X. A Change of Approach

It is my belief that the failure of economists to reach correct conclusions about the treatment of harmful effects cannot be ascribed simply to a few slips in analysis. It stems from basic defects in the current approach to problems of welfare economics. What is needed is a change of approach.

Analysis in terms of divergencies between private and social products concentrates attention on particular deficiencies in the system and tends to nourish the belief that any measure which will remove the deficiency is necessarily desirable. It diverts attention from those other changes in the system which are inevitably associated with the corrective measure, changes which may well produce more harm than the original deficiency. In the preceding sections of this article, we have seen many examples of this. But it is not necessary to approach the problem in this way. Economists who study problems of the firm habitually use an opportunity cost approach and compare the receipts obtained from a given combination of factors with alternative business arrangements. It would seem desirable to use a similar approach when dealing with questions of economic policy and to compare the total product yielded by alternative social arrangements. In this article, the analysis has been confined, as is usual in this part of economics, to comparisons of the value of production, as measured by the market. But it is, of course, desirable that the choice between different social arrangements for the solution of economic problems should be carried out in broader terms than this and that the total effect of these arrangements in all spheres of life should be taken into account. As Frank H. Knight has so often emphasized, problems of welfare economics must ultimately dissolve into a study of aesthetics and morals.

A second feature of the usual treatment of the problems discussed in this article is that the analysis proceeds in terms of a comparison between a state of laissez-faire and some kind of ideal world. This approach inevitably leads to a looseness of thought since the nature of the alternatives being compared is never clear. In a state of laissez-faire, is there a monetary, a legal or a political system and if so, what are they? In an ideal world, would there be a monetary, a legal or a political system and if so, what would they be? The answers to all these questions are shrouded in mystery and every man is free to draw whatever conclusions he likes. Actually very little analysis is required to show that an ideal world is better than a state of laissez-faire, unless the definitions of a state of laissez-faire and an ideal world happen to be the same. But the whole discussion is largely irrelevant for questions of economic policy since whatever we may have in mind as our ideal world, it is clear that we have not yet discovered how to get to it from where we are. A better approach would seem to be to start our analysis with a situation approximating that which actually exists, to examine the effects of a proposed policy change and to attempt to decide whether the new situation would be, in total, better or worse than the original one. In this way, conclusions for policy would have some relevance to the actual situation.

A final reason for the failure to develop a theory adequate to handle the problem of harmful effects stems from a faulty concept of a factor of production. This is usually thought of as a physical entity which the businessman acquires and uses (an acre of land, a ton of fertiliser) instead of as a right to perform certain (physical) actions. We may speak of a person owning land and using it as a factor of production but what the land-owner in fact possesses is the right to carry out a circumscribed list of actions. The rights of a land-owner are not unlimited. It is not even always possible for him to remove the land to another place, for instance, by quarrying it. And although it may be possible for him to exclude some people from using "his" land, this may not be true of others. For example, some people may have the right to cross the land. Furthermore, it may or may not be possible to erect certain types of buildings or to grow certain crops or to use particular drainage systems on the land. This does not come about simply because of government regulation. It would be equally true under the common law. In fact it would be true under any system of law. A system in which the rights of individuals were unlimited would be one in which there were no rights to acquire.

If factors of production are thought of as rights, it becomes easier to understand that the right to do something which has a harmful effect (such as the creation of smoke, noise, smells, etc.) is also a factor of production. Just as we may use a piece of land in such a way as to prevent someone else from crossing it, or parking his car, or building his house upon it, so we may use it in such a way as to deny him a view or quiet or unpolluted air. The cost of exercising a right (of using a factor of production) is always the loss which is suffered elsewhere in consequence of the exercise of that right— the inability to cross land, to park a car, to build a house, to enjoy a view, to have peace and quiet or to breathe clean air.

It would clearly be desirable if the only actions performed were those in which what was gained was worth more than what was lost. But in choosing between social arrangements within the context of which individual decisions are made, we have to bear in mind that a change in the existing system which will lead to an improvement in some decisions may well lead to a worsening of others. Furthermore we have to take into account the costs involved in operating the various social arrangements (whether it be the working of a market or of a government department), as well as the costs involved in moving to a new system. In devising and choosing between social arrangements we should have regard for the total effect. This, above all, is the change in approach which I am advocating.

NOTES

Note: This article, although concerned with a technical problem of economic analysis, arose out of the study of the Political Economy of Broadcasting which I am now conducting. The argument of the present article was implicit in a previous article dealing with the problem of allocating radio and television frequencies ("The Federal Communications Commission," 2 *J. Law & Econ.* [1959]) but comments which I have received seemed to suggest that it would be desirable to deal with the question in a more explicit way and without reference to the original problem for the solution of which the analysis was developed.

1. Coase, "The Federal Communications Commission." 2 *J. Law & Econ.* 26–27 (1959).

2. G. J. Stigler, *The Theory of Price,* 105 (1952).

3. The argument in the text has proceeded on the assumption that the alternative to cultivation of the crop is abandonment of cultivation altogether. But this need not be so. There may be crops which are less liable to damage by cattle but which would not be as profitable as the crop grown in the absence of damage. Thus, if the cultivation of a new crop would yield a return to the farmer of $1 instead of $2, and the size of the herd which would cause $3 damage with the old crop would cause $1 damage with the new crop, it would be profitable to the cattle-raiser to pay any sum less than $2 to induce the farmer to change his crop (since this would reduce damage liability from $3 to $1) and it would be profitable for the farmer to do so if the amount received was more than $1 (the reduction in his return caused by switching crops). In fact, there would be room for a mutually satisfactory bargain in all cases in which change of crop would reduce the amount of damage by more than it reduces the value of the crop (excluding damage)—in all cases, that is, in which a change in the crop cultivated would lead to an increase in the value of production.

4. See Coase, "The Nature of the Firm." 4 *Economica,* New Series, 386 (1937). Reprinted in *Readings in Price Theory,* 331 (1952).

5. For reasons explained in my earlier article, see *Readings in Price Theory,* n. 14 at 337.

6. Pigou, *The Economics of Welfare,* 192–4, 381, and *Public Finance* 94–100 (3d ed. 1947).

RALPH TURVEY

On Divergences Between
Social Cost and Private Cost

This paper summarizes some important ideas in Coase's work as well as contributions appearing in several other papers on externalities. Ralph Turvey agrees with Coase that the divergence between private and social costs resulting from externalities should not in all cases be eliminated by a device such as a tax. He emphasizes that each situation involving an externality must be considered individually in developing public policy. Of the alternative ways of controlling the externality, the control technique desirable on efficiency grounds maximizes the difference between benefits and costs (including the cost of regulation).

QUESTIONS TO GUIDE THE READING

Assume it has been determined that smoking indoors harms nonsmokers.

1. What alternative control strategies are possible?
2. How would you go about evaluating each of these techniques? What data would be useful?

The notion that the resource-allocation effects of divergences between marginal social and private costs can be dealt with by imposing a tax or granting a subsidy equal to the difference now seems too simple a notion. Three recent articles have shown us this. First came Professor Coase's "The Problem of Social Cost," then Davis and Whinston's "Externalities, Welfare and the Theory of Games" appeared, and, finally, Buchanan and Stubblebine have published their paper "Externality."[1] These articles have an aggregate length of eighty pages and are by no means easy to read. The following attempt to synthesize and summarise the main ideas may therefore be useful. It is couched in terms of external diseconomies, i.e., an excess of social over private costs, and the reader is left to invert the analysis himself should he be interested in external economies.

Ralph Turvey, "On Divergences Between Social Cost and Private Cost," *Economica* (August 1963), 309–13. Reprinted by permission of the author.

Ralph Turvey is Director of the Bureau of Statistics, International Labor Office, Geneva, Switzerland.

The scope of the following argument can usefully be indicated by starting with a brief statement of its main conclusions. The first is that if the party imposing external diseconomies and the party suffering them are able and willing to negotiate to their mutual advantage, state intervention is unnecessary to secure optimum resource allocation. The second is that the imposition of a tax upon the party imposing external diseconomies can be a very complicated matter, even in principle, so that the *a priori* prescription of such a tax is unwise.

To develop these and other points, let us begin by calling A the person, firm or group (of persons or firms) which imposes a diseconomy, and B the person, firm or group which suffers it. How much B suffers will in many cases depend not only upon the *scale* of A's diseconomy-creating activity, but also upon the precise *nature* of A's activity and upon B's *reaction* to it. If A emits smoke, for example, B's loss will depend not only upon the quantity emitted but also upon the height of A's chimney and upon the cost to B of installing air-conditioning, indoor clothes-dryers or other means of reducing the effect of the smoke. Thus to ascertain the optimum resource allocation will frequently require an investigation of the nature and costs both of alternative activities open to A and of the devices by which B can reduce the impact of each activity. The optimum involves that kind and scale of A's activity and that adjustment to it by B which maximises the algebraic sum of A's gain and B's loss as against the situation where A pursues no diseconomy-creating activity. Note that the optimum will frequently involve B suffering a loss, both in total and at the margin.[2]

If A and B are firms, gain and loss can be measured in money terms as profit differences. (In considering a social optimum, allowance has of course to be made by market imperfections.) Now assuming that they both seek to maximise profits, that they know about the available alternatives and adjustments and that they are able and willing to negotiate, they will achieve the optimum without any government interference. They will internalize the externality by merger,[3] or they will make an agreement whereby B pays A to modify the nature or scale of its activity.[4] Alternatively,[5] if the law gives B rights against A, A will pay B to accept the optimal amount of loss imposed by A.

If A and B are people, their gain and loss must be measured as the amount of money they respectively would pay to indulge in and prevent A's activity. It could also be measured as the amount of money they respectively would require to refrain from and to endure A's activity, which will be different unless the marginal utility of income is constant. We shall assume that it is constant for both A and B, which is reasonable when the payments do not bulk large in relation to their incomes.[6] Under this assumption, it makes no difference whether B pays A or, if the law gives B rights against A, A compensates B.

Whether A and B are persons or firms, to levy a tax on A which is *not* received as damages or compensation by B may prevent optimal resource allocation from being achieved—still assuming that they can and do negoti-

Figure 1

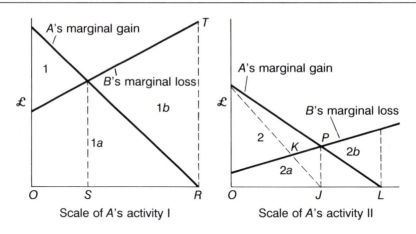

ate.[7] The reason is that the resource allocation which maximises A's *gain less B's loss* may differ from that which maximizes A's *gain less A's tax less B's loss*.

The points made so far can usefully be presented diagrammatically (Figure 1). We assume that A has only two alternative activities, I and II, and that their scales and B's losses are all continuously variable. Let us temporarily disregard the dotted curve in the right-hand part of the diagram. The area under A's curves then gives the total gain to A. The area under B's curves gives the total loss to B after he has made the best adjustment possible to A's activity. This is thus the direct loss as reduced by adjustment, plus the cost of making that adjustment.

If A and B could not negotiate and if A were unhampered by restrictions of any sort, A would choose activity I at a scale of *OR*. A scale of *OS* would obviously give a larger social product, but the optimum is clearly activity II at scale *OJ*, since area 2 is greater than area 1. Now B will be prepared to pay up to (1a + 1b − 2a) to secure this result, while A will be prepared to accept down to (1 + 1a − 2 − 2a) to assure it. The difference is (1b − 1 + 2), the maximum gain to be shared between them, and this is clearly positive.

If A is liable to compensate B for actual damages caused by either activity I or II, he will choose activity II at scale *OJ* (i.e., the optimum allocation), pay 2a to B and retain a net gain of 2. The result is the same as when there is no such liability, though the distribution of the gain is very different: B will pay A up to (1a + 1b − 2a) to secure this result. Hence whether or not we should advocate the imposition of a liability on A for damages caused is a matter of fairness, not of resource allocation. Our judgment will presumably depend on such factors as who got there first, whether one of them is a non-conforming user (e.g., an establishment for the breeding of maggots on putrescible vegetable matter in a residential district), who is richer, and so on. Efficient resource allocation requires the imposition of a liability upon *A* only if we can show that inertia, obstinacy, etc. inhibit *A* and *B* from reaching a voluntary agreement.[8]

We can now make the point implicit in Buchanan-Stubblebine's argument, namely that there is a necessity for any impost levied on *A* to be paid to *B* when *A* and *B* are able to negotiate. Suppose that *A* is charged an amount equal to the loss he imposes on *B;* subtracting this from his marginal gain curve in the right-hand part of the diagram gives us the dotted line as his marginal net gain. If *A* moves to point *J* it will then pay *B* to induce him to move back to position *K* (which is sub-optimal) as it is this position which maximises the *joint* net gain to *A* and *B* together.

There is a final point to be made about the case where *A* and *B* can negotiate. This is that if the external diseconomies are reciprocal, so that each imposes a loss upon the other, the problem is still more complicated.[9]

We now turn to the case where *A* and *B* cannot negotiate, which in most cases will result from *A* and/or *B* being too large a group for the members to get together. Here there are certain benefits to be had from resource re-allocation which are not privately appropriable. Just as with collective goods,[10] therefore, there is thus a case for collective action to achieve optimum allocation. But all this means is that *if* the state can ascertain and enforce a move to the optimum position at a cost less than the gain to be had, and *if* it can do this in a way which does not have unfavourable effects upon income distribution, then it should take action.

These two "ifs" are very important. The second is obvious and requires no elaboration. The first, however, deserves a few words. In order to ascertain the optimum type and scale of *A*'s activity, the authorities must estimate all of the curves in the diagrams. They must, in other words, list and evaluate all the alternatives open to *A* and examine their effects upon *B* and the adjustments *B* could make to reduce the loss suffered. When this is done, if it can be done, it is necessary to consider how to reach the optimum. Now, where the nature as well as the scale of *A*'s activity is variable, it may be necessary to control both, and this may require two controls, not one. Suppose, for instance, that in the diagram, both activities are the emission of smoke: I from a low chimney and II from a tall chimney. To induce *A* to shift from emitting *OR* smoke from the low chimney to emitting *OJ* smoke from the tall chimney, it will not suffice to levy a tax of *PJ* per unit of smoke.[11] If this alone were done, *A* would continue to use a low chimney, emitting slightly less than *OR* smoke. It will also be necessary to regulate chimney heights. A tax would do the trick alone only if it were proportioned to losses imposed rather than to smoke emitted, and that would be very difficult.

These complications show that in many cases the cost of achieving optimum resource allocation may outweigh the gain. If this is the case, a second-best solution may be appropriate. Thus a prohibition of all smoke emission would be better than *OR* smoke from a low chimney (since 1 is less than 1*b*) and a requirement that all chimneys be tall would be better still (giving a net gain of 2 less 2*b*). Whether these requirements should be imposed on existing chimney-owners as well as on new ones then introduces further complications relating to the short run and the long run.

There is no need to carry the example any further. It is now abundantly clear that any general prescription of a tax to deal with external diseconomies is useless. Each case must be considered on its own and there is no *a priori* reason to suppose that the imposition of a tax is better than alternative measures or indeed, that any measures at all are desirable unless we assume that information and administration are both costless.[12]

To sum up, then: when negotiation is possible, the case for government intervention is one of justice not of economic efficiency; when it is not, the theorist should be silent and call in the applied economist.

NOTES

1. *Journal of Law and Economics,* Vol. III, October, 1960, *Journal of Political Economy,* June, 1962, and *Economica,* November, 1962, respectively.
2. Buchanan-Stubblebine, pp. 380–1.
3. Davis-Whinston, pp. 244, 252, 256; Coase, pp. 16–17.
4. Coase, p. 6; Buchanan-Stubblebine agree, p. 383.
5. See previous references.
6. Dr. Mishan has examined the welfare criterion for the case where the only variable is the scale of *A*'s activity, but where neither *A* nor *B* has a constant marginal utility of income. Cf. his paper "Welfare Criteria for External Effects," *American Economic Review,* September, 1961.
7. Buchanan-Stubblebine, pp. 381–3.
8. Cf. the comparable argument on pp. 94–8 of my *The Economics of Real Property,* 1957, about the external economy to landlords of tenants' improvements.
9. Davis-Whinston devote several pages of game theory to this problem.
10. Buchanan-Stubblebine, p. 383.
11. Note how different *PJ* is from *RT,* the initial observable marginal external diseconomy.
12. Coase, pp. 18, 44.

ELIZABETH HOFFMAN AND
MATTHEW L. SPITZER

Experimental Tests of the Coase Theorem with Large Bargaining Groups

Many studies have investigated the conditions under which the Coase theorem is valid. This paper contains the results of controlled experiments designed to test Coase's proposition that agents will bargain to a joint profit-maximizing outcome. The authors find that Coase's contention is supported in group-bargaining situations even when participants do not have full information.

QUESTIONS TO GUIDE THE READING

1. What possible problems exist in transferring laboratory results such as these to the real world?
2. What implications do the results here have for a judge's choice of remedies in the area of nuisance law?

I. Introduction

In his path-breaking paper "The Problem of Social Cost"[1] Ronald Coase posited that a change in a liability rule will leave agents' production and consumption decisions both unchanged and economically efficient within the following (implicit) framework: (1) two agents to each bargain, (2) perfect knowledge of one another's (convex) production and profit or utility functions, (3) competitive markets, (4) zero transactions costs, (5) costless court system, (6) profit-maximizing producers and expected-utility maximizing consumers, (7) no wealth effects, and (8) agents will strike mutually advantageous bargains in the absence of transactions costs. While the theorem is "true" given these assumptions, criticism has focused on its applicability in a wider environment in which the assumptions are generally not met.

In a recent paper,[2] we reported the results of experimental tests of the

Elizabeth Hoffman and Matthew L. Spitzer, "Experimental Tests of the Coase Theorem with Large Bargaining Groups," *Journal of Legal Studies* 15, (January 1986), 149–71. Reprinted by permission of The University of Chicago and the authors.

Elizabeth Hoffman is Professor of Economics at the University of Arizona. **Matthew L. Spitzer** is Professor of Law at the University of Southern California.

Coase Theorem in situations in which there were either two or three parties to a bargain. Some experiments were conducted on a "full-information" basis, where the subjects were provided with both their own and the other subject's payoff schedules. Other experiments were conducted on a "limited-information" basis, in which subjects were only shown their own payoff schedules.[3] The results for all the two-person experiments and the three-person experiments with full information provided strong support for the Coase Theorem. Subjects chose the joint-profit-maximizing outcome over 92 percent of the time in each of the three experimental treatments. However, the results of the three-person experiments with limited information gave less support.

These results are important because they establish that agents will strike mutually advantageous bargains within the simple framework first proposed by Coase. Moreover, they suggest that simply relaxing the assumption of two parties to a bargain will not immediately lead to bargaining breakdown. On the other hand, the erosion of efficiency with three agents and incomplete information suggests that the Coase proposition's policy applications might not be as wide as its supporters claim.

In this paper we extend our previous work in order to examine the operation of the Coase Theorem when there are many parties to a bargain. As a theoretical matter, there is reason to believe that the parties will likely fail to exhaust the gains from voluntary trade of the number of parties increases, because the problem with holdouts becomes more acute. The easiest way to see the point is to assume that the population contains two types of persons, greedy and reasonable. Greedy people try to extract far more than "their share" of the surplus from any bargain and sometimes cause bargaining breakdown if the others do not give in. In the extreme situation, the presence of a single greedy person will block the formation of advantageous trades. As the number of persons needed to complete trades increases, the likelihood that one or more greedy persons will block the transaction should increase. This theoretical argument thus tends to point to a Hobbesian, not a Coasian, view of the world.[4]

The literature contains, however, very little empirical work on this general proposition. This paper is an effort to fill that gap. It reports the results of experiments designed to test the Coase Theorem for large groups. Using an experimental design similar to that in our previous work, we conducted experiments with both four and ten parties to a bargain under full and limited information, and with twenty parties to a bargain under limited information. The results provide continued overwhelming support for Coase's proposition. Overall, 93 percent of the decisions were efficient and there was no deterioration as the bargaining groups got larger. If anything, efficiency improved with larger groups. On the other hand, there was some deterioration in moving from full to limited information. Virtually 100 percent of the full-information bargains were efficient, but efficiency was closer to 90 percent with limited information.

These results provide significant implications for property, tort, and contract law. In the traditional language of political economy, the Coase Theorem is the cornerstone of a laissez-faire legal and economic policy governing contract and property law. One implication of our results is that policymakers should recognize the power of voluntary agreements to overcome externality problems, even in the absence of government intervention. More specifically, these results produce a presumption in favor of the Coase Theorem for disputes involving substantial numbers of parties. By a "presumption in favor of the Coase Theorem" we mean that a judge or legislator who is considering choosing a rule to govern a dispute in tort, contract, or property that involves as many as thirty-eight parties should assume that the parties can and will exhaust the gains from trade by voluntary agreement. One who would show that bargaining breakdown is likely must bear the burden of proof.

II. Experimental Design

A. General

In all the experiments[5] the subjects bargained "face-to-face" in public[6] for more money than most students can earn for an hour's work in their next best alternative employment. Side payments were allowed, and contracts were in writing and strictly enforced. All payments were made in public. Subjects were given no motivational instructions, in that they were not told what their objectives should be in choosing a number or in forming contracts.

We placed each bargaining group in a separate room (with the monitor being the only other person present) and randomly assigned payoff charts to the subjects. The monitor provided the subjects with the instructions that are given in the appendix. The subjects first read the instructions silently and then listened as the monitor read them aloud.

These instructions told subjects that they would be divided into two groups and that they had to choose one of a given set of numbers. They would be paid different amounts of money, in cash, depending on which number was chosen. In the full-information experiments each subject was given payoff information for all other subjects. In the limited-information experiments each subject was only given his own payoffs. Each set of payoff schedules had a unique and clearly identifiable joint-profit-maximizing number. If the subjects chose that number and reallocated the payoffs through side payments, each participant could make at least one dollar more than at the next best alternative.

In this formulation the numbers that the subjects choose are analogous to pollution levels in an externality problem. For example, one group of subjects preferred higher numbers and might represent upstream factories that pollute a river. The other group preferred lower numbers and might represent downstream users who need clean water.

The subjects were told that one of the two groups would be chosen "joint controllers." Joint controllers could choose a number in the following manner. If all joint controllers agreed on a number, then that agreed-on number was chosen. However, if any joint controller disagreed with the others, he might choose the number by himself. For example, if ten subjects, placed in the position of pollutees, were joint controllers and had to choose a number (pollution level), then any one of the joint controllers could insist on a lower number (level of pollution) than the other joint controllers wished. Even if the other nine joint controllers were willing to choose a higher number (to tolerate a higher level of pollution), the subjects outside the controlling group would not be helped unless the tenth joint controller also agreed to choose the higher number (to tolerate the pollution). If the tenth joint controller chose a lower number, the lower number controlled as the group's choice. If the subjects in the position of polluters were joint controllers, the number was chosen in exactly the same fashion, except that individual subjects could force the group to choose higher numbers. The "joint controllers" arrangement models a right to pollute (for polluters) or a right to an injunction forbidding pollution and guaranteeing clean water (for pollutees).

The subjects were also allowed to transfer, by contract, payoffs from any party to any other party.[7] This feature of the experiment directly mimics the contract mechanism that is central to the Coase Theorem.

After reading the instructions and examining their payoffs, subjects were tested on their understanding of the rules and the consequences of any decisions they might make.[8] After all the subjects in a particular experiment had answered all the questions correctly, and after the monitor had answered all the subjects' remaining uncertainties about the rules of the game, the monitor used one of the mechanisms described below for choosing joint controllers. The subjects were then instructed to proceed with the experiment (by choosing a number).

B. Four-Person, Coin-Flip Experiments

We began this experimental project as an extension of the experimental design we had used for the two- and three-person experiments in our previous work.[9] We used four parties to a bargain, either two against two (2×2) or one against three (1×3), and the right to be joint controllers was decided by a coin flip. Each grouping was run under both full and limited information, and each group made three decisions together, sequentially. Table 1 summarizes the number of experimental sessions of three decisions each we conducted under each of the four treatments.

C. Game-Trigger Experiments

The subjects in the experiments described above almost always chose the joint-profit maximum, thereby strongly supporting Coase. But they seldom chose payoff divisions that gave the controller or controllers at least their individual maxima—the amount controllers could make without cooperating with anyone else. More than half the time the subjects split the payoffs

Table 1   Four-Person, Coin-Flip Experimental Treatments

	Joint Controllers	
	2×2	1×3
Full information	3	25
Limited information	15	18

Table 2   Participants in Two-Person, Game-Trigger Experiments

	Information	
	Full	Limited
Sequential	11	10
Nonsequential	24	18

equally, as though controllers were not self-regarding, a point we have ana-lyzed elsewhere.[10]

In order to elicit more self-regarding payoff divisions, we developed a new experimental design and set of instructions. We hypothesized that sub-jects who won the coin flip did not feel they had the morally justifiable right to exercise the entitlement of the controller's position, which led them to bargain as if they were in a symmetric game and chose an equal split of the payoffs—the Nash solution. We then induced feelings of moral justification in the controller by making that individual "earn" the entitlement by winning a simple game. We also told the controller he or she had actually earned that right by winning the game.

1. *Two-Person* (1×1) *Experiments*. We first tested this new experimental design in the basic two-person setting. We ran two-person experiments with both full and limited information, each with both sequential deci-sions and nonsequential decisions. In the sequential decisions two sub-jects made two decisions together. In the nonsequential decisions each pair of subjects only made one decision together. Table 2 summarizes how many pairs of subjects participated in each treatment.

2. *Three-Person* (1×2) *Nonsequential*. We next tested this new experi-mental design with three-person (2×1) experiments. We were partic-ularly interested in replicating these experiments because the limited-information environment was likely to be quite unfavorable to the Coase Theorem, given our previous results. To put additional stress on the Coase Theorem, we also ran these experiments in the nonsequential mode. In other words, each group of three people (who did not know one another) made only one decision together. Thus there was no incen-tive for controllers just to behave altruistically and split the payoffs equally in hopes of receiving similar treatment in subsequent decisions.

Twenty-four experimental decisions were made under full information and twenty-four were made under limited information.

3. *Four-Person, Nonsequential*. The next three sets of experiments simply extended the three-person experiments to four parties to each bargain. We ran 1×3 joint controllers with both full and limited information and 2×2 joint controllers with only limited information. We only ran limited information for the 2×2 joint controllers because the full-information, symmetric experiments had been almost 100 percent efficient. Since 1×2 joint controllers had presented some problems, we ran the 1×3 with full as well as limited information. Twelve full-information and twelve limited-information decisions were made with 1×3 joint controllers; twelve limited-information decisions were made with 2×2 joint controllers.

4. *Ten-Person, Sequential*. We then conducted experiments with ten subjects to see if the Coase Theorem remained robust in large groups. Here we returned to the sequential experimental design. First we ran experiments with five subjects on each of two teams (5×5 experiments). The teams were organized similarly to the 2×2 teams in the four-person experiments. Six groups of ten subjects made two decisions each under full information, and five groups made two decisions each under limited information. Then we ran 1×9 joint controllers with both full and limited information. Five groups of ten subjects made two decisions each under full information, and five groups made two decisions each under limited information.

5. *Twenty-Person, Sequential*. Having completed the ten-person experiments, it was clear that the Coase Theorem was quite robust, even in moderately large groups. We then doubled the group size once again and focused only on the treatment showing any deviation from complete efficiency: one controller against many controllers under limited information. On the basis of the four- and ten-person experiments, we concluded that if the Coase Theorem was robust under that experimental treatment, we could be reasonably certain it would be robust with equal-size bargaining groups or full information. We planned to conduct the experiments in the outer treatment cells only if this cell failed to support the Coase Theorem. Four groups of twenty subjects made two decisions each using 1×19, limited-information experimental instructions.

D. Subjects

Subjects were undergraduate economics and management majors and management graduate students at Purdue University; upper-level undergraduate economics majors at Northwestern University; and law students, undergraduate arts and sciences students, and university staff at the University of Southern California. They were recruited in classes and by telephone and told only that they would participate in an economics decision. They were promised $4.00 per hour plus their earnings. Extra subjects were recruited in case of no-shows and paid at least \$2.00 just for showing up. All subjects were inexperienced in this particular kind of experiment, and friends were not allowed to participate together. After each experiment we explained the nature of the experiment and the scientific importance of not telling their friends about it. Later subjects appeared to be as naive about the experiment as earlier subjects had been, and there did not seem to be a time trend in the results.

III. Experimental Results

Table 3 summarizes the results of all 445 experimental decisions. For all sizes of bargaining groups, the results strongly support the Coase Theorem. If anything, larger bargaining groups were more likely to choose the joint-profit maximum than small groups were. Overall, 93 percent of the experimental decisions chose the profit-maximizing outcome; 98 percent of the ten- and twenty-subject decisions chose it. Efficiency is somewhat lower (91 percent) with limited than with full information (94 percent), but—critically—it is at least 90 percent for all but a few experimental treatments. Surprisingly, the only deviations from nearly 100 percent efficiency are among the four-person coin-flip experiments, which had the highest proportions of equal-split payoff divisions. In fact, these results strongly suggest that, in general, efficiency is compatible with self-regarding payoff divisions. The game-trigger experiments were more efficient (94 percent) than the coin-flip experiments (91 percent). The game-trigger experiments also yielded far more (81 percent) self-regarding divisions than the coin-flip experiments (only 33 percent).

It is possible to hazard an explanation for the seemingly anomalous situation in which the large groups cooperated more effectively than small ones. Subjects in large experiments created ad hoc institutions to help the transacting process. In the twenty-person experiments, for example, the nineteen people always shared information about payoffs with one another. They tended to caucus and select two or three of their number to deal directly with the single opponent. After some discussions the representatives would report back to the rest of their group, and then return to speak with the single opponent. In essence, the group of nineteen devised an informal institution that allowed them to overcome the problems of large numbers. By organizing themselves they were able to exhaust the gains from trade in fairly short order. The longest of these experiments took no more than two hours.

IV. Implications of the Results for Analysis of Nonlaboratory Environments

In this section we explore the applicability of our results to nonlaboratory settings and then consider some implications of our findings for the choice of common-law remedies, such as damages or injunctions.

A. Applicability of Results

To what extent do our experimental results supporting the Coase Theorem extend to nonlaboratory environments, assuming they could be replicated? To answer this question we will explore two different types of reasons for not using these results. First, subjects might not behave in the laboratory as they do in naturally occurring environments. Second, the experimental treatments used might not capture essential aspects of nonlaboratory environments.

1. *Laboratory Effects.* One important set of issues concerns the transferability of our results from the laboratory to the world at large. In a fundamental sense this problem is asymmetrical. If our experimental results had indicated substantial departures from efficiency, we would be able to say that the Coase Theorem was not supported and was, perhaps, wrong. If a theory cannot work in a laboratory that has been designed to focus on the assumptions underlying the theory, it is unlikely the theory will work in a naturally occurring environment, except by chance. If the Coase Theorem had failed in the laboratory setting, then we would have no cause to believe it would be valid in the field.

   The more difficult inferences run in the opposite direction, as several reasons might be suggested why our results would not be as robust in

Table 3   Results

Experiment	N	N_1	N_2	N_3	N_4
I. Coin flip					
A. Two-person					
1. Sequential*					
a. Full information	12	12	12	0	0
b. Limited information	8	8	6	2	0
2. Nonsequential					
a. Full information	12	11	5	7	0
b. Limited information	12	11	6	4	2
B. Four-person sequential					
1. 3 × 1 Controllers					
a. Full information	75	75	49	15	11
Single controller	41	41	25	6	10
Joint controller	31	31	21	9	1
No flip	3	3	3	0	0
b. Limited information	54	42	28	20	6
Single controller	23	18	8	10	5
Joint controller	28	21	17	10	1
No flip	3	3	3	0	0
2. 2 × 2 Controllers					
a. Full information	9	6	1	6	2
b. Limited information	45	42	16	20	9
Coin flip totals	227	207	123	74	30
Percentages		91	54	33	13

Table 3   *(continued)*

Experiment	N	N_1	N_2	N_3	N_4
II. Game trigger					
A. Two-person					
1. Sequential					
a. Full information	22	21	7	15	0
b. Limited information	20	18	7	11	2
2. Nonsequential					
a. Full information	24	20	2	21	1
b. Limited information	18	18	0	10	8
B. Three-person nonsequential					
1. Full information	24	23	1	23	0
Single controller	8	8	0	8	0
Joint controller	15	14	0	15	0
No game	1	1	1	0	0
2. Limited information	24	23	3	18	3
Single controller	5	5	1	3	1
Joint controller	19	18	2	15	2
C. Four-person nonsequential					
1. 3×1 Controllers					
a. Full information	12	12	1	11	0
Single controller	6	6	1	5	0
Joint controller	6	6	0	6	0
b. Limited information	12	10	1	10	1
Single controller	2	2	0	1	1
Joint controller	10	8	1	9	0
2. 2×2 Controllers					
a. Limited information	12	12	0	12	0
D. Ten-person sequential					
1. 5×5 Controllers					
a. Full information	12	11	0	12	0
b. Limited information	12	12	0	11	1
2. 9×1 Controllers					
a. Full information	8	8	0	7	1
b. Limited information	10	10	1	8	1
E. Twenty-person, sequential, limited information	8	8	0	7	1
Game-trigger totals	218	206	23	176	19
Percentages		94	11	81	8
Grant totals	445	413	146	250	49
Percentages		93	33	56	11
Full information	210	199	78	117	15
Percentages		95	37	56	7
Limited information	235	214	68	133	34
Percentages		91	29	57	14

Note.—N = total number of decisions; N_1 = number of joint profit maximums; N_2 = number of equal splits $\pm$ \$1.00; N_3 = number of individually rational divisions; N_4 = other payoff divisions.

*From Elizabeth Hoffman & Matthew L. Spitzer, Entitlements, Rights, and Fairness: An Experimental Examination of Subjects' Concepts of Distributive Justice, 14 J. Legal Stud. 259 (1985).

the field as they are in the laboratory. In particular, in a laboratory setting, subjects might regard money differently, or they might take different attitudes toward bargaining generally. These differences might be produced either by observer effects or by some substantial difference between our subject pool (mainly young, well-educated adults) and the population at large.

In order to explore this hypothesis it is useful to ask at the outset whether any evidence of laboratory effects appears in the data. The non-self-regarding nature of many of the controller's decisions might be taken as evidence of these effects, given the common assumption that people generally act in a self-regarding manner in naturally occurring environments. Two considerations suggest that this possibility should not present problems for the applicability of our results. First, the degree of self-regarding behavior increased markedly when we switched the experimental treatment from coin flip to game trigger, suggesting that the laboratory setting (as distinct from a naturally occurring setting) was not producing that behavior. Second, the results of the experiments with self-regarding controllers supported the Coase Theorem just as strongly as did the experiments with non-self-regarding controllers. Thus, even if people are, on average, less self-regarding in the laboratory than in naturally occurring environments, it seems to pose no threat to our test of the Coase Theorem. The theorem is quite robust with regard to differences in subjects' willingness to be self-regarding in a laboratory environment.

Despite the theorem's robustness in the laboratory, however, observer effects and differences between the subject pool and the population at large could render our results inapplicable in naturally occurring environments. Subjects might bargain to efficient outcomes merely because of a desire to appear to be "nice" because they were being watched by the experimenter. But if simply being observed could drive people to bargain to efficient outcomes, our results would apply to many nonlaboratory settings. Little "real-world" bargaining takes place in absolute secrecy. The results, and often the bargaining process itself, of virtually all important business deals are scrutinized by management, boards of directors, stockholders, or governmental organizations.

The subject pool in our experiments is also quite similar to the group of people who make the kind of business deals and get involved in the kind of lawsuits the Coase Theorem models. These subjects, who tended to be juniors, seniors, and graduate students between twenty and twenty-five years of age, will be the business leaders and propertied individuals of the next generation. We do not think that our subjects were too young and inexperienced in bargaining to provide a model for bargaining behavior. Most of the subjects were management students and law students, and both groups get instruction and practice in bargaining. They all seemed to take the experiments very seriously, and the results suggest that they did. Only if our subjects were to become less

able to contract to efficient outcomes as they grew older and more experienced would one question their usefulness for a test of the Coase
Theorem. But why expect people to be less likely to contract to the
efficient outcomes as they grow older and more experienced? Forcing a
bargaining breakdown is self-defeating behavior. An experienced nego-
tiator learns over time to get as much as possible from a bargain, not to
assure the bargain's failure.

2. *Experimental Treatment Effects.* A policy analyst might hesitate to trust
   our conclusions, however, on the ground that our experiments failed to
   incorporate enough of the naturally occurring phenomena. In particular,
   we have not modeled three crucial sources of bargaining breakdown.

   First, certain important bargaining and coordination costs were absent in our experiments. We only went up to twenty parties to a bargain
   and we brought them together face-to-face for the purpose of bargaining
   with one another. We did not forbid them to make joint-maximizing
   deals including side payments. We have no reason to believe they dis-
   liked the task of bargaining with one another. And we included institutions, such as standard form contracts and an hourly wage for bargainers, that undoubtedly reduced the costs of bargaining and facilitated the
   achievement of efficient outcomes.

   Naturally occurring bargains may not occur or be efficient if large
   groups cannot get organized to sit down together or if government regulations forbid them to do so. If they were to sit down together, they
   might not reach an efficient outcome if they could not enforce their
   agreements or if the bargaining took a great deal of time and the bargainers were not being paid. In addition, if the parties hate each other
   so much that they either will not talk or they prefer to hurt one another
   instead of maximizing jointly, no efficient bargaining is likely to take
   place. For such reasons, our results may not be applicable in a pollution
   dispute involving hundreds of unorganized homeowners (very large
   numbers), a price-fixing deal between large corporations (legally unen-
   forceable agreement), or a divorce settlement (animosity between parties).

   Second, informational deficiencies or asymmetries might also produce inefficient outcomes. Our experiment did not model situations in
   which parties did not know their own profit functions or could not learn
   how their own activities interfered with others' profits. In such situations individuals might try to joint maximize, given their information,
   but still be unable to do so. In some sense, however, one could argue
   that such behavior does not violate the spirit of the Coase Theorem. We
   simply need to reformulate the theorem with informational constraints,
   just as standard economic welfare theory[11] and bargaining theory[12] are
   being reformulated subject to those constraints. The theorem's predictions would undoubtedly be different, however, and we would want to
   test the new predictions with a limited-information set.

Third, we modeled no significant wealth effects in our experiments. Large changes in a consumer's wealth can cause substantial variations in the amount the consumer would be willing to pay for a "good," such as freedom from pollution. Usually, the wealthier he is the more he will pay for a good. In our experiments, when one side or the other gained the controller's position, its wealth was increased. However, our experiment did not change the subjects' payoffs according to which side became the controller. By keeping the payoffs constant, we kept wealth effects out of the experiment. If we had changed payoffs, thereby modeling large wealth effects on consumer demand, the payoff changes alone should have led to different outcomes. In this way, large wealth effects on consumer demand preclude application of the invariance result of the Coase Theorem.

Despite all these precautionary statements, however, we still believe that our results produce a presumption in favor of a Coase Theorem—type mechanism in a substantial class of conflicts. Such a class would include at least situations where bargaining and enforcement costs are low, where there are few informational problems, and where no more than twenty people are involved. Would this class of conflicts extend to disputes with more than twenty people? We think so. First, note that the Coase Theorem worked perfectly with 1×19 joint controllers. Second, note that it also worked perfectly in the ten-person, 5×5 experiments. If these results are not idiosyncratic, then we should expect the Coase Theorem to work in a 19×19 setting. Hence, our range of confidence should probably extend to disputes involving as many as thirty-eight parties. This is quite a substantial number, and it allows us to extend the presumption in favor of the Coase Theorem to a substantial class of disputes, such as landowner disputes involving rights to light and air, small nuisances, such as dog kennels, neighborhood aesthetics, such as ugly houses and funeral parlors, and contractual claims involving a number of people.

What do we mean by a "presumption in favor of the Coase Theorem"? We suggest that in choosing a legal rule to govern disputes such as those listed above, a judge or a legislator should start his analysis by presuming that the parties can and will, in general, exhaust the gains from trade through private bargaining. Someone who claims the opposite, that bargaining breakdown will generally occur in some particular setting, must bear the burden of proof. He must point to some phenomenon, such as very high transactions costs, and show how the phenomenon is likely to prevent contracting between the parties. Only if the person who predicts bargaining breakdown makes his case should the judge or legislator act with the presumption of bargaining breakdown.

This placement of the burden of proof, and the resultant framing of work on disputes, represents a substantial step forward. Previously, discussions had avoided dealing with disputes with twenty or thirty parties either by always assuming 1,000 or more parties in a large dispute[13] or by simply referring to "many" without specifying how many. Assuming our results can be replicated, we have provided a first step in using the Coase Theorem in the analysis of a substantial class of disputes. Henceforth, "many" may still be read to include 1,000 parties, but it probably will not include thirty-eight.

B. Examples of the Use of Our Results for Legal Policy

Our results may provide implications for the law of remedies in property, tort, and contract, where they support a preference for injunctive remedies as opposed to damages.[14]

1. *Nuisances Involving Relatively Few Parties*. The law of nuisance is re-plete with cases in which relatively few parties may and need bargain among themselves over the reassignment of property rights. In disputes between a kennel owner and nearby homeowners, for example, the par-ties can easily locate each other, so that the possible outcomes reduce to a familiar set of four. There are two injunctive remedies: (1) kennel's right—the kennel may emit noise and odors, and (2) homeowner's right—any homeowner is entitled to an order of the court enjoining the kennel to emit no noise or odors.

The court may also choose from two damages remedies: *(a)* kennel's right—the homeowners may obtain an order of the court directing the kennel to emit no noise and odors if and only if the homeowners pay the kennel all damages it suffers from reducing its level of pollution, or *(b)* homeowner's right—the kennel may pollute at any level it chooses, but it must pay homeowners for any damage caused by the noise and odors.

The great risk of either injunctive remedy is commonly thought to arise from the risk that, where the court assigns the right to the party who values it least, voluntary negotiations will not be able to correct the original allocative error. Alternatively, damage remedies impose considerable administrative costs on the courts and may not be entirely accurate. Our results suggest that the choice should be between rule 1 and rule 2 because risk of breakdown in voluntary negotiations is ordi-narily low, perhaps even if there are as many as thirty-eight parties to the dispute. Where the kennel is not enjoined as a nuisance, then the homeowners can by agreement pay the kennel operator money to re-duce the pollution. Where the kennel operation is so enjoined, the op-timal level of pollution can be achieved, this time with payments from the kennel operator to the homeowners.

The strength of these results may depend in part on the nature of the participants to the dispute. If the homeowners are relatively homoge-neous in their income and preference, the dispute may be more easily resolved than it would be if they differed among themselves in these respects. In addition, our results do not tell us anything about disputes involving, for example, a factory and hundreds or thousands of land-owners who may not even know of each others' existence. In such a situation, contracting to a Pareto optimum may still be unlikely, and the court may prefer to choose a damages entitlement. If the factory is a nuisance, the court may choose rule *b*, which allows the factory to pollute at any level as long as it pays landowners all judicially determined amounts of damage. Such a rule would prevent the landowners from holding out, and would encourage the factory to take into account the cost of its pollution. It might, however, suffer from possible inaccuracies in the court's valuation of damages from pollutants.

If the factory is not a nuisance, choosing a damage rule becomes more problematic. Rule *a* would allow the factory to pollute until the land-owners paid it an amount equal to the added costs it would incur from reducing its pollution. Unfortunately, such a rule might be plagued by substantial holdout problems. Unless some incentive-compatible taxation scheme were devised to get money from the landowners, such a rule would probably fail to produce worthwhile reductions in pollution. Hence, a court that was interested in efficiency might prefer to find the factory a nuisance and choose rule *b*.

2. *Enforcement of Old Servitudes*. Other legal rules may be analyzed in an entirely analogous fashion. Consider the enforcement of old servitudes that burden some parcels of land. Neighboring landowners frequently execute agreements, called equitable servitudes, to restrict in advance the right of any landowner to use his land in ways injurious to other landowners. For example, a group of landowners might all promise to use their land only for single family dwellings. If any landowner were to attempt to use his property in a manner inconsistent with his promise, any of the other landowners could go to court and get an injunction forbidding the inconsistent use. In this manner the landowners become "joint controllers" with respect to inconsistent uses; all landowners must consent to any one owner's inconsistent use of land before the inconsistent use will be permitted.

Many years after the creation of equitable servitudes, the nature of the neighborhood may change so much that the original servitudes have lost their utility. For example, the neighborhood adjacent to the single family homes that are restricted to that use may now include a large feedlot operation that emits a great deal of noise and odor. If one of the single family homeowners were to open a dog kennel, the extra noise and odor might matter little, if at all, to the neighbors.

If one of the neighbors sues to stop the dog kennel, a court must choose between injunctive and damages remedies. The two injunctive remedies, analogous to those discussed within nuisance, are (1) kennel's right ("doctrine of changed conditions")—the kennel may exist, and the court will refuse to enforce the servitude, and (2) homeowner's right—the homeowner is entitled to an order of the court enjoining the kennel's existence. There are also two damages remedies: *(a)* kennel's right—the homeowner may obtain an injunction against the kennel's existence if and only if the homeowner pays the world-be kennel owner all damages he suffers from the injunction, and (b) homeowner's right—the kennel owner must pay the homeowner all damages the homeowner suffers from the kennel's existence.

Again, where risk of bargaining breakdown is very small, the court should choose between rules 1 and 2. Subject to the caveats noted in the nuisance example, our experimental data again suggest that the risk of contractual breakdown in small where there are up to thirty-eight parties to the servitude arrangement. Where the numbers are larger, the increased risk of bargaining breakdown points to the increased desirability of damage remedies.

3. *Treatment of Secured Creditors in Bankruptcy.* Our analysis may be extended beyond the traditional common-law areas of tort, contract, and property. In particular, it might prove to be of special importance in determining the property treatment of secured creditors in bankruptcy. Generally a secured creditor has the right to invoke the power of the court to seize the pledged assets, to sell them, and to use the proceeds of the sale to satisfy the debt and necessary expenses, refunding any excess proceeds to the debtor. In contrast, general creditors must respect the priority of secured claims when they seek the aid of the court for the collection of their claims, and they cannot seize or sell pledged property in ways that destroy or prejudice the interests of secured creditors. One important question is whether the priorities of secured creditors should be altered in bankruptcy so that the secured creditor must release some alternative payment, such as a right to a stream of payment over several years, which may or may not be secured by the original pledged assets.[15]

Why might the law do such a thing? Thomas Jackson has argued as follows. A court may choose two different entitlements to protect a creditor's security interest: (1) secured creditor's property rights—the secured creditor can invoke the power of the court to sell the pledged asset and use the proceeds to satisfy the debt, or (2) secured creditor's damages right—the trustee in bankruptcy can stop the secured creditor from exercising his right to sell the asset, but must award the creditor a right to a set of payments worth the amount of the debt.[16] Selling the asset will often be economically inefficient, either because the asset may have a higher value within the debtor's business than outside, or because selling the asset may destroy the existence of the debtor's business, which destroys goodwill.

If the court chooses rule 1 and enforces the creditor's right to sell the assets, the creditor will have to agree not to sell the asset so as to avoid the economic loss. The debtor and its other creditors must persuade the secured creditor, probably by paying it some of the savings from not selling the asset, a loss that otherwise falls on the other creditors. In this situation the secured creditor may behave strategically and demand a large share of the savings from not selling the asset and thereby produce a large chance of bargaining breakdown and the attendant economic inefficiency. To avoid this result the court can choose rule 2, and give the secured creditor a damages right.

Our results suggest that the fear of bargaining breakdown, at least where there are relatively few creditors, may be overemphasized in such an analysis. If the risk of bargaining breakdown is small, then perhaps the law should enforce security interests in bankruptcy with a property entitlement[17] and allow the creditors to work things out, selling the asset in exactly those situations where it is efficient to do so. Once again, the law could utilize a presumption in favor of the Coase Theorem, leaving it to the other creditors to show that bargaining is difficult in any particular case in their attempt to persuade the court to use rule 2.

Of course, our experiments have little to say about bankruptcies involving hundreds of creditors. In such proceedings, the risk of bargaining breakdown may be very high, and the law should choose rule 2, and, if the law cannot choose different rules for cases involving few parties and many parties, then perhaps it should choose rule 2 for all cases. But the law need not choose 2 for all cases because of an excessive fear of bargaining breakdown in cases involving few parties.

4. *Litigation and Settlement.* There are some recent data on dispute resolution that suggest that our experimental support for the Coase Theorem is correct. When litigants sue each other there are strong incentives to settle the case before it gets to trial. Trial is very expensive for all sides involved in a dispute. If all parties to a lawsuit agree on the probabilities of one side or another prevailing, and the parties are motivated by money, then a group agreement to settle the litigation can make all parties better off by saving litigation expenses for everyone. Through side payments in the settlement agreement this saving can be distributed in any manner among the litigants. Of course, litigants may have an incentive to hold out, behave strategically, and threaten to cause bargaining breakdown. The empirical question arises, How often, and under what circumstances, will litigants settle before trial?

Marc Galanter reports that approximately 90 percent of all lawsuits are settled before trial.[18] Further, he gives a breakdown of those that do not settle. They are almost all suits whose description clearly places them outside the theoretical bounds of the Coase Theorem. Such non-settling suits:

1. cannot be settled, such as divorce cases, because a judicial decree is needed before the suit can end;
2. are very cheap to process, thereby providing little saving from settling;
3. involve a special value from a judicial decree, either because one of the parties wants the court to take moral responsibility for the action, wants to signal to a principal that there has been no shriking, or wants to establish a reputation with adversaries in future suits;

4. involve a special value from a judicial decree, because one of the parties wants to effect a change in the rule of law for future cases;

5. involve a "fundamental value" that the parties cannot monetize with ease; or

6. involve high transactions costs of settlement relative to the gains of doing so.

In sum, then, Galanter's results on litigation and settlement tend to reinforce our experimental results.

5. *Land Assembly*. There is, however, other real-world evidence that suggests that the problem of bargaining failure may well be more difficult. Steven N. S. Cheung recounts the failure of Hong Kong landlords and tenants to agree to vacate old uneconomic buildings, tear down the structures, and build new and larger apartment buildings.[19] Because post-World War II rent control statutes in Hong Kong gave tenants property rights—in essence making tenants joint controllers—landlords had to negotiate with dozens of tenant families to secure unanimous agreement among tenant families to move out. Cheung reports that conversations with people who remember the 1947–55 period suggest that holdouts always produced bargaining breakdown. Cheung could find no record of a successfully negotiated deal.

Cheung's work is intriguing, but for several reasons it cannot show that our experiments are inapplicable to the natural world. First, it is unclear how many parties were involved in these landlord and tenant negotiations. Cheung's own figures suggest that many of the negotiations could involve more than fifty parties. Second, Cheung's data are all anecdotal, and give no clue as to the "true" subjective values involved. Therefore, we cannot be sure that deals that were not consummated would have been value-increasing. Anecdotes from those involved in trying to assemble sites for large scale developments in the United States indicate that the fiercest holdouts are old people who have strong emotional ties to their dwelling places.[20] In such cases the old people cannot be made better off by a deal. Third, direct payments to tenants in exchange for their promise to leave were technically illegal (although Cheung indicates this may not have been a practical problem). On balance, Cheung's data should prompt us to question with care, but not totally to reject, our experimental data.

6. *Economic Efficiency as a Legal Norm*. Our results also change the tenor of the current jurisprudential debate about economic efficiency as a norm in the law. As used in the literature, which has grown around Richard Posner's various defenses of his "wealth maximization" norm, economic efficiency has been equated with the Hicks-Kaldor compensation criterion.[21] One of the central difficulties with the Hicks-Kaldor version of economic efficiency is that the criterion directs some to be made worse off, while some are made better off, merely because everyone could (but will not be) made better off. Where a judge must choose one of two allocations of a property right, and where bargaining is too

expensive, the rights will remain where they are judicially placed. The criterion of economic efficiency leads the judge to imagine a world in which bargaining, coordination, and enforcement costs are zero, to predict which of the claimants would purchase the right at auction, and then to actually award the right to that claimant.[22] Richard Posner defends such an approach by arguing that economic efficiency can be equated with Pareto superiority in the long run. This position has been attacked on many different grounds.

Regardless of the ultimate success of the arguments for and against Posner's version of the economic efficiency criterion, however, our experimental results should affect the tenor of the arguments. One who is arguing for the use of the efficiency norm may now claim that the norm describes that parties to a bargain will decide to do for themselves. The judge, then, is simply facilitating an inevitable process and is justifiably concerned about promoting economic efficiency. But simply choosing the efficient outcome, the judge merely saves society the legal costs that would be incurred during a long bargaining process.

Those who argue against economic efficiency as a norm may also find support in our results. After all, if the parties can be trusted to contract an efficient solution by themselves, a judge may ignore efficiency concerns and concentrate instead on effecting a "fair" distribution of income or on setting a precedent for an appealing theory of rights. Only in circumstances in which the Coase Theorem cannot be applied with confidence should economic efficiency have any claim on judicial attention.

In general, therefore, the form of the debate alters when one is fairly certain that the Coase Theorem is applicable. Our experimental results show that the Coase Theorem shifts the tone of the debate in a substantial number of cases.

V. Conclusions

Our experimental results provide very strong support for the Coase Theorem as a tool for analyzing decisions of groups of twenty persons or fewer, when bargaining, coordination, and enforcement costs are low and there are few information problems. We suggest they can be extended to similar groups of thirty-eight persons. Although a policy analyst should be quite careful about applying these results to a nonlaboratory setting, where he may do so with some confidence he can produce substantial implications for the law of remedies in tort, contract, and property.

NOTES

*Helpful comments were provided by Richard Craswell, Glenn Harrison, Peter Ordeshook, Alan Schwartz, Barbara White, and the participants in workshops at UCLA and Washington University. Research assistance was provided by

Gary Adler, Faye Anderson, Lee Ann Duffy, Felipe Prestamo, and Ellen Roth. The authors reluctantly accept responsibility for any errors. The financial support of National Science Foundation grant no. SES-8200266 is gratefully acknowledged.

1. R. H. Coase, The Problem of Social Cost, 3 J. Law & Econ. 1 (1960).

2. Elizabeth Hoffman and Matthew L. Spitzer, The Coase Theorem: Some Experimental Tests, 25 J. Law & Econ. 73 (1982).

3. For full details of the experimental procedure, see *id*.

4. Robert Cooter, The Cost of Coase, 11 J. Legal Stud. 1 (1982).

5. Instructions for all experiments are available in an appendix on request from the authors.

6. The monitors observed the bargaining.

7. Payoff sheets are included with the instructions.

8. Tests are included with the instructions.

9. Hoffman and Spitzer, *supra* note 2.

10. *Id*.

11. See, for example, Milton Harris and Robert M. Townshend, Resource Allocation under Asymmetric Information, 49 Econometrica 33 (1981).

12. Roger Myerson, Two-Person Bargaining Problems with Incomplete Information, 52 Econometrica 461 (1984).

13. See, for example, Richard A. Posner, Economic Analysis of Law 45 (2d ed. 1977) (1,000 parties); and Guido Calabresi and A. Douglas Melamed, Property Rules, Liability Rules and Inalienability: One View of the Cathedral, 85 Harv. L. Rev. 1089 (1972) (100,000 citizens).

14. We assume the law is, or should be, concerned at least in part with economic efficiency, but we also recognize that the proper jurisprudential role of economics is controversial. See text at notes 36–39 *infra*. Resolution of this controversy lies well beyond the scope of this paper.

15. Thomas H. Jackson, Bankruptcy, Non-bankruptcy Entitlements, and the Creditor's Bargain, 91 Yale L. J. 857, 872–77 (1982).

16. *Id*. at 868–71.

17. Of course, even a small risk of bargaining breakdown may be unacceptable if there is a very large loss when such a breakdown occurs. If one were certain that assets were *always much more valuable* in the debtor's going concern than on the open market, then rule 2 might be appropriate. However, Jackson does not seem to believe that this is the case, for he spends several pages attacking the failure to grant secured creditors full damages because sometimes it is efficient to sell the asset on the open market, rather than retain it in the debtor's going concern. *Id*. at 874–77.

18. Marc Galanter, Reading the Landscape of Disputes: What We Know and Don't Know (and Think We Don't Know) about Our Allegedly Contentious and Litigious Society, 31 UCLA L. Rev. 4, 28–30 (1983).

19. Steven N. S. Cheung, Rent Control and Housing Reconstruction: The Postwar Experience of Prewar Premises in Hong Kong, 22 J. Law and Econ. 27, 31–32 (1979).

20. Joanne Lipman, The Holdouts, Wall St. J., May 22, 1984, at 1, col. 1.

21. See, for example, Richard A. Posner, Utilitarianism, Economics, and Legal

Theory, 8 J. Legal Stud. 103 (1979). We neither defend nor attack this criterion as a norm in this paper. Instead, we show how the Coase Theorem, and our results, might affect the nature of the debate.

22. Richard A. Posner, The Ethical and Political Basis of the Efficiency Norm in Common Law Adjudication, in Symposium on Efficiency as a Legal Concern, 8 Hofstra L. Rev. 485, 485–771 (1980).

SELECTION 12

JOSEPH FARRELL

Information and the Coase Theorem

Joseph Farrell points out that the Coase theorem is unconvincing as a general argument against active government policy to control externalities, since it is valid only in the absence of barriers to efficient bargaining. Bargaining is inefficient when one bargainer has relevant information that another does not, such as his gain from a successful agreement. In such cases, the use of central authority may improve efficiency.

QUESTIONS TO GUIDE THE READING

1. How does the evidence on bargaining qualify the Coase theorem?
2. Why may people not readily reveal private information?
3. What are the benefits of having a central authority make decisions?
4. What are the costs of such centralization?

Every economist kept awake by noisy neighbors must have relieved the tedium of counting sheep by pondering the social institutions that make this kind of thing happen. A classical answer is that Pareto-efficiency normally requires competitive markets, and since there is obviously no such market for "quiet in my house tonight," inefficiency should be no surprise. In 1960, Ronald Coase's seminal paper "The Problem of Social Cost" challenged that view. Its claim is that complete competitive markets are not necessary for efficiency. Rather, if the market outcome is inefficient, then people will get together and negotiate their way to efficiency.

Although Coase was concerned with how negotiation can repair externalities, the argument is much broader. It says that if nothing obstructs efficient bargaining then people will negotiate until they reach Pareto-efficiency. This claim is far more ambitious than the traditional competitive-equilibrium welfare theorems. For instance, as Calabresi (1968) pointed out, it implies that we should not worry about monopoly or the provision of public goods either: people can negotiate their way to efficiency.

Joseph Farrell, "Information and the Coase Theorem," *The Journal of Economic Perspectives* 1 (Fall, 1987), 113–29. Reprinted by permission of the author and the publisher.

Joseph Farrell is Visiting Assistant Professor of Economics at the University of California, Berkeley.

Of course, it is a tautology that *if* people negotiate efficiently *then* every outcome will be efficient (else people would negotiate something better). The Coase theorem is important only if we believe that efficient negotiation is likely. Some economists think the Coase theorem implies a lot about the proper scope of government intervention in the economy and about the welfare consequences of laissez-faire. Others see it as a mere tautology: of course we can attribute inefficiencies to "bargaining imperfection," but it may not be useful to do so. Such attitudes sometimes seem to depend more on ideology than on reason. This article gives one economist's reasoned view.

The Coase Theorem as a Decentralization Result

Statements like, "If such-and-such conditions hold, then selfishly optimal individual decisions will lead to efficient aggregate outcomes," are called *decentralization results*. For instance, the familiar "welfare theorem" says that any competitive equilibrium with complete markets is Pareto-efficient. But no real economy has the required competitive markets in every good (indexed by time, place, and state-of-the-world). Some of the structural causes of this (like economies of scale) are straightforward, and so economists understand fairly well when the welfare theorem applies and when it does not.

On first acquaintance, the Coase theorem seems much more robust. Like the welfare theorem, it says that if everything is tradeable then Pareto-efficient outcomes result. Unlike the welfare theorem, it makes no strong assumptions about convexity, price-taking, and complete markets. Instead, a one-line argument says that, absent barriers to contracting, all must be well!

But as the U.S. Postal Service warns its customers, "If it seems too good to be true, it probably is." The Coase theorem dispenses with the heavy assumptions of perfect competition, but replaces them with the strong assumption that no mutually beneficial agreement is missed. So while it economizes on formal institutions, it demands a lot of coordination and negotiation. We can see this sharply by rephrasing the welfare theorem: in competitive markets, if a market-clearing outcome is Pareto-inefficient, then some agent (consumer or firm) is not at a maximum. That is, *unilateral* action can improve on anything inefficient. Without competitive markets, even when each individual is maximizing, the outcome is often inefficient. Improvements demand joint action, which requires coordination and negotiation. In this sense, competitive markets solve our coordination problems.

Looking at things this way suggests that we try to assess the difficulty of coordination and negotiation between the people who must get together to improve on inefficient outcomes. For instance, if many people must cooperate, it is harder than if only a handful are involved. Getting many people to negotiate successfully about supplying a public good is hard. (And one could argue that government is the right institution to deal with such problems, so that the Coase theorem loses its decentralization bite.) In this article, for simplicity, I will deal only with problems involving pairs of people—the bilateral externality problems of a pair of neighbors, for instance.

How, then, can we evaluate the claim that in bilateral negotiations rational economic people are likely to emerge with relatively efficient outcomes? Most expositions of Coase's argument focus on the inefficiencies that arise if tradeable property rights are not clearly established, and then suggest that any other inefficiencies must result from imperfections in bargaining, due perhaps to holdouts or to transactions costs. But these vague terms are not very helpful, and, in practice, bargaining problems may be as important a bar to efficiency as missing property rights. We ask, then, what are the causes of imperfections in bargaining, how policy affects transaction costs, and when these problems are severe compared with some alternative such as central direction.

Recently, many economists have analyzed the efficiency of bargaining. The so-called "cooperative" or "axiomatic" theory of bargaining is not helpful here, since one of its axioms is that outcomes are efficient! But a large literature has developed on "non-cooperative" models of bargaining, formalizing the process of offers and counteroffers that we see in real negotiations. The main conclusion of these models (recently surveyed by Sutton, 1986) is that bargaining is typically inefficient when, as is likely, each bargainer knows something relevant that the other does not, such as his payoff from a successful agreement. The inefficiencies consist of bargains not struck that should be, excessive delay and other direct costs of bargaining. Typically, each bargainer incurs and imposes real costs to change the likely price to his advantage.

If everyone knew all about everyone else, it is hard to envision how negotiation could drag on or break down. This intuition that bargaining will be efficient when everyone's tastes and opportunities are common knowledge is borne out by some recent studies. For instance, Rubinstein (1982) shows that, in one natural bargaining game with symmetric information, bargaining ends at once with one agent making an offer that the other is (just) willing to accept. Roth and Murnighan (1982) report experiments confirming that when bargainers' payoffs are common knowledge, little disagreement results. But when people don't know one another's tastes or opportunities, then experience, theory and experimental evidence all confirm that negotiations may be protracted, costly and unsuccessful. A potential buyer may value a house more than its prospective seller does, but less than the seller believes "most" buyers do. He would then have trouble persuading the seller to lower the price enough to make the deal. Exactly the same is true if it is quiet, rather than a house, that is being bought and sold.

So we cannot assume that all mutually beneficial contracts are signed, unless we assume that everyone knows everything about everyone, which they do not. The strong form of the Coase theorem—the claim that voluntary negotiation will lead to fully efficient outcomes—is implausible unless people know one another exceptionally well. As I shall argue, that case is not only unlikely, but is also the case where decentralization is least useful.

Why Are Decentralization Results Interesting?

Decentralization results are of interest for at least three reasons. First, as Adam Smith emphasized, they are surprising. Analyzing (in game theory) the aggregate results of individuals' selfishly-optimal choices, we find that those results are typically not Pareto-efficient. It is remarkable that a model with any resemblance to our economy predicts efficiency. Second, decentralization results give us a taxonomy of inefficiency: for instance, the welfare theorem lets us classify inefficiencies as due to monopoly, externalities, and so on. This helps us to understand and perhaps to solve such inefficiencies, just as a doctor's diagnosis (what is different about this patient from a healthy patient?) is part of treatment. Third and perhaps most important, people often use decentralization results—expecially the Coase theorem—as arguments against government intervention. They might claim, for instance, that the neighbors should be expected to reach an efficient outcome through private negotiations, without outside intervention.

As arguments against active government policy, the welfare theorem and the Coase theorem are unconvincing. They say that, in ideal circumstances, the laissez-faire outcome is no less Pareto-efficient than the ideal government-dictated outcome. But they do not claim that it is better; further, centralization has some obvious advantages, as in problems of equity. Why, then, do so many economists see the welfare theorem and the Coase theorem as powerful arguments against intervention? Presumably they think that the market process in practice comes closer to ideal performance than does the actual process of government. But this belief cannot be proven by analyzing models of the market and of government intervention that both give efficient outcomes. Instead, the imperfections of each system must be modelled.

A common complaint about centralized decisions is that they cannot properly adjust to the special circumstances of each case, as decentralized decisions can. Formally, people have private information that should affect decisions, and that for some reason is not available to a central authority. Hayek (1945) was perhaps the first to emphasize such informational problems. He argued that the problem solved by the welfare theorem is "emphatically *not* the economic problem which society faces." Society's problem is to make the best use of its knowledge, which "never exists in concentrated or integrated form, but solely as the dispersed bits of incomplete . . . knowledge which all the separate individuals possess." The challenge of decentralization is "whether we are more likely to succeed in putting at the disposal of a single central authority all the knowledge which ought to be used . . . or in conveying to the individuals such additional knowledge as they need." From Hayek's point of view, the Walrasian "decentralization" result is no such thing, since the central auctioneer must collect all (or a vast amount of) the economy's information to set market-clearing prices, and such an economy is thoroughly centralized. True decentralization consists in delegating decisions to those who know more about them. If there were no private information, to take an extreme version of Hayek's view, decentralization would have no point: a central authority would be perfectly able to take fully efficient decisions. Coase points out that decentralized negotiation would also work well then, but that is not a very exciting observation. It is much more instructive to compare how different systems do when private information does exist. Modern analysis of bargaining under incomplete information shows that property rights and negotiation will not lead to fully efficient outcomes in that interesting case (Samuelson, 1985). So the Coase theorem's strong claim, viewed as a decentralization result, is false when it is most interesting. But before dismissing the argument, let us be clearer about what is being compared.

Mechanism Design: Getting Private Information Revealed

Property rights and negotiation will not yield first-best outcomes when there is important private information, and that case is the one that should be examined. So property rights do not give fully efficient decentralization in real or interesting problems. But perhaps first-best efficiency is too demanding a standard; perhaps no social arrangement is that good when private information is important and people's goals differ. If so, then it would be silly to berate property rights for their failure.

Private information poses more than one problem for efficient choice. We shall return below to Hayek's view that no central authority can cope with the complexity of all the relevant information. Before doing so, we discuss another problem of central decision making, one which Hayek ignored: one must give people incentives to reveal what they know, assuming (contrary to Hayek) that the central authority can cope if they do so. The study of such incentives is the theory of *mechanism design*. Mechanism design captures some important virtues of central authority but misses its flaws.

People with private information may not readily reveal it, especially if they know that it will be used in a decision that affects them. Unless everyone shares the same goals, people typically have incentives to lie. For instance, suppose the government asks people how much they would value a public project, and plans to do the project if people seem keen enough. Then anyone who values the project more than he expects to be taxed for it will be tempted to exaggerate his enthusiasm, so as to maximize the chance that the government will go ahead; others (who would value it, but not enough) will pretend that they don't want it at all. Is there some way to make people's tax payments depend on their declared values and thus to cure those incentive problems? In order words, can one persuade people to tell the truth when they know how the information will be used? That is the subject of mechanism design.[1]

The formal framework is this. There is a central authority, whom I will call the king. He must make some decision, and to make a good decision he needs some facts that other people (his "subjects") know. Because the subjects care about the decision, but their goals differ from his, he must give them incentives to tell the truth. To do so, the king can commit himself to an incentive scheme: formally, this scheme specifies how the decision, and perhaps some money payments, will depend on the reported information.

Sometimes, to elicit important information, the king may have to promise to do things that he may not want to do once the information comes out, and so the assumption that he can commit himself is important. For instance, in an early incentive problem, Solomon had to decide which of two women was in fact the mother of a living infant boy whom they both claimed. (The other's son had died.) His solution is reported in First Book of Kings, Chapter 3, as follows:

> Then the king said, "The one says, 'This is my son that is alive, and your son is dead'; and the other says, 'No; but your son is dead, and my son is the living one.'" And the king said, "Bring me a sword." So a sword was brought before the king. And the king said, "Divide the living child in two, and give half to the one, and half to the other." Then the woman whose son was alive said to the king, because her heart yearned for her son, "Oh, my lord, give her the living child, and by no means slay it." But the other said, "It shall be neither mine nor yours; divide it." Then the king answered and said, "Give the living child to the first woman, and by no means slay it; she is its mother." And all Israel heard of the judgment which the king had rendered; and they stood in awe of the king, because they perceived that the wisdom of God was in him, to render justice.

Solomon's solution worked because the impostor apparently would have preferred a dead child to ceding it, or perhaps because she failed to see what the king was doing. Otherwise she would have done better to say what the real mother said, and take a chance of getting the boy. So perhaps Solomon was lucky. Or could he rely on finding some clever scheme?

Mechanism design theory answers this question for us, and broadly the answer is yes. A wise king like Solomon can find schemes to get the first-best outcome in trickier problems than the disputed baby. In general, doing so requires some *side payments,* which help establish people's true willingness to pay for particular outcomes, and thus show what decision would maximize net benefits. For instance, if the boy's mother values him more than does the impostor, then Solomon could have got him to the right mother by confiscating him and then auctioning him off! In much more general problems, Groves and Ledyard (1977), d'Aspremont and Gerard-Varet (1979), and others have shown how Solomon can set up a cunning scheme that makes side payments depend on reported information, so as to achieve fully efficient outcomes without losing the incentives to tell the truth.

The idea is that when you claim to want something very much, that claim will very likely make Solomon do what you ask. For instance, if you claim that tonight of all nights is an especially good time to turn up the Talking Heads, Solomon is likely to say "OK." But since that may be the opposite of what other people want, you should pay for the effect on them of this increased chance of the decision going your way; you should pay the *expected externality* that you create by your claim of intense preference. This is not for reasons of justice or equity (though those may apply too); it is because only if you must make such a payment will you have the right incentives to claim intense preference when, and only when, you feel it. By paying for the effects of your claim on others' expected welfare, you internalize the whole social problem when you report your private information, so it's not surprising that you have all the right incentives then. In this example, if you must pay for your neighbor's lost sleep, you will only tell Solomon you *must* have a party when in fact your urge is especially intense; similarly, your neighbor will only claim that he *must* get a good night's sleep when in fact he really needs it, since he must pay for your lost party.

Another way of looking at this problem is that each person can (by changing his report) get the others to give in to him in some way, by paying an amount just equal to their true reservation price for giving in; that is what the expected externality measures. So the scheme amounts to an idealized process of bargaining, stripped of strategic holdout problems: that is, a process in which everyone makes concessions at cost. Of course, such a process leads to efficient outcomes. But while Coase suggested that the efficiency of ideal bargaining means that everything can be decentralized, the mechanism-design view is that it means the opposite: centralization lets us have such a process (through an expected-externality scheme) while we know that decentralized bargaining is imperfect when there is private information.

This analysis of centralized authority, then, is optimistic about what a wise and benevolent central planner can do with suitably cunning schemes. What can we say for decentralization? There are two kinds of decentralization, each of which has important advantages in reality, but in this model they only impair efficiency. First, under *administrative decentralization,* instead of sending all information to the center (the king), we delegate some decisions to "princes" who have only partial information. In the mechanism-design model, such delegation cannot possibly be useful; anything the princes can do, the king can at least as well. (If the king gets all the information that the princes would get, then he can work out what they would do, and do the same. And if people are not tempted to lie to the princes, then they will not lie to the king if he promises to do that.) Thus decentralization becomes a mere subset of centralization, and is at best harmless. For instance, Solomon might be willing to delegate to the music-lover the choice of Mahler versus Bruckner. But if it were Scarlatti versus the Stones, it might affect how late Solomon would want to let you play music, so delegation might be troublesome. In general, since the social decision problem can't be split up into chunks with no interdependence, such administrative decentralization is not harmless. Of course, this observation points up the idealized view that mechanism-design takes of the central administrator; we will return to this point below.

A second, more radical, concept is *political decentralization,* in which people are always free to choose whether to participate in any relationship with others. Voluntary trade has a good press among economists (see for instance Friedman and Friedman, 1979), and it may be surprising that it often mars efficiency. The reason is a little more subtle than the obvious drawback to administrative decentralization that we just described, and it is closely related to the timing of commitments.

If people make voluntary agreements when they know nothing that is not common knowledge, then the freedom to leave just ensures that everyone shares in the benefits from cooperation: voluntarism has only distributional effects. Distributing the ex-ante gains somehow, people can sign contracts that bind them to essentially the same schemes that Solomon would impose on them. There is really no difference between such ex-ante contracts and central authority; indeed, voluntary contracts can include the appointment of a mediator to collect and process information, and to say what should be done.

But if people sign voluntary contracts *already knowing something that others do not know,* then things are different. In that case, voluntary contracts must not only be designed to prevent cheating, but also must give every "type"[2] of person positive surplus, or else he won't participate; and in general it is costly to efficiency if some types refuse to play. For instance, the confiscate-and-auction solution to the problem of who-should-get-it runs into trouble here; the owner either loses his object or else has to buy what he already had, so he'd rather just walk off. Similarly, Solomon's scheme to allocate the baby would not have worked if the impostor could not have been forced to the king's court.

A contract that makes every player willing to participate *once he knows his own private information* is called "individually rational." By definition, voluntary schemes must respect this constraint, but schemes imposed by the king need not. Since it imposes an extra constraint on the available schemes, this political decentralization obviously could damage efficiency. But it is perhaps surprising just how widespread that damage is. For instance, Myerson and Satterthwaite (1983) have shown that, in a class of bargaining problems, the first-best outcome is not attainable in any individually rational contract. That is, if people come to bargaining already knowing their private values for a good, then no arrangement exists that will lead them to trade precisely when they should, given that each can choose to walk away. So the king's power to coerce really helps to achieve efficiency.

For instance, suppose the problem is which of two people should have an indivisible object, a "seller" (who originally has it) or a "buyer." The efficient solution is that whoever in fact values it more should have it, with perhaps some payment to the other. (That is, every Pareto-efficient outcome has this form.) The king can easily achieve this outcome using an incentive-compatible scheme if participation is compulsory: for example, he can confiscate the item from the "seller" and then auction it off, dividing the revenues equally between the two people. But this solution is not feasible with voluntary trade; the seller may prefer to keep the object rather than to participate and risk having to repurchase (or lose) something he already has. A lump sum payment to the seller could solve that problem, but then the buyer (who would have to make that payment) might prefer to withdraw. And payments to encourage participation conditional on reported "type" (value) would upset the incentive properties of the confiscation/auction scheme. Myerson and Satterthwaite, in fact, show that there is *no* individually rational incentive-compatible scheme that always yields efficient outcomes in such a problem if it is unknown who values the object more. The same argument applies to our difficult neighbors: since we cannot say a priori what time people should go to sleep, voluntary bargaining cannot reproduce the good results that Solomon could get with a compulsory-participation scheme.

Thus the fact that voluntary exchange must make every type of participant better off actually hurts its ex-ante efficiency. Allowing some chance of harming one party can make each party substantially better-off in expected value. Political decentralization finds no favor in this mechanism-design outlook. . . .

NOTES

Note: The author thanks Patrick Bolton, Robert Gibbons, Paul Milgrom, James Mirrlees, Barry Nalebuff, Suzanne Scotchmer, Carl Shapiro, and Joseph Stiglitz for helpful comments.

1. For an introduction, see, for instance, Sonnenschein (1983), or for a more complete survey, Laffont and Maskin (1982).
2. A "type" of person is the possible participant who knows that his private information takes a particular value. For example, in a bargaining problem where the seller's reservation price is known to him alone, one type of seller is the seller who knows that his reservation price is $5.

REFERENCES

d'Aspremont, Claude, and Louis Gerard-Varet, "Incentives and Incomplete Information," *Journal of Public Economics,* 1979, 11, 25–45.

Calabresi, Guido, "Transaction Costs, Resource Allocation, and Liability Rules," *Journal of Law and Economics,* April 1968, 67–74.

Coase, Ronald, "The Nature of the Firm," *Economica,* 1937, 4, 386–405.

Coase, Ronald, "The Problem of Social Cost," *Journal of Law and Economics,* 1960, 1, 1–44.

Farrell, Joseph, "Rigidity Versus License," *American Economic Review,* March 1987, 77, 195–197.

Friedman, Milton, and Rose Friedman, Free to Choose, New York: Harcourt Brace Jovanovich, 1979.

Groves, Theodore, and J. Ledyard, "Optimal Allocation of Public Goods: A Solution to the Free Rider Problem," *Econometrica,* 1977, 45, 783–810.

Hayek, Friedrich, "The Use of Knowledge in Society," *American Economic Review,* September 1945, 35, 519–530.

Laffont, Jean-Jacques, and Eric Maskin, "The Theory of Incentives: An Overview." In Hildenbrand, Werner, ed., *Advances in Economic Theory.* Cambridge: Cambridge University Press, 1982.

Myerson, Roger, and Mark Satterthwaite, "Efficient Mechanisms for Bilateral Trading," *Journal of Economic Theory,* 1983, 29, 265–281.

Roth, Alvin, and J. Murnighan, "The Role of Information in Bargaining: An Experimental Study," *Econometrica,* 1982, 50, 1123–42.

Rubinstein, Ariel, "Perfect Equilibria in a Bargaining Model," *Econometrica,* 1982, 50, 97–110.

Samuelson, William, "Comments on the Coase Theorem." In Roth, Alvin, ed., *Game Theoretic Models of Bargaining.* New York: Cambridge University Press, 1985, pp. 321–340.

Sonnenschein, Hugo, "The Economics of Incentives: An Introductory Account," Nancy L. Schwartz Memorial Lecture, Northwestern University, 1983.

Sutton, John, "Noncooperative Bargaining Theory: An Introduction," *Review of Economic Studies,* 1986, 53, 709–724.

Economics of Public Goods

When justifying the existence of the government sector within a market economy, economists often cite the inability of private markets to provide an efficient level of a public good. For example, given a large number of citizens, an individual's private purchase of national defense will not affect significantly the level of national defense available to everyone. This creates an incentive for each person to "free ride," to attempt to benefit from others' purchases of national defense without paying. To induce citizens to reveal the benefits they would receive as well as to pay a share of the cost of the public good, a political process of preference revelation through voting is combined with compulsory taxation.

As pointed out in the first reading of this section, however, public goods have not always been included in the economic theory of public expenditures. Economists have debated the exact nature of a public good and have argued over which goods, services, or activities can be classified as public goods. Present-day disagreements are clear from the different treatments accorded the subject in public sector textbooks. In some texts, the theory of public goods is taught as a separate topic of public sector economics, while in others, the public good is presented as a pure externality and the theory as an extension of externality theory. Furthermore, disagreements still arise over how to provide an efficient level of particular public goods as well as over why the market system fails in the first place.

Public Goods as a Market Failure

The following three selections discuss the nature of public goods and proposed solutions to this market failure.

SELECTION 13

JOHN G. HEAD

Public Goods and Public Policy

John Head describes Paul Samuelson's basic theory of the nature of a public good and the set of conditions that must hold for the allocation of a public good to be Pareto optimal. He then investigates the characteristics of commodities that qualify as public goods. Finally, he considers the relationship between public goods and earlier justifications for public sector activities, such as externalities, natural monopoly, and income redistribution.

QUESTIONS TO GUIDE THE READING

1. How do the Pareto-optimal conditions for a public good differ from those for a private good? Which characteristic of the pure public good causes the change in the Pareto conditions? How?

2. How was the definition of "jointness' modified after debate among economists?

3. How can the concepts "external economies" and "impossibility of exclusion" be reconciled?

4. What is the basis for Head's argument that both decreasing cost industries and the unemployment/inflation concerns of Keynesian economics fall under Samuelson's definition of a public good?

1. Introduction

One of the most interesting developments in the Anglo-American public finance literature of recent years has been the appearance, under the formidable aegis of Professor Samuelson, of a prescriptive theory of public expenditure based on the alien Continental concept of a "public good."[1]

John G. Head is Professor of Economics at Monash University, Clayton Victoria, Australia.

John G. Head, "Public Goods and Public Policy," pp. 164–183, reprinted in John G. Head, ed. *Public Goods and Public Welfare*, Duke University Press, 1974. Reprinted by permission of the author.

The concept of a "public good," which first flourished in the Italian, German and Scandinavian literature on public expenditure theory of the late nineteenth century,[2] never really penetrated the English-speaking countries, where prescriptive theories of public expenditure and economic policy generally were founded on such concepts as external economies and diseconomies and consequent divergences between private and social cost-benefit calculations, imperfections of competition including those due to decreasing cost phenomena, and inequities in the distribution of income. The main lines of this largely independent English development can be found very firmly laid down in Pigou's great classic, *The Economics of Welfare*. Although the occasional article did appear in which the "public good" concept was employed or referred to,[3] its precise relationship to its more familiar Pigovian rivals was barely discussed, let alone made clear, and it remained, for most of the English-speaking economic world, yet another mystery in the Pandora's box of Continental esoterica.

Stimulated by the researches of Professor Musgrave, Samuelson has now opened this still far-from-empty box, and has set loose upon an ill-prepared literature a fully fledged mathematical theory of public expenditure, based upon this concept alone. This theory, it is probably fair to say, is still, eight years and two reexpositions later, something of an enigma to most economists, though it is nevertheless felt to be of considerable importance. In the course of his three articles, Samuelson refers to external economies, along with certain other considerations, as important elements in any completely general theory of public expenditure, but, except perhaps to the specialist, the precise relationship between the various concepts remains unclear.

It is the aim of this article to examine the meaning of the public good concept as it appears in Samuelson's theory, and relate it to the more familiar Pigovian and Keynesian theories of public policy. In this way we hope to be able to show the place and importance of the concept in a general prescriptive theory of public policy.

We shall begin (section 2) with a brief outline of Samuelson's theory. Then (section 3) we shall set out in some detail the main characteristics of the public good concept on which the theory is based. Finally (section 4) we shall try in various ways to relate these characteristics, both to one another and to the more familiar concepts of modern theories of market inefficiency.

2. Samuelson's Theory of Public Expenditure

In the following quotation from his original mathematical exposition in 1954, Samuelson provides what appears to be a singularly clear definition of the public good concept, which is to provide the foundation of his normative theory of public expenditure, viz.,

> "I explicitly assume two categories of goods: ordinary *private consumption goods* $(X_1, \ldots, X_n)$ which can be parcelled out among different individuals $(1, 2, \ldots, i, \ldots, s)$ according to the relations

$$X_j = \sum_1^s X_j^i;$$

and *collective consumption goods* $(X_{n+1}, \ldots, X_{n+m})$ which all enjoy in common in the sense that each individual's consumption of such a good leads to no subtraction from any other individual's consumption of that good, so that

$$X_{n+j} \overset{\underline{\cdot}}{=} X_{n+j}^i$$

simultaneously for each and every i^{th} individual and each collective consumption good."[4]*

In his geometrical reexposition in 1955 we find a similar definition of a "public consumption good," which "differs from a private consumption good in that each man's consumption of it . . . is related to the total by a condition of *equality* rather than of summation."[5]

On the basis of this definition, and making the usual convexity assumptions, Samuelson shows algebraically and geometrically that the familiar Pareto-optimum condition of welfare economics, requiring equality between marginal rates of substitution and marginal rates of transformation, no longer holds. Where, in the case of two private goods and two individuals 1 and 2, the condition was $MRS^1 = MRS^2 = MT$, what is now required, where one of the two goods is "public," is equality between the marginal rate of transformation and the *sum* of the marginal rates of substitution, i.e., $MRS^1 + MRS^2 = MT$.

Thus, given the same "New Welfare" value judgment, that the goal of economic life should be a situation in which it is impossible to make someone better off without making someone else worse off, i.e., a Pareto optimum, the characteristic features of the allocation of resources which will achieve this goal will change with the introduction of public goods.

Samuelson points out that this change in the Pareto-optimum conditions with the introduction of public goods has disastrous implications for "duality," i.e., for the ability of a competitive market to compute these conditions, even under otherwise ideal circumstances. In particular, charging individuals a common price equal to the marginal cost of producing a unit of the good (or even "average marginal cost" per individual served by that unit) will not be efficient in the case of public goods. Highly idealized multiple pricing will be required if output of these goods is to be optimal, but "no decentralized pricing system can serve to determine optimally these levels of collective consumption."[6]

Furthermore, circumstances are otherwise far from ideal. As Samuelson expresses it, "one could imagine every person in the community being indoctrinated to behave like a 'parametric decentralized bureaucrat' who *re-*

---

*Editor's note: The subscript j denotes a commodity.

veals his preferences by signaling in response to price parameters or Lagrangean multipliers,** to questionnaires, or to other devices. But . . . by departing from his indoctrinated rules, any one person can hope to snatch some selfish benefit in a way not possible under the self-policing competitive pricing of private goods."[7] "It is in the selfish interest of each person to give *false* signals, to pretend to have less interest in a given collective consumption activity than he really has."[8] In short, even with ideal multiple pricing, the market will fail because true preferences will not be revealed.

It is, therefore, in somehow promoting adequate provision of these public goods, that at least some of the proper economic functions of government are to be found. Samuelson warns, however, that these functions are not likely to be easy to perform efficiently, and emphasizes in particular that the benefit theory offers no perfect practical solution.

3. The Characteristics of a Public Good

Turning now to detailed consideration of the public good concept on which this theory is based, it appears that Samuelson's public good has two main characteristics, "jointness of supply," "indivisibility" or "lumpiness" on the one hand, and external economies on the other.

3.1 "Jointness"

The first and most obvious implication of the equal consumption requirement ($X_{n+j} = X^i_{n+j}$ for each and every individual) is that Samuelson's public good is in joint supply, in the special sense that, once produced, any given unit of the good can be made equally available to all. Extension of the supply to one individual facilitates its extension to all. Supply of a given unit to one individual, and supply of the same unit to other individuals, are clearly joint products.[9] Alternatively we could describe this characteristic as a special type of lumpiness or indivisibility of product.[10] As we shall see,[11] it is this "jointness" which alone accounts for the change in the Pareto-optimum conditions and the consequent need for a highly idealized system of multiple pricing referred to above, a need which a competitive market cannot meet.

Are there many goods which would appear to fall into this category? In his first article Samuelson offers no example. In the second, he instances an outdoor circus and national defense. In the third, a battleship and a television program are mentioned. None of these, nor any of a host of other traditional governmental activities seems, however, to satisfy this very stringent requirement to perfection. "Capacity limits" are usually met well before the good has become equally available to all, this applying alike to roads, bridges, hospitals, courts, police, and even flood control measures,

---

**Editors' note: *Lagrangean multiplier* refers to a mathematical optimization technique which in this context could give information about true preferences.

irrigation, national defense, and public health schemes such as vaccination programs and draining of malarial swamps. Furthermore, even before capacity limits in any strict sense are encountered, quality variations usually occur. Crowded roads and other facilities are usually regarded as giving inferior service to that provided by the same "goods" less fully utilized.

Under pressure on this particular point from such critics as Enke and Margolis,[12] Samuelson admits in his second article that his public good concept is properly to be regarded only as an "extreme polar case," which the student of public expenditure can set against the "logically equally extreme category of a private good," in order to bring out the essence of the case for government activity. Accordingly he reformulates the theory with this change of emphasis, to avoid the apparent overstatement of the original article.

It is, however, no more than a change of emphasis. "To deny that most public functions fit into my extreme definition of a public good is not to grant that they satisfy the logically equally extreme category of a private good . . . Indeed I am rash enough to think that in almost every one of the legitimate economic functions of government that critics put forward there is to be found a blending of the extreme antipodal models."[13]

"Jointness" thus remains an essential characteristic of a public good, though it is now to be understood in the less extreme sense that a given unit of the good, once produced, can be made at least partially available, though possibly in varying degrees, to more than one individual. Only beyond a point does additional consumption by one person imply the need for a corresponding reduction in consumption by others.

The presence of public good elements in this sense is quite sufficient to cause the change in the Pareto-optimum conditions and consequent failure of market catallactics described in section 2.[14] Modified in this way, the public good concept, and hence the theory of public policy based on it, thus becomes much more realistic and important. A whole host of activities, including all those listed earlier and many more, can be found which will satisfy this less demanding requirement.

3.2 External Economies

The second important characteristic of Samuelson's public good is that it gives rise to external economies. In his first article he speaks of the "external economies or jointness of demand intrinsic to the very concept of collective goods" and the "external effects basic to the very notion of collective consumption goods." Describing his theory in the second article, he states that "it explicitly introduces the vital external interdependencies that no theory of government can do without," and in the third that it "is the natural model to formulate so as to give strongest emphasis to external effects."

There are indications at various points in his articles that Samuelson may be using the term "external effects" in a rather broader sense than is now usual, and possibly even as a generic term to cover all causes of market inefficiency. To make quite sure that we do not get trapped in a semantic snarl, it may therefore be wise to begin with a brief discussion of the meaning of external economies and diseconomies.

In its narrowest modern sense the concept of external economies and diseconomies, applied to a given good, indicates that a change in the production and/or consumption of that good will affect the utility and/or production functions for other goods. The "reason" usually given by economists for the existence of these external economies or diseconomies is perhaps most succinctly described by Ellis and Fellner[15] as "the divorce of scarcity from effective ownership," i.e., imperfections in property titles. Following Sidgwick,[16] we might describe the problem as one of "nonappropriability," it being impossible for private firms and individuals, through ordinary private pricing, to appropriate the full social benefits (or be charged the full social costs) arising directly from their production and/or consumption of certain goods. An identical concept to be found in the important works of Bowen and Musgrave is "impossibility of exclusion," meaning that it is impossible for private firms and individuals, through private pricing, to exclude other firms and individuals from at least some part of the benefits (or be charged the full social costs) arising directly from their production and/or consumption of certain goods. The extramarket benefits in question are here to be interpreted narrowly in terms of use or enjoyment of the product itself.

The effect of these external economies and diseconomies is to create divergences between private and social costs and benefits, and thus to prevent the satisfaction of the optimum conditions. Some economic units can enjoy some of the benefits of certain activities without having to pay for them, and it would of course be grossly unrealistic to expect them to contribute voluntarily. These activities will therefore be underexpanded, and government expansion of them is justified. Similarly, where the full social costs cannot be charged to an economic unit through the pricing process, again voluntary contributions by way of compensation or expenditures to reduce the costs in question cannot reasonably be expected. Overexpansion of these activities is therefore likely, and their restraint is a legitimate economic function of government.

But for these ownership difficulties encountered by the consumer or producer of the good in physically excluding other users, there is no reason inherent in the external economies concept, why a competitive market could not ensure optimum output of it. The external economies concept in this sense is clearly not a generic term covering all causes of market inefficiency.

Do Samuelson's public goods exhibit external economies in this sense? Perhaps the easiest way of seeing that they do, is to notice the resemblance between Samuelson's definition and the Bowen and Musgrave concepts of goods for which price-exclusion is completely impossible,[17] and which therefore exhibit external economies to an extreme degree. These goods are referred to by Bowen as "social goods" and by Musgrave as goods satisfying "social wants." According to Musgrave, "Social wants are those wants satisfied by services that must be consumed in equal amounts by all. People who do not pay for the services cannot be excluded from the benefits that result; and since they cannot be excluded from the benefits, they will not engage in voluntary payments. Hence the market cannot satisfy such wants."[18]

In this definition the equal consumption requirement and the impossibility of exclusion appear side by side. Samuelson on the other hand does not explicitly refer in his definition to the possibility or otherwise of price-exclusion. On reflection, however, it should be clear that impossibility of exclusion is a direct implication of his formulation of the equal consumption condition for public goods. The latter is clearly to hold by definition in all situations, optimal and nonoptimal alike; public goods, once produced, not only *can* but *must* be made equally available to all. If exclusion were possible, however, consumption would not be equal for all individuals in innumerable nonoptimal situations of private pricing, since those unwilling to pay the inefficient private price would be excluded.

The second implication of the equal consumption requirement which defines Samuelson's public good is therefore that such a good exhibits external economies, i.e., exclusion or appropriability difficulties, to an extreme degree. As we shall see, it is this characteristic alone which accounts for the failure of the market mechanism to ensure revelation of true preferences.

Are there many goods which would appear to exhibit this characteristic? The answer would seem to be that there are none. Exclusion is never completely impossible, even in such obvious cases as national defense, flood control and public health programs.

Samuelson does not explicitly consider this question. Both Bowen and Musgrave appear, however, to employ the concept only to emphasize the essential feature of this particular market weakness. A less extreme usage is fairly clearly indicated, if perhaps underemphasized, in both cases.

There are in fact innumerable goods which will pose price-exclusion problems, and thus exhibit external economies (and diseconomies) in the less restrictive sense without approaching complete impossibility of exclusion. A theory of public expenditure based on this less restrictive, and hence more realistic and important concept, is itself correspondingly more realistic and important, with the general conclusion still justified, that, because of exclusion difficulties, true preferences will be understated, and the market will therefore fail to secure optimum production and consumption of the goods in question.

4. The Relationship Between Jointness, External Economies, and Other Concepts in the Theory of Public Policy

We have distinguished two important properties of Samuelson's public goods, namely jointness and external economies. Are they, however, conceptually quite distinct, or are they related in some way, or perhaps even identical? And what is the relationship between them and the various concepts of the more familiar theories of public policy? We shall consider these two questions in turn.

4.1 Jointness and External Economies

In the light of Samuelson's own definition and that of Musgrave, quoted earlier, and indeed of the whole traditional public good literature, in all of which the two characteristics appear to be merged, it is clearly important to ask whether they are in fact independent, somehow related, or one and the same.

4.1.1. We shall begin by considering whether the existence of jointness necessarily implies the existence of external economies and thus of price-exclusion problems. In other words, does it follow from the fact that a good *can* be made equally available to all, that it *must* be made equally available to all? Most public good concepts exhibit both characteristics, but does the one necessarily entail the other in this manner?

It is certainly true that some of the best examples of goods with jointness characteristics also pose the most difficult exclusion problems. National defense, flood control and public health programs are excellent examples of goods exhibiting both characteristics to a high degree.

The fact remains, however, that goods and services with jointness aspects may, and in fact often will, pose no price-exclusion problems. Bus, train and tram fares are too obvious to need comment, though in each case elements of jointness in the public good sense certainly exist.[19] Tolls are common in the case of roads and bridges. Fees are charged in the case of the courts, postal and telephone services, hospitals, etc., and could easily be extended, if necessary, to a host of similar services. Concerts, football matches and circuses (even outdoor ones!) can usually be fenced off and admission charges levied. Unscrambling devices may be perfectly feasible in the case of television and radio programs and the services of lighthouses. In short, the existence of jointness in no way necessarily entails the existence of price-exclusion problems. This point is explicitly recognized by both Samuelson and Musgrave.[20]

This is not of course to suggest that the imposition of charges will not occasionally, or even frequently, be extremely costly to the private firm and/or inconvenient to the user. In these cases it is perfectly possible that a socially superior service could be provided "free" by the government. We would therefore agree that there are often important exclusion problems co-existing with jointness, which may enormously reinforce the case for government intervention, without conceding that exclusion is the only problem involved, or, for that matter, that exclusion is in any literal sense "impossible."

4.1.2. Although joint supply or indivisibility in our present sense in no way necessarily implies the existence of price-exclusion difficulties, it is important to recognize that it does create a very similar problem for the effective functioning of political choice or voting mechanisms.

We have seen that there is no necessary problem in principle of ensuring, under a price system, that individuals will reveal their true preferences for goods exhibiting Samuelsonian jointness characteristics. Market inefficiency arises here because of the independent phenomenon of jointness.

If, however, the government steps in to promote, by extramarket means, more adequate provision of the service in question, the problem of determining true preferences immediately becomes acute. Whatever the nature of the political system, individuals and small groups will know that, if prices are not to be charged, the supply to them of this service "equally available to all" will depend overwhelmingly upon what the rest of the community is induced or forced to contribute, and to only the slightest extent on their own contributions. Each therefore has an enormous incentive to try to minimize his own contribution by understating his true preferences in public statements, bargaining, voting or other political activity relevant to the determination of the sharing of the burden. With large numbers behaving in this way, there is clearly a grave danger of underexpansion of the service when provided "free" by government.

This is precisely Wicksell's overwhelming objection to even the relatively refined benefit theory of Mazzola as a practical solution to the problem of securing adequate provision of public goods,[21] and the same point is also to be found in the articles by Benham, Musgrave, Bowen, and Peacock referred to in section 1. Samuelson also emphasizes in all three articles "the inherent *political* difficulty of ever getting men to reveal their tastes" for public goods.

It is important to stress again that this difficulty is a consequence of jointness, and arises whether price-exclusion is possible or not, and it applies to almost any conceivable voting mechanism, including that suggested by Wicksell. The problem is, however, considerably exacerbated where price-exclusion is impossible, since this removes the possibility of using previous market choices as some check on true preferences in the political activity following the switch to "free" government provision of the service.

4.1.3. If joint supply does not necessarily entail price-exclusion problems, why do writers such as Bowen and Musgrave bring the equal consumption requirement with its implications of jointness into the forefront of definitions of public goods, the essential characteristic of which is apparently intended to be complete impossibility of price-exclusion?

The answer suggested by Musgrave[22] is that, although jointness does not necessarily entail exclusion problems, the existence of exclusion problems does imply the existence of elements of jointness. If no economic unit can be price-excluded from any part of the good, it follows ipso facto, that each unit of the good is, and hence can be, made equally available to all, i.e., we have Samuelsonian jointness.

In many cases of extreme exclusion difficulties, it is true, as we have already noted, that joint supply is also involved. It is far from clear, however, that the exclusion problems in any way necessarily imply the existence of jointness. Oil wells drawing on a common pool would appear to be a case in point. New wells in the neighborhood of a strike may drastically reduce output from the original well, with the firm which made the original strike possibly quite unable to price-exclude others from peacefully expropriating a significant part of its "property." The good in question, oil, is however strictly "private" in Samuelson's sense of being "like bread whose total can be parcelled out among two or more persons with one man having a loaf less if another gets a loaf more." If one economic unit gets more oil, there is a corresponding reduction in the quantity which can be made available to others. Other similar examples could be cited. It is of course perfectly true, that all can take part in the scramble for the scarce supply, but this is the only sense in which "equal potential availability" can be claimed. In a sense, that is, the good is "indivisible," in so far as secure property titles to the individual units of it are difficult to grant, and this problem of parcelling out the total for purposes of legal ownership has doubtless contributed to the misunderstanding. Such "equal availability" or "indivisibility" is clearly in no way related to Samuelsonian jointness.

From the above analysis we can conclude that jointness and external economies are conceptually quite distinct properties of Samuelson's public good, and are in no way related. A clear differentiation between them is therefore extremely important to preserve.

4.2 Jointness, External Economies, and Other Concepts

Finally, let us consider possible relationships between these two characteristics of a public good and the more familiar concepts of Pigovian and Keynesian theories of public policy. We have already seen that the external economies which characterize the public good are simply an extreme category of external economies in the narrowest modern sense. The precise nature of jointness, however, requires further examination, as does the relationship between both these characteristics and the other elements which go to make up modern theories of market inefficiency.

4.2.1. What, first of all, is the precise relationship between jointness, which is the distinguishing characteristic of the Samuelson concept,[23] and these other theories of public policy?

The answer seems to be the obvious one suggested by the occasional use of the term *indivisibility* in this connection, namely that we are dealing here with a special case of decreasing costs.

This is perhaps most easily seen by recognizing that one of the most traditional examples of decreasing cost problems discussed in the public finance literature dealing with pricing policies for nationalized industries,[24] namely that of a bridge, is a perfect example of a good exhibiting jointness characteristics. Up to a point it is possible for some individuals to have more, without the need for anything like a corresponding reduction in the service available to others.

With a uniform toll being charged in a given period, as under private pricing, to (say) cover average cost in that period, it is quite likely that the bridge would not be used to "capacity," and some individuals who would be willing to pay marginal social cost would be excluded by the average cost price. As has been pointed out again and again in the literature, this is not Pareto-efficient pricing and, in a world in which all other optimum conditions are satisfied, the position could be substantially improved by lowering the uniform price towards the true marginal social (opportunity) cost of supplying the service to the last user. In the case of the bridge this will be zero if we neglect wear and tear, and lowering price to this level will therefore necessarily result in substantial losses, since overheads will be uncovered. Clearly these losses are due to spectacularly decreasing costs. In the absence of government action in the form of a subsidy or complete takeover, this financially disastrous but socially ideal pricing policy can clearly not be expected of a private firm. Whatever the form of the action taken, the losses should be covered by non- (or not too-) distorting taxation.

Alternatively, and this is the familiar verbal conclusion which Samuelson has effectively demonstrated mathematically and geometrically in his articles, a system of multiple pricing or multipart tariffs could be employed, mulcting the consumer surplus of intramarginal users to cover overhead. Under this system, each user would be charged a price which would equate his individual demand for the service with the fixed supply equally available to all. This is of course nothing more than a careful application of the general rule, familiar from the pricing debates referred to above, that where all other optimum conditions are satisfied, price, in the particular industry under consideration, should be set at marginal social cost and equate supply with demand. It is also familiar, at least by implication, from this branch of the literature, that no decentralized pricing system can compute this multiple pricing solution, and indeed that only the very roughest approximation to such a solution such as a two- or few-part tariff could, let alone would, be attempted by a central (private or public) pricing authority.[25] It has always been clear, in addition, that this problem is in no way related to exclusion difficulties in the narrow external economies sense.

The case of a bridge is only one of a number of cases of decreasing costs discussed in the literature, which are basically examples of Samuelsonian jointness. Wicksell[26] lists roads, ports, canals, railways, postal services, and public squares as well as bridges. Little,[27] writing more than fifty years later, mentions museums, parks, passenger trains and buses, broadcasting, water supply, and roads. In all these cases the decreasing cost problem is due very largely to elements of jointness, in the sense that at least up to a point, once a given unit of the good has been produced, additional consumption by one individual does not imply a corresponding reduction in the quantity which can be made available to others.

The decreasing cost implications of Samuelson's public good concept should indeed be evident on reflection from his definition, which implies very directly, even if it does not state, that the opportunity cost of supplying more of the service, and more specifically of supplying the same unit to more users, is zero. Modified in the direction of realism to take account of capacity limits, quality variations, and minor wear and tear effects due to additional use, the essential point remains, that opportunity cost is likely to be almost negligible and certainly very low in relation to average cost, i.e., we have sharply decreasing costs. In all these Samuelsonian cases, as long as any individual is excluded who has paid or is willing to pay any necessary "marginal customer cost" (the cost of installation of the telephone, the price of the television or radio receiver or vehicle, etc.), and who is also willing to pay the relatively small marginal social cost due to wear and tear (zero in the extreme Samuelson case), price to such users should be lowered. It is unlikely that even a private firm in a monopoly position could do this without incurring losses, and in the absence of public policy it would therefore never be done.

These are not of course the only examples of decreasing cost industries. Other cases traditionally quoted, such as steel and other heavy industries, are due to indivisibility of factors with no elements of jointness of product in our sense. There can be little doubt, however, that Samuelsonian cases are amongst the most numerous and important. It is also clear, both from the theory and from practical experience, that the resulting economic function of government is likely to be far from easy to perform efficiently even without price-exclusion difficulties.

It seems then that in terms of the usual theories of public policy, what is perhaps the essential characteristic of Samuelson's public good, namely its jointness of supply or indivisibility in the sense of equal potential availability, gives rise to a very important category of decreasing cost problems. It is interesting to observe the growing appreciation of this crucial point in his three articles. In the original mathematical exposition there is no mention whatever of decreasing costs. In the geometrical version we find, in the penultimate paragraph, the completely enigmatic statement that "whether or not I have overstated the applicability of this one theoretical model to actual governmental functions, I believe I did not go far enough in claiming for it relevance to the vast area of decreasing costs that constitutes an important part of economic reality and of the welfare economics of monopolistic competition."[28] Finally, in the third article, in the course of developing, with reference to television programs, the argument that impossibility of exclusion is far from the be-all and end-all of his public good concept, and under the general heading "Decreasing-cost phenomena," we find a brief but clear and explicit exposition of this basic point.[29]

4.2.2.   We have now seen that the first characteristic of Samuelson's public good, viz., jointness or indivisibility, accounts for an important part of the familiar concept of decreasing costs. The second characteristic, namely complete impossibility of exclusion, is a special and extreme case of the modern external economies concept.

Is there not, however, a sense in which decreasing costs and external economies are related? And is there perhaps some general relationship between these and the other major elements which go to make up modern theories of market inefficiency?[30]

4.2.2.1. Referring back to our earlier summary of the explanations which have been offered for the existence of external economies and diseconomies, we defined nonappropriability as that property of a good which makes it impossible for private economic units to appropriate, by ordinary private pricing, the full social benefits from their production and/or consumption of that good. So far, following the mainstream of the modern external economies doctrine, we have interpreted these "full social benefits" in a very narrow sense to refer only to use or enjoyment of the product itself. By price-exclusion problems we have therefore simply meant difficulties in physically excluding, from use or enjoyment of the product itself, other economic units who have not paid for the privilege.

Interpreting these full social benefits in the widest sense, however, it is clear that nonappropriability or impossibility of exclusion accounts for all decreasing cost problems as well as external economies in the narrow modern sense. By lowering price from (say) average cost to marginal cost in a situation in which all other optimum conditions are satisfied, a decreasing cost monopolist could provide resource-allocation benefits such that, as a result, it would be possible to make someone better off without making anyone else worse off. The firm could not, however, as a general rule, charge for these social benefits, and the individual beneficiaries could not be expected to contribute voluntarily. The possibly quite substantial losses that would be incurred by the monopolist through the lowering of price would not therefore in general be covered by other means, even though it would be possible for the community, by cooperative action, to compensate him and still enjoy a net benefit, with some members better off and none worse off than before. Since such spontaneous and voluntary cooperation cannot be relied upon, the average cost price and consequent misallocation will persist in the absence of government, and the reason is precisely the nonappropriability of these potential resource-allocation benefits. Exactly the same general argument applies to Samuelsonian as to other forms of lumpiness, and indeed to the much more general category of imperfections of competition from whatever cause (including decreasing cost phenomena).

4.2.2.2. It is interesting to notice that, in this more general sense, nonappropriability or impossibility of exclusion also accounts to a considerable extent for Keynesian and post-Keynesian vagaries of aggregate demand and supply and their associated inefficiency concepts of unemployment "equilibrium" and inflation. An economic unit increasing its consumption- or investment-spending, or accepting a substantial money-wage cut in a situation of unemployment equilibrium, can by no means appropriate to itself, through private pricing, the full social benefits in the form of multiplier and real balance effects on the incomes and profits of other economic units. Instead, the individual consumption-spender risks severe later hardship and insolvency; the investment-spending firm risks heavy losses and ultimate bankruptcy; the single trade union or employee accepting a wage cut loses both absolutely and relatively to less socially minded employee groups; and the small nation risks international insolvency and consequent further employment difficulties. With the signs changed, a similar argument applies to the inflation case, where again the full benefits from reduced inefficiencies of all sorts are not appropriable. The nonappropriability case for government activity in the stability field is therefore clear.

Again, in the case of suboptimal economic growth, the full benefits in terms of rising real wages from growth-promoting behavior, such as thrift, risk-bearing, dividend- and wage-restraint, are seldom anything like fully appropriable from the point of view of the economic unit which must bear the full cost of such behavior. Competitive depreciation and tariff and export-subsidy wars, including beggar-my-neighbor remedies for unemployment, provide further examples of cases in which socially responsible behavior fails to receive anything like its just reward.

In all these cases it would be possible for the community, by means of voluntary cooperative action, to compensate potential losers from socially desirable changes, and still enjoy a net benefit with some members better off and none worse off. Such cooperative effort will seldom be forthcoming in the absence of coercion and the inefficiency due to nonappropriability will therefore persist.

In a broad but very real and important sense then, domestic and international economic stability, domestic and international allocation of resources in accordance with consumers' wishes and an optimal rate of growth can all quite properly be regarded as public goods, for adequate provision of which public policy must be relied upon.

4.2.2.3.   Of the most important elements in the usual theories of market inadequacy only such slippery, though undoubtedly vital, concepts as inequitable income distribution (including therefore important aspects of economic stability and growth), imperfect knowledge and irrational motivation remain outside this wider nonappropriability net, and even here some part of the problem can undoubtedly be ascribed to exclusion difficulties.

The most important of these concepts, namely the gross inequalities of income which result from the free functioning of the market, is a concept which is largely alien to the New Welfare ethical foundations on which the whole of the above theory is based.

In our account we have adopted a goal of economic organization in the Kaldor-Hicks "hypothetical-compensationist" tradition of a situation in which it is impossible to make someone better off without making someone else worse off, and have regarded any resulting redistributions of income as of negligible importance. Alternatively, in the "actual-compensationist" tradition we could have postulated the same goal, but insisted at the same time that losers from any policy leading to the goal be compensated in costless lump-sum fashion, thus making the policy implications of the theory "more generally acceptable." Following this latter approach still further, we could insist in addition that the government's first policy act be to correct any initial (prepolicy) inequities in the distribution of income. A further extension of this approach would be the Bergson-Samuelson formulation, under which it is the post-policy distribution of income in the "bliss state" which is to be made ideal (or "swung to the ethical observer's optimum") using costless lump-sum taxes and subsidies. Finally, in the limit, we could demand that the government ensure that the initial distribution of income is ideal, and also that, in implementing the policies necessary for "efficiency," incomes be simultaneously redistributed to maintain an ideal income distribution throughout the process.

In other words, it is possible in various ways to graft considerations of income distribution on to the formal framework of a basically New Welfare theory of public policy. The operation is, however, rather artificial, and the crucial questions regarding the appropriate distribution of income are either ignored or begged, in accordance with the fundamental tenet of New Welfare that the economist qua economist has little to contribute on this important but controversial subject.

NOTES

1. P. A. Samuelson, "The Pure Theory of Public Expenditure," *Review of Economics and Statistics*, 1954; "Diagrammatic Exposition of a Theory of Public Expenditure," *Review of Economics and Statistics*, 1955; and "Aspects of Public Expenditure Theories," *Review of Economics and Statistics*, 1958.

2. Extracts from some of the most important contributions by Mazzola, Wicksell, Sax and others can be found in English translation in R. A. Musgrave and A. T. Peacock, eds., *Classics in the Theory of Public Finance* (London and New York, 1958).

3. See, for example, F. Benham, "Notes on the Pure Theory of Public Finance," *Economica*, 1934; R. A. Musgrave, "The Voluntary Exchange Theory of Public Economy," *Quarterly Journal of Economics*, 1938–39; H. R. Bowen, "The Interpretation of Voting in the Allocation of Economic Resources," *Quarterly Journal of Economics*, 1943–44, and *Toward Social Economy* (New York, 1948), Chap. 18; and (in French) A. T. Peacock, "Sur la théorie des dépenses publiques," *Economie Appliquée*, 1952.

4. Samuelson (1954), p. 387.

5. Samuelson (1955), p. 350. For one of the clearest of many similar definitions in the traditional Continental public good literature, see that of Sax, in Musgrave and Peacock, p. 183.

6. Samuelson (1954), p. 388.

7. Ibid., p. 389.

8. Ibid., pp. 388–89.

9. Samuelson uses the term *joint supply* only once, on p. 355 of his second article, to describe this property. He also refers to *jointness of demand*, traditionally reserved for "bacon and eggs" type phenomena. Musgrave uses the term *joint consumption*. I have preferred *jointness of supply* which is closest to traditional usage. Lindahl (see Musgrave and Peacock, p. 221) uses a joint supply analogy to good effect in his derivation of the "optimum conditions" for the public good case.

10. This is common usage in traditional public good discussions. Mazzola, Sax and Bowen, for example, all use the term *indivisibility* to describe public goods.

11. See below, sec. 4.2.1.

12. S. Enke, "More on the Misuses of Mathematics in Economics: A Rejoinder," *Review of Economics and Statistics,* 1955; and J. Margolis, "A Comment on the Pure Theory of Public Expenditures," *Review of Economics and Statistics,* 1955.

13. Samuelson (1955), p. 356.

14. See Samuelson (1955), p. 350 and especially n. 1.

15. H. S. Ellis and W. Fellner, "External Economies and Diseconomies," *American Economic Review,* 1943, p. 511.

16. Henry Sidgwick, *Principles of Political Economy,* 3rd ed. (London, 1883), pp. 406–7.

17. H. R. Bowen, *Toward Social Economy,* pp. 172–73; and R. A. Musgrave, *The Theory of Public Finance* (New York, 1959), pp. 8–9. Our definition of "impossibility of exclusion" above is less restrictive than this.

18. Ibid., p. 8.

19. The last bus can be made available to sixty people, etc.

20. Samuelson (1954), p. 389, and (1958), p. 335; and Musgrave, p. 10, n. 1.

21. Wicksell, in Musgrave and Peacock, pp. 81–82.

22. Musgrave, p. 10, n. 1.

23. In contrast, as we have seen, to the superficially very similar concepts of Bowen and Musgrave where impossibility of exclusion is the essential feature.

24. This literature dates back at least to Jules Dupuit's celebrated article of 1844, now reprinted in English translation in *International Economic Papers,* no. 2. The lively controversy of the 1940s was sparked off by Hotelling's classic, "The General Welfare in Relation to Problems of Taxation and of Railway and Utility Rates," *Econometrica,* 1938. For an excellent critical summary of this controversy, see I. M. D. Little, *A Critique of Welfare Economics,* 2nd ed. (Oxford, 1957), chap. 11. Also Nancy Ruggles, "Recent Developments in the Theory of Marginal Cost Pricing," *Review of Economic Studies,* 1949–50. Wicksell's brilliant 1896 discussion (for which see Musgrave and Peacock, pp. 97–105) is another landmark which is well worth attention.

25. Wicksell, pp. 99–100.

26. Little, p. 195.

27. Samuelson (1955), p. 356.

28. Samuelson (1958), p. 335.

29. The analysis of this section is based upon the highly suggestive extensions of the external economies concept contained in W. J. Baumol, *Welfare Economics and the Theory of the State* (London, 1952).

SELECTION 14

MANCUR OLSON, JR.

The Logic

This reading summarizes and extends the arguments in Mancur Olson's book *The Logic of Collective Action.* The logic of collective action may more accurately be described as the paradox of group inaction. Olson clearly demonstrates that the larger the number of individuals with a common interest, the larger the probability that nothing will be done by those same individuals to further that interest.

The "let George do it" philosophy is, of course, known to the student of public finance as the free rider problem. However, private groups, organized around collective interests, cannot rely upon the same means as governments to solve the problem of free riders. Yet such private groups exist. Olson describes the circumstances under which collective action by private organizations can be successful and when collective action will not be likely.

QUESTIONS TO GUIDE THE READING

1. What is the nature of the benefit-cost calculation that leads members of large groups to choose (rationally) not to act in the interest of the group?
2. How do selective incentives used by private organizations substitute for compulsory taxation used by governments?
3. Under what circumstances are social selective incentives available to a group?
4. How does the concept of "rational ignorance" explain the effectiveness of lobbying, acts of terrorism, and the existence of government policies that are seemingly inconsistent with the egalitarian goals of a democracy?
5. When is collective action more likely to occur in small groups than in large ones?

. . . It has often been taken for granted that if everyone in a group of individuals or firms had some interest in common, then there would be a ten-

Mancur Olson, "The Logic," in *The Rise and Decline of Nations: Economic Growth, Stagflation, and Social Rigidities,* Yale University Press (1982), 17–35. Reprinted by permission of Yale University Press.

Mancur Olson, Jr. is Professor of Economics at the University of Maryland.

dency for the group to seek to further this interest. Thus many students of politics in the United States for a long time supposed that citizens with a common political interest would organize and lobby to serve that interest. Each individual in the population would be in one or more groups and the vector of pressures of these competing groups explained the outcomes of the political process. Similarly, it was often supposed that if workers, farmers, or consumers faced monopolies harmful to their interests, they would eventually attain countervailing power through organizations such as labor unions or farm organizations that obtained market power and protective government action. On a larger scale, huge social classes are often expected to act in the interest of their members; the unalloyed form of this belief is, of course, the Marxian contention that in capitalist societies the bourgeois class runs the government to serve its own interests, and that once the exploitation of the proletariat goes far enough and "false consciousness" has disappeared, the working class will in its own interest revolt and establish a dictatorship of the proletariat. In general, if the individuals in some category or class had a sufficient degree of self-interest and if they all agreed on some common interest, then the group would to some extent also act in a self-interested or group-interested manner.

If we ponder the logic of the familiar assumption described in the preceding paragraph, we can see that it is fundamentally and indisputably faulty. Consider those consumers who agree that they pay higher prices for a product because of some objectionable monopoly or tariff, or those workers who agree that their skill deserves a higher wage. Let us now ask what would be the expedient course of action for an individual consumer who would like to see a boycott to combat a monopoly or a lobby to repeal the tariff, or for an individual worker who would like a strike threat or a minimum wage law that could bring higher wages. If the consumer or worker contributes a few days and a few dollars to organize a boycott or a union or to lobby for favorable legislation, he or she will have sacrificed time and money. What will this sacrifice obtain? The individual will at best succeed in advancing the cause to a small (often imperceptible) degree. In any case he will get only a minute share of the gain from his action. The very fact that the objective or interest is common to or shared by the group entails that the gain from any sacrifice an individual makes to serve this common purpose is shared with everyone in the group. The successful boycott or strike or lobbying action will bring the better price or wage for everyone in the relevant category, so the individual in any large group with a common interest will reap only a minute share of the gains from whatever sacrifices the individual makes to achieve this common interest. Since any gain goes to everyone in the group, those who contribute nothing to the effort will get just as much as those who made a contribution. It pays to "let George do it," but George has little or no incentive to do anything in the group interest either, so (in the absence of factors that are completely left out of the conceptions mentioned in the first paragraph) there will be little, if any, group action. The paradox, then, is that (in the absence of special arrangements or circumstances to which we shall turn later) large groups, at least if they are composed of rational individuals, will *not* act in their group interest.

This paradox is elaborated and set out in a way that lets the reader check every step of the logic in a book I wrote entitled *The Logic of Collective Action*. That book also shows that the evidence in the United States, the only country in which all powerful interest groups were considered, systematically supported the argument, and that the scattered evidence that I was aware of from other countries was also consistent with it. Since the present book is an outgrowth of *The Logic of Collective Action* and in large part even an application of the argument in it, the most serious critics or students of the present book should have read that one. For the many readers who naturally would not want to invest the time needed to do so without knowing what might be gained, and for those with a more casual interest, the first part of this chapter will explain a few features of the argument in *The Logic* that are needed to understand the rest of the present volume. Other parts of the chapter, however, should not involve any repetition.

II

One finding in *The Logic* is that the services of associations like labor unions, professional associations, farm organizations, cartels, lobbies (and even collusive groups without formal organization) resemble the basic services of the state in one utterly fundamental respect. The services of such associations, like the elemental services or "public goods" provided by governments, if provided to anyone, go to everyone in some category or group. Just as the law and order, defense, or pollution abatement brought about by government accrue to everyone in some country or geographic area, so the tariff obtained by a farm organization's lobbying effort raises the price to all producers of the relevant commodity. Similarly, as I argued earlier, the higher wage won by a union applies to all employees in the pertinent category. More generally, every lobby obtaining a general change in legislation or regulation thereby obtains a public or collective good for everyone who benefits from that change, and every combination—that is, every "cartel"— using market or industrial action to get a higher price or wage must, when it restricts the quantity supplied, raise the price for every seller, thereby creating a collective good for all sellers.

If governments, on the one hand, and combinations exploiting their political or market power, on the other, produce public or collective goods that inevitably go to everyone in some group or category, then both are subject to the paradoxical logic set out above: that is, the individuals and firms they serve have in general no incentive voluntarily to contribute to their support. It follows that if there is only voluntary and rational individual behavior,[1] then for the most part neither governments nor lobbies and cartels will exist, unless individuals support them for some reason *other* than the collective goods they provide. Of course, governments exist virtually everywhere and often there are lobbies and cartelistic organizations as well. If the argument so far is right, it follows that something *other* than the collective goods that governments and other organizations provide accounts for their existence.

In the case of governments, the answer was explained before *The Logic of Collective Action* was written; governments are obviously supported by compulsory taxation. Sometimes there is little objection to this compulsion, presumably because many people intuitively understand that public goods cannot be sold in the marketplace or financed by any voluntary mechanism; as I have already argued, each individual would get only a minute share of any governmental services he or she paid for and would get whatever level of services was provided by others in any event.

In the case of organizations that provide collective goods to their client groups through political or market action, the answer has not been obvious, but it is no less clear-cut. Organizations of this kind, at least when they represent large groups, are again not supported because of the collective goods they provide, but rather because they have been fortunate enough to find what I have called *selective incentives*. A selective incentive is one that applies selectively to the individuals depending on whether they do or do not contribute to the provision of the collective good.

A selective incentive can be either negative or positive; it can, for example, be a loss or punishment imposed only on those who do *not* help provide the collective good. Tax payments are, of course, obtained with the help of negative selective incentives, since those who are found not to have paid their taxes must then suffer both taxes and penalties. The best-known type of organized interest group in modern democratic societies, the labor union, is also usually supported, in part, through negative selective incentives. Most of the dues in strong unions are obtained through union shop, closed shop, or agency shop arrangements which make dues paying more or less compulsory and automatic. There are often also informal arrangements with the same effect; David McDonald, former president of the United Steel Workers of America, describes one of these arrangements used in the early history of that union. It was, he writes, a technique

> which we called . . . visual education, which was a high-sounding label for a practice much more accurately described as dues picketing. It worked very simply. A group of dues-paying members, selected by the district director (usually more for their size than their tact) would stand at the plant gate with pick handles or baseball bats in hand and confront each worker as he arrived for his shift.

As McDonald's "dues picketing" analogy suggests, picketing during strikes is another negative selective incentive that unions sometimes need; although picketing in industries with established and stable unions is usually peaceful, this is because the union's capacity to close down an enterprise against which it has called a strike is clear to all; the early phase of unionization often involves a great deal of violence on the part of both unions and anti-union employers and scabs.

Some opponents of labor unions argue that, since many of the members of labor unions join only through the processes McDonald described or through legally enforced union-shop arrangements, most of the relevant workers do not want to be unionized. The Taft-Hartley Act provided that impartial governmentally administered elections should be held to determine whether workers did in fact want to belong to unions. As the collective-good logic set out here suggests, the same workers who had to be coerced to pay union dues voted for the unions with compulsory dues (and normally by overwhelming margins), so that this feature of the Taft-Hartley Act was soon abandoned as pointless. The workers who as individuals tried to avoid paying union dues at the same time that they voted to force themselves all to pay dues are no different from taxpayers who vote, in effect, for high levels of taxation, yet try to arrange their private affairs in ways that avoid taxes. Because of the same logic, many professional associations also get members through covert or overt coercion (for example, lawyers in those states with a "closed bar"). So do lobbies and cartels of several other types; some of the contributions by corporate officials, for instance, to politicians useful to the corporation are also the result of subtle forms of coercion.

Positive selective incentives, although easily overlooked, are also commonplace, as diverse examples in *The Logic* demonstrate. American farm organizations offer prototypical examples. Many of the members of the stronger American farm organizations are members because their dues payments are automatically deducted from the "patronage dividends" of farm cooperatives or are included in the insurance premiums paid to mutual insurance companies associated with the farm organizations. Any number of organizations with urban clients also provide similar positive selective incentives in the form of insurance policies, publications, group air fares, and other private goods made available only to members. The grievance procedures of labor unions usually also offer selective incentives, since the grievances of active members often get most of the attention. The symbiosis between the political power of a lobbying organization and the business institutions associated with it often yields tax or other advantages for the business institution, and the publicity and other information flowing out of the political arm of a movement often generates patterns of preference or trust that make the business activities of the movement more remunerative. The surpluses obtained in such ways in turn provide positive selective incentives that recruit participants for the lobbying efforts.

III

Small groups, or occasionally large "federal" groups that are made up of many small groups of socially interactive members, have an additional source of both negative and positive selective incentives. Clearly most people value the companionship and respect of those with whom they interact. In modern societies solitary confinement is, apart from the rare death penalty, the harshest legal punishment. The censure or even ostracism of those who fail to bear a share of the burdens of collective action can sometimes be an important selective incentive. An extreme example of this occurs when British unionists refuse to speak to uncooperative colleagues, that is, "send them to Coventry." Similarly, those in a socially interactive group seeking a collective good can give special respect or honor to those who distinguish themselves by their sacrifices in the interest of the group and thereby offer them a positive selective incentive. Since most people apparently prefer relatively like-minded or agreeable and respectable company, and often prefer to associate with those whom they especially admire, they may find it costless to shun those who shirk the collective action and to favor those who oversubscribe.

Social selective incentives can be powerful and inexpensive, but they are available only in certain situations. As I have already indicated, they have little applicability to large groups, except in those cases in which the large groups can be federations of small groups that are capable of social interaction. It also is not possible to organize most large groups in need of a collective good into small, socially interactive subgroups, since most individuals do not have the time needed to maintain a huge number of friends and acquaintances.

The availability of social selective incentives is also limited by the social heterogeneity of some of the groups or categories that would benefit from a collective good. Everyday observation reveals that most socially interactive groups are fairly homogeneous and that many people resist extensive social interaction with those they deem to have lower status or greatly different tastes. Even Bohemian or other nonconformist groups often are made up of individuals who are similar to one another, however much they differ from the rest of society. Since some of the categories of individuals who would benefit from a collective good are socially heterogeneous, the social interaction needed for selective incentives sometimes cannot be arranged even when the number of individuals involved is small.

Another problem in organizing and maintaining socially heterogeneous groups is that they are less likely to agree on the exact nature of whatever collective good is at issue or on how much of it is worth buying. All the arguments showing the difficulty of collective action mentioned so far in this chapter hold even when there is perfect consensus about the collective good that is desired, the amount that is wanted, and the best way to obtain the good. But if anything, such as social heterogeneity, reduces consensus, collective action can become still less likely. And if there is nonetheless collective action, it incurs the extra cost (especially for the leaders of whatever organization or collusion is at issue) of accommodating and compromising the different views. The situation is slightly different in the very small groups to which we shall turn shortly. In such groups differences of opinion can sometimes provide a bit of an incentive to join an organization seeking a collective good, since joining might give the individual a significant influence over the organization's policy and the nature of any collective good it would obtain. But this consideration is not relevant to any group that is large enough so that a single individual cannot expect to affect the outcome.

Consensus is especially difficult where collective goods are concerned because the defining characteristic of collective goods—that they go to everyone in some group or category if they are provided at all—also entails that everyone in the relevant group gets more or less of the collective good together, and that they all have to accept whatever level and type of public good is provided. A country can have only one foreign and defense policy, however diverse the preferences and incomes of its citizenry, and (except in the rarely attainable case of a "Lindahl equilibrium") there will not be agreement within a country on how much should be spent to carry out the foreign and defense policy. . . . Heterogeneous clients with diverse demands for collective goods can pose an even greater problem for private associations, which not only must deal with the disagreements but also must find selective incentives strong enough to hold dissatisfied clients.

In short, the political entrepreneurs who attempt to organize collective action will accordingly be more likely to succeed if they strive to organize relatively homogeneous groups. The political managers whose task it is to maintain organized or collusive action similarly will be motivated to use indoctrination and selective recruitment to increase the homogeneity of their client groups. This is true in part because social selective incentives are more likely to be available to the more nearly homogeneous groups, and in part because homogeneity will help achieve consensus.

IV

Information and calculation about a collective good is often itself a collective good. Consider a typical member of a large organization who is deciding how much time to devote to studying the policies or leadership of the organization. The more time the member devotes to this matter, the greater the likelihood that his or her voting and advocacy will favor effective policies and leadership for the organization. This typical member will, however, get only a small share of the gain from the more effective policies and leadership: in the aggregate, the other members will get almost all the gains, so that the individual member does not have an incentive to devote nearly as much time to fact-finding and thinking about the organization as would be in the group interest. Each of the members of the group would be better off if they all could be coerced into spending more time finding out how to vote to make the organization best further their interests. This is dramatically evident in the case of the typical voter in a national election in a large country. The gain to such a voter from studying issues and candidates until it is clear what vote is truly in his or her interest is given by the difference in the value to the individual of the "right" election outcome as compared with the "wrong" outcome, *multiplied by the probability a change in the individual's vote will alter the outcome of the election*. Since the probability that a typical voter will change the outcome of the election is vanishingly small, the typical citizen is usually "rationally ignorant" about public affairs. Often, information about public affairs is so interesting or entertaining that it pays to acquire it for these reasons alone—this appears to be the single most important source of exceptions to the generalization that *typical* citizens are rationally ignorant about public affairs.

Individuals in a few special vocations can receive considerable rewards in private goods if they acquire exceptional knowledge of public goods. Politicians, lobbyists, journalists, and social scientists, for example, may earn more money, power, or prestige from knowledge of this or that public business. Occasionally, exceptional knowledge of public policy can generate exceptional profits in stock exchanges or other markets. Withal, the typical citizen will find that his or her income and life chances will not be improved by zealous study of public affairs, or even of any single collective good.

The limited knowledge of public affairs is in turn necessary to explain the effectiveness of lobbying. If all citizens had obtained and digested all pertinent information, they could not then be swayed by advertising or other persuasion. With perfectly informed citizens, elected officials would not be subject to the blandishments of lobbyists, since the constituents would then know if their interests were betrayed and defeat the unfaithful representative at the next election. Just as lobbies provide collective goods to special-interest groups, so their effectiveness is explained by the imperfect knowledge of citizens, and this in turn is due mainly to the fact that information and calculation about collective goods is also a collective good.

This fact—that the benefits of individual enlightenment about public goods are usually dispersed throughout a group or nation, rather than concentrated upon the individual who bears the costs of becoming enlightened—explains many other phenomena as well. It explains, for example, the "man bites dog" criterion of what is newsworthy. If the television newscasts were watched or newspapers were read solely to obtain the most important information about public affairs, aberrant events of little public importance would be ignored and typical patterns of quantitative significance would be emphasized; when the news is, by contrast, for most people largely an alternative to other forms of diversion or entertainment, intriguing oddities and human-interest items are in demand. Similarly, events that unfold in a suspenseful way or sex scandals among public figures are fully covered by the media, whereas the complexities of economic policy or quantitative analyses of public problems receive only minimal attention. Public officials, often able to thrive without giving the citizens good value for their tax monies, may fall over an exceptional mistake striking enough to be newsworthy. Extravagant statements, picturesque protests, and unruly demonstrations that offend much of the public they are designed to influence are also explicable in this way: they make diverting news and thus call attention to interests and arguments that might otherwise be ignored. Even some isolated acts of terrorism that are described as "senseless" can, from this perspective, be explained as effective means of obtaining the riveted attention of a public that otherwise would remain rationally ignorant.

This argument also helps us to understand certain apparent inconsistencies in the behavior of modern democracies. The arrangement of the income-tax brackets in all the major developed democracies is distinctly progressive, whereas the loopholes are more often tilted toward a minority of more prosperous taxpayers. Since both are the results of the same democratic institutions, why do they not have the same incidence? As I see it, the progression of the income tax is a matter of such salience and political controversy that much of the electorate knows about it, so populist and majoritarian considerations dictate a considerable degree of progression. The details of tax laws are far less widely known, and they often reflect the interests of small numbers of organized and usually more prosperous taxpayers. Several of the developed democracies similarly have adopted programs such as Medicare and Medicaid that are obviously inspired by the concerns about the cost of medical care to those with low or middle incomes, yet implemented or administered these programs in ways that resulted in large increases in income for prosperous physicians and other providers of medical care. Again, these diverse consequences seem to be explained by the fact that conspicuous and controversial choices of overall policies become known to the majorities who consume health care, whereas the many smaller choices needed to implement these programs are influenced primarily by a minority of organized providers of health care.

The fact that the typical individual does not have an incentive to spend much time studying many of his choices concerning collective goods also helps to explain some otherwise inexplicable individual contributions toward the provision of collective goods. The logic of collective action that has been described in this chapter is not immediately apparent to those who have never studied it; if it were, there would be nothing paradoxical in the argument with which this chapter opened, and students to whom the argument is explained would not react with initial skepticism. No doubt the practical implications of this logic for the individual's own choices were often discerned before the logic was ever set out in print, but this does not mean that they were always understood even at the intuitive and practical level. In particular, when the costs of individual contributions to collective action are very small, the individual has little incentive to investigate whether or not to make a contribution or even to exercise intuition. If the individual knows the costs of a contribution to collective action in the interest of a group of which he is a part are trivially small, he may rationally not take the trouble to consider whether the gains are smaller still. This is particularly the case since the size of these gains and the policies that would maximize them are matters about which it is usually not rational for him to investigate.

This consideration of the costs and benefits of calculation about public goods leads to the testable prediction that voluntary contributions toward the provision of collective goods for large groups without selective incentives will often occur when the costs of the individual contributions are negligible, but that they will *not* often occur when the costs of the individual contributions are considerable. In other words, when the costs of individual action to help to obtain a desired collective good are small enough, the result is indeterminate and sometimes goes one way and sometimes the other, but when the costs get larger this indeterminacy disappears. We should accordingly find that more than a few people are willing to take the moment of time needed to sign petitions for causes they support, or to express their opinions in the course of discussion, or to vote for the candidate or party they prefer. Similarly, if the argument here is correct, we should not find many instances where individuals voluntarily contribute substantial sums of resources year after year for the purpose of obtaining some collective good for some large group of which they are a part. Before parting with a large amount of money or time, and particularly before doing so repeatedly, the rational individual will reflect on what this considerable sacrifice will accomplish. If the individual is a typical individual in a large group that would benefit from a collective good, his contribution will not make a perceptible difference in the amount that is provided. The theory here predicts that such contributions become less likely the larger the contribution at issue.

V

Even when contributions are costly enough to elicit rational calculation, there is still one set of circumstances in which collective action can occur without selective incentives. This set of circumstances becomes evident the moment we think of situations in which there are only a few individuals or firms that would benefit from collective action. Suppose there are two firms of equal size in an industry and no other firms can enter the industry. It still will be the case that a higher price for the industry's product will benefit both firms and that legislation favorable to the industry will help both firms. The higher price and the favorable legislation are then collective goods to this "oligopolistic" industry, even though there are only two in the group that benefit from the collective goods. Obviously, each of the oligopolists is in a situation in which if it restricts output to raise the industry price, or lobbies for favorable legislation for the industry, it will tend to get half of the benefit. And the cost-benefit ratio of action in the common interest easily could be so favorable that, even though a firm bears the whole cost of its action and gets only half the benefit of this action, it could still profit from acting in the common interest. Thus if the group that would benefit from collective action is sufficiently small and the cost-benefit ratio of collective action for the group sufficiently favorable, there may well be calculated action in the collective interest even without selective incentives.

When there are only a few members in the group, there is also the possibility that they will bargain with one another and agree on collective action—then the action of each can have a perceptible effect on the interests and the expedient courses of action of others, so that each has an incentive to act strategically, that is, in ways that take into account the effect of the individual's choices on the choices of others. This interdependence of individual firms or persons in the group can give them an incentive to bargain with one another for their mutual advantage. Indeed, if bargaining costs were negligible, they would have an incentive to continue bargaining with one another until group gains were maximized, that is, until what we shall term a *group-optimal outcome* (or what economists sometimes call a "Pareto-optimal" outcome for the group) is achieved. One way the two firms mentioned in the previous paragraph could obtain such an outcome is by agreeing that each will bear half the costs of any collective action; each firm would then bear half the costs of its action in the common interest and receive half the benefits. It therefore would have an incentive to continue action in the collective interest until the aggregate gains of collective action were maximized. In any bargaining, however, each party has an incentive to seek the largest possible share of the group gain for itself, and usually also an incentive to threaten to block or undermine the collective action—that is, to be a "holdout"—if it does not get its preferred share of the group gains. Thus the bargaining may very well not succeed in achieving a group-optimal outcome and may also fail to achieve agreement on any collective action at all. The upshot of all this, as I explain elsewhere, is that "small" groups can often engage in collective action without selective incentives. In certain small groups ("privileged groups") there is actually a presumption that some of the collective good will be provided. Nonetheless, even in the best of circumstances collective action is problematic and the outcomes in particular cases are indeterminate.

Although some aspects of the matter are complex and indeterminate, the essence of the relationship between the size of the group that would benefit from collective action and the extent of collective action is beautifully simple—yet somehow not widely understood. Consider again our two firms and suppose that they have *not* worked out any agreement to maximize their aggregate gains or to coordinate their actions in any way. Each firm will still get half the gains of any action it takes in the interest of the group, and thus it may have a substantial incentive to act in the group interest even when it is acting unilaterally. There is, of course, also a *group external economy,* or gain to the group for which the firm acting unilaterally is not compensated, of 50 percent, so unilateral behavior does not achieve a group-optimal outcome. Now suppose there were a third firm of the same size— the group external economy would then be two thirds, and the individual firm would get only a third of the gain from any independent action it took in the group interest. Of course, if there were a hundred such firms, the group external economy would be 99 percent, and the individual firm would get only 1 percent of the gain from any action in the group interest. Obviously, when we get to large groups measured in millions or even thousands, the incentive for group-oriented behavior in the absence of selective incentives becomes insignificant and even imperceptible.

Untypical as my example of equal-sized firms may be, it makes the general point intuitively obvious: other things being equal, *the larger the number of individuals or firms that would benefit from a collective good, the smaller the share of the gains from action in the group interest that will accrue to the individual or firm that undertakes the action. Thus, in the absence of selective incentives, the incentive for group action diminishes as group size increases, so that large groups are less able to act in their common interest than small ones.* If an additional individual or firm that would value the collective good enters the scene, then the share of the gains from group-oriented action that anyone already in the group might take must diminish. This holds true whatever the relative sizes or valuations of the collective good in the group. . . .

The number of people who must bargain if a group-optimal amount of a collective good is to be obtained, and thus the costs of bargaining, must rise with the size of the group. This consideration reinforces the point just made. Indeed, both everyday observation and the logic of the matter suggest that for genuinely large groups, bargaining among all members to obtain agreement on the provision of a collective good is out of the question. The consideration mentioned earlier in this chapter, that social selective incentives are available only to small groups and (tenuously) to those larger groups that are federations of small groups, also suggests that small groups are more likely to organize than large ones.

The significance of the logic that has just been set out can best be seen by comparing groups that would have the same net gain from collective action, if they could engage in it, but that vary in size. Suppose there are a million individuals who would gain a thousand dollars each, or a billion in the aggregate, if they were to organize effectively and engage in collective action that had a total cost of a hundred million. If the logic set out above is right, they could not organize or engage in effective collective action without selective incentives. Now suppose that, although the total gain of a billion dollars from collective action and the aggregate cost of a hundred million remain the same, the group is composed instead of five big corporations or five organized municipalities, each of which would gain two hundred million. Collective action is not an absolute certainty even in this case, since each of the five could conceivably expect others to put up the hundred million and hope to gain the collective good worth two hundred million at no cost at all. Yet collective action, perhaps after some delays due to bargaining, seems very likely indeed. In this case any one of the five would gain a hundred million from providing the collective good even if it had to pay the whole cost itself; and the costs of bargaining among five would not be great, so they would sooner or later probably work out an agreement providing for the collective action. The numbers in this example are arbitrary, but roughly similar situations occur often in reality, and the contrast between "small" and "large" groups could be illustrated with an infinite number of diverse examples.

The significance of this argument shows up in a second way if one compares the operations of lobbies or cartels within jurisdictions of vastly different scale, such as a modest municipality on the one hand and a big country on the other. Within the town, the mayor or city council may be influenced by, say, a score of petitioners or a lobbying budget of a thousand dollars. A particular line of business may be in the hands of only a few firms, and if the town is distant enough from other markets only these few would need to agree to create a cartel. In a big country, the resources needed to influence the national government are likely to be much more substantial, and unless the firms are (as they sometimes are) gigantic, many of them would have to cooperate to create an effective cartel. Now suppose that the million individuals in our large group in the previous paragraph were spread out over a hundred thousand towns or jurisdictions, so that each jurisdiction had ten of them, along with the same proportion of citizens in other categories as before. Suppose also that the cost-benefit ratios remained the same, so that there was still a billion dollars to gain across all jurisdictions or ten thousand in each, and that it would still cost a hundred million dollars across all jurisdictions or a thousand in each. It no longer seems out of the question that in many jurisdictions the groups of ten, or subsets of them, would put up the thousand-dollar total needed to get the thousand for each individual. Thus we see that, if all else were equal, small jurisdictions would have more collective action per capita than large ones.

Differences in intensities of preference generate a third type of illustration of the logic at issue. A small number of zealots anxious for a particular collective good are more likely to act collectively to obtain that good than a larger number with the same aggregate willingness to pay. Suppose there are twenty-five individuals, each of whom finds a given collective good worth a thousand dollars in one case, whereas in another there are five thousand, each of whom finds the collective good worth five dollars. Obviously, the argument indicates that there would be a greater likelihood of collective action in the former case than in the latter, even though the aggregate demand for the collective good is the same in both. The great historical significance of small groups of fanatics no doubt owes something to this consideration.

VI

The argument in this chapter predicts that those groups that have access to selective incentives will be more likely to act collectively to obtain collective goods than those that do not, and that smaller groups will have a greater likelihood of engaging in collective action than larger ones. The empirical portions of *The Logic* show that this prediction has been correct for the United States. More study will be needed before we can be utterly certain that the argument also holds for other countries, but the more prominent features of the organizational landscape of other countries certainly do fit the theory. In no major country are large groups without access to selective incentives generally organized—the masses of consumers are not in consumers' organizations, the millions of taxpayers are not in taxpayers' organizations, the vast number of those with relatively low incomes are not in organizations for the poor, and the sometimes substantial numbers of unemployed have no organized voice. These groups are so dispersed that it is not feasible for any nongovernmental organization to coerce them; in this they differ dramatically from those, like workers in large factories or mines, who are susceptible to coercion through picketing. Neither does there appear to be any source of the positive selective incentives that might give individuals in these categories an incentive to cooperate with the many others with whom they share common interests. By contrast, almost everywhere the social prestige of the learned professions and the limited numbers of practitioners of each profession in each community has helped them to organize. The professions have also been helped to organize by the distinctive susceptibility of the public to the assertion that a professional organization, with the backing of government, ought to be able to determine who is "qualified" to practice the profession, and thereby to control a decisive selective incentive. The small groups of (often large) firms in industry after industry, in country after country, are similarly often organized in trade associations or organizations or collusions of one kind or another. So, frequently, are the small groups of (usually smaller) businesses in particular towns or communities. . . .

NOTES

1. *Rational* need not imply *self-interested*.

SELECTION 15

T. NICOLAUS TIDEMAN AND GORDON TULLOCK
A New and Superior Process for Making Social Choices

The demand-revealing process solves the free rider problem
associated with the efficient provision of public goods. It uses a
two-part tax: (1) a share of the cost of the good, assigned without
reference to individual voter demand; and (2) a "Clarke tax,"
which guarantees that voters will be worse off if they misrepresent
their preferences than if they tell the truth.

   The process works because neither the assigned share of the
cost nor the Clarke tax is based directly upon a voter's reported
demand. Further, because an individual's Clarke tax is equal to any
disutility other voters may suffer because of that individual's vote,
the process comes close to guaranteeing Pareto efficiency.
Essentially, truth is the best option. If voters lie to minimize Clarke
taxes, they will suffer, because the outcome will be further from
their most preferred choice than before. If they lie to change the
choice from the Pareto efficient outcome, Clarke taxes will be
larger, because total voter disutility is larger when social surplus is
smaller.

QUESTIONS TO GUIDE THE READING

1. In what way does the demand-revealing process own the
   "property rights" to the consequences of each individual's vote?

2. If a decision not to vote is equivalent to lying about one's
   preferences, how might the demand-revealing process increase
   voter participation?

3. How would you expect the current distribution of income (after
   taxes) in the United States to differ if all citizens voted using the
   demand-revealing process as opposed to direct majority rule?

4. Why is it necessary to form a coalition with other voters in order
   to benefit from cheating on the demand-revealing process?

Nicolaus T. Tideman and Gordon Tullock, "A New and Superior Process for Making Social
   Choices," *Journal of Political Economy 84* (December 1976), 1145–59. Reprinted by permission of the authors and The University of Chicago.

T. Nicolaus Tideman is Professor of Economics at the Virginia Polytechnic Institute and State
University. **Gordon Tullock** is Karl Eller Professor of Economics and Political Science at the
University of Arizona.

This paper describes a new process for making social choices, one that is superior to other processes that have been suggested. The method is immune to strategic maneuvering on the part of individual voters. It avoids the conditions of the Arrow theorem by using more information than the rank orders of preferences, and selects a unique point on or "almost on" the Pareto-optimal frontier, one that maximizes or "almost maximizes" the consumer surplus of society. Subject to any given distribution of wealth, the process may be used to approximate the Lindahl equilibrium for all public goods.[1]

These are strong claims, and it is therefore only sensible to begin this paper by pointing out that the process will not cure cancer, stop the tides, or, indeed, deal successfully with many other problems. As far as we know, all existing social-choice processes are subject to exploitation by suitably designed coalitions. This process is no exception. In addition, as in all democratic voting processes, voters are undermotivated to invest time and effort in a comparative evaluation of alternatives. The motives they are given for making sensible decisions are somewhat stronger than those for persons engaging in voting under majority rule, but voters will be asked to do more in the way of expressing their preferences than simply saying yes or no. Therefore, it is not clear whether the lack of an incentive to vote is more or less of a handicap for this process than it is for ordinary voting processes.

The process may be described most generally as a demand-revealing process. It relies on what might be called an incomplete compensation mechanism that appears to have been first described by Vickrey (1961) in the context of optimum counterspeculation policy for a socialist economy. The essence of the mechanism is that each person is paid for the benefits (or pays the costs) of his actions, but no one is charged (or credited) as required for budget balance. Vickrey showed that it would be possible to motivate individuals to reveal their true supply and demand schedules for a private good by paying each person the net increase in the sum of the producer and consumer surpluses of other persons in the market that resulted from the supply or demand schedule that the one person reported. Vickrey noted that there would be a problem of financing such a system, since it would generate a deficit. He did not discuss the potential application of such a system to public goods.

Two persons who were unaware of each other's work or Vickrey's discovered the applicability of a similar compensation mechanism to the problem of motivating individuals to reveal their true demands for public goods. The first to publish was Edward Clarke (1971, 1972), whose papers until now have made very little impact on the economics profession. The lack of impact can be attributed partly to the nature of the idea that Clarke put forward, which is counterintuitive to almost any welfare economist, and partly to Clarke's difficult writing style. The second person was Theodore Groves. In one paper (Groves 1973) he offered a mathematically rigorous treatment of a procedure like Vickrey's for allocating scarce private goods within an organization. More recently Groves and Loeb (1975) published a procedure isomorphic to Clarke's for selecting the optimal quantities of public goods.

Our objectives in this paper are to provide a clear explanation of the demand-revealing process as it applies to public goods and to extend the understanding of the process on several fronts.

While, as Bowen (1943) showed, majority rule is efficient if the intensity of voters' preferences is distributed symmetrically, the demand-revealing process does not require for its efficiency any restriction on the distribution of intensities of voters' preferences. Unlike the voting processes proposed by Thompson (1965), Dreze and de la Vallee Poussin (1971) and Tideman (1972), the demand-revealing process requires no special beliefs on the part of voters. Basically, it provides an environment in which each voter is motivated to reveal his preferences correctly. This is accomplished by the use of a special—indeed, bizarre—tax mechanism which rewards truthful presentation of preferences and penalizes concealment or falsification.

In order to explain the process, we start not with the problem with which Clarke's first paper dealt, the choices of the optimal amount of a single-dimensional public good, but with the simpler case of a choice among discrete options, which Clarke's second paper discussed cryptically. For simplicity, we shall start with two alternatives, which may be conceived of as two policies or two candidates. We shall then show how the process can be extended to more than two options. Having introduced the subject with these simple examples, we shall then turn to the choice of the optimal amount of a public good.

Choice Between Two Options

Suppose that a collective choice must be made between two options, designated A and B. The rule we describe involves asking each individual to state which option he prefers and the amount of money he is willing to pay to secure his preferred option instead of the other. We shall show shortly why he would have an incentive to respond truthfully. In table 1, we show the "votes" of each of three voters for the two options. Option A is worth a total of $70 to the persons who prefer it and is chosen by the rule because B is worth less to its proponent.

We now turn to why the voter is motivated to correctly state his preferences. There is a "Clarke Tax" to be levied, and, as we said before, it is a bizarre tax. We inquire with respect to each voter what the outcome would have been if he had not voted. For example, if voter 1 had not voted, then the outcome would have been that alternative A would have received $40 total and alternative B $60; hence, alternative B would have won. We charge voter 1 $20, the amount necessary to bring the "votes" for A up to equality with the "votes" for B. By the same line of reasoning, voter 3 pays a tax of $30. Voter 2 pays no tax because his vote did not change the outcome. Note that, had voter 1 understated his preference for A by an amount less than $10, he would have paid exactly the same tax as he did. If he had understated his preference for A by more than $10, B would have been selected. And voter 1 would prefer having A at the price of $20 to having B. Similarly, if a

Table 1   Aggregating Preferences for Two Options (in Dollars)

	Differential Values of Options	
Voter	A	B
1	30	0
2	0	60
3	40	0
Total	70	60

voter overstates his preferences, either the overstatement makes no difference in what is selected or what he pays or else (e.g., if voter 2 said B was worth $100 to him) he changes the result by his action and pays more for his choice than it is worth to him.

To describe the decision rule generally, define S_A as the sum over all voters who state a preference for A over B of the amounts they offer to pay to have A instead of B. Define S_B similarly. The collective-choice rule will be to choose A if $S_A > S_B$, choose B if $S_B > S_A$, and flip a coin to decide if $S_A = S_B$. The incentive to respond truthfully is generated by a "Clarke tax," a rule that a voter must pay a portion of his offer if and only if his vote changes the outcome. Any voter who changes the outcome must pay $|S_A - S_B|$, calculated without his vote. In the case of a tie that is decided by a coin toss, every voter on the side that wins the toss is regarded as having changed the outcome. If the result without a person's vote is a tie, he pays nothing.

In effect, this rule gives each voter the choice of (1) leaving the outcome where it would be without his vote or (2) changing it at a price of the reported net loss to other voters. If the value to a voter of his preferred outcome is less than the net value of the alternative to others, then he prefers (1), which occurs if he responds truthfully. If his value is greater than the aggregate net value to others, then he prefers (2), which again is what occurs upon a truthful response. If his value exactly balances the net value reported by others, then he is indifferent between the two possibilities, and we flip a coin if he responds truthfully. A nontruthful response cannot benefit the respondent, and it carries a risk of making him worse off than he would have been with the truth. If he understates his value, he may pass up an opportunity to obtain the result he desires at an attractive price. If he overstates his value, he may wind up paying more than it is worth to him to have his choice.

To characterize the rule in terms of property rights, one might call it "entitlement to the consequence of one's abstention," since the result that occurs if a voter abstains costs him nothing; while if his vote changes the collective choice, he must pay. This has a certain family resemblance to majority rule, where the voter's only entitlement is to what a majority of persons other than himself want, except that, if all others tie, he can decide the issue.

Any money collected from voters in this system must be wasted or given to nonvoters to keep the incentives correct. If voters received the money collected, the possibility of increasing their shares would distort their incentives. However, if the revenue were simply divided equally among all voters, the effective distortion would be minimal if there were more than 100 or so voters; with a large number of voters, it is most likely that no one vote will change the outcome, so that in most cases no taxes for voting will be collected. We will discuss the significance of the lack of budget balance in more detail in the context of decisions about continuous variables.

A serious problem in all voting systems is the weakness of the incentive to vote. The demand-revealing process is no exception. The only wholly instrumental reason for a person to vote is the possibility that his vote will be decisive. Failure to vote carries a risk of passing up a chance to alter the outcome at a favorable price, but the probability of being decisive is usually small enough so that people might still reasonably conclude that voting is not worth the effort. Even if people do decide to vote, they are normally not motivated to give any serious study to their vote in collective decision processes, because the probable gain from acquiring further information or simply reflecting on the information already at hand is usually less than the cost. Thus, ill-informed voting is to be expected. The demand-revealing process is no exception to this general rule put forward by Downs (1957).

It may seem that a person who sustains a large loss when his preference is not followed deserves compensation, but this cannot be given without motivating an excessive statement of differential value. If a voter expected to lose, an offer to compensate his loss would motivate a statement from him of a larger loss. In regard to the uncompensated losses that are produced, the demand-revealing process is similar to majority rule. In the latter, every voter must live with the choice of the majority. His only opportunity to be decisive on the issue is if there is an equal number of other voters on each side. Similarly, in the demand-revealing process, every voter must live with a finding that the aggregate value placed by others on the alternatives is opposed to his own interest, provided that he is not willing to pay enough to give his preference the higher aggregate value.

It might be objected that the demand-revealing process would permit confiscatory action. If there is a proposal to tear down one person's house and make the site a park, and if others report a greater gain from the park than the occupant's loss, then the latter loses his property. The demand-revealing process would indeed have this confiscatory characteristic if there were no constitutional limits on the proposals that could be considered. In this respect, the system is again like majority rule, which has a similar confiscatory potential. It is reasonable to expect that people making collective choices by the demand-revealing process would desire constitutional restrictions that would limit the potential for overt redistribution. For instance, a

Table 2   Aggregating Preferences for Three Options (in Dollars)

Voter	Differential Values of Options			Tax	Net Benefit of Voting
	A	B	C		
1	50	20	0	30	20
2	0	60	20	0	0
3	40	0	50	30	10
Total	90	80	70	. . .	. . .
Total Without Indicated Votes					
For 1: 2 + 3	40	60	70	. . .	. . .
For 2: 1 + 3	90	20	50	. . .	. . .
For 3: 1 + 2	50	80	20	. . .	. . .

proposal that a person's property be taken for a public purpose might be admissible only if he would be given reasonable compensation.

Choices among Several Discrete Options

We now show how a demand-revealing process operates when there are more than two discrete options. In table 2 there are three voters, indicated by numbers, and three options, indicated by letters. The numbers in table 2 have been obtained by simply adding a third option, C, to the two shown in table 1, while leaving the differential the voter is willing to pay for a choice between A and B the same as it was in table 1. The difference between the numbers associated with any two options is interpreted as the amount of money the voter is willing to pay to have the one option with the higher number instead of the other. Whether or not this is a legitimate interpretation will be discussed below.

It may be noted that the rank-order preferences generate cyclic choices when majority rule is used. To determine the collective choice by the demand-revealing process, we simply sum the columns and select the option with the highest total, which in this case is A. There is no cycle, nor could there be, although a tie would be possible.

The tax for each voter is calculated from the lower portion of table 2. For the tax on voter 1, add up the sum of the other individuals' votes. Option C would have been chosen with $70. The tax on voter 1 would be $70 minus $40, or $30, and voter 1 is better off by $20 ($50 − $30) than he would have been by abstaining. Note that if he had understated his preferences enough to avoid being taxed, for instance, if he had reported that A only benefited him $25, C would have been selected and voter 1 would have been worse off than he was by correctly presenting his preferences. In the case of voter 2, there is no tax because his vote does not change the outcome; and in the case of voter 3, there is a tax of $30 ($80 − $50), and he obtains a net benefit of $10 ($40 − $30). These taxes are fairly substantial, but that is because we have only a small number of voters. With many voters, the probability is high that the total tax would be relatively miniscule if not zero.

We next inquire whether the proposed method produces results that are "independent of irrelevant alternatives." If option C is dropped from the example in table 2, what difference would it make? Consider voter 1 first. He reports a differential value of $30 for A over B in table 2. If C were dropped from consideration, voter 1 would no longer have to offer $50 for A instead of C. He would be richer, and he might spend some of his additional wealth to increase his offer with respect to A instead of B, say, from $30 to $32. Such wealth effects could conceivably change the result.

We do not, however, think that this is what is normally meant by a dependence on irrelevant alternatives. Option C is relevant because its presence or absence affects the wealth of voter 1. If A owns a pizza den and is negotiating with B for its sale and C builds another pizza restaurant directly across the street, this will clearly affect the bargain between A and B. However, we do not think that it would be proper to say that this was a situation which "lacked independence of irrelevant alternatives." In view of the general controversies surrounding this particular criterion of the Arrow theorem, however, we should like to simply discuss the wealth effect in the demand-revealing process rather than attempt to clear up the linguistic problem.

To put the matter another way, when we insist that each voter arrange the options on a linear scale, so that the difference between the numbers on the scale for any pair of options represents what he is willing to pay to have one option instead of the other, we leave no room for wealth effects. It may be that voter 1's true willingness to pay is $22 for B instead of C and $32 for A instead of B, but only $50 (rather than $54) for A instead of C, because if he has to pay $22 to get from C to B, he is poorer than if he starts at B. With his lower wealth, it is not irrational for him to be willing to spend only $28 rather than $32, at that point, to get from B to A. The linear scale does not permit voter 1 to report these wealth effects, so he compromises by reporting the values in table 2.

It might be proposed that voters be asked to report their preferences among all pairs so that wealth effects could be taken into account in the decision process. However, to do that would be to reintroduce a possibility of cycles. Consider the two voters shown in table 3.

Table 3   The Possible Cycle in Three Options (in Dollars)

	A against B		B against C		A against C	
1	32	0	22	0	50	0
2	0	31	0	21	0	51

Voter 1 has the preferences described earlier. Voter 2 has preferences in the opposite order, of approximately the same magnitude but with less non-linearity from wealth effects. When the preferences are summed, we find a collective choice for A over B and B over C, but also for C over A. This problem of intransitivity might be resolved by applying some analytic device such as the "tournament matrix" described by Moon and Pullman (1970), but it is not clear how the Clarke tax would then be calculated. Furthermore, as long as there were cycles, there would be incentives for strategic misstatements. Therefore, it may be best to require each voter to submit a linearized statement of his preferences, letting him make the necessary approximations there. Then if he can guess which option would be selected without his vote, it will be in his interest to present comparisons with respect to that option truthfully.

A Simple Continuous Application

We now proceed with the specific case Clarke presented in his *Public Choice* article (1971). Assume there is some public good which can be purchased in any desired quantity. For the purpose of graphic ease, we assume that it is sold in units which cost $1, no matter how many are purchased, so that the line at $1/unit on figure 1 represents the social cost schedule for purchasing different quantities. The first stage in Clarke's process is to assign to each voter his share of the total cost. Let us temporarily assume this share is assigned arbitrarily, and for the ith voter the share is the line shown at P_i. Later we will discuss how it is possible to approximate the Lindahl condition in the allocation of these shares.

The voters are now asked to state their demand curves for the public good. Voter i's curve is shown as D_i. These curves are then summed vertically to get the aggregate demand (aggregate willingness to pay) curve AD. The point where the sum crosses the cost curve, that is, the $1/unit line, is the efficient quantity of public good to purchase. This is, of course, the Samuelson equilibrium and has many fine properties, although not as many as the Lindahl equilibrium, toward which we shall move shortly.

How do we motivate voter i, and indeed all of the other voters, to correctly reveal their true demand curves? The answer is by telling each voter he will be subject to a Clarke tax, calculated as follows. When all the ballots are received, the tax for voter i will be calculated by summing (vertically) the demand curves of all of the voters other than i, generating the curve AD-D_i, and finding the intersection between that curve and the line $1-$P_i$, which is the share of the tax cost that all voters other than i will pay. The intersection in figure 1 occurs at quantity A. This is the quantity of the public good that would be purchased if i reported a perfectly elastic (i.e., horizontal) demand schedule, identical to his cost share. Such a vote, offering to pay one's assigned share of whatever quantity others desire to purchase, is the analogue for continuous choices of abstaining in discrete choices. With voter i "abstaining," the revealed demand (of others) would intersect their

Figure 1

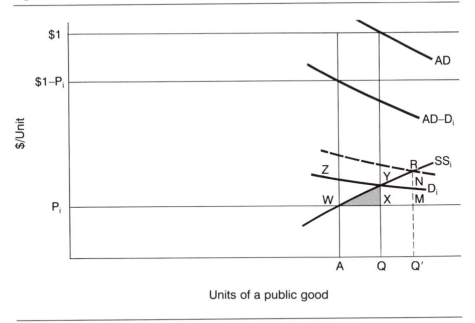

Units of a public good

The Tax on a Person Whose Benefit Exceeds His Assigned Tax Share

share of cost at A, and i's payment would be the rectangle to the left of A and below P_i. In order to compute i's tax when he does not "abstain," we determine from the curve AD-D_i the amount of compensation that voter i would have to pay to keep all other voters indifferent to any change from quantity A. The required compensation per unit at any quantity is the difference at that quantity between the total cost and the aggregate willingness of others to pay. We call the schedule of such amounts, calculated as $1 - (AD - D_i)$, a synthetic supply schedule. It can be thought of as the net marginal social cost of supplying i with additional units of the public good after allowing a credit against the gross cost for the value of the good to others. This schedule is shown as line SS_i in figure 1. The schedule SS_i is a mirror image of AD-D_i. In this example, we assume that i has a higher willingness to pay than his cost share at A. This implies that the effect of including his demand is to increase the quantity. The intersection of the synthetic supply curve and i's demand is at the quantity Q, and that is the optimal amount of the public good, because that is also the quantity where AD intersects the $1 line.

The amount that would have to be paid to individuals other than i in order to make them indifferent to the move from A to Q is represented by the area under SS_i, while the gain to voter i is the area under his demand curve. Voter i pays a composite tax which is the standard payment if he abstained plus the Clarke tax area under SS_i from A to Q. The total tax is equivalent to his assigned share of the cost of Q units of the public good (the rectangle to the left of line Q and below P_i) plus the shaded triangle WXY. The sum of such rectangles for all voters is enough to pay the total cost of the public good; the shaded triangle and corresponding amounts for other voters must be wasted or given to nonvoters to keep all the incentives correct.[2]

Suppose that voter i had misstated his demand curve in an effort to increase his net benefit. The benefit he has obtained from voting is the triangle WYZ. Clearly, stating his demand as less than it actually is would reduce the size of his triangle. On the other hand, if he stated his demand schedule as higher than it actually is, so that the quantity chosen would be, say, Q', his additional taxes would be $QQ'RY$ while his additional benefits would be only $QQ'NY$. He is best off correctly presenting his demand curve.

It must be mentioned that there is a very slight conceptual problem in the specification of these demand curves. Quantity demanded depends on income as well as price, and one determinant of a person's income is the Clarke tax he must pay. Since one person's Clarke tax depends on the demand curves specified by others, each person could logically say that he could not specify his demand curve until all others had done so. This is not a practical problem, however, because the Clarke tax, as we show below, is very small, and in most cases the uncertainty in the Clarke tax is very small, since it depends only on the elasticity of the aggregate willingness to pay of other voters, and in any event people can simply be directed to report demand curves that reflect their best guesses about their incomes.

In figure 2, we assume that j, given his tax share, wants less than that amount of the public good which the other voters would choose. As in figure 1, D_j represents his true demand for the public good, and quantity A represents the amount which would be purchased if he chose to abstain, that is, the point where the sum of the demand curves of all the other voters intersects the sum of their shares of the tax price. Line SS_j in this case, as in figure 1, represents the rate of compensation per unit which it would be necessary to pay the other voters to compensate them for any change from point A in the amount of the public good. To the left of point A, SS_j may be interpreted as the rate of reduction in taxes for j that can be granted while reducing the quantity of the public good and reducing taxes for others by the full amount of the loss of income that they experience. As in figure 1, this compensation is not actually going to be paid, but voter j will be taxed this amount.

Once again, the point of intersection between j's demand curve and the synthetic supply curve represents the optimal quantity of the public good, Q, which is also the quantity at which AD intersects the \$1/unit line. In this case, Q is less than would be chosen if voter j abstained. Voter j then pays a tax which is equal to the rectangle to the left of line Q and below his tax share, plus the shaded triangle. The rectangle is enough to pay his share of the cost of provision of the public good; the shaded triangle, once again, is wasted or given to nonvoters. We will leave to the reader the demonstration

Figure 2

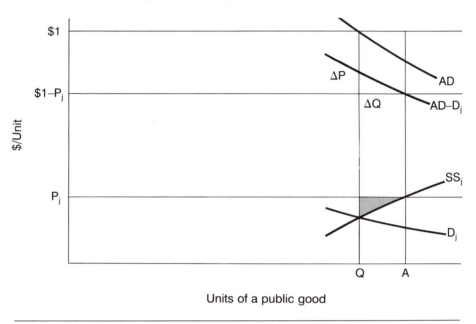

The Tax on a Person Whose Benefit Is Less than His Assigned Tax Share

that the correct presentation of his demand curve will maximize his welfare under these circumstances. It is essentially the same as the demonstration for figure 1.

What is true for voters i and j is true for all voters. They are motivated by this peculiar tax procedure to present accurately their true demand curves. The motivation, however, represented by triangle WYZ in figure 1, would normally be very small, about the same as the area of the shaded triangle.

To see how small the Clarke taxes would be, note that the shaded triangle in figure 2 is a mirror image of the one with sides labeled ΔP and ΔQ. If the elasticity of $AD - D_j$ is η, then $\Delta Q = \eta Q \Delta P/(1 - P_j)$, so that the area of the triangle is $1/2\eta Q(\Delta P)^2/(1 - P_j)$. The denominator approaches 1 as the number of voters increases, so that if η is on the order of magnitude of 2, then each voter's Clarke tax is roughly $Q(\Delta P)^2$. The values of ΔP would be related to the number of voters (N); it would be implausible for the average value of $(\Delta P)^2$ to be greater than $1/N^2$. Thus, the typical voter, whose share of the resource cost is Q/N, has a Clarke tax on the order of magnitude of $1/N$ times his resource cost, and the sum of all Clarke taxes is on the order of magnitude of one voter's taxes. Thus, if the citizens of the United States were voting on the annual federal budget, the grand total of all the Clarke taxes charged would be in the neighborhood of $2,000, or about one-thousandth of a penny per person.

As the triangles go to zero, the motivation for taking the trouble to present one's demand curve goes to zero. The method is cheat-proof and generates the socially optimal quantity of the public good when every voter maximizes his self-interest, but when N is large the Downs paradox is present: voters have almost no incentive to vote.

Since the excess revenues generated by the process are so very small, and certainly less than the administrative cost for any situation with more than a very small number of persons, the excess revenues deserve to be ignored. This may be rather untidy, but it is normal in welfare economics to ignore the cost of reaching a decision. If the Clarke tax is considered as part of the cost of making the decision, then it should be ignored. Contrarily, if it is not ignored, the cost of the processes of reaching decision rules by other processes should also be included. We feel that our suggestion of simply wasting the extra revenue rather than searching for some complex budget-balancing process which might or might not achieve the same result is an important contribution. It is also one of the reasons why it is so hard for welfare economists (ourselves included) to feel at home with the process.

So far, we have generated the Samuelson equilibrium; we now indicate how the Lindahl equilibrium may be approximated. To this point, we have simply assigned the base share of the total expenditure for the individual in an arbitrary manner. Suppose that, instead of assigning it arbitrarily, we appoint someone to do this, with the stipulation that from his pay we are going to subtract some multiple of the sum of the triangles for all of the voters.[3] The person assigning the fixed shares would be motivated to try to minimize the triangles. In the limit, if he were able to perfectly achieve his goal, there would be no triangles and no loss; we would have a perfect Lindahl equilibrium, with each voter paying for public goods according to his marginal evaluation.

It is unlikely that the official allocating the shares could do this perfectly, but he might be able to do quite well with advanced econometric methods. It should be emphasized, however, that there is one piece of information he cannot use in assigning the tax share of any individual: that individual's performance on previous choices. The voter, in making his choices on each individual decision, must not be able to offset against the optimality conditions for that particular choice the prospect of changing his base tax share in the future, because this would motivate him to misstate his demand curve.

As in all voting methods, there is a possibility for coalitions to distort the result. In particular, consider the strategy for a coalition of N persons whose equal benefits are greater than their equal tax shares. In figure 3, the demand schedule or voter i, D_i, is shown as a horizontal line because changes in the height would generally be negligible over the range of potential effects he and his coalition could have. The higher line, D_c, represents the demand that i would express taking account of the benefit of $D_i - P_i$

Figure 3

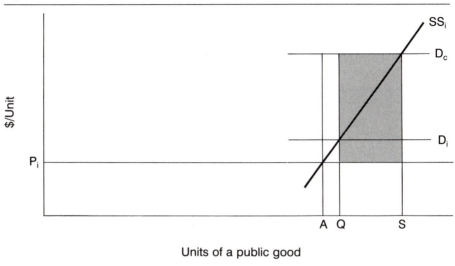

The Strategic Calculation of a Coalition

that each member of his coalition would receive for each unit increase in the quantity chosen. The distance from A to S is N times as far as the distance from A to Q, where the outcome would have been moved by an honest vote. With N persons in the coalition voting this way, the effect is to move the choice $N(N - 1)$ times the distance from A to Q, compared with honest voting. The gross benefit of the coalition activity to each member, in terms of benefits not paid for by his standard tax share, is $N(N - 1)(D_i - P_i)(Q - A)$, which is the area of the shaded rectangle. Each member's extra tax from coalition activity, apart from his standard tax share, is that portion of the shaded rectangle that is below the synthetic supply schedule. Thus, the net benefit of coalition activity to each member is a triangle like that in the upper left corner of the shaded rectangle, the area of which is proportional to $(N - 1)^2$ and to $(D_i - P_i)^2$. Thus, the benefit of forming coalitions varies with the square of the errors in tax shares and with the square of the number of members minus one. Voters whose tax shares overstate their benefits have a similar opportunity to form coalitions that multiply the understatements of their demands.

In this example, we have assumed that the only thing chosen is the unidimensional quantity of one public good. One of the convenient characteristics of the demand-revealing process is that it is not necessary to restrain voting to one issue at a time. A multidimensional public good or several public goods or public goods *plus* candidates can all be dealt with simultaneously. In general, it is much harder to organize coalitions in cases where the choice is not unidimensional. This is not to say that it is impossible. Still, we suspect that the demand-revealing process is rather less susceptible to coalition distortion than most voting methods.

The extension of the voting method to choices for more than one good is straightforward if the chosen quantity of one public good has no impact on demands for other public goods. However, if the chosen quantity of some goods affects the demands for other goods, a simultaneous solution is needed. One could ignore the interactions in the choice procedure and rely on individuals to make estimates of the quantities of other goods that would be chosen in reporting their demand schedules, but any misestimates by voters would lead to unnecessary inefficiencies.

At a conceptual level, one could ask all voters to report their marginal valuation schedules for each good at every combination of quantities of other public goods, although the data problem if this were really attempted would be unmanageable. If it were not impossible to obtain and operate on the data, the identification of an equilibrium where the appropriate marginal conditions were all satisfied simultaneously would be essentially no different from calculating a competitive equilibrium for private goods. Groves and Ledyard (1975) developed the theoretical foundations of such a system in detail.

In later publications,[4] we propose to apply the process to a number of other problems such as income redistribution, badly behaved demand curves, and use as a welfare indicator. We will also discuss its practical application in realistic government structure. The purpose of this paper, however, has been to explain the system and to demonstrate that it solves a number of problems previously thought to be unsolvable. The process does not violate the Arrow theorem, but it avoids the problems of the Arrow theorem by not meeting Arrow's assumptions. However, it seems to us that, if the Arrow theorem is considered as a result that suggests that a good voting process cannot be devised, then the real problem raised by Arrow is solved by this process.

NOTES

1. The method is also applicable to decisions about income and wealth redistribution, instead of leaving that issue aside in the conventional manner. It can be used to ensure the competitiveness of markets, and it provides a welfare criterion superior, in our opinion, to Pareto optimality. All of these matters must be deferred for later publication.

2. One possibility for avoiding waste would be for pairs of communities to agree to exchange their collections of these excess revenues.

3. Probably the best way of selecting the "tax setter" would be to solicit bids. Precautions against bribery would, of course, be necessary.

4. Mimeographed preliminary drafts are available on request.

REFERENCES

Bowen, H. R. "The Interpretation of Voting in the Allocation of Economic Resources." *Q.J.E.* 58 (November 1943): 32–42.

Clarke, E. H. "Multipart Pricing of Public Goods." *Public Choice* 11 (Fall 1971): 17–33.

———. "Multipart Pricing of Public Goods: An Example." In *Public Prices for Public Products,* edited by S. Mushkin. Washington: Urban Inst., 1972.

Downs, A. *An Economic Theory of Democracy.* New York: Harper & Row, 1957.

Dreze, J. H., and de la Vallee Poussin, D. "A Tâtonnenment Process for Public Goods." *Rev. Econ. Studies* 38 (April 1971): 133–50.

Groves, T. "Incentives in Teams." *Econometrica* 41 (July 1973): 617–33.

Groves, T., and Ledyard, J. "Optimal Allocation of Public Goods: A Solution to the 'Free Rider Problem.'" Discussion paper 144. Center Math. Studies Econ. and Management Sci., Northwestern Univ., May 1975.

Groves, T., and Loeb, M. "Incentives and Public Inputs." *J. Public Econ.* 4 (August 1975): 211–26.

Moon, J. W., and Pullman, N. J. "On Generalized Tournament Matrices." *SIAM Rev.* 12 (July 1970): 389–94.

Thompson, E. "A Pareto Optimal Group Decision Process." *Papers on Non-Market Decision Making* 1 (1965): 133–40.

Tideman, T. N. "The Efficient Provision of Public Goods." In *Public Prices for Public Products,* edited by S. Mushkin. Washington: Urban Inst., 1972.

Vickrey, W. "Counterspeculation, Auctions, and Competitive Sealed Tenders." *J. Finance* 16 (May 1961): 8–37.

Public Goods Issues

The following three selections give a number of examples to illustrate the nature of public goods—open trading systems, information, and the lighthouse.

SELECTION 16

CHARLES P. KINDLEBERGER

International Public Goods Without International Government

The term *public good* often carries with it a jurisdictional dimension, because the provision of the service is associated with a particular government unit. However, some public goods, such as world peace and an open trading system, must be provided through international cooperation. Kindleberger expresses his concern that indifference or free riders may prevent the production of these goods.

QUESTIONS TO GUIDE THE READING

1. What problems arise in attempting to define an optimal political unit?
2. What are the views of the "realists" and the "institutionalists" on the production of public goods?
3. According to Kindleberger, why has U.S. international policy recently changed?
4. What does the author believe happens to "hegemons"?

When the word of my prospective elevation to this exalted position first circulated at MIT at the end of March 1983, I happened to encounter Peter Temin in the library. He offered congratulations, and added: "In your presidential address, skip the methodology. Tell them a story." This is the technique that he and Paul David used to great effect in the session on economic history at Dallas a year ago. I choose, however, to follow the lead of another

---

Charles P. Kindelberger, "International Public Goods Without International Government," *American Economic Review* 76 (March 1986), 1–13. Reprinted by permission of the author and the publisher.

Charles P. Kindleberger is Ford Professor of Economics, Emeritus, Massachusetts Institute of Technology.

economic historian, Donald McCloskey, who maintains that economics should be a conversation (1983).

In a recent paper, unpublished I believe, George Stigler discussed "the imperialism of economics," which, he claims, is invading and colonizing political science—through public choice theory and the economic theory of democracy—law, and perhaps especially sociology, where our soon-to-be president-elect, Gary Becker (1981), has extended the reach of economics into questions of the family, marriage, procreation, crime, and other subjects usually dealt with by the sociologist. "Imperialism" suggests super- and sub-ordination, with economics on top, and raises the question whether as a profession we are not flirting with vainglory.

My interest has long been in trade, and I observe that economics imports from, as well as exports to, its sister social sciences. In public choice, we can perhaps explain after the event whose interest was served by a particular decision, but we need political science to be able to forecast which interest is likely to be served, whether that of the executive, the legislature, the bureaucracy, some pressure group—and which pressure group—or, in the odd instance, the voters. Individuals act in their own interest, let us grant, but a more general motive of emulation may be drawn from sociology as Adam Smith was aware in the *Wealth of Nations* (1776, p. 717), as well as in *The Theory of Moral Sentiments* (1759 (1808), I, p. 113). I want today to borrow one or two ideas from political philosophy, and to conduct a conversation with a new, impressive, and growing breed of political scientists working on international economic questions. The discussion falls into two loosely connected halves—the first dealing with what economists can, perhaps should, and to some extent do, import from political philosophy and sociology; the second dealing more especially with international public goods.

I

That sharp and sometimes angry theorist, Frank Graham (1948), thought it a mistake to think of trade between nations. Trade took place between firms, he insisted. The fact that they were in different states was irrelevant so long as economic policy was appropriately minimal, consisting perhaps of free trade, annually balanced budgets, and the gold standard. But states may differentiate between firms, through such measures as tariffs, embargos, monetary, fiscal, and exchange rate policy which affect all firms within a given space, and this adds a political dimension (see my 1978 study). The essence may go deeper. In an early graduate quiz, I asked for the difference between domestic and international trade, expecting a Ricardian answer on factor mobility. One paper, however, held that domestic trade was among "us," whereas international trade was between "us" and "them." The student who wrote this (now escaped from economics and teaching international law at a leading university) had come from Cambridge University and a course with Harry Johnson. We go beyond this simple statement today in saying that nations are groups of people with common tastes in public goods

(Richard Cooper, 1977). Geography discriminates between countries, as a hypothetical customs union between Iceland and New Zealand would demonstrate, and so do governments. Behind and alongside of governments, people discriminate.

Public goods, let me remind you, are that class of goods like public works where exclusion of consumers may be impossible, but in any event consumption of the good by one consuming unit—short of some level approaching congestion—does not exhaust its availability for others. They are typically underproduced—not, I believe, for the Galbraithian reason that private goods are advertized and public goods are not—but because the consumer who has access to the good anyhow has little reason to vote the taxes, or pay his or her appropriate share. Unless the consumer is a highly moral person, following the Kantian Categorical Imperative of acting in ways which can be generalized, he or she is apt to be a "free rider." The tendency for public goods to be underproduced is serious enough within a nation bound by some sort of social contract, and directed in public matters by a government with the power to impose and collect taxes. It is, I propose to argue in due course, a more serious problem in international political and economic relations in the absence of international government.

Adam Smith's list of public goods was limited to national defense, law and order, and public works that it would not pay individuals to produce for themselves. Most economists are prepared now to extend the list to include stabilization, regulation, and income redistribution (Cooper, 1977), even nationalism (Albert Breton, 1964), and standards that reduce transaction costs, including weights and measures, language, and money. Public goods were popular a decade ago. There is something of a tendency today, at least in political science, to draw back and claim that such institutions as open world markets are not public goods because countries can be excluded from them by discrimination. One monetarist goes so far as to maintain that money is not a public good, arguing, I believe, from the store-of-value function where possession by one individual denies possession by others, rather than from the unit-of-account function in which exclusion is impossible and exhaustion does not hold (Roland Vaubel, 1984).

II

Before addressing international public goods, I want to digress to suggest that there are other limits to the imperialist claims of economics. Social goods are not traded in markets, for example—honor, respect, dignity, love. In his address to the Columbia University Bicentennial Assembly, Sir Dennis Robertson asserted that what economists economize is love (1955, pp. 5–6). Michael Walzer (1983, pp. 101–102) has compiled a list of "things" that contemporary moral philosophy will not tolerate being bought and sold: human beings, political power, criminal justice, freedom of expression, marriage and procreation rights (*pace* Becker), the right to leave the political community, exemptions from military service and jury duty, political office, basic services like police protection, desperate exchanges such as permission for women and children to work fourteen hours a day, prizes and honors, love and friendship, criminally noxious substances such as heroin. The inclusion of a number of items on the list is debatable, and history reveals that most of them have been traded on occasion in some cultures. The market, moreover, strikes two lawyers as a dubious device for making "tragic choices," like those in which scarcity confronts humanistic moral values, for example, allocating food in famine, children available for adoption, or organ transplants (Guido Calabrese and Philip Bobbit, 1978). It is difficult to dissent from Walzers's conclusion that a radically *laissez-faire* economy would be like a totalitarian state, treating every social good as if it were a commodity (1983, p. 119). There is, moreover, a similar remark from a founder of the Chicago school, Frank Knight, who said that the extreme economic man, maximizing every material interest, and the extreme Christian, loving his neighbor as himself, were alike in that neither had any friends.[1]

To admit social goods, not traded in markets, into our economic calculus does not call for altruism. Economists are reluctant to depend on self-denial to any degree (Kenneth Arrow, 1975, p. 22), and moral philosophers are not far behind. To a modern student of ethics, James Fishkin (1982, ch. *ii*), obligations to others fall into three categories: minimal altruism, where the benefit to the receiver is substantial and the cost to the altruist low—the acts of a cheap Samaritan; acts of heroic sacrifice that are not called for; and a robust zone of indifference where one has no cause to be concerned over the effects of one's acts on others. This is for positive actions. Acts that harm others are proscribed by the Golden Rule. Adam Smith expressed the same viewpoint forcefully: "Every man is, no doubt, by nature first and principally recommended to his own care" (1759 (1808), I, p. 193), but goes on: "Although the ruin of our neighbor may affect us less than a very small misfortune of our own, we must not ruin him to prevent that small misfortune, or even to prevent our own ruin" (ibid., p. 194). Does this prohibit us from playing zero-sum games or negative non-zero-sum games? In international trade, must we refrain from levying the optimum tariff? The optimum tariff works to self-interest mainly in the absence of retaliation, and if Adam Smith excludes hurting our neighbor, he recognizes that "as every man doth, so shall it be done to him, and retaliation seems to be the great law of nature" (ibid., p. 191).

Note parenthetically that today's moral philosophers cover a wide territory either side of Fishkin, from Peter Singer (1972) at one extreme whose criterion of justice requires successive acts of altruism until the welfare of the recipient has risen to that of the giver which has fallen, to Robert Nozick (1974) at the other who believes that self-interest rules out altruism almost altogether.

III

Self-interest then is legitimate over a large zone of indifference provided that justice is served by our not hurting others. But the robust zone of indifference applies to strangers, and not to those with whom we have a special relationship, sharing collective goods. It does not apply in the family, the neighborhood, in clubs, in the tribe, racial or religious group, or in the nation. There is some uncertainty whether it applies in regions within a country—New England, the West, the South—or to arrangements between countries short of the world level such as North America or the European Common Market. Collective goods involved here are distributed by mechanisms different from the market: gifts, grants, unequal exchange, sharing through a budget according to need, interest-free loans, inheritance, dowries, alimony, and the like all have a place. Membership in these groups is decided in various ways: by birth, by choice—as in moving into a certain neighborhood or migrating between countries, by application for admission and acceptance. Walzer defends the right of countries to keep out would-be immigrants motivated by economic self-interest, but not those subjected to persecution: "The primary good that we distribute to one another is membership in some community" (1981; 1983, ch. *ii*, p. 1). He argues, however, that states lack the right to keep members from emigrating if there is some other community ready to take them in. Clubs discriminate against outsiders. Neighborhoods are more complex, being presumably open to anyone able to afford and find a place to live, but, in sociological reality, often exhibiting tendencies to attract their own kind and repel others, including harassment or unwritten or even legal restrictions against property ownership. The groupings are amorphous, but they exist.

The nature of the positive bonds that link families, neighborhoods, tribes, regions, and nations is usually taken for granted and left unexplored, but the consequences are not. Albert Hirschman (1970), for example, makes a distinction between voice and exit: voice—speaking up and trying to persuade—being the appropriate action when one disagrees with the course followed by a group to which one belongs; and exit—resigning or refusal to buy the good or service—as a response to what one dislikes in the market. Adam Smith minimizes the difference between families and strangers, suggesting that affection is little more than habitual sympathy produced by propinquity; despite the greater thickness of blood than water, he claims that siblings educated at distances from one another experience a diminution of affection (1759 (1808) II, pp. 68–70). In arguing against Walzer's view that countries owe immigrants the right to become citizens, Judith Lichtenberg (1981) echoes Smith's view in saying that the crucial difference between members and strangers lies between those with whom one has face-to-face contact and those with whom one does not. An accident that kills someone in one's town or a neighboring community is likely to be more moving than a catastrophe at the other end of the world in which hundreds or thousands die. Adam Smith goes further, comparing the loss of a little finger with a catastrophe that swallowed up China: ". . . if he lost his little finger he could not sleep, but for China he can snore . . . provided he has never seen them" (ibid., I, p. 317).

Some years ago in a book on the brain drain, Harry Johnson (1968) argued in favor of a cosmopolitan solution, encouraging emigration, and Don Patinkin (1968) for a national one. In discussing the Bhagwati scheme for taxing professional emigrants earning more abroad than at home, for the benefit of the poor sending country—saying this was akin to paying alimony in a divorce case for breaking a social taboo—I suggested (1977) that the Johnson position was equivalent to saying that a person should go where he or she could earn the highest return, while Patinkin said that people should stay where they belonged. Patinkin chided me privately for this interpretation, and it is admittedly oversimplified. But the difference between the Johnson and the Patinkin positions, both emanating from Chicago, suggests the line between market and nonmarket areas in economics is shadowy.

In writing about the multinational corporation, I have from time to time suggested that host countries resist the intrusion of strangers because ". . . man in his elemental state is a peasant with a possessive love of his own turf; a mercantilist who favors exports over imports; a Populist who distrusts banks, especially foreign banks; a monopolist who abhors competition; a xenophobe who feels threatened by strangers and foreigners" (1984, p. 39), usually adding that it is the task of international economics to extirpate these primitive instincts and to teach cosmopolitanism. The fact that some of these reactions remain at a late stage in the educational process can be tested by the device of asking students on examinations, *seriatim,* a series of questions:

> Do you advocate free trade, or at least is there a strong presumption in its favor?
> Do you advocate the free international movement of portfolio capital?
> . . . of corporate capital in foreign direct investment?
> . . . free migration of students and professional labor?
> . . . immigration of relatives of persons permanently resident in this country?
> . . . free migration for all?

(It is desirable to feed these questions to the victims one at a time, without revealing the whole list before the first answer is given, and to take up the replies to the first questions so that there is no chance to go back and amend early answers.) There will be sophisticated answers expatiating on the second, third, and fourth-best if the marginal conditions for a Pareto optimal solution are not met, and I would particularly excuse a James Meade (1955) solution that would limit immigration from countries that have not accomplished their Malthusian revolution, on the ground that their emigrants will be replaced, so that free immigration will reduce world income per capita, if not world income as a whole. Most economists and noneconomists alike would agree, however, that goods are less intrusive than money, money less so than corporations with control over *our* economic decisions.[2] Intellectuals with whom we identify are hardly intrusive at all. Most of us grant that relatives must be permitted to come together. On the other hand, free migration of labor in general poses a threat to the national identity. The Swiss cut off immigration, despite the appeals of business for more labor, when immigrants constituted one-third of the labor force. In Germany, separate localities felt threatened and stopped inward migration when immigrants reached 12 percent of the resident population. Feelings differed, of course, depending upon the origin of the migrants and their appearance, language, and religion.

One early venture of international economics into this line of investigation was Robert Mundell's "optimum currency area" (1961), initiating a discussion of how large the area for a single currency should be, that can readily be extended to economics in general and to other social sciences. Mundell defined an optimum currency area as one where labor moved freely within the area, but not between it and other areas, taking us back to the Ricardian criterion distinguishing domestic from foreign trade: factor mobility within but not between countries. In neither case is the discontinuity in mobility explained. Perhaps something is owed to low transport costs, but additionally, factor mobility requires a group with such strong social cohesion that those moving are willing to shift, and those at the receiving end are content to receive them.

Ronald McKinnon (1963) offered a different criterion: an optimum currency area was one that traded intensively at home, but only to a limited extent abroad. This implied that tastes within a country are homogeneous for traded goods (as well as for public goods), and that regionally specialized production had grown up to serve those tastes. The Mundell and McKinnon criteria do not necessarily converge: on Mundell's standard, Canada is too big to be an optimum currency area, because of limited movement between Quebec and the English-speaking parts of Canada, and the comparative isolation of the Maritimes and Vancouver. On McKinnon's criterion, however, it was too small because so much of its trade is with the United States.

If one broadens the issue from the optimum currency area to economics more generally and to the other social sciences, anomalies arise from the divergence between the optimum economic area, which on efficiency grounds I take to be the world, and the optimum social unit, one that gives the individual a sense of belonging and counting—which is much smaller. In shifting to the optimum political unit, at least two problems arise, one related to the nature of the ties, the other to the ambitions of its members. To take the second point first, for a nation bent on glory—led by a Bismarck or a de Gaulle—bigger is better; whereas if one is merely trying to get along without trouble, like, say, Denmark, small is beautiful enough.

On the first issue, political ties vary widely. There are leagues, alliances, commonwealths, confederations, federations, provinces, states, principalities, kingdoms. Some lesser units are "united" in varying degrees, as in the United Provinces of the Netherlands, the United States of America, the United Kingdom of Great Britain, and Northern Ireland. The North in the American Civil War was a union, as the Union of Socialist Soviet Republics asserts it is. The small amount of literature I have explored in examining the differences among these forms is not very conclusive, but perhaps the main distinction is between a single state that is centralized, and federations that are loosely joined, with greater powers at the local level. Designations are not always congruent with reality: the Federal German Republic is highly unified, despite the efforts of the occupation powers after World War II to spread political power widely; the Federal Reserve System was created as a loose agglomeration of twelve regional money markets but quickly fused into a single system in World War I. Centralization and federalization have reflections in demography and in finance. City populations in unified states follow a Pareto-skewed distribution with a single dominant city like London, Paris, or Vienna, and no close rival among the tail of smaller cities and towns. In federations the distribution of cities is log normal (Brian Berry, 1961). Parallel to the demographic division is the financial. Paris has 91.3 percent of French bank clearings; London 87 percent of those for Britain. The contrast is with Canada: Toronto, 37.3 percent; Montreal, 25.5 percent; Vancouver, 6.5 percent. Between these extremes lies Japan with Tokyo 51.2 percent and Osaka 19.7 percent (Jean Labasse, 1974, pp. 144–45).

One explanation for differences between centralized and federal states is historical: where larger states were formed later from unification of lesser units, administrative and financial functions were already being discharged at the local level, reducing the need for centralized services. This hypothesis faces the difficult counterexamples of Italy and Germany, unified out of smaller units in the second half of the nineteenth century, that quickly centralized administrative and financial functions, in Rome and Milan for Italy, and in Berlin for Germany. Another explanation runs in terms of size, with larger states necessarily federal because of the difficulty of providing administration to local units over long distances. This fits Canada, Australia, the United States, perhaps India, but fails to account for Switzerland, unless size is a proxy for maintaining a dense network of communication, and division of valleys by high mountains produces barriers equivalent to those of continental states. If the mathematically minded among you need an analogue, think of federal states as decomposable matrices.

The difference between a single state and a federation may be illustrated with two examples. Some years ago, Seymour Harris (1952) wrote a book on New England in which he claimed that the area got a raw deal from the rest of the country because it paid more in taxes to the federal government than it received in federal expenditure. This thesis implicitly violated the distinction between a budget and a market: in a market equal values are exchanged. A budget, on the other hand, is a device expressing the cohesion of a sharing group with monies raised according to one standard, perhaps ability to pay, and expenditure distributed according to another, some combination of efficiency and need. The other example, equally shocking to an international trade economist, was the notion of the *juste retour*, or fair return, propounded by France in connection with expenditure for joint projects in Europe. France insisted that all monies contributed by her be spent in France. Tied sales are a third- or fourth-best device to limit balance-of-payments deficits for a given contribution to joint efforts, or to maximize the contribution for a given deficit. They are inefficient rather than fair.

IV

But I want to move on to the geopolitical unit that produces public goods. It is a cliché that these have increased in size as costs of transport and communication have declined. Under the eighteenth-century Poor Law in England, the parish resisted immigration from neighboring parishes because of reluctance to share with outsiders. Fernand Braudel (1982) and Sir John Hicks (1969) have each expatiated on the rise of the size of the economic unit from the city-state to the nation-state. National and international markets for goods and money grew slowly, with entrepot centers that intermediated between buyers and sellers surviving in money—cheap to move in space—and largely disappearing for goods where costs of transport were high and could be saved by direct selling, rather than relaying goods through fairs in the Middle Ages and later through cities such as Amsterdam, Hamburg, Frankfurt, and London. The hub-and-spoke system recently discovered in airplane travel and still in place for money has long been superceded in goods. Caroline Isard and Walter Isard's (1945) point that the most pervasive changes in the economy came from innovations in transport and communications remains valid: contemplate the rudder (in place of the steering oar), fore-and-aft sails; the turnpike; canal; railroad (despite Robert Fogel, 1964); the steamship; iron-clad ship; telegraph; telephone; refrigerator ship; radio; airplane; bulk carrier; jet airplane; satellite television. The numbers of people brought into face-to-face contact across continents and hemispheres has increased exponentially. It is true, to be sure, as was said about a well-known governor and presidential candidate, that it was impossible to dislike him until one got to know him, and increases in mobility and communications have been accompanied by separatism: of the Walloons from the Flemish in Belgium, of Scotland and Wales in the United Kingdom (to pass over the troubled Irish question), and of the *Québecois* in Canada.[3] But it is easier than in Adam Smith's day to imagine ourselves in the circumstances of the Chinese, the inhabitants of the Sahelian desert in Africa, or the tornado-struck islands of Bangladesh as we see them nightly on our television screens via satellite. Do wider communication and transport change the production and distribution of public goods?

Conflicts between economics and political science abound, and many arise from the fact that goods, money, corporations, and people are mobile, whereas the state is fixed. The increase in mobility produced by innovations in transport and communication during and after World War II led some of us to conclude that the nation-state was in difficulty. A reaction occurred in the 1970s. It is significant that Raymond Vernon's influential book *Sovereignty at Bay* (1971), showing the multinational corporation ascendant over the state, was followed by his *Storm over Multinationals* (1977) in which the position is reversed. Cooper's *The Economics of Interdependence* (1968) was followed by an upsurge of interest in national autonomy, decoupling, and pluralism among political scientists, most of whom approve the nation-state and have as heroes, if they will forgive me, not Adam Smith and Woodrow Wilson, but Otto von Bismarck and perhaps even Charles de Gaulle. The tension remains, however. Mobility limits the state's capacity to enforce its writ in taxation, in foreign policy, in standards on such matters as antitrust, pure food and drugs, insider trading in securities, and the like. Mobility undermines social cohesion through the easy intrusion of different nationalities, races, religions, and traditions into the body politic.

V

I come at long last to international public goods. The primary one is peace. Economists are poorly qualified to discuss how, after war, peace is restored and maintained. Most of us reject the Marxian view that war grows directly out of capitalism, and as ordinary citizens and amateur students of history are prepared to agree that peace may be provided by a dominant world power—Pax Romana or Pax Britannica—or by balance-of-power maneuvering, although that seems accident prone. Among the more audacious economists producing an economic theory or set of theories on war is Walt Rostow (1960, pp. 108 ff.). There are views that ascribe war to population pressure, to ambitious rulers aggressively seeking power, and to complex miscalculation. How these are to be avoided or contained is a question primarily for political science.

In the economic sphere, various international public goods have been identified: an open trading system, including freedom of the seas, well-defined property rights, standards of weights and measures that may include international money, or fixed exchange rates, and the like. Those that have interested me especially in a study of the 1929 depression and other financial and economic crises have been trading systems, international money, capital flows, consistent macroeconomic policies in periods of tranquility, and a source of crisis management when needed. By the last I mean the maintenance of open markets in glut and a source of supplies in acute shortage, plus a lender of last resort in acute financial crisis (see my 1973 book, revised 1986, forthcoming).

Public goods are produced domestically by government, unless the governmental agenda is blocked in stalemate among competing distributional coalitions as described by Mancur Olson (1982). Voluntary provision of public goods is plagued by the free rider. In the international sphere where there is no world government, the question remains how public goods are produced. Ralph Bryant is one of the few economists who has discussed the public good element in international cooperation. His vocabulary is different from that of the political scientists: their "regimes" are his "supranational traffic regulations" (1980, p. 470), and he expects leadership in cooperation in monetary and fiscal policy from supranational institutions such as the International Monetary Fund (p. 481). I find this doubtful on the basis of the interwar record of such institutions as the League of Nations.

Political science in this field has produced two schools: the realists who hold to a national-interest theory of international politics, and the moralists, whom Robert Keohane prefers to call "institutionalists" (1984, p. 7). Realists maintain that international public goods are produced, if at all, by the leading power, a so-called "hegemon," that is willing to bear an undue part of the short-run costs of these goods, either because it regards itself as gaining in the long run, because it is paid in a different coin such as prestige, glory, immortality, or some combination of the two. Institutionalists recognize that hegemonic leaders emerge from time to time in the world economy and typically set in motion habits of international cooperation, called "regimes," which consist of "principles, norms, rules and decision-making procedures around which the expectations of international actors converge in given issue areas" (Stephen Krasner, 1983, p. 1). Under British hegemony, the regimes of free trade and the gold standard developed more or less unconsciously. With subsequent American hegemony, a more purposeful process of institution making was undertaken, with agreements at Bretton Woods, on tariffs and trade, the Organization for Economic Cooperation and Development, and the like. Political scientists recognize that regimes are more readily maintained than established since marginal costs are below average costs; as hegemonic periods come to an end with the waning of the leading country's economic vitality, new regimes needed to meet new problems are difficult to create. Cooper (1985) has written of the eighty years it took to create and get functioning the World Health Organization despite the clear benefits to all countries from controlling the spread of disease. And it takes work to maintain regimes; in the absence of infusions of attention and money, they tend in the long run to decay.

I originally suggested that the 1929 depression was allowed to run unchecked because there was no leading country able and willing to take responsibility for crisis management, halting beggar-thy-neighbor policies from 1930, and especially acting as a lender of last resort to prevent the serious run on the Creditanstalt in May 1931 spreading, as it did, to Germany, Britain, Japan, the United States, and ultimately to the gold bloc. Britain, the leading economic power of the nineteenth century, was unable to halt the run; the United States, which might have had the ability, possibly assisted by France, was unwilling. This view has been rejected by one economic historian who holds that the troubles of the interwar period were more deep-seated, and that what was needed was more fundamental therapy than maintaining open markets and providing a lender of last resort, something, that is, akin to the heroic public good after World War II, the Marshall Plan (D. E. Moggridge, 1982). That may have been true, though there is no way

I see that the issue can be settled. Leadership at an earlier stage in the 1920s, presumably furnished by the United States with some cost in foregone receipts on war-debt account, might have resolved the war-debt-reparations-commercial-debt tangle that proved so destabilizing after the 1929 stock market crash. I conclude that the existence of an international lender of last resort made the financial crises of 1825, 1836, 1847, 1866, and 1907 more or less ephemeral, like summer storms, whereas its absence in 1873, 1890, and 1929 produced deep depressions—shortened in the 1890 case by the *deus ex machina* of gold production from the Rand. Again there is room for disagreement.

The point of all this is that after about 1971, the United States, like Britain from about 1890, has shrunk in economic might relative to the world as a whole, and more importantly, has lost the appetite for providing international economic public goods—open markets in times of glut, supplies in times of acute shortage, steady flows of capital to developing countries, international money, coordination of macroeconomic policy and last-resort lending. The contraction of concern from the world to the nation is general, and applies to economists as well as to politicians and the public. In reading recent books on macroeconomic policy by leading governmental economists under both Democratic and Republican administrations, the late Arthur Okun (1981) and Herbert Stein (1984), I have been struck by how little attention the authors paid to international repercussions. The same observation has been made by Ralph Bryant (1980, p. *xviii*) and by the British economist R. C. O. Matthews, reviewing Arjo Klamer's *Conversations with Economists* . . . (1985, p. 621). There has been a recent upsurge of interest in the international dimension because of the connections among the federal deficit, the exchange rate for the dollar, and the balance-of-payments deficit, but the focus of this interest is almost exclusively on what the connections mean for U.S. interest rates, industrial policy, growth, and wealth. The international impact is largely ignored, bearing out the truth in former German Chancellor Helmut Schmidt's statement that "the United States seems completely unconscious of the economic efforts of its policies on the Alliance" (1984, p. 27).

Some of the discussion of international regimes by political scientists verges on what my teacher, Wesley Clair Mitchell, used to call "implicit theorizing," that is, convenient *ad hoc* theoretical explanations to fit given facts that lack generality. Charles Lipson (1985), for example, suggested that the slippage in U.S. hegemony in the 1970s resulted in a loss of the international public good of secure property rights and therefore in the widespread nationalization of foreign direct investment. He went on to say that the reason less developed countries (*LDC*s) did not default on their debts to bank syndicates was that bank lending was "better institutionalized," "a smaller group," "better protected by legal remedies" (pp. 136, 158, 170). He was surprised that the decline of British hegemony in the interwar period did not result in more *LDC* aggression against foreign property (p. 191), but failed to observe the widespread default on foreign bonds in the 1930s, de-

spite the organization of international finance. In my judgment Keohane exaggerates the efficacy and importance of the international regime in oil that
was formed after the first OPEC oil shock of 1973 (see his ch. 10). The crisis
caused by the Yom Kippur embargo of the Netherlands was to my mind
shockingly mishandled by governments, and the public good of crisis management was left to the private multinational oil companies. The formation
of the International Energy Agency was a classic operation in locking the
barn door after the horse had been stolen.

Between national self-interest and the provision of international public
goods, there is an intermediate position: indifference to both. An interesting
contrast has been observed in the 1930s between Britain which forced Argentina into a bilateral payments agreement (the Roca-Runciman Agreement
of 1933) in order to take advantage of its monopsony position, and the
United States that had a similar opportunity vis-à-vis Brazil but ignored it
(Marcelo de Paiva Abreu, 1984).

It is fairly clear from the historical record that economic hegemony runs
down in decay—in the British case after 1913 and the United States about
1971—leading Felix Rohatyn (1984) to say that the American century lasted
only twenty years. The Nixon shock of 1973 in cutting off soya bean exports
to Japan—a significant harm to an ally for a small gain to this country—was
the act of a bad Samaritan. The import surcharge of the same year may have
been required to move the dollar out from the position of the nth currency
when only $n - 1$ countries are free to fix their exchange rates, but it would
have been possible to start with the later attempt at cooperation that resulted
in the Smithsonian agreement. This is especially true when so much of the
case against the 1971 exchange rate was the result of the easy-money policy
of the Federal Reserve System under Chairman Arthur Burns, at a time
when the Bundesbank was tightening its money market/go-it-alone policies
of both banks that flooded the world with dollars.

The present U.S. administration claims to be working for open trade
and does fairly well in resisting appeals for protection. The positive push for
a Reagan round of trade liberalization in services and agriculture, however,
is in pursuit of a national and not an international public good. The regime
in capital movements—the World Bank, the regional development banks and
that in-last-resort lending orchestrated by the IMF—seems to be working,
with bridging loans and an *ad hoc* purchase of oil from Mexico for the U.S.
stockpile in 1982 when the IMF finds itself unable to move fast enough. But
there are signs of dissension that may spell trouble. The June 1985 bridging
loan for Argentina was declined by Germany and Switzerland on the
grounds that Argentina had not been sufficiently austere and that its problems were not a threat to the world financial system (*New York Times,* June
15, 1985, p. 1). The Japanese contribution, moreover, was said to have been
small, although no figures were given.

What I worry about mostly is exchange policy and macroeconomic coordination. The U.S. Treasury under Donald Regan was committed to the
policy of neglect, presumably benign, but in any event ideological. And the

commitment to consultative macroeconomic policies in annual summit meetings of seven heads of state has become a shadow play, a dog-and-pony show, a series of photo opportunities—whatever you choose to call them—with ceremony substituted for substance. The 1950s and 1960s, when serious discussions were held at the lowly level of Working Party No. 3 of the O.E.C.D., were superior because the United States and other countries took them seriously.

I am a realist when it comes to regimes. It seems to me that the momentum set in motion by a hegemonic power—if we must use that expression, I prefer to think of leadership or responsibility—runs down pretty quickly unless it is sustained by powerful commitment. The IMF and World Bank were agreed at Bretton Woods largely as a result of the U.S. Treasury: the forms were international, the substance was dictated by a single country (Armand van Dormel, 1978). In the early days of the IMF, Frank Southard told me, if the United States made no proposal, nothing happened. Today the same is true of the European Economic Community: unless Germany and France see eye to eye, which is infrequent, nothing happens. Proposals of great technical appeal from individuals or small countries are not welcomed as the preparatory phases of the World Economic Conference of 1933 demonstrated (see my 1973 book, pp. 210–14). There needs to be positive leadership, backed by resources and a readiness to make some sacrifice in the international interest.

The leadership role is not applauded. When the United States accused the rest of the world of being free riders, Andrew Shonfield countercharged the United States of being a "hard rider," "hustling and bullying the Europeans," "kicking over chairs when it did not get its way" (1976, pp. 86, 88, 102). Furnishing the dollar to the world as international money has brought the United States an accusation of extracting seignorage, although the facts that the dollar is not a monopoly currency and that foreign holdings earn market rates of interest deflect that criticism in sophisticated quarters.

Neglect can verge on sabotage. When the European central banks collaborated to hold the dollar down at the end of February 1985, the conspicuous failure of the United States to participate on a significant scale encouraged speculators not to cover long positions. A former trader for the Federal Reserve Bank of New York has expressed concern that the habits of central bank cooperation and U.S. official intimacy with the workings of the foreign-exchange market that have been built up over thirty years are being squandered for ideological reasons (Scott Pardee, 1964, p. 2).

Regimes are clearly more attractive in political terms than hegemony, or even than leadership with its overtones of the German *Führerprinzip* or of Italy's *Il Duce,* if not necessarily more so than responsibility. Polycentralism, pluralism, cooperation, equality, partnership, decoupling, self-reliance, and autonomy all have resonance. But it is hard to accept the view, so appealing to the political right, that the path to achieve cooperation is a tit-for-tat strategy, applied in a repetitive game, that teaches the other player or players to cooperate (Robert Axelrod, 1984). As Tibor Scitovsky demonstrated years ago (1937), this path can readily end by wiping out trade altogether. Hierarchical arrangements are being examined by economic theorists studying the organization of firms, but for less cosmic purposes than would be served by political and economic organization of the production of international public goods (Raj Sah and Joseph Stiglitz, 1985).

Minding one's own business—operating in the robust zone of indifference—is a sound rule on trend when macroeconomic variables are more or less stable. To the economist it means reliance on the market to the extent that the conditions for a Pareto optimum solution are broadly met. But the fallacy of composition remains a threat, and one cannot count on the Categorical Imperative. Markets work most of the time, as a positive-sum game in which the gain for one does not imply a loss for another. Experience teaches, however, that crises may arise. When they do, the rule changes from government and public indifference to the production of public goods by leadership or by a standby regime.

Leadership or responsibility limited to crises encounters another problem: how to keep the machinery for handling crises from obsolescence. In crisis one needs forceful and intelligent people, capable of making decisions with speed under pressure. It is sometimes said that the Japanese practice of decision by consensus with ideas coming up from below, makes it hard for that country to discharge in timely fashion the responsibilities of world leadership. In Marcus Goodrich's *Delilah* (1941), the amiable practice of fraternization between a watch officer and enlisted men on the bridge of the destroyer proved dangerous in a typhoon since the men had fallen into the habit of discussing the officer's orders. The paradox is that the attributes needed in crisis tend to atrophy in quiet times; for example in the control room of a Three Mile Island nuclear power plant.

Let me conclude by emphasizing once again my concern that politicians, economists, and political scientists may come to believe that the system should be run at all times by rules, including regimes, not people. Rules are desirable on trend. In crisis the need is for decision. I quote once more the letter of Sir Robert Peel of June 1844 a propos of the Bank Charter Act of that year:

> My Confidence is unshaken that we have taken all the Precautions which Legislation can prudently take against the Recurrence of a pecuniary Crisis. It may occur in spite of our Precautions; and if it be necessary to assume a grave Responsibility, I dare say Men will be found willing to assume such a Responsibility.
>
> [Parliamentary Papers,
> 1857, 1969, p. *xxix*]

NOTES

Note: This paper was delivered as a presidential address at the ninety-eighth meeting of the American Economic Association, December 29, 1985, New York, NY. I have benefited from comments and suggestions on an earlier draft from Susan Okin, Walt

W. Rostow, Walter S. Salant, and Robert M. Solow. A paper with the same title before translation, but with a different coverage was written in 1980, and has appeared in French (1985).

1. This at least is oral tradition. I have been unable to find a specific reference in Knight (1936), or Knight and Thornton Merriam (1947).

2. If the intrusiveness of goods is less than that of corporations from abroad, it is perhaps anomalous that the standard of friendly international dealings exemplified in treaties of Friendship, Commerce, and Navigation is less hospitable for goods than for corporations. Foreign corporations in theory are given national treatment; goods only that of the most-favored nation. In practice, many countries ignore the commitment to national treatment and discriminate both against foreign corporations as a class, and among those of different nationality.

3. Tastes in public goods can of course differ within countries. A striking comparison is furnished in E. Digby Baltzell's *Puritan Boston and Quaker Philadelphia* (1979). Boston is characterized as intolerant, extremely homogenous, ascetic, philanthropic, and devoted to social and political responsibility. Philadelphia, on the other hand, was an ethnic and religious melting pot, materialistic, believing in money making, and shunning power and responsibility. Boston produced four presidents of the United States, including one non-Puritan affected by the values of the city. Philadelphia none. Social scientists are wary of ascribing social responses to national (or urban) character. There may nonetheless be occasions when it is inescapable.

REFERENCES

Arrow, Kenneth, J., "Gifts and Exchanges," in Edmund S. Phelps, ed., *Altruism, Morality and Economic Theory,* New York: Russell Sage Foundation, 1975.

Axelrod, Robert, *The Evolution of Cooperation,* New York: Basic Books, 1984.

Baltzell, E. Digby, *Puritan Boston and Quaker Philadelphia: Two Protestant Ethics and the Spirit of Class Authority and Leadership,* New York: Free Press, 1979.

Becker, Gary, *A Treatise on the Family,* Cambridge: Harvard University Press, 1981.

Berry, Brian J. L., "City-Size Distribution and Economic Development," *Economic Development and Cultural Change,* July 1961, 9, 573–88.

Braudel, Fernand, *Civilization and Capitalism* (15th–18th Century), Vol. 2, *The Wheels of Commerce,* translated from the French by Sian Reynolds, New York: Harper and Row, 1982.

Breton, Albert, "The Economics of Nationalism," *Journal of Political Economy,* August 1964, 72, 376–86.

Bryant, Ralph C., *Money and Monetary Policy in Independent Nations,* Washington: The Brookings Institution, 1980.

Calabrese, Guido and Bobbitt, Philip, *Tragic Choices,* New York: W. W. Norton, 1978.

Cooper Richard N., *The Economics of Interdependence: Economic Policy in the Atlantic Community,* New York: McGraw-Hill, 1968.

———, "World-Wide vs Regional Integration: Is There an Optimal Size of the Integrated Area?," in Fritz Machlup, ed., *Economic Integration: Worldwide, Regional, Sectoral,* New York: Halstead, 1977.

————, "International Economic Cooperation: Is It Desirable? Is It Likely?," *Bulletin*, American Academy of Arts and Sciences, November 1985, 39, 11–35.

de Paiva Abreu, Marcelo, "Argentina and Brazil During the 1930s: The Impact of British and American Economic Policies," in Rosemary Thorp, ed., *Latin America in the 1930s: The Role of the Periphery in World Crisis*, London: Macmillan, 1984.

Fishkin, James S., *The Limits of Obligation*, New Haven: Yale University Press, 1982.

Fogel, Robert W., *Railroads and American Economic Growth: Essays in Econometric History*, Baltimore: Johns Hopkins Press, 1964.

Goodrich, Marcus, *Deliah*, New York: Farrar & Rinehart, 1941.

Graham, Frank D., *The Theory of International Values*, Princeton: Princeton University Press, 1948.

Harris, Seymour E., *The Economics of New England: Case Study of an Older Area*, Cambridge: Harvard University Press, 1965.

Hicks, John R., *A Theory of Economic History*, London: Oxford University Press, 1969.

Hirschman, Albert O., *Exit, Voice and Loyalty*, Cambridge: Harvard University Press, 1970.

Isard, Caroline and Isard, Walter, "Economic Implications of Aircraft," *Quarterly Journal of Economics*, February 1945, 59, 145–69.

Johnson, Harry G., "An 'Internationalist' Model," in Walter Adams, ed., *The Brain Drain*, New York: Macmillan, 1968.

Keohane, Robert O., *After Hegemony: Cooperation and Discord in the World Political Economy*, Princeton: Princeton University Press, 1984.

Kindleberger, Charles P., *The World in Depression, 1929–1939*, Berkeley: University of California Press, 1973.

————, "Internationalist and Nationalist Models in the Analysis of the Brain Drain: Progress and Unsolved Problems," *Minerva*, Winter 1977, 15, 553–61.

————, "Government and International Trade," *Essays in International Finance*, No. 129, International Finance Section, Princeton University, 1978.

————, *Multinational Excursions*, Cambridge, MIT Press, 1984.

————, "Des biens public internationaux en l'absence d'un gouvernement international," in *Croissance, échange et monnaie en économie international, Mélange en l'honneur de Monsieur le Professeur Jean Weiller*, Paris: Economica, 1985.

Knight, Frank H., *The Ethics of Competition and Other Essays*, London: George Allen & Unwin, 1936.

———— and Merriam, Thornton W., *The Economic Order and Religion*, London: Kegan Paul, Trend, Trubner, 1947.

Krasner, Stephen D., *International Regimes*, Ithaca: Cornell University Press, 1983.

Labasse, Jean, *L'espace financier: analyze geographique*, Paris: Colin, 1974.

Lichtenberg, Judith, "National Boundaries and Moral Boundaries," in Peter G. Brown and Henry Shue, eds., *Boundaries: National Autonomy and Its Limits*, Totowa: Rowman and Littlefield, 1981.

Lipson, Charles, *Standing Guard: Protecting Foreign Capital in the Nineteenth and Twentieth Centuries*, Berkeley: University of California Press, 1985.

McCloskey, Donald N., "The Rhetoric of Economics," *Journal of Economic Literature*, June 1983, 21, 481–517.

McKinnon, Ronald I., "Optimum Currency Areas," *American Economic Review*, September 1963, 53, 717–25.

Matthews, R. C. O., Review of Arjo Klamer, *Conversations with Economists . . .*, 1983, *Journal of Economic Literature*, June 1985, 23, 621–22.

Meade, James E., *The Theory of International Economic Policy*, Vol. II, *Trade and Welfare*, New York: Oxford University Press, 1955.

Moggridge, D. E., "Policy in the Crises of 1920 and 1929," in C. P. Kindleberger and J.-P. Laffargue, eds., *Financial Crises: Theory, History and Policy*, Cambridge: Cambridge University Press, 1982.

Mundell, Robert A., "A Theory of Optimum Currency Areas," *American Economic Review*, September 1961, 51, 657–65.

Nozick, Robert, *Anarchy, State and Utopia*, New York: Basic Books, 1974.

Ohlin, Bertil, *Interregional and International Trade*, Cambridge: Harvard University Press, 1933.

Okun, Arthur M., *Prices and Quantities*, Washington: Brookings Institution, 1981.

Olson, Mancur, *The Rise and Decline of Nations: Economic Growth, Stagflation and Social Rigidities*, New Haven: Yale University Press, 1982.

Pardee, Scott, "The Dollar," address before the Georgetown University Bankers Forum, Washington, D.C., September 22, 1964.

Patinkin, Don, "A 'Nationalist' Model," in Walter Adams, ed., *The Brain Drain*, New York: Macmillan, 1968.

Robertson, Sir Dennis, "What Do Economists Economize?," in R. Leckachman, ed., *National Policy for Economic Welfare at Home and Abroad*, New York: Doubleday, 1955.

Rohatyn, Felix G., *The Twenty-Year Century: Essays on Economics and Public Finance*, New York: Random House, 1984.

Rostow, Walt W., *The Stages of Economic Growth: A Non-Communist Manifesto*, Cambridge: Cambridge University Press, 1960.

Sah, Raaj Kumar and Stiglitz, Joseph E., "Human Fallibility and Economic Organization," *American Economic Review Proceedings*, May 1985, 75, 292–97.

Scitovsky, Tibor, "A Reconsideration of the Theory of Tariffs," reprinted in AEA *Readings in the Theory of International Trade*, Homewood: Richard D. Irwin, 1949.

Shonfield, Andrew, *International Economic Relations of the Western World*, Vol. I, *Politics and Trade*, New York: Oxford University Press, 1976.

Singer, Peter, "Famine, Affluence and Morality," *Philosophy and Public Affairs*, Spring 1972, 1, 229–43.

Smith, Adam, *The Theory of Moral Sentiments, or An Essay Toward an Analysis of the Principles by which Men Naturally Judge Concerning the Conduct and Character First of the Neighbours and then of Themselves*, 11th ed., Edinburgh: Bell and Bradfute, 1759; 1808.

———, *An Inquiry into the Nature and Causes of the Wealth of Nations*, Canaan ed., New York: Modern Library, 1776; 1937.

Schmidt, Helmut, "Saving Western Europe," *New York Review of Books*, May 31, 1984, 31, 25–27.

Stigler, George J., "Economics—The Imperial Science?," mimeo., 1984.

Stein, Herbert, *Presidential Economics: The Making of Economic Policy from Roosevelt to Reagan and Beyond,* New York: Simon and Schuster, 1984.

Van Dormel, Armand, *Bretton Woods: Birth of a Monetary System,* New York: Holmes and Meier, 1978.

Vaubel, Roland, "The Government's Money Monopoly: Externalities or Natural Monopoly?," *Kyklos,* 1984, 27, 27–57.

Vernon, Raymond, *Sovereignty at Bay,* Cambridge: Harvard University Press, 1971.

———, *Storm Over Multinationals,* Cambridge: Harvard University Press, 1977.

Walzer, Michael, "The Distribution of Membership," in Peter G. Brown and Henry Shue, eds., *Boundaries: National Autonomy and Its Limits,* Totowa: Rowman and Littlefield, 1981.

———, *Spheres of Justice,* New York: Basic Books, 1983.

Parliamentary Papers: Monetary Policy, Commercial Distress, Shannon: Irish University Press, 1957, 1969.

SELECTION 17

KENNETH J. ARROW

Information and Economic Behavior

Kenneth Arrow discusses the role of information in a private market economy and, in particular, the effects that lack of information, or uncertainty, can have on economic decision making. He argues that information itself can best be described as a commodity with the same characteristics as a public good. Thus, there is no guarantee that an optimal level of information will be produced or acquired in a private market economy. However, the ramifications of this market failure are more severe than for most public goods, because information itself is a necessary input for the efficient provision of goods and services in numerous other markets.

QUESTIONS TO GUIDE THE READING

1. How is uncertainty a property both of decisions that affect only the present and of decisions that affect future choices?
2. What are some examples of signals that might be used to predict quality or future prices?
3. Why do variables other than price or quantity become important in an economy characterized by uncertainty?
4. How does information conform to the characteristics of a public good?
5. Why might the need to process information efficiently explain the organization of firms better than classical economic theory does?
6. How can the presence of "adverse selection" or "moral hazard" cause insurance markets to fail?

The members of an economy—the firms, the consumers, the investors, and the government—make choices. To give a common name to them all, I will refer to them as agents, for indeed their most salient characteristic is that

Kenneth J. Arrow, "Information and Economic Behavior," lecture presented to the Federation of Swedish Industries, Stockholm (1973), reprinted in Volume 4 of *Collected Papers of Kenneth J. Arrow: The Economics of Information,* The Belknap Press of Harvard University Press (1984), 136–152. Reprinted by permission of the author.

Kenneth J. Arrow is Joan Kenney Professor of Economics and Professor of Operations Research at Stanford University. He received a Nobel Prize in Economics in 1972.

they act. That they make choices implies that they have alternatives, that what was chosen was not inevitable but was in fact only one in a range of opportunities. The opportunities available to a consumer are determined by the income he has and the prices he has to pay for commodities of different use-values. The opportunities available to a firm might be all the technologically feasible combinations of inputs and outputs, in the present and in the future; this description allows for time lags between input and output and for durable producers' goods whose product is realized over a period of time. The opportunities available to an investor are basically returns over the future from alternative present portfolios. If the investor plans to use his returns for consumption in the future, or, for that matter, for reinvestment, then the true meaning of his opportunities is understood only in terms of the consumer goods or investment opportunities that will be available in the future and the prices which they will command on the open market.

I have referred repeatedly to the future in the description of the opportunities open to individual economic agents. Certainly a most salient characteristic of the future is that we do not know it perfectly. Our forecasts, whether of future prices, future sales, or even the qualities of goods that will be available to us for use in production or consumption, are surely not known with certainty, and they are known with diminishing confidence as the future extends. Hence, it is intrinsic in the decision-making process, whether in the economic world or in any other, that the opportunities available, the consequences of our decisions, are not completely known to us.

But it is important to note that uncertainty is a property of many decisions which do not extend into the future or at least only into the immediate future. For example, if I wish to purchase some good, especially one I have not bought recently, I may not know its price. Of course, I can ascertain it, but only by the expenditure of time and other scarce resources. I will in general end up making a purchase without the prices of all possible substitutes; it would be too costly to find them out.

Perhaps even more significant than uncertainty about prices is uncertainty about the nature of the goods being purchased, about their quality. This is most striking and obvious when it comes to the hiring of labor, at all levels up to and perhaps most especially including the highest executive and academic levels. Any university professor who has participated in making appointments knows how difficult it is to evaluate the research and teaching potential of junior faculty, and the same considerations hold for the hiring of most other forms of labor. Indeed, the same uncertainty occurs at every promotion opportunity, for previous experience is almost never a sure guide to future performance in new circumstances. Again, consider many complex durable goods, such as automobiles. A genuine evaluation by the buyer in individual cases can really only be made, if ever, after considerable experience. The performance of an automobile or producers' durable, its durability, its need for repairs, are surely uncertain. Because of random variation from item to item, even previous experience does not permit confident generalization to new cases, though it does reduce the degree of uncertainty. It is perhaps sufficient for me to mention the securities market to recognize an area in which considerations of uncertainty dominate.

One remark should, however, be made at this stage. In many cases of quality uncertainty, the economic effect is major only because of some degree of irreversibility or time lag. If the quality of a worker were displayed immediately upon being hired and could be recognized without undue cost and if the act of hiring were costless, the uncertainty about labor quality would have little economic significance; the worker could be fired if unsatisfactory, with little lost to the employer. Similarly, the purchase of a complex machine is risky because second-hand prices tend to be considerably lower than new prices, and therefore the machine can be resold only with loss if it proves unsatisfactory. I should make clear at this stage that in many cases, these irreversibilities are themselves the indirect result of the prevalence of uncertainty; but I must defer explanation of this remark for a bit.

The general effects of uncertainty on economic decision making have been the object of intensive research for some time; the risk aversion of the average economic agent and its implications for such matters as portfolio selection, choice among alternative kinds of producers' durable goods, the choice between saving and consumption, and the capital structure of firms have been analyzed theoretically at considerable length and some significant empirical applications made.

It is not the general theory of behavior under uncertainty that I wish to discuss here but a particular aspect which has only recently begun to receive analytic attention. When there is uncertainty, there is usually the possibility of reducing it by the acquisition of *information*. Indeed, information is merely the negative measure of uncertainty, so to speak. Let me say immediately that I am not going to propose a quantitative measure for information. In particular, the well-known Shannon measure which has been so useful in communications engineering is not in general appropriate for economic analysis because it gives no weight to the value of the information. If beforehand a large manufacturer regards it as equally likely whether the price of his product will go up or down, then learning which is true conveys no more information, in the Shannon sense, than observing the toss of a fair coin. The Shannon measure may, however, be a useful measure of the cost of acquiring information.

I will think rather of information as a general descriptive term for an economically interesting category of goods which has not hitherto been accorded much attention by economic theorists. One finds occasional discussions of the effects of changes in information, usually given some name like "expectation," in the old business-cycle literature, which seems to have been largely displaced by post-Keynesian developments; of course, practical economic forecasters have always realized the importance of expectational information and indeed place increasing reliance on it as the quality of those data has improved. Albert Hart's pioneering work (1942) on flexibility in the choice of capital goods and other aspects of capital structure was based on a recognition that the firm would acquire new information over time. Statistical theorists and communications engineers have gone the farthest in stressing the value of information. Statistics is, indeed, the science of extracting information from a body of data. More specifically, in the theory of design of experiments, R. A. Fisher, Jerzy Neyman, Abraham Wald, and a long line of successors have grappled with the problem of allocating scarce resources to maximize the information attained.

The statisticians' model of information seems appropriate for our purposes. The economic agent has at any moment a probability distribution over possible values of the variables interesting to him, such as present and future prices or qualities of goods. Call these his *economic variables*. He makes an observation on some other variable; call it a *signal*. The distribution of the economic variables given the signal is different from the unconditional distribution. The decisions made depend, of course, on the distribution of economic variables; but if this distribution is in turn modified by the signals received, then economic behavior depends not only on the variables we usually regard as relevant, primarily prices, but also on signals which may themselves have little economic significance but which help reduce the uncertainty in predicting other as yet unobserved variables.

Let me give some examples of signals for economic variables. In forming a probability distribution for future prices we may use as information not merely current prices but also past prices; there is information in the development of the prices over time. This particular argument is familiar and has long been used in justifying the role of distributed lags in prices in the explanation of supply or investment (for an excellent review, see Nerlove, 1972). Though a cardinal point in the teaching of economics is that "bygones are forever bygones" and past prices should have no effect on future actions, nevertheless it is clear that they may convey information about the future and therefore affect present actions.

But signals can be even less direct. In many circumstances, past quantity movements may be signals for the distribution of future prices. If sales of a commodity have been declining, this may easily be taken as an indicator that its price will not rise, or more precisely, that the probability of a rise is lower than it would have been if sales had been rising. An example, familiar to business analysts but a stranger to formal economic theory, is the signaling role of government economic policy. A tax cut in a recession may have an effect not merely directly in terms of released purchasing power, but as a signal which raises the probability distribution of sales and therefore increases the incentive to invest.

Thus, at a very minimum, recognition of the concept of information and its possible changes over time implies a considerable revision of the theory of general economic equilibrium in the form in which it has evolved over the last century and which has reached such a high level of power and depth at the hands of Hicks, Samuelson, Debreu, and others in the last several decades. In this theory the economic behavior of individuals is governed primarily by prices. From the viewpoint of the society as a whole, prices are signals by which information about scarcities is transmitted among the members of society. The informational role of prices in resource allocation has especially been stressed by writers on the theory of socialism, from Barone through Lange and Lerner; the most sophisticated and general statement is that of Hurwicz (1960). The existence of uncertainty need not, in and of itself, destroy the primary role of prices in resource allocation, if markets exist not only for goods but for insurance against alternative possible outcomes. The basic contract to which a price attaches becomes one for delivery of a good contingent on the occurrence of some state of affairs.[1] Some such markets do exist, as for insurance and, in a modified form, for equities. Part of the reason that more do not exist derives from the existence and distribution of economic information, as will be discussed subsequently.

But in any case the presence of information, the existence of signals and the expectation of future signals, implies that, as we have already seen, actual economic behavior is partly governed by nonprice variables. This proposition at least opens the door for explaining the importance of quantity variables in the Keynesian system.[2] It also agrees to some extent with Janos Kornai's critique (1971) of general equilibrium theory for exaggerating the role of prices as compared with quantities in determining the behavior of firms in any decentralized economy, whether socialist or capitalist. I should add that I am far from regarding the allocative functions of prices as negligible; the demonstrable power of investment credits, tariffs, and excise taxes to influence the flow of resources does not allow that inference.

I have so far brought out one implication of the presence of information which reduces uncertainty, the economic relevance of nonprice signals. But there are two more implications, which are, I think, of even more fundamental importance in a reorientation of economic theory: (1) that information or signals have economic value and therefore are worth acquiring and transmitting even at some cost; (2) that different individuals have different information. In the rest of this chapter I will argue that these two rather simple observations taken together are potentially rich in implications for the working of an economic system.

I should stress the word "potentially." This is a report on a line of research, the bulk of which took place in the 1960s. Some theoretical results were obtained; very little empirical analysis was attempted. The initiators were Jacob Marschak (1959) and George Stigler (1961), with subsequent contributions by many writers but perhaps especially Armen Alchian (1969), Roy Radner (1961), Jack Hirshleifer (1971), Michael Rothschild (1973), and A. Michael Spence (1973), together with some contributions of mine (Arrow, 1971, chaps. 5–10, 12; 1973a; 1974). These works do not form a coherent stream; they start from different points of view, deal with different aspects, and use different terminologies. It is of some doctrinal interest to observe that they all come out of the much-criticized neoclassical tradition, though they certainly represent developments of it; that is, they start from some concept of individual advantage seeking in a world in which each agent has little market power, and they assume the equilibrium allocations which are arrived at are such that expectations are not falsified. A general definition of equilibrium in this context has been given by Hahn (1973, especially pp. 18-20). To be sure, the "expectations" are probability distributions rather than points, so that what is meant is that individual agents learn whatever it is that they could learn given their opportunities to observe.

The economic value of information offers no great mysteries in itself. It is easy to prove that one can always do better, whether as a producer or as a consumer, by basing decisions on a signal, provided the signal and the economic variables are not independently distributed. But this remark has an implication for economic decisions; the economic agent is willing to pay for information for signals.

We must now recognize that the signals available to an economic agent are not given to him but can be added to. The space of possible decisions has been enlarged to include the acquisition of information in addition to production and consumption. The research engineer can be thought of as eliciting signals from nature, analogous to the miner who draws minerals from the earth; research is a form of production. Information about the behavior of other economic agents, especially customers or workers, or about future or even present prices or qualities of goods are more straightforward examples of information whose acquisition is both possible and desired.

Clearly, firms do engage in information gathering. They spend resources on engineering and market research. Moreover, there are large and significant exchanges of information through the market—newspapers, business advice, and, in a somewhat modified sense of market, all of education—in short, the whole realm of the production and distribution of knowledge, which Fritz Machlup (1962) has so carefully measured. Thus, information is not merely a good that is desired and acquired but is to some extent a commodity like others whose markets we study.

But even though information can be a commodity, it is one only to a limited extent. The presumption that free markets will lead to an efficient allocation of resources is not valid in this case. If nothing else, there are at least two salient characteristics of information which prevent it from being fully identified as one of the commodities represented in our abstract models of general equilibrium: (1) it is, by definition, indivisible in its use; and (2) it is very difficult to appropriate. With regard to the first point, information about a method of production, for example, is the same regardless of the scale of the output. Since the cost of information depends only on the item, not its use, it pays a large-scale producer to acquire better information than a small-scale producer. Thus, information creates economies of scale throughout the economy, and therefore, according to well-known principles, causes a departure from the competitive economy.

Information is inappropriable because an individual who has some can never lose it by transmitting it. It is frequently noted in connection with the economics of research and development that information acquired by research at great cost may be transmitted much more cheaply. If the information is, therefore, transmitted to one buyer, he can in turn sell it very cheaply, so that the market price is well below the cost of production. But if the transmission costs are high, then it is also true that there is inappropriability, since the seller cannot realize the social value of the information. Both cases occur in practice with different kinds of information.

But then, according to well-known principles of welfare economics, the inappropriability of a commodity means that its production will be far from optimal. It may be below optimal; it may also induce costly protective measures outside the usual property system.

Thus, it has been a classic position that a competitive world will underinvest in research and development, because the information acquired will become general knowledge and cannot be appropriated by the firm financing the research (see, for example, Nelson, 1959, and Arrow, 1971, chap. 6; for a somewhat critical view, see Demsetz, 1969). But Hirshleifer (1971) has pointed out that, if secrecy is possible, there may be overinvestment in information gathering; each firm may secretly get the same information, either on nature or on each other, although it would of course consume less of society's resources if they were collected once and disseminated to all.

To dramatize the issue, let me give an example where information is socially useless but privately valuable. Imagine an economy of gatherers of different kinds of food. Weather is uncertain, and some types of food are in relatively greater supply in some kinds of weather than in others. There is an opportunity for mutually advantageous insurance contracts. Those who are relatively better off in one situation can pay the others then, in return for commitments to compensate in those weather situations in which the first group is relatively worse off. But now suppose that an opportunity arises for the accurate prediction of weather, though at some cost. Given the insurance market, it clearly pays any individual to buy the information and keep it a secret. He can then make large gains by betting on the weather that will in fact take place. But under the assumptions made there is no social gain; what is produced will be produced in any case. If the receivers of the weather information are small on the scale of the market, then there will be neither social gain nor social loss on the risk-sharing contracts. But if enough individuals buy the information, the market for risk trading is destroyed, for competition will change the odds to those conditional on the information received, which, if accurate enough, will leave little opportunity for insurance against unfavorable risks. Hence, there is a double social loss—the resources used unnecessarily in acquiring information and the destruction of a market for risk sharing.

This example has been extreme, because it has, by assumption, excluded any possible gains in production. Ordinarily, we would assume that a knowledge of future weather would permit a reallocation of resources to activities which would be relatively more productive under the forecast weather. In that case, the signal has a positive effect on welfare. But this does not blunt the essential point, that there will very likely be an overinvestment in the acquisition of information whose private value is to gain at the expense of others. One would suppose that the securities markets and the extensive apparatus for private information gathering there would exemplify this point. Further, the very acquisition of this information is apt to make the securities market less valuable as a means of risk sharing.

When information is unequally distributed, there are incentives not only to acquisition of information but also to the emission of signals. If I know something about my product which will make it more attractive to others, or if my (low) price is not generally known, I will be willing to incur costs to transmit this information to the outside world. Advertising is an obvious example of the emission of signals, but not the only one. I want to abstract here from the emission of false signals, of deception, because in long-run statistical equilibrium the receivers of the signals will have had enough experience to know the statistical distribution of the economic variables (price or qualities) conditional on the signal. However, it is hard to define the process by which a signal gets to be recognized as such and how the receiver learns to discriminate among them. It would seem that in many cases, at least, collective action is needed to define signals. Suppose, for example, that one firm labeled different qualities of its product according to some scheme. This signal might have little effect in a market with many competitors, because the consumers would not find it worthwhile to expend the intellectual resources needed to learn the signaling scheme. However, a grade-labeling scheme adopted by collective agreement of the entire industry would be worth learning. It would become easier to observe the signals and correlate them with factual observations.

This argument was used by Kaysen (1949, pp. 294–295) to explain the then-current use of the basing-point system for pricing in steel and other industries. It is not easy to give a conventional economic explanation for this system, and even less for the agreement among steel producers that price differentials among different grades of steel be fixed. But if the steel industry is thought of as an oligopoly forbidden, however, from engaging in explicit collusion, it becomes very important for the attainment of a mutually satisfactory equilibrium that each firm may be able to observe the prices of other firms. If not, each firm will have the possibility of cutting prices without retaliation. If, in fact, the prices for every point of delivery and every grade are freely variable, then the capacity of the firms to observe each others' price behavior is very limited compared with their possible scope. But if relative prices of locations and qualities are fixed, then each firm's entire behavior is summarized in one number, and mutual observation becomes possible.

The educational system has become, partly inadvertently, an industry which sells signals for individuals to emit to the world. Its primary intended function is the acquisition of knowledge. But in the course of its own internal measuring of its success in this function, it automatically generates signals of ability in education. If it is in fact the case, or at least believed to be the case, the ability to produce is correlated with ability to absorb education, then the educational system does produce signals about productive ability. I have already argued that the observation of the productive quality of labor is costly to employers. Hence, it pays them to use signals emitted at no cost to them. In turn, however, this creates an incentive for the student to continue his education beyond that level which he would otherwise desire and beyond the level which is socially desirable.

The welfare analysis of the signaling function of education is similar to that of the private demand for weather information in the previous example. It may be, for example, that the educational system simply identifies individuals who are generally more able. They might be equally productive whether or not they are recognized. In that case, as in the simple case where weather information has no productive value, the screening would produce a redistribution of income among individuals but no increase in total product. The resources devoted to education beyond that desired as a consumption good would be simply wasted socially; further, if there is any aversion to risk about one's own abilities, the screening reduces welfare in the aggregate. If, however, individuals have differing advantages in different positions in the economy, then education may serve as a sorting process which will increase total product. This sorting process may, by the way, operate on both sides of the market; not only do employers know more about potential workers, but the latter may learn more about their own abilities. But note that the social productivity of screening has to do with identification of comparative, not absolute, advantages. Since educational attainment inevitably signals the latter as well as the former, there is almost bound to be a socially excessive demand for education if offered at cost with adequate credit facilities for the student investing in his future earnings.

We have now seen that the differentiation of information among individuals together with the existence of costs of acquiring information may lead to the emission of signals to others. But, as already suggested, the creation of new types of signals which can be understood and believed in is by no means a simple task. The education system yields ability signals as a by-product of its main activities; it was not developed for that purpose. Creating a credible screening device *de novo* will in general be more difficult.

Let me turn to two other kinds of responses to the differentiation and the costs of acquisition of information: (1) adaptations to improve efficiency of information processing may arise; (2) markets may fail to exist or else they may perform their functions in ways different from those usually assumed.

Let us take up the first point. How can a firm, for example, become more efficient in the acquisition of information? Now there are many elements in the cost of information acquisition, but surely the most fundamental is the limitation on the ability of any individual to process information. No matter how much the technology of information processing is improved, the ability of the human mind and senses to absorb signals will be a permanent limitation. Clearly, one strategy for increasing the input of information is to increase the number of individual receptors. One can have many individuals linked together in a firm or other organization, each making different observations on the world. (There is no value in having them observe the same signals, provided they are observed without error.) Indeed, the market system as a whole has frequently been considered as an organization for the allocation of resources; the typical argument for its superiority to authoritative central allocation has been the greater intake of information through having many participants.

But multiplicity of observers creates a new problem, that of coordination. The items of information are typically complementary in value and have to be pooled in some way for best use. There is a need for communication channels, and these are costly. Clearly, if every signal received by each observer had to be transmitted to another, the total amount of information handling would be greater than in the absence of organization. Economy arises only if the signals transmitted within the organization are summaries of the information received. The theory of sufficient statistics suggests one instance of economy; in certain contexts, all the information in a sample of many observations can be transmitted as two numbers, a statistic and an indicator of its reliability. Thus, the costs of transmission are much lower than those of acquisition, and it is possible that joining the observers into a single organization can represent a new economy. (See Radner, 1961, for some aspects of the design of information structures for organizations.)

However, the establishment of a system of many observers linked by communication channels has long-run dangers of petrifaction. A communication system has some cost of initial investment which is irreversible. In particular, a communication channel is used to greatest capacity when it has an optimal code for transmitting messages. This "code" need not be interpreted literally; the term refers to all patterns of communication and interaction within an organization, patterns which make use of conventional signals and forms which have to be learned. Once learned, however, it is cheaper to reuse the same system than to learn a new one; there is a payoff on the initial learning investment but no way of liquidating it by sale to others. If external conditions change, an originally optimal communication system may no longer be the one that would be chosen if the organization were to begin all over again. Eventually the communication system may be very inefficient at handling signals, and the firm may vanish or undergo a major reorganization.

To put it another way, the firm's organization is designed to meet a more or less wide variety of possible signals. The wider the range planned for, the greater is the flexibility of the firm in meeting the unforeseen (that is what flexibility means), but the less efficient it is in meeting a narrower range of possibilities, as Hart (1942) pointed out.

I see the communication-economical point of view as explanatory of the internal structure of firms and more generally of other economic organizations. The assumptions about the firm made in classical economic theory will have to be altered. It is assumed there to be a point; instead, it is an incompletely connected network of information flows. Thus, a change in the price of, say, a factor of production may be observed in some parts of the firm but not in the rest. The response will surely be different in general than if the firm reacted by altering its entire plan immediately.

Indeed, the whole idea of a firm with definite boundaries cannot be maintained intact. For example, the customers of a firm are, to some extent, part of it, as Chester Barnard (1938, p. 77) has maintained. There are direct information flows from customers in the form of complaints, requests for product alteration or special services, or threats to change to another firm, in addition to the anonymous alterations of demand at a given price which constitute the sole information link between a firm and its market in neoclassical theory. Some employees of a firm will have closer links to customers than to at least some of the other employees.

Finally, let me note that the fact of differential information as between contracting parties will prevent some efficient contracts from being made. The best examples are those in which uncertainty enters explicitly into the nature of the contract, various types of insurance being the most obvious instances. The most striking category of market failure due to differential information is that known in the insurance literature as *adverse selection*. Suppose a population at risk, for example, in life insurance, is divided into strata with differing probabilities of an untoward event. Suppose further that each individual desiring insurance knows which stratum he belongs to and hence the probability of risk for him, but the insurers cannot distinguish among the insured according to risk and therefore are constrained to make the same offer to all. At any given price for insurance the high-risk individuals will buy more, the low-risk individuals less, so that the actuarial expectations will become more adverse than they would be with equal participation by all or than they would be in an ideal allocation with different premiums to different strata. The resulting equilibrium allocation of risk bearing will be inefficient, at least relative to that which would be attainable if information on risks were equally available to both sides.

What is more, the patent fact of inefficiency under adverse selection may lead to altering the nature of the market transactions. The insurance company may find it profitable to engage in information-gathering activities to reduce the extent of adverse selection, for example, by medical examinations. Since there is a mutual gain to be made, such activities may become general even in a competitive market. But then the parties to a transaction have closer links than the simple impersonal exchange of money for services; the information must be gathered on identified individuals, not on anonymous customers.

Adverse selection in insurance is relatively transparent, but the same phenomenon is at work elsewhere in the economic system. George Akerlof (1970) has called our attention to this question with regard to the sale of used automobiles, where the seller will in general have more information about the properties of the object sold than the buyers; again, something like adverse selection can seriously impair the operations of the market.

I would mention the whole capital market as another and very important example. Virtually all extension of credit involves some risk of default. Hence, indebtedness can never be in the form of anonymous promises to pay interest and principal. The purchaser of credit instruments buys them from specific individuals who are responsible; and in general he gathers information about the potential debtors. A good part of the activity of a bank is precisely in performing these tasks.

Closely related to adverse selection is the occurrence of "moral hazard," that is, the difficulty of distinguishing between decisions and exogenous uncertainty. (The adjective "moral" is misleading in many contexts but is hallowed by long use.) An insurance policy, for example, may induce the insured to change his behavior, therewith the risks against which the insurance is written. Thus, insurance against fire will lead a rational individual to be less careful if care is at all costly. "Health insurance," more precisely insurance against medical costs, is a currently important illustration; the insurance, once taken out, is equivalent to a reduction of the price of medical care, and therefore the rational individual will increase his consumption, which increases the amount of medical insurance payments and ultimately causes an increase in the premiums. This is a social cost, since an increase in medical expenditures by any individual increases the premium for all, and thus the use of both the services of risk bearing and those of medical care is inefficient (see Pauly, 1968; Arrow, 1971, chaps. 5, 9).

Again, economic institutions may compensate by introducing nonmarket informational devices. In the case of fire insurance, a company may inspect the premises and demand that certain precautions be taken as a condition for the policy, or, at least, adjust the premium according to the observed safety standards. In the case of health insurance, it is theoretically possible to investigate medical treatments to see if they are really necessary, and there has indeed been a trend toward peer review, at least.

It is important to observe that the problem of "moral hazard" is one of differential information. Consider the case of fire insurance. For simplicity, suppose there are three possible conditions not under the control of the insured: fire regardless of the insured's precautions; a condition which could create fire if the insured were careless but not otherwise; or no fire in any case. If the insurance company could observe which of these states has occurred, it would be possible for it to insure separately against the first two cases. The rational buyer would purchase insurance against the first according to simple principles of risk aversion; with regard to the second, however, he would weigh the costs of insurance against those of the alternative of being more careful. Such an insurance market would lead to an efficient allocation. It is the cost of determining the occurrence of these states which leads the insurance company to write policies against fire as such, which is less efficient in terms of resource allocation but cheaper in terms of information. Similarly, an efficient health insurance system would be possible if the insurer could observe some measure of the severity of illness and simply pay a sum determined by that measure and independent of actual expenditures by the insured.

The general principle underlying these last few examples has been set forth by Radner (1968). An insurance contract (in the most general sense, including any situation in which the final payoffs to the participants have an uncertain component) can be made only if the conditions under which the contract is to be executed can be observed by both parties. If one will observe a condition but not the other, then the contract cannot hinge on that condition's being satisfied, even though it would be in the interests of both parties to make such a conditional contract if it could be credibly enforced. Whenever some markets are barred from existence, there is inefficiency, which is frequently reflected in strains on other markets.

It is important to note that if the informational inequality is regarded as an irremovable condition, there will in general be substitutes for competitive markets which will increase welfare, though not to the point achievable under full equality of information. One possibility is that of nonlinear price systems, where the premium paid for an insurance policy is not proportional to the amount of the policy. Roughly, the idea is that individuals who seek to buy more insurance are more apt to be high risks and hence should pay a higher marginal premium. The formal structure of these problems is analogous to that of imposing taxes on income as a substitute for the theoretically superior imposition of a tax on innate ability, the point being that income is partly a result of an individual's labor-leisure choice; see Mirrlees (1971, 1972).

One adaptation of the economic system to differential information is scarcely mentioned in our models; it is the development of ethical codes and the internalization of certain values (see Arrow, 1973b). Every profession, such as the medical, owes its economic function to the inequality of information between the professional and his client; what the latter is buying is most of all the superior knowledge of the former. But this is just the situation in which it is most difficult to expect a market to function, as just explained. The patient has little protection against the physician's recommendation of unnecessarily costly treatments. It is probably no coincidence that ethical constraints on economic behavior are so strongly developed in the professions; they serve as an alternative to equal information, the physician's ethical motivation for the client's welfare being relied on to replace contracts which the latter could not enforce due to lack of knowledge.

In fact, ethical elements enter in some measure into every contract; without them, no market could function. There is an element of trust in every transaction; typically, one object of value changes hands before the other one does, and there is confidence that the countervalue will in fact be given up. It is not adequate to argue that there are enforcement mechanisms, such as police and courts; these are themselves services brought and sold, and it has to be asked why they will in fact do what *they* have contracted to do. In any case, the cost of enforcement becomes bearable only if most transactions take place without attempts at fraud, force, or cheating. Further, in transactions of any complexity, it would be too costly to draw up contracts which would cover every contingency. Some aspects have to be left for interpretation when needed, and it is implicitly understood that it will be possible to agree on the meaning of the contract, even though one party loses.

I expect that ethical codes and informal nonprice organizations will continue to evolve where needed, for example in the control of product quality, to permit transactions which would be impossible because of differential information in markets where all individuals behaved in a purely selfish manner. The evolution of ethical codes is facilitated by the fact that productive units are organizations, not individuals, and individuals are mobile among these organizations. Hence, ethical codes held by individuals, perhaps derived as part of business education, may survive even though detrimental to the profits of the firms because the managerial element can accept a trade-off between profits, which only partly inure to it, and learned ethics, which have been found to facilitate business in general.

These remarks are merely preliminary to a genuine study of the development of ethical codes in the economic world. The basic question is how best to emit those signals which will lead to accepted and understood ethical and authority relations and the conditions for their stability. The latter depends on some combination of perceptions and of the reality of mutual self-interest.

NOTES

1. For the theory of contingent markets, see Arrow (1971, chap. 4 [Chapter 3 in Volume 2 of these Collected Papers]); Debreu (1959, chap. 7).
2. See especially the interpretation of Leijonhufvud (1968).

REFERENCES

Akerlof, G. 1970. The market for "lemons": Qualitative uncertainty and the market mechanism. *Quarterly Journal of Economics* 84:488–500.

Alchian, A. 1969. Information costs, pricing, and resource unemployment. *Western Economic Journal* 7:109–128.

Arrow, K. J. 1971. *Essays in the Theory of Risk-Bearing*. Chicago: Markham, and Amsterdam: North-Holland.

Arrow, K. J. 1973a. Higher education as a filter. *Journal of Public Economics* 2:193–216. [Chapter 10 of this volume.]

Arrow, K. J. 1973b. Social responsibility and economic efficiency. *Public Policy* 21:303–318. [To appear in a later volume of these Collected Papers.]

Arrow, K. J. 1973c. The agenda of organizations. In R. L. Marris and A. Wood (eds.), *The Corporate Economy: Growth Competition and Innovative Power.* London and Basingstoke: Macmillan. Chapter 7, pp. 214–234. [Chapter 13 of this volume.]

Arrow, K. J. 1974. *The Limits of Organization*. New York: Norton.

Barnard, C. 1938. *The Functions of the Executive*. Cambridge, Mass.: Harvard University Press.

Debreu, G. 1959. *Theory of Value*. New York: Wiley.

Demsetz, H. 1969. Information and efficiency: Another viewpoint. *Journal of Law and Economics* 12:1–22.

Hahn, F. 1973. *On the Notion of Equilibrium in Economics*. Cambridge: Cambridge University Press.

Hart, A. G. 1942. Risk, uncertainty and the unprofitability of compounding probabilities. In O. Lange, F. McIntyre, and T. O. Yntema (eds.), *Studies in Mathematical Economics and Econometrics*. Chicago: University of Chicago Press. Pp. 110–118.

Hirshleifer, J. 1971. The private and social value of information and the reward to inventive activity. *American Economic Review* 61:561–574.

Hurwicz, L. 1960. Optimality and informational efficiency in resource allocation processes. In K. J. Arrow, S. Karlin, and P. Suppes (eds.), *Mathematical Methods in the Social Sciences, 1959*. Stanford, Calif.: Stanford University Press. Pp. 27–46.

Kaysen, C. 1949. Basing point pricing and public policy. *Quarterly Journal of Economics* 63:289–314.

Kornai, J. 1971. *Anti-Equilibrium*. Amsterdam: North-Holland.

Leijonhufvud, A. 1968. *On Keynesian Economics and the Economics of Keynes*. New York: Oxford University Press.

Machlup, F. 1962. *The Production and Distribution of Knowledge in the United States*. Princeton, N.J.: Princeton University Press.

Marschak, J. 1959. Remarks on the economics of information. In *Contributions to Scientific Research in Management*. Los Angeles: Western Data Processing Center, University of California. Pp. 79–98.

Mirrlees, J. 1971. An exploration in the theory of optimum income taxation. *Review of Economic Studies* 38:175–208.

Mirrlees, J. 1972. Notes on welfare economics, information, and efficiency. Unpublished, Oxford University.

Nelson, R. R. 1959. The simple economics of basic scientific research. *Journal of Political Economy* 67:297–306.

Nerlove, M. 1972. Lags in economic behavior. *Econometrica* 40:221–252.

Pauly, M. 1968. The economics of moral hazard. *American Economic Review* 58:531–537.

Radner, R. 1961. The evaluation of information in organizations. In J. Neyman (ed.), *Proceedings of the Fourth Berkeley Symposium on Mathematical Statistics and Probability*, vol. 1. Berkeley and Los Angeles: University of California Press.

Radner, R. 1968. Competitive equilibrium under uncertainty. *Econometrica* 36:31–58.

Rothschild, M. 1973. Models of market organization with imperfect information: A survey. *Journal of Political Economy* 81:1283–1308.

Spence, A. M. 1973. *Market Signaling*. Cambridge, Mass.: Harvard University Press.

Stigler, G. J. 1961. The economics of information. *Journal of Political Economy* 69:213–225.

RONALD H. COASE

The Lighthouse in Economics

The lighthouse has often been cited as an example of a public
good: once the light is produced, it is available to any ship in the
region, and consumption (use of the light) by one ship does not
diminish the amount of light available to other vessels. Also, it has
been argued that these characteristics make it difficult for private
lighthouse operators to collect fees from ships benefiting from their
services, thereby making public production and financing
necessary. Coase provides a history of the British lighthouse system,
pointing out that economists who have argued along those lines
have ignored some facts. British lighthouses were constructed,
operated, and owned privately. The role of government was limited
to the establishment and enforcement of charges for lighthouse
services collected by port agents.

QUESTIONS TO GUIDE THE READING

1. In recent years, how have the British financed their lighthouses?
2. In the 1600s, how did the private provision of lighthouse
   services develop in Britain?
3. Why were private lighthouses purchased by Trinity House?
4. "The British experience from 1610 to 1820 shows that
   economists have been wrong in depicting the lighthouse as a
   prime example of a public good." Do you agree? Explain.

I. Introduction

The lighthouse appears in the writings of economists because of the light it
is supposed to throw on the question of the economic functions of government. It is often used as an example of something which has to be provided
by government rather than by private enterprise. What economists usually
seem to have in mind is that the impossibility of securing payment from the
owners of the ships that benefit from the existence of the lighthouse makes
it unprofitable for any private individual or firm to build and maintain a
lighthouse.

Ronald H. Coase, "The Lighthouse in Economics," *Journal of Law and Economics* 17 (October
 1974), 357–76. Reprinted by permission of the author and The University of Chicago.

Ronald H. Coase is Clifton R. Musser Professor Emeritus of Economics at the University of
Chicago.

John Stuart Mill in his *Principles of Political Economy,* in the chapter "Of the Grounds and Limits of the Laissez-Faire or Non-Interference Principle," said:

> . . . it is a proper office of government to build and maintain lighthouses, establish buoys, etc. for the security of navigation: for since it is impossible that the ships at sea which are benefited by a lighthouse, should be made to pay a toll on the occasion of its use, no one would build lighthouses from motives of personal interest, unless indemnified and rewarded from a compulsory levy made by the state.[1]

Henry Sidgwick in his *Principles of Political Economy,* in the chapter, "The System of Natural Liberty Considered in Relation to Production," had this to say:

> . . . there is a large and varied class of cases in which the supposition [that an individual can always obtain through free exchange adequate remuneration for the services he renders] would be manifestly erroneous. In the first place there are some utilities which, from their nature, are practically incapable of being appropriated by those who produce them or would otherwise be willing to purchase them. For instance, it may easily happen that the benefits of a well-placed lighthouse must be largely enjoyed by ships on which no toll could be conveniently imposed.[2]

Pigou in the *Economics of Welfare* used Sidgwick's lighthouse example as an instance of uncompensated services, in which "marginal net product falls short of marginal social net product, because incidental services are performed to third parties from whom it is technically difficult to exact payment."[3]

Paul A. Samuelson, in his *Economics,* is more forthright than these earlier writers. In the section on the "Economic Role of Government," he says that "government provides certain indispensable *public* services without which community life would be unthinkable and which by their nature cannot appropriately be left to private enterprise." He gives us "obvious examples," the maintenance of national defense, of internal law and order, and the administration of justice and of contracts and he adds in a footnote:

> Here is a later example of government service: lighthouses. These save lives and cargoes; but lighthouse keepers cannot reach out to collect fees from skippers. "So," says the advanced treatise, "we have here a divergence between *private* advantage and money cost [as seen by a man odd enough to try to make his fortune running a lighthouse business] and true *social* advantage and cost [as measured by lives and cargoes saved in comparison with (1) total costs of the lighthouse and (2) extra costs that result from letting one more ship look at the warning light]." Philosophers and statesmen have always recognized the necessary role of government in such cases

of "external-economy divergence between private and social advantage."[4]

Later Samuelson again refers to the lighthouse as a "government activit[y] justifiable because of external effects." He says:

> Take our earlier case of a lighthouse to warn against rocks. Its beam helps everyone in sight. A businessman could not build it for a profit, since he cannot claim a price from each user. This certainly is the kind of activity that governments would naturally undertake.[5]

Samuelson does not leave the matter here. He also uses the lighthouse to make another point (one not found in the earlier writers). He says:

> . . . in the lighthouse example one thing should be noticed: The fact that the lighthouse operators cannot appropriate in the form of a purchase price a fee from those it benefits certainly helps to make it a suitable social or public good. But even if the operators were able—say, by radar reconnaisance—to claim a toll from every nearby user, that fact would not necessarily make it socially optimal for this service to be provided like a private good at a market-determined individual price. Why not? Because it costs society *zero extra cost* to let one extra ship use the service; hence any ships discouraged from those waters by the requirement to pay a positive price will represent a social economic loss—even if the price charged to all is no more than enough to pay the long-run expenses of the lighthouse. If the lighthouse is socially worth building and operating—and it need not be—a more advanced treatise can show how this social good is worth being made optimally available to all.[6]

There is an element of paradox in Samuelson's position. The government has to provide lighthouses because private firms could not charge for their services. But if it were possible for private firms to make such a charge they should not be allowed to do so (which also presumably calls for government action). Samuelson's position is quite different from that of Mill, Sidgwick or Pigou. As I read these writers, the difficulty of charging for the use of a lighthouse is a serious point with important consequences for lighthouse policy. They had no objection to charging as such and therefore, if this were possible, to the private operation of lighthouses. Mill's argument is not, however, free from ambiguity. He argues that the government should build and maintain lighthouses because, since ships benefited cannot be made to pay a toll, private enterprise would not provide a lighthouse service. But he then adds a qualifying phrase "unless indemnified and rewarded from a compulsory levy made by the state." I take a "compulsory levy" to be one imposed on ships benefited by the lighthouse (the levy would be, in effect, a toll). The element of ambiguity in Mill's exposition is whether he meant that the "compulsory levy" would make it possible for people to "build lighthouses from motives of personal interest" and therefore for government operation to be avoided or whether he meant that it was not possible (or desirable) for private firms to be "indemnified and rewarded from a compulsory levy" and that therefore government operation was required. My own opinion is that Mill had in mind the first of these alternative interpretations and, if this is right, it represents an important qualification to his view that building and maintaining lighthouses is "a proper office of the government." In any case, it seems clear that Mill had no objection in principle to the imposition of tolls.[7] Sidgwick's point (to which Pigou refers) raises no problems of interpretation. It is, however, very restricted in character. He says that "it may easily happen that the benefits of a well-placed lighthouse must be largely enjoyed by ships on which no toll could be conveniently imposed." This does not say that charging is impossible: indeed, it implies the contrary. What it says is that there may be circumstances in which most of those who benefit from the lighthouse can avoid paying the toll. It does not say that there may not be circumstances in which the benefits of the lighthouse are largely enjoyed by ships on which a toll could be conveniently laid and it implies that, in these circumstances, it would be desirable to impose a toll—which would make private operation of lighthouses possible.

It is, I think, difficult to understand exactly what Mill, Sidgwick, and Pigou meant without some knowledge of the British lighthouse system since, although these writers were probably unfamiliar with how the British system operated in detail, they were doubtless aware of its general character and this must have been in the back of their minds when they wrote about lighthouses. However, knowledge of the British lighthouse system not only enables one to have a greater understanding of Mill, Sidgwick, and Pigou; it also provides a context within which to appraise Samuelson's statements about lighthouses.

II. The British Lighthouse System

The authorities in Britain which build and maintain lighthouses are Trinity House (for England and Wales), the Commissioners of Northern Lighthouses (for Scotland), and the Commissioners of Irish Lights (for Ireland). The expenses of these authorities are met out of the General Lighthouse Fund. The income of this Fund is derived from light dues, which are paid by shipowners. The responsibility for making the arrangements for the payment of the light dues and for maintaining the accounts is placed on Trinity House (whether the payments are made in England, Wales, Scotland, or Ireland) although the actual collection is made by the customs authorities at the ports. The money obtained from the light dues is paid into the General Lighthouse Fund, which is under the control of the Department of Trade. The lighthouse authorities draw on the General Lighthouse Fund to meet their expenditures.

The relation of the Department of Trade to the various lighthouse authorities is somewhat similar to that of the Treasury to a British Government Department. The budgets of the authorities have to be approved by the Department. The proposed budgets of the three authorities are submitted about

Christmastime and are discussed at a Lighthouse Conference held annually in London. In addition to the three lighthouse authorities and the Department, there are also present at the conference members of the Lights Advisory Committee, a committee of the Chamber of Shipping (a trade association) representing shipowners, underwriters and shippers. The Lights Advisory Committee, although without statutory authority, plays an important part in the review procedure and the opinions it expresses are taken into account both by the lighthouse authorities in drawing up their budgets and by the Department in deciding on whether to approve the budgets. The light dues are set by the Department at a level which will yield, over a period of years, an amount of money sufficient to meet the likely expenditures. But in deciding on the program of works and changes in existing arrangements the participants in the conference, and particularly the members of the Lights Advisory Committee, have regard to the effect which new works or changes in existing arrangements would have on the level of light dues.

The basis on which light dues are levied was set out in the Second Schedule to the Merchant Shipping (Mercantile Marine Fund) Act of 1898.[8] Modifications to the level of the dues and in certain other respects have been made since then by Order in Council but the present method of charging is essentially that established in 1898. The dues are so much per net ton payable per voyage for all vessels arriving at, or departing from, ports in Britain. In the case of "Home Trade" ships, there is no further liability for light dues after the first 10 voyages in a year and in the case of "Foreign-going" ships, there is no further liability after 6 voyages. The light dues are different for these two categories of ship and are such that, for a ship of given size, 10 voyages for a "Home Trade" ship yield approximately the same sum as 6 voyages for a "Foreign-going" ship. Some categories of ship pay at a lower rate per net ton: sailing vessels of more than 100 tons and cruise ships. Tugs and pleasure yachts make an annual payment rather than a payment per voyage. In addition, some ships are exempt from light dues: ships belonging to the British or Foreign Governments (unless carrying cargo or passengers for remuneration), fishing vessels, hoppers and dredges, sailing vessels (except pleasure yachts) of less than 100 tons, all ships (including pleasure yachts) of less than 20 tons, vessels (other than tugs or pleasure yachts) in ballast, or putting in for bunker fuel or stores or because of the hazards of the sea. All these statements are subject to qualification. But they make clear the general nature of the scheme.

The present position is that the expenses of the British lighthouse service are met out of the General Lighthouse Fund, the income of which comes from light dues. In addition to expenditures on lighthouses in Great Britain and Ireland, the Fund is also used to pay for the maintenance of some colonial lighthouses and to meet the cost of marking and clearing wrecks (to the extent that these are not reimbursed by a salvaging firm), although these payments amount to only a very small proportion of total expenditures. There are also expenditures on lighthouses which are not met out of the Fund. The expenses of building and maintaining "local lights," those which are only of benefit to ships using particular ports, are not paid for out of the Fund, which is restricted to the finance of lighthouses which are useful for "general navigation." The expenditures for "local lights" are normally made by harbour authorities, and are recovered out of port dues.

III. The Evolution of the British Lighthouse System

Mill, writing in 1848, and Sidgwick, in 1883, to the extent that they had in mind the actual British lighthouse system, would obviously be thinking of earlier arrangements. To understand Mill and Sidgwick, we need to know something of the lighthouse system in the nineteenth century and of the way in which it had evolved. But a study of the history of the British lighthouse system is not only useful because it helps us to understand Mill and Sidgwick but also because it serves to enlarge our vision of the range of alternative institutional arrangements available for operating a lighthouse service. In discussing the history of the British lighthouse service, I will confine myself to England and Wales, which is, presumably, the part of the system with which Mill and Sidgwick would have been most familiar.

The principal lighthouse authority in England and Wales is Trinity House. It is also the principal pilotage authority for the United Kingdom. It maintains Homes and administers charitable trusts for mariners, their wives, widows, and orphans. It has also many miscellaneous responsibilities, for example, the inspection and regulation of "local lights" and the provision of Nautical Assessors or Trinity Masters at the hearing of marine cases in the Law Courts. It is represented on a number of harbour boards, including the Port of London Authority, and members of Trinity House serve on many committees (including government committees) dealing with maritime matters.

Trinity House is an ancient institution. It seems to have evolved out of a medieval seamen's guild. A petition asking for incorporation was presented to Henry VIII in 1513 and letters patent were granted in 1514.[9] The charter gave Trinity House the right to regulate pilotage, and this, together with its charitable work, represented its main activity for many years. It did not concern itself with lighthouses until much later.

There seem to have been few lighthouses in Britain before the seventeenth century and not many until the eighteenth century. There were, however, seamarks of various kinds. Most of these were on land and were not designed as aids to mariners, consisting of church steeples, houses, clumps of trees, etc. Buoys and beacons were also used as aids to navigation. Harris explains that these beacons were not lighthouses but "poles set in the seabed, or on the seashore, with perhaps an old lantern affixed to the top."[10] The regulation of seamarks and the provision of buoys and beacons in the early sixteenth century was the responsibility of the Lord High Admiral. To provide buoys and beacons, he appointed deputies, who collected dues from ships presumed to have benefited from the marks. In 1566 Trinity House was given the right to provide and also to regulate seamarks. They had the responsibility of seeing that privately owned seamarks were maintained. As an example, a merchant who had cut down, without permission, a clump of trees which had served as a seamark, was upbraided for "preferring a tryfle of private benefitt to your selfe before a great and generall good to the publique."[11] He could have been fined £100 (with the proceeds divided equally between the Crown and Trinity House). There seems to have been some doubt as to whether the Act of 1566 gave Trinity House the right to place seamarks in the water. This doubt was removed in 1594, when the rights of beaconage and buoyage were surrendered by the Lord High Admiral and were granted to Trinity House. How things worked out in practice is not clear since the Lord High Admiral continued to regulate buoyage and beaconage after 1594 but gradually the authority of Trinity House in this area seems to have been acknowledged.

Early in the seventeenth century, Trinity House established lighthouses at Caister and Lowestoft.[12] But it was not until late in the century that it built another lighthouse. In the meantime the building of lighthouses had been taken over by private individuals. As Harris says: "A characteristic element in Elizabethan society were the promoters of projects advanced ostensibly for the public benefit but in reality intended for private gain. Lighthouses did not escape their attention."[13] Later he says: "With the completion of the lighthouse at Lowestoft, the Brethren rested content and did no more . . . when in February 1614 they were asked to do something positive, and erect lighthouses at Winterton in response to a petition by some three hundred shipmasters, owners and fisherman, they seem to have done nothing. Failure to respond to demands of this sort not only shook confidence in the Corporation; since there was a prospect of profit, it was tantamount to inviting private speculators to intervene. They soon did so."[14] In the period 1610–1675, no lighthouses were erected by Trinity House. At least 10 were built by private individuals.[15] Of course, the desire of private individuals to erect lighthouses put Trinity House in a quandary. On the one hand it wanted to be recognized as the only body with authority to construct lighthouses; on the other, it was reluctant to invest its own funds in lighthouses. It therefore opposed the efforts of private individuals to construct lighthouses but, as we have seen, without success. Harris comments: "The lighthouse projectors were typical of the speculators of the period: they were not primarily motivated by considerations of public service. . . . There was a strong foundation of truth in what Sir Edward Coke told Parliament in 1621 'Proiectours like wattermen looke one waye and rowe another: they pretend publique profit, intende private.'"[16] The difficulty was that those who were motivated by a sense of public service did not build the lighthouses. As Harris says later: "Admittedly the primary motive of the lighthouse projectors was personal gain, but at least they got things done."[17]

The method used by private individuals to avoid infringing Trinity House's statutory authority was to obtain a patent from the Crown which empowered them to build a lighthouse and to levy tolls on ships presumed to have benefited from it. The way this was done was to present a petition from shipowners and shippers in which they said that they would greatly benefit from the lighthouse and were willing to pay the toll. Signatures were, I assume, obtained in the way signatures to petitions are normally obtained but no doubt they often represented a genuine expression of opinion. The King presumably used these grants of patents on occasion as a means of rewarding those who had served him. Later, the right to operate a lighthouse and to levy tolls was granted to individuals by Acts of Parliament.

The tolls were collected at the ports by agents (who might act for several lighthouses), who might be private individuals but were commonly customs officials. The toll varied with the lighthouse and ships paid a toll, varying with the size of the vessel, for each lighthouse passed. It was normally a rate per ton (say ¼d or ½d) for each voyage. Later, books were published setting out the lighthouses passed on different voyages and the charges that would be made.

In the meantime, Trinity House came to adopt a policy which maintained its rights while preserving its money (and even increasing it). Trinity House would apply for a patent to operate a lighthouse and would then grant a lease, for a rental, to a private individual who would then build the lighthouse with his own money. The advantage to a private individual of such a procedure would be that he would secure the co-operation rather than the opposition of Trinity House. . . .

We may understand the significance of the part played by private individuals and organizations in the provision of lighthouses in Britain if we consider the position at the beginning of the nineteenth century. The 1834 Committee on Lighthouses stated in their report that at that time there were in England and Wales (excluding floating lights) 42 lighthouses belonging to Trinity House, 3 lighthouses leased by Trinity House and in charge of individuals; 7 lighthouses leased by the Crown to individuals; 4 lighthouses in the hands of proprietors, held originally under patents and subsequently sanctioned by Acts of Parliament; or 56 in total, of which 14 were run by private individuals and organizations.[18] Between 1820 and 1834, Trinity House had built 9 new lighthouses, had purchased 5 lighthouses leased to individuals (in the case of Burnham, replacing the one purchased by building two lighthouses not counted in the 9 new built lighthouses) and had purchased 3 lighthouses owned by Greenwich Hospital (which acquired the lighthouses by bequest in 1719, they having been built by Sir John Meldrum about 1634). The position in 1820 was that there were 24 lighthouses operated by Trinity House and 22 by private individuals or organizations.[19] But many of the Trinity House lighthouses had not been built originally by them but had been acquired by purchase or as the result of the expiration of a lease (of which the Eddystone Lighthouse is an example, the lease having expired in 1804). Of the 24 lighthouses operated by Trinity House in 1820, 12 had been acquired as a result of the falling in of the lease while one had been taken over from the Chester Council in 1816, so that only 11 out of the 46 lighthouses in existence in 1820 had been originally built by Trinity House while 34 had been built by private individuals.

Since the main building activity of Trinity House started at the end of the eighteenth century, the dominance of private lighthouses was even more marked in earlier periods. Writing of the position in 1786, D. A. Stevenson says: "It is difficult to assess the attitude of Trinity House towards the English coastal lighthouses at this time. Judging by its actions and not by its protestations, the determination of the Corporation to erect lighthouses had never been strong: before 1806, whenever possible it had passed on to lessees the duty of erecting them. In 1786 it controlled lighthouses at 4 places: at Caister and Lowestoft (both managed in virtue of its local buoyage dues), and at Winterton and Scilly (both erected by the Corporation to thwart individuals keen to profit from dues under Crown patents)."[20]

However, by 1834, as we have seen, there were 56 lighthouses in total and Trinity House operated 42 of them. And there was strong support in Parliament for the proposal that Trinity House purchase the remaining lighthouses in private hands. This had been suggested by a Select Committee of the House of Commons in 1822, and Trinity House began shortly afterwards to buy out certain of the private interests in lighthouses. In 1836, an Act of Parliament vested all lighthouses in England in Trinity House, which was empowered to purchase the remaining lighthouses in private hands.[21] This was accomplished by 1842, after which date there were no longer any privately owned lighthouses, apart from "local lights," in England.

The purchase by Trinity House between 1823 and 1832 of the remainder of the leases that it had granted for Flatholm, Ferns, Burnham and North and South Forelands cost about £74,000.[22] The rest of the private lighthouses were purchased following the 1836 Act for just under £1,200,000, the largest sums being paid for the Smalls lighthouse, for which the lease had 41 years to run and for three lighthouses, Tynemouth, Spurn, and Skerries, for which the grant had been made in perpetuity by Act of Parliament. The sums paid for these four lighthouses were: Smalls, £170,000; Tynemouth, £125,000; Spurn, £330,000; Skerries, £445,000.[23] These are large sums, the £445,000 paid for Skerries being equivalent (according to a high authority) to $7–10 million today, which would probably have produced (owing to the lower level of taxation) a considerably higher income than today. Thus we find examples of men who were not only, in Samuelson's words, "odd enough to try to make a fortune running a lighthouse business," but actually succeeded in doing so. . . .

There can be little doubt that the main reason why the consolidation of lighthouses under Trinity House received such strong support was that it was thought that it would lead to lower light dues. The suggestion was, of course, made that lighthouses should be paid for out of the public treasury,[24] which would lead to the abolition of light dues, but this was not done and we need not discuss it here.

It is not apparent why it was thought that the consolidation of lighthouses under Trinity House would lower light dues. There is some basis for this view in the theory of complementary monopolies, but Cournot did not publish his analysis until 1838 and it could not have affected the views of those concerned with British lighthouses even if they were quicker to appreciate the significance of Cournot's analysis than the economics profession itself.[25] In any case, there were good reasons for thinking that little, if any, reduction in light dues would follow the consolidation. Since compensation was to be paid to the former owners of lighthouses, the same amount of money would need to be raised as before. And, as was pointed out by Trinity House, since "the Dues were mortgaged as security for the repayment of the money borrowed . . . the Dues cannot be taken off until the debt shall be discharged."[26] In fact, the light dues were not reduced until after 1848, when the loans were paid off.[27]

Another way in which some reduction in light dues could have been achieved would have been for Trinity House not to earn a net income from the operation of its own lighthouses. This money was, of course, devoted to charitable purposes, mainly the support of retired seamen, their widows and orphans. Such a use of funds derived ultimately from the light dues had been found objectionable by Parliamentary Committees in 1822 and 1834. The 1834 Committee, noting that 142 persons were supported in almshouses and that 8,431 men, women and children received sums ranging from 36 shillings to 30 pounds per annum, proposed that all pensions cease with the lives of those then receiving them and that no new pensioners be appointed, but this was not done.[28]

In 1853, the Government proposed that the proceeds of the light dues no longer be used for charitable purposes. Trinity House responded, in a representation to Her Majesty, claiming that this income was as much its property as it was for private proprietors of lighthouses (to whom compensation was paid). . . .

The use of the proceeds of the light dues for charitable purposes ceased in 1853. As a result, some reduction in the light dues was made possible, price moved closer to marginal cost and numerous ancient mariners and their families, unknown to the law and to us, were worse provided for. But it will be observed that it was not necessary to have a consolidation of all lighthouses under Trinity House to bring about this result.

This change was part of the reorganization which, in 1853, established the Mercantile Marine Fund, into which the light dues (and certain other monies) were paid and out of which the expenses of running the lighthouse service and some other expenses incurred on behalf of shipping were met.[29] In 1898, the system was again changed. The Mercantile Marine Fund was abolished and the General Lighthouse Fund was set up. The light dues (and only the light dues) were paid into this fund, which was to be used solely for the maintenance of the lighthouse service. At the same time, the system for computing the light dues was simplified, the charge made on each voyage no longer depending, as it had before, on the number of lighthouses which a ship passed or from which it could be presumed to derive a benefit. What was established in 1898 was essentially the present system of lighthouse finance and administration described in Section II. There have, of course, been changes in detail but the general character of the system has remained the same since 1898.

IV. Conclusion

The sketch of the British lighthouse system and its evolution in Sections II and III shows how limited are the lessons to be drawn from the remarks of Mill, Sidgwick and Pigou. Mill seems to be saying that if something like the British system for the finance and administration of lighthouses is not instituted, private operation of lighthouses would be impossible (which is not how most modern readers would be likely to interpret him). Sidgwick and Pigou argue that if there are ships which benefit from the lighthouse but on which tolls cannot be levied, then government intervention may be called for. But the ships which benefit from British lighthouses but do not pay would presumably be, in the main, those operated by foreign shipowners which do not call at British ports. In which case, it is not clear what the character of the required government action is or what governments are supposed to act. Should, for example, the Russian, Norwegian, German, and French governments compel their nationals to pay the toll even though their ships do not call at British ports or should these governments take action by paying a sum raised out of general taxation into the British General Lighthouse Fund? Or is the British government supposed to take action by raising revenue out of general taxation to be paid into the Lighthouse Fund to offset the failure of these foreign governments to compel their nationals to contribute to the Lighthouse Fund?

Now consider what would be likely to happen if support out of general taxation were substituted for the light dues (which seems to be what Samuelson would like). First of all, it would increase the extent to which the British Government and particularly the Treasury would feel obliged to supervise the operations of the lighthouse service, in order to keep under control the amount of the subsidy. This intervention of the Treasury would tend to reduce somewhat the efficiency with which the lighthouse service was administered. And it would have another effect. Because the revenue is now raised from the consumers of the service, a committee has been established, the Lights Advisory Committee, representing Shipowners, Underwriters, and Shippers, which is consulted about the budget, the operations of the service and particularly about new works. In this way, the lighthouse service is made more responsive to those who make use of its service and because it is the shipping industry which actually pays for additional services, they will presumably support changes in the arrangements only when the value of the additional benefits received is greater than the cost. This administrative arrangement would presumably be discarded if the service were financed out of general taxation and the service would therefore become somewhat less efficient. In general, it would seem to be a safe conclusion that the move to support the lighthouse service out of general taxation would result in a less appropriate administrative structure. And what is the gain which Samuelson sees as coming from this change in the way in which the lighthouse service is financed? It is that some ships which are now discouraged from making a voyage to Britain because of the light dues would in future do so. As it happens, the form of the toll and the exemptions mean that for most ships the number of voyages will not be affected by the fact that light dues are paid. There may be some ships somewhere which are laid up or broken up because of the light dues, but the number cannot be great, if indeed there are any ships in this category. It is difficult for me to resist the conclusion that the benefit which would come from the abandonment of the light dues would be very unimportant and that there would be some loss from the change in the administrative structure.

The question remains: how is it that these great men have, in their economic writings, been led to make statements about lighthouses which are misleading as to the facts, whose meaning, if thought about in a concrete fashion, is quite unclear, and which, to the extent that they imply a policy conclusion, are very likely wrong? The explanation is that these references by economists to lighthouses are not the result of their having made a study of lighthouses or having read a detailed study by some other economist. Despite the extensive use of the lighthouse example in the literature, no economist, to my knowledge, has ever made a comprehensive study of lighthouse finance and administration. The lighthouse is simply plucked out of the air to serve as an illustration. The purpose of the lighthouse example is to provide "corroborative detail, intended to give artistic verisimilitude to an otherwise bald and unconvincing narrative."[30]

This seems to me to be the wrong approach. I think we should try to develop generalizations which would give us guidance as to how various activities should best be organized and financed. But such generalizations are not likely to be helpful unless they are derived from studies of how such activities are actually carried out within different institutional frameworks. Such studies would enable us to discover which factors are important and which are not in determining the outcome and would lead to generalizations which have a solid base. They are also likely to serve another purpose, by showing us the richness of the social alternatives between which we can choose.

The account in this paper of the British lighthouse system does little more than reveal some of the possibilities. The early history shows that, contrary to the belief of many economists, a lighthouse service can be provided by private enterprise. In those days, shipowners and shippers could petition the Crown to allow a private individual to construct a lighthouse and to levy a (specified) toll on ships benefiting from it. The lighthouses were built, operated, financed and owned by private individuals, who could sell the lighthouse or dispose of it by bequest. The role of the government was limited to the establishment and enforcement of property rights in the lighthouse. The charges were collected at the ports by agents for the lighthouses. The problem of enforcement was no different for them than for other suppliers of goods and services to the shipowner. The property rights were unusual only in that they stipulated the price that could be charged.

Later, the provision of lighthouses in England and Wales was entrusted to Trinity House, a private organization with public duties, but the service continued to be financed by tolls levied on ships. The system apparently favored by Samuelson, finance by the government out of general taxation, has never been tried in Britain. Such a government-financed system does not necessarily exclude the participation of private enterprise in the building or operation of lighthouses but it would seem to preclude private ownership of lighthouses, except in a very attenuated form and would certainly be quite different from the system in Britain which came to an end in the 1830s. Of course, government finance would be very likely to involve both government operation and government ownership of lighthouses. How such governmental systems actually operate I do not know. Bierce's definition of an American lighthouse—"A tall building on the seashore in which the government maintains a lamp and the friend of a politician"[31]—presumably does not tell the whole story.

We may conclude that economists should not use the lighthouse as an example of a service which could only be provided by the government. But this paper is not intended to settle the question of how lighthouse service ought to be organized and financed. This must await more detailed studies. In the meantime, economists wishing to point to a service which is best provided by the government should use an example which has a more solid backing.

NOTES

Note: It is with great pleasure that I acknowledge the helpfulness of members of Trinity House and of officials in the Department of Trade and of the Chamber of Shipping in providing me with information on the British lighthouse system. They are not, however, in any way responsible for the use I have made of this information and should not be presumed to share the conclusions I draw.

1. John Stuart Mill, Principles of Political Economy, in 3 The Collected Works of John Stuart Mill 968 (ed. J. M. Robson, 1965).
2. Henry Sidgwick, The Principles of Political Economy 406 (3rd ed., 1901). In the first edition (1883), the sentence relating to lighthouses is the same but the rest of the wording (but not the sense) is somewhat changed.
3. A. C. Pigou, Economics of Welfare 183–84 (4th ed. 1938).
4. Paul A. Samuelson, Economics: An Introductory Analysis 45 (6th ed. 1964). All references to Samuelson's Economics will be to the 6th edition.
5. Paul A. Samuelson, *supra* note 4, at 159.
6. *Id.* at 151.
7. Compare what Mill has to say on tolls in *supra* note 1, at 862–63.
8. 61 & 62 Vic., c.44, sch.2.
9. G. G. Harris, Trinity House of Deptford 1515–1660, at 19–20 (1969). My sketch

of the early history of Trinity House is largely based on this work, particularly ch. 7, Beacons, Markes and Signes for the Sea and ch. 8, An Vncertaine Light.

10. *Id.* at 153.

11. *Id.* at 161.

12. *Id.* at 183–87.

13. *Id.* at 180–81.

14. *Id.* at 187.

15. D. Alan Stevenson, The World's Lighthouses Before 1820, at 259 (1959).

16. G. G. Harris, *supra* note 9, at 214.

17. *Id.* at 264.

18. See Report from the Select Committee on Lighthouses, in Parl. Papers Sess. 1834, vol. 12, at vi (Reports from Committees, vol. 8) [hereinafter cited as "1834 Report"].

19. *Id.* at vii.

20. Stevenson, *supra* note 15, at 65.

21. An Act for vesting Lighthouses, Lights, and Sea Marks on the Coasts of England in the Corporation of Trinity House of Deptford Strond, 6 & 7 Will. 4, c.79 (1836).

22. 1834 Report, at vii.

23. Report from the Select Committee on Lighthouses, in Parl. Papers Sess. 1845, vol. 9, at vi [hereinafter cited as "1845 Report"].

24. For example, the Select Committee on Lighthouses of 1845 recommended "That all expenses for the erection and maintenance of Lighthouses . . . be henceforth defrayed out of the public revenue. . . ." 1845 Report, at xii.

25. See Augustin Cournot, Researches into the Mathematical Principles of the Theory of Wealth 99–104 (Nathaniel T. Bacon trans., 1897). See also Marshall's discussion of Cournot's analysis, 1 Principles of Economics 493–95 (9th (Variorum) ed., 1961).

26. 1845 Report, at vii.

27. T. Golding, Trinity House from Within 63 (1929).

28. 1834 Report, at xiii.

29. The Merchant Shipping Law Amendment Act of 1853, 16 & 17 Vic., c.131 §§ 3–30.

30. William S. Gilbert, "The Mikado."

31. Ambrose Bierce, The Devil's Dictionary 193 (1925).

Distributional Equity

The following three selections discuss Rawls's theory of justice and the Marxist perspective of distributive equity.

SELECTION 19

KENNETH J. ARROW

Some Ordinalist-Utilitarian Notes on Rawls's Theory of Justice

Simply because any government expenditure or tax policy will affect the distribution of income, it can be argued that the question of distributive equity must be addressed by members of a democratic society. On the other hand, a more direct argument for a policy of distributive equity is often made: justice is a public good, and as such, an efficient level will not be provided by the private market. Once again, though, the conclusion is the same: the issue of distributive justice cannot be ignored.

Stressing that his perspective is necessarily that of an economist, Kenneth Arrow provides a critical assessment of the philosopher John Rawls's theory of justice. Arrow first summarizes the two axioms of Rawls's theory and illustrates how the concept of "original position" is used by Rawls to assert that any rational individual will choose these two axioms of distributive justice. He then raises questions about the validity of interpersonal comparisons of utility and the information requirements of the theory. Finally, Arrow discusses the tax and savings policies that he believes would be required to institute Rawls's theory of justice.

QUESTIONS TO GUIDE THE READING

1. How has utilitarianism influenced economic theory and policy?

2. In what ways do you think the rule of choice, with full knowledge of circumstances or behind the veil of ignorance, would affect the probability that a society would choose to distribute benefits on the basis of the "productivity principle"?

3. Under what conditions does the assumption of close-knittedness

---

Kenneth J. Arrow, "Some Ordinalist-Utilitarian Notes on Rawls's Theory of Justice," *Journal of Philosophy* Vol. LXX, No. 9 (May 10, 1973), 245–63. Reprinted by permission of the author and The Journal of Philosophy.

Kenneth J. Arrow is Joan Kenney Professor of Economics and Professor of Operations Research at Stanford University. He received a Nobel Prize in Economics in 1972.

imply that the maximin principle will lead to the same policies
as utilitarianism?

4. Why might the inability to make interpersonal comparisons of
   utility render both Rawls's theory of justice and utilitarianism
   inoperable?

5. How do you believe incentive or disincentive effects of
   redistribution are likely to affect the final outcome of Rawls's
   maximin principle?

Rawls's major work [*A Theory of Justice* (Cambridge, Mass: Belknap Press,
Harvard University Press, 1971)] has been widely and correctly acclaimed
as the most searching investigation of the notion of justice in modern times.
It combines a genuine and fruitful originality of viewpoint with an extraordinary systematic evaluation of foundations, implications for action, and
connections with other aspects of moral choice. The specific postulates for
justice that Rawls enunciates are quite novel, and yet, once stated, they
clearly have a strong claim on our attention as at least plausible candidates
for the foundations of a theory of justice. The arguments for accepting these
postulates are part of the contractarian tradition, but have been developed
in many new and interesting ways. The implications of these postulates for
specific aspects of the institutions of liberty, particularly civil liberty, and
for the operations of the economic order are spelled out in considerable and
thoughtful detail. (As an economist accustomed to much elementary misunderstanding of the nature of an economy on the part of philosophers and
social scientists, I must express my gratitude for the sophistication and
knowledge which Rawls displays here.) Finally, the relations between justice
of social institutions and the notion of morally right behavior on the part of
individuals is analyzed at considerable and intelligent length.

It will become clear in what follows that I have a number of questions
and objections to Rawls's theory. Indeed, it is not surprising that no theory
of justice can be so compelling as to forestall some objections; indeed, that
very fact is disturbing to the quest for the concept of justice, as I shall briefly
note toward the end of this chapter. These questions are a tribute to the
breadth and fruitfulness of Rawls's work.

My critical stance is derived from a particular tradition of thought: that
of welfare economics. In the prescription of economic policy, questions of
distributive justice inevitably arise. (Not *all* such questions arise, only some;
in particular, justice in the allocation of freedoms rather than goods is not
part of the formal analysis of welfare economics, though some economists
have made strong informal and unanalyzed commitments to some aspects of
freedom.) The implicit ethical basis of economic policy judgment is some
version of utilitarianism. At the same time, descriptive economics has relied
heavily on a utilitarian psychology in explaining the choices made by con-

sumers and other economic agents. The basic theorem of welfare economics—that under certain conditions the competitive economic system yields
an outcome that is optimal or efficient (in a sense which requires careful
definition)—depends on the identification of the utility structures that motivate the choices made by economic agents with the utility structures used
in judging the optimality of the outcome of the competitive system. As a
result, the utility concepts which, in one form or another, underlie welfare
judgments in economics as well as elsewhere (according to Rawls's and
many other theories of justice) have been subjected to an intensive scrutiny
by economists. There has been more emphasis on their operational meaning,
but perhaps less on their specific content; philosophers have been more
prone to analyze what individuals should want, where economists have been
content to identify "should" with "is" for the individual (not for society).

    I do not mean that all economists or even those who have concerned
themselves with welfare judgments will agree with the following remarks,
but I do want to suggest the background from which these concerns originated.

    I begin by highlighting the basic assumptions of Rawls's theory and
stress those aspects which especially intersect my interests. I shall be brief,
since by now the theory is doubtless reasonably familiar to the reader. Next,
I raise some specific questions about different aspects of the theory, in particular, the logic by which Rawls proceeds from the general point of view of
the theory (the "original position," the "difference principle" in its general
form) to more specific implications, such as the priority of liberty and the
maximum principle for distribution of goods. In the central section of this
chapter I raise a number of the epistemological issues that seem to me to be
crucial in the development of most kinds of ethical theory and in particular
Rawls's: How do we know other people's welfare enough to apply a principle of justice? What knowledge is assumed to be possessed by those in
Rawls's original position when they agree to a set of principles? I continue
by stating more explicitly what may be termed an *ordinalist* (epistemologically modest) version of utilitarianism and argue that, in these terms,
Rawls's position does not differ sharply. I briefly discuss the role of majority
and other kinds of voting in a theory of justice, especially in light of the
earlier discussion. Next, I turn to a different line, an examination of the
implication of Rawls's theory for economic policy. In the final section some
of the preceding discussions are applied and extended to raise some questions about the possibility of any theory of justice; the criterion of univer-
salizability may be impossible to achieve when people are really different,
particularly when different life experiences mean that they can never have
the same information.

Some Basic Aspects of Rawls's Theory

The central part of Rawls's theory is a statement of fundamental propositions about the nature of a just society, what may be thought of as a system
of axioms. On the one side, it is sought to justify these axioms as deriving

from a contract made among rational potential members of society; on the other side, the implications of these axioms for the determination of social institutions are drawn.

The axioms themselves can be thought of as divided into two parts: one is a general statement of the notion of justice, the second a more detailed elaboration of more specific forms.

The general point of view is a strongly affirmed egalitarianism, to be departed from only when it is in the interest of all to do so. "All social values—liberty and opportunity, income and wealth, and the bases of self-respect—are to be distributed equally unless unequal distribution of any, or all, of these values is to everyone's advantage" (p. 62; parenthetical page references hereafter are to Rawls's book). This *generalized difference principle,* as Rawls terms it, is no tautology. In particular, it implies that even natural advantages, superiorities of intelligence or strength, do not in themselves create any claims to greater rewards. The principles of justice are "an agreement to regard the distribution of natural talents as a common asset and to share in the benefits of this distribution" (101).

Personally, I share fully this value judgment; and, indeed, it is implied by almost all attempts at full formalization of welfare economics.[1] But a contradictory proposition—that an individual is entitled to what he creates—is widely and unreflectively held; when teaching elementary economics, I have had considerable difficulty in persuading the students that this *productivity principle* is not completely self-evident.

It may be worth stressing that the assumption of what may be termed *asset egalitarianism* (that all the assets of society, including personal skills, are available as a common pool for whatever distribution justice calls for) is so much taken for granted that it is hardly argued for. All the alternatives to his principles of justice that Rawls considers imply asset egalitarianism (though some of them are very inegalitarian in result, since more goods are to be assigned to those most capable of using them). The productivity principle is not even considered. It must be said, on the other hand, that asset egalitarianism is certainly an implication of the "original position" contract. (The practical implications of asset egalitarianism are, however, severely modified in the direction of the productivity principle by incentive considerations.)

But Rawls's theory is a much more specific statement of the concept of justice. This consists in two parts. First, among the goods distributed by the social order, liberty has a priority over others; no amount of material goods is considered to compensate for a loss of liberty. Second, among goods of a given priority class, inequalities should be permitted only if they increase the lot of the least well off. The first principle will be referred to as the *priority of liberty,* the second as the *maximin* principle (*max*imizing the welfare at its *min*imum level; Rawls himself refers to this as the *difference principle*).

Rawls argues for these two principles as being those which would be agreed to by rational individuals in a hypothetical *original position,* where they have full general knowledge of the world, but do not know which individual they will be. The idea of this "veil of ignorance" is that principles of justice must be universalizable; they must be sure as to command assent by anyone who does not take account of his individual circumstances. If it is assumed that rational individuals under these circumstances have some degree of aversion to uncertainty, then they will find it desirable to enter into an insurance agreement, that the more successful will share with the less, though not so much as to make them both worse off. Thus, the original-position argument does lead to a generalized view of justice. Rawls then further argues that his more specific principles (priority of liberty and the maximin principle) also follow from the original-position argument, at least in the sense of being preferable to other principles advanced in the philosophical literature, such as classical utilitarianism.

Two final remarks on the general nature of Rawls's system: (1) The principles of justice are intended to apply to the choice of social institutions, not to the actual allocative decisions of society separately. (2) The principles are supposed to characterize an ideal state of justice. If the ideal state is not achieved, they do not in themselves supply any basis for deciding that one nonideal state is more or less just than another. "Questions of strategy are not to be confused with those of justice . . . The force of opposing attitudes has no bearing on the question of right but only on the feasibility of arrangements of liberty" (231). It is intended of course that a characterization of ideal or optimal states of justice is a first step in a complete ordering of alternative institutional arrangements as more or less just.

The Derivation of Rawls's Specific Rules

From the viewpoint of the logical structure of the theory, a central question is the extent to which the assumption of the original position really implies the highly specific forms of Rawls's two rules. Let me take the priority of liberty first. This is given a central place in the presentation, and at a number of points the fact that the theory puts such emphasis on liberty is used to distinguish it favorably from utilitarianism; the latter, it is argued, might easily lead to sacrificing the liberty of a few for the benefit of many. "Each person possesses an inviolability founded on justice that even the welfare of society as a whole cannot override. For this reason justice denies that the loss of freedom for some is made right by a greater good shared by others" (3–4).

Despite its importance, the definitive argument for the priority of liberty is postponed to very late in the book (541–548). The key argument is that the priority of liberty is desired by every individual. In technical terms, each individual has a *lexicographical* (or "lexical," in Rawls's simplification) ordering of goods of all kinds, with liberty coming first; of any two possible states, an individual will always prefer that with the most liberty, regardless of other goods (such as income), and will choose according to income only among states with equal liberty. "The supposition is that . . . the persons . . . will not exchange a lesser liberty for an improvement in their economic well-being, at least not once a certain level of wealth has been attained . . . As the conditions of civilization improve, the marginal significance for our good of further economic and social advantages diminishes relative to the interests of liberty" (542).

The argument is clearly an empirical judgment, and the reader can decide for himself how much weight it will bear. I want to bring out another aspect, the relation to utilitarianism. If in fact each individual assigns priority to liberty in the lexicographical sense, then the most classical sum-of-utilities criterion will do the same for social choice; the rule will be for society to maximize the sum of individuals' liberties and then, among those states which accomplish this, choose that which maximizes the sum of satisfactions from other goods.

Let me now turn to the maximin rule (this is to be applied separately to liberty and to the nonpriority goods). The justification appears most explicitly on pages 155–158; it is mainly an argument for maximin as against the sum-of-utilities criterion. It should first be noted that the original-position assumption had also been put forth by the economists W. S. Vickrey[2] and J. C. Harsanyi;[3] but they used it to supply a contractarian foundation to a form of utilitarianism (discussed at considerable length by Rawls, 161–175). They started from the position, that of F. P. Ramsey, and J. von Neumann and O. Morgenstern, that choice under risky conditions can be described as the maximization of expected utility. In the original position each individual may with equal probability be any member of the society. If there are n members of the society and if the ith member will have utility u_i under some given allocation decision, then the value of that allocation to any individual is $\Sigma u_i(1/n)$, since $1/n$ is the probability of being individual i. Thus, in choosing among alternative allocations of goods, each individual in the original position will want to maximize this expectation, or, what is the same thing for a given population, maximize the sum of utilities.

Rawls, however, starting from the same premises, derives the statement that society should maximize min u_i. The argument seems to have two parts: first, that in an original position, where the quality of an entire life is at stake, it is reasonable to have a high degree of aversion to risk, and being concerned with the worst possible outcome is an extreme form of risk aversion; and, second, that the probabilities are in fact ill defined and should not be employed in such a calculation. The first point raises some questions about the meaning of the utilities and does not do justice to the fact that, at least in Vickrey and Harsanyi, the utilities are already so measured as to reflect risk aversion (see some further discussion below). The second point is a version of a recurrent and unresolved controversy in the theory of behavior under uncertainty; are all uncertainties expressible by probabilities? The view that they are has a long history and has been given an axiomatic justification by Ramsey[4] and by L. J. Savage.[5] The contrary view has been upheld by F. H. Knight[6] and by many writers who have held to an objective view of probability; the maximin theory of rational decision making under uncertainty was set forth by A. Wald[7] specifically in the latter context. Among economists, G. L. S. Shackle[8] has been a noted advocate of a more general theory which includes maximin as a special case. L. Hurwicz and I[9] have given a set of axioms which imply that choice will be based on some function of the maximum and the minimum utility.

It has, however, long been remarked that the maximin theory has some implications that seem hardly acceptable. It implies that any benefit, no matter how small, to the worst-off member of society will outweigh any loss to a better-off individual, provided it does not reduce the second below the level of the first. Thus, there can easily exist medical procedures which serve to keep people barely alive but with little satisfaction, and which are yet so expensive as to reduce the rest of the population to poverty. A maximin principle would apparently imply that such procedures be adopted.

Rawls considers this argument, but rejects it on the ground that it will not occur in practice. He fairly consistently assumes that the actual society has the property he calls *close-knittedness:* "As we raise the expectations of the more advantaged the situation of the worst off is continuously improved . . . For the greater expectations of the more favored presumably cover the costs of training and encourage better performance" (158). It is hard to analyze this argument fairly in short compass. On the face of it, it seems clearly false; there is nothing easier than to point out changes that benefit the well-off at the expense of the poor, including the least advantaged, for example, simultaneous reduction of the income tax for high brackets and of welfare payments. Rawls holds that one must consider his principles in their totality—in particular, a strongly expressed demand for open access to all positions. But even with perfect equality of opportunity, there will presumably remain inequalities due to biological and cultural inheritance (Rawls nowhere advocates abolition of the family) and chance events, and once inequalities do exist, the harmony of interests seems to be less than all-pervasive. In any case, the assumption of close-knittedness undermines all the distinctions that Rawls is so careful to make. For if it holds, there is no difference in policy implication between the maximin principle and the sum of utilities; if all satisfactions go up together, the conflict between the individual and the society disappears.

Epistemological Issues in the Theory of Justice

Many theories of justice, including both Rawls's and utilitarianism, imply that the social institutions or their creators have access to some kinds of knowledge. This raises the question whether they can in fact or even in principle have such knowledge. In this section two epistemological questions are raised, though there are others: (1) How can interpersonal comparisons of satisfaction be made? and (2) What knowledge is available in the original position?

1. The problem of interpersonal comparison of utilities seems to bother economists more than philosophers. As already indicated, utility or satisfac-

tion or any other similar concept appears in economic theory as an explanation of individual behavior, for example, of a consumer. Specifically, it is hypothesized that the individual chooses his consumption so as to maximize his utility, subject to the constraints imposed by his budget. But for this purpose a quantitatively measurable utility is a superfluous concept. All that is needed is an ordering, that is, a statement for each pair of consumption patterns as to which is preferred. Any numerical function over the possible consumption patterns having the property that it assigns larger numbers to preferred bundles could be thought of as a utility function. Clearly, then, any monotonic transformation of a utility function is also a utility function.

To turn the matter around, it might be asked, how can we have any evidence about the magnitude of utility? The only evidence on an individual's utility function is supplied by his observable behavior, specifically the choices he makes in the course of maximizing the function. But such choices are defined by the preference ordering and must therefore be the same for all utility functions compatible with that ordering. Hence there is no quantitative meaning of utility for an individual. (This *ordinalist* position was introduced into economics by V. Pareto and I. Fisher and has become fairly orthodox in the last thirty [now forty] years.)

If the utility of an individual is not measurable, then a fortiori the comparison of utilities of different individuals is not meaningful. In particular, the sum-of-utilities criterion becomes indefensible as it stands. Rawls's maximin criterion also implies interpersonal comparison, for we must pick out the least advantaged individual, and that requires statements of the form "Individual *A* is worse off than individual *B*." Unlike the sum-of-utilities approach, however, it does not require that the units in which different individuals' utilities are measured be comparable, only that we be able to rank different individuals according to some scale of satisfaction. However, we do not have any underlying numerical magnitude to use for this purpose, and the question still remains, what is the operational meaning of the interpersonal comparison?

If one is to take the sum-of-utilities criterion seriously, then it would have to be considered possible for individuals to have different utility functions; in particular, they might derive different amounts of satisfaction from the same increments to their wealth. Then the utilitarian would have to agree that the sum of utilities would be increased by shifting wealth to the more sensitive individuals. This does not occur in Rawls's theory, but something parallel to it does. Consider an individual who is incapable of deriving much pleasure from anything, whether because of psychological or physical limitations. He may well be the worst-off individual and therefore be the touchstone of distribution policy, even though he derives little satisfaction from the additional income.

In the usual applications of the sum-of-utilities approach, the problem of differing utilities is dodged by assuming it away; it is postulated that everyone has the same utility function. This avoids not only what may be thought of as the injustice of distributing income in favor of the more sensitive, but also the problem of ascertaining in detail what the utility functions are, a task which might be thought impossible, as argued above, or at least very difficult in practice, if the ordinalist position is not accepted. Rawls criticizes this utilitarian evasion, though cautiously; he does not wish to reject interpersonal comparisons (90–91). But in fact he winds up with a somewhat similar approach. He introduces the interesting concept of *primary goods,* those goods which are needed whatever an individual's preference relation ("rational plan of life," in Rawls's terms) is. These might be liberties, opportunities, and income and wealth. Then, even though individuals might have very different uses for these primary goods, we need consider only some simple index of them for purposes of interpersonal comparison. The fact that one individual was satisfied with water and soy flour, while another was desperate without prephylloxera clarets and plovers' eggs, would have no bearing on the interpersonal comparison; if they had the same income, they would be equally well off.

If this comparison appears facetious, consider the hemophiliac who needs about $4,000 worth per annum of coagulant therapy to arrive at a state of security from bleeding at all comparable to that of the normal person. Does equal income mean equality? If not, then, to be consistent, Rawls would have to add health to the list of primary goods; but then there is a trade-off between health and wealth which involves all the conceptual problems of differing utility functions.

The restriction to some list of primary goods is probably essential. I have but two comments: (a) so long as there is more than one primary good, there is an index-number problem in commensurating the different goods, which is in principle as difficult as the problem of interpersonal comparability with which we started; (b) if we could resolve the problem of interpersonal comparability in Rawls's system by reducing everything in effect to a single primary good, we could do the same in the sum-of-utilities approach. To the last statement, however, there is a qualification: the maximin criterion requires only interpersonal ordinality, whereas the classical view requires interpersonally comparable units; to that extent, the Rawls system is epistemologically less demanding.

2. Let us turn from the epistemological problems of the current decision maker for society to those in the original position. Individuals are supposed to know the laws of the physical and the social worlds, but not to know who they are or will be. But empirical knowledge is after all uncertain, and even in the original position individuals may disagree about the facts and laws of the universe. For example, Rawls argues for religious toleration on the grounds that one does not know what religion one will have, and therefore one wants society to tolerate all religions. Operationally, a Catholic would have to recognize that in the original position he would not know he would be a Catholic and would therefore have to tolerate Protestants or Jews or whatever, since he might well have been one. But suppose he replies that in fact Catholicism is the true religion, that it is part of the knowledge which

all sensible people are supposed to have in the original position, and that he insists on it for the salvation of all mankind. How could this be refuted?

Indeed, just this sort of argument is raised by writers like Marcuse, not to mention any totalitarian state and, within wider limits, any state. Only those who correctly understand the laws of society should be allowed to express their political opinions. I feel I know that Marxism (or laissez-faire) is the truth; therefore, in the original position, I would have supported suppressing other positions. Even Rawls permits suppression of those who do not believe in freedom.

I hope it is not necessary to say that I am in favor of very wide toleration. But I am not convinced that the original position is a sufficient basis for this argument, for it transfers the problem to the area of factual disagreement.

There is another kind of knowledge problem in the original position: that about social preferences. Rawls assumes that individuals are egoistic, their social preferences being derived from the veil of ignorance. But why should there not be views of benevolence (or envy) even in the original position? All that is required is that they not refer to named individuals. But if these are admitted, then there can be disagreement over the degree of benevolence or malevolence, and the happy assumption that there are no disagreements in the original position disappears. . . .

Economic Implications of Rawls's Principles

Rawls's views have implications most directly for the redistribution of income, both among contemporaries and across generations. The maximin rule would seem on the face of it to lead to radical equalization of income. Indeed, so would the sum-of-utilities rule, if it is assumed that all individuals have the same utility function which displays decreasing marginal satisfactions from additional increments of income. Rawls, however, holds that the close-knittedness of members of the society means that perfect equality of income is not to the advantage of the least well-off, but that typically they will benefit by an increase in income to some higher up on the income scale.

Rawls is rather brief on why one might expect this kind of relation, but economists have laid considerable stress on the *incentive* effects of taxation. Assume that each individual can produce a certain amount per hour worked, but that this productivity varies from individual to individual. In the absence of taxation, the least productive individual will be the worst off. Therefore, a Rawlsian (or even an old-fashioned utilitarian) may advocate a tax on the income of the more able to be paid out to the less able. This is, in fact, essentially the widespread proposal for a negative income tax. However, since the effort to produce may in itself detract from satisfaction, an income tax will lead individuals to reduce the number of hours they work and therefore the amount they produce. If the tax rate on the more able is high enough, the amount of work will go down so much that the amount collected in taxes for redistribution to the worst off will actually decrease. It is at this stage that the economy becomes close-knit.

The conflict between incentive and equity occurs in a utilitarian framework and was already noted by Edgeworth (who was really very conservative and was glad to escape from the rigorous egalitarianism to which his utilitarianism led). The mathematical problem of choosing a tax schedule to maximize the sum of utilities, taking account of the adverse incentive effects, is a very difficult one; it was broached by Vickrey in his 1945 paper and analyzed by J. A. Mirrlees,[10] R. C. Fair,[11] and E. Sheshinski,[12] among others. More recently, the tax implications of the Rawls criterion have been analyzed along similar lines in papers by Atkinson, Phelps, and Sheshinski. The practical implications of this research are as yet dubious, primarily because too little is known about the magnitude of the incentive effects, particularly in the upper brackets.

As I have indicated, Rawls is inexplicit about the incentive effects and so does not give clear guidance to the determination of tax rates. On pages 277–279 he argues for progressive income and inheritance taxes to achieve justice, but there is no indication how the rates should be chosen. Clearly, the philosophy of justice is under no obligation to tell us what the rates should be in a numerical sense; but it is supposed to define the rule that translates any given set of facts into a tax schedule. The maximin rule would, on the face of it, lead to perfect equalization, that is, 100-percent taxation above a certain level, with corresponding subsidies below it. As far as I can see, it is only the incentive question that prevents us from carrying this policy out.

The incentive question raises another issue with regard to the obligation of an individual to perform justice. (Rawls has much to say on the notion of duties and obligations on individuals, though I have slighted that discussion in this review.) If each individual revealed his productivity (the amount he could produce per unit of time), it would be possible to achieve a perfect reconciliation of justice and incentives; namely, tax each individual according to his ability, not according to his actual output. Then he could not escape taxes by working less, and so the tax system would have no adverse incentive effects. Practical economists would reject this solution, because it would be taken for granted that no individual would be truthful if the consequences of truth telling were so painful. But Rawls, like most social philosophers, takes it for granted that individuals are supposed to act justly, at least in certain contexts. For example, as legislators or voters, it is an obligation or duty to judge according to the principles of justice, not according to self-interest. If, then, an individual is supposed to assess his own potential for earning income, is there an obligation to be truthful?

One of the most difficult questions in allocative justice is the distribution of wealth over generations. To what extent is one generation obligated to save, so as to increase the welfare of the next generation? The traditional economic problem has been the general act of investment in productive land, machines, and buildings which produce goods in the future; more recently, we have become especially concerned with preservation of undisturbed environments and natural resources. The most straightforward utilitarian answer is that the utilities of future generations enter equally with those of the present. Since the present generation is a very small part of the total number of individuals over a horizon easily measurable in thousands of years, the policy conclusion would be that virtually everything should be saved and very little consumed, a conclusion which seems offensive to common sense. The most usual formulation has been to assert a criterion of maximizing a sum of *discounted* utilities, in which the utilities of future generations are given successively smaller weights. The implications of such policies seem to be more in accordance with common sense and practice, but the foundations of such a criterion seem arbitrary.

Rawls argues that the maximin criterion, properly interpreted, can be applied to the determination of a just rate of savings (284–292). In the original position, individuals do not know which generation they belong to and should therefore judge a just rate on that basis. That is, they agree to leave a fixed fraction of their income to the next generation in return for receiving an equal fraction of the previous generation's income. There are two difficulties with this argument: (1) Why should they agree on a *fraction* rather than some more complicated rule—for example, an increasing fraction as wealth increases? (2) More serious, it would appear that the maximin rule would most likely lead to zero as the agreed-on savings rate; for the first generation would lose under any positive savings rate, whereas the welfare of all future generations would increase. This point is reinforced strongly if one adds the empirical fact of technological progress, so that even in the absence of savings the successive generations are getting better off. Then a maximin policy would call for improving the lot of the earlier generations, which can only be done by negative saving (running down existing capital equipment) if at all possible. (To be precise, the above argument is valid only in the absence of population growth. If population is growing, then zero saving would mean less capital per person and therefore a falling income per capita. Hence, a maximin rule in the absence of technological progress would call for positive saving; it can easily be shown that the rule would be that the rate of savings equals the rate of population growth multiplied by the capital-output ratio.)

Rawls, however, modifies the motivations in the original position at this point in the argument. "The parties are regarded as representing family lines, say, with ties of sentiment between successive generations" (292). This is a major departure from the egoistic assumptions held up to this point about behavior and choice in the original position. It should be noted that so long as fathers think more highly of themselves than of their sons, or even more highly of their sons than of subsequent generations, the effect of this modification is very much the same as that of discounting future utilities. Although my guess is that any justification for provision for the future will run somewhat along these lines, it cannot be said that the solution fully escapes all difficulties. (1) It introduces an element of altruism into the original position; if we introduce family sentiments, why not others (nations, tribal)? And why not elements of envy? (2) One might like a theory of justice in which the role of the family was derived rather than primitive. In a reexamination of social institutions, why should the family remain above scrutiny, its role being locked into the original assumptions? (3) Anyway, the family argument for saving has an implication that should be displayed and possibly questioned. Presumably the burden of saving should fall only on those with children and perhaps in proportion to the number of children. Since education and public construction are essentially forms of saving, taxes to support them should fall only on those with children. In the original position this is just the sort of contract that would be arrived at if the concern for the future were based solely on family ties.

A Critical Note on the Possibility of Justice

Rawls's work is based on the hypothesis that there is a meaningful universal concept of justice. If there is, it surely must, as he says, be universalizable in some sense, that is, based on principles that are symmetric among the particular accidents that distinguish one individual's position from another. But as I look around at the many conflicts that plague our humanity, I find many for which I can imagine no argument of a symmetric nature which would convince both sides.

One problem is that any actual individual must necessarily have limited information about the world, and different individuals have different information. Hence, they cannot possibly argue themselves back into an original position with common information, even if they succeed in "forgetting" who they are. Indeed, one of the most brilliant passages in Rawls's book is that on what he calls "social union" (520–530). He argues that no human life is enough to encounter more than a small fraction of the experiences needed for completeness, so that individuals have a natural complementarity with one another (a more mundane version of this idea is Adam Smith's stress on the importance of the division of labor). The social nature of man springs from this variegation of experience. But precisely the same differentiations imply differing and incompletely communicable life experiences and therewith the possible impossibility of agreeing on the just action in any concrete situation.

Indeed, the thrust of Rawls's work, particularly in its latter passages, is highly harmonistic; the principles of justice are stable, according to Rawls, because the moral education they induce reinforces them. But if the specific application of the principles is judged to be different according to different life experiences (and of course different genetic experiences), even as between parent and child, then the needed concordance of views may evaporate.

To put the matter somewhat differently, many sociologists would hold that in a world of limited information, conflict unresolved by appeal to commonly accepted principles may have a positive value; it is the means by which information about others is conveyed. In its own sphere, this is the role assigned to competition by economists; if everyone attempted to act justly at every moment in his economic life, it might be difficult ever to find out what the true interests of anyone were.

To the extent that individuals are really individual, each an autonomous end in himself, to that extent they must be somewhat mysterious and inaccessible to one another. There cannot be any rule that is completely acceptable to all. There must be, or so it now seems to me, the possibility of unadjudicable conflict, which may show itself logically as paradoxes in the process of social decision making.

NOTES

1. See A. Bergson, *Essays in Normative Economics* (Cambridge, Mass.: Harvard, 1966), chap. 1; P. A. Samuelson, *The Foundations of Economic Analysis* (Cambridge, Mass.: Harvard, 1947), pp. 230–248; or F. Y. Edgeworth, *Mathematical Psychics* (London: Kegan Paul, 1881), pp. 56–82.

2. "Measuring Marginal Utility by Reactions to Risk," *Econometrica*, 13 (1945):319–333, p. 329; "Utility, Strategy, and Social Decision Rules," *Quarterly Journal of Economics*. 74 (1960): 507–535.

    Vickrey's 1945 statement has been overlooked by all subsequent writers—not surprisingly, since it received relatively little emphasis in a paper overtly devoted to a seemingly different subject. I read the paper before I was concerned with the theory of social choice; the implications for that theory were so easy to overlook that they did not occur to me at all when they would have been relevant.

3. "Cardinal Utility in Welfare Economics and the Theory of Risk-Taking," *Journal of Political Economy*, 61 (1953): 434–5; "Cardinal Welfare, Individualistic Ethics, and Interpersonal Comparisons of Utility," ibid., 63 (1955): 309–321.

4. "Truth and Probability," in *The Foundations of Mathematics and Other Logical Essays* (London: K. Paul, Trench, Trubner, 1931), pp. 156–198.

5. *The Foundations of Statistics* (New York: Wiley, 1954).

6. *Risk, Uncertainty, and Profit* (New York: Houghton Mifflin, 1921).

7. "Contributions to the Theory of Statistical Estimation and Testing Hypotheses," *Annals of Mathematical Statistics*, 10 (1939): 299–326.

8. *Expectations in Economics* (Cambridge: University Press, 1949) and subsequent works.

9. "An Optimality Criterion for Decision-making under Ignorance," in C. F. Carter and J. L. Ford, eds. *Uncertainty and Expectation in Economics* (Oxford: Basil Blackwell, 1972), pp. 1–11.

10. "An Exploration in the Theory of Optimal Income Taxation," *Review of Economic Studies*, 38 (1971): 175–208.

11. "The Optimal Distribution of Income," *Quarterly Journal of Economics*, 85 (1971): 551–579.

12. "The Optimum Linear Income Tax," *Review of Economic Studies*, 39 (1972): 297–302.

JOHN RAWLS

Some Reasons for the Maximin Criterion

John Rawls delivered this defense of his maximin criterion at the American Economic Association meetings in December 1973. The ground rule he proposes for deciding between different rules of justice is social contract theory's conception of original position. If this basis for choice is accepted, Rawls goes on to argue, not only is his complete theory of justice (which includes both the priority of liberty and the maximin principle of inequality) superior to the utilitarian criterion of maximizing average utility but also the maximin principle, when considered alone, is still preferable to maximal average utility.

QUESTIONS TO GUIDE THE READING

1. Can you conceive of a definition of original position in which the voters might not unanimously agree upon a rule of justice?
2. If, as Rawls asserts, individuals in the original position desire basic liberties, how could the criterion of utilitarianism result in a society with less than those basic liberties?
3. How do the information requirements of Rawls's maximin criterion differ from those of utilitarianism?
4. Do you believe that individuals are more likely to favor pattern criteria when choosing a policy of social justice?

Recently the maximin criterion of distributive equity has received some attention from economists in connection with the problem of optimal income taxation.[1] Unhappily I am unable to examine the merits of the criterion from the standpoint of economic theory, although whether the criterion is a reasonable distributive standard depends importantly on the sort of examination that only economists can undertake.

John Rawls, "Some Reasons for the Maximin Criterion," *American Economic Review* 64 (May 1974), 141–6. Reprinted by permission of the author and the publisher.

John Rawls is the James Bryant Conant University Professor of Philosophy at Harvard University.

What I shall do is to summarize briefly some of the reasons for taking the maximin criterion seriously. I should emphasize that the maximin equity criterion and the so-called maximin rule for choice under uncertainty are two very different things. I shall formulate the reasons for the equity criterion so that they are completely independent from this rule.

In *A Theory of Justice* I have considered the maximin criterion as part of a social contract theory. Here I must assume a certain familiarity with this conception.[2] One feature of it might be put this way: injustice exists because basic agreements are made too late (Richard Zeckhauser). People already know their social positions and relative strength in bargaining, their abilities and preferences, and these contingencies and knowledge of them cumulatively distort the social system. In an attempt to remedy this difficulty, contract theory introduces the notion of the original position. The most reasonable principles of justice are defined as those that would be unanimously agreed to in an appropriate initial situation that is fair between individuals conceived as free and equal moral persons.

In order to define the original position as fair in this sense, we imagine that everyone is deprived of certain morally irrelevant information.[3] They do not know their place in society, their class position or social status, their place in the distribution of natural assets and abilities, their deeper aims and interests, or their particular psychological makeup. Excluding this information insures that no one is advantaged or disadvantaged in the choice of principles by natural chance or social contingencies. Since all are in this sense similarly situated and no one knows how to frame principles that favor his particular condition, each will reason in the same way. Any agreement reached is unanimous and there is no need to vote.

Thus the subject of the original agreement is a conception of social justice. Also, this conception is understood to apply to the basic structure of society: that is, to its major institutions—the political constitution and the principal economic and social arrangements—and how they fit together into one system. The application of the maximin criterion to optimal income taxation is, then, perfectly in order, since an income tax is part of the basic structure. But the maximin criterion is not meant to apply to small-scale situations, say, to how a doctor should treat his patients or a university its students.[4] For these situations different principles will presumably be necessary. Maximin is a macro not a micro principle. I should add that the criterion is unsuitable for determining the just rate of savings; it is intended to hold only within generations (Rawls, sec. 44, pp. 291–92, Kenneth J. Arrow, 1973a, and Robert M. Solow).

But what alternative conceptions are available in the original position? We must resort to great simplifications in order to get our bearings. We cannot consider the general case where the parties are to choose among all possible conceptions of justice; it is too difficult to specify this class of alternatives. Therefore we imagine that the parties are given a short list of conceptions between which they are to decide.

Here I can discuss only two pair-wise comparisons. These are designed to reflect the traditional aim of contract theory, namely, to provide an account of justice that is both superior to utilitarianism and a more adequate basis for a democratic society. Therefore the first choice is between a conception defined by the principle that average utility is to be maximized and a conception defined by two principles that express a democratic idea of justice. These principles read as follows:

1. Each person has an equal right to the most extensive scheme of equal basic liberties compatible with a similar scheme of liberties for all.
2. Social and economic inequalities are to meet two conditions: they must be (a) to the greatest expected benefit of the least advantaged members of society (the maximin equity criterion) and (b) attached to offices and positions open to all under conditions of fair equality of opportunity.

I assume that the first of these takes priority over the second, but this and other matters must be left aside. (For more on this, see Rawls, pp. 40–45 and 62–65.) For simplicity I also assume that a person's utility is affected predominantly by liberties and opportunities, income and wealth, and their distribution. I suppose further that everyone has normal physical needs so that the problem of special health care does not arise.[5]

Now which of these conceptions would be chosen depends on how the persons in the original position are conceived. Contract theory stipulates that they regard themselves as having certain fundamental interests, the claims of which they must protect, if this is possible. It is in the name of these interests that they have a right to equal respect and consideration in the design of society. The religious interest is a familiar historical example; the interest in the integrity of the person is another. In the original position the parties do not know what particular form these interests take. But they do assume that they have such interests and also that the basic liberties necessary for their protection (for example, freedom of thought and liberty of conscience, freedom of the person, and political liberty) are guaranteed by the first principle of justice.

Given these stipulations, the two principles of justice would be chosen. For while the principle of utility may sometimes lead to a social order securing these liberties, there is no reason why it will do so in general. And even if the principle often does, it would be pointless to run the risk of encountering circumstances when it does not. Put formally, each must suppose that the marginal utility of these fundamental interests is infinite; this requires anyone in the original position to give them priority and to adopt the two principles of justice.

This conclusion is strengthened when one adds that the parties regard themselves as having a higher-order interest in how their other interests, even fundamental ones, are regulated and shaped by social institutions. They think of themselves as beings who can choose and revise their final ends and who must preserve their liberty in these matters. A free person is not only one who has final ends which he is free to pursue or to reject, but also one whose original allegiance and continued devotion to these ends are formed under conditions that are free. Since the two principles secure these conditions, they must be chosen.

The second pair-wise comparison is far more difficult. In this case the choice is between the two principles of justice and a variant of these principles in which the utility principle has a subordinate place. To define this variant, replace the second principle by the following: social and economic inequalities are to be adjusted so as to maximize average utility consistent with fair equality of opportunity. The choice between this variant and the two principles is more delicate because the arguments from liberty can no longer be made, at least not so directly. The first principle belongs to both conceptions, and so the operation of the utility principle is hedged by basic rights as well as fair equality of opportunity.

One reason favoring the two principles of justice is this. From the standpoint of the original position, the parties will surely be very considerably risk-averse; if we ask how risk-averse, we might say not less than that of most any normal person. Of course, this is extremely vague; but if we assume that utility is estimated from the standpoint of individuals in society and represents, as the classical utilitarians believed, a quantity ascertainable independent of choices involving risk, then, given the crucial nature of the decision in the original position, the claims of the utility principle seem quite dubious. On the other hand, if we suppose that utility is measured from the original position and takes account of risk, the utility criterion may not differ much from maximin. The standard of utility approaches maximin as risk aversion increases without limit (Arrow, pp. 256–57). So, either way, the original position pushes us toward maximin. However, in weighing the second pair-wise comparison, I assume that, based on considerations of risk aversion alone, there is a significant difference between the two conceptions. Thus the problem is to identify other attractive features of the maximin criterion that tip the balance of reasons in its favor.

First, much less information is needed to apply the maximin criterion. Once the least-favored group is identified, it may be relatively easy to determine which policies are to their advantage. By comparison it is much more difficult to know what maximizes average utility. We require a fairly precise way of comparing the utilities of different social groups by some meaningful standard, as well as a method of estimating the overall balance of gains and losses. In application this principle leaves so much to judgment that some may reasonably claim that the gains of one group outweigh the losses of another, while others may equally reasonably deny it. This situation gives those favored by existing inequalities an opportunity to exploit their advantage so that, as a result, inequalities are likely to be excessive, undermining the justice of the system.

A further consideration is this: a distributive criterion is to serve as a public principle. Citizens generally should be able to understand it and have some confidence that it is realized. Pattern criteria, those that require the actual distribution to exhibit certain ascertainable features, do well by the test of publicity. Of these, strict equality (equal division) is the sharpest principle. The trouble with pattern criteria is that sharpness is not the only desideratum, and they often have little else to commend them. On the other hand, the utility principle is not sharp enough: even if it were satisfied, there could be little public confidence that this is indeed the case. The maximin criterion has sufficient sharpness; at the same time it is efficient while strict equality is not.

Another ground supporting the maximin criterion is based on the strains of commitment: in the original position the parties are to favor those principles compliance with which should prove more tolerable, whatever their situation in society turns out to be. The notion of a contract implies that one cannot enter into an agreement that one will be unable to keep. By this test, also, maximin seems superior, for the principles chosen would regulate social and economic inequalities in the basic structure of society that affect people's life-prospects. These are peculiarly deep and pervasive inequalities and often hard to accept.

Looking first at the situation of the less advantaged, the utility principle asks them to view the greater advantages of others who have more as a sufficient reason for having still lower prospects of life than otherwise they could be allowed. This is an extreme demand psychologically; by contrast, the maximin criterion assures the less favored that inequalities work to their advantage. The problem with maximin would appear to lie with those who are better situated. They must accept less than what they would receive with the utility principle, but two things greatly lessen their strains of commitment: they are, after all, more fortunate and enjoy the benefits of that fact; and insofar as they value their situation relatively in comparison with others, they give up that much less. In fact, our tendency to evaluate our circumstances in relation to the circumstances of others suggests that society should be arranged so that if possible all its members can with reason be happy with their situation. The maximin criterion achieves this better than the principle of utility.

I have noted several reasons that support the maximin criterion: very considerable normal risk-aversion (given the special features of the original position), less demanding information requirements, greater suitability as a public principle, and weaker strains of commitment. Yet no one of them is clearly decisive by itself. Thus the question arises whether there is any consideration that is compelling. I want to suggest that the aspirations of free and equal personality point directly to the maximin criterion.

Since the principles of equal liberty and fair equality of opportunity are common to both alternatives in the second comparison, some form of democracy obtains when either alternative is realized. Citizens are to view themselves as free and equal persons; social institutions should be willingly complied with and recognized as just. Presumably, however, certain social and economic inequalities exist, and individuals' life-prospects are significantly affected by their family and class origins, by their natural endowments, and by chance contingencies over the course of their lives. We must ask: In the light of what principles can free and equal moral persons permit their relations to be affected by social fortune and the natural lottery? Since no one deserves his place in the distribution of talents, nor his starting place in society, desert is not an answer. Yet free and equal persons want the effects of chance to be regulated by some principle, if a reasonable principle exists.

Now when the maximin criterion is followed, the natural distribution of abilities is viewed in some respects as a collective asset. While an equal distribution might seem more in keeping with the equality of free moral persons, at least if the distribution were a matter of choice, this is not a reason for eliminating natural variations, much less for destroying unusual talents. To the contrary, natural variations are recognized as an opportunity, particularly since they are often complementary and form a basis for social ties. Institutions are allowed to exploit the full range of abilities provided the resulting inequalities are no greater than necessary to produce corresponding advantages for the less fortunate. The same constraint holds for the inequalities between social classes. Thus at first sight the distribution of natural assets and unequal life-expectations threatens the relations between free and equal moral persons. But provided the maximin criterion is satisfied, these relations may be preserved: inequalities are to everyone's advantage and those able to gain from their good fortune do so in ways agreeable to those less favored. Meeting this burden of proof reflects the value of equality.

Now the maximin criterion would conform to the precept "from each according to his abilities, to each according to his needs" if society were to impose a head tax on natural assets. In this way income inequalities could be greatly reduced if not eliminated. Of course, there are enormous practical difficulties in such a scheme; ability may be impossible to measure and individuals would have every incentive to conceal their talents. But another difficulty is the interference with liberty; greater natural talents are not a collective asset in the sense that society should compel those who have them to put them to work for the less favored. This would be a drastic infringement upon freedom. But society can say that the better endowed may improve their situations only on terms that help others. In this way inequalities are permitted in ways consistent with everyone's self-respect.

I have attempted a brief survey of the grounds for the maximin criterion. I have done this because historically it has attracted little attention, and yet it is a natural focal point between strict equality and the principle of average utility. It turns out to have a number of attractive features. But I do not wish to overemphasize this criterion: a deeper investigation covering more pairwise comparisons may show that some other conception of justice is more reasonable. In any case, the idea that economists may find most useful in contract theory is that of the original position. This perspective can be defined in various ways and with different degrees of abstraction and some of these may prove illuminating for economic theory.[6]

NOTES

Note: I am grateful to Robert Cooter and Richard Zeckhauser for their very instructive comments which enabled me to improve these remarks and saved me from several mistakes.

1. See A. B. Atkinson, Martin Feldstein, Yoshitaka Itsumi, and Edmund S. Phelps.
2. In economics this sort of theory was reintroduced by James Buchanan and Gordon Tullock.
3. A similar idea is found in J. C. Harsanyi (1953).
4. This affects the force of Harsanyi's counterexamples (Harsanyi, 1973).
5. Part of the justification for these assumptions given by the notion of primary goods. See Rawls, sec. 15. Of course, there are still difficulties (Arrow, 1973b, p. 254).
6. See Zeckhauser for an illustration of the use of this sort of framework.

REFERENCES

K. J. Arrow, "Rawls's Principle of Just Saving," Instit. for Math. Stud. in the Soc. Sciences, Stanford, tech. rep. no. 106, Sept. 1973a.

———, "Some Ordinalist-Utilitarian Notes on Rawls's Theory of Justice," *J. Phil.*, May 1973b, 70, 254.

A. B. Atkinson, "How Progressive Should Income Tax Be?" in J. M. Parkin, ed., *Essays in Modern Economics,* London 1973.

J. Buchanan and G. Tullock, *The Calculus of Consent,* Ann Arbor 1962.

M. Feldstein, "On the Optimal Progressivity of the Income Tax," Harvard Instit. of Econ. Res., disc. pap. 309, July 1973.

J. C. Harsanyi, "Cardinal Utility in Welfare Economics and in the Theory of Risk Taking," *J. Polit. Econ.,* Oct. 1953, 61, 434–35.

———, "Can the Maximin Principle Serve as a Basis for Morality?" Center for Res. in Manage. Sc., Berkeley, work. pap. no. CP-351, May 1973, 8–9.

Y. Itsumi, "Distributional Effects of Income Tax Schedules," *Rev. Econ. Stud.,* forthcoming.

E. S. Phelps, "The Taxation of Wage Income for Economic Justice," *Quart. J. Econ.,* Aug. 1973, 87, 331–54.

J. Rawls, *A Theory of Justice,* Cambridge, Mass. 1971.

R. M. Solow, "Intergenerational Equity and Exhaustible Resources," dept. of econ., work. pap. no. 103, Cambridge, Mass. Feb. 1973.

R. Zeckhauser, "Risk Spreading and Distribution," in H. M. Hochman and G. E. Peterson, eds., *Political Economics of Income Distribution,* New York 1974.

DUNCAN K. FOLEY

State Expenditure from a
Marxist Perspective

Duncan Foley examines public sector activities from a Marxist
perspective, which he argues is more realistic than the
oversimplistic approaches of reductionism or functionalism. In
general, Marxist theory attempts to understand state expenditures
within a historical and dynamic context of change. Within this
framework, capitalism is a social force influencing government
activities in order to protect its interests and to foster its expansion.
In contrast, Foley asserts, neoclassical economic theory is unable
to explain the true relationship between capitalism and present-day
government activities, because this theory takes into account only
individual wants and endowments.

QUESTIONS TO GUIDE THE READING

1. How does Foley's analysis avoid the fallacies of a reductionist
   Marxist view and of Marxist functionalism?

2. How might education viewed as a socialization mechanism be
   consistent with the neoclassical theory of education as a public
   good?

3. Under what circumstances is it to the advantage of a capitalist
   society to maintain both unemployment and welfare programs,
   including unemployment compensation?

4. Why is it possible for a large public sector to reflect the goals of
   capitalism as opposed to being a sign of a move toward
   socialism?

1. Introduction

This paper develops a theory of State expenditure on a Marxist basis. It
argues that we can understand the determinants of modern State expenditure in relation to the historical development of capitalism. If we adopt this
theoretical point of view we can see specific links between particular categories of State expenditure and the historical dynamics of capital accumu-

Duncan K. Foley, "State Expenditure from a Marxist Perspective," *Journal of Public Economics*
9 (1978), 221–38. Reprinted by permission of Elsevier Science Publishers.

Duncan K. Foley is Professor of Economics at Barnard College.

lation. We can locate spending on the military, education, and welfare, for example, in relation to the problems that have emerged with the dominance of capitalism in modern society and the expansion of capital to a world scale.

I argue that it is possible to think of these systematic links between capitalism and State expenditure without falling into the fallacies of reductionism or functionalism. A reductionist Marxism would see the State as no more than the expression of the capitalist class dominance over the working class in modern capitalist society. A Marxist functionalism tries to explain phenomena by showing that they meet a need of the capitalist system as a whole or of the capitalist class in particular. In this paper I try to construct a theory in which the State has a certain autonomy, where the capitalist class interest is usually decisive in shaping State policy, but only through the outcome of real struggle, and which treats the determinants of State action as a problem separable from that of the effects of State policy on profitability and capital accumulation. The problems of capital have created the agenda for the modern State's expenditures and the conflict between classes and class fractions the primary pressures on State decisions.

In section 2, I develop very briefly the basic theoretical ideas that underlie this view of the State. Section 3 takes up three central sectors of State expenditure, the military, education, and welfare and unemployment policy and tries to establish their links with particular aspects of capitalist production. Section 4 outlines some explanations of the growth of modern State expenditure which are compatible with the overall Marxist theory. . . . Section 6 contains some concluding remarks on what we know and don't know about the modern State.

The main purpose of the paper is to give an overview of this theory, so that specific points are treated briefly, with references to more complete discussions in the Marxist literature. This discussion does not develop any mathematical models to represent the theoretical ideas but it is my hope that this kind of theoretical discussion at an abstract level will facilitate the creation of such models, and my suspicion that this kind of discussion is a necessary step toward such models.

2. The State in a Marxist Perspective

The philosophical and methodological basis of Marxist economics is historical materalism. This point of view emphasizes that the categories of social existence (for example, commodities or property) are not absolute prior ahistorical givens, but relations between people that emerge in particular historical circumstances. Society at any period is seen as a mutually conditioned totality of such relations. The study of any social category, like the State, within a historical materialist framework centers on the conditions of reproduction of that category within the system of relations, and its effects on other relations. Furthermore the reproduction of social relations is from a historical materialist viewpoint *contradictory* in the sense that a certain relation may tend to destroy the conditions for its own reproduction. The competition of many capitals, for instance, may through the cost of advantages and market power accruing to large scale lead to its opposite, the centralization and concentration of capital.

This notion of reproduction becomes a central tool in Marxist theoretical analysis, in some ways like the notion of equilibrium for bourgeois economics. In fact the idea of equilibrium can be understood as a partial treatment of reproduction which emphasizes the ability of a certain social configuration to reproduce itself without violating some limited set of conditions (like individual profit or utility maximization, for example). Equilibrium concepts cannot very well represent the contradictory development of a social form, however, because equilibrium begins by looking for a state of the system free from contradiction within a certain defined area of analysis. The point of view of reproduction, on the other hand, searches for those ways in which a social configuration tends to destroy the given, 'exogenous' state on which it rests, and for the mechanisms by which certain forms propagate themselves in spite of these contradictions.

The State within this framework has no general determination. In any historical period the State will have a particular content related to the development of relations of production in that period. The central questions for the Marxist study of the State are: what are the central relations of the society in question (e.g., capitalist relations, or some others?); how is the State linked to those relations (e.g., a bourgeois State or a worker's State?); what developments in the relations of production are shaping and altering the State (e.g., is the disappearance of competition leading to regulation?); what effects are State activities having on the conditions of reproduction of other elements of the society (e.g., is the State suppressing the small competitive sector, stabilizing the market demand for commodities, altering the degree of competition in the labor market?).

The theory of State expenditure developed in this paper is Marxist in two senses. First, it operates within the historical materialist framework. Second, it accepts Marx's answers to the first question posed in the last paragraph, that the dominant relation of modern society is the capital–labor relation, so that the State in capitalist society has to be understood first of all in relation to the reproduction and accumulation of capital, and to the class relations of workers and capitalists.

It is necessary, however, if we take up a Marxist perspective, to avoid two related fallacies. The first is what might be called a reductionist Marxist view which represents all relations under capitalism as nothing but the class relation between workers and capitalists expressing itself in various ways. From a reductionist perspective the State must be simply an expression of the domination the bourgeoisie exercises over the proletariat in capitalist society. This idea leads easily to theories of conscious conspiratorial direction of the State by, and in the class interests of the bourgeoisie, theories which are oversimple and cannot account for a huge range of contractory evidence.

A second fallacy that must be avoided is a Marxist functionalism, which explains particular relations in capitalist society by showing that these relations meet a "need" of the system as a whole. This functionalist argument (which is often implied rather than explicitly stated) claims that if we can show that a certain State action helps to reproduce capitalist social relations, then we have given a good explanation for why the action did in fact occur. This argument would be valid only if there were some general law that whatever is necessary for the reproduction of the capitalist system will in fact happen, a principle of functionalism which is inadequate both because the set of "what is necessary for the reproduction of the system" is not well defined and because it offers no explanation of the mechanism by which "needs" are transformed into actions, which is presumably the heart of a theory of fiscal politics. This functionalism also tends to obscure the contradictions inherent in State policy and the real struggles over State policy carried on by particular classes and class fractions.

It seems to me that a Marxist account must locate the State in relation to class struggle and the accumulation of capital, but with a certain autonomy.[1] The aim of the analysis must be to see how State policy has its determinants in the contradictory development of capitalism, and to show the effects of State action on the conditions for capital accumulation, as two separable problems. The State is in this perspective an analytical category different from the capitalist class, and can be thought of as moving in contradiction at times to that class or parts of it. But the dynamics of the capital–labor relation establish the main agenda for State policy and the capitalist class as the primary appropriator of surplus value is the class in the best position to influence and control State policy in its class interest. Thus we would expect to see a certain continuing tension and struggle over State policy as it affects class relations in capitalist society, a struggle which capital generally wins. This formulation avoids the fallacy of reducing the State to a mere expression of capitalist interest, while acknowledging the generally decisive role capitalists as a class play in controlling State policy. Within this framework the State appears as an arena of conflict in which various fractions of capital struggle to shape State policy to strengthen their own conditions of existence as they perceive them, and in which working class interests, although they never emerge in advanced capitalist societies as dominant, are more or less vigorously represented and help to shape the outcome.

The exact mechanisms by which capitalists as a class exercise a pervasive power over State policy differ depending on historical and institutional realities.[2] In many important capitalist countries the struggle over the control of State power involves the forms of electoral politics. From a Marxist point of view we note two important aspects of electoral politics. First, State policy itself is decided in elections only in rare and marginal instances. Whatever group or fraction holds State power, the great mass of State policy is determined within the administrative apparatus of the State, a bureaucracy in which an intense struggle for influence among emergent interests constantly manifests itself. In the few instances where policy depends on the political leaders themselves, the electorate is given a choice of administrations whose policies have been determined in party struggles in which money and allied forms of influence have a disproportionate power. Thus the struggle over State policy is largely located outside the electoral process itself. Second, elections in modern capitalist States are very much determined by the organization and financial strength of the contending parties, since, whatever the conscious position of some parts of the electorate, the election itself is decided mostly by who turns out to vote and the propagandizing of marginal groups of voters. Thus elections appear in this light more as a peaceful method of struggle between classes and class fractions over State power without resorting to civil war than as a coherent expression of the individual preferences of the electors.

In extreme cases in advanced capitalist countries and routinely in the "underdeveloped" countries capitalist influence on State policy is exercised through coercion, violence and sabotage. Direct links between military dictatorships and local or international strata of the capitalist class are apparent in many recent historical junctures. In a typical case of class struggle in Chile under Allende we can see the orchestration of economic sabotage and military force (within a context of what appeared from a capitalist point of view to be economic mismanagement and political ineptitude on the part of a left-wing regime) to ensure a pro-capitalist shift in State policy.

In all modern capitalist states capitalist class influence on State policy is also fostered by certain widely shared conceptions and beliefs, which tend to coordinate State decisions in a line favorable to the class interests of capital. There is a strong tendency promoted by educational and journalistic practice and by political rhetoric to identify the "national interest" with the interest of national capital. We measure economic success by indicators that weight capitalist production and profitability heavily. Society is represented as happy when capitalist production is thriving and when social disputes have been settled on terms favorable to the profitability of capital. These shared beliefs tend to coordinate State decisions into policies acceptable to the capitalist class, to establish in Gramsci's phrase the ideological hegemony of capital. They are an important channel through which the capitalist class influences and controls State policy.[3]

From a Marxist point of view, then, the modern State and its expenditures can be explained only by locating them in relation to the historical development of capitalism. The agenda for State action and the major pressures on State policy grow out of the conflict between the capitalist and working classes over the appropriation of surplus value, and out of conflicts within the capitalist class over the distribution of surplus value. While capitalists in general and large capital in particular have a generally decisive advantage in these struggles, there is no reason to reduce the State and its policies to a simple expression of the dominance of the capitalist class or one fraction of it in modern society. The mechanisms through which classes struggle over State policy are complex and historically specific, and the particularity of those mechanisms plays a real role in determining outcomes.

With these points in mind we can proceed to look more closely at various forms of modern State expenditure and the growth of the State in advanced capitalist countries.

3. Armies, Schools, the Dole

As we examine particular aspects of State expenditure, the force of the general propositions outlined in the last section will become clearer. I will concentrate on three areas of State spending, the military, education, and transfers to the poor and unemployed, as examples.

From a Marxist viewpoint the central questions about State military expenditure involve the ways in which choices about the extent, shape and use of military power have social consequences for particular class interests.[4] How does State military policy contribute to the expansion of capitalist social relations in general, to the strengthening of particular capitals in competition with others, to the defense of capitalism against the threats posed by revolutionary socialist movements, and to the stabilization of market demand for commodities? Issues like competitive arms races and the use of military power for purely strategic purposes appear in this perspective to be secondary phenomena. Every strategic intervention can be made in many ways, and the choice of exactly what military steps to take to secure a given objective involves political and class-oriented considerations, which are the underlying determinants of the policy.

We can analyze the use of military power in the service of capitalist interests (a phenomenon often discussed under the general topic of imperialism) in relation to three central conditions for the appropriation and accumulation of profits: access to cheap labor, markets for products, and sources of raw materials.

Profitability of capitalist production rests on the availability of labor at a sufficiently low wage. In the Marxist analysis of capitalism the major force preventing wages in any sector from rising too rapidly is the competition or potential competition of a pool of labor outside that sector living in conditions that make wage employment in the sector attractive. The accumulation of capital in a sector tends to draw this reserve labor into employment in that sector. This tendency of accumulation to produce pressures to bring new labor into production is a central aspect of the struggle between workers and capitalists that capitalist production creates and re-creates.

The degree of competition on any labor market depends on both the entry of labor through migration (and training) and on the ability of capitalists to relocate production to exploit new sources of labor. The ability to influence both of these processes through State policy is a fundamental strategic advantage the capitalist class enjoys in its struggle with workers. The State directly affects domestic labor markets through its policies on migration and the importation of foreign labor on a temporary basis. Political conditions in areas where pools of reserve labor exist that foster capitalist investment and emigration are also favorable to the maintenance of reserve labor on a world scale. Thus a problem of securing the cooperation of foreign governments in the investment and labor recruitment programs of capital emerges in the course of accumulation. This in turn creates pressures for the creation and use of military, intelligence, and diplomatic apparatuses in the metropolitan capitalist countries capable of securing this cooperation.

A more dramatic instance of the imperialist use of State military power in the present century has been the attempt of some capitals to gain control of labor, markets, or sources of raw materials in competition with other capitals. This type of imperialist rivalry pits large modern military forces against each other in confrontations that have led in some instances to world crises and wars. The Marxist theory attempts to base an explanation of these events in the logic of capital accumulation and competition, to establish that the content of modern wars is a struggle over surplus value and the possibility of appropriating surplus value, though the form of war is, of course, far older than capitalism.

A Marxist account of military expenditure roots that expenditure in the logic of reproduction of the capitalist economic system itself. Although diplomatic and military issues appear to involve the clashes of particular nations and their "national interests," the Marxist conception locates these national conflicts in relation to class divisions that cut across national boundaries. The scale of military expenditure in this perspective will change as the size and concentration of capital changes, and as the conflicts between classes and class fractions express themselves in particular historical conjunctures.

The problem of State expenditures on education is a central and troublesome topic for both Marxist and bourgeois economic theories.[5]

From a Marxist viewpoint education touches on the reproduction of capitalist social relations at many different levels. Some part of the technical skills and knowledge necessary for production are provided by formal State-financed education. However, these skills are not the primary content of State-financed education, which spends a lot of time in producing certain attitudes and beliefs about the world in its students, in reinforcing certain traits of personality and classifying people according to the traits they exhibit, and in acting as a kind of gate or sorting device which regulates access to high-paying and high-status jobs.

Conservative bourgeois theory emphasizes the first (the reproduction of skills) and the last (access to high-paying jobs) of these aspects and links them through the concept of human capital, arguing that it is in fact the acquisition of particular skills that guarantees access to high-paying jobs. The high pay in this theory is a rent arising from competition among employers in circumstances where the market for labor with various kinds of skills clears in some sense.

This theory raises some difficult problems. It cannot explain why the State is so deeply involved in education in all modern capitalist countries. Competing private profit making educational institutions would be necessary to explain a cost-determined supply schedule for human capital. It is impossible to define the clearing of markets for labor of different skills without such a supply schedule. In fact the great bulk of education is carried on by State-supported and administered schools, colleges and universities whose pricing policies bear only a tenuous relation to costs. Corollary to this institutional anomaly is the question of what the clearance of markets for differently skilled labor actually means. If the education system acts to meet needs for various skill levels and always has a reserve capacity to create more labor with any particular skills, then the productivity of those skills is not in any practical sense the determinant of relative wages. Techniques will be chosen by employers to equalize the marginal productivity of particular skilled labor to the wages of that class of labor.

Liberal bourgeois theory rationalizes the strong State role in education by positing some substantial externality to education, often expressed as "good citizenship." This argument is not adequate to explain the actual role of the State in education because at most it suggests a subsidy to education as a privately produced commodity, not a full-scale State-regulated or administered educational system. (It also involves the functionalist fallacy I discussed in the last section, since it begs the question of what mechanism might actually respond to the existence of an externality in education.)

Within the Marxist and radical tradition in economic theory education is seen as reproducing class relations by influencing the attitudes and beliefs of students about the world, especially the society in which they live (in Marxist language by reproducing ideology) and by channeling students into different sectors of the labor market. "Ideology" in this context is viewed not simply as notions of what are "good" or "bad" for individuals and society as a whole, but as involving the structure of concepts through which people try to grasp their relation to society. The concept of the "individual" itself from this point of view is an ideological category, and thinking in terms of an opposition between "individual" and "society" will produce certain biases and blind spots in people's thought about the world.

From this Marxist perspective it is somewhat easier to see why the State is so centrally involved in education in capitalist society. The reproduction of ideology is inherently a social process, and emerges as a problem only at a level more global than that of particular capitalist firms. If human capital theory were adequate to give a complete account of education, in that individual knowledge and skills were in fact the prime content of education, then this problem of the emergent aspect of ideology would never arise.

The observation that education reproduces ideology and regulates supplies of labor onto different strata of the labor market, however, does not constitute a complete explanation of how the State educational apparatus comes into existence and reproduces itself. The State educational apparatus does not always succeed in performing its functions smoothly; it has itself an autonomy and the possibility of a development in contradiction to the reproduction of capitalist relations of production (as we saw in many capitalist countries in the 1960s). Furthermore, in many capitalist countries the educational apparatus has emerged as an autonomous structure with its own ideology and dynamics of change expressed through bureaucracies, political organizations, unions, and so on. An important part of what happens in education probably must be explained in the context of an account of this educational apparatus.

State expenditure on welfare and unemployment compensation are from a Marxist viewpoint closely related to education.[6] The major theme in both cases is the inadequacy of capitalist relations of production to reproduce one of their own vital requirements, exploitable labor power. The reproduction of labor power generally involves factors that lie outside the wage-labor relation itself. The State through its educational apparatus more or less guarantees the skills and attitudes of the labor force, and through its welfare and unemployment programs tries to regulate in broad terms the supply of labor power in the aggregate. The major effect of these programs in a Marxist perspective is to maintain a reserve of unemployed, not to eliminate unemployment. Unemployment and welfare policy operate between the horns of a dilemma. On the one hand these programs must be large enough and generous enough to assure on average the survival and political docility of workers disemployed in large numbers in the periodic crises and recessions which are characteristic of capitalist development. On the other hand, generous welfare programs may attract too many people into the fringes of the labor market from outside capitalist production, and weaken the competitive pressure on wages by providing a tolerable alternative to work.

The Marxist basis for a positive theory of the levels of welfare support and unemployment compensation is the notion that these policies are determined primarily by a struggle over the desirable tightness of the labor market among different classes and class fractions. This theory would look in a very different direction from theories that focus on measures of income distribution or concepts of distributive justice for the determinants of levels of welfare programs. It would look for ways in which welfare and unemployment compensation vary in different stages of the business cycle and in response to changes in the availability of pools of reserve labor.

Certain common themes appear in these Marxist analyses of different areas of State expenditure. In each case the occasion for State expenditure arises where the accumulation and concentration of capital have run into contradictions which the system of competitive capital cannot overcome. Welfare relief and unemployment compensation emerge as central State activities only when the process of capitalist expansion has created a class of unemployed and semiemployed workers as an incident in the alternate exhaustion and replenishment of pools of reserve labor. As capitalism comes to require workers with differentiated skills and particular ideological stances, general public schooling becomes an issue for State action. The military–diplomatic apparatus begins to protect property and manage markets on a world scale at a point when capital itself has developed to a world scale and is so concentrated that the profitability of particular capitals has a direct relation to these large political–economic questions.

These areas of State expenditure can be seen as aspects of monopoly capital, understood as the stage of accumulation and concentration of capital where particular capitals are so large and the capitalist system so pervasive that the profitability of production no longer can be assured by the spontaneous action of the market and the conditions created by other modes of production. At this stage the boundary conditions for profitable production, the pool of reserve labor, the stability of market demand, the attitudes of workers, and so on, become a central concern of the State.

4. The State in Advanced Capitalist Society

The object of Marxist work on the determinants of State expenditure is not to give a single theoretical account of government or public spending in an ahistorical sense, but to arrive at an explanation of the shape and growth of State activities in advanced capitalist society. In this perspective a major problem is to explain the growth of the State sector in most capitalist countries over the last seventy years.[7] This fact cannot be seen as an accident, nor as a policy choice (or mistake) but must be explained in relation to changes in the scale and organization of capitalist production on a world scale. What pressures arising from the dynamics of accumulation have created this rapid relative growth of the State? Have these pressures relented at this point in capitalist development or will they continue to operate? What contradictions are inherent in this rapid growth of the State, and how do they revise the terms on which political and economic class struggle will take place?

Though it is common in political and economic debate to refer to the growth of the State as a tendency toward socialism, most Marxist writers do not identify State intervention in the market per se as a step toward socialism. From a Marxist perspective the critical question is the nature of class dominance or hegemony in a society, not the formal relations between the State and capital.[8] A strong tendency in the Marxist tradition is to see State power and the conquest of State power as the means by which the working class can carry class struggle to the point of destroying capitalist relations of production, but the important element in this vision is working class control over State power, not the raw fact of State intervention in production. The expansion of State power itself does not necessarily strengthen the working class, and can often weaken it if State power expands under the firm control of the capitalists.

Working-class movements may see an expansion of State power as a means to their end of altering the social relations of production. But all capitalists see some use of State power as necessary for the maintenance of capitalist relations of production, and certain strata or fractions of the capitalist class may want a decisive increase in State power at certain historical junctures as a means to their particular class aims.

There is evidence suggesting, for example, that in the late nineteenth and early twentieth centuries large U.S. firms in certain sectors, especially transportation, saw State intervention in the form of regulation as a way of stabilizing cartel-like arrangements in those sectors, and exerted themselves to achieve this growth of State intervention.[9] Since the Second World War we have seen in almost every major capitalist country pressures from large capital operating on a national or international scale of the State to take responsibility for regulating labor supply, smoothing out cyclicality of demand, and coordinating the competitive efforts of national capitals on the world market. Each of these examples shows the State undertaking to manage a problem that emerges for a particular segment of capital in the course of capitalist development.

The Marxist analysis suggests two explanations for the modern expansion of the State. The first locates the growth of the State in relation to the concentration and centralization of capital and to conflicts between larger and smaller capitals over State policies which favor the profitability of one or the other. The second links the growth of the State to the growing severity of capitalist crisis in advanced capitalism and the tendency for the State to intervene to secure the basic conditions for the continued viability of capitalism as a system. Both of these approaches suggest that the determinants of the growth of the State are to be sought in the dynamics of capitalist accumulation itself.

The first line of discussion begins with the observation that capital accumulates unevenly, with a few large and many small capitals coexisting at any time. One of the advantages large capitals have is that for them certain necessary conditions of production, like labor supply, market for output, financing of working capital, and supplies of raw materials emerge as global, strategic problems which they can use State policies and other nonmarket means to manage. Thus in the structure of accumulation a certain conflict between capitals is built-in, so to speak, with some capitals eager to support certain types of State intervention and expenditure as a way of gaining a competitive advantage.

There are segments of capital which will support State expenditures to regulate labor supply (including education, welfare, and unemployment compensation programs), to ensure stable political and social environments for foreign investment, and to secure markets and access to raw materials. Large capital may be liberal in U.S. political terms, or even "statist," supporting an active foreign policy and a strong military establishment. These fractions of capital are not sorry to see the State grow domestically so long as that growth tends to unify and homogenize national and international markets for labor and produced commodities.

One explanation for the growth of the State, then, is the pressure brought on it to strengthen the conditions of existence of large and centralized capitals. This type of State growth is not socialist in a Marxist sense, since it is shaped not by the emergent needs of society as a whole, nor even by the aims of the working class, but by the strategic imperatives of profitability for large concentrations of capital.

The Marxist analysis also explains the growth of the State in advanced capitalist society as a response to crises of the capitalist system as a whole which are rooted in the struggle between capitalists and workers.[10] As these crises became more and more severe during the 1930s and 1940s with the Great Depression and the Second World War, the State began to come under pressure to prevent or alleviate collapses of market demand by expanding its own spending. This argument suggests that those contradictions, like an imbalance between accumulation and labor supply, or an overly competitive structure of capital, which produced depressions without State intervention now produce pressures and conflicts over State economic policy. For instance, there may be a contradiction inherent in the Keynesian policy of managing aggregate demand so as to maintain low levels of unemployment if long periods of low unemployment strengthen labor's bargaining position and lead to an erosion of profits.[11] This in turn, though it may not produce a major recession or depression as in the past, creates a struggle at a political level over how vigorous the State should be in reducing unemployment, how long it should allow recessions to continue and so on.

The recent phenomenon of chronic and sometimes accelerating inflation of money prices of commodities is in some Marxist analyses linked to the emerging monopoly power of big capital and the State's attempts to manage labor markets and aggregate demand in the context of this concentration of capital. The mechanisms that explain this linkage have not been worked out very precisely in the Marxist literature. A major lacuna is the lack of a systematic, generally agreed-upon theory of the formation of money wages and money prices in capitalist production when the link between the credit system, including the State's own credit, and commodity money, like gold, have become vestigial.[12]

Despite the lack of a precise account of the mechanism of money wage and price determination the Marxist literature does suggest that a systematic result of the State's attempts to regulate the labor market will be pressures on the State to intervene in the process of money wage and price setting as well. The crisis of capitalism, though its manifestations as a decline in aggregate demand and explosive growth of unemployment have been to some degree suppressed by State policies, re-emerges as a struggle over the level of real incomes (often explicitly over a State incomes policy), a conflict in which the class struggle that produced the crisis to begin with shows itself openly.

To sum up, this second line of Marxist analysis sees the growth of the State in the last seventy years as fundamentally determined by the fact that capitalist crisis has become the dominant social problem in advanced capitalist countries. The agenda for State action thus has come to include the global management of the conditions for profitable capitalist production. The State grows as it responds to pressures to secure first one, then another of these contradictory conditions.

It seems only reasonable to me, however, to correct these views which emphasize the problems of capital as a whole or of certain fractions of capital as determinants of State policy, by remembering that State policy is also a locus of class conflict. In the areas we have discussed, welfare and unemployment policy, for instance, there is an inevitably ambiguous thrust of policy in class terms. Welfare programs, for example, serve to strengthen workers' bargaining power in certain situations as well as to regulate the pressures on the labor market. The demand for State support of education reflects working-class aspirations as well as capitalist manipulation. In the past forty years it has been workers, through unions and left-wing political parties who have put forward most of the major reforms and innovations in State policy. It appears to me that workers have put forward these proposals, for social insurance, socialized medicine, public housing, public education, and so forth, as attempts to achieve within the capitalist State some of the goals of socialism. But these reforms have always been adopted as partial measures since they have not touched the social relations of production themselves, and as partial measures have been shaped and administered so as to strengthen the reproduction of the fundamental social relations of capitalism. It seems very important, however, to recognize the element of class struggle in the formation of capitalist State policy, rather than sliding into the one-sided view that the capitalist State is "nothing but" the capitalist class getting its way by other means than its direct control over production. This is important even if we also recognize that without an alteration of the underlying social relations of production the hegemony of capital will in almost every case express itself by blunting partial reforms and shaping them for its own ends.

Marxist economic theory, because it represents the capitalist system of production as a specific, historically limited system which has particular concrete preconditions for its reproduction, can see systematic determinations for phenomena like the growth of the State. But to achieve convincing explanation Marxist theory faces two major hurdles. First, at point after point, clear models of the mechanisms through which relations of production influence other aspects of economic life (clear models of the operation of money, labor markets, price formation, political influence, for example) are lacking. This leaves important gaps in the general arguments, since very often the thrust of an explanation depends critically on the details of some mechanism. It is impossible for instance to sustain an argument that the state creates recessions to discipline the labor force without a model of how the State can in fact control aggregate demand, and an understanding of the limits of that control. If we are to have convincing accounts of the links between production and State policy, we need a better understanding of the modern dynamics of accumulation. What is the relative importance of investment in the third world and in advanced capitalist countries? What are the relations between big and small capital and how are they expressed? Only on the basis of such an improved understanding can we feel secure about such historical explanations.

On the basis of Marxist analysis we would expect pressures for the growth of State expenditure and regulation to increase. The form of this enlarged State will, in this view, depend on the class relations that lie beneath the politics. We can imagine strong states very much under the thumb of large capital where the content of planning and state activity is the strengthening of national capital in competition on a world scale and the suppression of militant working-class movements. We can also imagine enlarged States where capital has had to concede much ground to militant working-class organizations and where the content of State planning is the compromising of vigorous class struggle, in which working-class interests play an important part. It seems unlikely on the basis of the Marxist analysis that there will be a dismantling of the State apparatus on a large scale, or a return to reliance on the market as the chief regulator of economic life. . . .

6. Conclusion

To construct an analysis of State expenditure on Marxist foundations is above all to locate the modern State historically in the specific context of capitalist development. The accumulation of capital entails changes in the qualitative structure as well as the scale of capitalist production. At each stage the accumulation of capital threatens to destroy certain of the conditions for the reproduction of capitalism as a system, and the political mechanisms of the modern State come under pressure to do something about the resulting problems.

When we constitute the problems of State expenditures in these terms we can proceed in a methodologically straightforward way to attack them. We must first identify and understand the dynamic of the accumulation process that produce the contradiction in question (for example, the processes by which reserves of labor are exhausted and replenished in the case of unemployment compensation). This establishes the space within which the State must act. In the course of grounding the State's policy in the specific dynamics of the accumulation process we will also begin to identify the pressures and limitations on State action that will shape the final outcome (for example, the effects unemployment compensation will have on competition on the labor market).

We can from the Marxist perspective know the most important truths about the modern State and its spending. The State is a human creation, but not the creation of everyone interacting equally. People come to the political process already partly determined by their roles in production. They come not as abstract individuals but as workers or capitalists. They come not as equals, but burdened by the asymmetries and inequalities reproduced by capitalist production itself. To understand the modern State we must see it in the context of these class relations, shaped by the struggles of classes, not by an abstract logic of collective choice. The constituency of the modern State is not a collection of abstract individuals, but classes and class fractions created and re-created by capitalist relations of production. It is not surprising or mysterious when we understand these things that States should, for instance, more consistently and tenaciously pursue the health of capitalist production than the health of their people.

Knowledge of these basic facts also forces us to recognize how much we don't know about the modern State. The ways in which contradictory pressures are in the end resolved into a State policy need concrete study. In only a few cases do we have a very exact idea of the roles of ideology, extortion and coercion in this resolution.

Above all it is our rudimentary image of the world of capital itself that limits our knowledge of the State and State spending. The only adequate knowledge of an unevenly developed phenomenon is concrete knowledge; averages or typical cases give inevitably distorted representations of such phenomena. What is the exact structure of capital in terms of size, competition and concentration? How are large and small capitals linked to each other in production and exchange? On what lines do the conflict between these fractions of capital emerge most sharply? A more exact and textured knowledge of the structure and dynamics of capital will at each step clarify and deepen our understanding of the State and its spending.

NOTES

Note: An earlier version of this paper was presented to the International Seminar on Public Economics in Namur, Belgium in November, 1976, where I benefited from the ensuing discussion and particularly the comments of R. A. Musgrave and James Buchanan. I would like to thank Professor Baba, Jens Christiansen, Suzanne de Brunhoff, Helene Foley, Don Harris, Deborah Milenkovitch, Bridget O'Laughlin, A. M. Thompson III, the Political Economy Seminar at Stanford University, and an anonymous referee of this journal for help and comments on this work. The responsibility for errors of fact, argument, and judgment remain with me.

1. An extended discussion of the problems mentioned in the last two paragraphs at a high level of abstraction can be found in Althusser (1970).
2. Miliband (1969) discusses these questions in considerable detail.
3. See Althusser (1971) for an extraordinary outline of the theory of ideology.
4. More complete discussions of the relation of military spending to capitalist production can be found in Baran and Sweezy (1966), Mattick (1969), O'Connor (1973).
5. See Althusser (1971) and Bowles and Gintis (1976) on education in advanced capitalist society.
6. For more complete discussions of welfare and unemployment compensation programs, see O'Connor (1973) and de Brunhoff (1976).
7. This problem is a central theme in Baran and Sweezy (1966), de Brunhoff (1976), Mattick (1969) and O'Connor (1973).
8. This point is explained very clearly in Sweezy and Bettelheim (1971).
9. See Kolko (1963).
10. Baran and Sweezy (1966), de Brunhoff (1976), Mattick (1969), and O'Connor (1973) all develop this argument.
11. See Boddy and Crotty (1975) and Kalecki (1971).
12. The best discussions of these monetary questions from a Marxist point of view known to me is de Brunhoff (1973).

REFERENCES

Althusser, L., 1970, For Marx (Vintage Books, New York).

Althusser, L., 1971, Ideology and ideological State apparatuses, in: Lenin and philosophy (Monthly Review Press, New York).

Baran, P., and P. Sweezy, 1966, Monopoly capital (Monthly Review Press, New York).

Boddy, R., and J. Crotty, 1975, Class conflict and macro-policy: The political business cycle, Review of Radical Political Economics 7(1), 1–19.

Bowles, S., and H. Gintis, 1976, Schooling in capitalist America (Basic Books, New York).

de Brunhoff, S., 1976, Etat et capital (Maspero, Paris).

de Brunhoff, S., 1973, La Monnaie chez Marx (Editions Sociales, Paris) (English translation: Marx on money (Urizen Press, New York) 1976).

Kolko, G., 1963, The triumph of conversatism: A reinterpretation of American history, 1900–1916 (Free Press of Glencoe, New York).

Kalecki, M., 1971, Selected essays on the dynamics of the capitalist economy (Cambridge University Press, New York).

Mattick, P., 1969, Marx and Keynes: The limits of the mixed economy (Porter Sargent, Boston).

Miliband, R., 1969, The State in capitalist society (Basic Books, New York).

O'Connor, J., 1973, The fiscal crisis of the State (St. Martin's Press, New York).

San Francisco Bay Area Kapitalistate Group, 1975. The fiscal crisis of the State: A review. Kapitalistate 3, 149–57.

Sweezy, P., and C. Bettelheim, 1971. On the transition to socialism (Monthly Review Press, New York).

Economics of the Political Process

One explanation of the expansion of public sector economics is that economists have turned to applying their box of tools to the political process. Surprisingly, a public choice system (based on one person, one vote) does not often act like the private market system (based on one dollar, one vote). A perfectly competitive market can reach a unique, Pareto-efficient equilibrium, yet if the same market participants vote in a political system, there is no guarantee of either uniqueness or Pareto efficiency.

Economists are also intrigued by the influence of the political process on the implementation of economic policy recommendations. For instance, sometimes efficient policy recommendations are not adopted. Also, policies that are adopted often do not perform as desired. Therefore, some of the readings in this section reflect the efforts of economists to (1) understand the influence of the political process, and (2) assess the effectiveness of past government tax and expenditure programs in meeting the programs' goals.

Collective Decision Making

The following three selections illustrate how voting systems can fail to be efficient and discuss the only circumstances under which a voting system is guaranteed to reach unique Pareto efficient outcomes.

SELECTION 22

LYNN ARTHUR STEEN

Election Mathematics: Do All Those Numbers Mean What They Say?

Using illustrations drawn from U.S. presidential campaigns, Lynn
Steen describes the contradictions or irrationalities inherent in a
variety of voting schemes. It is certain that collective decision
making is not analogous to individual decision making. Each
individual voter may be rational, with decisive and transitive
preferences, but as Steen shows, there is no guarantee that a voting
mechanism that aggregates individual preferences will be decisive
or transitive. Steen begins with a discussion of the possible
consequences of using direct majority rule to choose among more
than two candidates or policies. He then contrasts plurality voting
with runoff voting, point voting, and approval voting.

QUESTIONS TO GUIDE THE READING

1. In general, what type of presidential candidate do you believe
   would be in favor of a two-party system? Who would support
   the right of third-party candidacy?
2. How is it possible for minorities to win under direct majority
   rule?
3. What might be the consequences of sophisticated voting?
4. In Steen's example, why do the results of approval voting differ
   from those of plurality voting and point voting?

Lynn A. Steen, "Election Mathematics: Do All Those Numbers Mean What They Say?" as published in *Scientific American*, Vol. 243 (Oct. 1980), 16–26B. Reprinted by permission of the
author.

Lynn A. Steen is Professor of Mathematics at St. Olaf College.

Over the past year the prospect of a three-way race for president of the United States has focused public attention on the importance of strategies for voting and on the special vagaries of the electoral college. Although the complications imposed by the electoral college are unique to presidential elections, other uncertainties imposed by three-way contests for public office are not. When the public must choose among more than two alternatives, the task of making the choice is frustratingly difficult. The source of both the difficulties and the possible solutions is to be found in the little-known mathematical theory of elections.

The social contract of a democracy depends in an obvious and fundamental way on a simple mathematical concept, namely the concept of a majority. Barring the unlikely event of a tie, in any dichotomous ballot one side or the other must receive more than half of the votes. When there are three or more choices of approximately equal strength, however, it is unlikely that such a ballot will yield a majority decision. It is primarily for this reason that many people believe the two-party system is essential to the stability of democracy in the U.S., even though that system is neither mandated nor recognized by the Constitution.

Mathematical theory and political idealism notwithstanding, quite often the public does face a choice among three or more significant alternatives. The same problem that this year appeared as Carter v. Reagan v. Anderson has developed in other years. Such multiple-candidate contests are difficult to resolve fairly if there is no clear-cut majority, but they can easily arise in any free election. Indeed, it follows from some simple mathematics that there are practically no positions candidates in a two-way contest can take that are invulnerable to attack by a third or a fourth candidate.

If each issue in a two-candidate election is represented by a rating of voter preference on a one-dimensional scale, then regardless of the distribution of attitudes among the voters the optimal position for each candidate is the median: the point that divides the electorate into two camps of equal size. The same is true whether public opinion is distributed normally (so that the graph of position v. number of supporters has a single, centered hump), is split bimodally (so that the graph has two approximately equal humps), is skewed sharply to one side or is divided in a highly irregular way. An example of each of these distributions, with the median marked, is given in the accompanying illustration [page 310].

Consider a two-candidate contest in which one candidate adopts a position a little to the left of the median and the other candidate begins with a position at about the middle of the right half of the population. This would be typical of a centrist candidate C running against a moderate right-wing candidate R. In this case it is reasonable to assume that as far as this particular issue is concerned the voters whose preference lies to the left of the position held by the centrist candidate C will favor C, the voters whose preference lies to the right of candidate R will favor R, and the voters whose preference lies in between will be divided about evenly between the two

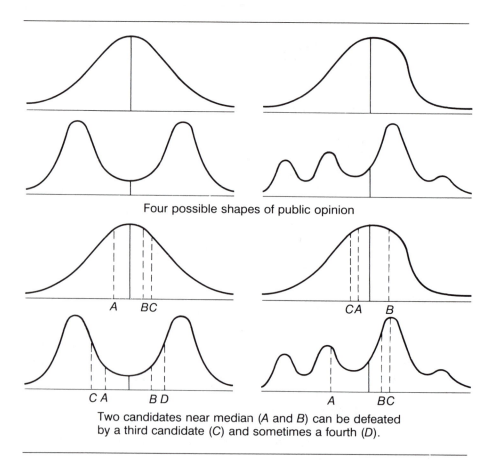

Four possible shapes of public opinion

Two candidates near median (*A* and *B*) can be defeated
by a third candidate (*C*) and sometimes a fourth (*D*).

candidates. Under these circumstances, in a preelection poll the centrist candidate would receive a majority of the votes.

The only way for candidate *R* to improve his standing in the poll (on this single issue) is to shift his position toward the middle of the distribution, to ensure that more voters will be to his right. Moving toward the center, or to the left, will always be advantageous for the right-wing candidate. Similarly, a left-leaning candidate can improve his standing with the voters by moving toward the center, or to the right. The median position is the only one that cannot be improved on by further shifting on the part of either candidate.

There is, of course, nothing very novel about this analysis. It is part of our common experience in presidential politics. Candidates representing the right or the left tend to begin distinctly to the right or to the left and then move progressively closer to the center as they attempt to appeal to a greater number of voters. The appeal of the median position in a two-candidate contest, however, is precisely what makes such a contest vulnerable to assault from either side by a third or a fourth candidate. In any contest with two candidates near the center a third candidate entering on the left or the right can always gain a plurality. Indeed, for practically any distribution of the electorate there are no positions in a two-candidate contest where at least one of the candidates cannot be beaten by a third. As is shown in the [figure on page 310], there is always a place along the one-dimensional continuum where a new candidate can position himself to displace one or more nearby candidates.

A single issue rarely plays a deciding role in an election. Hence election analyses based on single issues are not very helpful, unless they can be combined to show how to design a platform that will ensure a candidate's election. Shaping a winning platform is a complex business, however, because it is possible for a platform consisting entirely of winning, or majority, planks to be defeated. The reverse side of the coin is that a majority platform can be constructed from minority planks. Hence a majority can be formed from a coalition of minorities.

To see how this paradox can arise consider the simplest possible case: a ballot to decide two unrelated, dichotomous issues, represented by resolutions A and B. In this case the voters actually have four options:

I. Approve A and B.

II. Approve A and defeat B.

III. Defeat A and approve B.

IV. Defeat A and B.

The voters who favor both A and B would choose option I as their first choice, option IV as their fourth choice and option II as their second or third choice, depending on whether they feel more strongly about A or about B. The voters who favor A but object to B might rank the four options in the order II, I, IV, and III (or II, IV, I, and III). In general each voter will have a preference ranking for one of the $4 \times 3 \times 2 \times 1$, or 24, possible permutations of the four available options. (The rankings are by no means equally likely; it would be hard to imagine circumstances under which many people would rank the options in the order of preference I, IV, II, III.)

Now, for the sake of simplicity suppose 500 voters (say at a party convention) are divided into three caucuses as follows: caucus X, with 150 votes, ranks the four options in the order I, II, III, IV; caucus Y, with 150 votes, ranks them II, IV, I, III, and caucus Z, with 200 votes, ranks them III, IV, I, II. In this case caucuses X and Y, with 300 votes, favor the approval of resolution A, whereas caucuses X and Z, with 350 votes, favor the approval of resolution B. Because there are different voters making up these majorities, however, the platform consisting of the planks "Approve A" and "Approve B" will be defeated by the 350-vote block of caucuses Y and Z!

This surprising phenomenon is a special case of the well-known anomaly of cyclic majorities: If three voters respectively prefer A to B to C, B to C to A, and C to A to B, then any candidate can be defeated by some other candidate by a vote of two to one in a two-candidate contest. When the

Three caucuses voting on two platform planks create cyclic majorities

Options

     I. Approve resolutions A and B.

     II. Approve resolution A and defeat resolution B.

     III. Defeat resolution A and approve resolution B.

     IV. Defeat resolutions A and B.

Caucus	Policy	Votes	Order of Preference
X	Favors A strongly and favors B mildly	150	I, II, III, IV
Y	Opposes B strongly and favors A mildly	150	II, IV, I, III
Z	Opposes A strongly and favors B mildly	200	III, IV, I, II

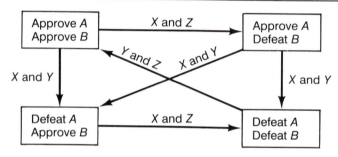

issues in an election create cyclic majorities, no set of positions on the issues is invulnerable to assault by a new coalition of minorities, another factor that encourages third- and fourth-party candidates.

The diagram above shows how the four options from which party planks in the example must be constructed create a variety of cyclic majorities, thereby explaining how a platform consisting of majority planks can represent the will of only a minority. The arrows joining various platforms depict voting dominance: the platform to which an arrow points will always lose to the platform at which the arrow originates in a dichotomous contest. The winning caucuses in each case appear beside the corresponding arrow. As this distribution demonstrates, any possible platform can be defeated by some other platform, and so a real convention whose divisions resemble the ones given in this example could become mired in an unending sequence of platform motions, with each motion defeating the one before.

The phenomenon of cyclic majorities is also responsible for the most famous election paradox, Kenneth J. Arrow's 1951 proof that certain generally accepted desiderata for voting schemes are logically inconsistent. If there are only two candidates, no problems arise. If three or more candidates appear on a single ballot, however, chaos reigns.

There are diverse schemes other than plurality voting for determining the winner in an election. Many were suggested by 18th-century scholars concerned about implementing the democratic ideals of the French Revolution. Although some of these proposals are so complex as to be completely impractical, several are still in common use, in particular the method of assigning points that reflect degrees of preference to the candidates in a contest (where the candidate receiving the most points is the winner) and various methods of holding runoff elections. Yet as Arrow has shown, none of these schemes—indeed, no method other than a rational benevolent dictatorship—satisfies such commonsense rules as: If A is preferred to B, and B is preferred to C, then A should be preferred to C. Cyclic majorities reduce all voting schemes to unpredictable mystery. (For a discussion of Arrow's proof see *Scientific American*, October, 1974.)

Another important problem with voting in three-option contests is that in many circumstances a vote for the candidate a person prefers most will increase the likelihood that the candidate he prefers least will be elected. (This dilemma was the one often seen in Anderson's candidacy. Many voters who preferred Anderson to Carter and Carter to Reagan believed most Anderson votes would be at Carter's expense.) The anomaly frequently leads thoughtful voters to what is called (depending on a voter's point of view) insincere or sophisticated voting.

If sophisticated voting is widely practiced, it can lead to a state of serious confusion where no one votes for his first choice, and so the public will is effectively camouflaged. An Anderson backer for whom Carter was a second choice might have voted for Carter instead of for Anderson in order to prevent the election of Reagan. If there were enough Anderson backers who reasoned this way, of course, some Reagan supporters might have begun to support Anderson to prevent Carter's reelection. The process of second-guessing the voting strategies of other segments of the electorate can quickly lead to an absurd hierarchy of insincerity in which the votes cast fail to reflect real preferences. Such a process, which it should be added is more a part of game theory than of classical voting theory, rarely gives a legitimate mandate to the victor.

Arrow's theorem shows there is no "perfect" voting scheme for multi-candidate elections. The procedure known as approval voting, however, manages to reflect a popular will without inducing anyone to vote insincerely. In approval voting each voter marks on the ballot every candidate who meets with his approval, and the candidate who receives the most votes of approval is the winner.

With this system it is never to a voter's advantage to withhold a vote for his first choice while voting for a less preferred candidate. Indeed, if most candidates seem to have an equal chance of winning, a rational voter should vote for all the candidates he believes are above the average of those running. To vote for more candidates would give unnecessary support to individuals the voter does not endorse, whereas to vote for fewer candidates (say to vote only for one's first choice) is to withhold support from an acceptable compromise candidate and to risk victory by an unacceptable candidate.

Comparison of voting methods for a three-way race

Order of preference	Total votes	Approval votes	
		First choice	First and second choices
A, B, C	30	20	10
A, C, B	5	5	0
B, A, C	20	10	10
B, C, A	5	5	5
C, A, B	10	5	5
C, B, A	30	20	10
Total	100	65	35

Plurality voting	Runoff voting	Point voting	Approval voting
A 35	A 35 + 20 = 55	A 35 (3) + 30 (2) + 35 = 200	A 25 + 10 + 15 = 50
B 25	C 40 + 5 = 45	B 25 (3) + 60 (2) + 15 = 210	B 15 + 10 + 20 = 45
C 40		C 40 (3) + 10 (2) + 50 = 190	C 25 + 15 + 0 = 40

Steven J. Brams, professor of politics at New York University, has described approval voting with the phrase "One man, *n* votes." It is an apt description because approval voting is merely a way of letting a person cast as many votes as he wishes, one for each acceptable candidate. It is easy to count votes that have been cast under this system, and no runoff elections are needed. For both theoretical and practical reasons approval voting is a good compromise between the single-vote ballot that encourages insincerity and the complete preference ordering whose complexity renders it useless in any practical situation.

The illustration above shows how approval voting might compare with plurality voting, runoff voting and point voting in an entirely hypothetical three-way contest. The number of voters supporting each of the six possible rankings of candidates are listed in the column "total votes," and since C would receive the largest block of first-choice votes, he would win in a plurality contest. In a runoff election B would be eliminated, and A would pick up enough second-choice votes (from those who had first voted for B) to defeat C by 55 votes to 45. In the simplest system of point voting first choices are assigned three points, second choices two points and third choices one point. Because of the large number of voters (60) for whom B is the second choice, with this voting scheme B, who was eliminated in the runoff, would be the winner.

The results of approval voting depend on whether voters find only their top choice acceptable or whether they could accept some other choices as well. (Because there are only three candidates in this example it is assumed that no one votes for all three; such a vote is legal, but it would be wasted since it would raise each candidate's total by the same amount.) In this case, with 65 voters approving only their first choice, A would receive 50 votes of approval and win the election. If some voters choose to approve two of the three candidates, however, *B* stands to gain most because of the large number of people who rank him as their second choice. With approval voting a shift in the number of candidates meeting the approval of even a small number of voters can easily change the outcome of the election. Hence the implementation of this voting scheme would necessitate a transformation of campaign strategies, from trying to convince voters that a candidate is the best choice to trying to convince them that he is acceptable. . . .

Elections will always remain a matter of passion more than of logic, based on belief more than on reason. As these examples demonstrate, however, the mathematics of elections can have subtle and unexpected consequences. As in many other realms of human experience, naive expectations can be shattered by simple mathematical structures disguised as paradoxes and anomalies. . . .

SELECTION 23

ALLAN FELDMAN

Manipulating Voting Procedures

Democratic governments, most voters would agree, should be egalitarian. No one individual or set of individuals is supposed to be able to control the outcomes of a voting rule. Allan Feldman asserts, however, that egalitarianism cannot be guaranteed: the only voting rule (or social decision function) that is immune to manipulation is a dictatorship. After surveying the research that led to this surprising result, Feldman proceeds to show how preferences can be misrepresented in order to manipulate, among others, plurality voting, majority voting, and approval voting.

QUESTIONS TO GUIDE THE READING

1. Why does the possibility of cycles imply that direct majority rule is an incomplete, i.e., insufficiently decisive, voting scheme?
2. Under what circumstances would you feel comfortable accepting a voting scheme that is "only intended for honest men," as de Borda asserted about his method of marks?
3. How does a social welfare function (SWF) differ from a social decision function (SDF)?
4. What constitutes a satisfactory social decision function?
5. How do approval voting and the random mixed decision scheme violate the technical definition of a social decision function? Why is it possible to conclude that neither is manipulable?
6. How does the notion of a dictatorial SDF differ from the everyday usage of the term *dictatorship*?

I. Introduction

The French Enlightment left Western Civilization with, among other things, the first systematic analyses of the properties of elections. These analyses grew out of the then blossoming interest in democratic institutions and the

Allan Feldman, "Manipulating Voting Procedures," *Economic Inquiry* 27 (July 1979), 452-74. Reprinted by permission of the author and the publisher.

Allan Feldman is Associate Professor of Economics at Brown University.

democratic or egalitarian state. However, French political philosophers, particularly Rousseau, de Borda, and Condorcet, may have raised as many questions as they answered about the nature of elections as expressions of the general will. The questions they raised are with us still, because, unfortunately, elections are logically imperfect. The purpose of this paper is to discuss in a relatively nontechnical way the nature of logical imperfections of elections.

Let us begin near the beginning, with the Marquis de Condorcet (1743–1794). (For a detailed exposition of Condorcet's theory, as well as most other historically important voting theories, see Duncan Black (1958).) In the *Essai sur l'Application de l'Analyse à la Probabilité des Decisions Rendues à la Pluralité des Voix* (Paris, 1785) he set out to solve the following problem in probability theory: A jury is to decide, by voting, between two alternatives A and B (which might be, say, the guilt or innocence of a defendant). One alternative is right, and the other is wrong. The members of the jury, however, are imperfect. When they vote they may err. Given particular probabilities of each member's voting correctly or incorrectly, what is the probability that the jury's decision is right? This is not difficult to calculate; naturally it depends on the numbers of jury members voting for A and B. However, the analysis becomes more complicated when there are three (or more) alternatives, say, A, B, and C. Again, one alternative is right, and the others are wrong. If votes are taken by the jury between pairs of alternatives, what is the probability that the jury's decision is correct? The question is meaningful when the voting results are consistent, for example, if A gets more votes than B in a contest between the two, if B gets more votes than C in a contest between those two, and if A gets more votes than C in a contest between those two. In this case the jury's decision is A, and the probability that this decision is right can be calculated in a straightforward manner.

However, there are cases in which the voting between pairs of alternatives *cycles*. In such cases there do exist straightforward ways to calculate the probabilities of correctness of each of the alternatives, but these might all be distressingly small. In fact, the cycling cases prompted Condorcet to switch from obvious probability calculations to a somewhat an *ad hoc* judgment, the essence of which is this: if an alternative X is decisively defeated by another alternative Y, X cannot be the right alternative. This judgment is not terribly satisfactory and will not play an important role in what follows. However, the cycling or "paradoxical" cases of Condorcet still provide the simplest examples of voting imperfections, so we turn to one now:

Assume there are seven voters of three types, and three alternatives, A, B, and C. There are three type one voters, and each type one voter prefers A to B to C. There are two type two voters, each of whom prefers B to C to A. There are two type three voters, each of whom prefers C to A to B. These assumptions are illustrated below:

		Type 1	Type 2	Type 3
Order	↑	A	B	C
of		B	C	A
Preference		C	A	B
		(3 voters)	(2 voters)	(2 voters)

In a vote between A and B, A wins, five votes (from type 1 and 3 voters) to two (from type 2 voters). In a vote between B and C, B gets five votes (from type 1 and 2 voters) and C gets two (from type 3 voters). In a vote between A and C, however, C gets four votes (from type 2 and 3 voters) and A gets three (from type 1 voters). Thus there is a cycle in the voting results: A defeats B, B defeats C, but C defeats A. In terms of the jury problem, a cyclical structure like this might result in unacceptably small (correctly calculated) probabilities of rightness for *every* alternative. Condorcet's *ad hoc* judgment would be to discard B and C, since each of these is defeated five to two, while A is (at worst) defeated four to three.

But if this judgment strikes us as unacceptably arbitrary, or if the probability analysis is fundamentally unacceptable because a "correct" choice is unknown, unknowable and/or non-existent, then *majority voting between pairs fails as a method for making social choices.*

There are, however, other methods. Jean-Charles de Borda (1733–1799) published his *Memoire sur les Élections au Scrutin* (see De Grazia (1953)) four years before Condorcet's *Essai.* In it de Borda developed a "method of marks." Each elector ranks the alternatives according to his order of preference (ignoring the possibility of ties). If there are k alternatives, an elector's first choice is assigned k points, his second $k-1$ points, and so on down to his last choice, which is assigned one point. The total vote for an alternative is the sum of the points assigned it by the various electors, and the winner (barring ties) is the alternative with the highest sum.

For the example above, the de Borda votes are:

$$3 \times 3 + 2 \times 1 + 2 \times 2 = 15 \text{ for A}$$
$$3 \times 2 + 2 \times 3 + 2 \times 1 = 14 \text{ for B}$$
$$3 \times 1 + 2 \times 2 + 2 \times 3 = 13 \text{ for C}$$

so A wins. Clearly, de Borda's method escapes the cycling possibility of pairwise majority voting, since the vote totals of the alternatives cannot cycle. However, the method *is* problematic.

The problem we focus on, which is relayed secondhand by Black (1958, p. 182) and noted by Satterthwaite (1975), is that of deliberate misrepresentation of their preferences by the electors. De Borda is quoted as saying "my scheme is only intended for honest men." To illustrate just how appropriate this remark is, we modify the example by adding two alternatives, D and E, and assuming the following structure of preferences:

Type 1	Type 2	Type 3
A	B	C
B	C	A
C	A	B
D	D	D
E	E	E
(3 voters)	(2 voters)	(2 voters)

Now the de Borda counts are:

$$3 \times 5 + 2 \times 3 + 2 \times 4 = 29 \text{ for A}$$
$$3 \times 4 + 2 \times 5 + 2 \times 3 = 28 \text{ for B}$$
$$3 \times 3 + 2 \times 4 + 2 \times 5 = 27 \text{ for C}$$
$$3 \times 2 + 2 \times 2 + 2 \times 2 = 14 \text{ for D}$$
$$3 \times 1 + 2 \times 1 + 2 \times 1 = 7 \text{ for E}$$

and A wins again. However, if one of the type 2 electors had falsely declared

$$
\begin{array}{c}
B \\
C \\
D \\
E \\
A \\
\end{array}
$$

as his preference ordering, the de Borda counts would have been 28 for B, 27 for C and 27 for A, and B would have won. This elector would have been better off than when he voted honestly: *the method provides a temptation for misrepresentation of preferences, or "strategic" voting.*

The possibility of manipulating the result of an election through the misrepresentation of preferences was not seriously considered by either de Borda or Condorcet. The Rev. C. L. Dodgson gave it some passing consideration almost a century later, especially in Chapter I, Section 5 of "A Discussion of the Various Methods of Procedure in Conducting Elections" (1873), reprinted in Black (1958). Dodgson's "method of marks" procedure (which differs from de Borda's) works as follows:

A certain number of marks is fixed, which each elector shall have at his disposal; he may assign them all to one candidate, or divide them among several candidates, in proportion of their eligibility; and the candidate who gets the greatest total of marks is the winner.

Dodgson writes the method would

> be absolutely perfect, if only each elector wished to do all in his power to secure *that candidate who should be the most generally acceptable*

(his italics); however,

> we are not sufficiently unselfish and public-spirited to give any hope of this result being attained.

Each elector would attempt to manipulate the results by assigning all of his votes to his own favorite candidate. In fact, this is not quite correct, as a voter might assign all his marks to his second choice if he thought his first could not win, but the method is obviously easily manipulable. Although Dodgson was aware of the potential of election manipulation through voter misrepresentation of preferences, there is no reason to believe he thought the problem inescapable, and the question lay dormant for most of yet another century.

The modern surge in interest in properties of voting procedures began in the late 1940s and early 1950s with two results, one modest and one profound. In 1948 Duncan Black "solved" the cyclical voting paradox by deriving conditions under which pairwise majority voting cannot cycle. However, this interesting result had limited ultimate bearing on the question of election manipulation, or strategic voting. (Limited bearing is not no bearing; see Blin and Satterthwaite (1976).) The profound result, which ultimately did bear heavily on the question of manipulability of elections, was Kenneth Arrow's 1951 impossibility theorem for preference aggregation procedures (Arrow (1963)).

At least in its early incarnations, Arrow's theorem was not technically about voting procedures. Voting procedures generate single alternatives (winners) from among sets of alternatives; Arrow's theorem is on its surface about procedures which generate orderings of the entire set of alternatives. To be more precise, we need to introduce some terminology. It is assumed that each person in society has an ordering, or ranking, of the set of alternatives. A specification of all people's orderings is called a *preference profile*. For example, in the Condorcet voting paradox example,

Type 1	Type 2	Type 3
A	B	C
B	C	A
C	A	B
(3 voters)	(2 voters)	(2 voters)

is a preference profile.

What we have called voting procedures are rules for transforming preference profiles into winners, or mappings from the set of possible preference profiles into the set of alternatives. For each preference profile the mapping produces a single winning alternative. Technically such a mapping is called a *social decision function,* or SDF. An SDF takes a preference profile, digests it, and produces a winning alternative. (A more generally defined SDF maps preference profiles into *sets* of winning alternatives, rather than single winners. See, e.g., Sen (1970) and (1977). This paper, however, is only about single-winner SDFs.) In contrast, the rules Arrow first studied, which are now called *social welfare functions* or SWFs, are rules for transforming preference profiles into social preference orderings or rankings. An SWF takes a preference profile, digests the list, and produces a social ordering. Obviously, there are procedures which can be viewed as either SWFs or as SDFs; de Borda voting is one.

The question Arrow asked is whether or not there exists a "satisfactory" SWF. The answer naturally depends on what is incorporated into criteria, which have been somewhat modified and refined over the years, were basically as follows:

1. The SWF must produce a social *ordering,* that is a complete reflexive and transitive social preference relation. This requirement excludes majority voting between pairs, which can give rise to (intransitive) cycles.

2. The SWF must always work, no matter what (finite) set of alternatives and preference profiles are given to it.

3. The SWF must respond positively to individual preferences. Loosely speaking, if x is socially preferred to y at the start, and x gains support, x must remain preferred to y at the end.

4. The SWF cannot be imposed. That is, if all individuals prefer x to y, the SWF must yield a social ordering which ranks x above y.

5. The SWF must show "independence of irrelevant alternatives." This means that the social ranking of x vis-à-vis y must depend *only* on individual rankings of x vis-à-vis y, not on the strengths of feelings, not on rankings of x vs. z or y vs. w or z vs. w, or any other such "irrelevancy." It is not difficult to see that de Borda's method violates independence, as does Dodgson's method of marks.

6. There must be no dictator, no single person whose individual preference ordering always defines the social preference ordering.

In his remarkable theorem, Arrow showed that *no "satisfactory" SWF exists.*

This negative answer might seem to shadow the search for a perfect voting procedure, or SDF. If there is no satisfactory way to aggregate individual preferences into a social preference ordering, perhaps there is no satisfactory way to aggregate individual preferences into an election winner. But the connection is really not so obvious. In its original form, Arrow's theorem is about generating social preference relations. Although the theorem can be, and has been, translated into a collection of theorems about what we would call generally defined SDFs (see, e.g., Sen (1977), pp. 71–75), there are hurdles in the translation. For example, it is not immediately clear that an SDF, a procedure which merely generates winners, can be adapted in some way that accommodates Arrow's requirements (1), (3), (4) or (5), or that those requirements can be adapted in a way which makes sense for SDFs. Moreover, it seems intuitively reasonable that generating single alternatives (winners) ought to be less of a *strain* on a decision procedure than generating whole lists, or orderings, of the alternatives, so if the latter is impossible the former might not be.

In fact, Arrow's theorem profoundly affected the search for an ideal SDF in three ways. First, its negative conclusion (there is *no* satisfactory SWF) generated an enormous intellectual storm, prompting some to try to show what Arrow did wrong, and others to show how the results could be generalized. Some of the storm's electricity leaked to the analysis of SDFs. Second, Arrow's theorem was actually used as a tool by some in proving the impossibility theorem concerning SDFs which will occupy us below (Gibbard (1973); and Schmeidler and Sonnenschein (forthcoming), proof I). Third, and perhaps most important, Arrow's theorem suggests two questions about SDFs which are analogous to the questions Arrow raised about SWFs: What is a "satisfactory" SDF? Does a "satisfactory" SDF exist?

What then is a "satisfactory" SDF? The remarks about manipulation of the de Borda and Dodgson rules suggests one possible criterion: An SDF ought to be immune to manipulation through the misrepresentation of preferences. Moreover, common sense suggests that a "satisfactory" SDF shouldn't be a dictatorship. These two requirements may not seem like much in light of the six occasionally complex requirements Arrow imposes on SWFs. In fact, however, several authors conjectured around 1960 (Dummett and Farquharson (1961) and Vickrey (1960)) that any nondictatorial voting procedure is manipulable, and finally in the 1970s Allan Gibbard (1973) and Mark Allen Satterthwaite (1973, 1975) independently proved this is the case. *If a satisfactory social decision function is one which is always immune to manipulation and which is nondictatorial, there is no satisfactory social decision function.*

This paper provides, in Section II, a number of detailed examples of manipulation. . . .

II. More Examples of Manipulability and Non-Manipulability

In this section several voting procedures are analyzed to discover whether or not they are manipulable. The first four procedures fit the technical definition for SDFs: each takes every voter's preference ordering (the preference profile) as inputs, and produces a single, certain winner as its output. The fifth is not an SDF; it takes every voter's set of acceptable or approved alternatives as inputs, and produces a certain winner as its output. (A voter's acknowledgement that "X, Y, and Z are acceptable, whereas W, U, V, . . . are unacceptable" is not quite the same thing as his declaring

Y
Z
X
U
W
•
•
•

as his preference ordering.) The sixth procedure is a lottery type mechanism. It takes every voter's preference ordering as its inputs, and produces *odds* for the alternatives as an output. The actual winner is then chosen randomly. Now to the examples:

The first procedure is the *plurality voting* rule. There are many candidates or alternatives. Each elector casts one vote for one candidate. The candidate with the highest total wins.

This is a common practice, typically used in U.S. party primary and general elections, for example. It also is common that a voter would like to see a candidate with an extreme or "pure" position win, but does not vote for the candidate because to do so would be tantamount to "throwing his vote away." To make one's vote *count,* one votes for a candidate who has a good chance of winning. However, the reluctance to throw one's vote away implies, in our terms, the desire to manipulate. For example, suppose there are three types of voters with the following preferences:

Type 1	Type 2	Type 3
A	B	C
B	C	B
C	A	A
(10 voters)	(9 voters)	(2 voters)

In a sincere election, type 3 voters cast their votes for C, but A wins the plurality. If type 3 voters anticipate this result, they can vote for B instead; that is, they can vote as if their preferences were

B
C
A

and by so doing guarantee that B, whom they prefer to A, is elected. Naturally, type 3 voters would be apt to deny that they are "manipulating" anything; they would say that they are simply not wasting their votes.

Let me note at this point that two voters are manipulating here. Manipulation by a group rather than a single individual is technically called *coalitional* manipulation, and this and several subsequent examples involve coalitional manipulation. In all these examples of coalitional manipulation, however, it is possible to make modifications to transform them into cases of manipulation by individuals. Unfortunately, the modified examples are slightly inelegant, as they involve tie votes and the resolution of ties by chairmen. (For example, in the case above, if there were 10 type 1 voters and 10 type 2 voters, and if one of the type 1 voters were chairman, then a sincere election would entail 10 votes for A, 10 for B, and 2 for C, and the chairman would break the A-B tie in favor of A. One type 3 voter could then manipulate the election by casting his vote for B, in which case A would get 10, B would get 11, and B would win.) The Gibbard-Satterthwaite theorem of Section III will establish that it is impossible to devise a nondictatorial SDF which is immune to manipulation by *individuals,* and it clearly follows that it is impossible to devise a nondictatorial SDF which is immune to manipulation by coalitions.

The second procedure to look at is *majority voting,* modified by the introduction of an agenda. Because of the possibility of cycling, majority voting between pairs may not give an unambiguous winner, unless the pairwise comparisons are restricted through the use of agendas or other devices. With the preference profile of the voting cycling example, that is,

Type 1	Type 2	Type 3
A	B	C
B	C	A
C	A	B
(3 voters)	(2 voters)	(2 voters)

it has already observed that sincere pairwise majority voting produces a cycle: A defeats B; B defeats C; but C defeats A. Now suppose that A is the "status quo," while B is a motion to change the status quo and C is an amended version of that motion. A typical committee practice (called Procedure α in Black (1958)) is to hold a vote between B and C (the motion and the amended version), and place the winner of that vote against A (the status quo). If voters are sincere, Procedure α produces B on the first round (the amendment is defeated) and A on the second (the bill is defeated).

But under these circumstances, type 2 voters could misrepresent their preferences as

C
B
A

If they did, C would win the first round (the amendment would pass) and then C would defeat A (the amended bill would be adopted). This outcome would be preferred by type 2 voters to A, so they could manipulate the procedure to their benefit.

A second committee practice (called Procedure β in Black (1958)) pits each motion against the status quo, and then selects from among those which defeat the status quo one which defeats the others. In our example, C defeats the status quo while B does not, so C is adopted, provided the voters vote sincerely. But under Procedure β, type 1 voters have an opportunity to gain by misrepresentation. If they vote as if their preferences were

B
A
C

both B and C would defeat the status quo in the first round. In the second, B would defeat C, and type 1 voters would have manipulated the choice of B, which they prefer, over C.

Now we turn to somewhat more complex and less often used election rules. The third procedure we consider is the method of *exhaustive voting*, which works in stages. In stage 1, each elector casts a vote for his *least* preferred candidate. The candidate with the largest number of (no-confidence) votes is eliminated from the list. In stage 2, each elector votes for his least-preferred candidate, from the list of remaining candidates. The candidate with the largest number of (no-confidence) votes is again eliminated. The process continues until only one candidate remains, and the one remaining candidate (barring ties) is the winner. For example, suppose the preferences of the electors are as follows:

Type 1	Type 2	Type 3	Type 4	Type 5
A	B	D	C	D
C	C	C	B	C
B	A	B	D	A
D	D	A	A	B
(10 voters)	(7 voters)	(5 voters)	(3 voters)	(4 voters)

The voting goes this way: In stage 1, D is eliminated. In stage 2, A is eliminated. In stage 3, B is eliminated. Therefore, C wins the election when everyone votes sincerely.

The voting could be manipulated by type 1 electors. If they voted as if their preferences were

A
D
B
C

then in stage 1, C would be eliminated, in stage 2, B would be eliminated, and in stage 3, D would be eliminated. A would be left as the social choice, making type 1 voters better off than they are when they are honest.

The fourth procedure to consider is the method of the *single transferable vote*. This is another staged procedure, in which, at each stage, voters cast votes for their *most* preferred candidates. In stage 1, each voter casts one vote for his favorite. Then the candidate with the fewest votes is eliminated. In stage 2, each elector casts a single vote for his favorite among the remaining candidates. The candidate with the fewest votes is eliminated. The process continues until one candidate remains: the last remaining candidate is the winner.

With the preferences above, the process works as follows: In stage 1, C, with 3 votes, is eliminated. In stage 2, D, with 9 votes, is eliminated. In stage 3, A, with 14 votes, is eliminated, and B is the ultimate winner. However, the procedure could be manipulated by the type 5 voters. If they voted as if their preferences were

C
D
A
B

in stage 1, D would be eliminated. In stage 2, B would be eliminated. In stage 3, A would be eliminated, and C would be the winner. And type 5 voters prefer C to B.

The fifth procedure is *approval voting*. (For a detailed analysis, the interested reader should see Brams and Fishburn (1977).) Approval voting works this way: each voter is faced with m candidates, say A, B, C, D, . . . He may cast 0, 1, 2, . . . or even m votes, by assigning a single vote to each candidate he *approves,* and none to each candidate he *disapproves*. The candidate with the highest total wins. For example, consider a simple voting paradox case with three electors. Assume that person 1 is the chairman: if there are ties for first place, he breaks them.

1 (Chairman)	2	3
A	B	C
B	C	A
C	A	B

Each elector may cast 0, 1, 2, or 3 votes. Casting votes for none or all of the candidates are equally foolish options, which may safely be ignored. Elector 1 might cast one vote for A, one vote for B, and none for C, or one vote for B and none for A or C; and so on. The first two voting strategies involve voicing approval for the top one-third or top two-thirds of his list by person 1, whereas the third strategy involves his approving B but *not* approving A, whom he really prefers to B. The first strategies are, therefore, analogous to SDF electors declaring true preferences, and the last is analogous to SDF electors declaring false preferences. Consequently the first two strategies are called *sincere* by Brams and Fishburn. Person 2's sincere strategies are one vote for B and none for C and A; and one vote for B, one vote for C, and none for A. Person 3's sincere strategies are one for C, none for A or B; and one for C, one for A, and none for B.

The question asked about each of the first four procedures was this: Can an example be constructed in which it is advantageous for some person(s) to falsely represent his (their) preferences, *given what the other people are doing?* Let us ask the analogous question for approval voting: Can an example be constructed in which it is advantageous for some person(s) to vote insincerely, given what the other people are doing? The answer is obviously yes. Using the above preferences, suppose each voter casts one vote for his favorite. The results are: one for A, one for B, and one for C. The chairman (person 1) breaks the tie in favor of A. If 2 voted insincerely here, by casting one vote for C and none for B or A, the results would be: one for A, and two for C. So C would win, and two prefers C to A.

In this sense, approval voting *is* manipulable. On the other hand, 2 could also adopt a sincere strategy to secure the desired outcome: if he were to cast one vote for B, one for C and none for A, the results would be: one for A, two for C, one for B, so C would *again* win. In fact, the following proposition is rather obvious: Suppose all voters but *i* have declared their strategies. Then there exists a *sincere* strategy that will produce the best outcome for *i* possible, given the strategies of the others. In this sense, approval voting is *not* manipulable.

(Brams and Fishburn discuss manipulability in yet another sense. Given that a voter does not know what the other voters' strategies are, might he vote insincerely in order to hedge, or minimize the risk of an especially bad election outcome? In general, when there are four or more alternatives, the answer is yes.)

Our sixth election procedure is a random one. Given a preference profile, an SDF chooses a single, certain winner. It is a deterministic rule. If a SDF decides twice with the same preference profile, it will produce the same winner both times. Suppose determinism is abandoned. What can be said of a lottery-type social decision mechanism?

Such mechanisms are called *mixed decision schemes,* and the simplest MDS, mentioned, for example, in Gibbard (1973), is a probabilist version of plurality voting: Each voter casts one vote (for his favorite candidate, if he is sincere). Let p_j = the fraction of the vote received by alternative j. Then the winner is *randomly drawn,* with the probability that j wins equal to p_j.

As an example, let the preference profile again be:

Type 1	Type 2	Type 3
A	B	C
B	C	B
C	A	A
(3 voters)	(2 voters)	(2 voters)

Now $p_A = 3/7$, $p_B = 2/7$, and $p_c = 2/7$. A random drawing is performed, in which A's probability of winning is 3/7, B's is 2/7, and C's is 2/7.

That the randomized plurality scheme is immune to manipulation by individuals can be seen as follows: Each voter attempts to maximize an expected utility function

$$EU = p_A \, U(A) + p_B \, U(B) + \cdots$$

where $U(A)$ is the utility to the voter of outcome A, and so on. When the voter casts his vote he affects EU by increasing the relative size of one of the probabilities, and it is clear that EU is increased most when the voter casts his vote for the outcome X for which $U(X)$ is largest. But this implies sincere voting; $U(X)$ is largest for the X the voter likes best.

There is then at least one MDS which is "satisfactory," in the sense that it precludes manipulation. But an MDS won't do, for *randomness per se might be objectionable.* Do we want an election procedure which produces an outcome by a roll of dice? Often not. (Peter Fishburn (1976) has a rather nice discussion, with examples, of unobjectionable social choice lotteries; e.g., the following verse is from the Book of Proverbs in the Bible: "The lot puts an end to disputes and decides between powerful contenders" (18:18). Also see Barberá (1977) and Gibbard (1977) for technical approaches).

Moreover, the particular MDS discussed above has some other problems: It assigns the largest likelihood of choice to A, even though in a pairwise election A would be defeated either by B or by C, and in a de Borda election A would be defeated by B.

This completes our casual survey of some manipulable (and nonmanipulable) voting procedures. The first four procedures, all genuine SDFs, are all occasionally liable to manipulation through misrepresentation of preferences. The fifth procedure, approval voting, might or might not be liable to manipulation, depending on the definition of manipulation one adopts. But this procedure is not a genuine SDF. The sixth procedure cannot be manipulated by individuals, but it is a random procedure, and therefore, not a true SDF.

The purpose of this section has been twofold: First, to flesh out the idea of manipulating voting procedures, and second, to show that well-known (and not-so-well-known) SDFs are at least occasionally liable to manipulation through misrepresentation of preferences. . . .

IV. Conclusion

The impossibility theorem of Gibbard and Satterthwaite is so definitive that it ought to cap a 200-year-old search for an ideal voting procedure: There is no ideal voting procedure. However, it will not stop the search. It will raise and is raising hosts of questions just as Arrow's theorem did: What non-SDF procedures (like random plurality voting) are not manipulable (Barberá (1977), Fishburn (1976), Gibbard (1977))? What restrictions might be placed on allowable preference profiles and/or ballots to escape the theorem (Blin and Satterthwaite (1976))? What about the sizes of manipulating coalitions? What happens when the number of voters is very large (Pazner and Wesley (1978)) (in which case the probability that one person's manipulation will affect the outcome is effectively zero)? What can be said about the manipulation of those more general SDFs that map preference profiles into *sets* of best alternatives, rather than singleton winners (Kelly (1977))?

The questions will go on and on, because at issue is the fundamental nature of democratic decision processes, and this issue is obviously profound. But the result that it is logically impossible to escape deficiencies in voting procedures, which first surfaced in Condorcet and de Borda, will, inevitably, remain. . . .

NOTE

Acknowledgments: Peter Fishburn, Allan Gibbard, Elisha Pazner, and David Schmeidler made helpful comments on an earlier draft. Mark Grimm assisted with some of the examples.

REFERENCES

Arrow, K. J., *Social Choice and Individual Values,* 2nd ed., Wiley, New York, 1963.

Barberá, S., "The Manipulability of Social Choice Mechanisms that Do Not Leave Too Much to Chance," *Econometrica, 45,* October 1977, 1573–1588.

Black, D., "On the Rationale of Group Decision Making," *The Journal of Political Economy, 56,* 1948, 23–34.

———, *The Theory of Committees and Elections,* Cambridge University Press, Cambridge, England, 1958.

Blin, J. M., and Satterthwaite, M. A., "Strategy-Proofness and Single-Peakedness," *Public Choice,* 1976, 51–58.

Brams, S. J., and Fishburn, P. C., "Approval Voting," mimeo., 1977.

De Grazia, A., "Mathematical Derivation of an Election System," *Isis, 44,* June 1953, 42–51.

Dummett, A., and Farquharson, R., "Stability in Voting," *Econometrica, 29,* 1961, 34–44.

Feldman, A. M., "A Very Unsubtle Version of Arrow's Impossibility Theorem," *Economic Inquiry,* 1974, 534–546.

Fishburn, P. C., "Acceptable Social Choice Lotteries," *Proceedings of the International Symposium on Decision Theory and Social Ethics,* Bavaria, 1976.

Gibbard, A., "Manipulation of Voting Schemes: A General Result," *Econometrica, 41,* July 1973, 587–601.

———. "Manipulation of Schemes that Combine Voting with Chance," *Econometrica, 45,* April 1977, 665–681.

Kelly, J. S., "Strategy-Proofness and Social Choice Functions Without Singlevaluedness," *Econometrica, 45,* 1977, 439–446.

Pazner, E., and Wesley, E., "Cheatproofness Properties of the Plurality Rule in Large Societies," *The Review of Economic Studies,* February 1978, 85–92.

Satterthwaite, M. A., "The Existence of a Strategy Proof Voting Procedure: A Topic in Social Choice Theory," Ph.D. Dissertation, University of Wisconsin, 1973.

———, "Strategy-Proofness and Arrow's Conditions: Existence and Correspondence Theorems for Voting Procedures and Social Welfare Functions," *Journal of Economic Theory, 10,* 1975, 187–217.

Schmeidler, D., and Sonnenschein, H., "The Possibility of a Cheat Proof Social Choice Function: A Theorem of A. Gibbard and M. Satterthwaite," Discussion Paper No. 89, Center for Mathematical Studies in Economics and Management Science, Northwestern University, Evanston, Illinois, 1974.

———, "Two Proofs of the Gibbard-Satterthwaite Theorem on the Possibility of a Strategy-Proof Social Choice Function," *Proceedings of a Conference on Decision Theory and Social Ethics,* Reidel Publishing Co., forthcoming.

Sen, A. K., *Collective Choice and Social Welfare,* Holden-Day, Inc., San Francisco, 1970.

———, "Social Choice Theory: A Re-examination," *Econometrica, 45,* No. 1, 1977, 53–90.

Vickrey, W., "Utility, Strategy, and Social Decision Rules," *Quarterly Journal of Economics, 74,* 1960, 507–535.

DOUGLAS H. BLAIR AND ROBERT A. POLLAK
Rational Collective Choice

An impossibility theorem is an enigma frustrating to researchers.
Normally counterintuitive, it describes circumstances under which
something cannot be accomplished, and thus blocks anyone who
was working toward a solution. Kenneth Arrow's famous theorem
proving the impossibility of a 'rational' voting rule has been no
exception. After first attempting, and failing, to prove Arrow wrong,
researchers have focused on determining what the implications are
for voting rules if Arrow's requirements are not met. Douglas Blair
and Robert Pollak provide a summary of the results of this line of
research, concluding that, however unsettling it may be, Arrow's
requirements define limits to collective rationality that cannot easily
be extended.

QUESTIONS TO GUIDE THE READING

1. How is it possible for an individual to become a dictator under
   direct majority rule simply by being in control of an agenda?
2. Why does Arrow's theorem apply to all voting procedures, not
   just direct majority rule?
3. When could voting in presidential elections violate the axiom of
   Pairwise Determination?
4. How does the replacement of Arrow's requirement for R-
   transitivity by P-transitivity change the conclusions of the
   theorem?
5. How might the implications of an acyclic constitution describe
   day-to-day political decision making in America?

Can a system of voting be devised that is at the same time rational, decisive
and egalitarian? Studies of this question by philosophers, political scientists
and economists (including the two of us) suggest that the answer is no. These
characteristics of an ideal system are in fact incompatible. A method of voting may avoid arbitrariness, deadlock or inequality of power, but it cannot
escape all three. The continuing analysis of this dilemma has led to a deeper

Douglas H. Blair and Robert A. Pollak, "Rational Collective Choice," *Scientific American 249*
(August 1983), 88–95. Copyright © 1983 by Scientific American, Inc. All rights reserved.

Douglas H. Blair is Associate Professor of Economics at Rutgers University. **Robert A. Pollak** is
Charles and William Day Professor of Economics at the University of Pennsylvania.

understanding of existing voting systems and may lead in time to the discovery of better ones.

The axiomatic analysis of rational voting procedures was initiated some 33 years ago by the economist Kenneth J. Arrow of Stanford University. He advanced five intuitively appealing axioms that any procedure for combining or aggregating the preferences of individuals into collective judgments should satisfy, and he proved that the only procedures obeying all of them concentrate all power in the hands of a single individual. No nondictatorial method satisfying all Arrow's axioms can be found, not for want of ingenuity but because none exists. In part for this work Arrow shared the Nobel prize in economics in 1972.

Over the past 15 years investigators have reexamined Arrow's axioms in an effort to circumvent his "impossibility theorem" by relaxing his requirements. The problem has attracted widespread interest because it is closely linked with central questions in philosophy, political science and economics. Philosophers face it, for example, in analyzing the practical implications of utilitarianism, the ethical doctrine holding that the rightness of actions depends on their consequences for people's happiness and hence requiring a method for aggregating the preferences of individuals. Political scientists encounter it in designing or evaluating rules of voting for committees or legislatures. Economists confront it in analyzing rationing and other nonmarket methods of allocating resources. This task is an important one in normative economics, because in determining the appropriate scope for intervention by the government in the operations of a free-market economy it is crucial to understand the potential performance of the alternatives to laissez-faire.

Majority rule deserves first consideration among procedures for aggregating individuals' preferences; its virtues include simplicity, equality and the weight of tradition. Majority rule is essentially a procedure for ranking pairs of candidates or alternatives. When more than two alternatives must be ranked, however, majority rule encounters a difficulty the Marquis de Condorcet recognized nearly 200 years ago.

The difficulty pointed out by Condorcet is now known as the "paradox of voting." Suppose a committee consisting of Tom, Dick and Harry must rank three candidates, x, y and z. Tom's preference ranking of the candidates is x, y, z. Dick's is y, z, x and Harry's is z, x, y. Majority voting between pairs of candidates yields a cycle: x defeats y, y defeats z and z defeats x, all by two votes to one. This voting cycle is the simplest example of Condorcet's paradox of voting.

Political scientists have identified many historical cases of voting cycles. For example, William H. Riker of the University of Rochester argues that the adoption of the 17th Amendment, providing for the direct election of U.S. senators, was delayed for 10 years by parliamentary maneuvers that depended on voting cycles involving the status quo (the appointment of senators by the state legislature) and two versions of the amendment.

When more than two alternatives are feasible, some new principle is needed for generating choices for pairwise rankings. The preference config-urations that induce the paradox of voting create difficulties for each natural approach. The simplest method chooses an alternative that is undefeated by any other. In a paradox-of-voting situation, however, no such alternative exists, because each alternative or candidate loses to another.

A second method for proceeding from pairwise rankings to choices is to specify an agenda, listing the order in which pairs of alternatives will be taken up. For example, the agenda might call for an initial vote on x, v. y, followed by a second stage in which the winner is matched against z. Under this agenda our three-member committee would first vote for x over y and at the second stage z would defeat x. It is easy to verify that under each of the three possible agendas in this situation the alternative taken up last emerges as the victor: the agenda determines the result. Voting cycles there-fore present substantive difficulties as well as aesthetic ones. When a cycle occurs, the choice of an ultimate winner is at best arbitrary (if the agenda is selected randomly) and at worst determined by the machinations of the agenda setter.

Further opportunities for strategic maneuvering arise if a voter can alter the agenda by introducing new alternatives. Suppose (with the same com-mittee) z represents the status quo and y is an alternative embodied in a motion that has been introduced. With only these two alternatives available y will defeat z, and Harry (who prefers z to y) will be disappointed. If he can introduce an amendment x to the motion y, however, x will defeat y on the initial vote, and at the second stage x will lose to z. Harry thus will obtain the enactment of his favored alternative.

Even if new alternatives cannot be introduced and the agenda cannot be manipulated, opportunities may still exist for voters to profit by misrepre-senting their preferences. Consider again the agenda in which z is taken up last. If each member of the committee votes his true preference on each ballot, the winning alternative, z, is the least desirable one for Tom. Sup-pose, however, Tom votes for y instead of x on the initial ballot; then y prevails, going on to defeat z in the second stage. By this stratagem he has blocked the choice of the alternative he liked least.

Cyclic collective preferences present problems of arbitrary outcomes and strategic behavior. These difficulties arise whether the preferences are generated by majority rule, as in our example, or by some other voting pro-cedure. Arrow was therefore led to ask: Do inconsistent collective prefer-ences arise only under majority rule and closely related methods or are they inherent in all voting systems? To answer the question he might have assem-bled a list of voting procedures and for each procedure checked whether any configurations of individuals' rankings gave rise to cycles or to collective preferences with some other unacceptable feature. The difficulty is that he would have had to consider an immense number of aggregation procedures, differing widely in the roles they assign to particular voters and in the criteria they employ in ranking particular pairs of alternatives.

Of necessity Arrow chose an axiomatic approach instead. He formulated the problem as the choice of a constitution, that is, a rule assigning a collective ranking of the alternatives to each configuration of individuals' rankings. A constitution specifies whether each alternative stands as preferred, inferior or indifferent to every other one. (Two alternatives are indifferent if society regards them as being equally attractive.) Arrow narrowed the field of possible constitutions by imposing five requirements that (he argued) are necessary properties of any ethically acceptable method of aggregation. He then characterized the class of constitutions that satisfy all five properties.

The first of Arrow's axioms, Universal Scope, requires that a constitution be capable of aggregating every possible configuration of voters' preferences. Since one cannot predict all the patterns of conflict that will arise over the life of a voting rule, Arrow argued, a society should not adopt a constitution that will break down when certain configurations of voters' preferences arise. He contended that the society should instead insist on a constitution sufficiently general to resolve all possible controversies.

Arrow's second axiom, Unanimity, governs the operation of a constitution when there is no disagreement among voters. It specifies that for preference configurations in which every individual prefers x to y the collective ranking must put x above y. If one accepts the view that a society's ranking should reflect its members' preferences, it is difficult to quarrel with the Unanimity condition, which resolves what surely are the easiest problems of preference aggregation.

Arrow's third axiom, Pairwise Determination, requires that society's ranking of any pair of alternatives depend only on individuals' rankings of those two alternatives. No matter how the preferences of individuals for other alternatives may change, as long as each individual's ordering of x and y remains invariant the collective ranking of x and y does also. This condition implies, for example, that the collective ranking of Ronald Reagan and Jimmy Carter is independent of how individuals rank Edward Kennedy with respect to those two or to Walter Mondale.

A constitution satisfying Pairwise Determination limits the information about individuals' rankings required to determine the collective ranking of a pair of alternatives. In particular, information about the preferences of individuals for unavailable options is irrelevant to the collective ranking of the available ones; this is an advantage when it is difficult or costly to elicit individuals' preference rankings. Without the condition of Pairwise Determination the constitution must specify what other alternatives are relevant to the determination of the collective ranking of x and y and how the preferences of individuals for those alternatives affect the collective ranking of x and y.

One common procedure, rank-order voting, violates Pairwise Determination. (It is the system normally employed by newspaper wire services to determine the ranking of college athletic teams.) When there are three alternatives, this constitution assigns each individual's first choice three points, his second two points and his third one point; the collective ranking is then found by summing the scores for each alternative and ranking them according to their total scores. In the three-member committee we have described each candidate receives a score of six, and so the committee is indifferent among the three candidates.

Suppose, however, Tom's preference ranking changes from x, y, z to x, z, y. Although no voter has changed his ranking of x and y, rank-order voting now yields a collective ranking of x over y, since x still receives a score of six but y now gets five. Hence under rank-order voting the collective ordering of x and y depends not only on how individuals rank them but also on the relative positions of other alternatives such as z.

Arrow's fourth and fifth axioms are best discussed using a shorthand notation. P denotes a strict collective preference (analogous to the relation "greater than" between a pair of real numbers), I denotes collective indifference (analogous to equality) and R denotes a weak collective-preference relation (analogous to "greater than or equal to"). Thus the expression xRy stands for "x is collectively at least as good as y," that is, either xPy or xIy.

Arrow's fourth axiom is Completeness: for every pair of alternatives x and y it must be true that xRy or yRx (or both, in which case x and y are indifferent). This axiom compels the aggregation procedure to rank every pair of alternatives. As long as the constitution has the option of declaring any pair of alternatives indifferent, Completeness seems to be a relatively innocuous requirement.

The fifth axiom, R-transitivity, requires that a weak collective preference be transitive: formally, if xRy and yRz, then xRz. Transitive relations involving pairs of real numbers include "greater than" ($>$), "equal to" ($=$) and "greater than or equal to" ($\geq$). Hence if a number x is greater than y and y is greater than z, x must be greater than z. In economic analysis Completeness and R-transitivity are conventional assumptions, and individuals whose preferences obey these axioms are said to be "rational." By extension Arrow employed the term "collective rationality" to describe constitutions satisfying both Completeness and R-transitivity. He imposed R-transitivity to ensure that the chosen alternative would be independent of the agenda or path by which it is reached.

Having defined and defended this set of five desirable properties, Arrow proved that the only constitutions satisfying all of them share a simple and startling defect: each constitution is dictatorial. A dictator is a person with the power to impose on the society his strict preference over any pair of alternatives. Arrow stated his theorem in a slightly different way. He added a sixth axiom, nondictatorship, and proved that no constitution exists that obeys all six axioms. For this reason Arrow's result is often described as an "impossibility theorem."

Thus the designer of voting procedures for legislatures, committees and clubs who accepts these conditions as necessary properties of constitutions is simply out of luck. Arrow's apparently modest requirements have powerful and unpalatable implications. As his impossibility theorem demonstrates, the five axioms are highly restrictive; although they are attractive singly, they are pernicious in combination. Voting theorists have devoted much effort to reexamining the axioms, seeking a way around Arrow's unhappy conclusion.

A plausible argument can be made that Universal Scope is too ambitious a requirement. Not every logically possible configuration of preference rankings is equally likely. Since some configurations may be extremely unlikely, requiring a constitution to aggregate consistently every logically possible configuration into a collective ranking seems unnecessarily strong.

The commonest strategy in relaxing this requirement has been to focus on a particular procedure, usually majority rule, and to look for restrictions that rule out preference configurations implying intransitive collective preferences. For example, if only preference configurations in which there is no disagreement among individuals could arise, the Unanimity axiom would determine collective preferences and the problem of intransitivity could not arise. The best-known nontrivial restriction is single-peaked preferences, discovered in the 1940s by the British economist Duncan Black.

Single-peakedness arises when all individuals evaluate alternatives according to some single criterion and, in any pairwise choice, each individual votes for the alternative closer to his own most preferred position. For example, each voter might rank candidates according to how close they were to his own position on the political spectrum from liberal to conservative. Hence if x is more liberal than y and y is more liberal than z, a society with single-peaked preferences that contained liberals (x, y, z), conservatives (z, y, x), and moderates $(y, x, z$ or $y, z, x)$ could not contain individuals for whom the middle alternative is ranked below both extremes $(x, z, y$ and $z, x, y)$. If single-peakedness could be expected to hold in practice, the case for majority rule would be compelling. Usually, however, people rank alternatives by multiple criteria and so single-peakedness will fail.

More generally, the strategy of imposing restrictions on preference configurations can be fruitful only if the restrictions are plausible in terms of a theory of preference formation or preference structure. Social scientists, however, have not succeeded in formally modeling either the role of socialization in the development of tastes and values or the degree of similarity of preferences needed for social stability. Therefore, notwithstanding a great deal of effort, no characterization of possible patterns of rankings has yet been formulated that is broad enough to encompass voters' actual preferences and at the same time narrow enough to evade the dictatorship conclusion.

The possibility of abandoning the Unanimity axiom has generated little enthusiasm. On reconsideration, Unanimity still seems to be a mild requirement to impose on mechanisms for aggregating individuals' preferences into collective rankings. Furthermore, Robert Wilson of Stanford University has shown that the only additional constitutions satisfying Arrow's other axioms but violating Unanimity are even less appealing than dictatorships. In particular there are two new possibilities. The first possibility is universal indifference, the rule that makes every pair of alternatives perpetually indifferent regardless of how individuals rank them. The second is inverse dictatorship, a rule under which some particular individual's preference ranking is reversed to form the collective ranking. This method would serve an orderly society only if a voter with infallibly bad judgment could be found.

Pairwise Determination drew heavy fire in the first decade after Arrow published his work, but criticism of this axiom has subsided. Arrow's original defense of the condition was that constitutions satisfying it can be implemented without the burden of collecting large amounts of preference information. To rank the alternatives x and y it is never necessary to ascertain the position of z in individuals' rankings. Constitutions that violate this axiom are generally cumbersome, at least when there are many alternatives, because much preference information must be obtained to rank even a small number of feasible alternatives. Moreover, since the collective ranking of x and y under constitutions violating this axiom is sensitive to individuals' rankings of third alternatives, it is often possible for voters to manipulate the outcome on x and y by misrepresenting their preferences about other alternatives.

Arrow's least defensible requirement is probably R-transitivity. To avoid Arrow's conclusion theorists of voting have examined the consequences of several less restrictive conditions. It is not difficult to show that R-transitivity is equivalent to the conjunction of two weaker conditions, P-transitivity (the transitivity of the strict collective-preference relation P) and I-transitivity (the transitivity of collective indifference). Therefore a straightforward way to weaken Arrow's rationality requirement is to retain one of these conditions while abandoning the other.

I-transitivity is particularly vulnerable to criticism, since studies by psychologists have shown that individuals in experimental situations often exhibit intransitive indifference. For example, an individual who expresses indifference between x and y and between y and z will often prefer x to z. Thus the analogy between individual preference and collective preference yields little support for requiring collective rankings to be I-transitive.

The economist and philosopher Amartya K. Sen of the University of Oxford showed that abandoning I-transitivity while retaining P-transitivity provides an escape from Arrow's dictatorship result. He offered an example of a nondictatorial constitution satisfying Arrow's first four axioms and P-transitivity. His procedure, which might be called the rule of consensus, yields xPy if and only if every individual ranks x as being at least as good as y and at least one individual strictly prefers x to y. Therefore when two individuals disagree over x and y, the result is xIy. Each individual has a veto that enables him to block a strict collective preference opposite to his own. To see that collective indifference need not be transitive consider a committee with two members, one with a preference y, x, z and the other with a preference x, z, y; the rule of consensus gives xIy and yIz but xPz.

The phenomenon of intransitive individual indifference may reflect the inability of individuals to distinguish among alternatives that are close together. For example, in judging political conservatism candidates x and y

may seem equally conservative to an individual because their policy positions are indistinguishably close, and the same may seem true of y and z. Yet candidates x and z may be far enough apart for the individual to perceive that x is more conservative than z and hence to prefer one to the other.

The psychologist R. Duncan Luce of Harvard University has proposed a notion of consistency called the semiorder to model situations entailing such thresholds of perception. Semiordered preferences exhibit P-transitivity but allow intransitive indifference. If collective choice is seen as a process of aggregating the policy judgments of individuals to form collective policy judgments, the notion of imperfect discrimination can be applied to collective preferences as well as to individual ones.

The semiorder, however, is a stronger rationality requirement than P-transitivity alone, a fact that has important consequences for preference-aggregation procedures. As we have demonstrated elsewhere, requiring that a constitution yield semiordered collective preferences and satisfy Arrow's other axioms still implies dictatorship. Thus the perception-threshold justification for weakening R-transitivity, although it is appealing and plausible, does not avoid Arrow's dismal conclusion.

Arrow's principal justification for R-transitivity was that the choice from some set of alternatives should be independent of the agenda or path by which the choice is made. Remarkably, the desire for path independence leads directly to an argument for P-transitivity alone as the appropriate rationality requirement for collective-preference rankings. Charles R. Plott of the California Institute of Technology has proposed a formal definition of path independence and has shown that all constitutions satisfying this condition are P-transitive. Furthermore, any P-transitive constitution satisfies path independence. Therefore, although Arrow's original collective rationality condition guarantees path independence, a less restrictive condition would accomplish the same objective.

Sen's rule of consensus shows that nondictatorial P-transitive constitutions exist. As Sen recognized, however, the rule of consensus is not an appealing solution to Arrow's problem because it is so often indecisive. Whenever any two individuals have opposing strict preference rankings of a pair of alternatives—surely a ubiquitous form of conflicting interests—the rule of consensus declares the two alternatives to be indifferent. A constitution that yields collective indifference whenever individuals' rankings conflict is virtually useless.

Can more attractive P-transitive constitutions be discovered? The philosopher Allan Gibbard of the University of Michigan has shown that they cannot. Gibbard proved that under every P-transitive procedure obeying Arrow's remaining axioms there exists a privileged set of individuals he called an oligarchy. This oligarchy as a group has the power to impose on the entire society its unanimous strict preference over any pair of alternatives. Moreover, each member of the oligarchy as an individual has the power to veto strict collective preference opposite to his own: whenever any oligarch strictly prefers x to y, yPx is impossible. Thus a dictator is an oligarchy of one, whereas the rule of consensus implies an oligarchy consisting of the entire society.

Not all oligarchic constitutions distribute power unequally, as the rule of consensus demonstrates. As more members are installed in the oligarchy the distribution of power becomes more nearly equal. Yet a large oligarchy increases the probability of indecisiveness, since conflicts between oligarchs imply collective indifference. Because path independence requires P-transitivity, Gibbard's theorem implies that the attractive property of path independence can only be purchased at the cost of indecisiveness or inequality. To escape the dilemma of choosing between the inequality of small oligarchies and the indecisiveness of large ones, collective rationality must be weakened beyond P-transitivity.

P-transitive constitutions satisfying Arrow's other axioms have an additional drawback. They are inflexible in the sense that, except when all members of the oligarchy are indifferent, they cannot impose different requirements for strict collective preference on different pairs of alternatives. Instead they must treat pairs of alternatives in a neutral or symmetric fashion. Hence if Tom but neither Dick nor Harry has a stake in a change from policy y to policy x, it may be appropriate to give Tom the right to veto the ranking xPy. Yet it may be undesirable to give him such power over other pairs. P-transitive constitutions satisfying Arrow's other axioms, however, cannot exhibit this flexibility.

Under the oligarchic P-transitive constitutions satisfying Arrow's other axioms a group (or an individual) with the power to impose its will over one pair of alternatives must have the same power over all pairs. Similarly, an individual or a group with veto power over one pair of alternatives must also have that power over every pair. If a particular configuration of preferences between x and y implies that x is collectively preferred to y (Pairwise Determination guarantees that no additional information about individuals' preferences figures in determining the collective ranking of x and y), the same configuration of individuals' preferences between z and w implies that z is collectively preferred to w. It is possible to treat pairs of alternatives in asymmetric or non-neutral ways under constitutions satisfying weaker rationality conditions than P-transitivity.

A less restrictive requirement than P-transitivity is acyclicity, the absence of cycles of strict collective preference regardless of their length. For example, with three alternatives the collective preference ranking xPy, yPz, xIz is acyclic (since it has no cycles of strict preference), but it violates P-transitivity (since the first two rankings would require xPz). Among the collective preferences ruled out by acyclicity is the three-alternative cycle encountered in the paradox of voting.

Acyclicity is an attractive property to demand of a constitution, particularly when the procedure adopted for converting pairwise collective rankings into choices is to select the alternatives that are undefeated by all others. Acyclicity guarantees that at least one such alternative always exists in every finite feasible set, and it is the least restrictive condition that does so.

In the acyclic example above, for instance, alternative x is not defeated by either of its competitors, whereas with the cyclic collective preference xPy, yPz and zPx each alternative loses to another one. Without acyclicity the appropriate collective choice is far from clear.

Acyclic constitutions satisfying Arrow's other axioms need not be neutral; they allow pairs of alternatives to be treated in an asymmetric fashion. Nonneutral procedures are quite common. In the U.S. Senate, to take one (sometimes cyclic) example, an ordinary bill passes with a simple majority, but a motion to limit debate requires three-fifths and a proposed constitutional amendment requires two-thirds. Whether or not neutrality is a desirable feature of a constitution depends on the nature of the alternatives. When candidates for office are being ranked, a neutral rule is more appealing than one favoring a particular candidate. When alternatives have asymmetric consequences, however, non-neutral rules biased against more drastic outcomes may be advantageous. The criminal-justice system provides examples at both ends of the spectrum: jury trials are not guaranteed in minor cases, and death sentences are automatically reviewed by appellate courts.

Relaxing the rationality requirement from P-transitivity to acyclicity makes possible many constitutions without oligarchies. All the new constitutions, however, share one of the principal drawbacks of oligarchic rules. All acyclic constitutions satisfying Arrow's other axioms grant some group or individual extensive veto power.

Typical of these additional acyclic constitutions was the voting rule in the United Nations Security Council until 1965. The Security Council then consisted of five permanent members and six nonpermanent ones. A motion succeeded if it received at least seven affirmative votes and no negative vote from any permanent member. Thus each permanent member of the Security Council had a veto; no motion could pass if any permanent member of the council opposed it. These five nations did not constitute an oligarchy, however, since additional support from nonpermanent members was required for strict collective preference.

Under acyclic constitutions an individual or a group may have veto power over some pairs of alternatives but not over others. The extent of veto power under such rules must therefore be described in terms of the number of pairs over which some individual or group exercises a veto. As we have recently shown, when the number of alternatives is large with respect to the number of individuals, at least one individual must be able to veto a large number of pairs of alternatives. More precisely, as the ratio of alternatives to voters increases without limit, the proportion of pairs of alternatives over which some particular individual must have a veto approaches unity.

Even when there are fewer alternatives than there are individuals, their ratio is critical. R-transitivity and P-transitivity are rationality conditions applying to triples of alternatives. Acyclicity, in contrast, rules out cycles of every possible length: the absence of cycles with three alternatives does not imply the absence of cycles with four. As the number of alternatives increases, longer cycles become possible.

With only two alternatives, x and y, majority voting cannot yield a cycle. A cycle would require both that more than half of the voters prefer x to y and that more than half of the voters prefer y to x; consequently at least one individual would prefer x to y and y to x, which is clearly impossible. When there are three or more alternatives, as the paradox of voting shows, no individual need agree with all the links in the collective-preference cycle, and so the cycle does not contradict the transitivity of any individual's preference ranking.

A five-member committee further illustrates the critical role of the ratio of alternatives to individuals. Consider the constitution requiring four affirmative votes for strict preference—a constitution intermediate between majority rule and the rule of consensus. Could the cycle xPy, yPz, zPx arise under the four-fifths-majority constitution? It could not, since each individual has transitive preferences and at least four voters must agree with each link in the collective ranking. With a five-member committee at least one member would have to agree with each of the three links in the collective-preference cycle, which is impossible.

With a five-member committee and three alternatives four-fifths-majority rule has advantages over both majority rule and the rule of consensus. Unlike majority rule, no cycle can occur. Unlike the rule of consensus, no member has a veto. These advantages, however, are won at a price. The four-fifths rule is less rational than the rule of consensus: although collective preferences are acyclic, they are not P-transitive and so are not path-independent. The rule is less decisive than bare majority rule: although no individual has a veto, any group of two voters can block a collective ranking of two alternatives that stands opposite to their own.

Under an acyclic constitution the size of the smallest group with veto power depends on the relative numbers of alternatives and individuals. When there are only two alternatives, as the case of majority rule makes clear, the smallest veto group needed is half of the electorate. When there are as many alternatives as there are individuals, under any acyclic rule there must exist at least one individual who, standing alone, has veto power over some pairs of alternatives. In intermediate cases, as the constitution stipulating a majority of four-fifths illustrates, some minority groups have veto power. Constitutions that grant veto power to a large number of small groups are likely to lead to deadlock rather than to decision.

An uncompromising egalitarian would argue that since some individuals must have veto power, all individuals should have it. The larger the set of vetoers, however, the more frequent the incidence of collective indifference, since indifference occurs whenever two individuals with veto power in appropriate directions rank x and y in opposite ways. The palatability of acyclic constitutions thus depends on the ratio of alternatives to individuals. When the number of alternatives is only slightly smaller than the number of individuals, "small" groups must be endowed with extensive veto power, although there need not be an individual with veto power. As the number of alternatives increases, the size of the smallest vetoing group required for acyclicity grows smaller. With as many alternatives as there are individuals, at least one individual must be able to veto some pairs. As the number of alternatives increases further, the proportion of pairs over which the individual has veto power approaches unity.

The "impossibility theorems" that began with Arrow's famous proposition define constraints on a society's choice of a rule for collective decision making. The constraints are severe. Three widely shared objectives—collective rationality, decisiveness and equality of power—stand in irreconcilable conflict. If society forgoes collective rationality, thereby accepting the necessary arbitrariness and manipulability of irrational procedures, majority rule is likely to be the choice because it attains the remaining goals. If society insists on retaining a degree of collective rationality, it can achieve equality by adopting the rule of consensus, but only at the price of extreme indecisiveness. Society can increase decisiveness by concentrating veto power in progressively fewer hands; the most decisive rule, dictatorship, is also the least egalitarian.

There is little comfort here for those designing ideal procedures for collective choice. Nevertheless, every society must make collective choices and devise voting procedures, however imperfect they may be. Axiomatic analysis, pursuing the line of investigation begun by Arrow 33 years ago, has yielded a richer understanding of existing voting methods and may eventually yield better ones. It also demonstrates that the opportunities for improvement are severely limited. Stark compromises are inevitable.

Public Decision Rules

The first of the following three selections presents benefit-cost analysis in the public sector, while the other two focus on natural monopoly—its definition and the Ramsey pricing rule.

SELECTION 25

KENNETH J. ARROW

Criteria for Social Investment

Benefit-cost analysis is a technique that has been increasingly utilized in the evaluation of government projects. Kenneth Arrow discusses issues in quantifying the benefits and costs of social investments. These include both the use of "shadow prices" in ascribing values to benefits and the choice of a proper social discount rate for future benefits and costs.

QUESTIONS TO GUIDE THE READING

1. Why may it be necessary to impute hypothetical prices in measuring the benefits of social investment?
2. What efficiencies can be obtained from nonzero prices for the output of a public project?
3. What is the importance of a discount rate to a benefit-cost analysis? What issues arise in choosing a particular discount rate?
4. What impact does the use of unemployed resources have on the measurement of costs?

Introduction

The following paper was originally prepared as an exposition of the general principles of social investment. It is clear, however, that it has been most strongly influenced by the United States' experience in investment in water

Kenneth J. Arrow, "Criteria for Social Investment" *Water Resources Research* 1 (1965), 1–8. Copyright by the American Geophysical Union. Reprinted by permission of the author and the publisher.

Kenneth J. Arrow is Joan Kenney Professor of Economics and Professor of Operations Research at Stanford University. He received a Nobel Prize in Economics in 1972.

resources. The three major problems treated are the discounting of future benefits, the measurement of benefits, and the measurement of costs; the last category, however, is much less complex than the first two. As will be seen, the problems of discounting relate to the general economy rather than to the particular project at hand; thus the discussion is as applicable to water investments as to any other investments. The different problems in the measurement of benefits are important for different classes of water projects. For example, the divergence between social and private costs and the problem of appropriability is liable to be most acute for water purification. On the other hand, issues relating to economies of scale and the difficulties that they raise for the evaluation of benefits are likely to be much more important in irrigation projects. The importance of consumption (as opposed to production) benefits is less in water resource problems than in health or education, but it is illustrated by recreation. Thus, all the issues raised in this paper have applicability to the water resources area.

Remarks on Investment in General

Investment is the allocation of current resources, which have alternative productive uses, to an activity whose benefits will accrue over the future. The benefits take the form of production of goods and services.

The cost of an investment is the benefit that could have been derived by using the resources in some other activity.

An investment, then, is justified if the benefits anticipated are greater than the costs. This, of course, is an optimality condition for any productive activity. It takes particular forms for investment activities and, more specifically, for the special class of activities referred to as social investment.

The central problem in the evaluation of investments in general is commensuration over time. Benefits accrue at different times from each other and from the costs. To add up the benefits, we must establish rates of exchange between benefits at different times, weights to be assigned to the benefits before adding them together; the same procedure must be followed for costs.

One possibility, indeed, is simply to add benefits without regard to time period, i.e., to weight the benefits in all future time periods equally with each other and with the present. This practice is, however, unsatisfactory for two reasons: (1) time preference and (2) the opportunity cost of capital.

1. It can be taken as a datum that, from almost any point of view, present benefits are preferred to equal future benefits, especially if they are sufficiently removed in time.

2. The given investment must be compared with other investments also capable of yielding deferred benefits. If there exists an alternative investment capable of yielding a benefit of, say, 1.10 units of benefit a year hence for a present cost of 1 unit, then the given investment, to be justified, must be capable of yielding at least as much. This proposition is a straightforward statement of technical efficiency and is independent of any value judgments

as to time preference. The most convenient way of expressing this demand is to define the present value of a future benefit as the current expenditure of resources which, if invested in the alternative manner, could yield the same benefit. If r is the rate of return on the alternative investment, then 1 unit of resources invested there could yield $1 + r$ units of benefit in 1 year, $(1 + r)^2$ units in 2 years (including reinvestment of the first year's return), and, in general, $(1 + r)^t$ units of benefits after t years. Hence, the present value of a benefit B_1 due in 1 year is

$$B_1/(1 + r)$$

The present value of a benefit B_t to occur in the tth year ahead is

$$B_t/(1 + r)^t$$

Finally, the total present value of an investment which will yield benefits B_1, $\cdots$, B_T in the first, $\cdots$, Tth year ahead, where T is the last year in which benefits are expected (the horizon), is

$$V = \sum_{t = 1}^{T} B_t/(1 + r)^t$$

The precise operational sense in which V is the present value of the given investment is now given. Suppose the amount V were invested today in the alternative investment. From the proceeds available at the end of 1 year, including recapture of some or all of the principal and additional income, withdraw benefits to the extent of B_1 and reinvest the remainder in the alternative investment. Repeat the process in each subsequent year, t. The result will be that precisely B_T can be withdrawn in year T with nothing else to reinvest. Thus, it can be seen that for an initial investment of the quantity of resources V in the alternative investment, it is possible to achieve the same benefits at each point of time as in the given investment. It follows that the given investment is justified (as against making an equal investment in the alternative) only if the cost C of the given investment is less than V. Thus, the condition that the present value of future benefits from a given investment, discounted by the rate of return on alternative investment opportunities, exceed cost is necessary for the efficient use of resources.

The efficiency or opportunity-cost interpretation of discounting is independent of any questions of time preference. In and of itself, however, it is only a partial solution to the determination of investment. If the present value of an investment, discounted at the rate of return of an alternative, falls short of the cost, it should certainly not be undertaken; if any investment at all is made, it should be in the alternative. On the other hand, if the alternative investment is in fact being made and if the present value of the given investment is greater than the cost, then the given investment should certainly be undertaken, at the expense of the alternative if necessary. But the opportunity-cost criterion is not an answer to the question of whether both the given and the alternative investment should be undertaken. The answer to this question depends on the aggregate volume of resources that will be devoted to investment as against current consumption and, hence, basically on the relative preferences for present and future benefits in relation to the rates of return on investments.

At an over-all optimum of the economy, therefore, the discount of future benefits according to opportunity costs must equal the discount according to time preference. However, in establishing criteria for a relatively limited body of investments, such as social investments will frequently be, the opportunity-cost criterion may be adequate if it can be presupposed that time preference has already been allowed to operate in the determination of the over-all volume of investment and, therefore, indirectly in the determination of the rate of return on alternative investments.

The Special Category of Social Investment

The majority of investments yield their benefits in the form of identifiable goods which can be marketed or withheld. These benefits are in a very natural way *appropriable,* in the sense that the organization producing them can without difficulty charge individual consumers for them, so that those who want and need the product can buy and others can refrain. The production of food and clothing provides, perhaps, the purest example of appropriable benefits. The future benefits from such an investment can be fairly measured by the output evaluated at the price at which it can all be sold less, of course, all current production costs (wages and materials).

But a wide and important class of investments yield benefits which, in their very act of production, inure to a wide class of individuals. They cannot be excluded from the benefit, and, hence, a price cannot be charged that will effectively discriminate between those who want the service and those who do not. Water purification provides a simple example; if it is decided to install equipment that will improve the purity of the water, all users will receive the benefits over the lifetime of the equipment, whether or not they would be willing to bear the cost in a free choice. (This choice is not only a matter of individual tastes for pure water; some of the uses of household water, such as gardening, have much lower purity requirements than others, so that some individual consumers may, in fact, derive very little additional benefit.) The price system is not operative, for it would require that each consumer be given the freedom to buy water at both the older and the newer levels of purity or, at the very least, be given his option between the two, with price differences reflecting cost differences. Water purification is really of the same order as the general run of collective services provided by government. In this context it is differentiated from the rest only in that there is an investment component; i.e., the benefits and costs do not accrue at the same point of time.

There are other instances in which pricing of benefits would be technically feasible, but for other reasons it is not regarded as performing an appropriate social function. Elementary, secondary, and, to a considerable extent, higher education have begun to belong to this category. The public schools could charge their pupils or their parents for the cost of education, but in the first place there may be a divergence of interest between the parents, who are capable of paying, and the children, who are receiving the benefit. This is part of a wider class of cases in which the beneficiaries are incapable of appreciating the benefit, either because of natural limitations of understanding (as in children or mental patients) or because the benefits would not really be understood until they have been experienced. The second reason, in the case of education, is that the benefits of education accrue not merely to the students but to the society of which they are a part.

In general, the line between appropriable and inappropriable cannot be drawn very sharply. There are very few acts, even of private consumption, which do not have some direct effect on the welfare of others. It is a matter partly of empirical and partly of value judgment as to when the external effects of benefits are sufficiently widespread to set aside the principle that the individual is the best judge of his own welfare.

There is another and very important reason rooted in the facts of technology for the treatment of wide-scale classes of benefits as inappropriable, even though it would be technically feasible to set prices, namely where there are increasing returns to the scale of operation. In that circumstance a collective agreement to undertake a productive enterprise and to share the costs in some way may benefit everyone, yet any ordinary pricing system would fail. For example, competition among electricity systems would certainly not ensure an optimal allocation of resources but instead would probably reduce the supply of electricity to small proportions. It is, to be sure, often possible, for example in irrigation to determine the benefits through a pricing calculation, but the supply must nevertheless be arranged through a monopoly; because of the dangers of monopoly in certain circumstances, the investment must actually be provided socially.

The remarks in this and the preceding section establish general outlines for the discussion to follow. In the next three sections we consider the following problems of evaluating the discounted benefits and costs: the measurement of benefits, the determination of the rate of discount, and the measurement of costs.

Problems in the Measurement of Benefits

The benefits derived from social investment are by nature more difficult to measure than benefits from private investment. There is inevitably some failure in the extent to which the price system will be adequate. The price system, however, even in its ordinary form does have an important role in the estimation of benefits, and, in a more extended sense, there really is no benefit calculation possible that is not based on a set of at least hypothetical prices.

In our discussion we will distinguish between market prices and accounting or shadow prices. Market prices are prices actually charged for the benefits, leaving each consumer free to use or not use them and thereby incur or avoid the price. In investments lacking a social character, the highest market price that will lead consumers to buy the entire output is an adequate measure of the benefit per unit of product, and aggregate benefits are appropriately measured by the volume of aggregate sales less, of course, the aggregate of current operating costs. The process of allocation still involves the nontrivial element of forecasting and its inevitable counterpart, uncertainty. But it would take us too far afield to discuss these questions here. Instead, we wish to concentrate on those problems in the measurement of benefits that specifically differentiate private from social investments.

The basic reason for the difficulty of relying entirely on market prices is, as we have seen, the inappropriability of some benefits, the impossibility or, at any rate, difficulty of separating the creation of benefits for individuals from the act of production or, at least, the act of consumption by others. For these instances we must make a calculating equivalent of the price system, and to this equivalent the name of shadow or accounting price has variously been given.

Uses and Limits of Market Prices

For many purposes, and probably for more purposes than now realized, it would be feasible and useful to market the benefits from a project at a suitable price, as when the benefits are fully appropriable and the reason for the social character of the investment is rather the existence of economies of scale. In effect, the enterprise, though publicly operated, is still being required in the long run to pay its way. One may equivalently suppose that the investment is given a separate organization which borrows the initial capital and has to repay it with interest. The condition is that, with these costs added to current operating costs, the enterprise will still cover these total costs over the life of the investment.

The obvious advantage to such a system is the pressure for efficiency and responsibility, both in the initial act of investment and in the subsequent operation. At least after the event, there is a clear-cut determination of the profitability of the enterprise. This not only helps in supplying a record for the future but also imposes caution on the determination of the investment, since it is known that there will be such a check and in what terms the check will be. Finally, by making the benefits definable in fairly straightforward operational terms, it should improve the ability to forecast the profitability and, therefore, the desirability. To the extent that market prices are used in the distribution of benefits, we may speak of them as being recoverable. Recoverability is not an all-or-none proposition, of course. It is perfectly possible to charge a price to a direct beneficiary and still argue that the benefits that are covered are less than the total benefits because of indirect effects. For example, fees are frequently charged for public higher education, yet they are very far below the costs. This practice is presumably justified on the basis of indirect benefits.

Although the efficiencies gained by full, or even partial, recoverability of benefits are considerable, too much emphasis should not be placed on recoverability as a condition for investment. Well-known propositions of welfare economics tell us that the product of any investment should be offered at marginal cost up to the limits of its capacity. These marginal costs may or may not be adequate to recover the cost of the original investment. This point is of particular importance when there are widespread economies of scale, for then the marginal cost is almost sure to be below the long-run average cost, and recovery through market prices is necessarily less than total. It might be possible to achieve a greater recovery with a price above marginal cost (depending, of course, on the elasticity of demand), but then the investment, in effect, is not being used from the social point of view as well as it might be. By increasing the volume of recoverable benefits through higher prices, the aggregate benefits, recoverable and otherwise, have been reduced.

Divergence Between Social and Private Benefits

A classic in economic theory is the case in which there is a direct beneficiary from whom the product can be withheld, but his act of consumption, or the act of production in order to achieve this consumption, yields benefits to other parties against whom no exclusion is possible. The water purification example cited above is an extreme case. To supply pure water to even one individual, it is necessary to supply it to everyone. Milder interactions are very common. Thus, treatment of infectious diseases is beneficial to the patient, but, in addition, the possibility of spread to other individuals is also reduced. Under these conditions it would be necessary to take into account the fact that the aggregate benefits are greater than the part that can be allocated privately with ease. Hence, to justify itself an investment in public health, including medical care of infectious diseases, need not expect to be fully made up from fees charged to patients.

Shadow Pricing

In the absence of market prices, it is necessary to impute value to the benefits. In the case of water purification, it might be asked what price, *if it could be charged,* would suffice to clear the market. More generally, the shadow price should be estimated for all beneficiaries, not only the primary ones. Computation replaces the market.

There is no difficulty with the concept of a shadow price; but there is the intensely practical problem of measuring it. Whereas market prices are operationally revealed in the market, shadow prices must be indirectly estimated, often by introspection on the part of a questionnaire-answering public or its governmental representatives. The difficulty of estimating a shadow price that represents the value of social, as opposed to private, benefits has led in practice to two opposite errors: (1) ignoring the additional benefits not representable by market prices and thus failing to make socially desirable investments, or (2) introducing nonprice and nonquantifiable justifications for projects which make difficult the rational weighing of alternatives (e.g., justifications such as the development of land as an end in itself or the provision of water as an absolute need).

Ultimately, a shadow price is a subjective valuation which must be made by individuals. In a democratic society it is perfectly proper that the valuation be made by the political process. It would, however, be a major improvement in the relevance of the discussion if the shadow price were the explicit subject.

Economies of Scale and Consumers' Surplus

Prices, shadow or market, strictly speaking are valuations only for small changes in quantities. Suppose, for example, it is contemplated to bring in a water supply for a desert region. The price in the absence of an aqueduct is prohibitive, but, once the aqueduct is installed, the marginal cost of water may be very small. If water is sold at its marginal cost, each individual will be better off than he would be if he had to pay the pre-aqueduct price; hence, there is a certain maximum lump sum payment (a fixed payment per year independent of the amount he consumes) which he could make and still be no worse off, according to his tastes and needs, than he was in the absence of the aqueduct. The benefits for the project are the aggregate of these hypothetical lump sum payments plus the benefits recovered from the marginal cost pricing less current operating costs. The measurement of these benefits for the purpose of making decisions about social investments is not necessarily tied to any attempt to recapture some or all of these benefits through taxes or a two-part price system.

The aggregate of lump sum payments is one of the many definitions of consumers' surplus. Although there are some conceptual difficulties that have been overlooked in this simplified exposition, the basic problem here, as with shadow prices, is one of measurement. All practical approximations are one form or another of the area under the demand curve as the price drops from its preproject to its postproject level. Considerations of this type are too well known to require further expansion here; it need only be remarked that they apply to shadow prices as well as to market prices. In each case the benefit per unit of output will lie between the preproject and postproject prices.

Production and Consumption Benefits

All benefits are, in the last analysis, benefits to individuals whom we may think of as consumers, but the relation may be direct or it may be indirect, through facilitating the production of goods desired by consumers. Most social investment activities yield benefits of both types. A highway increases the convenience of private automobile travel, a direct benefit to consumers; it also decreases the cost of trucking operations, which ultimately decreases the cost or increases the supply of consumers' goods.

Consumption benefits are those whose immediate beneficiaries are individuals in their capacities as consumers; production benefits are those whose immediate beneficiaries are economic units engaged in production for a market. The distinction has no significance from the point of view of determining the total benefits for evaluating a social investment project. The importance is rather that production benefits are far more easily measurable; in effect, the production unit imputes the market valuation of the final product back to the benefit yielded by the investment project. Thus, as a first approximation, the production benefit of a highway is the saving in cost on the volume of traffic originally carried. If the effect is large, the problem discussed in the preceding section arises, and some measure of surplus is needed; the cost saving will lead to a larger flow of traffic, and the benefit is measured instead by the cost saving on a volume of traffic intermediate between the original and final levels.

Hence, even if the production benefits are not recovered for one reason or another (in particular, under marginal-cost pricing of the benefits of a project with large economies of scale), they are fairly easily measurable. Any help in the measurement of benefits should be used. But there is a danger that the superior measurability of production benefits will lead to an underestimate or complete disregard of consumption benefits. A striking example has occurred in some discussions of the economics of public health. Benefits are measured in terms of the workdays saved, a production benefit, in complete disregard of the direct consumption benefit of prevention of or recovery from illness.

The Rate of Discount

The Measurement of the Opportunity
Cost of Capital

As has been seen, it is a straightforward implication of efficiency that the sum of benefits, discounted at the rate of return on alternative investments, exceed the cost. But which of the many other investments in an economy is *the* alternative?

If the economy as a whole were operating at perfect efficiency before considering a possible new social investment, the rates of return on all alternative investments would be equal (at least at the margin, i.e., for small additions to investment). Further, each individual in such an economy has full access to the capital market, so that his division of current income between consumption and saving has been made on the assumption that the rate of return on saving equals the common rate of return on all investments. In such a situation there can be no doubt of the proper rate of discount;

further, the mode of financing the social investment makes no difference either. If the resources are obtained by taxation, they are drawn either from consumption or from investment. A dollar drawn from private investment reduces aggregate output in future years by r dollars, where r is the rate of return; but an individual is, at the margin, indifferent between consuming and saving a dollar, which means that he is indifferent between consuming the dollar immediately and receiving a permanent income of r dollars per annum from it. Hence, the social investment must yield an equivalent income or be condemned as inefficient, whether the dollar invested came from investment or from consumption. Finally, if the money is borrowed, the rate of interest would have to be the same as the rate of return on private investment opportunities; otherwise no one would buy government bonds. Again the government would be confronted with the common rate of return on private investments as the appropriate discount rate to be applied to future benefits from a proposed social investment.

In free-enterprise societies it does not appear at first glance that the rate of return is, in fact, the same on all private investments. Savings-bank deposits, government bonds, and corporate bonds certainly yield different rates of return. Two interpretations of this observation have been offered: (1) Investments differ in riskiness, and the observed differences in rates of return are, in fact, compensations for these differences. It is argued in this interpretation that the risk-corrected rates of return are really the same. (2) There are imperfections and limitations of entry in capital and product markets so that rates of return really differ. Which of these explanations is in fact the better is an empirical question which cannot be dealt with here. The two hypotheses are not, of course, mutually exclusive, and both undoubtedly play a role in actuality—with what weights is certainly not easy to determine.

The two interpretations have very different implications for the determination of the opportunity cost of capital appropriate for discounting future benefits:

1. It remains true that the mode of financing has no influence on the appropriate discount rate, since each individual is presumed to have come into equilibrium as among consumption and the investments of varying degrees of riskiness. There is a uniquely defined pure rate of return, corresponding to riskless investments, which is usually taken to be the rate on government bonds of long maturity. Clearly, riskless social investment should be discounted at the pure rate of return under the hypothesis that observed rates of return differ because of riskiness. The implications for the rate of discount to be applied to benefits from risky social investments are less clear. According to one view, the rate to be applied is that which obtains in the private sector for investments of equal riskiness. Another position is that the government is necessarily in a better position to bear risks than any private investor. In fact, since it is involved with so many risky ventures, the law of large numbers ensures an aggregate certainty. It is therefore argued that the rate of discount should be the pure rate. The benefits to which

the discount rate should be applied are uncertain; this uncertainty is what is meant by saying that the investment is risky. The single number that should represent a benefit is the expected value.

2. If the view that differences in observed rates of return are due to market imperfections is correct, the mode of financing investments becomes important. The rate of discount is the rate on the alternative private investments available to the particular individuals from whom the money was drawn, whether taxpayers or bondbuyers. This alternative rate would be different for different individuals; thus the discount rate used by the government would have to be an approximate average.

It should be noted that the second view has implications not merely for the determination of the rate of discount but also for the preferred mode of financing. To the greatest extent possible, funds should be drawn from those individuals and fields of economic activity for which the rates of return on alternative investments are the lowest.

Social and Private Time Preference

As noted in a previous section, full optimality requires that the rate of time preference and the opportunity cost of capital be equal. This condition is, however, only of significance if the volume of social investment is not completely infinitesimal compared with private investment.

Suppose again that there is a perfect capital market; then for each individual, his rate of time preference equals the opportunity cost of capital. It has, however, been argued that even in this case it is not correct for society to be governed by the private rate. The government has an obligation to the future and, in particular, to unborn generations who are not represented in the current market. It should be made clear that this interest must be over and above the interest felt by individuals in the future welfare of their own heirs, born and unborn, for the latter is already reflected in individual time preference. This argument has been put in the form of divergence between private and social benefit. Each individual derives satisfaction from having wealth added to future generations. Each one can, by his own actions, add only infinitesimally to this wealth, but a collective agreement to do so will increase everyone's welfare.

If this argument is accepted, it does not necessarily lead to a special rate of discount for social investment. Indeed, the optimal solution would be to lower the required rate of return on all investment, private and social, for example by lending to private business at a lower rate than the market or by driving the rate of interest down through a budgetary surplus and debt retirement. More private investment would be undertaken, so that the marginal investment would have a lower rate of return and the opportunity cost of capital would be lower. Then, without changing the rule of discounting the benefits of social investment at the opportunity cost, the interest rate would be lowered.

If, however, it is accepted that there is an institutional limit on the extent to which the government can engage in direct or indirect financing of private investment, the social rate of time preference may remain below the common value of the opportunity cost of capital and the individual rate of time preference. It would clearly not be socially advantageous to withdraw resources from private investment to social investment with a lower rate of return, but it would be socially advantageous to withdraw some resources from consumption to social investment because of the divergence between social and individual time preference. Under these assumptions the appropriate rate of discount on future benefits from social investment will depend on the source of financing; it will be an average of the social rate of time preference and the opportunity cost of capital, with the weights depending on the extent to which resources are drawn from consumption or investment.

If we drop the assumption of a perfect capital market and admit differences in rates of return, we consider again the implications of the two alternative hypotheses of the preceding subsection. The first leads to much the same results as the case of a perfect market. The second hypothesis tends to reinforce the statements of the preceding paragraph.

The argument for a social rate of time preference distinct from individual rates is basically a matter of value judgment. Its validity and its importance, if valid, are both subject to considerable dispute.

The Measurement of Costs

The analysis of costs offers fewer difficulties than those of benefits and the rate of discount. For most purposes even a large volume of investment will have little effect on the costs of the inputs, so that evaluation at market prices is usually satisfactory. There are, however, two major qualifications, arising out of the possible presence of unemployment and out of neighborhood or amenity effects of certain classes of costs.

Unemployed Resources

During a period of unemployment of labor or capital, the market price of an input will exceed its true social cost. Putting the idle worker or machine to work costs society nothing, but there is a wage or other price to be paid. The government, as guardian of the nation's economic welfare, should properly reckon only with true social costs. Hence, during a depression the cost of an investment should exclude costs of labor and plant that would otherwise be unemployed. Even in times of generally high employment there may be local areas of unemployment; the same rules should hold for projects in such an area. The allowance for unemployment applies only to the initial investment cost; in estimating future operating costs to be deducted from future benefits, it should normally be assumed that full employment will prevail.

Amenity Costs

Just as there can be a divergence between private and social benefits, so there can be divergence between private and social costs. A highway may conduce to an increase in air pollution; it may also, through its noise, be a source of disutility to the neighborhood. Since social investment projects are frequently large in magnitude, they frequently are so physically large that they impinge upon human sensibilities in a major fashion. Although it is hard to frame any general statement about amenity costs, they should in principle be assigned shadow costs which should be deducted from benefits or added to costs in making a benefit-cost calculation.

EDWARD D. LOWRY

Justification for Regulation: The Case for Natural Monopoly

One rationale for government intervention in the private sector is
the existence of a natural monopoly. Edward Lowry summarizes the
development of the natural monopoly concept. He argues that
natural monopoly should be defined as a circumstance in which
one firm can supply a whole market at less cost than two or more
firms.

QUESTIONS TO GUIDE THE READING

1. What was the relationship between the development of the
   natural monopoly concept and the actual regulation of natural
   monopolies?

2. How can a natural monopoly market be defined more broadly
   than simply one exhibiting static economies of scale? Why may
   the broader definition be appropriate?

3. Can you think of any possibly "unnatural" monopolies—where
   several firms could provide a service less expensively than one
   firm but the government mandates a single (public or private)
   supplier?

Development of the Natural Monopoly Concept

Until the end of the nineteenth century, competition, or at least laissez-faire,
characterized our national policy. The first articulation of the notion of natural monopoly appears in John Stuart Mill's *"Principles of Political Economy"* (1848). Mill concluded that the gas supply industry in London seemed
to lie outside the realm of competition, for he felt that duplication of facilities
was wasteful:

> It is obvious, for example, how great an economy of labor would be
> obtained if London were supplied by a single gas or water company
> instead of the existing plurality. . . . Were there only one establish-

Edward D. Lowry, "Justification for Regulation: The Case for Natural Monopoly," *Public Utilities Fortnightly* (November 8, 1973), 17–22.

Edward D. Lowry is Staff Manager, Federal Regulatory, Bell Atlantic.

ment, it could make lower charges, consistently with obtaining the rate of profit now realized. . . .[1]

Following Mill's recognition of the problem, considerable attention was given to inherently noncompetitive industries. Drawing upon his numerous contacts with industry, Thomas Henry Farrer (Secretary of the Board of Trade in England) in his 1883 publication, *"The State in Its Relation to Trade,"* suggested that industries such as harbors, lighthouses, roads, railways, gasworks, and telegraphs were inherently monopolistic. Acknowledging that in some of these industries competition had been attempted and had failed, whereas others had been monopolies from their inception, he asserted: "But in none of them has competition proved to be completely successful. . . . it is only in those cases which competition does not regulate them, that the need for special state interference is felt."[2]

Farrer attempted to isolate *one* general characteristic which distinguished the inherently monopolostic undertakings from those governed by the ordinary law of competition.[3] He concluded that one cannot isolate any one specific characteristic inherent in monopolies. Instead they exhibit all of the following characteristics:[4]

1. What they supply is a necessity.
2. They occupy peculiarly favored spots or lines of land.
3. The article or service they supply is used at the place where and in connection with the plant or machinery by which it is supplied.
4. This article or service can in general be largely, if not indefinitely, increased without a proportionate increase in plant and capital.
5. The certainty and a well-defined harmonious arrangement, which can only be attained by unity, are paramount considerations.

Farrer's contribution to the theory of natural monopoly was the provision of these criteria to segregate industries which were inherently monopolistic from all others.

In 1887, Henry Carter Adams, who was a student of industry and economics (and received the first Doctorate in Political Economy awarded by The Johns Hopkins University), wrote a monograph, entitled "Relation of the State to Industrial Action." It stated that unrestricted freedom in private enterprise did not always lead to the greatest good for society. Instead, Adams argued that the benefits of an industrial monopoly could be superior to those of competition. To channel the benefits of monopoly to society, he advocated extending the duties of the state so that ". . . society should be guaranteed against the oppression of exclusive privileges administered for personal profit, while at the same time it should be secured such advantages as flow from concentrated organization."[5] Recognizing the difficulty of achieving the conflicting goals, Adams offered a policy guideline for private monopolies. According to Adams, industries should be classified in one of these categories: constant, decreasing, or increasing returns. The first two classes of industries were adequately controlled by competitive forces, while the third class required regulation by the state. In other words, industries with increasing returns, also called economies of scale, should be regulated monopolies.

Adams' monograph reads as if it were written today, when it describes the uniqueness of industries with declining unit costs:

> . . . where the law of increasing returns works with any degree of intensity, the principle of free competition is powerless to exercise a healthy regulating influence. This is true, because it is easier for an established business to extend its facilities for satisfactorily meeting a new demand than for a new industry to spring into competitive existence. . . . The control of the state over industries should be coextensive with the application of the law of increasing returns in industries. . . . *Such businesses are by nature monopolies.* . . . If it is for the interest of men to combine, no law can make them compete. (Emphasis added.)[6]

He concluded that in this case a monopoly established by law and managed in the public interest, rather than an irresponsible, extralegal monopoly was necessary.

Although Mill, Farrer, and Adams developed the basic theory underlying the natural monopoly concept, it was Richard T. Ely (professor of political economy at Johns Hopkins and founder of the American Economic Association) who labeled and widely disseminated this concept. In the 1880s, the *Baltimore Evening Sun* commissioned Ely to write a series of articles discussing current economic problems. During that time the Interstate Commerce Act was passed by Congress (1887) and state legislatures were involved in an active dialogue regarding the need for regulation.[7] The interest of Congress and state legislatures in regulation of industry generated considerable public awareness. Ely was the first to label industries requiring some form of regulation "natural monopolies." His articles, as well as three subsequent books, disseminated and popularized the notion of natural monopoly. According to Ely, natural monopolies depend for their existence on inevitable economic forces—that they develop independently of man's desire and sometimes even in opposition to it.[8]

In his 1937 textbook, Ely distinguished three classes of natural monopoly: (1) those dependent on special or unique limitations on the supply of raw materials (e.g., diamonds); (2) those based on secrecy or special privilege (patents); and (3) those arising from "peculiar properties" inherent in the business. The third class, considered by far the most important, included canals, railways, gas and water companies, telegraphs, and electric lighting. He pointed out the incompatibility of these industries with competition:

> Natural monopolies of this third class are, however, more often rooted in *conditions that make competition self-destructive.* These conditions are three in number, and the presence of all three is gen-

erally necessary to create monopoly: (1) The commodity of service rendered must be of such a nature that a small difference in price will lead buyers to purchase from one producer rather than from another. (2) The business must be of such a nature as to make the creation of a large number of competitive plants impossible. Either because the business is one in which special advantages attach to large-scale production or because there are actual physical difficulties in the way of the multiplication of competing plants, there must be fairly definite limits to the possible increase of the number of plants among which the business might be divided. (3) The proportion of fixed to variable expenses of production must be high.[9]

Ely indicated the unsuitability of competition in the case of public utilities sector. He noted that a similar pattern was followed whenever competition was introduced into this sector. A new "competitor" would enter the industry, creating a rate war with subsequent danger to the profitability of all firms concerned. The inevitable result was a merger or rate agreement.[10] Thus, by the late 1930s the economic theory of natural monopoly had been established, and most of the writers, from that time on, drew from various aspects of that well-developed theory.

In the two decades that followed, economists devoted little attention to public utility economics. For example, in 1950, Eli Clemens in his textbook reviewed the forces that worked irresistibly to make certain industries monopolies: conditions of space and geography, large capital investments, economies of decreasing costs, technical limitations of the market, and confirmation of an exclusive franchise.[11]

In 1957, Martin Glaeser described the economic and institutional foundations of regulated monopolies and concluded that public utilities are best conducted in a legal and regulated monopoly, since consolidation usually occurs when there are few competitors and since it is in the public interest to maximize street capacity. He cites the advantages of unified operations and of lower costs because of economies of large scale, and concludes that the operation should extend over as large a geographical area as is economically feasible.[12]

Examining exceptions to competitive policy in 1959, Carl Kaysen and Donald Turner expressed concern that regulation could easily expand beyond the scope appropriate to the conditions that first produced it; e.g., the need for safety regulations in air commerce does not necessarily require restrictions on freedom of entry. However, they agreed that there were situations in which competition was not a viable alternative. They defined such instances under the heading of natural monopoly. According to them, a natural monopoly was a monopoly which resulted from economies of scale so that a firm of efficient size could produce all or more than the market could take at a remunerative price, and could continually expand its capacity at less cost than that of a new firm entering the business. Therefore, competition might exist for a while, but only until bankruptcy or merger left the field to one firm. Hence, competition in any meaningful sense is self-destructive. They concluded: "Natural monopoly is traditionally the classic case for extensive regulation of the price, service, investment, and other management decisions of the industry concerned."[13]

Although they recognized the natural monopoly situation and the conditions under which it occurred, they expressed an uneasiness with the theory and with any policy that interferes with the free working of the marketplace. They noted that economies of scale is a relative concept, and that market definitions can vary widely. To them it seemed probable that for the telephone company, a natural monopoly existed in a market as large as the entire country, but they noted that local transportation monopolies have been largely eradicated.

Beginning with the sixties, there was a renewed interest in public utility economics. James Bonbright, one of the prominent economists in this field, refers to the theory of natural monopoly as an old and orthodox point of view and cautions against oversimplifying this theory by exclusively focusing on decreasing unit costs. He contends that the widespread assumption that a public utility must be producing on the declining cost part of its cost curve in order to justify its claim to acceptance as a natural monopoly is quite unwarranted. He based his conclusion on the fact that this assumption "ignores the point that even if the unit cost of supplying a given area with a given type of public utility service must increase with an enhanced rate of output, any specified required rate of output can be supplied most economically by a single firm or single system."[14]

Instead, he contends that what favors a monopoly status for a public utility is the "severely localized and hence restricted markets for utility services—markets limited because of the necessarily close connection between the utility plant on the one hand and the consumers' premises on the other. . . . Were it compelled to share its limited market with two or more rival plants owning duplicate distribution networks, the total cost of serving the city would be materially higher."[15]

Paul Garfield and Wallace Lovejoy attribute the fact that public utilities operate at lower unit costs under monopoly than under competition to the following reasons:[16]

1. Combination of utilities into monopolies makes possible the elimination of costly duplication of facilities.

2. Since service must be produced and delivered as it is demanded by consumers, this generally results in public utilities having proportionately heavier investment in fixed assets than other businesses (e.g., higher ratio of constant to total costs). In addition, the largely nonstorable nature of utility services accentuates this investment in order to assure the continuity of service.

3. Public utilities can achieve decreasing average unit costs as output increases due to the fact that they serve an entire market and as output

increases the constant costs are distributed more thinly to each unit of output.

Another economist writing about public utilities is Charles Phillips, Jr. He summarized the various economic characteristics of regulated monopoly this way:[17]

1. Economies of scale is the primary determinant of inherently noncompetitive market situation.
2. Economies of scale often require large-scale plant and large fixed investments and is an important characteristic of public utilities.
3. There is the problem of unused capacity, which results first from the diversity of consumer demand and second from engineering considerations, stemming from general policy requirement that utilities must have the necessary capacity to meet foreseeable increases in demand.
4. Diversity of demand is the result of consumers' demanding instantaneous and uninterrupted service. Thus the utility has to build capacity because it can neither store the service nor defer its purchase.
5. Most regulated firms' markets, as well as their customers' alternatives, are restricted by the necessity of the close connection between the utility's plant and consumers' premises.
6. Competition may be limited by the fact that equipment must be located below, upon, or over public property. These technical limitations suggest not only that competition would be a public nuisance if regulators allowed several companies to put in their own conduits, mains, and wires, but also that valuable space would be used up. . . .

Richard Posner in his article, "Natural Monopoly and Its Regulation," states that natural monopoly "does not refer to the actual number of sellers in a market but to the relationship between demand and the technology of supply."[18] He defines natural monopoly as the case where the entire demand within a relevant market can be satisfied at lowest cost by one firm rather than by two or more. If such a market contains more than one firm, either the firms will quickly reduce to one through mergers or failures, or production will continue to consume more resources than necessary. Thus, in the first case competition is short-lived and in the second it produces inefficient results.

More recently, Alfred Kahn, in his analysis of natural monopoly, contends that the essential prerequisite of a natural monopoly is the inherent tendency to decreasing unit costs over the entire market. The principal source of this tendency, he continues, is the necessity of making a large investment in order to serve customers on demand. According to Kahn, this tendency is created or accentuated by certain common or interrelated characteristics of many public utility services, such as (1) a fixed and essentially immovable connection between supplier and customer, (2) nonstorable nature of these services, (3) obligation of instantaneous supply upon demand, and (4) wide fluctuations in demands for service. Although he recognizes that these tendencies result in large fixed costs which make for declining cost in the short run within the limits of the existing capacity, he asserts that these conditions are not sufficient to explain the existence of natural monopoly.

Kahn goes on to point out that the phenomenon of natural monopoly is in some way related to the wastes that would arise, if in the presence of competition certain facilities would have to be duplicated, but, just as with fixed investment, he stresses that it is not the fact of duplication alone that makes for a natural monopoly. It is only when one firm can serve the entire demand most efficiently (lower total cost) than two or more firms that monopoly becomes natural. He concludes that the presence of declining unit costs is a necessary and sufficient condition that makes duplication wasteful.[19]

Conclusion

Although there has been a tendency by some economists to equate natural monopoly with economies of scale in a narrow static sense, our historical review indicates that a natural monopoly should be defined much more broadly. A more realistic definition of natural monopoly is that it exists when one firm can supply the entire market at less cost than can two or more firms. This definition precludes wasteful duplication of facilities. It also recognizes that utilities must be closely connected with the consumer and must provide service instantaneously upon demand. This service, moreover, is of such a nature that neither can it be stored, nor its purchase deferred. As a result, these conditions require a relatively large capital investment.

Thus, we arrive at the conclusion that neither the exhaustion, the absence, nor the unlikelihood of economies of scale, as defined in the traditional static sense, necessarily justifies entry or deregulation. Instead, the compelling force that demands a regulated monopoly structure is efficiency. When a one-firm industry can most efficiently provide a good or service, we have a natural monopoly condition. Then, it is in the public interest for government to impose regulation.

NOTES

Note: The author would like to thank Peter C. Manus and Leigh Tripoli for their comments. The views expressed in this article are those of the author and do not necessarily represent the policy or views of the Bell system.

1. *"Principles of Political Economy,"* by John Stuart Mill (London: Longmans, Green and Company, 1909 edition), p. 143.
2. *"The State in Its Relation to Trade,"* by Thomas Henry Farrer (London: Macmillan and Company, 1902), p. 96.
3. After examining various characteristics, Farrer found that

"It is not *large capital* for though most of them require large capital, some gas and water companies, which are complete monopolies, have capitals of not more than two or three thousand pounds; whilst other enterprises, with enormous capitals—e.g., banks, insurance offices, shipping companies—are not monopolies.

"It is not *positive law,* for few of them have a monopoly expressly granted or confirmed by law; and in most, if not all, of the cases where such a monopoly happens to have been so granted or confirmed, it would have existed without such grant or confirmation.

"They all agree in *supplying necessaries*. But this alone is no test, for butchers and bakers supply necessaries.

"Most, if not all, of them have *exclusive possession or occupation of certain peculiarly favorable portions of land;* e.g., docks, of the riverside; gas and water companies, of the streets. But this is only true in a limited sense of such undertakings as the post office, telegraphs, or even of roads and railway; and a mine, a quarry, or a fishery, has equally possession of specially favored sites without generally or necessarily becoming a monopoly.

"The article or convenience supplied by them is *local,* and cannot be dissevered from the possessor or user of the land or premises occupied by the undertaking. The undertaking does not produce an article to be carried away and sold in a distant market, but a convenience in the use of the undertaking itself, as in the case of harbors, roads, railways, post office, and telegraphs; or an article sold and used on the spot where it is produced, as in the case of gas and water.

"Again, in most of these cases the convenience afforded or article produced is one which can be *increased almost indefinitely,* without proportionate increase of the original plant; so that to set up a rival scheme is an extravagant waste of capital.

"There is also in some of these undertakings, and notoriously in the cases of the post office, of telegraphs, and of railways, another consideration; viz., the paramount importance of *certainty and harmonious arrangement*. In the case of most industries—e.g., in that of a baker—instead of several to choose from; but this consideration is in such a case not paramount to considerations of cheapness." (Ibid., pp. 96, 97.)

4. Ibid., p. 98.
5. "Relation of the State to Industrial Action," by Henry Carter Adams, reprinted in *"Two Essays by Henry Carter Adams,"* edited by Joseph Dorfman (New York: Augustus M. Kelly, 1969), p. 104.
6. Ibid., p. 109.
7. *"Problems of To-Day,"* by Richard T. Ely (New York: Thomas Y. Crowell & Company, 1888).
8. Ibid., p. 109.
9. *"Outlines of Economics,"* by Richard T. Ely (New York: The Macmillan Company, 1937, 6th edition), p. 628.
10. Ibid., pp. 629–631.
11. *"Economics and Public Utilities,"* by Eli Clemens (New York: Appleton-Century Crofts Inc., 1950), pp. 26–28.
12. *"Public Utilities in American Capitalism,"* by Martin Glaeser (New York: The Macmillan Company, 1957), pp. 74, 75.
13. *"Antitrust Policy,"* by Carl Kaysen and Donald Turner (Cambridge: Harvard University Press, 1959), p. 191.

14. *"Principles of Public Utility Rates,"* by James C. Bonbright (New York and London: Columbia University Press, 1961), pp. 14, 15.

15. Ibid., pp. 12, 13.

16. *"Public Utility Economics,"* by Paul J. Garfield and Wallace F. Lovejoy (Englewood Cliffs, New Jersey: Prentice Hall Inc., 1964), pp. 17, 18.

17. *"The Economics of Regulation,"* by Charles F. Phillips, Jr. *(Homewood, Illinois: Richard D. Crown Inc., 1969, revised edition), pp. 21–27.*

18. Richard A. Posner, op. cit., p. 548.

19. *"The Economics of Regulation: Principles and Institutions,"* by Alfred E. Kahn (New York: John Wiley & Sons, 1971), Vol. 2, pp. 119–123.

SELECTION 27

EDWARD E. ZAJAC

Basic Ramsey Prices in the Regulated Sector

Edward Zajac focuses on the problem of determining efficient prices for a multiproduct decreasing-cost public utility that by law is instructed to earn its shareholders a prescribed "fair" return on their investment. Such a utility cannot set price equal to marginal cost because of the resulting losses. Under Ramsey pricing, the firm levies markups (prices above marginal cost) that are inversely related to the absolute value of demand elasticity in each market it serves. Such pricing has often been applied as a way of covering the common or overhead costs associated with serving different markets.

QUESTIONS TO GUIDE THE READING

1. Why is marginal cost typically less than average cost where large fixed setup costs are present?

2. What price changes are necessary to satisfy the Ramsey formula if the absolute value of the price elasticity of demand for one product decreases?

3. Excise tax theory suggests on efficiency grounds that products with relatively inelastic demand be taxed. How is this suggestion similar to Ramsey pricing?

4. How can the pursuit of economic efficiency in public utility pricing lead to results contrary to the goals of equity?

> The only economic function of price is to influence *behavior*. This is a notion that traditional regulators have great difficulty accepting.
>
> A. E. KAHN IN "PUBLIC UTILITIES FORTNIGHTLY,"
> JAN. 19, 1978

3.1 Introduction

In a sense, the regulated sector of the economy is the mirror image of the market sector. The principal economic-theoretic concerns in the market sector, such as economic efficiency and the incentives that bring it about, the

Edward E. Zajac, "Basic Ramsey Prices in the Regulated Sector," in *Fairness or Efficiency: An Introduction to Public Utility Pricing,* Ballanger Publishing Co. (1978), 21–32. Reprinted by permission of the author.

Edward E. Zajac is Professor of Economics at the University of Arizona.

automatic sizing of firms, planning, bearing of uncertainty and risk—matters largely controlled automatically through the action of the "invisible hand"— are of tangential concern in the day-to-day workings of rate-base, rate-of-return regulation, and with the exception of economic efficiency, of tangential theoretical interest in the economic literature on regulation. On the other hand, matters of fairness and justness—of relatively little theoretical concern in the pure market economy—loom large, either explicitly or implicitly, and are of primary importance in regulatory proceedings.

The reasons for the differences between the market and regulated sectors are perhaps not surprising. Those who find the market place unjust by and large have no place to go to seek relief—the invisible hand is not only invisible in markets, it is invisible to those seeking the redress of grievances. On the other hand those who find regulated prices unjust, have the regulatory process to appeal to for remedy. The process has in fact many of the trappings of the judicial process, with the hearing of evidence and the issuance of rulings.

In spite of the realities of the concern for fairness, economists theorizing about public utility pricing have focused mainly on the question of economic efficiency. The next section reviews some of their research.

3.2 The Pricing Problem for the Regulated Firm

. . . Large shared or common economic costs give rise to "market failures," in particular, to the possibility of a single firm's dominating an entire industry, and thus having power to set the industry's prices at whatever level the firm chooses. In the United States, society has typically chosen governmental regulation as the method for coping with industries where large shared costs prevail. This allows society the advantage of avoiding duplication of common costs by having a single firm serve society's needs. It also allows the imposition of pricing constraints or price administration to prevent the single firm from earning exorbitant profits.

However, as already mentioned, if prices are constrained or administered, we can expect the supply-demand action of some markets to be impeded. This in turn means that with administered prices we do not necessarily expect prices automatically to adjust in the direction of economic efficiency. . . .

Furthermore, with administered prices and impeded market action, we do not expect the "invisible hand" automatically to fix the firms' boundaries, rather boundary setting must also be incorporated into the regulatory or administrative process. The boundary issue is in fact an important one which is discussed later. But for the present, it is convenient to focus on the price-setting problem, taking as given the services the regulated firm is to offer and the condition that no further rivals to the regulated firm are permitted.

An obvious approach to the problem of pricing in the regulated sector is price administration that does what one expects complete markets to do, that is, administration that sets prices to achieve economic efficiency. In fact this proposal has a long history and has been extensively discussed in the economics literature.

At equilibrium in the perfectly competitive economy, prices charged by producers for outputs are simply related to the producers' costs. The *price* for a unit of output equilibrates to the *marginal cost* or cost of producing an extra output unit. . . .

Since the perfectly competitive equilibrium is known to be economically efficient, a natural proposal to economists is to imitate theoretically ideal market action by having regulated prices also set equal to marginal costs, again where costs are forward looking.[1] However, this leads to difficulties in those regulated sectors in which the marginal cost is below average cost, as is typically the case where there are large fixed set-up costs. For then, with prices set at marginal cost, total revenues fall short of total costs. This in turn implies that the regulated firm will be unable to survive under private ownership unless it is subsidized by revenues raised in other parts of the economy. Alternatively, if it is desired to administer the regulated firm with prices at marginal costs and with the use of governmental subsidies, one must cope with the issue of how the subsidies are to be raised so as not to interfere with economic efficiency, an issue as difficult as regulating prices efficiently at the outset.

In the United States the theory of setting prices at marginal costs and subsidizing any consequent losses has not been followed. Rather, the legal precept is that the owners of a regulated firm are entitled to fair compensation by the regulated firm's customers for the use of the owners' capital. This precept requires that regulated firms operate at a zero profit, where all costs are considered. Put in other terms, the regulated firm is constrained to generate revenues that only cover operating costs and the "cost of capital," that is, that provide the same return to the shareholders that they would get in alternative investments of comparable risk. Revenues in excess of these total costs are not allowed. This "revenue requirement" or "budget" or "zero-profit" constraint generally precludes pricing at marginal cost, and we shall not discuss the price equals marginal cost proposal further.

The "total revenues = total costs" or "zero-profit" constraint complicates the problem of finding regulated, economically efficient prices. Nevertheless, the problem has been extensively dealt with in terms of theoretical models whose complexity varies, depending on assumptions made about the interactions of the firm and its regulators with the remainder of the economy.[2] A detailed discussion of all these efforts goes beyond the scope of this monograph. However, we can get insight into the results by considering special, simple cases. Because of the theory's importance, the next two sections, Sections 3.3 and 3.4, develop two different approaches to providing such insight in terms of the simplest model of the regulated firm first suggested by Ramsey in 1927. It is becoming more and more common to call this model's prices, "Ramsey prices," a practice that will be followed here. . . .

3.3 Ramsey Prices Preserve Quantity Ratios

Imagine that prices are initially set at marginal costs throughout the economy and consumers everywhere accordingly adjust their consumption patterns so as to maximize their individual satisfactions. Presumably, the regulated firm will find that with prices equal to marginal costs it is not meeting its zero-profit constraint of total revenues covering total costs. Imagine then that the regulated firm's prices are changed to cause satisfaction of the zero-profit condition, while prices are maintained at marginal costs throughout the rest of the economy; that the required price change is a small proportion of marginal cost; and that price changes in one of the firm's markets do not influence demands in the firm's other markets (i.e., independent demand schedules).[3] If the prices are changed so as to achieve economic efficiency, it turns out that they should *change all the regulated firm's outputs in the same proportion.* In symbols,

$$x_i^{mc}/x_j^{mc} = x_i/x_j \qquad (1)$$

where

$x_i^{mc}, x_j^{mc} =$ outputs in the firm's i^{th} and j^{th} markets when price equals marginal cost everywhere

$x_i, x_j =$ outputs in the firm's i^{th} and j^{th} markets when the firm's prices are adjusted to be economically efficient and at the same time to attain a zero profit

Equation (1) has an intuitively appealing interpretation in terms of the two-stage process we have imagined. In the first stage, prices set at marginal costs coordinate the economy to an efficient allocation of resources. At the conclusion of this stage, the attainment of economic efficiency means that there are no mutually advantageous exchanges in the quantities of goods consumed. For the regulated firm, the aggregate amount consumed of the ith good or service will be x_i^{mc} and the ratio of the ith to the jth output will be x_i^{mc}/x_j^{mc}. In the second stage, the change in the firm's prices causes output changes. Equation (1) says that if the output changes maintain the ratio x_i^{mc}/x_j^{mc} for *any* two markets i and j, then, after the price adjustment, there will again exist no possible mutually advantageous exchanges of the firm's outputs possible and economic efficiency will again result.

Note that Eq. (1) has the following implications for pricing. Say the demand for the ith good or service is very insensitive to changes in its price, (price *inelastic*) while the demand for the jth good in relatively sensitive to price changes (price *elastic*). Then to maintain the ratio x_i^{mc}/x_j^{mc} the price of the ith good or service will have to be raised comparatively higher with respect to its marginal cost than will be the price of the jth good or service. This fact emerges explicitly in the next section where we develop the variant of Eq. (1) that is expressed in terms of prices rather than outputs.

3.4 Ramsey Prices Balance Gains and Losses for Small Price Changes

Prices, not output levels are the control variables available to policy makers. Hence an explanation of Ramsey prices in terms of prices is more directly applicable to the pricing of regulated firms. To arrive at a price-oriented interpretation, we again restrict attention to the case of independent demands.[4] Let us consider first a price rise so small that it reduces demand for a commodity by one unit. Perhaps at a price of $10/unit, 10,000 units are consumed, and a price rise to $10.02 results in a demand of 9999 units. It is important to distinguish two effects. First is the effect on the *marginal* consumer, that is, the consumer who decides to forgo the consumption of one unit when the price is raised above $10. For this person, the price rise results in a standoff: he doesn't get the satisfaction of consuming the unit, but he also doesn't part with $10. Put in other terms, the refusal of the marginal consumer to buy the commodity when its price is raised from $10 to $10.02 indicates that the value to him of consuming one unit is somewhere between $10 and $10.02. In the extreme, knife-edge case, if the marginal consumer refuses to buy the additional unit for *any* price rise above $10, no matter how slight, his value of one unit is exactly $10. A price rise above $10 then means an exact trade of forgone consumption for retained income.

The second effect of the price rise is felt by the *infra-marginal* consumers, that is, those who continue to consume the 9999 units. Since they consume exactly the same number of units as they did at the $10 price, the aggregate effect on them of the price rise to $10.02 is a loss of 9999 × $0.02 or $199.98.

Clearly, a price decrease evokes symmetric effects. If a price of $9.99 means a demand of 10,001 units, the marginal demander values the additional unit somewhere between $10 and $9.99, and in the knife-edge case, the marginal demander has a value of exactly $9.99 for a unit. For the infra-marginal consumers, the price decrease represents an aggregate gain of 10,000 × $0.01 or $100.

Now imagine that a regulated firm's prices are initially such that the firm makes zero profit. Imagine further that the price of one service, say Service I, is slightly raised while that of a second service, say Service J, is compensatingly lowered so as to maintain the firm at zero profit. The amounts by which the services' prices must be adjusted depend of course on the firm's cost structure and the sensitivities of demands in the Ith and J^{th} markets to these markets' prices. In particular, in order to maintain zero profit, it may be necessary to raise the price of Service I so that the output demanded falls off by only one unit while lowering Service J's price so that its demand increases by several units. Whatever the relation between Service I's price rise and Service J's compensating price drop and the consequent output adjustments, the infra-marginal customers of Service I will lose and those of Service J will gain, while the marginal customers of both services will break even. If Service J gains exceed the Service I losses then, in principle, the Service J customers could compensate the Service I customers to accept the price adjustment and there would be money left over to be shared by both. Likewise, if Service I's losses exceeded Service J's gains, the directions of the price changes could simply be reversed. Then a price drop for Service I and a compensating price rise for Service J would allow Service I to compensate Service J and would leave a money surplus to be shared by both services. In either case the firm would presumably be indifferent between the initial prices and the adjusted prices because both sets of prices would allow it to realize its zero profit goal. However, from the standpoint of the customers of Services I and J, the adjusted prices are potentially preferable since in principle they allow both sets of customers to be better off.

For any two services, we can imagine such an exploration for a "Pareto superior" price adjustment, given any initial set of prices that has the firm at zero profit and given that prices throughout the rest of the economy are maintained at marginal costs. The Ramsey prices are *the zero-profit prices for which there is no Pareto superior adjustment.* That is, at the Ramsey prices the firm satisfies its zero profit constraint and, further, any slight price adjustment that maintains it at zero profit will result in aggregate gains being *exactly* equal to aggregate losses. Ramsey prices are thus economically efficient in the sense that there is no way that they can be adjusted to benefit some without harm to others.

In symbols, for any two of the firm's markets, say I and J, the Ramsey prices turn out to satisfy the formula.[5]

$$e_i[p_i^R - mc_i]/p_i^R = e_j[p_j^R - mc_j]/p_j^R$$

and the condition

$$Total\ Revenues = Total\ Costs$$

where

$$p_i^R, p_j^R = \text{Ramsey prices in the } I^{th} \text{ and } J^{th} \text{ markets}$$
$$mc_i, mc_j = \text{marginal cost in the } I^{th} \text{ and } J^{th} \text{ markets}$$
$$e_i, e_j = \text{elasticities of demand in the } I^{th} \text{ and } J^{th}$$
markets (elasticity of demand = percent change in output for a one percent change in price)

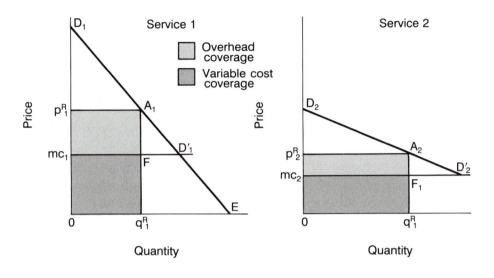

At Ramsey prices, $D_1A_1/A_1D_1' = D_2A_2/A_2D_1'$ and the sum of overhead coverages equals the overhead.

3.5 Diagrammatic Presentation of Ramsey Prices

A convenient diagrammatic interpretation of Ramsey prices is available when demand schedules in all the firm's markets are independent of one another and when marginal costs in all markets are constant. These assumptions are generally invalid, but they are often approximately true if relatively small price deviations from some set of initial prices are being considered.

To illustrate the diagrammatic construction, we need depict only two of the firm's markets, say Service 1 and Service 2, as shown in Fig. 1. Assume first that the demand schedules for the two markets are the straight lines $D_1A_1D'_1$ and $D_2A_2D'_2$ respectively, where prices are marked on the vertical axes and quantities on the horizontal axes. The constant marginal costs, mc_1 and mc_2, are also marked on the vertical price axes.

Ramsey prices are indicated by p_1^R and p_2^R. At Ramsey prices, demands fall on Points A_1 and A_2 of the demand schedules of Fig. 1, and the corresponding output levels are then q_1^R and q_2^R.

With prices at their Ramsey values, two geometric conditions are satisfied. First, if D' is the intersection of the demand schedule with the horizontal line at height mc, then the ratio DA/AD' is the same in all markets, so that for Services 1 and 2, $D_1A_1/A_1D'_1 = D_2A_2/A_2D'_2$. This condition by itself is obviously insufficient since it is satisfied by an infinite number of combinations of prices for the two markets. So a second condition relating to the firm's zero profit constraint is required. This is most easily stated in terms of *overhead coverages,* shown in Fig. 1. For example, at the price p_1^R and corresponding demand q_1^R, the firm obtains the revenue $p_1^R \times q_1^R$ from Service 1. In Fig. 1 this revenue is the sum of two cross-sectioned rectangles. The lower rectangle represents the portion of this revenue that covers the firm's *variable* cost, $mc_1 \times q_1^R$, that is, the cost that varies with the quantity that the firm sells in the Service 1 market. The upper rectangle represents the amount of revenue available to cover the firm's nonvariable costs or overhead, that is, the costs which do not vary with the quantities sold in the respective markets. To attain the firm's zero profit goal, the sum of the overhead coverages must equal the firm's overhead. Imposing this condition as well nails down the Ramsey prices in Fig. 1. To summarize, when prices are at their Ramsey values we have

1. $\dfrac{DA}{AD'}$ is the same in all markets.

2. The sum over all markets of overhead coverages equals the overhead.[6]

For convenience, straight line demand schedules have been assumed. However, the construction still applies if the straight line segments $D_1A_1D'_1$ and $D_2A_2D'_2$ are interpreted as *tangents* to bowed demand curves, with Points A_1 and A_2 being the points of tangency.

3.6 Cautionary Note

In this chapter I have tried to show the basic economic forces that are at the heart of theoretical models of economically efficient prices for public utilities. However, in Section 3.2, I mentioned that there are a number of such models; although they have in common the elements that led to the Ramsey formulas of Sections 3.3 and 3.4, they differ in the details of the descriptions of the firm's markets and the interactions of the firm with the rest of the economy. The reader is cautioned that these differences can be significant. For example, in the derivation of the Ramsey formula we assumed that a consumer's gains or losses depended only on the units of a commodity that he consumed and not on the units that others consumed (in economists' jargon, we assumed the absence of "consumption externalities"). However, having a telephone is obviously worthless unless someone else has a telephone, and, as one might suspect, consumption externalities play an important role in telephone pricing. In fact, the notion that the value of telephone service to me depends on the number of persons I can talk to is an important element in the "value of service" concept in traditional telephone rate making. When consumption externalities are important, the Ramsey formula of Sections 3.3 and 3.4 must be significantly modified (see note 3 at the end of the chapter).

Likewise, in deriving the simple Ramsey formula, we have assumed that prices outside of the regulated sector are everywhere equal to marginal costs. . . .

NOTES

1. See Samuelson [1973] for a discussion of the proposal to set the regulated firm's prices equal to marginal costs.

2. As the text indicates, the seminal paper is Ramsey [1927]. A survey of the literature prior to 1970 on the problem of pricing for a regulated firm is given by Baumol and Bradford [1970]. Some subsequent references are Diamond and Mirrlees [1971], Rohlfs [1976], and Atkinson and Stiglitz [1976].

3. To be more precise, we must in fact make several more assumptions in order for the theory to be correct. For example, we assume that the regulated firm acts as a "price taker" for the labor and raw materials it buys, that is, the firm is not large enough significantly to influence prices by virtue of its buying actions; and that its products do not exhibit "consumption externalities," that is, the enjoyment of any of the firm's products by a single customer does not depend on how much of its products are used by other customers. . . . In the case of telephone utilities the "no consumption externalities" assumption is violated, and the basic Ramsey formula must be modified to take consumption externalities into account. See Rohlfs [1974], Littlechild [1975], and Willig and Klein [1977] for a discussion of this issue and for further references to the literature.

4. Demands are independent if price changes in one of the firm's markets have no influence on demands in the firm's other markets.

5. For the analytically minded, note that $x_i dp_i$ is the inframarginal gain or loss in the ith market for a small price change, dp_i, and

$$x_i dp_i + x_j dp_j = 0 \qquad \text{(a)}$$

is the condition that there be no net inframarginal gain or loss for any two markets for price changes dp_i, dp_j. The ith market's overhead coverage is $(p_i - mc_i)x_i$, and the condition that there be no change in overhead coverage in two markets is

$$d[(p_i - mc_i)x_i] + d[(p_j - mc_j)x_j] = 0 \qquad \text{(b)}$$

Straightforward manipulations of Eqs. (a) and (b) yield the Ramsey formulas in the text.

6. The derivation of this diagrammatic construction follows easily from the fact that the elasticity of a point on a straight-line demand schedule is the negative of the ratio of the segment below to the segment above, i.e., in Fig. 1,

$$e_i = - A_1E/A_1D_1$$

By simple geometry

$$(p_1^R - mc_1)/p_1^R = A_1D'_1/A_1E$$

Hence,

$$e_1(p_1^R - mc_1)/p_1 = - A_1D'_1/A_1D_1$$

which by the Ramsey formula is constant in all markets. This constant has been called the *Ramsey number* (see Willig and Bailey [1977]). For a generalization of this diagrammatic construction see Zajac [1974]. Note also that strictly speaking, for the case shown in Fig. 1 there will be two price sets that satisfy Conditions (1) and (2). However, each price in one set will be higher than the corresponding price, market-by-market, in the second set. The higher prices are thus "Pareto inferior" to the lower prices and can be ignored.

REFERENCES

A. B. Atkinson and J. E. Stiglitz, 1976, "The Design of Tax Structure: Direct Versus Indirect Taxation," *Journal Public Economics,* 6, 55–70.

P. A. Diamond and J. A. Mirrlees, 1971, "Optimal Taxation and Public Production," *American Economic Review,* 61, 8–27 and 261–278.

A. E. Kahn, 1978a, "Applications of Economics to Utility Rate Structures," *Public Utilities Fortnightly,* 101, 13–17.

S. C. Littlechild, 1975, "Two-Part Tariffs and Consumption Externalities," *Bell Journal of Economics,* 6, 661–670.

F. Ramsey, 1927, "A Contribution to the Theory of Taxation," *Economic Journal,* 37, 47–61.

J. H. Rohlfs, 1976, "Evaluation of Changes in a Suboptimal Economy," *Review of Economic Studies,* 43(2), 359–362.

P. A. Samuelson, 1973, *Economics* (ninth edition), McGraw-Hill.

R. D. Willig and E. E. Bailey, 1977, "Income Distributional Concerns in Regulatory Policy Making" to appear in the Proceedings of NBER Research Conference on Public Regulation, Washington, Dec. 1977.

R. D. Willig and R. W. Klein, 1977, "Network Externalities and Optimal Telecommunications Pricing: A Preliminary Sketch," Proceedings of the Fifth Annual Telecommunications Policy Research Conference (available from the National Telecommunications Information Service, Washington, D.C.).

E. E. Zajac, 1974, "Note on an Extension of the Ramsey Inverse Elasticity of Demand Pricing or Taxation Formula," *Journal of Public Economics,* 3, 181–184.

Public Expenditure Issues

The following six selections use the standard of economic efficiency to evaluate the provision of goods and services through the political process. The last three readings focus on the operation of specific government programs.

SELECTION 28

ALICE M. RIVLIN

Economics and the Political Process

In recent years, economists have become increasingly involved in the federal budget process. Alice Rivlin, a former director of the Congressional Budget Office, examines attempts in the United States to improve the economic decision-making process within both executive and legislative branches of federal government. She focuses on the weaknesses in the economic policy process and offers suggestions for improvement.

QUESTIONS TO GUIDE THE READING

1. According to Rivlin, why did the United States create and fail to reduce the large structural budget deficit of the 1980s?
2. How did the creation of OMB and CEA enhance the President's ability to formulate economic policy? What problems were created?
3. What are the advantages of a "deficit-neutral" amendment rule?
4. What changes does Rivlin recommend to make the economic policy process more effective?
5. How can economists help to improve the policy-making process?

I want to use this once-in-a-lifetime opportunity for pontificating to the profession, to explore ways of improving the interaction between what economists do and the political process. Tension and conflict are, of course, in-

Alice M. Rivlin, "Economics and the Political Process," *American Economic Review 77* (March 1987), 1–10. Reprinted by permission of the author and the publisher.

Alice M. Rivlin is Director of Economic Studies at the Brookings Institution.

herent in political decisions, especially on economic policy. Nothing can make such decisions easy. Nevertheless, it is my contention that economic policymaking in Washington in the last decade has been more frustrating, muddled, and confusing than necessary. Some of the fault lies with economists and economics; some with politicians and the political process; some in the interactions. I want to offer some suggestions for modest improvements.

Most economists probably share my premise that economics ultimately ought to be more than just challenging intellectual gymnastics. It ought to help us understand how the economy works and provide a basis for intelligent political choices among economic policies. Even those who devote their energies to resolving purely theoretical issues imagine that somehow in the end their efforts will prove socially useful.

The dedicated, idealistic young economist who aspires to advise a government may well envision herself someday as the wise and impartial adviser to the philosopher queen. In this daydream, the adviser presents the best forecasts that can be made of the future course of the economy. She explains the macroeconomic policy options and what is likely to happen if each is undertaken. She elucidates why market solutions are efficient, when markets are likely to fail, and what can be done when this occurs. She identifies risks and uncertainties, which fortunately are not overwhelming. She represents the best professional judgment of her fellow economists, indicating the major respects in which most economists agree and scrupulously pointing out that in minor respects the views of some of her professional colleagues might differ from her own. She remains above the political fray, identifying any values or distributional biases that may creep into her judgments and eschewing identification with interest groups or ideological causes.

The queen for her part listens carefully and intelligently, asks thoughtful questions, and weighs the options. She may consult other experts on noneconomic aspects of the decisions, but these can be assumed not to be very important. She then makes final decisions—even very hard ones—and sticks to them. The decisions are carried out, the economy prospers, and a grateful nation applauds the wisdom of the monarch and her economist and the usefulness of economics.

But in the real world, both economics and politics are frustratingly unlike this picture. Both are pluralistic in the extreme and appear to be getting more so. Economists and political leaders not only miscommunicate, but each accuses the other of incompetence, obfuscation, self-serving motives, and antisocial behavior.

Economists, of course, do not wait for others to attack them; they do it themselves. Walter Heller said in his presidential address that the "chorus of self-criticism has risen to a new crescendo" (1975, p. 1), and the self-deprecation has not abated in the intervening decade. If a golden age of economists' self-confidence ever occurred, it is long past. Events of recent years have kept reminding us that our national economy is diverse and complex, battered by unpredictable shocks, and increasingly interconnected with the even more diverse and complex world outside our borders. Knowledge of how the domestic economy works and interacts with the rest of the world is imperfect. Economists keep coming up with ingeneous theories, but they have a hard time testing them. Data are inadequate and controlled experimentation nearly impossible. Modeling has greatly enhanced our understanding of the past, but shows few visible signs of improving the reliability of macroeconomic prediction. Forecasting even for short periods remains an uncertain art in which neither economists nor politicians can have much confidence.

Many of the most sophisticated and realistic members of the profession, conscious of all these difficulties, have abandoned the attempt to advise governments on policies in favor of the more manageable tasks of adding to the knowledge base. This may be understandable, but it deprives the economic policy debate of the input of some very good minds and runs the risk of leaving the job of interacting with the political arena disproportionately to those with strong ideological views.

I. Fragmentation of the Economic Policy Process

The pluralism of economics pales beside the pluralism of the political system that policy-minded economists aspire to assist. Even if one leaves aside the complexities of federalism, the process by which national economic policy evolves in Washington is so fragmented and complicated that it is almost impossible to explain to the uninitiated how it is supposed to work, let along how it does work.

A well-founded distrust of despots led our forefathers not only to opt for representative democracy, but to divide power among the executive and legislative and judicial branches, and between the House and the Senate. On matters of taxing and spending, they were especially protective of the power of the people's representatives, making it clear that while the president could propose taxing and spending, the ultimate authority lies with the Congress, subject only to presidential veto. This divided power creates a built-in hurdle to making and carrying out fiscal policy. The hurdle is low when the president is articulating a policy that has broad support in the country and in the Congress. It can lead to erratic shifts of policy when the president is indecisive, and to deadlock when the president is leading in a direction in which the public and its elected representatives do not wish to go. Deadlocks are rare, but can be serious. The failure to reduce the huge structural budget deficit of the mid-1980s largely reflects the fact that the president's solution—drastic reduction of the federal role in the domestic economy—does not command broad popular support.

The separation of powers between the Congress and the president is basic to our system of government and probably worth the price of occasional deadlock. The difficulties of making economic policy, however, are strongly compounded by the propensity of our pluralistic society to diffuse power and decision-making authority both within the executive branch and within Congress. With respect to taxing and spending policy, for example, the simple notion that the president proposes and the Congress disposes is greatly complicated by the fragmentation of power within each branch. Moreover, periodic efforts to make the policy process more coherent within each branch, while often temporarily successful, have added new power centers without consolidating the old ones.

In the executive branch, the trend since early in the century has been to centralize power in the White House in order to make it easier for the president to formulate and articulate taxing and spending policy, and to utilize the growing skills of the economics profession to that end. But this worthy goal has been accomplished in stages, with a new institution added at each stage. The creation of what is now called the Office of Management of Budget (OMB) in the 1920s made it possible for the president to review and evaluate spending requests and impose a set of priorities on his budget proposal to Congress reflecting his administration's view of the appropriate size and role of government. The creation of the Council of Economic Advisers (CEA) in the 1940s provided a focal point for bringing the advice of the economics profession into the service of presidential decision making and a locus for creating an official forecast of economic activity.

The creation of OMB and CEA improved the president's ability to formulate and articulate macroeconomic policy. It also left the president, in addition to his other impossible duties, with the job of resolving a built-in tension over responsibility for economic policy among the CEA, OMB, and the Treasury, not to mention the White House staff and the agencies with line responsibility for implementing various aspects of economic policy.

Presidents have tried various coordination mechanisms including "troika" arrangements and an almost infinite variety of broader councils and committees with varying membership, responsibilities, and leadership. The system works tolerably well or exceedingly creakily, depending on the president's personal style and the personalities involved. But it encourages battling over turf as well as substance, and is hardly designed to minimize the amount of presidential energy needed to evolve a coherent, explainable policy on taxing and spending. One might wonder whether it is not time to do what so many other countries do and give our president the equivalent of a responsible finance minister charged with the functions now diffused to our budget director, Council of Economic Advisers, and Treasury Secretary.

The fragmentation of power and responsibility is, of course, even more extreme in the Congress. The legislative branch also has a long history of attempts to make taxing and spending policy in a more coherent fashion by adding new coordinating institutions—appropriations committees, a joint economic committee, budget committees, a congressional budget office— without eliminating or consolidating any of the old ones.

The most recent attempt to improve congressional economic decision making—one in which I was an active participant—followed the Budget Reform Act of 1974 which created the budget committees and the Congressional Budget Office. These budget reforms succeeded in their main objective of focusing the attention of the Congress on overall budget policy, not just individual taxing and spending fragments. They have forced the Congress to fit the pieces together, to debate and vote on an overall taxing and spending plan—a budget resolution—to which specific taxing and spending matters must conform. No one can say that the Congress in the last few years has ignored fiscal policy! The creation of the Congressional Budget Office, moreover, has given Congress independent access to forecasts, projections, and analysis of economic options.

The downside of the budget reforms, however, was that the budget process was superimposed on the already complex responsibilities of authorizing, appropriating, and tax committees. It has added to the layers and stages of congressional policymaking without removing any of them, has made the process of budget decision making nearly impossible even for members of Congress to understand, and increased the workload so much that decisions are routinely made late and in an atmosphere of crisis. Moreover, Congress now frequently has to deal with two sets of estimates, those of the OMB and those of the Congressional Budget Office, which may differ because they are based on different forecasts of economic activity, or for even less obvious technical reasons.

Meanwhile, back in the separate world of the Federal Reserve, monetary policy is being decided and carried out. It is a curious paradox that a nation, which feels it needs many more hands on the tiller of fiscal policy than most countries regard as workable, is content to leave monetary policy to a central bank with fewer visible ties to the rest of the government than the central banks of most countries.

There is plenty of informal communication, of course, especially between the Federal Reserve and the hydraheaded economic establishment of the executive branch. More formal cooperation between the monetary and fiscal authorities, as in the United Kingdom, might contribute only marginally to making monetary and fiscal policy decisions part of a more coherent strategy for the economy—and at the cost of depriving the executive branch of the luxury of blaming the Federal Reserve when things go wrong. The love-hate relation between the Congress and Federal Reserve, however, warrants more attention. Despite occasional outbursts of anxiety over escalating interest rates, Congress has shown little inclination to control monetary policy, or even to inquire into the consistency of monetary and fiscal objectives. The Fed is required to report monetary growth targets to the banking committees, as though monetary policy were a matter of banking system regulation, but has little genuine interaction with the budget committees whose job is to debate and propose fiscal policy.

II. The Process under Stress

This whole complicated economic policy system has been subjected to enormous strain in recent years. Political economists like to harken back to the golden years of the 1950s and 1960s when economists got respect and the economic policy machinery functioned smoothly. The nostalgia is only partly a result of faulty memories. It's not hard to be satisfied with econo- mists and policy processes when the economy is growing, productivity marches steadily upward, and even the national debt is obligingly declining in relative importance. It's much harder when productivity growth plummets for reasons that no one honestly purports fully to understand, expectations of public and private consumers have to be cut back to fit with slower in- come growth, and inflation and interest rates are bouncing around at unfa- miliar levels.

Adjusting to the energy shocks and slower growth that began in the 1970s strained the economic policy processes of all industrial countries and made the participants feel frustrated and inadequate. It's not obvious, even with hindsight, that the fundamental difficulties facing the industrial world in the 1970s can credibly be blamed on economists or any particular struc- ture of government or economic policy responses, but all came in for their share of the understandable hostility.

The difficulties of the U.S. economy in the 1980s, by contrast, revolve heavily around an economic policy mistake: the creation of a large structural deficit in the federal budget. I do not believe that the structure of our eco- nomic decision process was the cause of the mistake. Blaming the deficit on inherent flaws in the policy process requires an explanation of why the pro- cess did not cause similar mistakes in the past. But the events of 1981 which produced the deficit illustrate several of the difficulties of economic policy- making which make mistakes harder to avoid:

- The uncertainty of macroeconomic forecasting;
- The isolation of monetary and fiscal policy;
- The contentiousness of economists and their tendency to let their ideo- logical positions cloud their judgments about the likely effects of partic- ular policies.

That a tax cut unmatched by comparable spending cuts would produce a deficit should have surprised no economist. That the deficit was so large reflected both economic and political miscalculations. The Reagan Admin- istration has been faulted for masking the deficit with a "rosy scenario," but the fact is that most of the forecasting community, including the Congres- sional Budget Office, expected positive real growth in the economy. The administration's official forecast differed from the rest only in its degree of optimism. Forecasters in and out of government were oversanguine about growth largely because they failed to realize how serious the Federal Re- serve was about reining in the money supply to control inflation. The Fed was not defying the administration, which was touting the efficacy of mon- etary stringency for controlling inflation, but hardly anyone seemed to re- member that the way tight money controls inflation is by slowing economic activity. Moreover, as our Association's President-elect, Robert Eisner, has pointed out (1986, p. 146), the economics community, unfamiliar with a world of high inflation rates, overestimated the stimulative effect of the existing deficit. Added to this was the enthusiasm of the ideological proponents of smaller government, some of whom exaggerated the possible effects of lower tax rates on supply and some of whom simply hoped that deficits would pressure Congress to cut back domestic spending. The size of the deficits was also masked by the assumption of unspecified future spending cuts, an assumption reflecting the view that the U.S. government was operating a lot of wasteful programs with little public support which Congress could soon be persuaded to reduce or eliminate.

Both in the administration and in Congress, decisions were made at a breakneck pace, in a highly charged political atmosphere, amid conflicting claims and competing forecasts, with little attention to the consistency of monetary and fiscal policy and mostly by people with little experience in evaluating the reasonableness of any set of economic estimates. (See David Stockman, 1986, ch. 3.) When the dust settled, we found ourselves with a serious recession that nobody expected, and an escalating structural budget deficit that nobody wanted. It was hardly economic policy's finest hour.

The agonizing—and so far only partially successful—struggle to correct the mistakes of 1981 have kept the economic policy process under stress and have continued to dramatize some of its weakest aspects. The struggle between the president and the Congress over deficit solutions illustrates the price we pay for the separation of powers. The fact that fiscal policy has become an exercise in damage control, while the Federal Reserve makes all the important decisions about the economy, underlines the separation of monetary and fiscal policy. The sensitivity of deficits to the pace of the economy advertises the unreliability of macroeconomic forecasts. The fact that all the actions that could be taken to correct the deficit are unpleasant ones drags out the annual agony of budget setting interminably and dramatizes how layered and cumbersome it has become.

Small wonder that the strains of the last few years, with a little help from the press, have reinforced the negative stereotypes that economists and political decision makers have of each other. Political decision makers see economists as quarrelsome folks who cannot forecast, cannot agree, cannot express themselves clearly, and have strong ideological biases. Economists return the favor by regarding politicians as short-sighted, interested only in what is popular with the electorate, and unwilling to face hard decisions. All of the stereotypes are partly right.

Politicians embody their stereotype in economist jokes. Economists have retaliated more massively by applying the tools of their trade to the political system itself. Public choice theory essentially asks the question: what would economic policy be like if our stereotype of politicians were entirely true? The answer provides considerable insight into observed political behavior and certainly helps explain why the idealistic economist so often fails to find the system simulating the public interest motivation of the philosopher queen.

III. Some Drastic Nonsolutions

Widespread concern that the economic policy process is not working well has spawned proposals for drastic change that move in two quite different directions: one toward circumscribing the discretion of elected officials by putting economic policy on automatic pilot and the other toward making elected officials more directly responsible to the voters for their policies.

The automatic pilot approach flows from the perspective of public choice theory that the decisions of democratically elected officials interested in staying in office cannot be counted on to produce economic policy in the social interest, but are likely to be biased toward excessive government spending, growing deficits, special interest tax and spending programs, and easier money. A way to overcome these biases is to agree in advance on strict rules of economic policy, such as a fixed monetary growth path or constitutionally required balance in the federal budget.

Even if one accepts the premises, however, firm rules are hard to define in a rapidly changing world—no one seems to know what "money" is anymore—and can easily lead to perverse results. Recent experience with trying to reduce the federal deficit along the fixed path specified by the Gramm-Rudman-Hollings amendment, for example, has given us a taste of some of the possible disadvantages of a balanced budget rule. There is danger that specific dollar targets for the deficit will require procyclical fiscal policy, perhaps precipitating a recession that would then make budget balance even less attainable. Moreover, the effort to reach the targets can induce cosmetic or self-defeating measures, such as moving spending from one fiscal year to another for no valid reason, selling assets to reduce a current deficit while exacerbating future ones, and accomplishing desired purposes by regulatory or other nonbudgetary means.

The Gramm-Rudman-Hollings experience, however, has suggested the usefulness of a different approach to deficit reduction than a balanced budget rule; namely, a deficit neutral amendment rule. If legislators advocating a tax preference are required to propose a rate increase to pay for it, special interest tax legislation may falter. Similarly, the requirement that a proposal for additional spending be accompanied by a simultaneous proposal to raise taxes or reduce another spending program may be an effective brake on deficits.

The other direction of reform reflects the contrasting view that the separation of powers and the diffusion of responsibility in our government make it too difficult for the electorate to enforce its will by holding officials responsible for their policies. The potential for deadlock would be reduced if the United States moved toward a parliamentary system, or found a way to hold political parties more strictly accountable for proposing or carrying out identifiable policies.

Casual examination of parliamentary democracies, such as the United Kingdom and Sweden, does not provide striking evidence of the superiority of parliamentary systems for making economic choices, even if one did not have two hundred years of tradition to contend with in changing our system.

The more modest notion that our system would work more smoothly if political parties had better defined positions and disciplined their elected members more strictly may well be right, but seems to fly in the face of current history. Voters are showing less strong party affiliation and more inclination to choose for themselves among candidates, while members of Congress tend increasingly to be pragmatists willing to work out nonideological compromises across party lines. These trends seem likely to be the irreversible consequences of greater education, sophistication, and exposure to public issues among voters and elected officials alike and to make a resurgence of party discipline and loyalty unrealistic.

IV. Making the Economic Policy System Work Better

My own proposals involve less drastic changes in the structure of our government. They reflect a strong faith in the ability of informed citizens and their elected representatives to make policy decisions for the common good, even to make substantial sacrifices and take political risks to further what they perceive as the long-run national interest—once they understand what the choices are. I also believe that the separation of powers between the executive and legislative branches works pretty well most of the time. It provides needed protection against overzealousness in either branch, albeit at some risk of occasional stalemate.

The main problem, it seems to me, is that our economic policy system has gradually become so complex, diffused, and fragmented that it impedes rather than fosters informed choices on major issues. The fragmentation imposes two kinds of costs. First, it makes the decision process itself exceedingly inefficient. Decisions are made too often, in too great detail, and reviewed by too many layers of decision makers in the executive branch and in Congress. Too much time is absorbed in procedure and in wrangling over details, not enough on major decisions. It's time to simplify the process, to weed out some of the institutions, and to tip the balance between substance and process back toward substance.

Second, decisions are made separately that ought to be made together, or at least with attention to their impact on each other. The separation of monetary and fiscal policy is one example; the separation of tax and spending decisions is another. Congress has made a good deal of progress in recent years in putting spending decisions together with their revenue or deficit consequences, but more could be done. I have seven steps to suggest that might make the economic policy process work more effectively.

First, seek out decisions that should be made less frequently and arrange to do so. This would economize decision-making time and enhance the chances of thoughtful, well-informed decisions. It would free up time and energy for managing the government enterprise more effectively, with a longer planning horizon. It would also reduce the inefficiency and sense of unfairness that goes with frequent changes of the rules. Making the federal budget every other year would be a major advance. Major revisions of the tax code should occur even less frequently. Big ticket acquisitions, such as major weapons systems, should be reviewed thoroughly at infrequent intervals and then put on a steady efficient track, not constantly revisited.

With a two-year budget, there would occasionally be major events, such as a sudden escalation of international tension or a sharp unexpected shift in the economic outlook, that would justify reopening the budget in midstream, but the temptation to tinker frequently should be strongly resisted. The argument that economists cannot forecast accurately two years in advance, while quite true, does not undermine the case for a multiyear budget. It simply reinforces the point that discretionary fiscal policy is hazardous and ought to be viewed with great skepticism whether the budget is annual or biennial.

Second, seek out decisions that need not be made at all and stop making them. Some spending programs could be consolidated into block grants or devolved to the states, not necessarily in the interest of smaller government, but in the interest of greater responsiveness to local needs and a less cluttered federal decision schedule. In other cases, the responsibility is clearly federal—as in defense—but Congress would be doing its job more effectively if it concentrated on major policy issues rather than on details of program management.

Third, in the executive branch, consolidate authority for tax, budget, and fiscal policy in a single cabinet department. The department could retain the name Treasury, but might better be called the Department of Economic Affairs. The Secretary of Economic Affairs should have a high-level chief economist or economic council with a strong professional staff. The chief economist should work closely with the budget director who also should report to the Secretary. The purpose would be to bring together economic decisions now made in OMB, CEA, and Treasury under one high-level responsible person, to relieve the president of the duty of adjudicating among so many potentially warring power centers, and to increase the chances of building a highly professional permanent economic staff one step removed from the short-run political concerns of the White House.

Fourth, streamline the congressional committee structure to reduce the number of steps in the budget process. The authorizing and appropriating functions should be combined in a single set of "program committees," one for each major area of public spending. This would imply a single defense committee, for example, and a social insurance committee. The tax committees should handle the revenue side—not additional spending programs as at present. The budget committees would be charged with considering fiscal policy and putting the spending and revenue sides together into a budget to be passed by the whole Congress. The Joint Economic Committee should celebrate the important contributions it made to economic understanding in the days before the budget process and then close up shop.

Fifth, bring monetary and fiscal policy into the same conversation. This end could be furthered by closer formal links between the central bank and the Department of Economic Affairs to dramatize the need for consultation and interaction. The Federal Reserve chairman should make a report to the budget committees of Congress laying out recommended short- and longer-run economic goals for the nation and discussing combinations of monetary and fiscal strategies to achieve them. The Fed's report should be an important input to congressional deliberations on fiscal policy.

Sixth, strive for a government-wide official economic forecast to be updated on a regular schedule. The main purpose of the common forecast would be to reduce the confusion generated by conflicting estimates, but the increased interaction between the Department of Economic Affairs, the Congressional Budget Office, and the Federal Reserve necessary to create such a forecast would increase mutual understanding of what is happening to the economy and what the goals of policy should be. Occasionally, it might be necessary for one of the agencies to dissent and explain why it disagreed with the forecast, but these occasions are likely to be infrequent. There should also be more attention than at present to the consequences for policy of the forecast being wrong.

Finally, bring choices explicitly into the decision process, both in executive branch deliberations and, especially, in Congress. Those proposing spending increases or tax reductions should routinely be required to specify what is to be given up and to offer both the benefit and its cost as a package. In other words, proposals should be deficit neutral.

V. What Economists Can Do

For their part, how can economists be more useful in the policy process? The press and politicians often sound as if they are telling us to work harder: go back to your computers and don't come out until you know how the economy really works and can give us reliable forecasts. But economists know that the economic system is incredibly complicated, and that increasing global interdependence and rapidly changing technologies and public attitudes are not making it easier to understand. It is not likely in our lifetimes that anyone will happen on a paradigm that explains everything, or even that forecasting will become appreciably more accurate. Like the medical profession, which also deals with an incredibly complex system, we economists just have to keep applying our imperfect knowledge as carefully as possible and learning from the results. Both doctors and economists need humility, but neither should abandon their patients to the quacks.

The objective of economists ought to be to raise the level of debate on economic policy, to make clear what they know and do not know, and to increase the chances of policy decisions that make the economy work better. Much of the time that means telling the public and politicians what they would rather not hear: hard choices must be made. We are stuck with being the dismal science.

Increased effort in three directions would make economics more useful in the policy process. First, *economists should put much more emphasis on their areas of agreement*. The press admittedly makes this difficult. Agreement is not news, and the press' stereotype of economists' diversity of views is so entrenched that they will go to great lengths to scare up a lonely dissenter to an almost universally held economic platitude and give her equal time.

Economists realize that the breakthrough insights around which "schools" are built are at best partial visions of the truth, but our training leads us to elaborate and differentiate these insights, to explain to ourselves and to others where they lead in different directions, not where they come together. Yet areas of agreement are wide—even in macroeconomics—and a major effort to make this clearer to ourselves and our audience would be useful.

Second, *economists should devote more serious attention to increasing the basic economic literacy of the public, the media, and the political community.* While the print media seem to me increasingly knowledgeable and sophisticated about economic issues, television, where most people get most of their information, lags far behind. Television coverage of the economy is heavily weighted to isolated economic statistics reported without context—the wholesale price index increased two-tenths of a percent in October—and talking heads disagreeing, briefly, for some obscure reason. Some of the best newscasters appear to have bad cases of economics phobia.

Media bashing is not the answer. The profession needs to take the lead in explaining more clearly what is happening to the economy, why it matters, and what the arguments are about or ought to be about. This means more than each of us taking a little time to make a luncheon speech, write an op ed piece, or appear on a talk show. It means sustained efforts on the part of teams of economists to figure out how to present economic ideas more interestingly and understandably, developing new graphics and other teaching tools and getting feedback from real audiences. The technology is available and the audiences exist—the number of people who will watch long hard-to-follow congressional debates and hearings on cable television is quite astonishing. We just need to devote the kind of effort and ingenuity that goes into explaining to audiences the complex, fast-moving, jargon-ridden game of football to our complex, fast-moving, jargon-ridden game of economics.

Third, *economists need to be more careful to sort out, for ourselves and others, what we really know from our ideological biases.* George Stigler pointed out in his presidential address (1965) that economists beginning with Adam Smith have not hesitated to make strong assertions, both positive and negative, about the effectiveness of government intervention without offering serious evidence to support their claims. For two hundred years, "the chief instrument of empirical demonstration on the economic competence of the state has been the telling anecdote" (pp. 11–12). In the more than two decades since Stigler presided over our Association, an enormous amount of useful empirical work has been done, as he predicted it would be, on the effectiveness of government programs, the costs and benefits of regulation, and so forth. Still the arguments among economists about the merits of larger vs. smaller government too often revolve around anecdotes or, worse, misleading statistics quoted out of context. My own anecdotal evidence would lead me to believe that liberals and conservatives are about equally guilty.

My concern is not with economists taking sides on policy issues or acting as advocates of particular positions. Indeed, I think many policy debates would be clarified if there were more formal and informal opportunities for economists to marshall the evidence on each side and to examine and cross-examine each other in front of some counterpart of judge or jury.

We economists tend to be uncomfortable in the role of partisans or advocates, preferring to be seen as neutral experts whether we are or not. Lawyers move more easily among roles; and the best are able to serve with distinction at different times as prosecutors, defenders, experts, and judges. The system works well when the roles are played competently and the rules of evidence strictly observed. Economists might increase their usefulness to the policy process if they made clear at any given moment which role they were playing. More important, we need to work hard to raise the standards of evidence, to make clear to the public and the participants in the political process what we are reasonably sure we know and how we know it, and where we are guessing or expressing our preferences.

NOTES

Note: This paper was delivered as the presidential address at the ninety-ninth meeting of the American Economic Association, December 29, 1986, New Orleans, Louisiana.

The views set forth here are solely my own and do not necessarily represent the opinions of the trustees, officers, or other staff members of the Brookings Institution. I am grateful for the insights and assistance of many colleagues, especially Robert D. Reischauer, Charles L. Schultze, Mary S. Skinner, and Valerie M. Owens.

REFERENCES

Eisner, Robert, *How Real is the Federal Deficit,* New York: Free Press, 1986.

Heclo, Hugh, "OMB and the Presidency—the Problem of 'Neutral Competence'," *The Public Interest,* 1975, 10, 80–89.

Heller, Walter, W., "What's Right With Economics," *American Economic Review,* March 1975, 65, 1–26.

Mueller, Dennis C., *Public Choice,* Cambridge: Cambridge University Press, 1979.

Okun, Arthur M., "The Economist and Presidential Leadership," in *Economics for Policy Making,* Joseph A. Pechman, ed., Cambridge: MIT Press, 1983, 577–82.

Porter, Robert B., "Economic Advice to the President: From Eisenhower to Reagan," *Political Science Quarterly,* Fall 1983, 98, 403–06.

———, "Organizing Economic Advice to the President: A Modest Proposal, *"American Economic Review Proceedings,* May 1982, 72, 356–60.

Schultz, George, "Reflections on Political Economy," *Challenge,* March/April 1974, 17, 6–11.

Schultze, Charles L., "The Role and Responsibilities of the Economist in Government," *American Economic Review Proceedings,* May 1982, 72, 62–66.

Stigler, George J., "The Economist and the State," *American Economic Review,* March 1965, 55, 1–18.

Stockman, David A., *The Triumph of Politics,* New York: Harper and Row, 1986.

Tufte, Edward R., *Political Control of the Economy,* Princeton: Princeton University Press, 1978.

SELECTION 29

ROBERT D. TOLLISON

Rent Seeking: A Survey

Rent seeking occurs as parties compete for profits that have been artificially contrived by government. Such competition can be wasteful. For example, in the case of competition for a government-protected monopoly franchise, rent seeking in the political arena can result in social waste exceeding the social cost of monopoly. The rent-seeking literature has focused both on the explanation of contrived rents and on the analysis of how people compete for such rents.

QUESTIONS TO GUIDE THE READING

1. What are the differences between profit seeking in the competitive price system and competition for artificially contrived rents?
2. Under what circumstances are monopoly rents wasted, from society's viewpoint?
3. What public policies do you think can serve to lower the social cost of rent seeking?

I. Introduction

The purpose of this essay is to survey the emerging theory of the rent-seeking society. The initial problem is to clarify terminology. Rent is a venerable concept in economics. Defined as a return in excess of a resource owner's opportunity cost, economic rent has played a prominent role in the history of economic analysis ("corn is not high because rent is paid, rent is paid because corn is high"). In this sense it is a fair guess that most economists would consider "rent seeking" to be equivalent to "profit seeking," whereby it is meant that the expectation of excess returns motivates value-increasing activities in the economy. Such excess returns (positive *and* negative) are typically viewed as short-lived (quasi-rents) because competition will drive them to normal levels.

The competitive dissipation of rents, however, is not what is meant by "rent seeking." Rents emanate from two sources. They arise *naturally* in

Robert D. Tollison, "Rent Seeking: A Survey," *Kyklos* 35 (Fasc. 4, 1982), 575–602.

Robert D. Tollison is the Duncan Black Professor of Economics and Director of the Center for Study of Public Choice at George Mason University.

the price system by, for example, shifts in demand and supply curves. The pursuit of rents under these circumstances in the sense in which rent seeking is equivalent to profit seeking. Rents can also be contrived *artificially* through, for example, government action. The fact that rents are contrived, however, does not mean that they are exempt from competition, and this is where rent seeking comes into play.

Consider the example of monopoly rents. The typical discussion depicts such returns as a transfer from consumers to a monopolist. Treated as such, monopoly rents embody no social costs. Yet if the process by which monopoly rents are contrived is subject to competition (e.g., lobbying), the analytical fiction of these rents as a pure transfer vanishes because resources spent in the pursuit of a transfer are *wasted* from society's point of view. These expenditures add nothing to social product (they are zero-sum at best), and their opportunity cost constitutes lost production to society.

The theory of rent seeking involves the study of how people compete for artificially contrived transfers. Like the rest of economic theory, rent seeking has normative and positive elements. Normative rent-seeking theory refers to the specification and estimation of the costs of rent-seeking activities to the economy. Are contrived rents dissipated by competition to capture them? Are they exactly dissipated by competitive rent seeking, or are there imperfections in rent-seeking processes such that expenditures to capture monopoly positions either exceed or fall short of the rents that inhere in them? What role does the consumer play in the theory of the rent-seeking society? What is the domain of rent-seeking behavior, that is, is government required for rent-seeking theory to be applicable or can rents be contrived and dissipated in private settings?

The positive side of rent-seeking theory is directed to the question of what explains the sources of contrived rents in a society. For example, in normal textbook presentations monopoly is introduced by drawing a downward sloping demand curve and its associated marginal revenue curve. The effects of monopoly are explained, but the issue of why some industries consist of pre-takers and others consist of price-searchers is largely begged. Positive rent-seeking theory goes behind the facade of microeconomic theory and attempts to explain why some sectors of the economy are sheltered and some not.

This essay will survey the economic theory of rent seeking. In Section II, a more detailed discussion of the differences between rent seeking and profit seeking is given. In Section III, normative rent-seeking theory and empirical measures are discussed. . . . Some concluding remarks are offered in Section V.

II. Rent Seeking versus Profit Seeking

In economic analysis the definition of economic rent is a payment to a resource owner above the amount his resources could command in their next best alternative use. An economic rent is a receipt in excess of the opportunity cost of a resource. It has been observed that it is not necessary to pay economic rents in order to procure an efficient allocation of resources. This argument, however, is based on a faulty perception of the dynamics of the competitive market process. Over time, the presence of economic rents provides the incentive for resource owners to seek out more profitable allocations of their resources. When competition is viewed as a dynamic, value-creating, evolutionary process, the role of economic rents in stimulating entrepreneurial decisions and in prompting an efficient allocation of resources is crucial [Kirzner 1973]. "Rent seeking" or "profit seeking" in a competitive market order is a normal feature of economic life. The returns of resource owners will be driven to normal levels (on both the intensive and extensive margins) by competitive profit seeking as some resource owners earn positive rents which promote entry and others earn negative rents which cause exit. Profit seeking and economic rents are inherently related to the efficiency of the competitive market process. Such activities drive the competitive price system and create value (e.g., new products) in the economy.

The task at hand is to distinguish what is meant by rent seeking from profit seeking. Consider a simple example in which the king wishes to grant a monopoly right in the production of playing cards. In this case artificial scarcity is created by the state, and as a consequence, monopoly rents are present to be captured by monopolists who seek the king's favor. Normally, these rents are thought of as transfers from playing card consumers to the card monopolist. Yet in the example, this can only be the case if the aspiring monopolists employ no real resources to compete for the monopoly rents. To the extent that real resources are spent to capture monopoly rents in such ways as lobbying, these expenditures create no value from a social point of view. It is this activity of wasting resources in competing for artificially contrived transfers that is called rent seeking. If an incipient monopolist hires a lawyer to lobby the king for the monopoly right, the opportunity cost of this lawyer (e.g., the contracts that he does not write while engaged in lobbying) is a social cost of the monopolization process. Moreover, the deflection of lawyers from productive to transfer-seeking pursuits will generate a disequilibrium in the market for lawyers, with the implication that there will be excessive entry into the legal profession. As will be presented in more detail in Section III, such rent-seeking costs must be added to the standard welfare-triangle loss associated with monopoly to obtain an estimate of the total social costs of monopoly and regulation.

"Real" rents are different from "government" or "fake" rents because rent seeking has productive implications in the first case but not in the second. Just to drive the point home, consider the following example. The return to professional baseball players includes some (inframarginal) rents which leads young children to play baseball rather than practice the piano. This increases the supply of baseball players tomorrow (because young children practiced today), and the amount and quality of baseball is altered (improved?). In the case of monopoly rents lobbying is the analogy to practicing, and lobbying does not increase output because output is fixed by definition. It is the restricting of output artificially that creates the rents.

Rent seeking is the expenditure of scarce resources to capture an artificially created transfer. The implications of the economic wastefulness of rent-seeking activity are difficult to escape once an artificial scarcity has been created [Buchanan 1980]. At one level the king can allow individuals to compete for the playing card monopoly and waste resources through such activities as bribery. Such outright venality is perhaps the simplest and most readily understood level of rent seeking. At a second level the state could sell the monopoly right to the highest bidder and put the proceeds at the disposal of government officials. In this case the monopoly rents will most likely show up in the wages of state officials, and to capture rents at this level individuals will compete to become civil servants. This competition might be thought of in terms of excess returns to bureaucratic agents where these returns are competed away by excessive expenditures on education to prepare for civil service examinations [Tullock 1980]. At still another level should the monopoly right be sold to the highest bidder and the resources dispersed through the state budget in terms of expenditure increases and/or tax reductions, rent-seeking costs will be incurred as individuals seek to become members of the groups favored by the tax-expenditure program. Rent-seeking costs are incurred in each case, and only the form that such costs take is influenced by how the government transacts its business in artificially contrived scarcity values.

III. The Welfare Analysis of Rent Seeking

The welfare analysis of rent seeking concerns the issue of how costly such activities are to the economy. It was, in fact, through an effort to assess the nature of these costs that Tullock [1967] first analyzed the concept of rent seeking. Subsequent research has concentrated on expanding Tullock's theoretical insight and on developing empirical measures of rent-seeking costs.

1. Competitive Rent Seeking

In Figure 1 a simple monopoly diagram is drawn ($Q_m = \frac{1}{2}Q_c$). This model is sufficient to yield all of the insights generated by competitive rent-seeking theory.

In the standard analysis of monopoly a competitive industry is *costlessly* transformed into a simple monopoly. This analysis is developed as if a snapshot of equilibrium conditions were taken at two instants of time. One photograph reveals P_cQ_c as the market equilibrium and the other P_mQ_m. In this conceptual experiment the welfare cost is the lost consumer surplus given by ABC. In its modern form this partial equilibrium analysis was pioneered by Harberger [1954], who developed a reduced-form equation for ABC and used it to measure the extent of such losses in the U.S. manufacturing sector *circa* 1929. His empirical results showed the welfare loss from monopoly to be a negligible proportion (less than 1 percent) of GNP. By modifying the

Figure 1

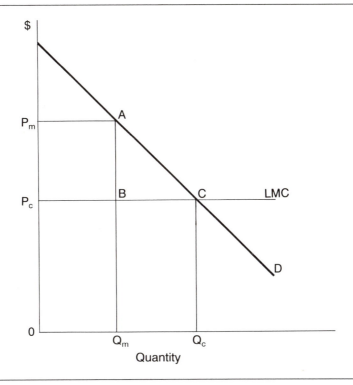

assumptions underlying the reduced-form for *ABC* (e.g., the elasticity of demand), a variety of subsequent estimates of welfare losses from monopoly have been published. These estimates generally follow the Harberger result in not constituting monopoly as an overwhelming social problem.[1]

Commenting upon the relatively low estimates of the welfare costs of monopolies and tariffs, Mundell [1962, p. 622] observed that "unless there is a thorough re-examination of the validity of the tools upon which these studies are founded . . . someone will inevitably draw the conclusion that economics has ceased to be important." Tullock rose to this challenge in a 1967 paper in the *Western Economic Journal* (now *Economic Inquiry*).[2] Tullock's insight was simple and straightforward. He argued that any resources spent to capture $P_m P_c AB$ were *also* a social cost of monopoly and that the conventional model of the welfare loss from monopoly, in which monopoly profits are treated as a lump-sum transfer from consumers to the monopolist, was incomplete if potential monopolists spent resources to capture the monopoly right. Since economists typically believe that competition is ever present, the relevance of Tullock's argument is apparent—monopoly rights will not generally be exempt from competition and expenditures to capture such contrived transfers are a social cost. The earlier application of this discussion to the employment of lawyer-lobbyist resources by monopoly-seekers need not be repeated here.[3]

What can be termed competitive rent seeking implies that the monopoly rents in Figure 1 (P_cP_mAB) are exactly dissipated. Tullock's original formulation of the problem was in these terms, as were the subsequent contributions by Krueger [1974] and Posner [1975]. Consider Posner's example of how competitive rent seeking might work in practice. A monopoly right is worth $100,000. There are ten risk-neutral bidders among whom there is no collusion. Each will bid $10,000 for the right, an expenditure which cannot be returned if theirs is not the winning bid. The result is that the monopoly returns are dissipated at a social level—$100,000 is spent to capture a transfer of $100,000.

Empirical work with the competitive rent-seeking model is relatively easy to implement. In effect the analyst must estimate the area of a trapezoid rather than just a triangle. Both Krueger [1974] and Posner [1975] have applied variations of such a model to derive estimates of rent-seeking costs. Krueger estimated that the value of rents in various parts of the Indian public sector constituted 7.3 percent of national income. She also estimated the rents in Turkish import licenses in 1968 to be approximately 15 percent of GNP. Posner has presented measures of rent-seeking costs in the U.S. economy. He asserts that such costs constitute roughly 3 percent of GNP, an amount which would have to be added to Harberger-type losses in the economy to obtain an estimate of the total social costs of monopoly and regulation. Rent-seeking analysis tends to magnify the problem of monopoly over and beyond the traditional measurements made by Harberger, rising to the challenge laid down by Mundell.

2. Rent Seeking and Consumers

In the usual presentation of the welfare costs of monopoly, whether of the Harberger- or the Tullock-Posner-type, the role of the consumer is entirely passive. No account is made of potential consumer activities to counter monopolization efforts by producers. This assumption of economic impotence is typically made on the basis of stylized facts which portray consumers as an unorganized, widely dispersed group without incentive to try to restrain the political monopolization process.

Two things can be said about this non-treatment of consumers. First, as an empirical issue, it is surely wrong. Since the 1960s there has been a rapid growth in the number and size of organized consumer groups; Evans [1980, p. 5] lists twenty-one major consumer organizations active in the U.S., including such familiar groups as Common Cause, the American Farm Bureau Federation, and the network of Nader organizations. The major groups concentrate on lobbying Congress and state legislatures, but there are also many smaller local groups which regularly appear in such mundane places as rate hearings to lobby for lower prices. Second, to the extent that welfare analysis does not include a role for consumer lobbying, it is lagging behind developments in the positive economic theory of rent seeking. Peltzman [1976], for example, offers a model in which a vote-maximizing regulator trades-off industry price and profits between consumer and producer forces. This formulation is squarely based on the idea that consumers impinge on political prices. As a corollary to Peltzman's contribution, it seems useful to expand the normative theory of rent-seeking to include a role for consumers. . . .

V. Concluding Remarks

Economic rent is not new to economists. Yet as this essay hopefully demonstrates, the full implications of the role of rents in the economy are just starting to emerge. In this sense rent seeking is an interesting intellectual innovation. As a rereading of Tullock's 1967 paper would convince virtually anyone, the insight that brought about the idea of rent seeking was exceedingly simple. Rents are competed for, and where rents are contrived, this competition has important normative and positive implications for economic analysis. The moral is perhaps that important advances in economics do not naturally have to flow from a highly mathematical or statistical approach to the subject. In this regard Tullock's original paper on rent seeking calls to mind Coase's [1960] seminal work on social cost.

NOTES

Note: Thanks go to James Buchanan, Robert McCormick and Dennis Mueller for helpful comments. The usual caveat applies.

1. Since this paper is concerned with rent seeking and not with the conventional welfare loss from monopoly, a review of the efforts to improve upon Harberger's original formulation of the latter problem is not pursued here. The interested reader may consult Scherer [1980, Ch. 17] and the references cited there.

2. Also see Tullock [1971, 1974] and Browning [1974].

3. One immediate implication of Tullock's insight, noted by Posner [1974], is that studies of the distributional effects of monopoly are misleading (e.g., Comanor and Smiley [1975]). Monopoly rents are *dissipated* (provided that lawyer-lobbyist earn normal returns) not *transferred*.

REFERENCES

Browning, Edgar K.: "On the Welfare Cost of Transfers," *Kyklos,* Vol. 26 (April 1974), pp. 374–377.

Buchanan, James M.: "Rent Seeking and Profit Seeking," in: Buchanan, Tollison and Tullock (Eds.), *Toward a Theory of the Rent-Seeking Society,* Texas A&M University Press, College Station, 1980, p. 3–15.

Coase, Ronald H.: "The Problem of Social Cost," *Journal of Law and Economics,* Vol. 3 (October 1960), pp. 1–44.

Comanor, William S. and Smiley, Robert H.: "Monopoly and the Distribution of Wealth," *Quarterly Journal of Economics,* Vol. 89 (May 1975), pp. 177–194.

Evans, Joel R. (Ed.): *Consumerism in the United States,* Praeger, New York, 1980.

Harberger, Arnold C.: "Monopoly and Resource Allocation," *American Economic Review,* Vol. 44 (May 1954), pp. 77–87.

Kirzner, Israel: *Competition and Entrepreneurship,* University of Chicago Press, Chicago, 1973.

Krueger, Anne O.: "The Political Economy of the Rent-Seeking Society," *American Economic Review,* Vol. 64 (June 1974), pp. 291–303.

Mundell, Robert A.: "Review of Jansenn's *Free Trade, Protection and Customs Union,*" *American Economic Review,* Vol. 52 (June 1962), pp. 621–622.

Peltzman, Sam: "Toward a More General Theory of Regulation," *Journal of Law and Economics,* Vol. 19 (August 1976), pp. 211–240.

Posner, Richard A.: "Taxation by Regulation," *Bell Journal of Economics and Management Science,* Vol. 2 (Spring 1971), pp. 22–50.

Posner, Richard A.: "Theories of Economic Regulation," *Bell Journal of Economics and Management Science,* Vol. 5 (Autumn 1974), pp. 335–358.

Posner, Richard A.: "The Social Costs of Monopoly and Regulation," *Journal of Political Economy,* Vol. 83 (August 1975), pp. 807–827.

Scherer, F. M.: *Industrial Market Structure and Economic Performance,* Rand McNally, Chicago, 1980.

Tullock, Gordon: "The Welfare Costs of Tariffs, Monopolies, and Theft," *Western Economic Journal,* Vol. 5 (June 1967), pp. 224–232.

Tullock, Gordon: "The Cost of Transfers," *Kyklos,* Vol. 24 (December 1971), pp. 629–643.

Tullock, Gordon: "More on the Cost of Transfers," *Kyklos,* Vol. 27 (April 1974), pp. 378–381.

Tullock, Gordon: "Rent Seeking as a Negative-Sum Game," in: Buchanan, Tollison and Tullock (Eds.): *Toward a Theory of the Rent-Seeking Society,* Texas A&M University Press, College Station, 1980, pp. 16–36.

SELECTION 30

THOMAS E. BORCHERDING, WERNER W. POMMEREHNE, AND
FRIEDRICH SCHNEIDER

Comparing the Efficiency of Private and Public Production: The Evidence from Five Countries

Frequently the issue of private versus public production of goods
and services takes on ideological overtones. The authors of this
reading provide a comprehensive, even-handed assessment of the
evidence on the comparative efficiency of private and public
production. They offer their own explanation for the frequent
finding that public sector production is "wasteful" relative to
private sector production: Public sector production may appear to
be relatively wasteful, either because it is utilized as a vehicle for
redistribution or because costs of contracting, controlling, and
monitoring private sector production are not counted.

QUESTIONS TO GUIDE THE READING

1. How can competition between private and public firms affect
   the relative efficiency of public firms?
2. How does the property rights approach differ from the public
   choice approach in studying the difference between private and
   public firms?
3. Why is public sector "waste" an economic puzzle? How can
   such waste be controlled?
4. How does redistribution through the political process explain
   part of the "waste" of public sector production?

Thomas E. Borcherding, Werner W. Pommerehne, and Friedrich Schneider, "Comparing the
Efficiency of Private and Public Production: The Evidence from Five Countries." From *Journal
of Economics* (1982, Suppl. 2), 127–56. Copyright Springer-Verlag 1982. Reprinted by permission of the authors and Springer-Verlag.

Thomas E. Borcherding is Professor of Economics at the Claremont Graduate School. **Werner
W. Pommerehne** is Professor of Public Finance, the Free University, Berlin, Federal Republic
of Germany. **Friedrich Schneider** is Professor of Economics, University of Linz, Linz-Auhof,
Austria.

> *Without exception, the empirical findings indicate that the same*
> *level of output could be provided at substantially lower costs if*
> *output were produced by the private rather than the public*
> *sector.*
>
> J. T. BENNETT AND M. H. JOHNSON [1980]

Our task, to survey the putative differential in efficiency between public and private sectors in the United States, the Federal Republic of Germany, and selected other countries is at once both simple and demanding. The easy though laborious part is the literature search; and much of the paper, found in Section I, will consist of synopsizing and criticizing these findings epitomized by Bennett and Johnson's quotation above. The harder part is to make economic sense of their passage. Put differently, it is one thing for scholars to detect empirically a uniformly higher efficiency of private counterparts of activities supplied by public units, it is quite another thing to explain this persistent social fact. We shall, therefore, both because of instruction from the conference organizer and because of space limitations, devote ourselves largely to the more tractable task of reporting. Nonetheless, we will deal with the positive economic implications of these findings in the final section, II, of the paper without systematically exploring our speculations.[1]

Three idiosyncracies should be noted before we launch into our survey. First, the study is largely about the "supply side" of public outputs. The questions examined deal with differences in production efficiencies with respect to alternative organizational types (of firms), private vs. public, holding the collective demand for the product or service as given. Second, only the choice of private vs. public firms is considered. The possibility of "regulatory public finance" [Posner, 1971] is largely ignored as a substitute (or complementary) policy instrument. Finally, although our conference mission was to report on U.S. and German studies alone, we have also included the few Australian, Canadian and Swiss cases on record to this date. These latter studies were incorporated because of the similarity of political and social institutions in these three countries with those in the United States and Germany and because they were not reported upon in the other sessions of the conference.

I. The Literature Survey

For at least the last century, economists have employed *positive* "neo-classical" economic theory to explore the implications of wealth maximization by private firms operating in private property contexts.[2] Only since the 1950s, however, has this neo-classical methodology begun to be applied in collective, non-market circumstances. Further, only very recently, since the late 1960s, have empirical studies detailing the behavior of publicly operated firms been undertaken. Nonetheless, a large number of studies over a variety of activities now exists and definite "patterns of attack" have emerged to study the question of how public firms differ from their private equivalents. Basically, two methods are employed, though we predict that in the future these will rapidly merge as they currently are doing in the "regulation" literature [Blankart and Faber, 1982; Borcherding, 1983].

The first, explored in Part Ia, is what we call the "property rights approach." It concentrates on the differences in the ease of captureability of economic surplus of a resource and the rights to direct an asset's use, alter its form or transfer its claims among existent and potential owners. In short, it explores the differences in incentives between public and private agencies caused by variation in the ability of owners to monitor management and the problems that emerge when the goals of "owners" and their agents, "managers," diverge [Alchian, 1961, 1965]. The second or "public choice approach" found in Part Ib concentrates on political coalitions and their effect on input usage and rewards and/or product characteristics. These studies are largely directed by the so-called theory of bureaucracy [Niskanen, 1971]. Of course, these two classifications are somewhat stylized and certain contribution listed in one part might by other narrators be put in the other category. All the cost differential studies are found in Part Ia, but other quantitative and qualitative studies with efficiency implications are included there as well. For Part Ib no empirical cost differences are indicated, but interesting implications for efficiency still arise.

Ia. The Property Rights Approach

Those who focus on property rights variations point out one crucial difference between private and public firms: the practical difficulties in transferring ownership rights among individuals in the public sector and the relative ease of such transactions with private assets which includes, of course, the ability of owners (citizens) to monitor their agents' (elected officials' and bureaucrats') behavior.

By now this approach pioneered by Armen Alchian is well known, but it is useful to recall his predictions, to wit: government managers will not organize the inputs under their direction in such a way as to maximize the wealth of the putative owners, the general citizenry. He and his followers predict, therefore, that public firms will be less efficient, their management will enjoy "quieter lives," and because of this the public will give them lower levels of discretion than their colleagues in private firms. . . .

Of the more than 50 studies, only three by Pier, Vernon and Wicks [1974] on garbage collection, Meyer [1975] on electricity utilities, and Lindsay [1975, 1976] on Veterans' hospitals indicate that public are less costly than private firms. The Lindsay study, however, clearly indicates that quality is lower in the public mode, a clear violation of the *ceteris paribus* requirement and the Meyer and Pier, Vernon and Wicks studies suffer from serious, but differing *ceteris paribus* violations as well according to Crain and Zardkoohi [1978] and Pommerehne [1976].

In only five other studies for North America—Caves and Christensen's study [1980] of Canadian railroads, the St. Louis refuse collection studies by Collins and Downes [1977] and Hirsch [1965], the Minneapolis refuse collection study by Savas [1977c] and the study on electric utilities by Spann [1977]—do the data indicate no difference. For West Germany the insurance study by Finsinger [1981] finds equal production efficiencies of public and private firms. To explain their findings for Canada's two major railroads, Caves and Christensen hypothesize that brisk competition (since 1965) between the two organizational modes (and with other types of transport) has forced the nationalized Canadian railroad to adopt very efficient techniques of service provision. Finsinger [1981] parallels this judgment as do Savas [1977c] and Spann [1977]. Of the two St. Louis refuse studies, Savas [1980] argues that they neglect to adjust for the variety of private supply devices that Stevens and he [1978] have elsewhere discovered. Private supply on a non-franchise, openly competitive basis is very inefficient, even less so than government supply, because of loss of billing and network economies, but this argument fails to explain why a single firm does not dominate the market, since they find it is the least-cost collection method.

These eight anomalous cases aside, there still remain 40 cases where private supply is unequivocally more efficient and two [Frech, 1979, 1980; Nicols, 1967] where attenuated private property is shown to be more inefficient than less attenuated private claims.

The literature . . . is much more varied than our gloss indicates. Space limitations do not permit a fuller discussion, but let us quickly cite these other findings.[3] Public, or as De Alessi [1980] calls them, political, firms adopt cost-saving devices and innovation more slowly, if at all; give managers longer periods of tenure; realize lower and more variable rates of return; price less closely to imputable costs and with less regard to peak-capacity problems; favor voters to non-voters, business to residential users and organized to non-organized political groups; and systematically exhibit larger Averch-Johnson effects, i.e., overcapitalize even more than private-but-regulated firms. For those firms engaged in market transactions requiring willing consumers, government firms survive in spite of large economic losses and their managements sometimes even thrive in conditions that would lead to the dismissal of their private counterparts, but, as mentioned before, such losses are inversely related to the presence of competitors (sometimes even other public firms).

To sum up the results so far: The literature seems to indicate that (a) private production is cheaper than production in publicly owned and managed firms, and (b) given sufficient competition between public and private producers (and no discriminative regulations and subsidies), the differences in unit cost turn out to be insignificant. From this we may conclude that it is not so much the difference in the transferability of ownership but the lack of competition which leads to the often observed less efficient production in public firms.

Ib. The Public Choice Approach

Though the public choice approach coincides in several aspects with the ideas of the property rights school, it differs insofar as its main emphasis lies on the lacking competition in the public sector compared to the private one. Therefore the mainstream of analysis deals not so much with public utilities (or even nationalized industries) but looks closer at the public institutions and public bureaucracies which operate these institutions. Thus it considers the presence of bureaucracy in a more direct manner than does the property rights literature (with two notable exceptions, De Alessi [1969, 1973, 1974a, 1974b] and Eckert [1973, 1979]). Essentially, this literature develops politically the Alchian and Kessel [1962] notion that public managers divert higher shares of their principals' wealth to their own ends than do their private colleagues.

The paradigm example of this approach is Niskanen's classic book, *Bureaucracy and Representative Government* [1971] which offers the following hypothesis: bureaucrats, like all of us, are interested in more pay, power and prestige. These "three *P*'s" are more closely correlated with public budgets than in private firms where "the bottom line" acts as a more binding constraint to such sales maximizing strategies. The result is that bureaucrats in public firms "push" their programs more strongly than would their private counterparts and join with those in the legislature who find such excess supplies congenial to their constituents' interests. Special interests, lack of competitive alternatives facing the so-called median voter and high transactions costs all feature prominently in the theoretical discussions of this literature.

Empirical tests of this model are not numerous, but a few can be mentioned. Ott [1980] found that the (absolute) shadow price elasticity for public service in 81 U.S. cities was not significantly different from one, the budget maximizing position on the demand curve. Studies summarized by Deacon [1977] and Pommerehne [1982] found, however, that in most other studies demand price elasticity was less than one, a pattern not in keeping with Niskanen's first model [1971], though it does with his second one [Niskanen, 1975] where he allows a trade-off between budget and "perks."

De Alessi [1969], anticipating Niskanen, also claims that public managers are growth, not wealth oriented. He argues and finds supporting evidence that this leads to larger staffs and, more importantly, higher capital-labor ratios, since excess capital makes managers' and their subordinates' productivity appear higher to their monitoring agents, the legislature. It also means bureaucrats will employ lower discount rates, a well-known phenomenon to those who study the U.S. Corps of Engineers.

Deacon's study [1979] of the Lakewood Plan in California—an institution where smaller governments purchase services such as, but not limited to, refuse collection and fire and police protection from larger nearby communities, under conditions that appear to be competitive—did find budgets systematically higher by 20 percent in non-Lakewood communities. Wagner

and Weber [1975] using indices of competition among local jurisdictions offer similar results. Whether this is because demand curves are "pushed out"
or because unit costs in public firms rise when competition is lessened, at
this time cannot be easily distinguished. Given the unit cost studies cited in
their Table 1 and our knowledge of shadow price elasticities, however, it is
possible to break out the "budget push" from "cost push" factors. Since
price elasticities appear to range between $-\frac{1}{2}$ and $-\frac{3}{4}$ and public firm unit
costs are 10 to 20 percent in excess of private suppliers, the residual left for
"budget push" ranges from zero to 20 percent.

Pursuing this latter effect, Borcherding, Bush and Spann [1977] argue
that public employees effectively coalesce through their organizations and
"capture" civil service commissions over time, altering rules in such ways
that the effective supply of competing labor to public firms becomes less
wage elastic than a free market buyer would otherwise face. This public
employee market power is enhanced, they claim, by the fact that public service employees contribute to the election of their ultimate "bosses," defi-
nitely not an option for a private sector union. In some sense then, public
employees can alter the position of the derived demand schedule for their
services by (a) "nudging" the final demand schedule for public services to
the right and (b) specifying rules which lower both the elasticity of substitution between themselves and rival cooperant factors and the elasticity of
supply of these close substitutes. Both (a) and (b) will tend to raise wages,
but they may raise employment too, since, in effect, the budget and tie-in
effects may offset the usual substitution effects one might derive out of neoclassical models of labor demand in the presence of a simple monopoly.
Borcherding, Bush and Spann [1977] successfully test this conception on
non-federal U.S. government spending data using as independent variables
the presence or absence of civil service or the number of years that an activity had been controlled by civil service.

Recently, however, Pommerehne and Frey [1978] and Courant, Gramlich and Rubinfeld [1980] show that this public employees-as-voters pressure
group theory is overstated. This is not surprising when one thinks of the
public employees as forming a coalition, since the monitoring costs of seeing
that public employees of agency X vote for candidates who support expansion of bureau Y, and *vice versa,* is excessively high given the institution of
secret ballot. Nonetheless, implicit log rolling, the tying of the interests of
X and Y together, can take place by clever political entrepreneurship mitigating free-ridership to some degree. The position of public unions in the
United States opposing constitutional spending limitations (e.g., California's
Proposition 13 on the reduction of the property tax) is also evidence that
public employees can act on such wider group interest [Shapiro and Sonstelie, 1982].

Borcherding, Bush and Spann [1977] also go on to suggest that since
elected officials respond to public employee oriented collective demand,
capital-labor ratios may be lower than in private contexts. Orzechowski
[1977] tests this against De Alessi's obviously conflicting forementioned hy-

pothesis [1969] by comparing state colleges and universities in Virginia against their private institutional equivalents. Orzechowski finds that capital-labor ratios are, indeed, lower in the state system. Of course, this could be true yet absolute capital intensities per unit of output might still be higher in public than in the private institutions. Unfortunately, output data or even good proxies for them were unavailable (a problem for almost all the studies save refuse). Orzechowski [1974] did find elsewhere, however, on the basis of very aggregate data, that the public sector is significantly more capital-intensive than the private service sector and, in fact, it is more capital-intensive than for the economy as a whole. If true, De Alessi's hypothesis would have to be accepted and Orzechowski's earlier hypothesis discarded. Orzechowski's findings are not entirely persuasive, however. First, as is well-known among trade theorists, aggregates mask industry and firm factor combinations. Secondly, the data are generated in an exceedingly unreliable way. Crain and Zardkoohi [1978] find, however, that public firms are more capital intensive than private firms in water utilities as does Moore [1970] for electric utilities. Pfister [1976] discovered on the other hand that the German public forestry firms were more labor intensive. In short, the evidence for input bias is mixed, if not entirely lacking in persuasiveness.

De Alessi [1974b] in yet another paper argues that given the relative loose monitoring of bureaucratic managers by the political review authorities, a rational position for the latter given the gain-sharing results of assiduous monitoring, managers will indulge their taste for security rather more than in private firms. He finds evidence consistent with this risk-avoiding hypothesis. Public managers' tenures are more secure, of a longer duration, and their fluctuations in real wages lower than their private counterparts. Even limited competitiveness would suggest, however, that they "pay" for this in slightly lower salaries or by pre-employment queuing or qualification costs [Frech, 1980]. Hendricks [1977], in fact, shows that profit-regulated electric utilities' firms are no more generous with their wages paid to their workers than the unregulated ones. Hendricks finds, however, that tightly regulated firms tend to pay more than do lightly regulated ones which is consistent with Alchian and Kessel [1962]. The opportunity cost of a wage increase is lower in the former category, since price can be raised nearer to the monopoly optimum as a result. A lightly regulated industry, on the other hand is already so near its optimum that a wage increase is very costly to it. If Hendricks is correct, we should expect that the incidence of militant unionism is more prevalent in the more highly regulated utilities than in the less profit-constrained ones. There is, to date, no evidence for or against this hypothesis.

All of this may also have implications for public employee compensation, since public corporations or government bureaus can be thought of as firms operating under severe profit constraints. We have discovered few persuasive empirical studies on this as yet, though Staats [1973], Orr [1976], Smith [1976, 1981], Adie [1977], Munnell and Connolly [1979] and Quinn [1979, 1982] have done rather interesting studies on wages in the U.S. public sector. They claim there is much excess of wages in public employment, perhaps as high as 10 to 20 percent. This is most interesting, since Borcherding [1966] in reviewing the evidence for the 1940s and 1950s in the U.S. found no such premium. Lentz [1981] using New York state and county level data argues that wage premia are not uniform, but reflect the differential political support and power of the employee groups in question.

All of these findings, drawn from fairly aggregative data, suffer from not holding crucial variables such as skill levels, education and age constant. Luckily, Gunderson [1979a, 1979b, 1979c] has carefully made such comparisons for Canada, and Smith [1977] for the United States, holding these quality variables constant. Gunderson finds that the public sector in Canada is currently paying wages about 10 percent more than does the private manufacturing sector for comparable jobs. Of that, only six percent can be viewed as a rent (though for women it is nine percent). The remaining four percentage points are explained by higher input quality characteristics having alternative market values. Smith finds for the United States that the wage advantage for employees at the federal level goes up to 20 percent in 1975 as compared to similar jobs in the private sector, ceteris paribus. However, for employees at the state and especially at the local levels this rent in some cases does not significantly differ from zero. Similar to the findings for Canada, female employees had at all governmental levels a positive and always higher wage advantage.

In conclusion, according to the public choice scholars, governmental agencies and firms have distinct biases leading to higher production costs, just as the property rights literature suggests, but excessive outputs as well. The latter obtains because the bureaucracy can affect demand more readily under monopoly public ownership by the strength of its members' votes and/ or lobbying efforts. The absence of a civil service and the constraint on strong unions under more competitive types of supply, public or private, is thought to reduce the ability of members of such bureaucracies to offer their services to the legislature on disadvantageous terms compared to potential competitors. On the other hand, the bureaucracy is not likely to have sole "capture" rights over the bureaus, but share their ownership claims with other interests.

Recent works by Fiorina and Noll [1978], Owen and Braeutigam [1979] and Aranson [1979] attempt to model the "Iron Triangle" between legislature, bureaucracy and interest group(s), but this richer context [Lowi, 1979; Wilson, 1974, 1980] is longer in descriptive reality and/or theoretical curiosities than in testable implications conforming to a wide range of observed situations. It is, nonetheless, quite promising, since it recognizes the multigroup nature of public pressure group, an improvement over the simple "capture" theory of government implicit in Niskanen's earlier model [Niskanen, 1971]. In any case, almost none of this latter political science oriented literature lends itself to summary statistics which address themselves to simple efficiency measurements.

To sum up this part: The public choice approach not only recognizes the differences in behavior between publicly owned and managed firms and private ones due to the limited transferability of ownership. It also considers the likely oversupply of public services due to the lack of competition in their provision and production.

II. "Waste" as an Economic Puzzle

The theme of this paper has been generally contrary to the view of efficient public supply through state owned firms. This puts an economist in a rather awkward position. Economists use as their organizing principle the notion that waste will be minimized, given the transaction costs of engaging in exchange. This means that inefficiency is a magnitude that rational economic actors will, mistakes and ignorance aside, attempt to reduce as far as it pays to do so. Why then would such a supply device be so often used if it is so inefficient? The answer must lie in a misinterpretation.

Thus the findings in Section I need critical re-examination and amendment. Excessively complex "red tape," rules against nepotism, the encouragement of bureaucratic "professionalism," sealed bids and open negotiations, line item budgets, zero based budgets, sunset legislation, overlapping jurisdiction, legislative reductions of managerial discretion between current and capital budgets must all be reconsidered, too. Far from being stupid or silly impedimentia generally absent in private organizations, they may well be defenses against even greater waste. For example, perhaps civil service rules reducing favoritism and encouraging tenure (which elongate the views of bureaucratic managers) have efficiency inducing aspects, while the use of political appointees in top directorships of public corporations and independent agencies should, as Wilson [1961] suggests, reduce monitoring costs. Even "moderate" corruption may have some desirable side effects [Banfield, 1975; Neugebauer, 1978].

It would be useful to consider the possibility, therefore, that transaction costs are such that some of the seemingly inefficient institutions represent least cost means of accomplishing productive as opposed to purely redistributive ends. Goldberg [1976a, 1976b] and Williamson [1976] have great insights on this with respect to their criticism of Demsetz's suggestion [1968] to control private utilities by contract management rather than by regulation or public ownership. Each of the former two authors focus on a significant cost of operating under a Demsetz-style contracting out. Goldberg emphasizes the difficulty in achieving efficient contracts because of the narrow self-interest of bureaucrats who must act as administrators or purchasing agents according to (often vague) instructions from elected officials.

According to Goldberg, the result is that bureaucrats externalize cost by their demand for excessive information and overly safe contractual terms. Williamson stresses the likelihood of the incidence of "opportunism" on the part of the private suppliers together with the difficulties of post-contractual risk-sharing and day-to-day adjustments to non-anticipated shocks. All of these difficulties clearly raise the cost of Demsetz's contract management regime. In short, Goldberg and Williamson hold that the subtle ends of public policy cannot always be efficiently realized by private contracts between the state and private firms.[4]

Furthermore, what in Parts Ia and Ib is loosely called waste may, in fact, be transfers. That they are arranged in-kind rather than as cash grants can be explained by the desire of the political authority to parcel them out effectively, i.e., at the least cost and to the right persons [Stigler, 1971; Pommerehne, 1979, 1980; Becker, 1981; Pommerehne and Schneider, 1982; Borcherding, 1983]. Further, a civil service setting is better at hiding this redistributional goal than a more open contract management scheme [Pommerehne, 1980; Borcherding, 1983]. Unfortunately no test has yet been devised to determine whether a policy is wealth enhancing or purely redistributive. No matter; both require public supplying agents to carry them out efficiently.

In a recent critique of the property rights and public choice group's verdict on the inefficiency of bureaucracy, Breton and Wintrobe [1979] state their case counter to Alchian, Davies, Niskanen et al. as follows:

> [A]lthough each bureau has, to a greater or lesser degree, a monopoly on the services it provides to citizens, bureaus are accountable to their political masters and there is certainly competition among political parties for office. Moreover, bureaus compete against each other for funds from the ruling government. Consequently, one would expect that inefficient bureaucrats would find themselves displaced by more efficient ones, either by transfers of personnel or by territorial encroachment. And a political party which tolerated inefficiency would find itself displaced from office. In short, if one is disposed to, one can in the competition among bureaucrats for funds or amenities, and in the competition among political parties for office, glimpse the operation of that same ghostly invisible hand which is said to insure efficiency in the private sector.

Again, as for Caves and Christensen [1980], competition is said to act as an efficient substitute for the absence of ownership transferability present in private sector exchanges. Any real differences in efficiency, must be explained, therefore, by differing "frictions," i.e., the differential transactions costs associated with different behavior under one institutional regime rather than another. Waste in a practical sense, then, cannot exist, unless there is persistent and remedial error in the choice of societal institutions. The latter possibility, willful ignorance, cannot readily be accepted, however, without seriously compromising the economist's commitment to the rational choice paradigm. If our paradigm is to be retained, the answer to the hypothesis that inefficiency is present is to suggest the accuser look instead for other explanations. What one (especially the uninformed outsider) might term waste might, in fact, be the best means of accomplishing an otherwise non-realizable end.

It seems, therefore, implausible (at least, to us) that unit costs could be anywhere from 10 to 50 or even 5000 percent higher for delivery of policies via public firms than they are under contracting-out systems. Our position is that much of these excess costs are, in fact, *transfers* taken in the form of higher wages, reduced intensity of effort, corruption, bribery, boondoggling and deliberate means of realizing some other redistribution. But one can also argue, as does Hettich [1969], that some of these costs represent the price for delivering desirable, but unique outputs whose characteristics would be provided in different amounts and ratios by private supply instruments. Alchian [1965] puts this quite well:

> The desire to avoid or suppress the effects of the profit making incentive is, however, often the reason society resorts to public ownership . . . If public ownership in some government activity were converted to private property, the method of achieving the government objectives would be changed.

The error in (most of) the early property rights and public choice approaches is in not recognizing that public policy and the specified public outputs to realize its ends have many and very subtle dimensions, whose revealed preferences are themselves functions of the supply institution chosen. Latter members of the property rights group, *all* directed intellectually by Coase's two fundamental papers, "The Nature of the Firm" [1937] and "The Problem of Social Cost" [1960], have recognized this for choices among private sector arrangements (Williamson, 1967, 1971, 1975, 1979; McManus, 1978a; Alchian and Demsetz, 1972; Klein, Crawford and Alchian, 1978; Barzel, 1979; Klein and Leffler, 1981; Acheson, 1973; McManus and Acheson, 1979). Lindsay [1975, 1976, 1979] has explicitly applied this notion that characteristics of commodities supplied by public firms will differ from privately provided goods of the same class because of monitoring economies. Baldwin [1975] in his excellent study of the Canadian Crown corporation Air Canada and its relationship to the Canadian Transport Commission declares as much as do Breton [1971], Wintrobe [1977], McManus [1978b], Acheson [1979], Acheson and Chant [1973], Chant and Acheson [1972] and Breton and Wintrobe [1980] in various other Canadian contexts.

It is this interaction of goals (ends) and institutional choice (means) that ought to direct our future attention as much as the continued study of differences in measured efficiencies. It is the understanding of the former that will shed light on the phenomenon of the costly public firm.

To conclude our paper: Government "waste" is after all a sick consideration, neglecting those sizeable costs of contracting, monitoring and controlling which may arise when private production is preferred over the public one. Also some part of the "waste" is the result of the political process of redistribution, where public production is used as an efficient means for selecting and discriminating. Thus we expect that the claim for "more market and less government" has no real address and that the chance of most proposals of how to decrease public production or to increase its efficiency is rather modest.

NOTES

Note: Presented to the International Seminar in Public Economics/Conference on Public Production, Bonn, in August, 1981 as two separate papers. These were revised and combined following the suggestion of the managing editor of the Zeitschrift für Nationalökonomie/Journal of Economics, Dieter Bös.

Borcherding wishes to thank Douglas T. Wills (Burnaby) for his assistance in preparing this report, the Simon Fraser University Programmes of Distinction for providing typing services, the Youth Employment Program (Summer financial assistance for Wills in 1981) and the Earhart Foundation of Ann Arbor, Michigan (assistance in the summer of 1980 when much of the data was originally gathered). Pommerehne and Schneider wish to thank Guy Gilbert (Paris) and Alexander Van der Bellen (Vienna) for helpful comments and suggestions. The paper was written while Pommerehne was a visiting scholar at the University of Paris-X-Nanterre/France, having been assisted financially in the preparation of this paper by the French Government. Both authors wish to acknowledge the support provided by the Swiss National Science Foundation (Grant 1.821-0.78).

1. Borcherding [1983] spends some time on this in Section IV of his paper on Canadian public enterprises, and Pommerehne and Schneider [1982] deal with it in Section 4 of their paper on private and public production in selected European countries.

2. "Classical" authors were much concerned with the collective choice behavior of governmental firms; see Backhaus [1980] and Borcherding [1983, Section III].

3. The text in the paper closely paraphrases De Alessi's summary [1974a].

4. It should be recognized, nonetheless, that perhaps 50 percent of public sector outputs in the U.S. and Canada are contracted-out to private suppliers.

REFERENCES

D. K. Adie [1977]: An Evaluation of Postal Service Wage Rates, Washington, D.C.

A. A. Alchian [1961]: Some Economics of Property Rights, Mimeo, Rand Corporation, Santa Monica.

A. A. Alchian [1965]: Some Economics of Property Rights, Il Politico 30, pp. 816–829.

A. A. Alchian and H. Demsetz [1972]: Production, Information Costs and Economic Organization, American Economic Review 62, pp. 777–795.

A. A. Alchian and R. A. Kessel [1962]: Competition, Monopoly and the Pursuit of Money, in: National Bureau of Economic Research: Aspects of Labor Economics, Princeton, pp. 157–183.

P. H. Aranson [1979]: The Uncertain Search for Regulatory Reform: A Critique of the American Bar Commission on Law and the Economy's Exposure Draft "Federal Regulation: Roads to Reform," Mimeo, University of Miami, Miami.

H. Averch and L. L. Johnson [1962]: Behavior of the Firm Under a Regulatory Constraint, American Economic Review 52, pp. 1052–1069.

J. Backhaus [1980]: Öffentliche Unternehmen, Frankfurt.

E. C. Banfield [1975]: Corruption as a Feature of Government Organization, Journal of Law and Economics 18, pp. 587–606.

G. S. Becker [1981]: A Theory of Political Behavior, Mimeo, University of Chicago, Chicago.

J. T. Bennett and M. H. Johnson [1980]: Tax Reduction Without Sacrifice: Private Sector Production of Public Services, Public Finance Quarterly 8, pp. 363–396.

C. B. Blankart and M. Faber (eds.) [1982]: Regulierung öffentlicher Unternehmen, Königstein.

T. E. Borcherding [1966]: The Growth of Non-Federal Public Employment in the United States, 1900 to 1963, Ph.D. thesis, Duke University, Durham.

T. E. Borcherding [1983]: Towards a Positive Theory of Public Sector Supply, in R. Prichard (ed.): Public Enterprise in Canada, Toronto, forthcoming.

T. E. Borcherding, W. C. Bush, and R. M. Spann [1977]: The Effects on Public Spending of the Divisibility of Public Outputs in Consumption, Bureaucratic Power, and the Size of the Tax-Sharing Group, in: T. E. Borcherding (ed.): Budgets and Bureaucrats: The Sources of Government Growth, Durham, N.C., pp. 211–228.

A. Breton and R. S. Wintrobe [1979]: An Economic Analysis of Bureaucratic Efficiency, Mimeo, University of Toronto, Toronto.

D. W. Caves and L. R. Christensen [1980]: The Relative Efficiency of Public and Private Firms in a Competitive Environment: The Case of Canadian Railroads, Journal of Political Economy 88, pp. 958–976.

J. N. Collins and B. T. Downes [1977]: The Effect of Size on the Provision of Public Services: The Case of Solid Waste Collection in Smaller Cities, Urban Affairs Quarterly 12, pp. 333–347.

P. N. Courant, E. M. Gramlich, and D. L. Rubinfeld [1980]: Why Voters Support Tax Limitations Amendments: The Michigan Case, National Tax Journal 33, pp. 1–20.

W. M. Crain and A. Zardkoohi [1978]: A Test of the Property Rights Theory of the Firm: Water Utilities in the United States, Journal of Law and Economics 21, pp. 395–408.

L. De Alessi [1969]: Some Implications of Property Rights for Government Investment Choices, American Economic Review 59, pp. 16–23.

L. De Alessi [1973]: Private Property and Dispersion of Ownership in Large Corporations, Journal of Finance 28, pp. 839–851.

L. De Alessi [1974a]: An Economic Analysis of Government Ownership and Regulation: Theory and the Evidence from the Electric Power Industry, Public Choice 19, pp. 1–42.

L. De Alessi [1974b]: Managerial Tenure Under Private and Government Ownership in the Electric Power Industry, Journal of Political Economy 82, pp. 645–653.

L. De Alessi [1980]: The Economics of the Property Rights: A Review of the Evidence, Research in Law and Economics 2, pp. 1–47.

R. T. Deacon [1977]: Private Choice and Collective Outcomes: Evidence from Public Sector Demand Analysis, National Tax Journal 30, pp. 371–386.

R. T. Deacon [1979]: The Expenditure Effect of Alternative Public Supply Institutions, Public Choice 34, pp. 381–398.

H. Demsetz [1968]: Why Regulate Utilities? Journal of Law and Economics 11, pp. 55–66.

R. D. Eckert [1973]: On the Incentives of Regulators: The Case of Taxicabs, Public Choice 14, pp. 83–100.

R. D. Eckert [1979]: What Do Regulators Maximize? Mimeo, University of California, Claremont.

J. Finsinger [1981]: Competition, Ownership and Control in Markets with Imperfect Information: The Case of the German Liability and Life Insurance Markets, Mimeo, International Institute of Management, Berlin.

M. P. Fiorina and R. G. Noll [1978]: Voters, Bureaucrats and Legislators: A Rational Choice Perspective of the Growth of Government, Journal of Public Economics 9, pp. 239–254.

H. E. Frech [1979]: Mutual and Other Nonprofit Health Insurance Firms: Comparative Performance in a Natural Experiment, Research in Law and Economics, Supplement to Vol. 1, pp. 61–73.

H. E. Frech [1980]: Property Rights, The Theory of the Firm, and Competitive Markets for Top Decision Makers, Research in Law and Economics 2, pp. 49–63.

V. Goldberg [1976a]: Regulation and Administered Contracts, Bell Journal of Economics 7, pp. 426–448.

V. Goldberg [1976b]: Toward an Expanded Theory of Contract, Journal of Economic Issues 10, pp. 45–61.

M. Gunderson [1979a]: Decomposition of Public-Private Sector Earnings Differentials, in M. W. Bucovetsky (ed.): Studies in Public Employment and Composition in Canada, Montreal, pp. 1–28.

M. Gunderson [1979b]: Earnings Differentials Between the Public and Private Sectors, Canadian Journal of Economics 12, pp. 228–242.

M. Gunderson [1979c]: Professionalization of the Canadian Public Sector, in M. W. Bucovetsky (ed.): Studies in Public Employment and Composition in Canada, Montreal, pp. 81–124.

W. Hendricks [1977]: Regulation and Labor Earnings, Bell Journal of Economics 8, pp. 483–496.

W. Z. Hirsch [1965]: Cost Functions of Urban Government Services: Refuse Collection, Review of Economics and Statistics 47, pp. 87–92.

B. F. Lentz [1981]: Political and Economic Determinants of County Government Pay, Public Choice 36, pp. 253–271.

C. M. Lindsay [1975]: Veterans Administration Hospitals: An Economic Analysis of Government Enterprise, Washington, D.C.

C. M. Lindsay [1976]: A Theory of Government Enterprise, Journal of Political Economy 87, pp. 1061–1077.

T. L. Lowi [1979]: The End of Liberalism, New York.

R. A. Meyer [1975]: Publicly Owned versus Privately Owned Utilities: A Policy Choice, Review of Economics and Statistics 57, pp. 391–399.

T. G. Moore [1970]: The Effectiveness of Regulation of Electric Utility Prices, Southern Economic Journal 36, pp. 365–375.

A. H. Munnell and A. M. Connolly [1979]: Comparability of Public and Private Compensation: The Issue of Fringe Benefits, New England Economics Review, 5, pp. 27–45.

G. Neugebauer [1978]: Grundzüge einer ökonomischen Theorie der Korruption, Zurich.

A. Nichols [1967]: Stock versus Mutual Savings and Loan Associations: Some Evidence of Differences in Behavior, American Economic Review 57, pp. 377–346.

W. A. Niskanen [1971]: Bureaucracy and Representative Government, Chicago and New York.

W. A. Niskanen [1975]: Bureaucrats and Politicians, Journal of Law and Economics 18, pp. 617–643.

D. Orr [1976]: Public Employee Compensation Levels, in: A. L. Chickering (ed.): Public Employee Unions: A Study of the Crisis in Public Sector Labor Relations, San Francisco, pp. 64–86.

W. Orzechowski [1974]: Labor Intensity, Productivity, and the Growth of the Federal Sector, Public Choice 19, pp. 123–126.

W. Orzechowski [1977]: Economic Models of Bureaucracy: Survey, Extensions, and Evidence, in: T. E. Borcherding (ed.): Budgets and Bureaucrats: The Sources of Government Growth, Durham, N.C., pp. 229–259.

M. Ott [1980]: Bureaucracy, Monopoly, and the Demand for Municipal Services, Journal of Urban Economics 8, pp. 362–382.

B. M. Owen and R. Braeutigam [1978]: The Regulation Game: Strategic Use of the Administrative Process, Cambridge, Mass.

W. Pfister [1976]: Steigende Millionenverluste der Bayerischen Staatsforstverwaltung: Ein Dauerzustand?, Mitteilungsblatt des Bayerischen Waldbesitzerverbandes 26, pp. 1–9.

W. J. Pier, R. B. Vernon, and J. H. Wicks [1974]: An Empirical Comparison of Government and Private Production Efficiency, National Tax Journal 27, pp. 653–656.

W. W. Pommerehne [1976]: Private versus öffentliche Müllabfuhr; Ein theoretischer und empirischer Vergleich, Finanzarchiv 35, pp. 272–294.

W. W. Pommerehne [1979]: Gebundene versus freie Geldtransfers: Eine Fallstudie, in: C. C. von Weizsäcker (ed.): Staat und Wirtschaft, Berlin, pp. 147–164.

W. W. Pommerehne [1980]: Real versus Monetary Transfers: Reflections on Some Lessons from the United States, Mimeo, University of Zurich, Zurich.

W. W. Pommerehne [1982]: Empirische Ansätze zur Erfassung der Präferenzen für öffentliche Güter, in: G. Bombach, B. Gahlen, and A. E. Ott (eds.): Möglichkeiten und Grenzen der Staatstätigkeit, Tübingen, forthcoming.

W. W. Pommerehne and B. S. Frey [1978]: Bureaucratic Behavior in Democracy: A Case Study, Public Finance 33, pp. 98–112.

W. W. Pommerehne and F. Schneider [1982]: Private and Public Production in Selected European Countries: Findings and Some Positive Economic Implications, Mimeo, University of Zurich, Zurich.

M. A. Posner [1971]: Taxation by Regulation, Bell Journal of Economics and Management Science 2, pp. 22–50.

J. F. Quinn [1979]: Wage Differentials Among Older Workers in the Public and Private Sectors, Journal of Human Resources 14, pp. 41–62.

J. F. Quinn [1982]: Compensation in the Public Sector: The Importance of Pensions, in: R. H. Haveman (ed.): Public Finance and Public Employment, Detroit, pp. 227–243.

E. S. Savas [1977c]: An Empirical Study of Competition in Municipal Service Delivery, Public Administration Review 37, pp. 717–724.

E. S. Savas [1980]: Comparative Costs of Public and Private Enterprise, in: W. J. Baumol (ed.): Public and Private Enterprise in a Mixed Economy, New York and London, pp. 234–294.

P. Shapiro and J. Sonstelie [1982]: Did Proposition 13 Stay Leviathan? American Economic Review, Papers and Proceedings 72, pp. 184–190.

S. P. Smith [1976]: Pay Differentials Between Federal Government and Private Sector Workers, Industrial and Labor Relations Review 29, pp. 179–197.

S. P. Smith [1977]: Equal Pay in the Public Sector: Fact or Fantasy, Princeton.

S. P. Smith [1981]: Public-Private Wage Differentials in Metropolitan Areas, in: P. Mieszkowski and G. E. Peterson (eds.): Public Sector Labor Markets, Washington, D.C., pp. 81–102.

R. M. Spann [1977]: Public versus Private Provision of Governmental Services, in: T. E. Borcherding (ed.): Budgets and Bureaucrats: The Sources of Government Growth, Durham, N.C., pp. 71–89.

E. B. Staats [1973]: Weighting Comparability in Federal Pay, Tax Review 24, pp. 1–6.

B. J. Stevens and E. S. Savas [1978]: The Cost of Residential Refuse Collection and the Effect Service Arrangements, Municipal Year Book 44, pp. 200–205.

G. S. Stigler [1971]: The Theory of Economic Regulation, Bell Journal of Economics and Management Science 2, pp. 137–146.

R. E. Wagner and W. E. Weber [1975]: Competition, Monopoly, and the Organization of Government in Metropolitan Areas, Journal of Law and Economics 18, pp. 661–684.

O. E. Williamson [1971]: The Vertical Integration of Production: Market Failure Considerations, American Economic Review, Papers and Proceedings 61, pp. 112–126.

O. E. Williamson [1975]: Markets and Hierarchies: Analysis and Antitrust Implications, New York and London.

O. E. Williamson [1976]: Franchise Bidding for Natural Monopolies in General and with Respect to CATV, Bell Journal of Economics 7, pp. 73–104.

O. E. Williamson [1969]: Transactions Cost Economics: The Governance of Contractual Relationships, Journal of Law and Economics 22, pp. 233–262.

G. W. Wilson and J. M. Jadlow [1978]: Competition, Profit Incentives, and Technical Efficiency in the Nuclear Medicine Industry, Mimeo, Indiana University, Bloomington.

J. Q. Wilson [1961]: The Economy of Patronage, Journal of Political Economy 69, pp. 369–380.

J. Q. Wilson [1974]: The Politics of Regulation, in J. W. McKie (ed.): Social Responsibility and the Business Predicament, Washington, D.C., pp. 135–168.

J. Q. Wilson [1980]: The Politics of Regulation, New York, N.Y.

R. Wintrobe [1977]: The Economics of Bureaucracy, Mimeo, University of Western Ontario, London.

C. Wolf [1979]: A Theory of Non-Market Failures, Public Interest 55, pp. 114–133.

M. Zumbühl [1978]: Privatisierung staatlicher Wirtschaftstätigkeit—Notwendigkeit und Möglichkeiten, Zürich.

Addresses of authors: Prof. Thomas E. Borcherding, Simon Fraser University, Department of Economics, Burnaby, B. C. Canada V5A 1S6; Dr. Werner W. Pommerehne and Dr. Friedrich Schneider, Institut für Empirische Wirtschaftsforschung der Universität Zürich, Kleinstrasse 15, CH-8008 Zurich, Switzerland.

JAMES TOBIN

The Future of Social Security: One Economist's Assessment

Today's workers finance today's retirees; current payroll taxes fund Social Security retirement benefits. Although the 1983 payroll tax increase enabled the Social Security Administration to predict a slight budget surplus over the next few decades, a continuation of low birth rates and low productivity, combined with increasing years lived past retirement, could lead to as much as a 20 percent rise in payroll taxes to ensure the continued solvency of the system.

James Tobin provides a critical analysis not only of the Social Security program and proposals for reform, but of the political and ideological issues that surround it, which must necessarily be taken into account if the "crisis" is to be understood. His analysis covers how Social Security got into trouble, possible economic implications of the current system of financing, reasons for compulsory participation, and a proposal for a fully funded system.

QUESTIONS TO GUIDE THE READING

1. What are the differences between the way the current system is funded and the proposal for a "fully funded" system?
2. How did Social Security get into trouble?
3. Under what circumstances might the Social Security program be acting as a damper on national savings? If true, what would be the economic implications?
4. What is the case for compulsory participation?
5. How could Social Security affect retirement decisions?

To most Americans, Social Security means federal pensions paid to old people, Old Age and Survivors Insurance (OASI) in technical lingo. That is my subject here. It is only one of the programs begun by the Social Security Act of 1935, which also established our federal-state systems of unemployment

James Tobin, "The Future of Social Security: One Economist's Assessment," from Theodore R. Marmor and Jerry L. Mashaw, eds., *Social Security in Contemporary American Politics.* Copyright © 1988 Princeton University Press. Reprinted by permission of the publisher.

James Tobin is Professor of Economics at Yale University. He received a Nobel Prize in Economics in 1981.

compensation, assistance to needy old people, and assistance to families with dependent children, as well as various social services. From the beginning, OASI differed from the other initiatives in several respects. It was to be a federal program, uniform across the nation. Like unemployment compensation, its benefits to persons eligible because of required payroll tax contributions were not conditioned on need but only on those contributions and on other personal circumstances, mainly age and substantial retirement. In several steps beginning in 1954, disability was added to those personal circumstances, and it is sometimes necessary to refer to the combined program, Old Age, Survivors, and Disability Insurance (OASDI). In 1965 health insurance for the elderly, Medicare, was added, and the comprehensive acronym became Old Age, Survivors, Disability, and Health Insurance (OASDHI). But OASI remains the giant Social Security program.

On its golden anniversary (1985) OASI was both successful, surely even beyond the dreams of its founders, and troubled. In the *1985 Economic Report of the President,* his Council of Economic Advisers credits OASI for the remarkably healthy economic position of the elderly. The other side of the same coin is the growth in the program's cost, a source of considerable anxiety and alarm. Panic in 1981 and 1982 about the imminent "insolvency" of the trust fund was dissipated by legislation in 1983, a bipartisan compromise package of future payroll tax increases and benefit cuts projected to keep the fund in the black for several decades. Nonetheless Social Security continues to be a candidate for federal budgetmakers seeking ways to cut deficits in the overall federal budget. Moreover, the 1983 package may not forestall another and more serious insolvency threat in the twenty-first century.

Major Issues Facing OASI

Any assessment of the future of OASI must face three interrelated issues: balancing contributions and benefits; erosion of confidence; and financing. I shall discuss each in turn.

Balancing Contributions and Benefits

The overriding long-run issue about OASI is the balance between the tax contributions of the young and the benefits of the old. The system is now geared to scale up benefits automatically so as to maintain the ratio of benefits to contemporaneous wages, the replacement ratio, at its historical level of roughly 40 percent. Payroll tax rates are the residual balancing item in the OASI financial equation. They have been raised steadily for years, and according to current projections they will have to be raised substantially next century if the replacement ratio is to be maintained. The generations involved, however, may at some point prefer to move to or toward a different option—freezing the tax rates and adjusting future benefits instead. This would mean that in the twenty-first century the benefit-wage ratio would fall: OASI benefits would still be rising in absolute purchasing power, but they would decline relative to the wages of active workers. It is not too soon to begin serious consideration of the options.

Erosion of Confidence

The confidence of young workers in Social Security has eroded in recent years. Some are worried that the system will go broke. Others perceive that their rate of return on the payroll tax contributions they and their employers make will be quite low, in contrast to the interest rates they observe in financial markets today. They wonder why participation in such a system should be compulsory. The link between the contributions of, or on behalf of, any individual participant and his or her eventual benefits is quite loose, and quite mysterious. The system is a hybrid, mixing social retirement insurance with some intragenerational redistribution in favor of workers with low earnings. This is bound to diminish the rates of return high-wage workers perceive they can earn through OASI.

Old issues return anew: Should OASI be made more purely an insurance program, letting the general federal budget handle redistribution via needs-tested transfers? Should the link between contributions and benefits be actuarially fair for individual participants? Should the benefit entitlements earned by past contributions be reported regularly and clearly to participants throughout their careers? Should compulsory participation be limited to defined levels of contributions and benefits? . . . The founders of Social Security confronted these questions and compromised. Compromises, even theirs, are not graven in stone. Times, circumstances, and attitudes change. At the end of this chapter I shall sketch, as an option worth considering, a system that links contributions and benefits more explicitly and tightly.

Financing Social Security

The issues just raised regarding the links between contributions and benefits for individual participants are related to questions about the financing of the system as a whole. Until now Social Security has been mainly a pay-as-you-go system, using its current receipts from workers' contributions to pay its current benefits. Its trust fund, as its reserves are called, has been deliberately kept small. Under the 1983 legislation, this fund will grow to unprecedented heights relative to annual outlays over the next fifteen to twenty years. Thereafter it is projected to decline, and to vanish after midcentury.

A case can be made on macroeconomic grounds for a funded system in preference to pay-as-you-go. Full funding would mean a trust fund commensurate to OASI's liabilities for the future benefits earned by the contributions previously paid in. The accumulation of such a fund, it can be argued, would add to national saving and investment enough productive capital to yield the promised benefits. That yield might well be a higher rate of return than pay-as-you-go can offer.

History cannot be rerun. A shift to full funding would take nearly a half century to accomplish. Moreover, the proposal inevitably raises the question of the relation between Social Security trust funds and the overall federal budget. I shall discuss these financial issues, and in my sketch of possible reforms for the next century I shall describe how the long transition to a fully funded system might be managed. . . .

How Social Security Got into Trouble

Why and how did so successful and popular a program run into financial difficulties and come to encounter distrust among its future beneficiaries? There are several reasons in recent history, some related to the general economic and political environment and some intrinsic to the OASI system.

Stagflation

Along with the economies of the rest of the world, the American economy went sour beginning in 1970. The period since then has been an era of stagflation, OPEC oil shocks, four recessions, and low productivity growth. The most important symptom relevant to our topic is that real after-tax wage incomes, instead of rising at 2.5 to 3 percent per year as they had in the two previous decades, actually declined. A young man starting work in 1963 or 1973 has not experienced the progress toward the American dream that his father rightly took for granted a decade or two earlier. Indeed, from 1973 to 1983 his real wage income went down. If young families nonetheless advanced their incomes during the 1970s, it was because both spouses worked and postponed or eschewed child-bearing. The commitment of today's young women to working careers in preference to motherhood also means that there will be few payroll taxpayers relative to OASI beneficiaries next century.

Meanwhile, the living standards of the elderly not only escaped the economywide setbacks but sharply improved. From 1970 to 1980, while average monthly real wages declined by 7.4 percent, average monthly OASI benefits rose in real terms by 37 percent. Generous improvements of benefits were enacted in the early 1970s, and were protected by automatic adjustment to the Consumer Price Index (CPI) beginning in 1973.

The Political Climate

The contrast of the stagnant 1970s with the prosperously growing 1960s was summarized by Lester Thurow in the term zero-sum society, implying intensified conflict over the distribution of a national pie that was no longer growing. Redistributions of income of all kinds via taxes and governmental transfers waned in popularity. Tax revolts mushroomed in local, state, and national politics. General trust in government was eroded by Vietnam and Watergate. Conservative economics and ideology gained influence. The public was receptive to the conservative diagnosis of the 1970s, which attributed the disappointing economic performance to the size and growth of government—expenditures, taxes, regulations—rather than to OPEC and other external misfortunes. The last two, maybe even three, presidential elections have been won on the slogan "government is not the solution, it is the problem."

Demographic Trends

The age distribution has turned adverse to Social Security. Aged workers retire sooner and live longer. Births, low in the 1920s and 1930s, zoomed after the Second World War, began to decline in the 1960s, and now hardly suffice to replace parents. . . . The ratio of persons aged 20 to 64 to persons aged 65 and over is falling, and so, of course, is the number of workers per OASI beneficiary.

These clouds have some silver linings. Official projections have gone wrong in the past, and the current ones may be unduly pessimistic. Lower natural population and labor force growth may open the doors to more legal immigrants, mostly young workers who will be paying into the trust fund. Greater scarcity of labor might lead to faster growth of real wages—though given present uncertainties about capital formation and technological progress, this is by no means a sure thing. In any case, workers with fewer children will be able to afford either higher payroll taxes or additional saving on their own retirement.

The Maturing of the System

Some difficulties endemic to the OASI system became salient in the less benign environment after 1970, especially after 1973. Even though the climate is now improving, these problems, once surfaced, will not go away. They have roots in the history of OASI.

OASI took a long time to reach maturity, and growing up was much easier than adulthood. The reach of the system, thus of the payroll tax, was gradually extended by legislation and by economic change (for example, migration from rural self-employment to nonfarm wage labor). Ratios of persons in covered employment any time during a year to average civilian employment for the year are indicative: they were 0.82 in 1950; 1.10 in 1960; 1.13 in 1984. During this long period of expanding coverage, the number of contributing active workers was growing more rapidly than the labor force, and of course the covered percentage of retired workers was always lagging behind. By the 1970s we were coming to the end of this road. The few remaining pockets of exempt private employment were being absorbed. State and local governments still have discretion; they are likely to continue successfully their resistance to compulsory inclusion.

Growth of coverage combined with growth of labor force and productivity to swell the proceeds of the payroll tax faster than the benefit payments committed by previous legislation. The surpluses might have been allowed to pile up in the OASI trust fund, the way an insurance company channels current premiums into reserves against its liabilities to future beneficiaries. But this was not done. Even so, the taxes and benefits set in the original act in 1935 would have built a substantial fund, estimated at that time to reach $47 billion in 1980 (equivalent to about 300 billion actual 1980 dollars—compared with 1980 benefit outlays of $105 billion). In fact, the trust fund was $23 billion in 1980. The 1939 amendments deliberately scaled down the fund's growth, aiming only at a modest contingency reserve. In addition, as surpluses loomed after 1950, Congress regularly increased the scope and size of benefits. The reforms were always very desirable improvements in the effectiveness and fairness of the system. Several generations of beneficiaries have, therefore, obtained excellent returns on their contributions, and I will, too. But as the system approached maturity, these enlarged benefits could be continued only by successive increases in payroll taxes. . . .

Indexation

In 1972 another fateful decision was made: the automatic indexing of benefits. At the same time, benefits were scaled up by 20 percent. Indexation was well intended. Indeed, it was an act of political abnegation by Congress. The setting of benefits (including, but in practice not confined to, adjusting them for inflation) was taken off the regular political agenda. Moreover, there was every reason in past experience to believe the move was financially prudent. OASDI revenues would grow with wages, benefits with prices. Wages grow faster than prices; anyway, they always had. Came the OPEC rise in oil prices, and the vanishing of productivity growth, and this relationship was reversed. In this way the stagflation of the 1970s hit OASI finances very directly. The blow was compounded by an inadvertent technical error in the 1972 legislation, which under the circumstances overindexed benefits; this was corrected in 1977.

In retrospect it is easy to see that indexing by the CPI is not a good idea, even in economic times less turbulent than the 1970s. It is not a good idea for government-paid benefits, and it is not a good idea for wage contracts. Such indexing immunizes the favored individuals from losses the nation as a whole cannot escape—in 1973–1974 and 1979–1980 the big rises in the cost of imported oil—and throws their costs onto unprotected fellow citizens. Likewise indexation in effect exempts its beneficiaries from paying the increased taxes embodied in the prices that compose the index; others must bear the burdens of the public programs financed by those taxes. It would be both possible and desirable to construct an index purged of these unintended implications and to mandate its use, not only in Social Security but wherever else indexed commitments are made; this should be done before the economy runs again into stormy weather like the 1970s.

Social Security and National Saving

The issue of pay-as-you-go versus funding is both more basic and more difficult than correcting for inflation. At the macroeconomic level the question is how OASI financing affects national saving and capital investment and, through them, future productivity and standards of living. It is obviously related to the similar question about overall federal fiscal policies.

Martin Feldstein has been the most prominent and insistent critic of pay-as-you-go financing. He argues that this system greatly diminishes aggregate national saving. Workers regard their payroll tax contributions as saving; the prospect of future OASI pensions spares them, at least in part, the need to provide for retirement on their own. But under pay-as-you-go, the government treats receipts from those taxes like any other revenues and spends them. They are not channeled, directly or indirectly, through the capital markets into investment in productive capital assets whose yields could pay the future pensions. Feldstein estimated the national capital stock to be trillions of dollars smaller than it would have been with a funded system.

Feldstein's argument overstates the problem, both theoretically and empirically. It probably is true that OASI taxes displace some voluntary saving. For example, some private pension plans, explicitly aiming at a target ratio of total retirement income to wage or salary, offset OASI improvements by lowering their own provisions. . . . However, many workers are so constrained by their current liquid resources that they cannot offset OASI taxes by consuming more and saving less on their own. Moreover, many elderly pensioners do not consume all their pensions during retirement, as the Feldstein scenario assumes they do. Their benefits wind up, in part, in larger bequests to their children. Middle- and upper-income retired individuals typically save actuarially excessive amounts against the risk of prolonged high medical and custodial expenses, knowing that any unneeded amounts will end up in their estates. Empirical studies provoked by Feldstein's work are inconclusive, but they indicate that the effects of unfunded OASI on voluntary private saving are at most much smaller than Feldstein asserted.

OASI Financing and Federal Fiscal Policy

The issue turns also on the effects of OASI financing on general federal fiscal policy and of that policy on the economy and its rate of capital accumulation. Would the overall "unified" budget deficit be smaller if, because of funding, OASI were in surplus? Or would the political and economic strategies that determine the budget offset the OASI surplus with a larger deficit in other transactions? A test may come in the 1990s and 2000s when, thanks to the 1983 legislation, the OASI trust fund is projected to grow to 10 to 20 percent of GNP with annual surpluses of 2 to 2.5 percent of GNP. Moreover, we are about to return to the pre-1968 practice of focusing official attention on the administrative budget and deficit, thus separating the trust funds from the budget that is presumptively supposed to balance.

My guess is that in the past the federal government would have run larger administrative deficits had the trust funds been raking in surpluses. Indeed this often would have been good macroeconomic policy because fiscal stimulus was needed to avoid or overcome recessions and keep the economy close to full employment. Fund surpluses, if not offset by administrative deficits or aggressively stimulative monetary policy, would frequently have meant greater unemployment rather than more capital accumulation. If we were to assume that nowadays Federal Reserve monetary policy calls the macroeconomic tune, so that national output and employment are always what the Fed wants and permits, irrespective of fiscal policy, then the situation would correspond more closely to Feldstein's assumptions. Conditional on monetary policy, we would get more capital formation the lower the federal deficit. And funding, combined with segregated accounting, probably would lower the overall deficit, although by less than the OASI surplus.

A truly funded system could be expected to yield on average a higher rate of return on participants' contributions. A mature pay-as-you-go system cannot do better than the rate of growth of real payrolls—that is, the sum of the rates of growth of employment and real wages. In the long run the growth of real wages is the growth of labor productivity. The formulas prescribed in the 1972 and 1977 legislation approximately guarantee that real benefits will grow along with real wages (that is, with productivity). That is how earnings replacement rates are maintained. The formulas ignore trends in labor force and employment, which also determine the growth in real payrolls and thus in OASI contributions. As those growth trends decline, it will not be possible to pay the benefits the formulas generate without raising payroll tax rates. To make the same point another way, in those circumstances it will not be possible to hold tax rates constant without lowering earnings replacement rates.

For the rest of the century, the growth of real payrolls should be about 3 percent per annum. Subsequently labor force growth will slow down. The baby-boomer bulge will subside, and the growth of the female labor force will decline as women's participation in the labor force approaches that of men. In official middle-range economic and demographic projections for the first half of the next century, real earnings per worker grow at about 1.8 percent per year and the covered labor force at 0.1 percent, implying growth of taxable payrolls at well below 2 percent. The major uncertainty is productivity growth. The sources of its decline in the 1970s are still a mystery to students of the subject. Should labor productivity take off next century, the returns on the contributions of younger persons currently working or entering the labor force will be much better than the estimates look now.

A funded system could in principle yield a rate of return equal to the economy's real interest rate, basically a reflection of the marginal productivity of capital. Social Security trust funds, invested in federal securities, actually earn a bit less because the federal government's borrowing rate is lower than rates on private securities. Those beneficiaries partially subject to income tax would earn still less, but this liability also reduces their return under pay-as-you-go. At present the pretax real rate appears to be 4 to 5 percent, thus higher than the current 3 percent growth rate of real payrolls. Over a working career, this difference compounds to a 20 to 50 percent advantage in benefits.

An advantage of this kind is not, however, an opportunity available to OASI participants without a long transitional period of extra saving to do the funding, at the expense of the consumption of taxpayers and/or beneficiaries. Moreover, the differential in favor of funding may not last. In the past, real rates of interest in financial markets have often been lower than the growth of real payrolls.

I shall return shortly to the funding issue, but first I must consider some basic questions about OASI that I mentioned at the beginning of this chapter: the compulsory nature of Social Security, and the relative roles of redistribution and insurance in the benefits provided.

Why Is Social Security Compulsory?

What is the rationale for compulsory universal participation? If yuppies think they could do better on their own, why not let them opt out? Why not let workers and their families arrange and finance their own retirements? Why not leave it to parents and children to define the obligations of generations to each other? In the polls previously cited, 56 percent favored voluntary Social Security, although 75 percent said they would participate anyway.

The perception that market returns are today higher than those likely to be earned on Social Security contributions is evidently a source of the disillusionment reported in polls: 58 percent of respondents say they could do better "at the bank," and only 22 percent think they could not do better on their own. Of course, many workers, including respondents who think they could provide better for their own retirement than by contributing to OASI, would not in fact succeed in doing so. Indeed, many would not in fact save the equivalent of their payroll taxes if they were free to choose.

There are several arguments for compulsion. The first is simple paternalism. It should not be lightly dismissed. Some citizens may not know what is good for them, or they may be too short-sighted or weak-willed to act. Young people find it difficult to save for that incredibly remote time of old age. When it does arrive, they will be grateful in retrospect if Uncle Sam has made them save. Many people like such discipline and prefer that money never pass through their hands.

The second is a paternalistic argument with a different twist—society's interest in having individuals provide for their own old age. Society will not let the aged starve and die in the street (I hope that is still true in the United States). Instead, society will use public resources to help the destitute even if their own past improvidence might be the reason for their plight, a possibility very difficult to substantiate in any individual case. Consequently, it is argued, the state has the right to protect society, as well as the individual, against such improvidence.

Third, there are what economists call externalities in universal participation. The government can provide a better retirement plan for most people than they could obtain on their own, provided everyone participates. Some individuals could possibly do better personally if allowed to opt out, but if everyone were free to do so few would do better. The government plan itself would be impaired by adverse selection—the withdrawal of the better risks and their premiums. Moreover, a universal and uniform plan has economies of scale that would be lost if participation were voluntary.

Fourth, a universal plan underwritten by the taxing and monetary powers of the central government can offer some guarantees that a decentralized system of private pensions and voluntary saving cannot. These include protection against internal inflation. A big advantage of OASI over private plans is that OASI is portable and vested; rights and benefits once earned are not lost by changing jobs or residences or by leaving the work force. The founders of Social Security were very wise to establish it as a nationally uniform system, centrally governed and administered. Thanks to their foresight, we avoided the distortions that a decentralized system would have introduced into workers' choices of jobs and residences and into employers' choices of locations. Such distortions occur because of differences among states and localities in unemployment compensation and welfare programs, and because of the incomplete portability and vesting of most entitlements to private pensions. . . .

Fifth, in a highly interdependent modern economy, the intergenerational social compact is not solely among blood relatives. We recognize a general social obligation for the welfare, education, and socialization of children, an obligation that extends to citizens who have no children and to parents with more than ample means to care for their own. Likewise, active workers have some responsibilities for the elders in the society as a whole, whatever they may give to or receive from their own parents. Intergenerational transfers are legitimate agenda of democratic politics.

Some may find these defenses of compulsion unconvincing; others may not have seen compulsion as problematic in the first place. I think there is a strong case for a compulsory system, but I do wonder whether it justifies compulsory accumulation of ever higher benefits, far above absolute minimal requirements for subsistence. OASI enthusiasts point with pride to the fact that its benefits now replace about the same percentage of the earnings of active workers as when the program began, about 40 percent. They use that statistic to counter critics who claim present benefits are too generous. But this same replacement ratio provides now, and in the next century, a much more comfortable retirement than it did half a century ago.

At some point the generations who will be working and retiring in the twenty-first century may wish to limit the growth of compulsory contributions and the benefits they buy, while inviting voluntary supplementary participation in OASI. Individuals, or employers and employees in concert, would be free to make additional voluntary contributions and obtain higher benefits. OASI could be an attractively simple channel for individuals' retirement saving and private retirement plans.

Insurance versus Redistribution

From its inception OASI was a carefully conceived compromise among several not wholly compatible objectives. Its overriding purpose, of course, was to enable older people to live decently and independently once they could no longer earn income from employment. OASI's reliance on contributions collected by taxing workers and their employers, and the absence of a means test for benefits, follow from the principle that participants earn benefits as a matter of right. The analogy to insurance benefits earned by premiums was deliberate; here the "risk" is living too long after wages stop, and the "premiums" buy "security" from destitution or dependence. But in fact the connection of benefits to contributions, within age cohorts and between them, has always been loose and uneven.

The variability of that connection comes from another objective. The system is intentionally redistributive among workers of any given birth date. (It is redistributive across generations, as already noted.) High wage earners receive significantly lower pensions per dollar of payroll tax contributions than do their lower wage contemporaries. . . .

The progressivity of the formula does not convey the full impact of the system on the distribution of income among contemporaneous participants. Some ancillary government policies enhance progressivity. At the low end of the income spectrum, Supplemental Security Income (SSI) is a federal means-tested assistance program for the elderly, financed not from the OASI trust fund but from general revenues. It is a "safety net" for old people whose entitlements to Social Security do not meet minimal needs. At the affluent end of the income spectrum, the 1983 provision for partial income taxation of OASI benefits makes Social Security per se more progressive. However, . . . low cumulative contributions may have resulted from loose connection to covered employment rather than from low incomes during working years.

A more important point is that beneficiaries with . . . lower monthly benefits relative to lifetime contributions tend to live longer and receive those benefits a longer time. On an actuarial basis, this longevity effect roughly, and serendipitously, offsets the progressivity of the . . . formula. OASI pays virtually nothing except to living primary beneficiaries and their spouses. The risk against which OASI insures is that of living too long, and it makes no distinctions among its beneficiaries with respect to life expectancy. . . .

As is usually the case, equity and efficiency conflict. Use of the system's revenues to improve the lots of the poorer retirees and their families can create some perverse incentives. Participants can retire and begin receiving benefits as early as age 62. The weight of evidence is that the system has significantly reinforced the trend toward earlier retirement. Although a worker can gain higher monthly benefits by continuing to work, the gain has been actuarially inadequate, especially for postponing retirement age beyond the long standard age of 65. Under the 1983 amendments, this bias is being gradually eliminated. The legislation also schedules a gradual increase after year 2000 in the normal retirement age in OASI calculus. These changes seem quite appropriate. As the health and longevity of senior citizens improve gradually, it is a service to them, to their younger tax-paying contemporaries, and to the economy at large to employ their services.

In the past, a severe disincentive to work by the elderly has been the consequent total or partial loss of OASI benefits. Now, however, from age 70 on, OASI beneficiaries may work without losing any benefits. If they do work, however, they still pay Social Security taxes. This anomaly betrays an official attitude that those payments are just like other taxes, rather than contributions to earn retirement benefits. Working OASI beneficiaries should be excused from further contributions, especially now that earned income may make them liable for personal income taxes on their benefits as well as on the earnings themselves.

Serious disincentives prior to retirement are inherent in the size and growth of payroll tax rates noted above. Further increases—two to five percentage points—are likely in the twenty-first century, to handle the midcentury demographic crunch if benefit-earnings replacement ratios are maintained. Health insurance is also financed from payroll taxes. Total payroll tax rates, including health insurance, have risen from 8.8 percent in 1967 to 14.1 percent now and are scheduled to be 15.3 percent after 1989, probably even higher after the financing of Medicare is seriously reviewed over the next few years. . . . In the middle of the next century total payroll taxes will have to be 21 to 26 percent of taxable payrolls, according to middle-range official projections.

Payroll taxes, to the extent they are regarded as ordinary taxes rather than as contributions which earn full value in future benefits, are disincentives to work by employees. For workers with annual earnings above the limit of the payroll tax, however, they are not a disincentive discouraging extra work. Likewise, if employers regard their payroll taxes as additional costs rather than as substitutes for wages, they are a disincentive to employment. High tax rates invite evasion and encourage substitution of capital and other inputs for labor, especially for low-wage and unskilled labor, all of whose earnings are taxable. If workers perceive no clear and fair link of contributions to benefits, the work and employment disincentives will be strong. But the disincentive to voluntary saving will be weak because distrust of Social Security might lead participants to make other provisions for retirement. . . .

Redistribution would then be accomplished by extra assistance to those in need, paid from general federal revenues, like SSI. This approach would eliminate from OASI the actuarial anomalies and disincentives incident to redistribution within the system, on the assumption that the redistribution could be handled more efficiently through the general budget.

The issues of intergenerational redistribution and equity are even more difficult. As explained above, they are especially acute right now. Present beneficiaries and participants who will retire before the turn of the century are getting high returns on their past contributions because of the past unsustainable growth of the system and the indexation of benefits in 1973. Many of them are much better off than many young payroll taxpayers are now or ever will be. Should the present fortunate elderly be asked to give up some of their windfalls either to enable payroll taxes to be reduced or to start building up a larger fund for the benefit of future retirees? Note that these purposes are intergenerational transfers within the OASI system. To accomplish them, deficit reduction targets for the remainder of the federal budget should remain unchanged. In any case, the problem is that immediate or early reduction of benefits, particularly so soon after the 1983 compromise, seems like a breach of contract, further weakening the trust of all generations in Social Security. Although further cuts of benefits could be phased in slowly, the windfalls of the luckiest cohorts of retirees would be untouched.

A Possible Funded System

No radical change of OASI is likely in the near future. The Greenspan compromise has assured its "solvency" well into the next century. No crisis is likely to return OASI to the urgent agenda of politics for a couple of decades, although it may continue to be vulnerable to budget cutters who try to resolve general fiscal imbalances without raising taxes or cutting defense. The trust fund surpluses anticipated in the 1990s might tempt Congress to sweeten benefits or lower payroll taxes, although the deficits anticipated some decades later should be an inhibition. The Greenspan Commission left unresolved the financial crunch projected between 2030 and 2040. The generations involved have the time and opportunity to choose among various ways of averting it. As a contribution to that debate, let me spell out what a funded system recast along purer insurance lines would look like. I shall draw in part on the proposals of Professors Boskin, Kotlikoff, and Shoven for "personal security accounts."

1. Every individual participant would have a funded account, which would vest him or her with rights to pensions and to ancillary insurance and benefits, from first covered job until actual retirement. The age of retirement (i.e., commencement of benefits) would be discretionary within a specified interval. Benefit claims would depend on the dates and amounts of contributions in the same way for all participants. The fund would grow during the participant's working career, not only by additional contributions but also by compound interest. The interest rate would vary with the government's borrowing rate, but it would never be less than the rate of inflation

of a suitable consumer price index (purged of the price effects of uninsurable shocks and indirect taxes).

2. At the time of retirement, this fund—less amounts charged to it for disability insurance, death benefits, and other ancillary items—will be converted actuarially into an indexed annuity, either for the life of the participant alone or with continuing payments to a surviving spouse, at the choice of the participant.

3. Contributions of married workers will be divided equally between the two spouses' accounts, as long as they are married. There will be no spousal benefits or benefits to a surviving spouse other than the optional survivor annuity mentioned above. But a married retired couple will receive all the benefits the two of them earned by working or by being married to a worker. Changes of this type are overdue. The present system does not do justice to working spouses or to divorcees.

4. During periods of registered unemployment, a participant's compulsory payroll contributions to OASI in his previous job will be credited to his account without payments by the participant or his previous employer. The government could also credit extra contributions to participants who worked at low wages or were registered as unemployed for, say, at least forty weeks of a year. These extra contributions could be proportional to the shortfall of earnings from, say, half the earnings cap for the year. Thus could some progressivity be built into the system.

5. The system will be funded in aggregate. The trust fund will both receive the payroll contributions and credits, and disburse the annuities and other benefits. The Treasury will pay the trust fund interest on its balance at the designated rates. Since the scheme is essentially a "defined contribution" plan, its solvency will not be a problem unless real interest rates are chronically so low as to bring into force the guarantees of purchasing power.

6. Transition to such a funded system could take place slowly, as follows. Following its adoption, only new participants below age 35 would play by the new rules. Their aggregate contributions and credits would build up a new trust fund, Trust Fund II. Everyone else would play out the game by the old rules, via existing Trust Fund I. That fund would be deprived of receipts from the Fund II participants. The Treasury would "borrow" those receipts from Fund II and pay them out as necessary to Fund I beneficiaries. At the end of some forty years of transition, Fund II would hold Treasury obligations equal in value to the accounts of its participants. From a macroeconomic standpoint, total receipts and payments throughout the transition would be virtually the same as if there were no new program. The difference would be simply that the government would now be acknowledging its liabilities to future beneficiaries, the Fund II participants. Present federal accounting does not reckon such liabilities as public debt, although they really are.

I do not want to be misunderstood. Accounting is not magic. It cannot produce the economic funding that Feldstein advocated unless the nation does some extra saving during the transition. This proposal does not assign that task to any particular generation, contributors or beneficiaries, but via the overall federal budget to the nation as a whole. Only if the gradual acknowledgment of the Treasury's debt to Fund II inspires presidents and congresses to lower their deficits on non-OASI transactions will the accounting reform have macroeconomic substance. At the end of the transition, OASI would be a funded system for its participants, but overall effects on national saving and capital formation would still depend on general fiscal and monetary policies.

This slow transition has the advantage of breaking the bad accounting news quite gradually. More important, it respects the legitimate expectations of everyone in the existing system. Faster transitions, under which many beneficiaries would receive benefits from both Funds I and II, would cause too many confusions, anomalies, and inequities.

The trade-off between workers' contribution rates and beneficiaries' earnings replacement rates is likely to be painful in the next century. The generations concerned have time to work out a solution. The present system biases the result to maintaining the replacement rate and raising payroll taxes as necessary to pay the ever higher benefits. The proposed new system would be an opportunity to choose other options. One option is to freeze the payroll tax and to adjust future benefits accordingly; there are many options in between.

The new system would be much less vulnerable to economic and demographic shocks of the kind that spawned recent "crises." Blind adherence to pay-as-you-go seems to result in raising taxes to cover previously committed benefits whenever adverse events threaten to deplete the fund. Even when problems are foreseen, action is postponed so long that benefits cannot be touched without violating commitments to those retired or about to retire. At the same time, the new system would give participants a fair, clear, and continuously reported link between their individual contributions and their benefit rights. Although the system as outlined could accomplish some redistribution in favor of poorer participants, that burden is placed mainly on the general federal budget.

Proposals of this kind are worth considering in the next national debate about Social Security. The questions they raise are not in my view liberal versus conservative or Democrat versus Republican issues. They are issues of pragmatic management. Aging is a common human fate, irrespective of politics, ideologies, and generations. How people choose to trade consumption when they are young for consumption when they are old should not bring them to the barricades. It should bring them to face squarely economic and demographic realities. I hope the generations who will work out the structure of the system in the next century will do so in this spirit.

In concluding I want to stress that Social Security is viable and affordable in its present form. In suggesting possible changes for consideration, I am in no way departing from either my conviction that the Social Security

Act was one of the greatest triumphs of political, social, and economic architecture in the history of the republic or my admiration for its original designers and builders and for those dedicated public servants, like Robert Ball, who have maintained, repaired, and improved the structure these many years. Social Security deserves celebration of its golden anniversary.

SELECTION 32

DAVID T. ELLWOOD AND LAWRENCE H. SUMMERS
Is Welfare Really the Problem?

David Ellwood and Lawrence Summers examine three major social
welfare programs in an attempt to evaluate their success or failure
in dealing with poverty in America. They find that essentially we
are getting what we have paid for. Poverty still exists, but there is
little evidence that it is maintained by government policies. After
showing how poverty rates have been tied directly to the
performance of the U.S. economy since the 1960s, Ellwood and
Summers go on to discuss both the social insurance programs
designed to provide a "safety net" for the middle class and the cash
assistance and in-kind programs designed to aid the official poor.

QUESTIONS TO GUIDE THE READING

1. In what ways is the economic condition of the nonelderly poor
   determined by the performance of the U.S. economy?
2. What percent of the poor are taken out of poverty by cash
   assistance programs? By the Food Stamp program? By
   Unemployment Insurance and/or Workers' Compensation?
3. What is the evidence presented by Ellwood and Summers to
   support their conclusion that disability benefits have not
   decreased labor force participation among recipients?
4. What is the case against the argument that the AFDC program
   encourages single-parent families?
5. Why is it unlikely that current welfare policies could directly
   provide poor black youth with disincentives to work?

The poverty issue is gridlocked. No one is satisfied with current policy, but
no alternative can generate much support. The sources of dissatisfaction are
well-illustrated in two recent tracts on the poverty problem: Charles Murray's *Losing Ground* and Michael Harrington's *The New American Poverty*.
Murray notes that poverty has increased in the last fifteen years while fed-

---

David T. Ellwood and Lawrence H. Summers, "Is Welfare Really the Problem?" *The Public
Interest* (Spring 1986), 57–78. © 1986 by National Affairs, Inc. Reprinted with permission of
the authors.

David T. Ellwood is Professor of Public Policy at the Kennedy School of Government, Harvard
University. **Lawrence H. Summers** is Nathaniel Ropes Professor of Political Economy at Harvard University.

eral social spending has ballooned. He argues for a poverty Laffer curve: Attempts to reduce poverty actually have made things worse. Harrington sees the problem of rising poverty as one caused by government inaction rather than action. He asserts that the War on Poverty was never really declared and argues that without a massive effort, there is no real chance of combatting poverty.

We have reviewed the existing policies and our national record in reducing poverty. Despite the haphazard evolution of these policies and their seeming lack of coherence, they function reasonably well. Our conclusion is that, given the resources devoted to fighting poverty, the policies have done as well as we could have hoped. There is logic to the broad outlines of the current "safety net." Categorical programs have provided financial support to the needy and probably have not caused an appreciable share of the current problems. It is true that current transfer policies do relatively little to help the poor achieve self-sufficiency or to ameliorate some of the serious social problems attending poverty, but a review of the record does not support the view they have caused them.

Measuring Poverty

Any discussion of trends in poverty must rely on some measure of the incidence of poverty. And any single poverty measure is bound to be misleading. We concentrate here on trends in the officially defined poverty rate: that fraction of the population living in families with incomes below the poverty line. It is important to understand that the poverty line is a fixed level of real income (which varies by family size) thought to be sufficient to provide a minimally adequate standard of living. It is adjusted each year only for changes in the cost of living. Changes in the poverty rate thus provide an indicator of society's success in alleviating hardship among those with relatively low incomes, and do not necessarily indicate changes in income inequality, which is quite another issue. It is also important to recognize that only cash payments are treated as part of family income in the official poverty measure. In-kind benefits such as medical care, food stamps, or housing assistance are not counted at all.

Figure I depicts the trends since 1959 in the poverty rate, defined as the percentage of all persons living in families with cash income below the poverty line. We have broken down the figures for the elderly and nonelderly separately. For those over sixty-five, there was dramatic and relatively continual progress up to 1974, some modest progress through 1978, and a relatively flat poverty level since that time. For the nonelderly there was a dramatic decline in the poverty rate between 1959 and 1969. Then progress halted. The rate moved up and down throughout the 1970s, finally turning up rather sharply in the 1980s. It is the dramatic halt to progress in reducing the poverty rate for the nonelderly which seemed to coincide with the onset of the Great Society programs that has sparked the current dissatisfaction with our antipoverty efforts. Throughout this article we focus primarily on

Figure I

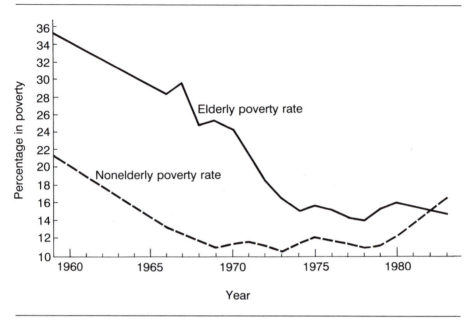

Official Poverty Rates for the Elderly and Nonelderly
Source: Official poverty statistics published annually by the U.S. Bureau of the Census (Current Population Reports, ser. P-60).

the nonelderly, since there appears to be less concern that our efforts at helping senior citizens were ineffectual or counterproductive.

Poverty and Economic Change

How much of the poverty rate can be explained by general economic developments? Figure II plots the nonelderly poverty rate along with the poverty threshold expressed as a fraction of median income. It is apparent that the curves dovetail almost perfectly. *Almost all of the variation in the poverty rate is tracked by movements in median family income. The poverty rate, and the poverty line as a fraction of total family income, move almost completely together.*

One does see a slight divergence of the trends in the 1980s. But here, it should be noted, the poverty rate is basically tracking the performance of the economy. In real terms, median family income in 1980 was no higher than it was in 1969. In the recession of 1982, it actually fell 5 percent below the 1969 level. Average families today have no more real income than they did almost fifteen years ago. It should not come as a great surprise, then, that poor families were not much better off either. And it seems reasonable to blame the same factors for the stagnation in the fortunes of both the poor and the nonpoor.

Figure II

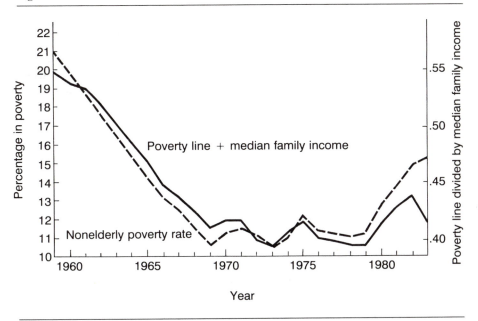

Relationship of Official Poverty Rate among Nonelderly Persons to Poverty Line as a Fraction of Median Family Income, 1959–1983

Source: Poverty rate data from U.S. Bureau of the Census (Current Population Reports, ser. P-60); median family income data from U.S. House of Representatives Subcommittee on Oversight and Subcommittee on Public Assistance and Unemployment Compensation, *Background material on poverty* (1983, p. 64).

The reasons for the lack of growth in median family income are not entirely clear. Real per capita disposable income did rise by 27.5 percent. Some of the explanations must therefore lie in demographic changes which were affecting both the poor and the nonpoor. There has been since the 1960s a large increase in the number of female-headed families, and average family size declined from 3.6 to 3.3. The share of income going to single individuals also increased substantially. But demographics alone cannot be the entire story. Median income of full-year, full-time male workers also declined between 1970 and 1980. Much of the blame must be placed on the productivity slowdown, which reduced the annual rate of growth of productivity to 0.8 percent in the 1970s after nearly two and a half decades of growth at almost 3 percent per year. Disposable income increased because more people were working, not because wages increased. Whatever the reasons for the decline, it would be absurd to blame changes in median family income on social welfare program mistakes. Making the poor better or worse off should not affect median income because the middle family in the income distribution would not be directly affected.

A brief consideration of the relevant magnitudes makes it clear why movements in average family incomes should be a dominant determinant of the fortunes of the poor. The bottom fifth of all families gets about 6 percent of total personal income. This figure has been remarkably stable for most of the past twenty years. At present, therefore, a 10 percent increase in disposable personal income would raise the amount of income flowing to the poor by $13 billion. A 25 percent increase, such as that achieved between 1961 and 1966, would increase the income of the bottom fifth by more than the total cost of all means-tested cash assistance programs plus Food Stamps.

There is an alternative way of seeing that the performance of the economy will be a dominant determinant of the economic condition of the poor. A majority of the nonelderly poor are in male-headed families. For this group, at least 75 percent of income results from earnings. Even among poor, female-headed families with children, fully 40 percent of all income comes from working. The fraction is much greater for families near the poverty line—the ones who will be drawn into or out of poverty as the economy swings.

Still, it is troubling to find that poverty rates have tracked median family income so closely. Expenditures on social welfare programs increased many times during the late 1960s and early 1970s. Shouldn't we have expected some improvement in poverty, if for no other reason than that transfers from the government should have pushed more people across the poverty line? This lack of progress seems to have fueled the current perception that the antipoverty programs were a failure. Charles Murray even argues that the growth in government programs induced the poor to stop relying on private sources of income and start relying on public sources, reducing their hopes for self-sufficiency. Let us examine this argument.

It is customary to break social welfare expenditures into three categories: social insurance; cash assistance; and in-kind benefits. The social insurance system is clearly geared to the middle class, designed to protect those who retire or who suffer some calamity such as total disability, unemployment, or work injury and therefore are unable to earn money. Medicare, which covers much of the medical care needs of the aged and totally disabled who receive Social Security, is usually classified as a social insurance program even though it provides in-kind benefits. Most workers are covered by these programs so long as they have worked a reasonable period. Far from being income-tested, these programs tend to give higher benefits to those who had higher earnings before retirement, disability, or unemployment. Thus the programs do protect some families from poverty, but they really are designed to protect middle-class incomes.

Benefits for the Poor

Cash assistance is offered to certain low-income groups. In most areas, only three groups really qualify for significant cash assistance: the aged; the totally disabled; and persons in single-parent families. Supplemental Security

Income (SSI) covers the first two groups while Aid to Families with Dependent Children (AFDC) covers the third. There is some assistance available for others. Most states offer a very modest General Assistance (GA) program, often for people who are partially disabled. Some states also offer an AFDC-Unemployed Parent (AFDC-UP) program for two-parent families. In fact, there are stringent restrictions on eligibility for AFDC-UP, and the program is extremely small, less than 5 percent of the total AFDC program. The cash transfer programs are explicitly income-tested and benefits decline as income rises.

Finally, there are a variety of in-kind benefits available. Food Stamps provide modest benefits per person in the form of vouchers, but the benefits are available, on a scale which varies by income, to all poor persons (except students and strikers). Medicaid provides medical benefits to the poor, but only to those who are aged, permanently disabled, or are in single-parent families. There are housing assistance programs and a number of other modest in-kind benefits, like Low Income Home Energy Assistance.

Table I shows the magnitude and the growth of these various programs. Expenditures are divided by major beneficiary group: the elderly; the totally disabled; and all others. Certainly the most prominent fact on the table is that the bulk of all expenditures and the bulk of the dollar growth has been in programs for the elderly. We would certainly expect to see, as we have seen, a very dramatic reduction in poverty among this group even in the 1970s, when growth was rather flat.

By almost any standard, expenditures on cash assistance programs specifically targeted at the poor are small. Taken together, all the cash assistance programs for the nonelderly totalled less than $20 billion in 1982. That is a considerable increase over 1960, when benefits were under $5 billion (in 1980 dollars). But it still represents much less than 1 percent of GNP. Federal expenditures for these programs are less than 2 percent of the federal budget.

These expenditures are too small to have very much effect on measured poverty. Cash assistance pushes just 5 percent of poor persons out of poverty. Spreading the $20 billion spent on cash assistance across all the 30.6 million nonelderly poor yields an average cash benefit of slightly over $50 per person per month. Benefits are actually concentrated on those persons who are single parents or disabled. But for single parents, benefits average only $100 monthly per person; for the disabled, they average roughly $220. These amounts just are not sufficient to push very many persons out of poverty.

Perhaps even more important, over the period when poverty rates were stable, there were only modest changes in expenditures for these programs. Between 1970 and 1980, cash assistance expenditures rose from $13.7 billion to $18.9 billion. Yet over the entire decade, *annual* expenditures per nonelderly poor person rose just $93! Such an increase would hardly be noticed in the poverty statistics. And even that figure overstates the significance of the increase. Nearly all of the growth in these programs came in the disability program, which reaches only two million persons.

**Table I   Costs of Major Public Assistance and Social Insurance
Programs for the Elderly, Totally Disabled, and All Others
(Billions of Constant 1980 Dollars)**

	1960	1970	1980
Programs for the Elderly			
Social Insurance			
Social Security, Old Age, and Survivor's	$29.2	$60.7	$104.7
Public Employee's and Railroad Retirement	9.7	21.9	44.3
Medicare[a]	0	16.8	29.1
Cash Assistance			
Supplemental Security Income (and Old Age Assistance	4.5	4.0	2.7
In-Kind Benefits			
Medicaid[a]	0	4.1	8.7
Food Stamps	0	0.2	0.5
Housing[b]	0.1	0.5	2.5
Programs for the Totally Disabled			
Social Insurance			
Social Security Disability[c]	1.6	6.5	15.4
Medicare[d]	0	0	4.5
Cash Assistance			
Supplemental Security Income (and Aid to the Disabled)	0.7	2.1	5.0
In-Kind Benefits			
Medicaid[a]	0	2.2	7.0

Programs which provide in-kind benefits, such as Food Stamps, housing assistance, or medical care, did grow considerably over the 1970s. But none of these gets counted as income for purposes of defining poverty, though they clearly reduce hardship.

The Food Stamp program comes closest to offering cash assistance, and benefits from the program should surely be counted as income in calculating poverty. Unlike almost every other major social program, Food Stamps are available to all poor families regardless of their characteristics. But average benefits are relatively low—less than $40 per month per person. Thus the program would not push very many people out of poverty even if its benefits were included as measured income. If Food Stamps were treated as income in 1982, the number of non-elderly poor would have fallen from 30.6 million to 29.1 million. Housing assistance is also available—in 1980, $4 billion was

Table I *Continued*

	1960	1970	1980
Programs for Others			
Social Insurance			
Unemployment Insurance	8.4	9.3	18.9
Workers' Compensation	3.6	6.5	13.6
Cash Assistance			
Aid to Families With Dependent Children (AFDC)	2.8	10.3	12.5
General Assistance (GA)	0.9	1.3	1.4
In-Kind Benefits			
Medicaid[a]	0	3.7	7.5
Food Stamps	0	1.1	8.6
Housing[b]	0.4	1.0	4.7

Sources: Social Security Bulletin, Annual Statistical Supplement 1982 (Washington: U.S. Government Printing Office), Tables 2, 18, 19, 154, 155, 160, 172, 192, 200. Also *Statistical Abstract 1984*. Tables 640, 643; and *Statistical Abstract 1978*, Table 549.

[a]Medicare and Medicaid began in 1966.

[b]Estimate based on fraction of persons receiving housing assistance who are elderly. (See Bureau of the Census, 1982).

[c]Social Security Disability Insurance program began in 1956.

[d]Medicare was extended to the disabled in 1974.

spent on the nonelderly. There are also a variety of child welfare, child nutrition, social services, and other programs. We do not have an exact total for these for the nonelderly, but it is probably between $5 and $10 billion.

Medical care falls into a special category. Persons who are in single-parent families or who are totally disabled and a few others can qualify for Medicaid. In 1980 the cost for single parents was $7.5 billion; for the disabled, $7 billion. It is less appropriate to think of medical care in the same way that cash assistance or food stamps are viewed. The poor never bought much health insurance prior to the start of the program in 1967 so provision for medical care was not really counted in determining the poverty level. Care was provided on a charity basis, in government-financed county hospitals, or it was simply not provided.

Because none of these in-kind benefits is counted in income, they cannot reduce statistically measured poverty. But there are indications that these programs have been at least partially successful in achieving their specific goals. Life expectancy in the U.S. rose more during the 1970s than during either the 1950s or 1960s. Perhaps more significantly, life expectancy rose more for nonwhites than whites: 4.2 years versus 2.7 years. Similarly, the nonwhite infant mortality rate declined almost twice as much in absolute terms as the white rate. And both caloric intake and protein consumption of the poor increased relative to the middle class. "Nutritional inequality" declined noticeably.

Benefits for the Middle Class

The really large growth in social benefits for the nonelderly came in the social insurance programs—the programs for the middle class. Unemployment Insurance (UI), Workers' Compensation (WC), Social Security Disability (DI), and Medicare for the disabled together cost $52 billion in 1980, up from $22 billion just a decade before.

These programs are not generally perceived by the public as being antipoverty programs, and rightly so. Their benefits go largely to the middle class. Only one-quarter of UI and WC funds go to persons who would otherwise be poor. Nonetheless, their significance in aiding the poor should not be understated. For those formerly poor persons lucky enough to receive UI or WC benefits, three-quarters are pushed out of poverty by them. Indeed, in some respects these programs probably do more to reduce poverty among the nonelderly than the cash assistance programs do. If UI and WC did not exist, at least 3 million more nonelderly people would be poor. (We have no comparable figures for the DI program.)

So it is not really surprising that measured poverty hardly improved during the 1970s. The single most important correlate with poverty—median family income—did not change. On government's side of the ledger, expenditures for cash assistance directed to the poor started small and did not increase very much. In-kind benefits increased dramatically, but they are not counted in income, so they could not improve measured poverty.

But whether or not government transfers were large enough to have a significant effect on poverty, concerns remain that government may actually be contributing to the poverty problem by discouraging work and encouraging single-parent family formation. We looked at three groups that figure prominently in any discussion of the disadvantaged in America. The first two are afforded the bulk of cash assistance—the disabled and those in single-parent families. For both of these groups, existing policies have been indicted as having important counterproductive influences. The third group, black youth, has at times been cited as an associated victim of the current welfare system. In all three cases, we considered whether or not transfer policies must bear significant responsibility for the problems faced by the groups.

The disability insurance (DI) portion of Social Security and Supplemental Security Income, which provides for those who are disabled and poor, grew enormously during the 1970s—both more than doubled during the decade. The combined cost of social insurance and cash assistance and in-kind benefits for the disabled was nearly $33 billion in 1980. Recently it has been charged that the program has reduced labor force participation of middle-aged men. The charge is serious, since the program is intended solely for those who cannot work.

The program's growth has indeed coincided with a significant decrease in labor force participation among men. In 1960, only about 4 percent of men aged forty-five to fifty-four were out of the labor force. By 1980, the figure had reached almost 9 percent. For black men the increases were even more dramatic: from 7 percent up to 16 percent. Motivated by these statistics, a need to cut budgets, and a host of anecdotes, the Reagan administration undertook a major tightening of eligibility rules under DI in the early 1980s, cutting several hundred thousand people and making eligibility more difficult to obtain. These policy developments coincided with increasing criticism within some academic circles of this antipoverty program for contributing to declining male labor force participation. The argument was that men who could work have been shifting to Disability Insurance. Thus Donald Parsons concluded in 1980 that the recent increase in nonparticipation in the labor force of prime-aged men can be largely explained by the increased generosity of social welfare transfers (though these findings have been disputed by other economists).

One approach to exploring the employability of those who received disability insurance is to look at the earnings patterns of those who applied but were denied. Certainly those who were denied assistance are on average considerably more employable than those granted benefits. Unfortunately, there are few data from recent years on the subsequent earnings of those denied disability benefits. However, the Social Security Administration (SSA) has examined the subsequent earnings experience of those denied benefits in 1967 and 1970. In assessing this evidence, it is important to recall that the fraction of disability applicants denied eligibility has risen steadily through time, from 49 percent in 1965 to 52 percent in 1975 to 66 percent in 1980. Thus rejections are even more common now than during that study period.

Yet in the late 1960s, virtually all of those who were rejected by the Disability Insurance program did little work in subsequent years. A SSA staff paper summarized the 1967 survey results by noting: "A large proportion of the denied applicants never returned to competitive employment despite many years of work prior to their disability and an administrative decision in 1967 that they were still able to do so." Further, "Four-fifths of these claimants who were initially denied in 1967 did not return to sustained competitive employment in the following five years."[1] Similar results were obtained in the 1970 survey.

Preliminary work by John Bound suggests that these basic conclusions hold in recent years even if one looks across the entire age distribution of persons under sixty applying for disability benefits. More than half do not return to sustained work. And those who do return to work suffer earnings losses of nearly 50 percent.

Since 1970 the DI program has doubled in size. Some of the increase is undoubtedly due to increased knowledge of the program and some may be due to increased benefit levels and some relaxation in standards. But even if the program now were taking people equivalent to the least-employable *four-fifths* of those rejected in 1970, it would still be taking a group which would have done no sustained work whether or not they had been accepted. And recall that in 1980, prior to the recently increased restrictions, 66 percent of applicants were denied entry to a program that is designed for the totally disabled. Those who apply are unlikely to be very healthy.

Disability programs appear to be one example where a carefully targeted program can give generous benefits without generating large adverse incentive effects. But the program succeeds largely because benefits are based on a relatively objective and difficult-to-alter set of physical conditions.

AFDC and Single-Parent Families

The mounting number of children being raised in single-parent households is commanding increased national attention. The apparent "crisis of the family" is noted most acutely with respect to black households, but the trends seem to extend to all racial and economic groups. The numbers are stark. By the time today's children turn eighteen, some 45 percent of whites and 85 percent of blacks are expected to have lived for some part of their life in a single-parent household. At a minimum those who live in single-parent households face financial hardship; there may be other adverse consequences as well.

Certainly the most troubling and potentially the most damning accusation leveled against the current welfare system is the charge that it encourages the formation and perpetuation of single-parent families. The specifics of the charges have changed over time, but not the basic message. Originally, it was suggested that we had developed a welfare system that rewarded single-parent families by denying benefits to families with two parents. More recently, in the wake of the negative income tax experiments, it is alleged that by relieving a family of the necessity of relying on two parents for income, welfare facilitates marital disruption.

Figure III plots the fraction of all children living in a female-headed household and the fraction of all children who have received AFDC since 1960. The fraction of all children living in a female-headed household started rising much faster in the late 1960s, at precisely the time when the number of children on AFDC rose sharply. But then the trends diverged—dramatically so.

Since 1972, the fraction of all children who live in a female-headed household has jumped quite dramatically, from 14 percent to almost 20 percent. During that same period, the fraction of all children who were in homes collecting AFDC held almost constant, at 12 percent. The figures are even more dramatic for blacks. Between 1972 and 1980 the number of black children in female-headed families rose nearly 20 percent. The number of black children on AFDC actually *fell* by 5 percent.

Figure III

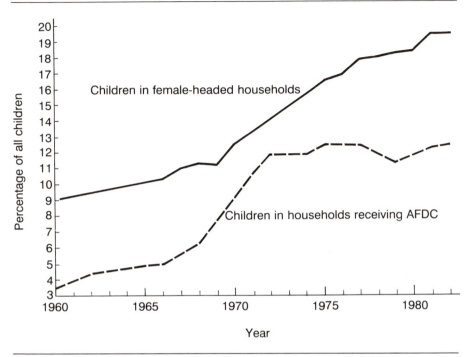

Comparative Percentages of Children in Female-Headed and AFDC Households, 1960–1982

Source: U.S. Bureau of the Census (Current Population Reports, ser. P-20), *Household and Family Characteristics,* various years; *Social Security Bulletin, Annual Statistical Supplement,* various years.

If AFDC were pulling families apart and encouraging the formation of single-parent families, it is very hard to understand why the number of children on the program would remain constant throughout the period in our history when family structures changed the most.

These figures are easy to understand in light of the fact that real AFDC levels fell by almost 30 percent between 1970 and 1980 in the median state. Even in some comparatively liberal states, benefits plummeted. In New York City, benefits dropped 33 percent in real terms over this period. Food Stamps mitigated the declines somewhat. But between 1971 and 1983, combined Food Stamps and AFDC benefits fell by 22 percent in real terms in the median state. A smaller and smaller fraction of children in single-parent families were receiving AFDC for a very simple reason—benefit levels, and therefore eligibility, were being sharply cut back.

Perhaps the impact of AFDC benefits was delayed, or perhaps once a threshold is reached, people do not react to changes in benefit levels. These explanations could explain why family structures continued to change even as benefits fell. But we can think of no story crediting AFDC with a very large part in inducing changed family structures which is consistent with a falling absolute number of children on the program.

And what about the sharp rise in the fraction of all births to unmarried black mothers? The birth rate to unmarried black women fell 13 percent between 1970 and 1980. But the birth rate among all married black women fell even more—by 38 percent—so the fraction of births to unmarried women rose. During the same period, the unmarried birth rate to whites rose by 27 percent. It seems difficult to argue that AFDC was a major influence in unmarried births when there was simultaneoulsy a rise in the birth rate to unmarried whites and a fall in the rate for unmarried blacks.[2]

Probably the most important lesson of the time-series analysis is that family structure changes just do not seem to mirror benefit level changes. We have already made rather Draconian cuts in benefit levels and family structure changes have not slowed appreciably. It seems hard to believe that further cuts would do much to hold families together.

A second approach also fails to find a strong connection between AFDC and family structure. Benefit levels vary widely from state to state. In Mississippi in 1980, a single-parent family of four could get a maximum of $120 per month in AFDC benefits, and that amount had been raised from $60 per month only a few years earlier. In California or New York, the same family could get $563 in benefits.

The gaps between states are not quite as large as they might seem, because the Food Stamps program is a federal one with uniform benefit levels nationally. As such it narrows the gaps in benefits between states. But even including Food Stamps, benefits vary by a factor of two to three. Food Stamps are available whether or not one is in a single-parent family, so their impact on family formation choices is unclear.

The obvious test is to compare the percentage of children living in female-headed households, or the divorce rate or the birth rate to unmarried women, with benefit levels across the states. Figure IV provides such a comparison for 1980. There is no obvious relationship between the percentage of children not living in two-parent families and AFDC benefit levels across states. The same holds for almost every other measure of family structure as well, including divorce rates and out-of-wedlock birth rates. More sophisticated regression techniques which control for differing socioeconomic characteristics across states typically also show little or no relationship.

Our conclusion is that AFDC has far less to do with changes in family structures than has been alleged. We suspect that the changes are probably better traced to changing attitudes toward welfare and heightened independence brought about by a host of forces that seemed to have come to a crescendo in the late 1960s. In the black community, family structure changes may have had more to do with the changing fortunes of black men than the availability of AFDC.

Figure IV

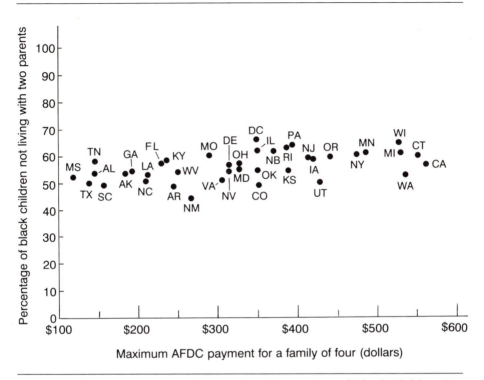

Relation of State AFDC Benefit Levels to Proportion of Black Children in Single-Parent Households, 1980.

Source: State volumes of the 1980 census; AFDC benefit amounts from U.S. House of Representatives Subcommittee on Oversight and Subcommittee on Public Assistance and Unemployment Compensation, *Background material on poverty* (1983, p. 83).

AFDC and Single Mothers

Unlike the disability program, there are undoubtedly some reductions in labor supply by female family heads induced by the current program. However, studies suggest that AFDC has had a modest effect in reducing work. Welfare mothers do not seem to be very sensitive to work incentives. Most recently, changes have been made in the AFDC program which essentially eliminate all work incentives. After four months, benefits are reduced at least $1 for each dollar the woman earns over $30. Yet available evidence indicates that there has been little change in the work of single mothers.

Concerns about AFDC run deeper than just a fear that short-term work incentives are distorted. There is a sense that long-term dependency has developed, that people have come to rely on welfare to meet needs that they could and would meet on their own if they had no alternative. Except for the case studies of sociologists, we know of no definitive work on the extent to which pathological dependency exists, or on the role that AFDC has had in creating such dependency.

But there is information on the duration of AFDC receipt which does shed some light on this issue. The evidence, as analayzed by Mary Jo Bane and David Ellwood for example, suggests two subgroups within the AFDC population. Most people who use AFDC stay on the program a relatively short time. At least 50 percent leave within two years, 85 percent leave within eight. Most women who ever use AFDC do not seem to get trapped by it. At the same time, the minority which does stay on a long time accumulates and thus ultimately receives most of the benefits that are paid out. That minority also accounts for a large fraction of people who are on the program at any one point in time. The 15 percent of new recipients who stay eight years or more on the program collect more than 50 percent of the benefits paid out. Further, certain women are at particular risk of long-term dependency. Unmarried mothers, high school dropouts, and nonwhites all tend to have much longer stays than others.

Thus the program does provide short-term relief to the majority of the people it touches, but the bulk of its expenditures goes to a group that is in fact dependent on welfare for an extended period. This dependent group is a legitimate source of concern. There is not any good evidence that they are trapped by welfare *per se*; we only know that they rely on it for at least part of their support. Such dependence is easily explained. Few single mothers get much child support from absent fathers, so there are just two routes to self-sufficiency—work and marriage. And both of these can be hampered by the presence of young children. Still, the fact that many are found in this state of dependence seems undesirable.

Knowingly or unknowingly we have been engaged in an experiment over the past ten years. This experiment has been carried out at the expense of single mothers and its results can be judged a failure. We have cut back AFDC benefits considerably, but there has been no noticeable effect on family structure or work. We can be sure the impact on the well-being of single mothers was noticed by the families. We have also conducted an experiment in allowing benefits to vary across states for years. Here, too, there is little evidence that these differences have had any noticeable effect on work or family structure.

Yet there are sources of concern. There is little evidence that the current system causes large changes in family structure. But there is reason to worry that massive widening of welfare benefits to other groups could have more serious disruptive effects. The negative income tax experiments suggested that a system which allowed a husband and wife to split up and each collect benefits independently increased marital splits among low-income families by as much as 40 percent more than was true under the existing system. These results, while not definitive (splits did not increase in one site, racial patterns differed across sites), do serve as a warning that major changes in incentives could have important consequences, at least for marital stability.

And dependency *is* a problem for some AFDC recipients, at least if dependency is defined as long-term welfare receipt. Such dependency is troubling, particularly since it seems to be greatest among groups that have considerable disadvantages to begin with. Our current welfare policies may have some influence on this dependence. There is a widespread hope that government could do something to help these women become self-sufficient.

Yet government has not shown much capacity to improve the situation very much. We know of no serious policy that encourages family formation. We have tried various programs that have had some success (particularly Supported Work) in helping long-term recipients and poor women generally, but gains have been quite modest. While the desire to pursue ways to improve the ability of single women to support themselves is widespread, few who have designed these programs have very optimistic expectations.

The peculiar nature of the welfare problem for single mothers is the fact that society generally recognizes and encourages mothers who stay home and care for children, but it also sees self-sufficiency as a virtue and it is increasingly unwilling to accept welfare dependence among single mothers in the way it accepts it among the disabled. Thus one cannot have a program of high benefits and no work incentives, as is offered the disabled. More complex regulations about work and child care are inevitable given social preferences. Diverse services must be offered.

Black Youth and the "Job Gap"

By every conceivable measure the labor market situation for young blacks is bad and getting worse. Figure V shows the unemployment rate among black and white youth aged sixteen to nineteen from 1955 to 1980. While the rate for white youth has been relatively steady throughout the period, the rate for blacks has risen almost continually, though it was during the 1970s that the gap really widened. If we look at the sexes separately, we see similar patterns for young men and women. Things get somewhat better as the youth age, but the gap between the races has been widening for those aged twenty to twenty-four as well. The magnitude of the problem cannot be overstated. In 1980, before the recession really hit, only one in three black teenagers out of school had any job.

What is all the more perplexing about this widening gap is the fact that the changes have come at a time when developments are occurring that might have been expected to narrow the racial gap. Civil rights legislation was passed in the 1960s which reduced overt discrimination in the workplace. The educational patterns of the races have been converging: Similar proportions of blacks and whites now complete high school. College is almost as common for nonwhites as whites. Blacks are also narrowing the racial gap in the more highly paid professions.

The fear of many conservatives is that the very social forces which predominated in the late 1960s, particularly the push for social welfare programs, lead to a destruction of traditional values and expectations that hard work pays off in the long run. We are not competent to judge the entire

Figure V

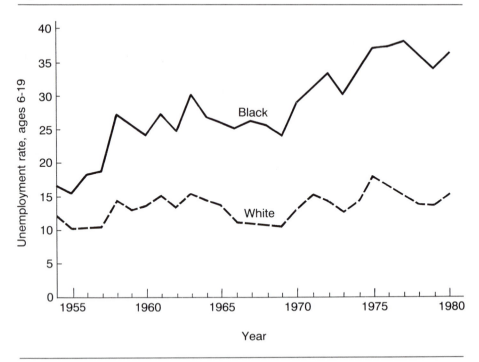

Unemployment among Teenaged Black and White Youth, 1954–1980
Source: U.S. Bureau of Labor Statistics, *Handbook of Labor Statistics* (1984).

sociological impact of public policy generally or to evaluate changing values in America's ghettos. But we can explore the logic of an assertion that the expansion of social welfare programs played a major role in the decline of work among black youth.

We will concentrate on employment of black male youth to avoid problems associated with childbearing among young women. Is it plausible that social welfare policies have caused a severe decline in the work ethic among young black men?

Certainly such policies have not removed incentives to work. Single men are eligible for very little in the way of federally sponsored welfare benefits. A youth living alone is eligible only for Food Stamps. In 1982, his benefits would have been $70 per month, hardly enough to live on. For the first $85 the youth earns, benefits are not reduced at all, then for every dollar he earned these benefits would be reduced by only 25 cents. If he found a full-time minimum-wage job he would earn $560 per month in gross earnings and at least $450 after taxes and expenses. It certainly seems hard to believe that the Food Stamp program would reduce the financial rewards to work much.

If the youth lives at home (as most do), the picture hardly changes. If he lives in a poor two-parent household, his family is likely to be collecting Food Stamps. His presence in the home increases the monthly stamp allotment by roughly $60 per month. This allotment is diminished by the same formula as above if he works. Contrary to popular belief, a child eighteen-years-old or over who is not in school cannot now and never could be counted as a part of an AFDC unit. That means that a family's AFDC benefits do not depend on whether the youth lives with the family or not, and benefits will not be reduced if he earns more.

Thus it is extremely unlikely that welfare programs have robbed young black men of an incentive to work with their direct effects. But there is a broader concern. Perhaps the whole structure of welfare has created a culture of nonwork and dependence. Such a possibility is very hard to test, but there are several facts which are hard to explain in light of such a hypothesis: Employment rates for young men living in two-parent families are not very different from those of youngsters living with one parent. In 1975, some 23 percent of young black men living with two parents and 21 percent of those living with one parent had jobs. For whites, the figures are closer to 50 percent for both family types. One would generally expect to find a difference by family type simply because youth jobs are typically found through informal networks and one would anticipate that those in fatherless homes would have less access to such networks. Moreover, though unemployment does fall among blacks as family income rises, the differential between whites and blacks is largely unchanged.

Black youth living in central cities do not seem to fare much worse than those living outside the ghettos. According to the 1980 Census, 32 percent of out-of-school black youth in central cities had jobs whereas 38 percent of those living in the suburbs were employed. Similarly only 35 percent of out-of-school nonwhites living in nonfarm rural areas were working. While the figures above differ slightly, they are all vastly lower than the 62 percent figure for whites. If black youth unemployment were concentrated in the ghettos, it would be easier to point to the culture of poverty hypothesis.

The fact that black/white youth unemployment differentials seem to persist for all geographic locations, for all family types, and for all income groups clearly suggests something more fundamental is to blame than the growth of welfare programs, which amount to less than 1 percent of GNP.

Among researchers who have looked at the problem, there is no consensus about what is happening. Most of the simple theories have been tried and they do not account for all of the widening differential between blacks and whites. There is considerable evidence of a job shortage for black youth. Kim B. Clark and Lawrence H. Summers have documented that black youth unemployment responds very strongly to aggregate demand,[3] but such an explanation can be only part of the story. Macroeconomic conditions did worsen over the 1970s, but not enough to explain the widening differential. And the racial gap widened somewhat even during the extraordinarily strong economy of the late 1960s. There are fewer jobs in the ghettos, but Ellwood has shown that nonghetto youth seem to fare just as badly as ghetto youth.[4] Nearly all researchers agree that the minimum wage lowers black youth employment, but the differential has continued to widen even during periods when the minimum wage did not change. Women entered the labor force in large numbers in the 1970s, but their entrance did not seem to hurt white youth. Taken together, the various explanations might explain half or more of the widening differential, but one gets the sense that something more fundamental has changed. Moreover, even if one places all the blame on job shortages, the explanation begs the question of why jobs are not being offered to young blacks when they are being offered to young whites.

And just as black youth joblessness defies easy explanation, it defies easy solution. Most careful experiments have shown disappointing long-term results. Public service employment increases youth employment, but when the public jobs end, employment rates seem to fall back to their previous levels. There just are not any good answers at the current time.

This is not the appropriate place to discuss what might be done to help such youth. But one thing is very clear: To expand welfare benefits to this group would have large adverse incentive effects. The negative income tax experiments showed that when income was afforded to youth aged sixteen to twenty-one, work fell by almost 50 percent below its already low rate. It is hard to imagine a policy with more deleterious effects on the long-run well-being of black youth.

The employment problems of black youth then cannot be blamed on current welfare policies. In large part, that is because we have avoided offering welfare to young people. While there is surely some financial suffering as a result, the fact that extending benefits to these persons would so dramatically reduce work is an overriding consideration.

Reaffirming the "Categorical" Welfare System

The analysis in this paper demonstrates that government policies cannot be blamed for a great deal of the problems of the disadvantaged. This reflects the design of current policy. Much aid is the in-kind form and programs are offered on a categorical basis.

The fact that the problems of the three groups we considered are so different and that the consequences of aid varied so greatly argues for a continued reliance on a categorical approach to offering aid to the disadvantaged. For the disabled, there is little concern with dependence or work incentives. This allows for liberal benefits and forces no compromises on work incentive. For single mothers, the need is quite real, and while there is little evidence that we have been overly generous in our benefits, there is evidence for some long-term dependency. Trying to balance the needs of children, the rights of mothers to care for their children, and the desire of society (and presumably the mothers themselves) to be self-sufficient suggests the need for a complex policy aimed at that group. For youth, the reduced work that would apparently accompany an extension of benefits is a crucial factor mitigating against an expansion of welfare in that direction.

More fundamentally, general economic principles suggest the desirability of a complex welfare system with different rules for different groups and partial reliance on in-kind benefits. The patchwork character of current policies *is* consistent with the goal of economic efficiency. The basic problem of welfare policy is to transfer income to those truly in need without sizeable adverse incentive effects and without diverting significant resources to those who are not truly in need. Seen in this light, prominent features of our current welfare system seem easily explainable. Efficiency in redistribution can be increased if payments are based on available indicators of true earning power.

Particularly desirable are indicators which are not easily altered, such as disability, and perhaps family status. Moreover, the use of any type of assistance which will help the truly poor, but be relatively unattractive to the nonpoor, will raise the amount that can be redistributed with a minimum of distortion. This may justify substantial reliance on some types of in-kind programs. People not in need are less likely to try to look poor in order to qualify for public housing than they are to qualify for cash assistance. Some administrative burdens on welfare recipients might also be defended as facilitating redistribution by increasing the government's ability to separate those in serious need.

Current policy may also be defended on philosophical grounds. It expresses the value society places on self-reliance. We expect those who can to help themselves. Benefits are provided only to those able to provide some evidence of their inability to support themselves. Most Americans regard the reasons for indigency as sharply influencing their willingness to offer aid. The disabled, single parents, and those injured or laid off from work can offer some evidence that their financial straits are not caused by an unwillingness to work.

While we see reasons for concern about the effects of reducing eligibility restrictions, we see little cause for concern about the effects of raising benefit levels under current programs. Restoring real AFDC benefits to the levels of a decade ago and reducing or eliminating regional disparities would do a great deal for people in need without much disincentive effect on work. Certainly there are equity considerations which would be served by allowing working poor families aid beyond Food Stamps. But there are strong arguments for the primary notion of categorical welfare, at least until we develop ways of attacking the fundamental social problems of the nation's poor directly and successfully.

NOTES

1. Ralph Tretel, "Appeal by Denied Disability Claimants," Social Security Administration staff paper No. 23 (Washington: U.S. Government Printing Office, 1976), pp. 22, 25.

2. See, for example, Mary Jo Bane and David T. Ellwood, "The Impact of AFDC on Family Structure and Living Arrangements," *Journal of Labor Research* (1986).

3. Kim B. Clark and Lawrence H. Summers, "The dynamics of youth unemployment," in *The Youth Labor Market Problem: Its Nature, Courses, and Consequences,* Richard B. Freeman, David A. Wise, eds. (Chicago: University of Chicago Press, 1982).

4. David T. Ellwood, "The Spatial Mismatch Hypothesis: Are There Teenage Jobs Missing in the Ghetto?" in *The Black Youth Employment Problem,* Richard B. Freeman, Kasey Ichniowsky, eds. (Chicago: University of Chicago Press, forthcoming).

SELECTION 33

GARY T. BURTLESS AND ROBERT H. HAVEMAN

Taxes and Transfers: How Much Economic Loss?

Are taxes and transfers causing the size of the economic pie to shrink? Or, to put it in different terms, is there less to go around because government policy significantly reduces the incentives to work both of the people paying taxes and the people receiving welfare transfers? In examining the evidence, Gary Burtless and Robert Haveman argue that the answer is more likely no than yes. This does not imply, however, that people like paying taxes; it just means that historical evidence does not support the conclusion that people work less in order to avoid paying taxes.

QUESTIONS TO GUIDE THE READING

1. What is the relationship between labor supply response and the excess burden of taxation?
2. How did the NIT experiments support the claim that welfare transfers reduce work effort?
3. What support did Hausman's study on the excess burden of income taxes provide for the "supply-sider" claim that the 1981 U.S. tax cut would raise tax revenues?
4. Why might an increase in taxes actually cause high-income earners to work more?
5. On what arguments do the authors base their claim that economic research in this area is far from complete or incontrovertible?

The burden of the U.S. tax and transfer system inevitably appears oppressive to individuals who pay taxes. Indeed, in recent years a large number of economists have come to share the view that the growing public sector is eroding the efficiency of the market economy through the disincentives and

Gary T. Burtless and Robert H. Haveman, "Taxes and Transfers: How Much Economic Loss?" *Challenge* (March-April 1987), 45–51. Reprinted by permission of publisher, M. E. Sharpe, Inc., 80 Business Park Drive, Armonk, New York 10504 USA.

Gary T. Burtless is Senior Fellow Economist at the Brookings Institution. **Robert H. Haveman** is John Bascom Professor of Economics and Director of the LaFollette Institute of Public Affairs at the University of Wisconsin.

distortions created by our tax and welfare systems. Reflecting that concern, Assar Lindbeck, writing in *Challenge* (January/February 1986), outlined the case that welfare states in Western industrial democracies have either exceeded or are about to "'go too far' and exceed their admittedly ill-defined limits."

These attitudes represent a dramatic departure from the prevailing views among economists in the 1960s and early 1970s when distortions of taxes and transfers were held to be modest. Today, public finance scholars, in particular, believe that taxes on labor income cause major distortions in worker behavior. Because labor taxes account for well over half of all government revenues, the distortions of work behavior have, they argue, important consequences for total labor supply and national welfare. In their efforts to measure the welfare costs of taxation, some researchers have generated new estimates of the effects of government tax and transfer programs on the supply of labor. From this literature there emerged public policy proposals calling for large supply-side tax cuts and dramatic cutbacks in income transfer benefits in order to reduce disincentives to work.

We argue here that the claims of some economists and political critics of the current U.S. tax-transfer system spring from a very selective reading of the evidence about that system's effects. The distortions appear, on balance, to be far less onerous than the critics claim, and the research is hardly a firm guide to public policy, much less a blueprint to overhaul the existing tax and transfer system.

The Theory of Tax Distortions

It is important at the outset to distinguish between several concepts of the effect or burden of taxes. To a taxpayer the burden of taxes might simply be the amount or fraction of income that must be paid out to tax authorities. But economists see the tax burden in a more complicated way. The total burden of a tax includes not only the money actually sent to tax authorities but the additional loss imposed on the taxpayer because taxes are not raised in the most efficient manner. This additional loss of economic welfare is measured in money terms and is referred to as the "excess burden" of the tax.

The most efficient tax, according to economists, is a lump-sum or head tax; it is efficient because it causes no distortion in prices and hence causes no loss in taxpayer welfare beyond the direct cost of the tax itself. An excise tax, by contrast, distorts the price system by driving a wedge between the price paid by a consumer and the price received by a producer. Because both the consumer and the producer face a distorted price, both will respond to an incorrect marginal incentive. The welfare loss caused by this distortion is the excess burden. Income and payroll taxes are equivalent to an excise tax on supplying work effort in the labor market. Because these two taxes can impose high combined tax rates on marginal earned income, the potential economic distortion is large.

The economists' concept of tax burden is a difficult one for most people to understand. Most citizens and taxpayers are probably more interested in knowing the effect of a tax on some simple measure of economic behavior, such as labor earnings or employment. If marginal tax rates are raised, does labor supply fall and, if so, by how much? Does the fall in taxable earnings cause tax receipts to fall by enough to offset the revenue gain from higher tax rates? The answers to these questions have practical policy significance and may help to determine whether policymakers prefer one tax policy over another.

There is, of course, a relationship between the work response to a tax change and the excess burden caused by that change. If taxpayers' work effort is highly responsive to small changes in net wage rates or after-tax income levels, the excess burden associated with a tax increase may be quite substantial. On the other hand, if taxpayers are unresponsive to large changes in net wages and after-tax income, the excess burden is small. The logic behind this proposition is straightforward. If taxpayer behavior is not much affected by a price distortion, the welfare of the taxpayer must be quite close to what it would have been if the same amount of revenue had been raised with a nondistorting, lump-sum tax.

A key to comprehending the recent shift in views about tax burdens is an understanding of the development of those views over time. Most of the relevant empirical studies have focused on behavior in the labor markets; that is, estimating what economists call the labor supply function. These estimates have in turn been used to gauge the excess burden associated with income and payroll taxes or, in a few studies, all taxes borne by labor.

Before 1970 the potential effects of taxes and transfers were widely recognized, but empirical estimates of their effects were rare. The earliest U.S. studies about how workers react to taxes were based on their responses in surveys to questions about the oppressiveness of high marginal taxes. This type of research was summarized by Joseph Pechman in his 1971 book, *Federal Tax Policy,* as follows:

> The evidence suggests that income taxation does not reduce the amount of labor supply by workers and managers. . . . Nearly all people who are asked about income taxation grumble about it, but relatively few state that they work fewer hours or exert less than their best efforts to avoid being taxed.

Not surprisingly, the excess burden of income taxes was believed to be commensurately small. Arnold C. Harberger (1974), in a celebrated study of the welfare effects of federal taxes, found that the income tax caused distortions in the worker's choice between labor and leisure that amounted to only $1 billion per year. This was less than 2.5 percent of the revenue raised by the personal income tax in 1961.

Starting around 1970, U.S. economists began investigating labor supply behavior using large-scale sets of microeconomic data that were just then becoming available. Readers of these early studies were frequently frustrated with the wide variation in the estimated size of income and gross wage effects. The largest estimates of a worker's response suggested that the potential effects of existing and proposed transfer programs would be substantial; smaller estimates, however, implied just the opposite.

NIT Experiments

Many economists undertook these early studies because they were interested in reforming the complex U.S. public welfare system. Those who proposed to reform the system found it essential to get reliable estimates of labor's responses to changing incentives. At the end of the 1960s, the federal government began the first of four negative income tax (NIT) experiments designed to improve previous estimates of labor supply response. Researchers designed experiments to test how workers would react to various alternative programs intended to replace the existing welfare system. Economists measured the responses of individual workers to variations in marginal tax rates and basic income support levels. From these responses, the analyst could develop an aggregate labor supply function for low-income workers.

There is little doubt that the NIT experiments reduced the amount of uncertainty about the responsiveness of low-wage workers to changes in taxes and income transfers. The results from the largest and most sophisticated of the NIT experiments showed that youths and women, in particular, cut back their activity in the labor market, especially if they were enrolled in the longer-term, five-year plans. Prime-aged men reduced their annual hours of work by 9 or 10 percent; their spouses reduced annual hours by 17 to 20 percent; and single women heading families reduced annual hours by more than 20 percent—by as much as 28 to 32 percent in the longer-duration plans. Much of the work reduction occurred in the form of withdrawals from employment or active labor force participation rather than in marginal reductions in weekly work effort. The NIT experiments provided convincing evidence of the potential magnitude of work reductions arising out of generous income transfers and sharply higher marginal tax rates on earnings.

Partly as a result of the resources invested in the NIT experiments, research on labor supply grew rapidly in depth, breadth, and technical sophistication over the 1970s. The NIT experiments, as well as a number of large-scale, highly detailed, longitudinal surveys, permitted economists to examine for the first time how the worker responds in the labor market over the life cycle in response to changes in wages, taxes, transfers, and other sources of unearned income.

In an exhaustive 1983 survey, Killingsworth noted several highlights of the most recent labor supply studies. As in the earlier studies, men were consistently less sensitive to variations in wage-rates and unearned income than were women. Furthermore, more recent studies found women to respond even more sensitively than the earlier studies suggested. Reporting on the nonexperimental studies, Killingsworth found only little progress in narrowing the range of estimated responsiveness, however. The recent estimates of response have occasionally been used to predict the effect of changes in the tax and transfer system on labor market behavior. Unfortunately though, the simulated effects reflect the same wide variations of responses—and the same potential biases—as do the estimates of the parameters themselves.

The New View

As the empirical studies grew more technically sophisticated and their results more widely used in national studies, some economists became persuaded that the adverse effects of taxes and transfers are large. The findings of the NIT experiments of course attracted wide attention, in part because the response estimates appeared simple to interpret and alarmingly high. Some critics of an NIT believed the adverse labor-supply responses were so large that they represented a serious threat to the national economy (Anderson 1978; Murray 1984). According to the experimental results, the earnings of a typical low-income family could fall by $0.25 to $0.60 for every $1.00 rise in income transfer support provided by the government; that finding must have been disturbing even for advocates of an NIT.

The major U.S. transfer programs have been a central focus of recent empirical research on labor supply. Some studies of the Social Security system have found very large effects of retirement benefits on work effort among the aged. The labor force participation of older U.S. men has fallen substantially in recent years: In the 30 years after 1950, the participation rate of men over 65 fell by more than half, from 46 percent to 20 percent. During that period, the rate for men aged 55 to 64 fell from 87 percent to 73 percent. Over the same 30-year interval, real Social Security benefits were rising rapidly and eligibility for benefits was extended to a much wider population. Some economists inferred causality and asserted that the rise in Social Security was the main factor behind the trend toward earlier retirement. It has also been claimed that increasingly generous Social Security disability benefits have caused a decline in older male labor force participation, particularly among blacks.

Some scholars studying the effects of public assistance programs have concluded that welfare benefits for single parents with children have led to a low labor force participation rate and sharply reduced hours of work among single women. Unemployment insurance has also been the subject of a large number of statistical studies, most of them concluding that the system contributed significantly to raising reported unemployment or reducing employment. One study has even claimed that generous unemployment pay was the main cause of high and persistent British unemployment during the Great Depression.

Some economists now deny that there is any theoretical ambiguity about the effect of tax changes on the aggregate supply of labor. According to the earlier, more conventional view, tax increases have an effect on labor supply that was theoretically indeterminate. Workers will want to reduce their work effort (this is the substitution effect) when a tax increase reduces their net pay for work; but because they have less after-tax income they may wish to work longer hours to make up the lost income (the income effect). Since the two effects may partly or wholly offset one another, the net result is ambiguous.

According to the new view emerging out of recent research, the two effects do not offset one another in the aggregate, because what some people lose in net income is returned to others (or to themselves) in the form of increased transfers or government goods and services. Only the substitution effect matters, they argue. Hence, the unambiguous effect of a tax increase must be to reduce aggregate work effort.

Further Evidence

Even more influential than this theoretical development was a new empirical study. In 1981 Jerry Hausman published a landmark paper on the effect of income taxes on the labor supply behavior of American adults. Hausman found that the disincentive effects of the income tax were quite large for men as well as for women. He estimated that prime-age husbands reduced their work effort by about 8 percent in comparison to their behavior in a no-tax world. Married and single women were estimated to have even larger labor supply responses than men.

The Hausman study also provided an estimate of the excess burden associated with the income tax system. For men, the excess burden associated with the new estimate of labor supply response is about 5 percent of pretax earnings. Stated another way, the deadweight loss arising from the existing progressive income tax system on men amounts to more than 20 percent of the value of the taxes raised. For women, who have larger labor supply responses than men, the welfare loss of the tax system is an even greater share of the collected revenue. These estimates exceed by a wide margin Arnold Harberger's earlier estimate of the excess burden associated with income taxes.

The new, very large estimates of labor supply distortions arising from income taxes have caused many economists to reconsider their assessment of the burden of taxes. In addition, other research projects have contributed to the impression that income taxes and income transfers greatly distort labor supply decisions. Studies of the effect of the Swedish tax system by Stuart (1981), of the U.S. tax system by Stuart (1984); Ballard, Shoven, and Whalley; and Browning (1985); and of the tax and transfer system by Browning and Johnson (1984) have substantially raised previous estimates of efficiency losses caused by government fiscal activity. Using a range of estimates of labor supply responsiveness, Browning (1985) concludes that the welfare loss from the existing tax system lies between 8 and 28 percent of the revenues collected, with his preferred estimate being 16 percent.

Of greater interest to some of these authors is the *marginal* welfare loss associated with taxes. The marginal loss is the added amount of excess burden caused by a slight proportional rise in existing tax rates. The recent studies conclude that, at the margin, the welfare loss from the U.S. tax system is in the range of at least 15 to 50 percent of the added revenues collected. Browning's (1985) preferred estimate is in the upper half of that range. Stuart (1984) estimates that the marginal welfare loss from an added dollar of tax revenue is $0.20–$0.24, based upon pre-1976 estimates of labor supply responsiveness. But he argues that this estimate of marginal loss must be more than doubled—to $0.57–$0.72—if we take into account the most recent, and higher, estimates of labor supply responsiveness.

The estimated distortion caused by taxes that are redistributed as transfers is even more alarming. Browning and Johnson have argued, for example, that the disposable income of the top three income quintiles is depressed by $9.51 for each $1.00 increase in income successfully transferred to the lowest two quintiles. It is depressed by this large amount because taxpayers substantially reduce their work effort; and in addition, because transfer receipts reduce their earnings, thus increasing the amount of money that must be transferred in order to raise recipients' incomes by $1.00. The marginal welfare loss in the top three quintiles caused by this redistribution is $3.49.

The implications of the new estimates of efficiency loss have not gone unnoticed. A primary motivation behind the 1981 U.S. tax cut was the new-found belief among policymakers and a few economists that high marginal tax rates were responsible for marked reductions in taxable earnings and tax revenue. Although it is arguable whether serious scholarly research played a very important role in this development, the new perception among economists of large efficiency losses from taxation probably lessened their initial criticism of the 1981 law. Welfare policy has also been influenced by the recent research. As mentioned above, the findings of the NIT experiments, as well as other studies, have been used to argue against improvements in the generosity of welfare and have even been used to argue for the wholesale abandonment of existing public assistance programs (see Murray 1984).

An Evaluation of the New View

The labor supply research of the past 15 years has illuminated a wide variety of subjects that were previously little understood. If the views of economists have changed, at least part of the reason is that there is now more knowledge about the subject than existed in the 1960s. However, contrary to the alarmist view that taxes and transfers impose intolerably high work effort and efficiency losses, we believe that much of the evidence points to a far less pessimistic conclusion. Our brief review leads us to conclude that aggregate labor supply in the United States has not been dramatically reduced by the combined impacts of government taxes and transfers, and that some new estimates of the excess burden of taxes and transfers are overdrawn and highly uncertain.

1. Not even statistical studies showing the largest labor supply responses support the most extreme claim about the disincentive effects of

taxes on work behavior; namely, that a reduction in present rates would result in an increase in tax revenues from labor income. Arthur B. Laffer is almost certainly correct in his belief that, at a sufficiently high marginal tax rate, further increases in the rate would depress government revenue by discouraging economic activity. However, no serious empirical research has shown that U.S. taxes actually are sufficiently high for that prediction to be true at current rates or at rates imposed any time in the past two decades. The failure of federal tax revenues to rise after 1981, as the supply-siders predicted, also casts strong doubt on their claims.

2. Contrary to the recent claim that income effects are irrelevant in computing the aggregate response to taxes, it turns out that the size and distribution of income effects are critical in evaluating the sign of the aggregate response. Consider, for example, an increase in positive income taxes used to finance an increase in transfer payments. It is usually the case that additional taxes will be levied on workers with high earnings while additional transfer benefits will be received by people with very low earnings (or no earnings at all). The additional income received by people with low earnings will induce them to reduce their hours of work, but the amount of hours reduction will be limited to the amount they already work—no one can work less than zero hours.

By contrast, higher-income earners, who suffer an after-tax income loss, will be induced by the income effect to work additional hours. Since there is no relevant limit to the amount of extra hours worked by taxpayers, the extra hours induced by the income effect on high-earnings workers may easily exceed the hours reductions experienced by low-earnings workers. If work disincentives of taxes and transfers are concentrated on the fraction of the population that is unable to make substantial work-effort reductions, and if work-incentive effects are concentrated on those who can substantially raise work effort, a tax rise that is used to finance more generous transfers may easily boost aggregate labor supply. Hence, the sign as well as the size of the aggregate response is indeterminate *a priori*.

3. A careful evaluation of the aggregate labor supply responses to taxes and transfers should rest on the full body of available evidence, and not only on the estimates from a few polar studies. When economists have attempted to provide an assessment of the labor supply responses to taxes and transfers from the published studies of such effects, they have arrived at far more modest numbers than those cited by advocates of the alarmist view. In the most frequently cited review of the effects of transfers, Danziger, Haveman, and Plotnick (1981) summarized the evidence on the labor-supply effects of Social Security, unemployment insurance, and welfare spending.

> [It] suggests that because of labor supply reductions by transfer recipients, total [desired] work effort in the economy was 3.3 percent lower than it would have been. Adding the reductions due to the other [transfer] programs . . . gives a total reduction of 4.8 percent. In an economy with involuntary unemployment, however, not all of

this supply would be employed. If the unemployment rate were 7.0 percent, and if the increased labor supply of transfer recipients would find employment at a rate equal to that of other workers, the net loss of employment time would be about 4.5 percent. Because those receiving transfer benefits tend to have below-average wage rates, the loss of total earnings is probably about 3.5 percent.

Browning and Johnson, whose 1984 study found very large welfare effects of marginal changes in taxes and transfers, estimate the total effect of a stylized version of the U.S. tax-transfer system to be a reduction in aggregate labor supply of about 5.2 percent. Even this may overstate the effect of the system, as we shall see below.

4. Although the results from the NIT experiments carry heavy weight in any overall evaluation of labor supply effects, because of the random assignment of observations and the controlled and systematic variation of treatment, we must use caution in inferring the actual effects of the tax-transfer system from them.

In spite of the apparently large *average* responses observed in some of the experiments, scholarly summaries of the results have usually reached the following conclusions: (1) the observed sensitivities of response (elasticities) fall well within the range that would have been predicted prior to the experiments; (2) the responses fall in the lower part of that range; and (3) the range of responses across the different NIT experiments was far narrower than the range of predicted responses that existed prior to the experiments. The findings from the experiments in fact imply that the marginal cost of raising transfer is much lower than the estimate of Browning and Johnson. Whereas Browning and Johnson estimate that the net income of the affluent must be reduced by $9.51 to raise the income of the poor by $1.00, findings from the largest NIT experiment suggest that the cost of aiding the working poor is actually less than $1.90. The cost of helping the poor who are too infirm to work is presumably much lower than $1.90.

5. The underpinnings of both the theory and empirical work on labor supply response are a source of much greater controversy than is generally recognized. This may be especially true of those studies showing the largest responses to taxes and transfers. Following are some of the major unsettled issues.

• While the 1981 study by Hausman is correctly regarded as the most important and innovative examination of tax effects on U.S. labor supply, it has not yet received the systematic scrutiny that is merited by its importance. Several economists have pointed to technical features of Hausman's model that require especially careful sensitivity analysis. Until this kind of analysis is performed, Hausman's findings will be regarded as provisional by most quantitative labor economists.

• Actual estimates of labor supply parameters (income and substitution effects) typically rely on untested assumptions about the attributes of work life: that the workday and the workweek are flexible; that the wage rate is exogenous to the choice of work effort; that there are no time and money costs associated with working; that the budget line is continuous, though perhaps nonlinear; and that disequilibrium and rationing are absent from labor markets. Any or all of these assumptions might be violated in practice, with unknown effects on the parameter estimates.

- There are a variety of technical issues in the econometric estimation of labor supply parameters that remain unresolved and on which little consensus exists.

- A number of additional estimation issues concern the modeling of responses to taxes and transfers. In the presence of tax evasion and welfare fraud, how can the "true" marginal wage rate be measured? How can the actual availability of public transfers be imputed? How can the relevant trade-off between work and income be accurately specified when particular tax and transfer programs are associated with a variety of tied benefits or characteristics which are difficult to measure, e.g., stigma, implicit subsidies for training and education, and guarantees or generous subsidies of medical care?

- A complete assessment of the aggregate responses to taxes must rest upon an accurate estimate of the work-effort effects of the government goods and services that are provided through taxes. These effects may be either positive or negative; at present their direction and size are a complete mystery.

In sum, the state of empirical work in this area remains unsettled, in spite of important advances in both theory and empirical estimation over the past decade. When we consider, in addition, the wide variation in existing estimates of labor supply responses to taxes and transfers, it seems to us that the evidence should be treated cautiously. Our available evidence is certainly not authoritative enough to support the calls for dramatic tax reductions or government retrenchment implicit in the writings of some critics of the current system.

6. While it may not be widely recognized, many of the more alarming findings about work response to taxes and transfers have not been confirmed upon subsequent reanalysis. For example, the majority of recent studies has found that Social Security retirement benefits contributed only modestly to the trend toward earlier retirement among U.S. men. This finding has been replicated in recent cross-sectional and time-series studies, most of which have been far more technically sophisticated than the earlier research on this subject. While the critics of Social Security are quick to note the sharp decline in older male labor force participation since World War II, they appear to forget that participation of men over 65 fell by over one-third between 1900 and 1940—well before Social Security could have affected labor supply. The alarmist view of the effects of disability insurance on labor force participation has also been called into serious question. The fact is that alarmist

results have generally been found in only a minority of studies, and most of those findings have not stood up well to careful reanalysis designed to improve on the earlier models or data.

7. An important point overlooked by some readers of recent studies is that the elimination or drastic reduction of existing taxes or the substitution of a lump-sum system are probably not appropriate alternatives with which to compare the existing system. Indeed, the authors of a few of the studies had a quite different alternative system in mind—usually, a tax system raising equal revenue but with less progressivity, a broader base, and lower marginal tax rates. Hausman was explicit in this, and he found that a proportional tax system with a $4,000 initial exemption would cause about half of the deadweight loss caused by the present system. That is, in comparison to a relatively feasible alternative tax system that raises the same amount of revenue, the present tax system induces economic distortion. The current system can be modified in order to improve its efficiency, but the efficiency gains are much smaller when moving to feasible alternative systems than when moving to a totally nondistorting system, or no system at all.

8. Finally we note one important kind of evidence that is sometimes forgotten. The historical trends in the U.S. labor supply do not appear to conform especially well to the predictions offered by the harshest critics of the welfare state. This seems to us a fundamental problem with the new view. It is well known that tax levels and transfer benefits have grown substantially over the past three decades. While it is true that the labor force participation of men, especially older men, has fallen over that period, this decline has been more than offset by a sharp rise in the labor force participation rate of American women. From 1948 to 1984, the participation rate of adult men fell by 10 percentage points, mostly due to a sharp decline at older ages, but the rate for adult women *rose* by 22 percentage points. The overall employment rate rose by 3 percentage points, and the participation rate by 5.5 points. Annual hours of work per person under 65 have risen—not fallen—in the United States since 1960. This growth in paid employment and hours hardly seems consistent with the view that the growing burden of taxes and transfers has markedly depressed labor supply.

Unconvinced

Our assessment of the recent literature on tax and transfer distortions leads us to be skeptical of the claim that these distortions have led to massive reductions in work effort. Even though the statistical evidence on work responses is imprecise and not always consistent, we believe historical experience has convincingly disproven the most extreme claims about the sensitivity of U.S. labor supply to tax and transfer policy. For example, neither history nor plausible statistical evidence is consistent with the claim that tax revenues would rise as a result of a reduction in marginal tax rates.

We are much more uncertain about the average and marginal excess burden associated with existing taxes. Excess burden, unlike labor supply, is not directly observed, so it is much more difficult to form a reliable estimate of its magnitude. It is conceivable that the average or marginal excess burden of taxes is very large, as several recent analysts have claimed, even though aggregate labor supply does not appear especially sensitive to large changes in the tax structure. But it is equally plausible to infer that the lack of aggregate responsiveness is an indication that the excess burden of taxes is small. The evidence on excess burden must be far more extensive, consistent, and reliable for it to be used as a firm guide to public policy.

REFERENCES

Taxation, Resource Allocation and Welfare in *Taxation and Welfare*. Arnold C. Harberger. Little, Brown & Co., Boston, 1974.

Welfare. Martin Anderson. The Hoover Institution Press, Stanford, Calif., 1978.

Labor Supply. Jerry A. Hausman in *How Taxes Affect Economic Behavior,* Henry Aaron and Joseph Pechman, editors. The Brookings Institution Press, Washington, D.C., 1981.

How Income Transfers Affect Work, Savings and the Income Distribution: A Critical Review. Sheldon Danziger, Robert Haveman, and Robert Plotnick in *Journal of Economic Literature,* September 1981.

Swedish Tax Rates, Labor Supply, and Tax Revenues. Charles E. Stuart in *Journal of Political Economy,* October 1981.

Labor Supply. Mark R. Killingsworth, Cambridge University Press, New York, 1983.

Losing Ground. American Social Policy, 1950–1980. Charles Murray. Basic Books, New York, 1984.

The Trade-Off Between Equality and Efficiency. Edgar K. Browning and William R. Johnson in *Journal of Political Economy,* April 1984.

Welfare Costs per Dollar of Additional Tax Revenue in the U.S. Charles E. Stuart in *American Economic Review,* June 1984.

On the Marginal Welfare Cost of Taxation. Edgar K. Browning (mimeo). Texas A&M University, College Station, 1985.

General Equilibrium Computations of the Marginal Welfare Costs of Taxes in the U.S. Charles L. Ballard, John B. Shoven, and John Whalley in *American Economic Review,* March 1985.

Limits to the Welfare State. Assar Lindbeck in *Challenge,* January/February 1986.

Economics of Taxation

The search for an optimal tax system is probably the longest lived of all research efforts in public sector economics, and it is showing no sign of concluding. Many criteria have been suggested over the years, including efficiency, equity, ease of compliance, and administrative cost. However, agreement on the criteria for judging a tax policy does not imply agreement on the relative importance of each requirement. In addition, the validity of most conclusions from optimal tax research depends upon the assumptions made about consumer and firm behavior, and unfortunately, unanimity has yet to be reached on these assumptions as well. The selected readings clearly illustrate the unsettled nature of this area of economics. Of particular interest is the lack of consensus about the effects of the 1986 tax reforms.

Optimal Taxation

The following four selections focus on major elements of the debate about optimal taxation: criteria for evaluating taxation, proposals for optimal taxation and the validity of underlying assumptions, and whether debt is equivalent to taxation.

SELECTION 34

R. W. HAFER AND MICHAEL E. TREBING

The Value-Added Tax: A Review of the Issues

Although major changes were instituted by the Tax Reform Act of 1986, tax reform still remains a controversial and relevant topic for debate in the United States. In the search for an ideal federal tax system, frequent reference is made to the experience of the European Common Market countries with the value-added tax (VAT). Some VAT proponents see this tax as a replacement only for the corporate income tax, while others view a national VAT as a viable alternative to the personal income tax as well.

    The authors of this reading illustrate how a value-added tax is calculated and explain how the VAT is administered in Europe. They then consider the advantages and disadvantages of the VAT in terms of the criteria of economic efficiency, equity, and cost of administration.

QUESTIONS TO GUIDE THE READING

1. Under what circumstances will the total tax revenue collected by a VAT be identical to that collected by a general sales tax?

2. How does the VAT achieve one of the major principles of optimal taxation—price neutrality? How might the VAT be structured to encourage or discourage certain economic activities (such as capital formation)?

3. Why might politicians claim that it would be politically advantageous to raise additional tax revenues through a value-added tax rather than by an increased retail sales tax?

R. W. Hafer and Michael E. Trebing, "The Value-Added Tax: A Review of the Issues," *Federal Reserve Bank of St. Louis Review* 62 (January 1980), 3–10.

R. W. Hafer is Research Officer at the Federal Reserve Bank of St. Louis. **Michael E. Trebing** is Assistant Vice-President at the Memphis Branch of the Federal Reserve Bank of St. Louis.

4. In terms of economic efficiency, what clear advantages does the VAT have over turnover taxes (used in Europe prior to the introduction of the VAT)?

Recently many groups have called for major tax reform. These groups maintain that the existing U.S. tax system has altered economic incentives and negatively influenced the performance of the economy. One possible solution to this problem is for the United States to adopt a value-added tax (VAT) similar to that used by European governments. This article provides a general economic framework for examining the current debate over the introduction of a VAT into the U.S. tax system.

Background

Value added is the difference between a firm's receipts from the sale of a product and the payment for the resources or raw materials used in producing it. In other words, value added is equivalent to a firm's payment to the factors of production—land, labor, and capital—in the form of rent, wages, interest, and profits. These payments represent the "base" to which a VAT would be applied.

A simplified example of how value-added can be determined is shown in Table 1, which illustrates a hypothetical four-step process of converting wheat into a loaf of bread. The miller purchases wheat from the farmer at a price of 10 cents and sells the resulting flour to the baker for 20 cents. Since one-half of the price to the baker represents the farmer's receipts, 10 cents of the miller's receipts represent the value added to the raw wheat during this stage of the production process. After converting the flour into bread, the baker sells the loaf of bread to the retailer for 30 cents. Since the cost of the flour was 20 cents, the value added at this stage (the baker's) is again 10 cents. Finally, out of the 40-cent retail price for the loaf, the remaining 10 cents represents the retailer's value added.

The usefulness of this example is twofold. First, it illustrates the fact that the *final retail price to the consumer is really nothing more than the sum of the value added at each stage of production*. Second, it provides a format by which a sales tax can be distinguished from a VAT. A sales tax involves a single payment by the consumer at the retail level and is levied at a constant rate on the purchase price. The VAT, on the other hand, is assessed at each stage of production. If the sales tax rate and the VAT rate are equal, the total tax revenue in the above example is the same irrespective of the collection process.

There are two basic methods of calculating the VAT. In the *additive* method, the tax base for the VAT is the sum of the firm's payments to the factors used in producing the good. Under this scheme, the VAT rate, say

Table 1   Calculating the Value Added

Stage							Receipts	Value-Added
1 Farmer	.10						.10	.10
2 Miller	.10	+	.10				.20	.10 (= .20 − .10)
3 Baker	.10	+	.10	+	.10		.30	.10 (= .30 − .20)
4 Retailer	.10	+	.10	+	.10	+	.10 = .40	.10 (= .40 − .30)

Final sales price to consumer = $.40
                Total value added = $.40

**Table 2   Calculating VAT Liability Via
                Additive Procedure**

Wages	$500,000
Interest	50,000
Rent	25,000
Profit	25,000
Total	$600,000

Value added = $600,000
Tax payable = $600,000 × 10% (VAT rate) = $ 60,000

Source: Richard W. Lindholm, *Value-Added Tax and Other Tax Reforms* (Chicago: Nelson-Hall, 1976), pp. 30–31.

10 percent, is applied to the firm's costs in terms of wages, interest, rents, and profits. Table 2 illustrates a hypothetical example of how the additive procedure is used to calculate the VAT due.

Table 3 provides the information needed to calculate the VAT payable under the second method, the *subtractive* procedure. Essentially, this approach makes the base to which the VAT rate is applied equal to the difference between a firm's sales receipts and its cost of production (again, its value added). The actual tax liability using this procedure is identical to that derived using the additive approach.

The Tax Base and Its Calculation

As noted before, the VAT base is usually calculated as the difference between a firm's sales receipts and its cost of purchases from other firms. A debate exists, however, over whether all of a firm's costs should be included in the calculation of the base or whether special exemptions should be made.

**Table 3   Calculating VAT Liability Via
               Subtractive Procedure**

Total sales of goods and services	$1,000,000
Total interest, dividends, and rents received	200,000
Total (A)	$1,200,000
Taxes	$ 200,000
Purchase of materials, services, power, and capital on which VAT has been paid	300,000
Interest, dividends, and rents paid to other firms	100,000
Total (B)	$ 600,000

Value added $= A - B$
$\qquad\quad = \$600,000$
Tax payable $= \$600,000 \times 10\%$ (VAT rate) $= \$\quad 60,000$

Source: Lindholm, *Value-Added Tax and Other Tax Reforms,*
pp. 30–31.

Exemptions from the tax base are important because they determine many of the economic effects of a VAT. Of particular concern is the treatment of capital goods. There are three general approaches to the treatment of capital goods: the gross product, the income, and the consumption approaches.

Under the gross product approach, firms are not permitted to deduct the purchase price of capital goods when calculating their VAT base, nor are they allowed to deduct the depreciation of existing capital. The tax base at each stage of production, therefore, includes wages, interest, rent, profits, *and* depreciation. Since there is no deduction for either capital goods depreciation or their purchase, the VAT applies to all income earned in the production of the firm's output. Thus, in an economy-wide sense, the tax base is associated with the value of gross national product—the total current market value of all goods and services produced or the total income derived from their production.

The income approach, on the other hand, *does* allow firms to deduct capital depreciation from their tax base. Since firms "use up" a percentage of their existing capital stock each year, this approach taxes firms on their *net* instead of gross income. The tax base of the income-type VAT is analogous, therefore, to the net national product of the economy.

The third approach to the treatment of capital goods, called the consumption approach, is the most widely used VAT. It is the type that much of Europe has adopted, that Congress is currently considering, and that will be analyzed for the remainder of this article. Under this scheme, each firm

Table 4   VAT Implemented

Country	Effective Year
Belgium	1971
Denmark	1967
France	1954
Ireland	1972
Italy	1973
Luxembourg	1970
Netherlands	1969
United Kingdom	1973
West Germany	1968

may deduct its capital expenditures on plant and equipment in addition to depreciation. The tax base becomes the firm's gross receipts less its purchases of materials and capital outlays (plant and equipment). In an aggregate sense, the VAT base under the consumption approach corresponds to the output of consumer goods or, equivalently, income earned in producing consumer goods.

VAT: The European Experience

The VAT is by no means a new idea. Following World War I, the possibility of implementing a VAT-type system was discussed in certain European countries and in the United States.[1] Although the debate continued over the next several decades, it was not until the 1950s that a VAT system was introduced in France and in the state of Michigan.

In an attempt to foster trade between its members, the Council of the European Economic Community (EEC) issued a directive on April 1, 1967, which required all member nations to establish a VAT system by January 1, 1970. Although the directive concerned only the current members—Belgium, France, Germany, Italy, Luxembourg, and the Netherlands—it was extended to the United Kingdom, Denmark, and Ireland upon their joining the EEC in 1973 (Table 4). Since most popular discussions of the VAT refer to the "European experience," it may be useful to briefly examine the basis of its adoption and its record to date.

The VAT was introduced in various European countries as an alternative to turnover taxes. These turnover taxes, sometimes referred to as cascading turnover taxes, are characterized by the payment of taxes at each level of production without regard to relief for the tax paid at a prior stage. Because of the way in which these taxes were implemented, there was considerable incentive for a firm to control all the stages of production (vertical integration). Also, there was a variety of rules and regulations about the

Table 5   Standard VAT Rates in EEC Countries

Country	Rate
Belgium	16.0%
Denmark	20.2
France	17.6
Ireland	20.0
Italy	14.0
Luxembourg	10.0
Netherlands	18.0
United Kingdom	8.0
Germany	12.0

Source: Value-Added Tax (Arthur Anderson & Co., 1979).

taxation of certain exports and imports, which reduced the foreign trade potential between the countries. The VAT provided for the general tax exemption of export goods and services. Thus, the goal of the EEC in introducing VAT was twofold: to "harmonize" the members' tax systems and to encourage intra-EEC trade.

While introduction of the VAT system has increased foreign trade among the EEC nations, harmonization of the various tax systems is still far from complete. As Table 5 indicates, the "standard" VAT rate varies considerably among the various EEC countries. Moreover, each country may choose to apply different rates to various groups of goods and services. For example, Belgium has two basic rates: a standard rate of 16.0 percent on necessities, and a 25.0 percent rate on luxury goods. Likewise, Germany and the United Kingdom each have different rates for necessity and luxury items.

In addition, each country exempts certain items from taxation. Although a complete listing would point out the wide diversity of possible exemptions, there are several areas commonly exempted from VAT. As mentioned earlier, exports are fully exempt from VAT. Also, sales of securities, stocks and bonds, doctors' services, financial services such as insurance and banking, and postal services are generally exempt.

Criteria for Evaluating the VAT

The effect of taxation on economic efficiency is linked to the concept of potential output. Potential output, as it relates to a market-type economy, may vary according to incentives available in the market-place. The economist defines these incentives in terms of income and relative prices. To the extent that taxes can alter economic incentives or the return to productive activity, they induce changes in economic behavior.

Economists use several criteria to judge the desirability of a given tax or tax system. These criteria involve both efficiency and equity considerations.

Neutrality

Price theory suggests that prices established in a competitive market are reflections of both consumer preference for goods and services and the least-cost combination of inputs used to produce those goods. A tax system is considered optimal if it does not interfere with the price allocation mechanism established in the market—that is, it is neutral toward economic behavior. Although all taxes distort or alter economic behavior to some degree, certain taxes can be judged "superior" on efficiency grounds. VAT proponents claim that the value-added tax would achieve the objectives of neutrality toward both economic behavior and allocative efficiency.

A tax on each firm's value added can be thought of as a proportional tax on the firm's use of the factors of production. If each firm combines land, labor, and capital in the most efficient (least-cost) manner, resources are bid into their most productive use. Payments to these factors in a competitive market are approximately equal to each factor's contribution to the market value of each firm's output. Thus, a uniform VAT on *all* firms imposes the same *proportional* tax cost—with respect to each firm's payments to the sum of factor payments (value added)—and is, therefore, neutral toward the choice of production methods or the use of productive resources.

A question remains regarding the neutrality of the consumption or the income approaches. Economic theory suggests that the consumption approach is less distorting since it does not alter the individual's choice between consumption and saving (i.e., current vs. future consumption). The income approach, however, discriminates against saving since capital expenditures are not deductible from the tax base.

Capital Formation and Growth

A common complaint about our tax system is that it discourages economic growth. VAT proponents claim that a consumption-type VAT would not. Since they believe that a reliance upon income taxation has altered individual consumption-savings choices through the income tax's impact on relative prices, proponents argue that the VAT would support both a higher level of savings and investment.[2] Behind this argument lies the "double-tax issue," one of the oldest controversies in economics. In other words, "Should taxes be based on consumption or on income?" Consumption-base tax advocates claim that a tax levied on income is also a tax on savings and is therefore inefficient because it raises the "price" of saving (future consumption) relative to current consumption. Since a saver eventually is taxed on the interest earned from present savings, some analysts argue that the income is taxed twice. Hence, the double-tax issue.

The exemption of capital expenditures with a VAT would offset the non-neutral aspects of the current tax system, which relies heavily on income taxation, and may result in a higher level of overall savings and investment.

In addition, VAT would directly affect labor supply.[3] Some analysts contend that existing income and social security taxes have altered the relative price of work and leisure. These taxes, they claim, have induced individuals to reduce their supply of labor at prevailing market wages below which might otherwise have been supplied without these taxes. Whether VAT would correct these distortions depends upon the relative responsiveness of labor to the removal or reduction of the existing taxes and the changes in relative commodity prices that may result from the VAT.

Distribution of the Tax Burden

Another question of interest is "Who bears the burden of taxation?" An economic examination of this issue can be made through what economists call "incidence analysis." Incidence is the change in an individual's real income (nominal income adjusted for changes in the price level) that results from the imposition of a tax.

The key to understanding incidence lies in distinguishing between statutory incidence (the legal liability of the tax) and economic incidence (the final burden of the tax). The sale tax provides a clear example of this distinction. Although its legal liability is imposed upon the retailer, the sales tax often is assumed to be fully passed on to the individual who purchases goods from the retailer. However, since the prices of the retailer's goods are now higher, the quantity demanded will be reduced, and the owner's income therefore will be changed. In this case, the economic incidence of the tax differs from the statutory liability since the former takes into account both the final resting point of the tax as well as the economic ramifications on others (the retailer, for example).

Tracing the final burden of a VAT is difficult because it ultimately depends upon the number of exemptions. Assuming that the tax is applied equally to all goods and services and is an "additional" tax, its burden would be fully shifted to consumers. If exemptions are allowed or if other taxes are reduced, however, there will be changes in relative prices and in the production mix of the economy.

Equity Criteria

Equity criteria are often used to evaluate different taxes (and thus incidence patterns). These criteria attempt to answer the questions, "Who should pay taxes?" and "How should the burden of taxation be distributed among different individuals?" Although objective economic analysis provides few answers to these questions, it can provide a perspective on relative costs and benefits and on the trade-offs between economic efficiency and equity considerations.

A principal equity concern is over the relative tax burden imposed on individuals of different income levels. The concept behind our income tax system, for example, is that those individuals who earn a higher income should pay a higher percentage of their income in taxes. This is a "progressive" tax system. A "regressive" tax, in contrast, takes a lesser proportion of income from individuals who earn a larger income.

Critics of the VAT claim that it would be a regressive tax since it taxes consumption and since lower income individuals spend a larger proportion of their incomes on consumption goods relative to higher income individuals. Although this argument is straightforward, its validity depends on several unsettled issues.

First, one might question the preceding analysis of regressiveness on the grounds that it ignores the benefit side of fiscal policy. In other words, the *net* benefits derived from government spending or transfer payments is not taken into account. Thus, a more meaningful evaluation would include the benefits received from government-related programs as well as the costs.

On the other hand, the regressiveness of the tax could be alleviated either by adjustments to the income tax rate and/or by special tax credits. For example, the exemption of necessity items such as food, shelter, clothing, and medical care has been proposed. These exemptions, however, would reduce the tax base and thus necessitate higher tax rates to insure the same yield as under a comprehensive base approach. In general, therefore, attempts to alleviate the regressiveness of the tax are likely to complicate the administrative problems and interfere with the neutrality criteria discussed earlier.

Administrative Costs

The cost of administration is another criterion for evaluating the merits of a tax system. The initial administrative costs of introducing a VAT (or any other tax for that matter) would be relatively high.

Perhaps the most important factor affecting the cost of using a VAT is the degree of complexity of the tax. The use of multiple rates and numerous exemptions, in contrast to a single uniform rate, would raise the administrative costs. Indeed, it has been estimated that if the VAT system used involves more than a single rate, administrative costs may rise by 50 to 80 percent.[4] Most of this increase would be due to increased personnel costs caused by a rise in the amount of paperwork required of both business and government.

Another consideration is whether the tax is used to replace part of an existing tax or as a supplementary source of government revenue. If the VAT replaces only part of an existing tax or is merely added to the present system, administrative cost savings may be negligible. In fact, adding a VAT may increase the current cost of the government's tax collecting apparatus. This can be seen by considering the influence on costs from a reduction in existing tax rates. Since the previous tax system still exists and since there is little or no change in collecting or reporting procedures, the time and manpower involved in collecting a 5 percent tax is essentially the same as that for a 10 percent tax.

Furthermore, adding a VAT to the existing array of taxes would have differential cost effects on business. For instance, soon after a VAT was introduced in Germany in 1968, small noncomputerized firms estimated that tax-related administrative costs increased up to 20 percent. Relatively large businesses, however, reported negligible administrative cost increases.[5]

The frequency of collection is also a significant cost factor. Most of the European countries currently using a VAT require monthly payments. In the United Kingdom, however, the collection period is quarterly. Although a monthly payment schedule may create cash-flow problems for some businesses, the European experience suggests that this frequency is feasible since most firms already record the data needed to calculate their VAT liability on a monthly basis.

Economic Effects of VAT

Price Effects

A major concern about the implementation of a VAT is the resulting price effects. The introduction of the VAT, it has been widely asserted, will lead to a one-time increase in the general level of prices. In fact, it can be easily demonstrated that, although a uniform VAT rate (an identical rate for all goods and services) applied without exemption will not alter *relative* prices within the economy, it will result in a one-time increase in the overall level of prices.[6] It should be noted, however, that this conclusion is based on several assumptions.

Perhaps the most important assumption is that all sellers raise their prices by the exact amount of the VAT, thus passing the additional cost on to the consumer. There are several reasons why this actually may not occur.

A VAT is usually applied with a varying rate structure—for instance, a 5 percent rate on food and a 10 percent rate on nonfood items—and/or with some items exempt from taxation.[7] If sellers face different cost increases due to the VAT, then it is uncertain that *all* prices will be raised by an equal amount. Since none of these conditions will lead to identical increases in all prices, the consequent relative price changes would induce a shifting in the pre-VAT pattern of demand for goods and services. In this way, the production (and employment) decisions of producers are affected by the introduction of a VAT.

Introducing a VAT may cause a one-time change in the level of prices if the tax is merely a supplement to existing taxes. It is generally assumed that firms face higher costs because of the VAT and, therefore, attempt to pass this on to consumers. However, if the tax burden is reduced in some other area—for instance, the reduction in firms' contributions to social security—then this assumption is unwarranted. To determine the final price effect of a VAT in this case requires knowledge of the trade-off between reductions in existing taxes (if any) and the cost to the firm of administering the VAT.

Finally, it is unlikely that a rise in the general level of prices can be maintained without an increase in the money stock held by the public or an increase in the velocity of the existing money stock (decline in real money balances). If neither of these situations occurs, then changes in production and employment will occur since consumers would not be able to maintain previous consumption levels at the higher level of prices. Thus, the reaction of the government to observed changes brought on by the initial price effects of a VAT may further complicate the foregoing analysis.

Interjurisdictional Intrusion

How VAT might interefere with existing state and local taxes is also an important issue. State and local governments likely will be apprehensive about a VAT, given that the tax appears to be an intrusion into an area upon which these governments traditionally have relied—namely, the sales tax. Continued use of the retail sales tax should not conflict with federal use of the VAT from an economic efficiency view, however. If the VAT is applied at a uniform rate, relative prices will not be affected.

Some have argued, however, that a VAT may change taxpayers' perceptions of the cost of government expenditures and may alter the level of public services demanded. If the tax is "invisible" or hidden in the price of goods, taxpayers may demand a higher level of public expenditures since the cost are not fully perceived. On the other hand, if the tax is fully perceived at the retail level (for example, if the VAT portion is stated separately at purchase), consumers may object to additional retail sales taxes, and state and local governments will find it more difficult to tax by this method.

Stabilization

An important feature of a tax system is its overall response to cyclical fluctuations in the economy. For a given set of tax rates, the growth of the tax base normally will change with the level of aggregate economic activity. Provided that the change in tax revenues does not affect the level of government spending, these changes will cause variations in the overall budget surplus or deficit. "Built-in flexibility" is said to exist if tax liabilities rise (and fall) at a faster rate than income. Our tax system, based primarily on a progressive income tax, posits that the overall federal budget has a stabilizing effect on the economy since the tax acts to dampen fluctuations in economic activity. A substitution from income and social security taxes to a VAT likely would reduce such built-in flexibility.

Summary

The purpose of this article has been to provide a general background for understanding the value-added tax. Recent examinations have narrowly addressed the tax's price effects and its potential to reduce the existing tax burden imposed by federal income and social security taxes. While these are indeed important issues, a complete analysis of VAT must go deeper, examining the tax base, its neutrality, regressiveness, incidence, and effects on capital formation. In addition, the administrative costs of the tax itself must be considered as well.

NOTES

1. The idea of the VAT originated with a German industrialist by the name of F. Von Siemens. In 1918 he advocated the substitution of the VAT for the newly implemented turnover tax. T. S. Adams suggested using such a tax in the United States in 1921. In the same year, the tax was included in an amendment to the Revenue Act of 1921 proposed by Sen. Reed Smoot. For a general discussion of the development of the VAT, see John F. Due, "The Value-Added Tax," *The Western Economic Journal* (Spring 1965), pp. 65–71.

2. Richard Musgrave and Peggy Musgrave, *Public Finance in Theory and Practice* (New York: McGraw-Hill, 1973), pp. 468–69.

3. Musgrave and Musgrave, *Public Finance,* pp. 483–88.

4. National Economic Development Office, *Value-Added Tax* (London: Her Majesty's Stationery Office, 1971), p. 41, cited in Dan Throop Smith, *et al., What You Should Know About the Value-Added Tax* (Homewood: Dow Jones-Irwin, Inc., 1973), p. 53.

5. See Alan A. Tait, *Value-Added Tax* (London: McGraw-Hill, 1972), p. 126.

6. Ann F. Friedlaender, "Indirect Taxes and Relative Prices," *Quarterly Journal of Economics* (February 1967), pp. 125–39.

7. See the section "VAT: The European Experience."

DAVID F. BRADFORD AND HARVEY S. ROSEN

The Optimal Taxation of Commodities and Income

David Bradford and Harvey Rosen summarize economic research into both the optimal taxation of commodities such as tobacco or alcohol and the optimal taxation of labor income. Economists often find it difficult to convince policy makers of the usefulness of formal mathematical models. We are asked: "Aren't reason and experience enough?" Well, no. At least, not always. There are times when intuition fails and no relevant past experience exists to guide policy. It is at these times that a mathematical framework can provide economic guidelines.

QUESTIONS TO GUIDE THE READING

1. How can the inverse elasticity rule be used to justify taxes on tobacco and alcohol?
2. Under what circumstances does taxation of labor income conform to the inverse elasticity rule?
3. What research evidence exists to suggest that Mirrlee's low marginal tax rates were the result of his specific mathematical formulation of the optimal income taxation problem?
4. How might horizontal equity play a role in the determination of rules for optimal taxation?

The last few years have seen a resurgence of interest in the old question of how best to raise tax revenue. Roughly speaking, two different problems have been studied. The first is to find a set of commodity taxes that is optimal given certain efficiency and (sometimes) equity considerations. In a second strain of the literature, it is assumed that the revenue system is based

David F. Bradford and Harvey S. Rosen, "The Optimal Taxation of Commodities and Income," *American Economic Review*, May 1976, Vol. 66, No. 2, 94–101. Reprinted by permission of the authors.

David F. Bradford is Professor of Economics and Public Affairs at the Woodrow Wilson School of Public and International Affairs, Princeton University. **Harvey S. Rosen** is Professor of Economics at Princeton University, and Research Associate at the National Bureau of Economic Research.

upon income rather than commodity taxation, and the problem is to determine the optimal degree of progressivity (or regressivity).[1]

The principal motivation of some writers in the optimal taxation literature seems to be the discovery of fairly simple rules which policy makers actually can implement. Others are more interested in theoretical exploration of the implications of alternative economic assumptions than in developing usable policy recommendations. Practically all the contributions, however, have been quite mathematical and thus inaccessible to many practitioners in the public finance area. The purpose of this essay is to discuss in a nontechnical way the methodology and principal conclusions of the optimal taxation literature.[2]

In Sections I and II are discussed the optimal commodity and income tax literatures, respectively. Following this are some observations on the accomplishments of optimal taxation research and on some open questions.

I. Optimal Commodity Taxation

Since the literature contains many and varied derivations of the principal theorems of optimal commodity taxation,[3] we shall not carry out detailed proofs here. We can point out, however, some of the variations in the way the problem is posed. Most commonly a revenue constraint is taken as a starting point, together with an assumption that the government must use per unit commodity taxes. Thus lump sum taxes are excluded. If x_i is the quantity of the ith good purchased by the household sector from the production sector (negative if the households are net sellers, as in the case of the commodity "leisure"), and T_i is the per unit tax, the revenue constraint is

$$\sum T_i x_i = R, \tag{1}$$

where R is the required revenue level.

The taxes are the difference between the prices, p_i, received by producers and P_i, paid by the consumers,

$$T_i = P_i - p_i. \tag{2}$$

It is frequently assumed that producer prices are fixed, so that by setting taxes we set consumer prices and hence consumer welfare. The problem is then to make the choice of taxes in such a way as to maximize the resulting consumer welfare, i.e., to minimize excess burden.

A typical approach is to assume there to be only one consumer (hence no distribution problem), with a utility function $U(\cdot)$ depending on consumption vector x. Thus the objective might be to choose P (a vector of consumer prices) and p (a vector of producer prices) to

$$\text{maximize } U(x(P)) \tag{3}$$

subject to

$$\sum_i x_i(P)P_i = 0$$

and to

$$U_i(x(P)) = aP_i. \tag{4}$$

Conditions (4) are the familiar first order implications of the household's optimization, with a being the Lagrangian multiplier. . . .

This leads to the famous Ramsey result on optimal commodity taxation:

$$\sum_i T_i S_{ik} = bx_k, \qquad k = 1, \ldots, m \tag{6}$$

where S_{ik} is the derivative of the demand for the ith good with respect to the kth price, other prices and utility being held constant, and b is independent of k. The left-hand side gives an estimate of the change in demand for the kth good which would occur if the taxes were removed. Hence (6) says that the proportional change in demand (thus estimated) should be the same for all commodities—the Ramsey result.

Conditions (6) can also be expressed in terms of elasticities. Probably the most familiar "optimal tax" result is the form which applies when the off-diagonal elasticities are zero. In this case the first order conditions associated with (3) lead to the "inverse elasticity rule":

$$t_r = \frac{d}{E_{rr}}, \qquad r = 1, \ldots, m. \tag{7}$$

where $t_r = T_r/P_r$, the percentage or ad valorem rate of tax, d is a constant, and E_{rr} is the elasticity of the ordinary (uncompensated) demand function for the kth good. This formula has certainly been of importance in forming economists' intuitions on tax and price regulatory questions. It underlies the notion of charging according to "what the traffic can bear" in transportation, for example, and is the basis for the acceptance on efficiency grounds of such taxes as those on tobacco and alcohol, the demand for which is presumed price inelastic.

An important application of the analysis is to the presumptive case for direct over indirect taxation. The classic Hotelling argument for marginal cost pricing seemed to some to support the conclusion that an "income tax" will involve no efficiency cost. When it was recognized, however, that the "income" of the tax system is not the "budget level" of the elementary theory of consumer demand, but rather the product of a certain price, the wage, and a demanded quantity (negative net purchase of leisure), the apparent a priori advantage of an income tax was lost. The analyses of W. J. Corlett and D. C. Hague, I. M. D. Little and Milton Friedman to this effect all are applications of the theory of optimal commodity taxation as is neatly shown by Sandmo.

While the extensive subsequent work has shown how difficult it is to sustain *any* simple rules for commodity taxation, the result of the spreading awareness of this work has been to make economists think about tax questions in a new way and to hasten the search for rules which are reasonably robust.

For example, as Stiglitz and Atkinson point out, optimal tax analysis makes it clear that there is no a priori assurance that the income tax is the single best instrument for income redistribution—such "commodity taxes" as are represented by housing subsidies or food stamps might contribute to an optimal program. Michael Boskin notes that, in view of the differences in the observed elasticities of household supply of the two types of labor (husband labor and wife labor), it is probably efficient to tax these "commodities at different rates." Martin Feldstein (1975) uses the same basic approach to examine the choice between "tax expenditures" and direct expenditure methods of achieving an increase in a specified activity.

A natural question in view of the interpretation of the income tax as a commodity tax is whether taxation of labor only (i.e., uniform taxation of commodities) is appropriate. Not surprisingly, the answer is that it will be so when labor is inelastically supplied. Sandmo shows that this in turn will follow if utility is separable between leisure and all other goods and homogenous in those goods. Intuitively this separability means that further efficiency cannot be gained by differential taxation of goods that are "related" to leisure. Several writers have noted an important consequence when this result is reinterpreted in an intertemporal context. If utility is a function of consumption and leisure at different dates and separability obtains, then no taxes on interest income should be levied—consumption is the appropriate tax base. This simply illustrates the challenge, implicit in the optimal tax approach, to the widespread acceptance of taxation on the basis of Haig-Simons income which has been emphasized by Feldstein (1976).

While an "income tax" can be regarded as a tax on the sale of labor (negative net purchase of leisure), there is a feature of actual income taxes which is slighted by such a point of view: it is institutionally feasible to assess taxes at different *rates* on different individuals; in particular, progressive taxation of earnings is possible. This means that the income tax and such related taxes as the expenditure tax are potentially important instruments for meeting distributional objectives. We now turn to the studies which consider the trade-off between such distributional objectives and economic efficiency.

II. The Optimal Income Tax Literature

The problem of optimal income taxation has a long history in economics.[4] However, most of the recent literature stems from a paper published by James Mirrlees in 1971. A natural way to organize our discussion, then, is to summarize Mirrlees techniques and conclusions, and then view the en-suing literature as an attempt to explain and modify some of his results.

In Mirrlees' model, society is composed of individuals who have iden-tical atemporal utility functions in after tax income and leisure. Individuals differ only in their earning abilities (wage per hour). The government must collect an exogenously determined amount of tax revenue. The problem is to find an income tax schedule (tax function) which maximizes the sum of individuals' utilities subject to this revenue constraint.

Using the tools of the calculus of variations to solve the constrained maximization problem, Mirrlees finds that the optimal tax function exhibits marginal tax rates between zero and one, and that when it is operative, part of the population does not work. Although these results may seem weak, they are really quite remarkable given the absence of specific functional forms for the key relationships in the problem.

In order to get more specific results, more specific assumptions must be built into the analysis. Mirrlees assumes that the utility functions are Cobb-Douglas, and considers both log normal and Pareto distributions of earnings abilities. With these assumptions, the following results emerge: (a) the op-timal tax function is approximately linear with a negative intercept, and (b) the optimal tax function is characterized by "low" marginal tax rates which *fall* somewhat with income. Atkinson's (1973) interpolations of Mirrlees' re-sults indicate rates in the neighborhood of 20 percent.

Mirrlees was surprised at how low the marginal tax rates were: ". . . I must confess that I had expected the rigorous analysis of income-taxation in the utilitarian manner to provide an argument for high tax rates. It has not done so." (A study by Ray C. Fair in the same year also generated fairly low implied marginal tax rates.) Apparently, those who read the Mirrlees paper also found the low marginal tax rates counterintuitive, for much of the literature appears to be an attempt to explain them.

One concern was the maximand of Mirrlees' problem, an unweighted sum of individual utilities, which implies that a "util" to a rich individual adds as much to social welfare as a "util" to a poor individual. To what extent would more egalitarian results (i.e., higher marginal tax rates) emerge if a social welfare function were used which weighted the utilities of the rich less than those of the poor? Atkinson and Feldstein (1973) consider social welfare functions of the form

$$W = (\sum U_i^v)^{1/v} \qquad v \leqslant 1. \qquad (8)$$

Clearly, when $v = 1$, welfare (W) is the simple sum of utilities (U_i). When v is less than 1, however, it can be shown that a given increment to the utility of a low utility individual adds more to W than if awarded to a high utility individual. It should be noted, however, that the specifications of the social welfare function and the individual utility functions are not really indepen-dent of each other. We could, for example, specify the utility of the ith in-dividual to be U_i^v and then write social welfare as the arithmetic sum of these utilities.

Atkinson focuses attention on the case in which v approaches minus infinity. Under such circumstances, it can be shown that maximizing W is equivalent to maximizing the utility of the worst off individual in society: the maximin case. This case has received considerable attention due to philosopher John Rawls's argument that it is particularly compelling as an ethical criterion. (A number of criticisms of Rawls's position are suggested by Alvin K. Klevorik.)

Atkinson uses a Rawlsian social welfare function in a model with a linear income tax, no net government revenue requirement (i.e., taxation for redistribution only), and a Pareto distribution of skills in the economy. He finds that optimal marginal tax rates range between 30 and 45 percent. Thus, one solution to the mystery of Mirrlees' low marginal tax rates is his formulation of the objectives of the government. Social welfare functions which are more egalitarian than the classical utilitarian variety may yield higher marginal rates.

Another potential explanation for Mirrlees' results is the Cobb-Douglas assumption on the form of individuals' utility functions. Stern has investigated this possibility by assuming that individuals have constant elasticity of substitution *(CES)* utility functions in leisure and income. Using results on the elasticity of labor supply from the econometric literature,[5] he finds that an elasticity of substitution of about .4 is more realistic than 1.0.[6] When a variant of Mirrlees' problem is solved using *CES* utility functions with this lower elasticity of substitution, the optimal marginal tax rates are substantially higher—without appeal to a more egalitarian social welfare function.

Reexamination of the social welfare function suggests another possible explanation for the low tax rates typically generated by optimal income tax studies. Our intuition about optimal income taxation may perhaps be conditioned on societal objective functions which are not utilitarian-individualistic. For example, the presence in the social welfare function of a variable parameterizing the "aesthetics" of the income distribution would lead to more egalitarian results.[7] Similarly Feldstein (1976) has shown that if interdependent utility functions are allowed for, very high marginal tax rates may be appropriate.

We now turn to a limitation of the Mirrlees model which is just beginning to receive attention, its atemporal setting. The appropriate taxation of capital income is one of the most controversial aspects of the tax system, yet the studies cited above for the most part ignore it. Janusz A. Ordover and Edmund S. Phelps examine the optimal mix of taxes on two factors of production (capital and labor) in a one sector neoclassical growth model. Their model is very general, and therefore no results on tax rates emerge which can be compared to those discussed above. Moreover, the only social welfare function they consider is the maximin case. Despite these limitations, explicit attention to the taxation of capital income in the optimal income tax framework is an important step which will no doubt stimulate further research.

We could continue to list additional aspects of the Mirrlees model which have been changed and expanded in order to ascertain their effects on optimal tax rates. However, the basic thrust of the literature should now be clear. An exogenously determined amount of tax revenue must be raised by income taxes on individuals whose economic choices are distorted by the presence of those taxes. Given technological and behavioral assumptions, the optimal tax schedule is that which leaves some social welfare function at a maximum after the tax is collected. The literature shows how various assumptions on these components lead to different conclusions regarding the shape of the optimal income tax schedule.

III. Concluding Remarks

The accomplishments of the optimal taxation research have been considerable. It has upset many comfortable rules of thumb and lent precision to many informal arguments. But there remains work to be done. Part of this work will, of course, consist of increasing the stock of variations on the basic problems for which solutions have been described. Another, and very important part will consist of the attempt to determine quantitatively which of these problems best describes the actual economy to be taxed—filling in all those empty boxes with real, estimated elasticities.

However, work of another kind is needed to advance the normative power of the analysis. Normatively the optimal tax literature rests on a utilitarian base. It is true that the optimal commodity tax results, or some of them at least, can be cast, in a form which says: if your tax system doesn't look like this, there is a potential bargain which can be struck among your citizens which would make all better off. However, these bargains are complex and their possibility tends to be eliminated by the very assumptions that require the use of second-best instruments in the first place. For practical application implicit interpersonal utility comparisons are required. The optimal income tax results are also dependent on such comparisons. The missing link is a welfare function, and the question is how does one persuade a legislature or an electorate to decide in accordance with some particular welfare function?

Asking the optimal tax researchers to resolve this is effectively to ask them to make welfare economics persuasive, obviously a tall order. But, interestingly, the tax literature has always appealed to non-utilitarian criteria as well.

Thus, missing from the optimal tax literature is the idea of horizontal equity, the notion that ". . . people in equal positions should be treated equally." (Richard A. Musgrave 1959, p. 160) (Customarily, "equal positions" are defined in terms of an observable index of ability to pay such as income, expenditure, or wealth.) In none of the studies discussed above has the injunction to treat equals the same appeared either as a constraint in the maximization problem, or as an argument in the objective function. Therefore, they will in general[8] fail to provide horizontal equity. In light of this, Musgrave (1976) and others have suggested that it is inappropriate to characterize such schemes as "optimal."

Defining horizontal equity in terms of income is inadequate because individuals with identical opportunity sets but different tastes will have different incomes. An alternative way to define equal position would be identical opportunity sets. However, it seems more in the spirit of the optimal taxation literature to define equal position in terms of utilities: individuals are "the same" only if they derive identical amounts of utility from their consumption and leisure bundles. The choice of a criterion for horizontal equity is important because when tastes differ between individuals, different criteria may lead to different conclusions as to the fairness of a given tax. For example, an income tax which is perfectly fair according to conventional notions of horizontal equity hurts an "income lover" more than a "leisure lover."

In an attempt to put the discussion of horizontal equity and the optimal taxation literature on the same plane, Feldstein (1976) has redefined the principle of horizontal equity in terms of utility rather than ability to pay.[9] However, complete integration of horizontal equity into the optimal tax framework remains to be done. Perhaps this could be accomplished by including some measure of departure from horizontal equity as an argument in the social welfare function, but this approach is bedeviled by conceptual difficulties in measuring departures from horizontal equity.[10]

It may well be that horizontal equity, ancient and honorable criterion of tax policy though it be, is not a helpful concept. However, apparent appeal of this nonoperational idea to practical people suggests the attractiveness of properties of a tax structure which are independent of the economy to which that structure is applied. To discover whether there are any such properties which significantly narrow the range of "good" tax structures might be a useful topic of research.

NOTES

Note: The authors would like to thank Roger Gordon for useful conversations and Jay Stuart for assistance in gathering material. An extended version of this paper is available upon request to the authors.

1. Although we shall focus upon these problems in this paper, the optimal tax literature has had a somewhat wider scope. For example, Peter A. Diamond and James A. Mirrlees consider the problem of optimal expenditure along with taxation.
2. Consult Nicholas Stern or Atkinson and Stiglitz for more technical surveys.
3. See, for example, Frank A. Ramsey, M. Boiteux, or Agnar Sandmo.
4. See especially F. Y. Edgeworth's important contribution.
5. These are measures of the elasticity of hours per year with respect to the wage, and thus do not take into account other, perhaps more important, dimensions of labor supply.
6. If the elasticity of substitution were zero, lump sum taxation would be possible. If the elasticity of substitution were infinite, no revenue could be raised.
7. Such a social welfare would be non-Paretian, but there is nothing to prevent a reasonable set of value judgments from allowing for such a possibility.

8. It can be shown that if all individuals have identical tastes and there is only one type of ability, then horizontal equity will be satisfied by virtually any broad-based tax. (See Feldstein, 1976.) Such assumptions, as we have seen, are built into a number of the optimal tax studies. For an exception, see Diamond and Mirrlees.

9. "If two individuals would be equally well off (have the same utility level) in the absence of taxation, they should be equally well off if there is a tax."

10. See Rosen for a discussion of these problems and some attempts to surmount them.

REFERENCES

A. B. Atkinson, "How Progressive Should the Income Tax Be?" in Longman's, *Essays on Modern Economics,* London 1973.

M. Boiteux, "Sur la gestion des monopoles publics astreint a l'equilib budgetaire," *Econometrica,* 1956, 24, 22–40, reprinted in translation by W. J. Baumol and D. F. Bradford, "On the Management of Public Monopolies Subject to Budgetary Constraints," *J. Econ. Theory,* Sept. 1971, 3, 219–40.

M. J. Boskin, "Optimal Tax Treatment of the Family," Stanford Univ., mimeo. 1973.

W. J. Corlett and D. C. Hague, "Complementarity and the Excess Burden of Taxation," *Rev. Econ. Stud.,* 1953–54, 21, 21–30.

P. A. Diamond and J. A. Mirrlees, "Optimal Taxation and Public Production: II," *Amer. Econ. Rev.,* June 1971, 41, 261–78.

J. Dupuit, *Traite theorique et pratique de la conduite et de la distribution des eaux,* Paris 1854.

F. Y. Edgeworth, "The Pure Theory of Taxation," *Econ. J.,* 1897, 7, 46–70.

R. C. Fair, "The Optimal Distribution of Income," *Quart. J. Econ.,* 1971, 85, 551–79.

M. Feldstein, "On the Optimal Progressivity of the Income Tax," *J. Polit. Econ.,* 1973, 2, 357–76.

———, "The Theory of Tax Expenditures," Harvard Univ., mimeo. 1975.

———, "On the Theory of Tax Reform," *J. Publ. Econ.,* July–August, 1976, 6, 77–104.

M. Friedman, "The Welfare Effects of an Income and an Excise Tax," *J. Polit. Econ.,* 1952, 60, 1–24.

A. K. Klevorick, "Discussion," *Amer. Econ. Rev. Proc.,* May 1974, 64, 158–61.

I. M. D. Little, "Direct vs. Indirect Taxes," *Econ. J.,* 1951, 61, 577–84.

J. A. Mirrlees, "An Exploration in the Theory of Optimum Income Taxation," *Rev. Econ. Stud.,* 1971, 38, 179–208.

R. A. Musgrave, *The Theory of Public Finance,* New York 1959.

———, "Optimal Taxation, Equitable Taxation and Second-Best Taxation," *J. Publ. Econ.,* July–August, 1976, 6, 3–16.

J. A. Ordover and E. S. Phelps, "Linear Taxation of Wealth and Wages for Intragenerational Justice: Some Steady-State Cases," *Amer. Econ. Rev.,* Sept. 1975, 65, 660–73.

F. P. Ramsey, "A Contribution to the Theory of Taxation," *Econ. J.*, 1927, 37, 47–61.

J. Rawls, "Some Reasons for the Maximin Criterion," *Amer. Econ. Rev. Proc.*, May 1974, 64, 141–46.

H. Rosen, "Income, Utility, and Horizontal Equity Under the U.S. Income Tax," Princeton Univ., mimeo. 1975.

P. A. Samuelson, "Theory of Optimal Taxation," unpublished, approx. 1952.

A. Sandmo, "A Note on the Structure of Optimal Taxation," *Amer. Econ. Rev.*, Sept. 1974, 64, 701–06.

J. S. Stamp, *Fundamental Principles of Taxation in the Light of Modern Developments*, London 1921.

MICHAEL J. BOSKIN

On Some Recent Econometric Research in Public Finance

The validity of economic theories must be tested, especially when they affect public policy. Econometric analysis, using regression as well as other statistical techniques, is one way that assumptions underlying theoretical propositions and the implications of those propositions can be tested for reliability (statistical significance) and robustness (dependence upon statistical technique).

Michael Boskin's advocacy of continued econometric research in the area of optimal taxation theory is easily understood: prescriptions for optimal taxation policy are based directly on many assumptions about consumer behavior. In this reading, Boskin surveys recent econometric research on the relationship between taxation and three consumer activities: charitable giving, labor supply, and savings. At the same time, he discusses the advances in econometric techniques that enabled researchers to perform these studies.

QUESTIONS TO GUIDE THE READING

1. What proof of the robustness of their results should policy makers demand of researchers?

2. Suppose the tax deduction for charitable giving were eliminated. Contrast the effect on charitable giving that would have been predicted by research prior to 1975 with that predicted by the 1975 and 1976 studies by Feldstein and his colleagues.

3. What advances have been made in research on labor supply responses? Why, then, is Boskin pessimistic about the validity of the conclusions that can be drawn from studies in this area?

4. How have the studies on taxation and savings cast doubt on "Denison's Law"?

Michael J. Boskin, "On Some Recent Econometric Research in Public Finance," *American Economic Review* 66 (May 1976), 102–9. Reprinted by permission of the author and the publisher.

Michael J. Boskin is Wohlsord Professor of Economics at Stanford University.

In a field like public finance which is intimately concerned with the formulation and evaluation of public policy, the continuing search for scientific information (upon which to base such policies) acquires a particularly large marginal social product. Yet, throughout the history of public finance there has been at times a harmonious blend of the analytical with the empirical and at other times a flagrant clash between them. From such clashes a synthesis frequently has been developed which gains widespread acceptance. The point is simply that scientific information is only acquired as the intersection of theoretical and empirical research. Once this is recognized, there are three basic ways in which we are able to improve our basic knowledge: we may develop new and better theoretical insights; we may obtain more data, or improved data, or both; and we may develop superior methods by which to analyze data.

In the last few years, a number of excellent examples of each type of progress in public finance have been produced. The purpose of the present paper is to discuss several examples of recent econometric work in order to indicate the enormous progress that has been made in obtaining vastly improved estimates of some of the key parameters with which we are concerned. In so doing, we shall also note how these empirical findings sometimes force us to abandon previously held beliefs and ways of thinking about certain problems.

Toward this end, Section I discusses some recent evidence on the effect of the charitable contributions deduction on giving to charity. This recent work is based on a variety of data sources and employs some relatively advanced econometric techniques to estimate the price and income elasticities of charitable giving. The estimated price elasticities are much larger than those which had been accepted previously and have strikingly different implications for public policy. Thus a reworking of what is basically a simple problem of estimating the demand for a single commodity has resulted in an enormous advance. Section II deals with recent advances in the analysis of the effects of taxes on the supply of labor. I include this topic both to illustrate my major point in an area of incredibly rapid technical progress and to demonstrate how public financiers also must rely on research from related fields. The conceptual and estimation problems in this area are much more complex than those for the analysis of tax incentives for charitable giving, but we are converging (slowly) on a better understanding of the ways in which taxes affect labor supply.

Section III reports on some recent research on the effects of taxes on saving behavior. Again, more and better data and advances in econometric techniques have led to empirical results which are forcing us to rethink some widely accepted propositions on the incidence and effects of taxation. Here the focus is on simple macroeconomic models and different types of data and estimation problems than in the examples cited above.

Finally, Section IV offers a brief summary and suggestions for future research.

I. The Effects of Tax Incentives on Giving to Charity

As an example of a wide range of problems in the analysis of the effects of tax deductibility of any particular item, consider the deductibility of charitable contributions in the income and estate taxes. For those persons itemizing deductions, deductibility lowers the cost of giving to $1 - r$, where r is the marginal tax rate. A frequently used measure of the efficiency of a tax deduction is the ratio of the induced increase in a particular activity (such as charitable giving) due to the deduction, to the revenue foregone by the Treasury. Obviously, this ratio is a key parameter in policy discussion and its size is a function of the price elasticity of demand for the commodity under consideration.

Until quite recently, it was thought that the charitable deduction had very little impact on giving. For example, William Vickrey (1962) concludes that ". . . the evidence would seem to indicate that while the deductibility may increase the gross amount of contributions, it does so by less than the tax relief granted." Further, Michael Taussig (1967) estimated that charities received only five cents for every dollar of revenue foregone by the Treasury. Unfortunately, Vickrey does not estimate a demand for giving equation and Taussig does so in a way that obscures the relationship between giving and after-tax cost.[1] Thus, their conclusions are not the sort of information upon which one would want to base tax policy toward charitable contributions.

In somewhat of a tour de force, Feldstein (1975a,b) and Feldstein and his collaborators (1975a,b, 1976) have examined several complementary data sources and estimated demand for charitable giving equations. The basic equation estimated in each of these studies is of the form

$$ln\ G_i = \alpha_0 + \alpha_1\ ln\ Y_i + \alpha_2\ ln\ P_i + \varepsilon_i$$

where G is charitable contributions, Y is income and P is net-of-tax price. The results indicated a price elasticity in excess of unity in virtually every case. Note that this result suggests that charitable organizations gain absolutely *more* than the Treasury loses in revenue, i.e., the deduction is more than fully efficient. Feldstein (1975a) also notes that eliminating the deduction would increase inequality in the after tax and giving distribution of income.

The most important thing to note about this work from a methodological point of view is the bringing to bear of a variety of different data sources to attempt to answer the same question: How large is the price elasticity of giving to charity? Feldstein and his collaborators use pooled aggregate statistics of income data by income class, individual tax return data from 1962 and 1970 tax returns and household survey data. Thus the advantages of several types of data have been exploited. For example, the household survey data include much information on demographic variables which influence charitable giving and these have been used as additional regressors in the basic equation; the pooled time series data are useful in dealing with the permanent-transitory income problem, etc.

Contrast this approach of examining several data sources in analyzing a particular problem with the typical approach in empirical work in public finance (and other fields of economics). Usually, we witness a sporadic series of difficult to compare studies produced over a long period of time using different data sources, econometric techniques and definitions of variables. Then someone writes a survey paper bemoaning the differences in the studies and heroically attempting to determine if the difference is due to the different data sources, the different techniques used to analyze the data or some change over time or across demographic groups in the underlying behavior. The policy maker frequently is left to choose from a bewildering array of conflicting studies.

While applying the same techniques to a variety of types of data sources will not always lead to virtually identical results, it frequently will be the case that knowledge of the advantages and limitations of the alternative data sources can be combined with econometric techniques to narrow substantially the confidence intervals we attach to estimates of key parameters.

A second major methodological feature of these studies is the attempt to examine a variety of functional forms, definitions of the variables and subsamples of the population in order to test the robustness of the basic results. For example, in addition to the basic constant elasticity demand equation described above, Feldstein et al. estimated equations in which the price elasticity was allowed to vary with price and the income elasticity with income; in which separate price elasticities were estimated for separate income classes and age and marital status groups; and in which alternative reasonable measures of price and income were used. Fortunately, the results supported the basic conclusion of a greater than unitary price elasticity.

Economic theory *generally* guides us to a set of structural relationships to study; it *sometimes* places meaningful restrictions on some of these relationships (non-negativity, symmetry, etc.); however, it *rarely* implies a precise functional form. Further, the available data usually do not contain information which enables us to conform exactly to our theoretical definitions of variables. Hence, it is important to explore the robustness of our results to alternative specifications. Combined with an analysis of alternative data sources, this approach in at least a subset of cases will lead to results which may be imbedded in the subsequent analysis and discussion of the problem under investigation. For example, the results of Feldstein et al. have replaced the earlier results and the simple cross-tabulations from tax data which have ignored these behavioral responses.

We shall see below that studies of the effects of taxes on labor supply suffer in the extreme from noncomparability of data source, estimation technique, functional form and variable measurement, whereas studies of saving behavior partly follow the pattern outlined above. Before turning to these studies, however, it is worth noting one more type of advance that has been made in the recent literature on taxes and charitable contributions.

A variety of recently developed econometric techniques are continually in the process of diffusion throughout the profession. One type which is becoming increasingly important in public finance and other fields which analyze data on individual households is the analysis of qualitative and limited dependent variables. These techniques are designed to deal with situations where the dependent variable in a relationship must take on one of a mutually exclusive set of discrete values or piles up at some limit. For example, a person chooses whether or not to be in the labor force, which college to attend, which transport mode to take to work, etc. In the analysis of data on charitable bequests, one is confronted with precisely such a problem. Only twenty percent of decedents leave anything to charity. Hence, in regressions such as those described above for charitable contributions under the income tax, of charitable bequests on wealth and price, eighty percent of the observations on the dependent variable are zeroes! Fortunately, techniques have been—and are being—developed to handle these problems. As an example of the potential difficulties involved, Stephen K. McNees (1973) estimated such an equation using ordinary least squares. His results predict that most estates bequeath negative amounts to charity.[2] I have reestimated his equations using the truncated normal regression model and have estimated substantial price elasticities of charitable bequests. We shall return to a discussion of these techniques below.

II. The Effects of Taxes on the Supply of Labor

The importance of estimates of the effects of taxes on the supply of labor to the making of intelligent tax policy is difficult to overemphasize. Answers to such structural questions as an appropriate unit of account for taxation and to such fundamental issues such as the optimal progressivity of the income tax depend crucially upon the effects of taxes on labor supply. Indeed, much recent theoretical and empirical research in public finance focuses on relaxing the assumption of fixed factor supplies. We deal with labor and capital in turn.

The last few years have witnessed an explosion of research on labor supply. It illustrates two other crucial types of (admittedly sporadic) progress being made in econometric research in public finance: the availability of new bodies of data potentially useful in the study of a wide variety of problems and major advances in econometric technique. New and important sets of data containing information on individual households have become increasingly available. This development in itself has enormous import for empirical work in public finance as it potentially frees us from exclusive reliance on time series data and its inherent problems. Examples include the 1966 and 1967 *Surveys of Economic Opportunity,* the *Panel Study of Income Dynamics,* and the *National Longitudinal Surveys*. These data allow us to follow the same households over several years; special methods for analyzing such data are now emerging. Finally, controlled social experiments are producing data which complement these other data sources in important ways.

All of these data sources have been used in attempts to estimate labor supply functions. Unfortunately, different techniques have been applied in each of these studies. For example, Boskin (1974) and Robert E. Hall (1974) use the Survey of Economic Opportunity to estimate labor supply for various groups as a function of after-tax income and wage rates. James J. Heckman (1975), using the National Longitudinal Survey, makes an important conceptual advance, but totally ignores taxes in measuring wage rates! Harvey S. Rosen (1973) reports results from this same body of data supporting the hypothesis that it is after-tax rather than gross wage rates that matter. It seems as if each paper has made an advance but generally ignores those made previously. Hence, the studies are extremely difficult to compare and no clear consensus on elasticities of labor supply has emerged. About all that can be said in surveying the studies is that the labor supply of wives seems to be more wage-elastic than that of husbands; while the latter (at least ignoring human investment on the job) appears to be relatively inelastic, estimates of the former range from well under one to well over two. Worse yet, every estimate I have seen is inconsistent in the statistical sense due either to econometric technique used or to measurement of the variables.

The study of labor supply also provides an excellent example of the interaction of data availability, policy relevance and conceptual advances. There is no question that the intellectual interest (not to mention financial support) in research on labor supply was stimulated by the debate over the labor supply effects of a negative income tax. A variety of successive and important conceptual advances have been made. For example, the typical labor supply study of several years ago merely regressed hours of work on wage rates and a measure of income. For groups of the population with labor force participation rates well below 100%, this procedure is inappropriate. Further, imputing wages to those not currently working by comparison with those who are may also lead to inconsistent estimates.[3] For example, Heckman points out that if

$$W_M = f(E, S)$$
$$W_A = f(C, A, W_s, H)$$

(where W_M is the market wage rate facing a potential worker, W_A is the asking wage, E is labor market experience, S is years of schooling, C is the number of children, A is assets, H is hours of work, and W_s is spouse's wage), hours of work will adjust so that $W_A = W_M$ for workers, whereas $W_M < W_A$ if hours of work in the market are zero. He uses this simple observation to build an econometric technique for estimating these two functions, which may be solved for the market labor supply function. The technique is a generalization of the truncated regression model (usually called Tobit analysis) discussed above. It solves many of the problems encountered in the previous work on labor supply.

Unfortunately, Heckman's estimates are not yet readily usable because he ignores taxes in the measurement of wage rates; hence his estimates are inconsistent. G. Hanoch (1975), in an excellent paper, has extended the Heckman notion in a variety of ways. However, nothing like a systematic combination of the improvements in measurement, in conceptualization, and in econometric technique has been used to analyze a variety of complementary data sources. From the point of view of the consumers of estimates of the effects of taxes in labor supply, such a synthesis is badly needed and long overdue.

III. Taxation and Saving

The recent econometric research in taxation and saving behavior has not been pushed forward primarily by new econometric techniques. Rather, it has been, marked by a more careful examination of the fundamental relationships, an attempt to incorporate potentially important missing elements and an examination of alternative data sources and functional forms. In addition to the obvious direct usefulness of this work, it is particularly important because the recent results are forcing us to reexamine widely held views on tax incidence.

The three most important lines of inquiry, in my opinion, have been the study of the relationship of corporate and personal saving, the social security system, and the interest elasticity of the saving rate and public and private marginal propensities to save.

The typical consumption or saving function related consumption or saving to private income after taxes, excluding retained earnings. Feldstein (1973) and Feldstein and G. Fane (1972) have extended this model to include the "components" of capital gains, including retained earnings. The estimates based on U.S. and British time series data, respectively, suggest that the marginal propensity to consume out of retained earnings is two-thirds that out of disposable income. Again, these results are derived from a variety of specifications of the basic relationship, including alternative measures of permanent income. They suggest that consumers see through the corporate veil and (partially) adjust their personal saving to changes in corporate saving.

A second line of work, also pioneered by Feldstein (1974a, 1975d), and contributed to by Alicia H. Munnell (1974), has been the study of the effects of social security on private saving. The enormous increase in social security benefits financed on a pay-as-you go basis has been one of the most important features of the postwar U.S. economy. It is conceivable that the expectation of social security payments during retirement, financed by the generation then working, leads to a decrease in private saving. Feldstein has examined two different types of data to attempt to answer this question. His studies of aggregate U.S. time series and an international cross section imply that an enormous substitution of expected social security benefits for private saving has occurred. Indeed, his best estimates are that the substitution is virtually dollar for dollar and that the U.S. private saving rate has been reduced by thirty percent or more by the social security program.

Finally, Boskin (1976) has reexamined the questions of the interest elasticity of the saving rate and differential marginal propensities to save publically and privately raised by Feldstein (1974a,b), Peter A. Diamond (1970), C. Wright (1969) and Warren E. Weber (1970, 1975). Paying particularly close attention to the measurement of saving and real after-tax rates of return, he estimates an interest elasticity of approximately .4; this estimate is much larger than that found in previous work. He also concludes that the marginal propensity to save out of private after-tax income is over twice that out of government revenue.

Again, as with the study of charitable contributions, these studies are marked by an attempt to bring several data sources to bear on the same question; to examine the robustness of the conclusions to alternative sample periods, definitions of the variables, and functional forms; and to apply the most reasonable econometric techniques warranted by the problem and the data. Unlike the studies of charitable contributions, the studies of taxation and saving have implications far beyond the particular problem addressed. For example, some widely held notions on the incidence of taxation *assume* that the policies under study do not affect saving, the capital-labor ratio, and hence the functional distribution of income. Indeed, much of the profession seems to give a behavioral interpretation to what has come to be called Denison's Law.[4] The studies mentioned above call this assumption into serious question. Feldstein's estimates of the impact of the social security system on private saving indicates that the *benefits* side of social security has sharply increased the rate of interest and decreased the wage rate. My estimates of the interest elasticity of the saving rate imply that the traditional view—embodied in virtually all empirical estimates of tax incidence—that a proportional income tax is borne in proportion to income is erroneous; labor bears more than its proportion of national income. Further, taxes on capital income are largely shifted onto labor; hence, the traditional views on the incidence of capital income taxes may need to be replaced.

IV. Conclusion

I have tried to illustrate in the brief space provided me the important advances that have occurred recently in econometric work in public finance. It seems to me we have entered a new era where both the quality and quantity of econometric research are improving rapidly. As noted above, there are several reasons for this state of affairs. First, a variety of new data sources have become available. Second, new techniques for analyzing that data have been developed. Third, a style of research placing heavy emphasis on exploiting alternative data sources and examining the robustness of the results to alternative specifications has emerged.

I have no doubt that while the particular studies mentioned will be improved by still more and better data and techniques, the methodological message they impart will serve to upgrade the quality of both the future empirical research in public finance and the information upon which sound public policies ultimately must be based.

NOTES

Note: This paper is part of a planned larger survey of empirical research in public finance. It is meant to illustrate the types of progress being made, not to survey the field comprehensively. Indeed, anything approaching a complete list of references would probably exceed my modest page limit! See G. F. Break (1974) for a partial survey.

1. See Martin Feldstein, 1975a.
2. See Boskin, 1976.
3. See J. Heckman, 1975.
4. See P. David and J. Scadding, 1974.

REFERENCES

M. Boskin, "The Economics of the Labor Supply," in G. Cain and H. Watts, eds., *Income Maintenance and Labor Supply,* New York 1974.

———, "Estate Taxation and Charitable Bequests," *J. Publ. Econ., Feb. 1976.*

———, "Taxation Saving and the Rate of Interest," National Bureau of Economic Research, Jan. 1976.

G. F. Break, "Taxation," in A. Blinder, et al., *The Economics of Public Finance,* Brookings Inst., Washington 1974.

P. David and J. Scadding, "Private Savings: Ultrarationality, Aggregation and Denison's Law," *J. Polit. Econ.,* Apr. 1974.

P. Diamond, "Incidence of an Interest Income Tax," *J. Econ. Theory,* Sept. 1970.

M. Feldstein, "Tax Incidence with Growth and Variable Factor Supply," *Quart. J. Econ.,* Nov. 1974a.

———, "Incidence of a Capital Income Tax with Variable Savings Rates," *Rev. Econ. Stud.,* Aug. 1974b.

———, "The Income Tax and Charitable Contributions: Part I," *Nat. Tax J.,* Mar. 1975a.

———, "The Income Tax and Charitable Contributions: Part II," *Nat. Tax J.,* June 1975b.

———, "Social Security, Induced Retirement and Aggregate Capital Accumulation," *J. Polit. Econ.,* Oct. 1974c.

———, "Social Security Programs and Private Savings: International Evidence in an Extended Life-Cycle Model," Harvard Institute for Economic Research, disc. pap., 1975c.

———, "Tax Incentives, Corporate Savings and Capital Accumulation in the United States," *J. Publ. Econ.,* Apr. 1973.

———— and G. Fane, "Taxes, Corporate Dividend Policy and Personal Savings: the British Postwar Experience," *Rev. Econ. Statist.*, 1974.

———— and C. Clotfelter, "Tax Incentives and Charitable Contributions in the United States: A Microeconometric Analysis," *J. Publ. Econ.*, Feb. 1976.

———— and A. Taylor, "Taxation and Charitable Contributions: An Analysis of Individual Tax Return Data for 1962 and 1970," Harvard Institute for Economic Research, disc. pap., 1975a.

———— and M. Boskin, "Effects of the Charitable Deduction on Contributions by Low and Middle Income Households: Evidence from the National Survey of Philanthropy," CREG memo no. 192, Stanford Univ., 1975b.

R. Hall, "Wages, Income and Hours of Work," in G. Cain and H. Watts, eds., *Income Maintenance and Labor Supply,* New York 1974.

G. Hanoch, "Hours and Weeks in the Theory of Labor Supply," Rand memo, 1975.

J. Heckman, "Shadow Prices, Market Wages, and Female Labor Supply," *Econometrica,* 1974.

S. McNees, "Deductibility of Charitable Bequests," *Nat. Tax J.*, Mar. 1973.

A. Munnell, "The Impact of Social Security on Personal Savings," *Nat. Tax J.*, Dec. 1974.

H. Rosen, "The Impact of U.S. Tax Laws on the Labor Supply of Married Women," unpublished dissertation, Harvard 1973.

M. Taussig, "Economic Aspects of the Personal Income Tax Treatment of Charitable Contributions," *Nat. Tax J.*, Mar. 1967.

W. Vickrey, "One Economist's View of Philanthropy," in F. Dickinson, ed., *Philanthropy and Public Policy,* National Bureau of Economic Research 1962.

W. Weber, "The Effect of Interest Rates on Aggregate Consumption," *Amer. Econ. Rev.*, Sept. 1970.

————, "Interest Rates, Inflation, and Consumer Expenditure," *Amer. Econ. Rev.*, Dec. 1975.

C. Wright, "Saving and the Rate of Interest," in A. Harberger and M. Bailey, *The Taxation of Income from Capital,* Brookings Inst., Washington 1967.

SELECTION 37

RANDALL G. HOLCOMBE, JOHN D. JACKSON,
AND ASGHAR ZARDKOOHI

The National Debt Controversy

"Is taxation equivalent to debt?" This question was argued by
David Ricardo and Adam Smith around the turn of the eighteenth
century and continues to be a controversial topic for debate today.
The authors of this reading survey the history of the debate and the
arguments used by economists on each side of the issue. The focus
of the discussion is on the equivalent question: "Who bears the
burden of the debt—current or future taxpayers?"

QUESTIONS TO GUIDE THE READING

1. How could the "burden of the debt" be shifted into the future?
2. Under what circumstances will taxation be equivalent to debt
   finance?
3. What effect might the fact that your heirs will be taxed to pay
   off the debt have on your decision to leave an inheritance?
4. If taxation is not the same as debt, what differences might you
   expect to see in the type of voters who would support one
   versus the other method of financing government expenditures?

One of the oldest controversies in economic theory concerns the shifting of
the burden of the national debt. Simply stated, one side of the argument
claims that the burden of the debt is borne at the time the debt is issued; the
other says that the burden of the debt is shifted forward in time. The debate
began before the publication of *The Wealth of Nations*, and still has not been
resolved. A large number of issues are involved, and many authors have
previously written with the intent of offering the final resolution to the controversy.[1] In view of the lack of success of those writers this paper has a
more modest ambition: to review and simplify some of the basic points of
disagreement. . . . Hopefully, this framework of analysis will lend some
clarity to the basic issues of the debate.

There are two basic issues that have been important in the history of the

---

Randall G. Holcombe, John D. Jackson, and Asghar Zardkoohi, "The National Debt Controversy," *Kyklos 34* (1981, Fasc. 2), 186–202.

Randall G. Holcombe is Professor of Economics at Florida State University. **John D. Jackson** is
Associate Professor of Economics at Auburn University. **Asghar Zardkoohi** is Associate Professor of Management at Texas A & M University.

national debt controversy. The first, loosely stated, is who bears the burden of the debt. The second is whether debt should be used to finance public expenditures. The simultaneous examination of these two questions has sometimes clouded the analysis of some fundamental issues. The general thrust of the question about who bears the burden of the debt centers on whether the debt can be shifted forward in time. While this is the starting point for most analyses, some writers have mixed an analysis of the desirability of debt finance along with an evaluation of who bears the burden, resulting in a sort of cost-benefit analysis of the debt-financed expenditures rather than a simple analysis of the shifting of the burden.[2] This line of analysis has brought some normative elements into the controversy, which has at times tended to obscure the fundamental question concerning whether the burden of the debt can be shifted. In order to avoid a cost-benefit analysis of the debt-financed expenditures and focus solely on the possibility of shifting the burden of the debt, the burden of the debt should be analyzed independently of the merits of debt finance, under the assumption that government expenditures are held constant. For purposes of theoretical analysis, the effect of financing a given level of expenditures by some mix of taxation and debt should be compared to financing the same expenditures by reducing taxes and replacing the tax revenue with debt. The burden of the debt question then asks whether taxation is equivalent to debt. This line of analysis can be traced back to Ricardo.[3]

I. Is Taxation Equivalent to Debt?

Before 1958, the distinction between internal and external debt was crucial to the debate, and Lerner's [1948] argument that internal debt is no burden because we owe it to ourselves can be traced back at least to 1735.[4] Adam Smith [1776, p. 881] took issue with this viewpoint, stating that "The practice of funding has gradually enfeebled every state which has adopted it."[5] Another way of viewing the "we owe it to ourselves" argument with respect to the internal debt is that the real cost of government spending is the opportunity cost, and current projects must be undertaken using currently available resources. Therefore, the opportunity cost must be paid when the debt is issued. The view that the burden of the debt is borne at the same time that the debt is issued was labeled "the new orthodoxy" by Buchanan [1958]. Buchanan attacked this position on the grounds that when the debt is issued, both the buyers and the sellers of the bonds engage in voluntary transactions, and so cannot be made worse off. When interest payments are made on the debt, however, tax rates must be higher than they otherwise would have been. The taxpayers who do not voluntarily agree to the higher taxes are made worse off; therefore, they bear the burden of the debt.

This basic argument was supported and developed by other writers,[6] and has become more sophisticated in the process of development. However, the mechanism behind the shifting of the burden is straightforward. The issuance of government debt competes for the same funds that would otherwise purchase private debt. The additional demand for funds (supply of bonds) causes the interest rate to rise, reducing the amount of loans demanded in the private sector. This reduces private sector capital accumulation, which lowers the consumption of the individual in the future. While it is true that the resources going into the public sector are present resources, the burden of the debt is still shifted forward in time. The issuance of debt reduces present investment, and therefore reduces future consumption.

This new and improved argument that the burden of the debt is shifted forward in time was met by a new defense. The issuance of debt implies that either the debt must be repaid in the future or the interest of the debt must be paid in perpetuity. In either case, taxpayers have a liability in the form of future tax payments which has a present value just equal to the present value of the government bonds sold. The creation of the asset of bonds is just offset by the creation of the liability of future taxes. Thompson [1967] discussed some of the implications of the creation of the tax liability, and a similar model was developed by Barro [1974]. Thompson's model relies on the artifact of infinitely long-lived people, whereas Barro arrives at the same conclusion by incorporating inheritances into a finite lives model.

Although the debate had been simmering since the publication of Buchanan's [1958] book, the publication of Barro's [1974] article heightened the controversy. Those who believe taxation and debt to be equivalent base their conclusion on a model in which inheritances link generations, as developed by Barro. Those who believe that the burden of debt financing is passed forward in time cite the shortcomings of the Barro model in depicting the actual process of debt issue or inheritance. . . . As presented in the literature, the issues sometimes tend to seem obscure, and frequently examine in a complex model only a small part of the controversy. The discussion that follows is intended to simplify these issues. . . .

II. Are Government Bonds Net Wealth?

Barro sets up a simple analytical model to evaluate the effect of the issuance of government bonds. The arguments in each individual's utility function are his own consumption and the utility of his heir in the next generation. Since his heir will have this same utility function, the effect is an individual who acts as if he has an infinite time horizon. Barro then performs an experiment by having the government issue bonds to finance a transfer payment to the present generation. The bonds will be redeemed later. The result of the experiment is that the present generation realizes that the future redemption of the bonds will impose a future tax liability with a present value just equal to the amount of bond issue. In order to compensate the next generation for the inheritance of the liability, the present generation will increase its bequest of assets to offset the future tax liability. Since the future tax liability is created at the same time as the bond assets, the issuance of bonds will simultaneously cause the current generation to increase their saving to finance the future tax liability. In this way, an addition to the national debt will cause an equal increase in saving, implying that the debt issue has no real effects.

The first thing to notice about the Barro model is that it does not model exactly the fundamental issue in the national debt controversy. The fundamental issue is whether taxation is equivalent to debt, yet Barro's comparative statics contrasts an initial equilibrium with a second equilibrium where debt is issued to finance additional government expenditures. The comparative statics experiment that would exactly model the controversy would hold government expenditures constant and replace some taxation with an equal amount of debt. Within the Barro model, it is apparent that this second experiment would show taxation to be equivalent to debt, but this difference between Barro's original model and the issue of subsequent debate is worth noting in order to make sure that at least the issue of the debate is clear. The question at issue is whether taxation has the same real effects as debt finance, and while Barro does not model this directly, his model is used as the foundation for the conclusion that the two methods of public finance are equivalent in their real effects.

The Barro model has been attacked on three primary grounds by those who believe that taxation and debt are not equivalent in their real effects. The first ground is that the generation that buys the bonds suffers from fiscal illusion. They fully capitalize the value of the bond assets at the time of issue, but the future tax liability associated with the bonds is not fully capitalized. The second ground for attacking the conclusions of the Barro model regards the interdependence of utility functions. This objection suggests that the interdependence of utility functions is not quite as specified in the Barro model. The third ground for objection to the Barro model is institutional. Even people with no fiscal illusion and possessing the utility function specified in the Barro model operate in a different institutional environment from that specified in the Barro model, and the institutional differences alter people's behavior from that specified in the model. These grounds will be discussed in turn, but it is important to note that none of them faults the logic inherent in the model. In all three cases, the objections are that the assumptions of the model misrepresent reality in such a way that the conclusions of the model do not apply to the real world.

III. Fiscal Illusion

Buchanan [1976] is the opponent of Barro's hypothesis who most visibly argues that fiscal illusion destroys the equivalency of taxation and debt. The bond assets are fully capitalized by the purchasers, but taxpayers do not fully account for the future tax liabilities at the time the debt is issued. As a result, the economy behaves as if the bonds were a net addition to wealth, and present consumption is increased. This reduces present investment, and the lower capital accumulation harms future generations.

This is the oldest facet of the national debt controversy, and both sides of the debate were clearly presented by Ricardo. In his *Principles,* Ricardo presented the essence of the Barro model in a very straightforward manner, causing Buchanan to label Barro's conclusion "the Ricardian equivalence theorem." O'Driscoll [1977] nicely summarizes the fiscal illusion debate using passages from Ricardo to illustrate not only that Ricardo saw both sides of the debate, but that he sided with Buchanan in believing that taxpayers suffer from fiscal illusion.

IV. Nature of Interdependent Utility Functions

The objection to the Barro model that the consumption patterns of individuals are best represented in a life-cycle model where bequests are peripheral is most associated with the work of Feldstein [1976a, 1976b]. Feldstein uses empirical evidence in the case of Social Security to demonstrate that individuals will reduce their private saving when the asset of promised Social Security payments is created and at the same time a Social Security tax liability of the same present value is created. Empirically, individuals capitalize the asset more fully than the liability. Both Barro and Feldstein agree that the promise to pay Social Security benefits is analytically equivalent to the issuance of bonds, so Feldstein argues that his empirical evidence on Social Security implies that the burden of the national debt is shifted to the future via lower saving rates.

While Feldstein's ultimate evidence is empirical, he develops his analysis within a life-cycle model which demonstrates that individuals will reduce their saving when it is possible to shift the burden of Social Security or debt to the future. Feldstein further argues that in a growing economy, the debt need never be paid off as long as the growth rate of the economy is at least as high as the interest rate. The debt can simply be refinanced. Even if the growth rate is not that large, some of the debt can be refinanced through growth, lowering the burden on future generations.

This objection to the Barro model might be labeled the life-cycle objection because it has been developed within the life-cycle hypothesis; but the objection more generally is that the Barro model does not accurately depict the way in which present generations are concerned about their heirs. Individuals save early in their lives in order to live off those savings in their later years, and would be likely to die with some assets simply because their time of death is uncertain and those assets that they possess at death are the hedge against the possibility of a longer life. If one's bequest was simply a method of passing purchasing power to one's heirs, then the existence of inheritance taxes alone would suggest that the individual choose a different method than dying with assets.

V. Institutional Differences

Another type of objection to Barro's model is that actual institutions differ in important ways from the institutions in the Barro model. Drazen [1978], for example, suggests that if investment in the human capital of the next generation is possible, the burden of the national debt could be shifted forward in time even in the absence of fiscal illusion and if individuals had the utility functions that Barro assumed. This is because older generations cannot recapture investments they make in the human capital of their heirs. The existence of the national debt provides a way that present generations could in effect charge their heirs for investments in human capital.

Perhaps the most significant institutional difference, however, is that the amount of debt incurred by the government is only a partial determinant of the burden that will be placed on an individual's heirs. If the Barro model had included many different families with heirs that would be earning many different incomes that could not be precisely predicted, then an individual in the present generation will have no way to know what would be the burden of the debt falling on his direct heirs. If the individual's heirs will have a small income, then their relative share of taxes (from which the debt will be repaid) will be low, and a smaller inheritance would be justified. Larger incomes of the heirs would imply a larger tax burden, and perhaps a larger inheritance. In this case, the larger tax burden would be due to a larger income, and a parent interested in his heir's utility level might feel it unnecessary to compensate the heir because he earns a higher income.

All of this is complicated by the fact that leaving a larger bequest increases the wealth of the heir and so his ability to be taxed. That is, a bequest to offset the burden of the debt will increase the heir's share of the burden. A smaller bequest would mean that the heir is responsible for less of the burden of the debt, because his wealth and therefore his tax share will be smaller. Thus, the mere act of leaving an inheritance increases the burden of the national debt placed on the individual's direct heirs.

VI. A Final Argument

These arguments against the equivalence of debt and taxation show the possibility of substantial shortcomings in the model purporting their equivalence. As Feldstein [1976a, p. 335] notes when evaluating the behavior of bequestors: "The subtlety of the required anticipations makes it unlikely that households actually do respond as Barro's model suggests. Since the economics profession has previously ignored the need to adjust bequests to compensate for future tax liabilities, it may be safe to assume that households also have not made the adjustment implied by the new theory." Perhaps the best reply to this comment and to the other criticisms of the equivalence theory is that individuals do not need to understand the subtleties involved; they only need to respond to prices in the market. More debt will lead to a higher interest rate, and a higher interest rate will induce the additional saving. Economists did not need to discover the invisible hand before it began working to allocate resources.

In brief summary, then, the argument that taxation and debt are equivalent in their real effects rests upon a model of intergenerational transfers that operates in a manner such that substituting a dollar of debt for a dollar of taxation will increase saving by one dollar in order to offset the future tax liability. The arguments for nonequivalence suggest that for a number of reasons the future tax liability will not be fully capitalized, so that the substitution of a dollar of debt for a dollar of taxation will not cause saving to increase by the amount of the newly issued debt. . . .

NOTES

Note: We are grateful to James Buchanan, Mark Fratrik, and Richard Saba for assistance and helpful comments.

1. See, for example, Modigliani [1961, p. 730], who says that his approach "leads to a consistent and yet straightforward answer to all relevant questions." West [1975, p. 179] claims that using his analysis, "the central features of the debate— are shown to disappear." See also Mishan [1963], whose title "How to Make a Burden of the Public Debt" conveys his view of the debate.
2. Some writers who have, at least to some extent, mingled these ideas are Mishan [1963], Modigliani [1961], and West [1975].
3. Ricardo [1821, p. 161].
4. See Melon [1735, Chapter XXIII].
5. Smith makes this statement after remarking, on page 879, "In the payment of the interest of the public debt, it has been said, it is the right hand which pays the left . . . It supposes that the whole public debt is owing to the inhabitants of the country . . . But that the whole debt were owing to the inhabitants of the country, it would not upon that account be less pernicious."
6. A frequently cited paper appearing shortly after Buchanan's book is Bowen, Davis and Kopf [1960]. A more recent proponent of this view is Martin Feldstein, whose paper [1976a] cites some relevant works. Modigliani [1961] also supports the shifting argument, as does Diamond [1965].

REFERENCES

Barro, Robert J.: "Are Government Bonds Net Wealth?," *Journal of Political Economy,* 82 (1974), Nov./Dec., pp. 1095–1117.

Bowen, W. G., Davis, R. G., and Kopf, D. K.: "The Public Debt: A Burden on Future Generations?," *American Economic Review,* 50 (1960), September, pp. 701–706.

Buchanan, James M.: *Public Principles of Public Debt,* Homewood, Illinois: Richard D. Irwin, Inc., 1958.

Buchanan, James M.: "Barro on the Ricardian Equivalence Theorem," *Journal of Political Economy,* 84 (1976), April, pp. 337–342.

Diamond, Peter A.: "National Debt in a Neoclassical Growth Model," *American Economic Review,* LV (1965), December, pp. 1126–1150.

Drazen, Allan: "Government Debt, Human Capital, and Bequests in a Life-Cycle Model," *Journal of Political Economy,* 86 (1978), June, pp. 505–516.

Feldstein, Martin: "Perceived Wealth in Bonds and Social Security: A Comment," *Journal of Political Economy,* 84 (1976), April, pp. 331–336 (1976a).

Feldstein, Martin: "Social Security and Private Savings: International Evidence in an Extended Life-Cycle Model," in *The Economics of Public Services,* edited by M. Feldstein and R. Inman, London: Macmillan, 1976 (1976b).

Melon, Jean François: *Essai Politique sur le Commerce,* Amsterdam: F. Changuion, 1735.

Mishan, E. J.: "How to Make a Burden of the Public Debt," *The Journal of Political Economy* LXXI (1963), December, pp. 529–542.

Modigliani, Franco: "Long-run Implications of Alternative Fiscal Policies and the Burden of the National Debt," *The Economic Journal* LXXI (1961), December, pp. 730–755.

O'Driscoll, Gerald P., Jr.: "The Ricardian Nonequivalence Theorem," *Journal of Political Economy,* 85 (1977), February, pp. 207–210.

Ricardo, David: *The Principles of Political Economy* (1821), London: J. M. Dent & Sons, Ltd., 1912.

Smith, Adam: *The Wealth of Nations* (1776), New York: Modern Library.

Theil, Henri: *Principles of Econometrics,* New York, John Wiley and Sons, 1971.

Thompson, Earl A.: "Debt Instruments in Both Macroeconomic Theory and Capital Theory," *American Economic Review* LVII (1967), December, pp. 1196–1210.

West, E. G.: "Public Debt Burden and Cost Theory," *Economic Inquiry* XIII (1975), June, pp. 179–190.

Tax Reform

The following three selections focus on economists' definition of income for tax purposes and the changes in personal and corporate taxation under the U.S. Tax Reform Act of 1986.

SELECTION 38

RICHARD GOODE

The Economic Definition of Income

The credibility of income as a basis for assessing a person's ability to pay taxes depends critically on the way income is defined. In a search for the most desirable definition of income for tax purposes, Richard Goode compares several alternatives. He argues that the Schanz-Haig-Simons definition is the most useful and examines various conceptual questions and problems associated with it. This definition has been most widely accepted by economists and, indeed, has served as a major impetus in tax reform efforts in the United States and abroad.

QUESTIONS TO GUIDE THE READING

1. Why do definitions of income that stress capital maintenance favor investor income or labor income?
2. Owners of baseball teams have been permitted to deduct a depreciation allowance for players under contract. Is this consistent with the Schanz-Haig-Simons definition of income?
3. Why might it be desirable to tax the imputed rental value of owner-occupied dwellings?
4. To what extent have recent reforms of the U.S. personal income tax moved in the direction of Schanz-Haig-Simons?

Richard Goode, "The Economic Definition of Income," in Joseph A. Pechman (ed.), *Comprehensive Income Taxation*, The Brookings Institute, 1977, 1–30. Reprinted by permission of the publisher.

Richard Goode is a part-time Professorial Lecturer at the School of Advanced International Studies, Johns Hopkins University.

Much of the discussion of the individual income tax in the United States over the past two decades has stressed inequities and economic defects due to the erosion of the tax base and has led up to recommendations for a broader-based tax. This approach implies that there is an income concept against which practice can be meaningfully appraised. While tax specialists have often stated a formal definition, they have not always paid heed to it in their policy prescriptions. Many other participants in the extensive talk and writing about the tax base appear to assume that everyone knows what income is, or that adjusted gross income as identified in the Internal Revenue Code or personal income as estimated by the Department of Commerce is a suitable measure.

Economic theorists have not agreed on the definition of income. There is an extensive and tedious literature on the subject, enlivened by a few notable contributions. Some of the keenest analysts have concluded that it may well be impossible to define income rigorously. Thus Henry Simons said: "That it should be possible to delimit the concept precisely in every direction is hardly to be expected"; in another passage he wrote about "insuperable difficulties to achievement of a rigorous conception of personal income."[1] Kaldor asserted that "the problem of *defining* individual Income, quite apart from any problem of practical measurement, appears in principle insoluble."[2]

But fortunately the total absence of ambiguity is not required to make a concept useful. If rigor were the ruling criterion, discourse on public policy would be short. Despite the difficulties, income is in practice measured and taxed, though unsatisfactorily in many respects. A premise of this paper is that individual income can be defined reasonably clearly in a sense that is relevant for taxation. If, as I believe is true, there is more than one definition that meets the requirements, a choice can be made by reference to general usage and, more important, to notions of justice and ability to pay. Measurability is also essential.

A good definition of income is an indispensable intellectual foundation for the evaluation of an income tax statute. It serves as a basis for the orderly consideration of specific questions about inclusions, exclusions, and deductions. Without such a basis, discussion is likely to be unnecessarily discursive and the ad hoc conclusions reached may lack force. But the definition should not be viewed as a Platonic ideal to which unquestioned deference is owed. Income, in the words of an able lawyer, is "a concept calling for creative elaboration to effectuate the practical implementation of the purposes of the [income] tax."[3] Few important issues can be resolved merely by appealing to a definition.

This paper is concerned with the economic definition of personal income for tax purposes. Definitions for use in the theory of capital, social accounting, and other fields may properly differ from that which is preferred for individual taxation. No systematic attention is given in the paper to special problems related to the definition and measurement of business income.

Proposed Definitions

This section reviews several definitions of income that have been advanced by economists, sometimes explicitly for taxation but more often for other purposes, and briefly indicates some of their implications. One of the definitions has received far more support—from American specialists at least—than the others for use in taxation, and I shall try to explain why this is so. The preferred definition, nevertheless, is subject to a number of conceptual and practical difficulties that will be considered in later sections.

Definitions Stressing Capital Maintenance

Since 1976 was the bicentennial of *The Wealth of Nations* as well as of the Declaration of Independence, the filial piety proper for an economist impels me to begin my survey with Adam Smith. He wrote:

> The gross revenue of all the inhabitants of a great country, comprehends the whole annual produce of their land and labour; the neat revenue, what remains free to them after deducting the expence of maintaining; first, their fixed; and, secondly, their circulating capital; or what, without encroaching upon their capital, they can place in their stock reserved for immediate consumption, or spend upon their subsistence, conveniences, and amusements.[4]

Smith's definition in form pertains to what would now be called national income or social income, but in content it resembles other definitions that are clearly intended to apply to individuals. While the two concepts are related and many common problems are involved in their quantification, important differences in purpose justify differences in coverage and in the treatment of particular items. In national income statistics the primary objective is to estimate the aggregate value of goods and services produced, whereas in individual income accounts the objective is to measure an individual's (or a family's) command over economic resources. It should not be expected that the summation of individual incomes, so conceived, will equal national income.

The concept of income as what a person can consume without impairing his capital is a persistent one. It still appeals to economists. For example, J. R. Hicks in his influential treatise *Value and Capital*, first published in 1939 and revised in 1946, is reminiscent of Smith in the following:

> The purpose of income calculations in practical affairs is to give people an indication of the amount which they can consume without impoverishing themselves. Following out this idea, it would seem that we ought to define a man's income as the maximum value which he can consume during a week, and still expect to be as well off at the end of the week as he was at the beginning. . . . I think it is fairly clear that this is what the central meaning must be.[5]

Behind Smith's dignified eighteenth-century prose and Hicks's self-consciously homely phrasing lie many complexities relating to the meaning of "encroaching upon . . . capital" or being "as well off at the end of the week as . . . at the beginning." Even the meaning and measurement of consumption are unclear on close examination, though this difficulty has received much less attention than has the problem of capital maintenance.

Moving out from the "central meaning" of income, Hicks elaborates three definitions, or approximations to the central concept, which differ in the interpretation of keeping capital intact. The third version—and the one he prefers but acknowledges to be imperfect—is "the maximum amount of money which the individual can spend this week, and still expect to be able to spend the same amount *in real terms* in each ensuing week."[6] By thus asserting that recurrence, or permanence, is an essential attribute of income, Hicks links his definition with an idea that has been common in Great Britain but less so in the United States. The idea, however, was endorsed in a presidential address to the American Economic Association entitled "The Concept of Income, as Recurrent, Consumable Receipts."[7]

Although the central meaning of income, as seen by Hicks, can be reconciled with what I regard as the best definition of income for tax purposes, his own elaboration is different. Basically, income as defined by Hicks is subjective, dependent on the expectations of the individual, and hence not usable as a tax base. If an effort is made to salvage the idea of recurrence or permanence by relating it to market values rather than to individual expectations, the outcome is not a measurable concept of income suitable for all individuals. What may be evolved is a rationalization for omitting capital gains and losses from income while including interest, dividends, and rent. A distinction between change in capital value and yield may be meaningful in an agricultural society with certain legal institutions, or in the world of abstract economic theory, but it does not fit contemporary reality. There is in fact no clear difference between the function of changes in the market value of assets and the interest, dividend, or rental payments associated with them. Nor is it possible to distinguish for tax purposes between recurrent and nonrecurrent or expected and unexpected changes in market value. Another objection to Hicks's interpretation of income is that it concentrates on the yield of capital and applies awkwardly, if at all, to earnings from personal effort, which make up the greater part of what is commonly regarded as income and are taxed as such.

Source and Periodicity Concepts

Akin to definitions incorporating the criterion of recurrence or permanence are definitions that would restrict income to periodic flows from continuing sources. This approach may have been influenced by the origin of income taxation in several European countries as partial taxes or groups of schedular taxes on income from particular sources, as distinguished from a unitary

tax on an individual's total income. The implications of the source and periodicity concepts are similar to those connected with Hicks's version of the
capital-maintenance concept: the exclusion of capital gains and losses and
"casual" receipts such as gambling or lottery winnings and various lump-
sum payments on retirement or loss of employment. The weaknesses are
also similar: the artificiality of the distinction between capital gains and
other investment yields, the inconsistent treatment of income from personal
effort and income from other sources, and—more generally—the omission
of items that contribute to the ability to pay taxes.

Fisher's Definition

Another definition that grew out of theorizing about capital and its yield is
that of Fisher. According to him, income is fundamentally "yield," consisting of the services rendered by property or persons. Since the only services
desired for themselves are those that satisfy consumers' wants, income, as
defined by Fisher, is what others call consumption.[8] Savings and increases
or decreases in the value of capital assets are explicitly excluded. Apart from
the saving decisions of owners, no provision is made for capital maintenance, and no attention is paid to the question of permanence or recurrence.
Income is equivalent to consumption, regardless of whether spending is financed out of current earnings or by using up capital.

Fisher developed his definition before the modern income tax was
adopted in the United States and, he assures us, independently of any views
that he came to hold on social policy and taxation.[9] He later, however, en-
thusiastically advocated its use for taxation and argued that an "income"
tax based on his definition would be fairer and economically superior to the
existing tax.

For a long time Fisher insisted that the meaning of income should be
restricted to his concept, but finally he gave up this point and conceded that
in addition to "services" or "yield" income, as he defined it, there was another useful concept, "enrichment" income or "accretion," consisting of
consumption plus capital increase (or minus capital decrease).[10] Indeed he
remarked: "While yield is the more fundamental concept, accretion is, for
some purposes (other than taxation), the more useful."[11]

Although Fisher's argumentation sometimes appears to be reducible to
the proposition that the correct base for the income tax must be "income"
as he defined it for another purpose—and in a sense different from common
usage—his writings are intellectually far superior to many others on the subject. When he does discuss tax policy Fisher makes a respectable case for
preferring an expenditure tax (personal consumption tax) to a conventional
income tax. He also deserves credit for addressing many of the practical
problems that would have to be solved in order to put into effect an expenditure tax. I am not persuaded that the expenditure tax is better than the
income tax, but I shall reserve for my discussion of the accretion concept

the few comments on the advantages of the income tax for which there is space in this paper.

The Schanz-Haig-Simons Definition

The income definition that has received most support from American tax specialists is usually called the Haig-Simons concept but more accurately and less parochially could be named the Schanz-Haig-Simons (S-H-S) concept or definition.[12] Developed explicitly for tax purposes, this is the accretion concept, which defines personal income as the sum of consumption and accumulation.

Haig stated that income is "the increase or accretion in one's power to satisfy his wants in a given period in so far as that power consists of (*a*) money itself, or, (*b*) anything susceptible of valuation in terms of money. More simply stated, the definition of income which the economist offers is this: Income is the *money value of the net accretion to one's economic power between two points of time.*"[13] He emphasized that the definition is in terms of the power to satisfy economic wants rather than the satisfactions themselves and pointed out that this means that income is received when the power is obtained and not when it is exercised. This is to say, income includes savings as well as consumption.

Simons defined personal income for tax purposes as "the algebraic sum of (1) the market value of rights exercised in consumption and (2) the change in the value of the store of property rights between the beginning and end of the period in question." He added, "In other words, it is merely the result obtained by adding consumption during the period to 'wealth' at the end of the period and then subtracting 'wealth' at the beginning."[14]

In an enumeration that may have appeared deliberately provocative in 1896 in the light of much doctrine and tax practice, Schanz made clear that his definition included not only ordinary profits but also the usufruct of property, gifts, inheritances, legacies, lottery winnings, insurance proceeds, annuities, and windfall gains of all kinds and that all interest paid and capital losses should be deducted.[15]

As noted above, the S-H-S definition can be reconciled with a concept going back at least as far as Adam Smith. Income is the amount that one could consume without experiencing any increase or decrease in his capital. The reconciliation is valid, however, only on the basis of a particular and relatively simple view of the meaning of maintaining capital intact: capital comprises only nonhuman wealth, and it is intact if its money value does not change within the period.[16] In this sense, capital is equivalent to what is commonly called net worth in accounting statements.

Adherents to definitions stressing capital maintenance, however, usually have in mind a quite different interpretation. Only rarely is this clearly stated, and reliance is frequently placed on figures of speech—often a harvest metaphor—rather than on accounting statements. The intention is to exclude from income capital gains and losses and many nonrecurrent accretions to capital. Hicks has provided the sophisticated version of this interpretation of maintaining capital intact. As argued above, Hicks's version is unusable for taxation because it cannot be objectively measured; even if it could be approximated its policy implications would be unacceptable. The emphasis on the permanence of the real level of consumption accords with the rentier's aspiration in a world of uncertainty and inflation. A parallel concept can hardly be applied to entrepreneurs or recipients of income from personal effort. A definition of taxable income that omits capital gains and nonrecurrent or "casual" receipts will favor investors and speculators in securities, real estate, and commodities.

The Fisher definition, in contrast, is objective and measurable in principle (although there would be practical difficulties in applying it). Concern about capital maintenance and permanence or recurrence drop out of the formal requirements, or more accurately, the tax authorities would accept whatever provision the individual thought it appropriate to make for capital maintenance. But I do not believe that legislators or the public thought that a direct tax on consumption was being imposed when the income tax was enacted.

The reasons for preferring the S-H-S concept to Fisher's concept are really the reasons for preferring an income tax to an expenditure tax. This is not the place to elaborate the arguments, but a brief statement is essential, even at the risk of dogmatism. As I see it the income tax is superior in principle to the expenditure tax, first because income is generally a better index of ability to pay than is consumption. Both the amount of income obtained and the amount consumed depend on the decisions and opportunities of the individual, but consumption reflects an additional choice, that is, the disposal of the power to consume that accrues to one within a period of time. It is intuitively appealing to say that an individual's ability to pay is measured by the whole set of his additional consumption opportunities rather than by the subset that he elects to utilize currently. Another reason for preferring the income tax is that accumulation itself is an objective and a source of satisfaction distinguishable from current or future consumption. To the extent that progressive taxation is reguarded as a means of preventing excessive inequality, total income or wealth is preferable to consumption as a tax base because accumulation enhances the economic and political power and the social status of the individual. The proposition sometimes advanced that a tax on consumption is superior because it is apportioned according to the use of resources rather than according to one's contribution to production is misleading. Savers and investors direct the use of economic resources no less than do consumers. Whether private consumption or private investment should be displaced to make room for government expenditure is an important question of economic policy that ought to be debated on its merits.

Although the S-H-S definition has been accepted by most American specialists as the best available for tax purposes, a number of conceptual and practical questions are encountered in trying to apply it. I turn now to some of these issues. Before doing so, however, I should like to emphasize that my concentration on issues relating to the S-H-S concept should not be taken to imply that the difficulties could be avoided by adopting one of the other definitions. Many of the problems to be discussed would arise in connection with the other definitions, and there would be some special difficulties as well.

Conceptual Questions about the S-H-S Definition

This section considers several questions related to the meaning or acceptability of the S-H-S definition; questions that mainly concern difficulties of administration and compliance are discussed in the next section.

Price-Level Changes

A leading cause of changes in the money value of net worth, and hence a source of positive or negative income according to S-H-S, is fluctuations in the average price level. This presents some conceptual questions and important issues of policy and administration. They are outside the scope of this conference, however, and will not be discussed here.[17]

Double Counting in Relation to Capital Gains

An objection to including in income changes in the value of capital assets, as required by the S-H-S definition, is that such gains and losses merely reflect future income increases or decreases and that including them in both present and future income results in double counting and in double taxation or double deductions.[18] This objection is closely related to the general argument that an income tax results in double taxation of savings but is narrower in scope.

If one accepts the proposition that in taxing income the objective is to apportion the liability with reference to accretions in the power to consume rather than actual consumption, there is no irrationality or inequity in taxing both a capital gain and the subsequent income that it foretells. These are distinct though not independent accretions to consumption power. Where the increase in yield is of finite duration—for example, where it relates to a building or a piece of machinery—a full accrual system should permit the gain to be written off over the remaining life of the asset through periodic valuations or increased depreciation allowances. Thus the decline in consumption power associated with the diminishing value of the asset will reduce taxable income. (Under a system that taxes capital gains only when realized, a similar result will obtain if the asset is sold and the buyer depreciates his cost over the remaining life.) Where the increased yield is for an asset with an unlimited, or indefinite, life—for example, a share of corporate stock—adjusting future income will be unnecessary unless the expected yield and market value of the asset change again.

A highly simplified illustration may help clarify the case of an unexpected increase in the yield of a depreciable asset, with full accrual accounting according to the S-H-S definition. Assume a discount rate of 15 percent a year and consider an asset with a two-year life that throws off its yield in equal installments of $50 on the last day of each of the two years. In a perfect market the cost of the asset on the first day of year 1 and an investor's expected gross yield, depreciation allowance (straight-line), and net taxable income in years 1 and 2 will be as shown in column 1 below (all columns are in dollars):

	1	2	3
Year 1			
Cost	81.29	81.29	81.29
Capital gain	. . .	81.29	. . .
Gross yield	50.00	100.00	100.00
Depreciation allowance	40.65	81.29	40.65
Net taxable income	9.35	100.00	59.35
Year 2			
Gross yield	50.00	100.00	100.00
Depreciation allowance	40.64	81.29	40.64
Net taxable income	9.36	18.71	59.36
Years 1 and 2			
Net taxable income	18.71	118.71	118.71

If on the second day of year 1 it is discovered that the yield of the asset will be twice what was expected on the previous day, the position of an investor who bought on the first day will be approximately as shown in column 2. Column 3 shows the outcome if capital gains are included in taxable income only when realized rather than when accrued. It will be seen that the aggregate taxable income is the same in columns 2 and 3, though distributed differently between the years.

Human Wealth

The S-H-S concept does not include human wealth in capital or net worth, and changes in the value of human wealth are not taken into account in measuring accumulation. Thus, for example, a professional athlete is not seen as having experienced a gain in net worth when his skill is "discovered" and his future earning power is enhanced, nor is he permitted to deduct a depreciation allowance to reflect the decrease of the capitalized value of his expected future earnings with the passage of time and the shortening of his remaining career. In contrast, the owner of a racehorse has a capital gain in analogous circumstances and is entitled to depreciation allowances. The difference arises from the political and legal system, which classifies as property a horse but not a human being. It is entirely appropriate that this fundamental distinction be reflected in the definition of taxable income. No one appears to have contested the exclusion of increases in the value of human capital, but depreciation allowances to cover the disappearance of human earning capacity have often been advocated. These, however, would be unjustified except for deductions to recoup the cost of education and training and other investments that add to earning power.

Interest Rate Changes

A frequent source of capital gains and losses is changes in the interest rate at which expected future yields are discounted. For example, if the relevant interest rate falls from 9 percent to 8 percent, a perpetual stream of yields of $100 a year will increase in value from $1,111 to $1,250. A bond with twenty years to run to maturity, bearing a coupon rate of 9 percent, will increase in value from $1,000 to $1,099. An increase in the interest rate from 9 percent to 10 percent will cause the value of the perpetual stream to fall to $1,000 and the value of the bond to fall to $914.

The S-H-S definition requires that these increases or decreases in capital values be included in taxable income, but the question arises whether this is correct, since by assumption there has been no change in the expected stream of future yields of the assets. Concentrating on the case of the increase in capital values due to a decline in interest rates, one notes that the increment represents an immediate increase in the consumption power of the owner in the sense that he could command more consumption goods if he liquidated his capital. But a person who decided to "realize" his additional income by selling part of his assets would find that, other things being equal, he would receive less money income in the future. Clearly, this is another aspect of the problem of capital maintenance and permanency.

Kaldor argued that an increase in capital value due to a decline in the interest rate is fictitious in the sense that it represents nominal capital accumulation rather than real capital accumulation. Real capital accumulation, he asserted, occurs only when an individual secures "increased command over both consumption goods and income yielding resources." It would not be possible to correct for this kind of fictitious capital increment, even if one wished to do so, because all that can be observed is changes in market values. These may reflect either a change in the expected future yields or a change in the relevant discount rate, and the two cannot be separated. It was these considerations that led Kaldor to the pessimistic conclusion that the problem of defining income is "in principle insoluble."[19]

If capital maintenance is interpreted in Kaldor's exacting way (in which he resembles Hicks), the considerations just recited constitute a damaging criticism of the S-H-S definition. I think, however, that such a stringent standard for capital maintenance is unnecessary. The immediate increase in consumption power that occurs when interest rates decline represents a new opportunity for asset owners that merits inclusion in the index of ability to pay. The capital gain obtained by those who invested before the decline in interest rates reflects a genuine advantage they enjoy that is not obtained by those who invest later or by other income recipients. To argue that this capital gain should be excluded from income is tantamount to saying that old investors should be allowed to retain in perpetuity a preferred position compared with that of new investors and of recipients of income from labor and other sources. Furthermore, capital gains and losses due to changes in the interest rate, as Kaldor noted, cannot be unambiguously distinguished from other gains and losses that represent clear additions to economic power.

Over time, some of the apparent anomalies associated with changes in capital values due to interest rate changes will disappear. Thus, for example, an investor who immediately consumes his capital gain that is due to an interest rate decline will have less taxable income in the future than another investor who refrains from doing so. In the case of a bond the increase in capital value will be temporary and will be gradually reversed as the maturity of the bond approaches.

Definition of Consumption

The definition of consumption presents a fundamental problem of such complexity as to elicit Simons's concession that a rigorous conception of personal income cannot be achieved.[20] There are two aspects of the problem: first, the distinction between consumption and the costs of obtaining income; and second, the treatment of goods and services produced and used within the household. In a broad sense a large fraction of what is called consumption may be considered a cost of production in that it is necessary in order to sustain an efficient labor force. The impossibility of distinguishing clearly between the part of household expenditure that serves to make possible further production and the part that constitutes, in Adam Smith's phrase, "the sole end and purpose of all production,"[21] raises philosophical questions. It means that income from personal effort cannot be measured as precisely as property income and suggests that costs are less fully deductible for the former than for the latter.

Generally the classification of an item as a cost of production or as consumption depends on the intention of the spender, supplemented in practice by rules based partly on custom but with arbitrary elements. Many administrative questions arise about travel and entertainment and other expenditures that may plausibly be viewed as either a source of immediate gratification or a means of obtaining additional income. The difficulties are particularly acute in connection with income from self-employment, but they exist also for salary and wage earners.

The performance of services for oneself or one's household, such as housekeeping, repairs, and gardening, provides a series of illustrations of the problem of identifying and valuing income and consumption that do not pass through the market. While these services have economic value, any effort to include this in taxable income would fail and would discredit the tax law and its administration. Unavoidable inequities and economic distortions arise when some people work at paid employment and use their money income to buy services that others perform for themselves. The widespread bartering of personal services, allegedly a growing practice in certain countries with high marginal tax rates, could result in similar or worse distortions.

Leisure is sometimes classified as consumption[22] and hence by implication as part of S-H-S income. While in a broad sense this is correct, it would be impossible to make any allowance for leisure in assessing income for taxation. To the extent, however, that the performance of services within a household competes with leisure rather than with outside work that is compensated by money payments, the distortions due to the taxation of the latter are mitigated.[23]

It should be emphasized that the defects of an income tax based on the S-H-S definition that are due to the difficulties just discussed could not be avoided by adopting any of the other definitions of income that have been proposed or by going over to an expenditure tax.

A specific point that may be noted here is the argument of Andrews that medical expenses may appropriately be deducted from taxable income, even if the S-H-S definition is accepted, on the grounds that these outlays are not really consumption. Differences in the amount spent for medical care, he argues, reflect differences in need rather than choices among gratifications.[24] Acceptance of this conclusion would require recognizing that in addition to consumption goods and services and capital goods, there is another category comprising final utilization of economic resources in ways that are not pleasurable. While agreeing with Andrews that most people may derive little conscious gratification from medical expenditures, I do not accept his conclusion. For one thing, the same is true of many other outlays that are classified as consumption expenditures. Thus one buys an umbrella not as a source of gratification per se but for the purpose of avoiding the unpleasantness of getting wet when it rains. Also, the distinction between trying to stay in good health, for example, by spending for a nutritious diet and by paying for periodic checkups by a physician is not as clear as either the Andrews argument or the present tax law implies. Furthermore, a considerable part of medical expenditures strictly defined reflects voluntary choices about the need for treatment and its nature and cost. The high fees paid to prestigious physicians for the treatment of fashionable illnesses resemble the outlays that the patients make for other services. My disagreement with Andrews's rationalization of the medical expense deduction does not pretend to demonstrate that the provision cannot be justified on other grounds.

Andrews also argues that charitable contributions should be deducted because they are not part of the donor's consumption and suggests that the interest deduction may be justifiable on the same grounds.[25] His reasoning is too complex to summarize briefly. As to charitable contributions, my view is that they should be included in adjusted gross income because they are part of the economic resources subject to the disposal of the taxpayer but that a personal deduction for them can be supported for traditional reasons of public policy. My comments on interest payments are given below.

Taxes and Government Expenditures

Curiously, the public finance literature on the definition of income contains only infrequent references to the treatment of government. The formal definition of income as equal to consumption plus accumulation takes no explicit account of direct or indirect taxes. Literally, the S-H-S definition applies to income net of direct personal taxes; however, it has generally been interpreted to mean income before personal taxes, or perhaps more accurately no account has been taken of the existence of personal taxes.[26] Presumably consumption goods and services are valued at market prices, including indirect taxes. The treatment of direct personal taxes poses no conceptual issue, though for policy reasons taxes other than the personal income tax and income taxes levied by other jurisdictions may be deducted or credited. The treatment of indirect taxes involves no special problems as long as the income tax is based on nominal values, but if an adjustment for price level changes were introduced, it would be necessary to decide whether fluctuations corresponding to changes in indirect taxes should be excluded.

The question whether the value of government services should be included in individual income is a conceptual issue. Bittker argues the consistent application of the S-H-S definition would require the inclusion of these items and that the failure to do so "compromises" the tax reformers' aim of "taxing all income alike." His conclusion is not that an effort should be made to value the benefits but that the impossibility of doing so is evidence for his judgment that a comprehensive tax base is not a feasible or desirable objective.[27] Musgrave agrees that "ideally" a comprehensive definition of income would include the imputed value of the benefits from public services, along with cash transfers received from government, but holds that the impossibility of doing so does not destroy the usefulness of the comprehensive income concept or justify the exclusion of cash transfers.[28]

The question of the treatment of the benefits from government services is, in my opinion, less important than it may seem when first encountered. Expenditures for national defense, general government administration, and other so-called public goods cannot be allocated to individual beneficiaries. They represent a part of the general social environment in the same way that climate is part of the physical environment. No inequity or inefficiency results from failure to take account of the substantial fraction of total government expenditures falling in this category.

In a number of areas, however, close substitutability exists between benefits in kind and cash transfers. Medical services and education are important examples. Strict adherence to the S-H-S definition, as usually interpreted, would require that the cash grants be included in income, but this may be unfair and inefficient so long as the in-kind benefits are ignored. Since many of the in-kind benefits cannot be accurately valued and taxed, the exclusion from taxable income of cash grants for similar purposes may be justifiable as a means of avoiding arbitrary differences in taxation.[29] This argument would not justify the exclusion of cash transfer payments, such as unemployment compensation and old-age and survivors' benefits, which the recipient may spend as he pleases and for which there are no close counterparts in the form of in-kind benefits. Public assistance payments can be used for many purposes, but their limitation to persons who pass a means test may justify their exclusion from taxable income.

Gratuitous Receipts

The S-H-S concept calls for including in income gratuitous receipts in the form of gifts and inheritances (also bequests and devises). Simons argued that the donor should not be allowed a deduction because making a gift presumably provides satisfaction to him and is a form of consumption by him.[30] Only a few tax specialists have agreed that these items should be included in the taxable income of the recipients. Generally transfers at death are subject to special taxation on the estate or the heir, and in the United States and some other countries inter vivos gifts are taxed.

One source of difficulty is the diverse nature of the transfers that legally qualify as gratuitous. Some of them appear to have an important element of quid pro quo and to be similar to transactions that are generally agreed to give rise to income. In the relatively trivial cases of tips, noncontractual bonuses and severance pay, and other voluntary payments by employers to employees, the present practice is to include the item in taxable income.

Many other gratuitous transfers, however, particularly those between family members, appear to be of a different nature. Often these transfers may accurately be viewed as a sharing of consumption power rather than the creation of new income. This is related to the question of the appropriate definition of the taxable unit.

Transfer taxes on donors may have some advantages over income taxes on gratuitous receipts. It can be argued that donors should be subjected to special taxation because gifts and bequests represent a significant exercise of economic power. Under the income tax, large differences in taxation might occur between cases where wealth is transferred by a series of gifts and cases where it is transferred in a lump sum at the death of the donor, a possibility that is generally considered to be a weakness of unintegrated transfer taxes. On both social and economic grounds, higher rates may be acceptable for transfer taxes than for the income tax. Estate and gift taxes apply to transfer to residents and nonresidents alike; if these taxes were replaced by income taxation, some special problems would arise in the treatment of nonresident beneficiaries, whose circumstances would not be known or easily verifiable by the domestic tax authorities.

Administration and Compliance Questions

This section identifies several items that pose difficulties in applying the S-H-S definition without involving conceptual issues of the same complexity as those reviewed in the preceding section. Space limitations allow only a cursory treatment.

Accrued Capital Gains and Losses

A major problem associated with the use of the S-H-S concept concerns the time at which capital gains and losses should be taken into account. Although the concept requires that changes in the value of capital assets be reflected annually on an accrual basis, the majority of experts think that this would not be feasible and are willing to settle, at least at present, for the recognition of capital gains and losses at the time of realization through sale, exchange, gift, or bequest. The application of the realization principle for capital gains and losses substantially reduces the equity and efficiency of the income tax, even if gains are taxed at regular rates and losses are fully deductible. The impairment of the income tax is of course greater when gains are taxed at lower rates than other income and limitations are imposed on the deductibility of capital losses. Under a realization system the taxation of many gains is postponed for a long time, and this greatly reduces the effective tax rate. Probably the inflation and high nominal interest rates prevailing in the recent past have stimulated economists to attach more importance to the effect of postponement.

Taxes on capital gains have been increased in recent years but remain below those on other income. Further increases in the taxation of capital gains would be the most important step that could be taken to lessen the tilt of the income tax in favor of property income. There is a strong case for full taxation of gains realized by a sale or other exchange and those constructively realized by gift or at death. Although in principle capital losses should be fully deductible, it may be expedient to continue limitations on their deductibility against ordinary income so long as capital gains are taxed only at realization, in order to prevent taxpayers from realizing their losses while deferring their gains. Further consideration needs to be given to the feasibility of measures that would reduce the advantages of deferring gains.

Imputed Income from Dwellings and Durables

A comprehensive income tax base would have to include the imputed rental value of owner-occupied dwellings. Substantial problems would be involved in estimating this item, but I think they could be coped with in a reasonably satisfactory way. Imputed rent is taxed in the Scandinavian countries, Germany, and some other countries, but in the United Kingdom the previous practice of including it in taxable income has been discontinued. In principle, owner-users of consumer durables should also have to reflect in their taxable income an imputed return on their equity. My judgment is that it would not be practicable to assess this latter item and that its omission must be accepted as a shortcoming of the income tax in comparison with an ideal one.

Life Insurance

The S-H-S definition indicates that life insurance death benefits should be included in the income of beneficiaries and implies that interest accruing on life insurance policy reserves should be included in the income of policyholders. In the United States at present both are omitted, though some interest earnings are taxed when insurance proceeds are paid for reasons other than the death of the insured (when a policy matures or is surrendered). Death benefits resemble bequests and other gratuitous receipts and should be treated in the same way as these. Interest accruing on policy reserves, in my judgment, should be currently taxed to policyholders, and I believe that this would be feasible, although so far as I know no country does so. Since casualty insurance usually does not involve substantial policy reserves, a comparable provision would not be needed for it.

Interest Paid

Interest payments may be either a cost of obtaining income or a consumption expense. In my opinion the former but not the latter payments should be deducted in computing income. There is, however, no fully satisfactory way of distinguishing between the two. One approach (followed in Canada) is to allow the deduction only of interest paid on debts formally connected with business operations, professional practice, or income-producing property. This is too narrow because an individual's economic power can be properly evaluated only by taking a comprehensive view of his income and outgo and his balance sheet. In a broad sense any interest he pays is a cost of obtaining the yield of any capital assets he holds, because by contracting the interest-bearing debt he avoids disposing of the income-yielding assets. Thus, for example, interest paid on consumer installment debt may be viewed as a cost of obtaining interest income on bonds owned by the same individual.

On the other hand, if the individual holds no income-yielding assets and is not engaged in business or professional activity, the interest paid on the installment debt appears to be part of the cost of consumer goods. It is similar to a price supplement paid for buying a consumer good early or to rental payments for a leased car or other durable consumer good. A complication arises because the yield of certain assets—for example, owner-occupied dwellings, consumer durables, and municipal bonds—is not included in taxable income in the United States. Interest paid to carry such assets should not be deductible.

All things considered, I think that the least arbitrary solution would be to allow interest to be deducted only against taxable property income, defined as investment income and the part of business and professional income attributable to capital according to conventional rules. Interest payments would no longer be deductible by persons who report only salary and wage income. The last feature would no doubt be criticized as discriminatory and regressive.

Costs of Earning Labor Income

In order to reduce differences in the treatment of labor income and property income, the liberalization and rationalization of the rules for deducting the costs of education and training that are intended to enhance earning capacity would be desirable. It would be hard—though in my judgment possible—to devise acceptable rules and procedures to distinguish these costs from other educational costs. Similar problems arise in classifying moving expenses as costs of earning income or as consumption. Some would argue that commuting expenses are also of a mixed nature and should be partly deductible.

Pension Rights

The expectation of receiving a pension on retirement has an important bearing on the economic welfare of employed persons, and the appropriate treatment of pensions poses difficult questions for the income tax or for a wealth tax. Many pension plans in the United States call for contributions by employees and employers to a trustee who is not currently taxable on the interest obtained by investing the reserves. Employees do not obtain a deduction for their contributions and are not required to include in their current income employers' contributions and interest accruals. They are taxable on the benefits when received but are allowed to recover their own contributions free of tax.

It seems clear that the accrual of a pension right is a form of accumulation and hence a part of income according to the S-H-S concept. Significant questions of interpretation arise, however. If the accumulation is attributed to the employee only to the extent that he acquires a fully vested right to it, arbitrary distinctions may be made between plans calling for vesting and other plans, and the former kind of plan may be discouraged. On the other hand, if vesting is not considered a criterion, individuals may be taxed on hypothetical benefits they never obtain. While legislation enacted in 1974 requires a greater degree of vesting for tax-exempt pension plans than was customary in the past,[31] vesting is far from universal.

Assessment Procedures

The S-H-S income definition is a conceptual guide, not an assessment formula. In practice, net income is measured primarily by reference to transactions classified according to accounting conventions and not by the aggregation of consumption and accumulation. The U.S. Internal Revenue Code, like other tax statutes, identifies taxable income by enumerating items to be included, excluded, or deducted; however, it goes on to say that income is not limited to the enumerated items but includes income "from whatever source derived."

Comprehensively defined income—which may be regarded as an approximation of S-H-S income—could be assessed as follows:

$$Y_c = G - E + S - K + A$$

where G = gross receipts other than the proceeds of sale of capital assets, E = costs of obtaining G, S = proceeds of sale of capital assets (plus the value of capital assets transferred by gift or bequest), K = the cost or other basis of capital assets sold (or otherwise transferred), and A = change in the value of capital assets held throughout the year. G should be interpreted to include the imputed rental value of owner-occupied dwellings and E to include interest, depreciation, maintenance, property taxes, and other expenses relating to such dwellings. G should also include certain income received in kind by employees and others. E should include interest paid up to the amount of nonlabor income received. If capital gains and losses are taxed only when realized, A is dropped from the equation above. According to Simons, G should include gifts and inheritances received, but many others who generally favor the S-H-S approach would exclude these items.

In comparing U.S. practice with the formula, it is helpful to distinguish between adjusted gross income and taxable income. Adjusted gross income is net of most allowable costs of obtaining income and may be compared with Y_c. Taxable income is adjusted gross income less personal deductions, P, and personal exemptions. If this distinction were carefully observed, P would not include the costs of obtaining income but would consist of allowances that are granted for policy reasons other than the improvement of the definition of income. While this is broadly true, P now includes some items that might properly be regarded as part of E: for example, certain interest payments, certain investment expenses, part of educational expenses, union dues, and miscellaneous employment expenses. A sharp distinction between P and E would help clarify discussion and would suggest the elimination of inequities that now arise when persons who elect the standard deduction are denied deductions for some items that would qualify as part of E.

In the present U.S. law, G omits imputed income receipts, interest on tax-exempt bonds, most transfer payments received from government, and other gratuitous receipts. E is understated because it fails to include most of the costs of education and training that contribute to earning capacity and certain other costs of earning labor income but may be overstated in regard to travel and entertainment expenses and perhaps some other items. S omits half of the proceeds of the sale of capital assets held for certain minimum time periods (for 1976, six months; for 1977, nine months; and for 1978 and later, twelve months) as well as the value of assets transferred by gift or bequest. K, on the other hand, is in effect understated in certain cases by virtue of the limitation on the deductibility of capital losses against other income (and because of inflation, which is not being covered in this paper). A is wholly omitted.

Tax Expenditures

Closely related to the question of how taxable income compares with comprehensively defined income is the concept of "tax expenditures." Proposed originally by Assistant Secretary of the Treasury Stanley Surrey in 1967 and soon quantified by the Treasury Department, the idea won rapid acceptance in public and congressional debates on taxation.[32] It was incorporated in the Congressional Budget Act of 1974, which requires a listing of tax expenditures in the annual budget.

In his 1967 speech Surrey spoke of "deliberate departures from accepted concepts of net income and . . . various special exemptions, deductions and credits" that he considered equivalent to government expenditures.[33] The Treasury study, published in the 1968 annual report of the secretary of the treasury, gave estimates of the revenue reductions due to "the major respects in which the current income tax bases [i.e., the corporation and individual tax bases] deviate from widely accepted definitions of income and standards of business accounting and from the generally accepted structure of an income tax."[34] The Congressional Budget Act of 1974 defines tax expenditures as "revenue losses attributable to provisions of the federal tax laws which allow a special exclusion, exemption, or deduction from gross income or which provide a special credit, a preferential rate of tax, or a deferral of tax liability."[35]

The estimates of tax expenditures prepared by the Treasury Department are based on a broad income concept but not on the S-H-S definition or a close approximation of it. The standard is vaguer and more pragmatic. Thus the list of tax expenditures comprehends the exclusion from taxable income of social security benefits and public assistance benefits but not the exclusion of food stamp and Medicaid benefits or private gifts and inheritances; the deduction of mortgage interest and property taxes on owner-occupied dwellings is classified as a tax expenditure, but the omission of imputed net rent is not so classified; the exclusion of interest accruing on life insurance policy reserves, but not the exclusion of death benefits, is considered a tax expenditure; the low tax rate on long-term capital gains is viewed as a tax expenditure, but not the failure to tax unrealized gains or gains constructively realized by transfer through gift or bequest.

Some of the differences between the official list of tax expenditures and a list based on a rigorous application of the S-H-S definition are due to estimating difficulties.[36] However, Surrey and Hellmuth, replying to criticism of the tax expenditure budget by Bittker,[37] explicitly denied that the Treasury Department followed the Haig-Simons definition of income. No effort was made to cover exclusions "where the case for their inclusion in the income base stands on relatively technical or theoretical arguments" such as those for including imputed net rent. Surrey and Hellmuth appeal to the idea of a broad consensus about tax equity and to the implication that a special provision is a departure from accepted equity criteria that "must be defended on terms other than its rightful place in the tax structure—terms that in essence make it a 'tax expenditure.'"[38]

The term "tax expenditure" has undoubtedly stimulated many people to think about certain tax issues and the budget in a new way, and the regular publication of tax expenditure estimates provides useful information. In my opinion, however, the present tax expenditure budget rests on a shaky conceptual foundation and for this reason is less convincing to skeptics than it would be if more rigorously derived. The Surrey-Hellmuth defense assumes a broader and more exact consensus on tax equity than I detect, and the tax expenditure estimates are less firmly based than would be desirable for official statistics.

Two alternatives to the present tax expenditure budget, either of which could be more easily defended in my judgment, would be (1) a broader tabulation showing, as far as feasible, the estimated effects on tax liability of all differences between S-H-S income and adjusted gross income and of all personal deductions and credits; or (2) a narrower tabulation including only those provisions for which there is evidence in the legislative history that the dominant motivation was to encourage or reward certain behavior or to compensate for a particular hardship by reducing income tax liability. The term "tax expenditure" could appropriately be reserved for the latter items. The test of motivation should be critically applied since there is hardly any provision that has not sometimes been supported on the grounds that it induces desirable behavior or relieves hardship. The examination of the legislative history, however, should not be confined to that of the original enactment but should extend to any later systematic consideration of the provisions by the congressional tax committees of the two houses.

Conclusion

This review leads me to the conclusion that the S-H-S definition of income is much better for tax purposes than other definitions. All definitions are subject to conceptual problems and practical difficulties of application that prevent the attainment of a fully accurate and noncontroversial measurement. The S-H-S definition, however, is more objective than definitions of the Hicks-Kaldor type, which depend on subjective factors in determining whether capital is being maintained. The latter definitions and the source and periodicity concepts place undue emphasis on recurrence and permanence and thus omit accretions to economic power that are highly significant in modern economies. They favor investors and speculators over recipients of income from personal effort. The Fisher definition avoids the difficulties to which the other definitions are subject in regard to capital maintenance and timing, but it relates to consumption and not to income as ordinarily conceived. For the reasons briefly stated above, I believe that an income tax should be preferred to a consumption tax.

The S-H-S definition is a valuable guideline for tax policy and administration. There is a presumption that in assessing the income tax all the constituents of income as identified by S-H-S should be brought into the calculations. But a definition is not enough to establish policy. Those who wish to depart from the S-H-S definition should be expected to advance persuasive arguments for doing so, but they need not be asked to carry an extraordinary burden of proof.

The principal departures from the S-H-S definition that seem to me to be warranted are the exclusion from adjusted gross income of gifts and inheritances received, life insurance proceeds, accrued but unrealized capital gains and losses, and government transfer payments that are either close substitutes for in-kind benefits or subject to a means test.

The S-H-S definition gives guidance with respect to inclusions and exclusions from adjusted gross income. It calls for the deduction of all costs of obtaining income but is not particularly helpful in identifying these. The definition implies that income should be taxed at the time when an accretion to economic power accrues, but its adherents have not consistently stressed this point. The formulators of the definition and its users, it seems to me, implicitly assume that the consumer unit and the income unit for tax purposes coincide. Otherwise, the importance attached to consumption power is hard to interpret, and the recommendations on the treatment of gifts and inheritances are untenable. On the other hand, the S-H-S definition in itself does not tell which personal deductions are advantageous for policy purposes (as distinguished from the allowance of costs of obtaining income). It has nothing to say about personal exemptions or tax rates.

If it is not possible to move all the way to a comprehensive concept of income, the question arises whether a clear gain would be obtained by moving part of the way. Partial measures could make matters worse. This might well be true of action to include in adjusted gross income some of the government transfer payments that are now excluded. It has been contended that the base-broadening actions that are likely to be taken would accentuate an alleged discrimination against earned income, compared with investment income, and would therefore be undesirable.[39]

One's reaction to this criticism depends in part on a political forecast of what measures are likely to be enacted and also on one's view of the role of experts. Although tax experts should not be oblivious to the harm that may be done by the partial adoption or modification of their recommendations, I think that this should cause them to redouble their efforts at explanation and persuasion rather than to give up the attempt to formulate proposals for a good income tax and a good tax system. Leaving aside the question of short-run political acceptability, my opinion is that the reforms needed to approach more closely the S-H-S version of a comprehensive income definition would not, on balance, discriminate against earned income. Prominent among these reforms are measures that would increase taxes on investment income, including the full taxation of capital gains on a realization basis and the inclusion in income of the imputed rental value of owner-occupied dwellings, interest earned on life insurance policy reserves, and interest on tax-exempt bonds. Furthermore, in appraising the relative taxation of income from labor and income from property, account should be taken not only of the individual income tax but also of the corporation income tax, the property tax, estate and gift taxes, and payroll taxes.

NOTES

Note: I gratefully acknowledge helpful comments received from Sijbren Cnossen, Federico Herschel, George E. Lent, Leif Mutén, Joseph A. Pechman, Stanley S. Surrey, and Vito Tanzi. They, of course, are not responsible for errors, omissions, or misjudgments, particularly since I did not—and could not—accept all their suggestions, which clashed on some points.

1. Henry C. Simons, *Personal Income Taxation: The Definition of Income as a Problem of Fiscal Policy* (University of Chicago Press, 1938), pp. 43, 110.
2. Nicholas Kaldor, *An Expenditure Tax* (London: Allen and Unwin, 1955), p. 70.
3. William D. Andrews, "Personal Deductions in an Ideal Income Tax," *Harvard Law Review,* vol. 86 (December 1972), p. 324.
4. *An Inquiry into the Nature and Causes of the Wealth of Nations,* Edwin Cannan, ed. (Modern Library, 1937), bk. 2, chap. 2, p. 271.
5. *Value and Capital: An Inquiry into Some Fundamental Principles of Economic Theory,* 2d ed. (Oxford: Oxford University Press, 1946), p. 172.
6. Ibid., p. 174.
7. Carl C. Plehn, *American Economic Review,* vol. 14 (March 1924), pp. 1–12.
8. See the following works by Irving Fisher: *The Nature of Capital and Income* (London: Macmillan, 1906): "Income," *Encyclopaedia of the Social Sciences* (Macmillan, 1932), vol. 7, pp. 622–25; "Income in Theory and Income Taxation in Practice," *Econometrica,* vol. 5 (January 1937), pp. 1–55; and "The Concept of Income: A Rebuttal," *Econometrica,* vol. 7 (October 1939), pp. 357–61.
9. *Constructive Income Taxation,* p. x; and "The Concept of Income," p. 360.
10. "The Concept of Income," p. 357; and *Constructive Income Taxation,* pp. 48–51.
11. *Constructive Income Taxation,* p. 50. Fisher said that accretion may be more

useful in that it conveys information about future yields as well as the yield of the period under consideration.

12. Georg von Schanz (1853–1931) was a German economist and founder and editor of *Finanz-Archiv*. His definition is set forth in his important article, "Der Einkommensbegriff und die Einkommensteuergesetze," *Finanz-Archiv*, vol. 13, no. 1 (1896), pp. 1–87. See the article on Schanz by Hans Teschemacher in *Encyclopaedia of the Social Sciences* (Macmillan, 1934), vol. 13, pp. 563–64. According to Leif Mutén (*On the Development of Income Taxation Since World War I* [Amsterdam: International Bureau of Fiscal Documentation, 1967], p. 25), Schanz was anticipated by David Davidson, writing in Swedish in 1889.

13. Robert Murray Haig, "The Concept of Income—Economic and Legal Aspects," in Haig, ed., *The Federal Income Tax* (Columbia University Press, 1921), p. 7, reprinted in Richard A. Musgrave and Carl S. Shoup, eds., *Readings in the Economics of Taxation* (Irwin for the American Economic Association, 1959), p. 59.

14. *Personal Income Taxation*, p. 50.

15. As quoted in ibid., p. 61.

16. Break, "Capital Maintenance and the Concept of Income."

17. See Henry J. Aaron, ed., *Inflation and the Income Tax* (Brookings Institution, 1976).

18. See Fisher, "Income in Theory and Income Taxation in Practice," p. 47.

19. Kaldor, *An Expenditure Tax*, pp. 54–78 (quotations on pp. 69 and 70).

20. Simons, *Personal Income Taxation*, pp. 110–24.

21. *Wealth of Nations*, bk. 4, chap. 8, p. 625.

22. Simons, *Personal Income Taxation*, p. 52.

23. Goode, *The Individual Income Tax*, pp. 142–43.

24. "Personal Deductions in an Ideal Income Tax," pp. 331–43.

25. Ibid., pp. 344–76.

26. See Henry Aaron, "What is a Comprehensive Tax Base Anyway?" *National Tax Journal*, vol. 22 (December 1969), pp. 543–49.

27. Boris I. Bittker, "A 'Comprehensive Tax Base' as a Goal of Income Tax Reform," *Harvard Law Review*, vol. 80 (March 1967), pp. 935–38, reprinted in Bittker and others, *A Comprehensive Income Tax Base? A Debate* (Federal Tax Press, 1968), pp. 11–14.

28. Richard A. Musgrave, "In Defense of an Income Concept," *Harvard Law Review*, vol. 81 (November 1967), pp. 54–55; reprinted in Bittker and others, *A Comprehensive Income Tax Base?* pp. 72–73.

29. See Aaron, "What is a Comprehensive Tax Base Anyway?"

30. *Personal Income Taxation*, pp. 125–47.

31. Employee Retirement Income Security Act of 1974 (Public Law 93-406).

32. William F. Hellmuth and Oliver Oldman, eds., *Tax Policy and Tax Reform, 1961–1969: Selected Speeches and Testimony of Stanley S. Surrey* (Commerce Clearing House, 1973), pp. 573–641; Stanley S. Surrey, *Pathways to Tax Reform: The Concept of Tax Expenditures* (Harvard University Press, 1973): and *Annual Report of the Secretary of the Treasury on the State of the Finances for the Fiscal Year Ended June 30, 1968*, pp. 322–40.

33. Hellmuth and Oldman, *Tax Policy and Tax Reform*, p. 576.

34. Ibid., p. 588; and *Annual Report of the Secretary of the Treasury, 1968, p. 327.*

35. Public Law 93-344, sec. 3(a)(3).

36. *Special Analyses, Budget of the United States Government, Fiscal Year 1977*, pp. 116–22.

37. Boris I. Bittker, "Accounting for Federal 'Tax Subsidies' in the National Budget," *National Tax Journal*, vol. 22 (June 1969), pp. 244–61.

38. Stanley S. Surrey and William F. Hellmuth, "The Tax Expenditure Budget—Response to Professor Bittker," *National Tax Journal*, vol. 22 (December 1969), pp. 529, 537.

39. Bittker, "A 'Comprehensive Tax Base' as a Goal of Income Tax Reform," p. 983. Economists should be embarrassed that it was left for a lawyer to introduce into the debate "the theory of second best."

SELECTION 39

JOSEPH A. PECHMAN

Tax Reform: Theory and Practice

Joseph Pechman argues that the goal of tax reform should be comprehensive income taxation, based on an economic definition of income. The Tax Reform Act of 1986 represents a major move in that direction. Pechman provides a clear explanation of these changes and of the probable effect on the distribution of the tax burden. He concludes by pointing out "mistakes and missed opportunities."

QUESTIONS TO GUIDE THE READING

1. What is meant by the phrase "shrinking of the tax base," and what led to its occurrence in the United States?
2. Why does Pechman believe tax reform was successful in 1986?
3. How would you support the claim that, although the general corporate tax rate fell from 46 to 34 percent, corporations as a group will be paying more taxes than before?
4. What does Pechman believe are the "mistakes and missed opportunities" of the 1986 tax reform?

The Tax Reform Act of 1986 is the most significant piece of tax legislation enacted since the income tax was converted to a mass tax during World War II. After decades of erosion, the individual and corporate income tax bases were broadened and the revenues were used to reduce tax rates. Loopholes and preferences that were formerly considered sacrosanct were eliminated or moderated despite the determined opposition of powerful pressure groups. Comprehensive income taxation, which had earlier been regarded as an impossible dream, carried the day with strong bipartisan support. . . .

The Shrinking of the Tax Base

Despite the efforts of the tax reformers, the trend of U.S. tax policy since the end of World War II had been to expand old preferences and to introduce new ones to achieve various economic and social objectives. The list is long.

Joseph A. Pechman, "Tax Reform: Theory and Practice," *Journal of Economic Perspectives 1* (Summer 1987), 11–28. Reprinted by permission of the author and the publisher.

Joseph A. Pechman is Senior Fellow at the Brookings Institution.

It includes provisions that were intended to promote investment in general—accelerated depreciation and the investment tax credit—as well as tax favors to particular industries and firms, such as the extension of percentage depletion to sand, gravel, oyster shells, and salt, taxation at preferential capital gains rates of livestock held for more than six months, unharvested crops sold along with land, and coal royalties, and extension of immediate expensing of development and exploration costs to minerals as well as oil and gas. Many of these provisions, combined with the deduction for interest expense, permitted wealthy people and large corporations to avoid payment of any tax.

Some relief provisions were even tailored to fit specific individuals, the most famous of which was the "Mayer amendment," enacted in 1951. This amendment provided capital gains treatment for a lump sum distribution to Louis B. Mayer on his retirement from the movie industry. To avoid identifying him by name, the amendment was worded to apply to a movie executive who (1) had been employed for more than 20 years, (2) had held his rights to future profits for 12 years, and (3) had the right to receive a percentage of profits for life or for a period of at least five years after the termination of his employment.

The situation became so bad that in 1976 the House approved an amendment submitted by Congressman James Burke of Massachusetts, perhaps tongue-in-cheek, to provide a 7 percent tax credit for the purchase of garden tools "to encourage the private production of food." Sanity prevailed, however, and the amendment was removed by the Senate and not restored in conference. Louis Mayer and garden tools are only two examples. There were others.

The proliferation of tax preferences was interrupted in 1969, partly in response to the revelation by Treasury Secretary Joseph A. Barr of the outgoing Johnson administration that 154 persons with adjusted gross incomes of more than $200,000 had not paid tax in 1966. The reform spirit lasted until 1975, when percentage depletion was denied to large corporations. Congress then reverted to its old habits in 1978, when the exclusion for long-term capital gains was raised from 50 percent to 60 percent, homeowners over 55 years of age were given a lifetime exemption of $100,000 for capital gains realized on the sale of a principle residence, the limits on tax-exempt industrial development bonds were liberalized, and the investment tax credit was extended to outlays for rehabilitation of old buildings. In 1981, President Reagan easily persuaded Congress to enact his across-the-board individual income tax rate reductions and the excessively generous accelerated cost recovery system (ACRS) for depreciation, which were major features of his election campaign platform in the previous year. Congress got into the spirit of the occasion by adding to the bill a raft of unnecessary and costly deductions of its own, including an annual deduction of up to $2,000 for amounts set aside in individual retirement accounts (even by employees already covered by private pension plans), an exclusion of $750 ($1,500 on joint returns) for reinvested dividends paid by public utilities from 1982 through 1985, an exclusion of $1,000 ($2,000 on joint returns) for interest on savings certificates purchased in 1981 and 1982 (to help bail out the savings and loan industry), an increase to $125,000 in the lifetime capital gain exemption for homeowners, and a new deduction for charitable contributions of nonitemizers.[1] In the same bill, Congress gutted the estate and gift taxes by tripling the exemption and lowering the top rate from 75 percent to 50 percent.

Gathering the Forces for Reform

In the light of this dismal history, . . . the passage of the Tax Reform Act of 1986 is indeed a remarkable event. Political scientists will be trying for years to come to explain why it happened in 1986. I offer the following observations in full recognition of my amateur status as a political analyst.

First, the large tax cuts and new preferences enacted in recent years undermined the confidence of the people in the tax system. The growing use of tax shelters by wealthy people to reduce or eliminate their tax liabilities was well-known. So were the names of giant corporations (General Dynamics, General Electric, etc.) which had not been paying any taxes. Low- and middle-income taxpayers resented paying higher effective tax rates on their incomes than many wealthy individuals and large profitable corporations. Furthermore, the tax system has become so complicated that millions of people were paying someone else to prepare their returns. Tax reformers were promising greater equity, efficiency, and simplicity in taxation and this message struck a responsive chord.

Second, the old tax reformers were joined by the new breed of supply-siders in promoting lower tax rates (for example, see Meyer, 1981). The original idea of comprehensive reform was to maintain a system of graduated rates, but at a reduced level. The supply-siders added a new wrinkle: instead of a multiple-rate system, they proposed the use of a single flat rate, and were willing to sacrifice many tax preferences to get it. The flat tax movement collapsed when it was shown in congressional hearings that a flat rate meant that people with very high incomes (those with incomes of about $50,000) would pay lower taxes, while those with lower incomes would pay higher taxes. But to their credit, many of the flat taxers continued to support tax reform at mildly graduated rates, but a low top rate. As it turned out, the coalition of liberals and conservatives favoring comprehensive reform and rate reduction prevailed in Congress.

Third, the Treasury and its supporters stressed the importance of allocating resources on the basis of economic, rather than tax, considerations from the very beginning. Although businessmen were split on the merits of tax reform, many influential corporate executives found the idea of a "level playing field" appealing and threw their support behind the tax bill. Even the financial community, which traditionally fought any increase in the capital gains tax, muted its opposition this time because of the attractiveness of the low top rate on other income. . . .

What the Reform Accomplished

The Tax Reform Act of 1986 is a major step toward comprehensive tax reform. I believe it will greatly improve the fairness of the tax system and remove major distortions from the economy. The many more improvements remaining to be made in the tax system do not detract from what has been achieved. The major accomplishments of the act are as follows:

1. By doubling the personal exemptions and increasing the standard deduction, the act removes 4,800,000 poor people from the tax rolls.[2] This step restores the principle (abandoned by Congress in 1978) that people who are officially defined as "poor" should not be required to pay income tax. The principle will be perpetuated by the resumption in 1989 of the automatic annual adjustment for inflation of the personal exemptions.

2. Significant increases were made in the earned income credit for wage earners with families.[3] These increases eliminated almost the entire social security tax (including the employer's share) for those eligible for the full credit and reduced the tax burden for many other low income workers, thus increasing the progressivity of the tax system.

3. Two tax rates—15 percent and 28 percent—were substituted for the earlier 14 rates, which rose to a maximum of 50 percent. However, counting the 33 percent rate created by phasing out the lowest tax rate and personal exemptions for high income taxpayers, the new rate structure will have four brackets, with rates of 15, 28, 33, and 28 percent. These lower marginal rates will reduce the attractiveness of tax shelters and the return to tax cheating and increase work and saving incentives. Some estimates of the supply response to changes in tax rates have been excessive, but the more responsible estimates suggest that there will be a modest improvement in work effort; the saving response is unclear (Bosworth, 1984, chapters 3 and 5).

4. The taxation of realized capital gains as ordinary income—the keystone of comprehensive tax reform—has finally been realized. This change will reduce the incentive to disguise ordinary income as capital gains, and thus make the tax code less complicated and simplify financial planning. Without this change, the act would have cut the taxes of the wealthy by large amounts and would have been grossly unfair. However, the continued exemption from the regular tax of accrued capital gains on assets transferred by gift or at death will increase the incentive of taxpayers to defer realizing gains until the assets are transferred to their heirs.

5. A good start was made on reversing the erosion of the individual income tax base. Unemployment benefits, which were previously taxable only if a married taxpayer's income exceeded $18,000 ($12,000 for single people), were made taxable regardless of the size of income. Deductions for state and local sales taxes and consumer interest were eliminated. Deductions for unreimbursed business expenses, costs incurred in earning investment income, and other miscellaneous costs were allowed only to the extent that they exceed a floor of two percent of income. The floor for the deduction of medical expenses was raised from 5 percent to 7.5 percent of income.

The exclusions for prizes or awards for scientific and other achievements and for scholarships and fellowships exceeding university tuition, books, and supplies, were eliminated. Perhaps most important, the deduction for investment interest of noncorporate taxpayers was limited to investment income. These changes and others will enlarge the tax base, reduce horizontal inequities, and simplify compliance by reducing the number of people who itemize their deductions.

6. The act makes a frontal assault on major loopholes and special benefits. Many tax shelters will no longer be profitable because of a new limitation on the deductibility of losses from passive investments,[4] tax subsidies for borrowing (other than for mortgages) will be eliminated by the limitation on the deduction for investment interest expense, the deduction for contributions to individual retirement accounts by persons already covered by private pension plans will be allowed only for taxpayers with incomes below $50,000 if married and $35,000 if single,[5] deductible business expense accounts for meals, travel and entertainment will be limited to 80 percent of outlays, tax preferences benefiting defense contractors, banks, and other industries will be eliminated or narrowed,[6] and the minimum tax for both individuals and businesses will be strengthened.

7. Contrary to Henry Simons' views about the corporate tax, the U.S. Congress believes that a separate, unintegrated corporate tax is essential for effective income taxation. A separate corporate tax prevents individuals from avoiding income tax by accumulating earnings in corporations, although some might question whether it is appropriate to tax corporations at a higher tax rate than the top bracket individual rate. Simons disregarded the tremendous value of tax deferral, which is possible when capital gains are taxed only when realized. The 1986 act reduced the general corporate tax rate from 46 percent to 34 percent, thus reducing the maximum tax on dividends at the margin by over a quarter (from 73 percent to 52.5 percent) in the top brackets. Nevertheless, the reform act increased corporate tax liabilities about 20 percent overall by eliminating the investment credit, reducing depreciation allowances for structures, and eliminating loopholes.

How the New Tax Burden Is Distributed

The distributional effect of the act is distinctly progressive, especially if the increases in corporate income tax liabilities are taken into account. I have calculated the change in average effective tax rates on the basis of the most recent distribution of tax burdens estimated from the Brookings MERGE file (Table 1). The combined federal corporate and individual income tax burden is increased for the top 10 percent of the income distribution, but reduced for the lower 90 percent. Total federal tax burdens also decline in the lower nine deciles and then rise in the top decile. The tax reductions in the lower deciles are the result of the increases in the personal exemptions, standard deduction, and earned income credit under the individual income

Table 1   Change in Individual and Corporation Income Tax Liabilities under the Tax Reform Act of 1986, by Income Decile

Income Decile[a]	Percent Change in	
	Federal Individual and Corporate Income Taxes[b]	Total Federal Taxes
Lowest	−44	−16
Second	−32	−11
Third	−24	−10
Fourth	−16	−7
Fifth	−12	−6
Sixth	−8	−4
Seventh	−7	−4
Eighth	−6	−3
Ninth	−6	−4
Highest	+3	+2
Top 5%	+4	+3
Top 1%	+5	+5

Source: Author's estimates based on the 1985 Brookings MERGE file.

[a]The classification is by a comprehensive definition of income, including imputed rent and corporate earnings allocated to stockholders, whether distributed or not.

[b]Assumes the corporate tax is a tax on capital in general.

tax. The increases at the top reflect the increase in corporation tax liabilities, which are assumed to fall on owners of capital in these calculations.

The major complaint against the reform is that corporations will be paying higher taxes than before, which will increase the cost of capital and reduce investment. The fact is that the corporate rate reductions will be almost as large as the revenues raised by the elimination of the investment credit, reductions in depreciation allowances, and other changes in the capital cost allowances. Practically all the *additional* tax to be paid by corporations will come from eliminating loopholes and other structural changes. These reforms will increase average, but not marginal, tax rates and are less likely to affect investment incentives.

Critics of the increase in corporate tax liabilities neglect to mention that many corporations will actually be paying lower taxes than before. These are the corporations which have been paying taxes on most of their economic income. By eliminating preferences, the act will improve the allocation of investment and increase economic efficiency. Higher taxes will be paid by capital-intensive firms such as steel, aluminum, and utility companies, but they are the nation's sluggish industries. The less capital-intensive but more innovative industries—computers, electronics, biomedicine, and so on—will pay lower taxes and will have higher after-tax profits to invest.

This redistribution of the corporate tax burden should have a favorable effect on growth.[7]

Mistakes and Missed Opportunities

Notwithstanding the accomplishments just enumerated, much remains to be done to reach the comprehensive reform target. In legislation as far-reaching and as complicated as the Tax Reform Act of 1986, some mistakes were inevitable and some real opportunities for improvement in the tax structure were ignored. Moreover, the bill contains the earmarks of numerous political bargains and compromises that make little economic or administrative sense.

Perhaps the most unsatisfactory feature of the act is the way it handles owner-occupied housing. Since the tax advantages of homeowners are regarded by politicians as untouchable, the act kept intact the exclusion of the rental value of owned homes from income, the deduction for interest on home mortgages, and the deduction for property taxes. At the same time, the deduction for consumer interest was eliminated and the deduction for investment interest was limited to the amount of reported net investment income. The public is already being bombarded by newspaper and magazine articles by so-called experts who advise taxpayers to increase their home mortgages as a device to generate deductible interest payments. The tax bill limits the extent to which this can be done, but the efforts to circumvent the law will be difficult to police.[8]

Even if the exemption of imputed rent and a deduction for mortgage interest are sacrosanct, it is possible to limit the borrowing subsidy without encouraging rearrangements of debt for tax purposes. The solution was first proposed by my colleague, Richard Goode, more than twenty years ago and the new law applies it to investment interest (Goode, 1976, p. 152). The idea is to allow deductions for interest payments up to the amount of investment income reported on an individual's return. To accommodate the political requirement that mortgage interest be deductible, the limit can be raised to new investment income plus an arbitrary amount, say $10,000 or $15,000. At a 10 percent interest rate, such generous limits would permit deductions for interest on mortgages of up to $100,000 or $150,000—more than enough to take care of the vast majority of homeowners. The limits would also remove the discrimination against borrowing for other purposes and the temptation to refinance home mortgages for the purpose of financing other consumption or investments.

A second unsatisfactory feature of the new law is the treatment of deductions other than interest. I interpret the Simons definition of income to include all sources of income, without any deductions for the uses of that income. For equity reasons, I believe it is appropriate to permit a deduction for unusual expenses which reduce the taxpayer's ability to pay, but they should be kept to a minimum. The law already contains deductions for unusual medical expenses, which are defined as medical payments in excess of 7.5 percent of income (up from 5 percent under the old law), and casualty losses, which are allowable to the extent they exceed 10 percent of income. The remaining deductions for state and local taxes and charitable contributions subsidize public services provided by state and local governments and provide an incentive for private charitable giving.

The Treasury I plan in 1984 recommended the complete elimination of the state-local tax deduction and the restriction of the charitable contribution deduction to amounts in excess of 2 percent of income. Congress retained the deduction for charitable contributions and eliminated the deduction for state and local sales taxes, but retained the deduction for income and property taxes. I do not believe that our federal system of government depends on the deductibility of state and local taxes, as some allege, and I agree with the Treasury that charitable giving would not be impaired if the deduction were limited to amounts given above a small floor. The revenue gained from restructuring all deductions as the Treasury proposed would be large (on the order of $40 billion in 1988) and could be used to finance further reductions in marginal tax rates or to reduce the federal deficit. In addition, further pruning of the personal deductions would reduce the record-keeping needed to prepare tax returns and simplify tax compliance and administration.

I find another feature of the new tax law bizarre. This is the telescoping of the schedule of fourteen rates into two, while concealing two additional brackets. The reduction in the number of rates is a response to the flat tax proposals which were being promoted when the tax reform bill began its journey through Congress. The simplifications from a single or double rate system are negligible, but the allure of the flat rate survived the legislative process, even though it was necessary to conceal two brackets to moderate the loss of revenue.

More important, I have serious reservations about the elimination of graduation at the top of the income scale. Surely there is a difference in ability to pay out of a marginal dollar at $30,000 than at $300,000 of taxable income, yet the 1986 act makes no distinction between the rates at these levels. Moreover, the 5 percent marginal rate increase in the phase-out range is an anachronism that should not be allowed to survive. I do not recommend going back to fourteen brackets, but I certainly believe that there is room for graduation beyond four brackets, especially when one of the brackets introduces an unsightly bulge into the rate structure.

The four-bracket structure led to two additional changes that I find objectionable. The first is the elimination of the deduction for two-earner couples and the second is the elimination of the privilege of averaging. Since graduation was reduced, Congress felt that the remaining penalties on marriage and on fluctuating incomes were tolerable. These penalties were reduced, but they were not eliminated entirely. The annual marriage penalty can be as large as 13 percent and the penalty on fluctuating income can be as high as 40 percent over a period of five years. Moreover, omitting these provisions will act as a deterrent to the introduction of more graduation.

Consequently, I hope that the two-earner deduction and averaging will be restored.

Another major neglected problem was the erosion of the tax base from the exclusion of employee fringe benefits. Congress has treated fringe benefits leniently because they benefit workers with moderate income, but in fact the largest per capita subsidy goes to the highest paid employees because of graduated tax rates. Moreover, loopholes for moderate income recipients are no more defensible than those for the rich. The Reagan administration proposed to limit the exclusion from the tax base for health insurance premiums paid by employers to a rather generous amount, but even this proposal was rejected by the Congress. The so-called "cafeteria plans," which give employees a choice between taking cash compensation or nontaxable benefits (for such things as medical and dental expenses, accident and health insurance, group term life insurance, and child care), were left untouched. The revenue leakage from these provisions has been growing rapidly and it is time to stop it.

Finally, the act continued the earlier practice of adjusting the personal exemptions, standard deduction, and rate bracket limits for inflation, but avoided adjusting the value of taxable assets. Economists agree that, of the two types of adjustment, the adjustment of asset values is by far the more important. Perhaps the major reason why the tax system was in such disrepute a few years ago was the discrimination against capital incomes inherent in a nominal tax system. Now that capital gains will be subject to full taxation and depreciation has been put on a more realistic basis, an inflation adjustment of the purchase price of assets to compute real gains and losses and real depreciation allowances is essential to avoid pressure to reinstate the ad hoc adjustments that did so much damage to the tax system.

The major inhibition against indexing the base is the difficulty of adjusting interest receipts and expenses for inflation. In 1984, the Treasury I report proposed an approximate plan. It assumed (incorrectly) that the inflation element in all interest payments was the same. Furthermore, the plan was defective when applied to banks and other financial institutions. The Treasury avoided calling for direct adjustments for inflation in each transaction for fear that many taxpayers would not be able to cope. I am not persuaded, however, that the problem is insuperable. Most interest payments are made by financial institutions which can easily calculate the necessary inflation adjustments. Individuals and small businesses might have a difficult problem in adjusting their interest payments, but it would be better to address these problems directly than to refrain from indexing altogether. . . .

NOTES

Note: This paper was delivered as the 1986 Distinguished Lecture on Economics in Government, Joint Session of the American Economic Association and the Society of Government Economists, New Orleans,

December 29, 1986. I am grateful to Henry J. Aaron, Edward F. Denison, Harvey Galper, Richard Goode, and Charles E. McLure, Jr. for helpful comments and suggestions, and to Charles R. Byce and Rob E. Luginbuhl for programming assistance.

1. The deduction was phased in from 25 percent of the first $100 of annual contributions in 1982 and 1983 to 100 percent of contributions in 1986.

2. The personal exemption is increased from $1,080 in 1986 to $1,900 in 1987, $1,950 in 1988, and $2,000 beginning in 1989. For married couples, the standard deduction is increased from $3,670 in 1986 to $3,760 in 1987 and $5,000 beginning in 1988; for single persons, it is increased from $2,480 in 1986 to $2,540 in 1987 and $3,000 beginning in 1988.

3. The earned income credit is increased from 11 percent to 14 percent of earnings, the maximum credit is raised from $550 to $800, and the phase-out range is lifted from $6,500–$11,000 to $9,000–$17,000. The maximum credit and the phase-out starting point will be adjusted for inflation.

4. Losses from passive activities will be deducted only against passive income. A passive activity is a trade or business in which the taxpayer (or spouse) does not materially participate. All rental activities are regarded as passive.

5. The IRA deduction is phased out between $40,000 and $50,000 of adjusted gross income for married couples and between $25,000 and $35,000 for single people.

6. For example, defense contractors are required to pay tax on at least 40 percent of income from long-term contracts, banks will be required to deduct actual losses on loans rather than set up loss reserves and will not be allowed to deduct interest incurred to purchase tax-exempt securities, and oil and mining firms will be required to amortize 30 percent of intangible drilling costs and exploration and development outlays (instead of 20 percent under the old law).

7. For an evaluation of the economic effects of the 1986 tax reform, see Pechman, ed. (1987).

8. Mortgage interest is deductible only on first and second homes and is limited to interest on mortgages up to the purchase price of the property plus the cost of any improvements and loans to pay educational or medical expenses.

REFERENCES

Bosworth, Barry P., *Tax Incentives and Economic Growth*. Washington: The Brookings Institution, 1984.

Goode, Richard, *The Individual Income Tax*. Rev. ed. Washington: The Brookings Institution, 1976.

Meyer, Lawrence H., ed., *The Supply-Side Effects of Economic Policy*. St. Louis: Center for the Study of American Business and the Federal Reserve Bank of St. Louis, 1981.

Pechman, Joseph A., ed., *Tax Reform and the U.S. Economy*. Washington: The Brookings Institution, 1987.

Simons, Henry C., *Federal Tax Reform*. Chicago: The University of Chicago Press, 1950.

Simons, Henry C., *Personal Income Taxation*. Chicago: The University of Chicago Press, 1938.

RICHARD A. MUSGRAVE

Short of Euphoria

Nothing is gained without paying a price. Richard Musgrave argues
that this economic truism applies to the Tax Reform Act of 1986.
The reading is divided into two main sections, analyzing the reform
of (1) the individual income tax and (2) the corporation tax.
Musgrave does not underestimate how impressive the changes
were, but at the same time he carefully points out what the tax law
failed to accomplish and the costs paid to purchase the reform.

QUESTIONS TO GUIDE THE READING

1. How was the Tax Reform Act of 1986 able to satisfy both those
   desiring tax relief and those who argued for closing down tax
   loopholes?

2. If one of the goals was to increase tax revenues by eliminating
   "tax expenditures," why was it predicted that the tax reform
   would accomplish only a 12 percent recoupment of pre-reform
   estimates of 1988 tax expenditures?

3. Why do you think Musgrave argues that the tax expenditures
   associated with deductions, such as homeowner mortgage
   interest, should be voted on by congressional appropriation
   committees instead of tax committees?

4. In what ways might the tax reform laws have caused income
   taxation to become less progressive than it was prior to 1986?

5. Which industries are likely gain from the changes in the
   corporation tax, and which industries are likely to lose?

6. Why does Musgrave argue for needed increases in revenue, and
   why might the 1986 Tax Reform Act have jeopardized our
   ability to raise them?

The Tax Reform Act of 1986 is the most sweeping reform since the early
1940s when the pressures of war finance forced the transformation of the
income tax into a mass tax, and made it the core of the federal tax system.
Since then many adjustments have been made, but the basic structure of the

Richard A. Musgrave, "Short of Euphoria," *Journal of Economic Perspectives 1* (Summer 1987),
   59–71. Reprinted by permission of the author and the publisher.

Richard A. Musgrave is H. H. Burbank Professor of Political Economy Emeritus, Harvard University, and Research Associate, Crown College, University of California, Santa Cruz.

tax has remained unchanged. Behind this nominal stability, however, a slow erosion of the tax base appears to have been at work (Minarik, 1984, pp. 30, 33). The widening of loopholes and emergence of high income shelters gained momentum in recent years and undermined the public's faith in the income tax. The compounding of the investment tax credit and accelerated depreciation diluted and distorted the base of the corporation tax. The current reform reverses these trends, a major accomplishment that all reformers will welcome. But the reform, measured against the "impossible dream" of a decade ago (Break and Pechman, 1979), is far from complete. Its base broadening goes only part of the way, and though substantial gains have been made, they have not come without a price. The pattern of rate reduction, involving a drastic flattening of bracket rates, signals retreat from the progressive taxation that was an essential feature of the income tax tradition. Further, focus on reform has diverted attention from meeting urgent revenue needs.

Reforming the Individual Income Tax

The reform of the individual income tax involves three major changes: (1) a sharp increase in the level of tax-free income; (2) an impressive closing of loopholes over the higher income ranges; and (3) a drastic flattening of bracket rates. Item (1) has cut low income liabilities sharply but only enough to restore the past pattern. Item (2) increases higher income liabilities, improves horizontal equity, and makes for more efficient capital allocation. Item (3) discards the multiple and progressive bracket rates of the past and takes a major step towards a flat rate system. As shown below, loophole closing and flattening of bracket rates have offsetting effects on the pattern of effective tax rates over the middle and upper range, with a moderate reduction at the top of the scale. The magic formula which has permitted legislative success was thus to combine in one basket the goodies of low-end tax relief, closing loopholes, and collapsing the structure of bracket rates. As an additional sweetener, the reform allows a slight overall rate reduction, with a revenue loss of 10 percent in the personal income tax. By offering this combination, the reform could call on support from otherwise conflicting views, some focusing on loophole closing and others on reducing upper bracket rates.

The anatomy of the reform is summarized in Table 1, which shows revenue changes resulting from its major provisions and their impact along the income scale. While the benefits from raising the tax-free floor accrue largely to low incomes, those from rate reductions accrue primarily to the upper ranges, the range which also contributes much of the increased revenue from base broadening. The reform may thus be described as low-end relief, financed by revenue loss, plus a swap of base broadening for rate reduction higher up.

This pattern follows the general path suggested in a string of earlier plans, beginning with the Treasury's *Blueprints for Basic Tax Reform* (1977)

Table 1   Distribution of Revenue Change by Major Reform Components (Fiscal Year 1988)

Percentage Contributed by	Revenue Gain from Base Broadening[a]	Revenue Changes Due to Rate Changes[b]	Revenue Loss from Increase in Exemptions and Standard Deduction[c]
AGI brackets			
0–10,000	0.7%	3.1%	−7.2%
10,000 < 20,000	3.6	7.5	−24.0
20,000 < 30,000	7.9	—	−24.8
30,000 < 50,000	23.7	−20.7	−35.5
50,000 < 100,000	30.1	−33.0	—
100,000 and over	34.0	−57.3	−9.2
Total	100.0	100.0	−100.0
Total Gain or Loss as % of Revenue under 1986 Reform[d]	+24.7%	−11.4%	−6.4%

Source: Brookings tax simulation model. Changes are here estimated separately for each column, while holding the other provisions constant; the outcome thus differs from that under simultaneous estimation. See note (d) below. I am indebted to Chuck Byce for providing the calculation.

[a]Exemptions and rate schedules including zero bracket of 1986 law (adjusted to 1988 levels) are applied to broadened 1988 base as provided by the reform.

[b]The rate schedule provided by the reform is applied to pre-reform base and exemptions. The post-reform standard deduction is reduced to pre-reform zero bracket amount.

[c]Pre-reform rates are applied to pre-reform base, with exemptions increased as provided by reform, and zero bracket amount increased to level of standard deduction under reform.

[d]Total revenue change under each column, as percent of 1988 revenue under present law, estimated at $421 billion (see *Economic and Budget Outlook: An Update,* Congressional Budget Office, August 1986, p. 55). Total gains and losses under the three columns suggest a net gain of 6.4 percent, or $24 billion, as against a loss of 10 percent or $41 billion under simultaneous estimation (Joint Committee on Taxation, *Conference Report,* September, 1986, *II,* 885). The difference arises because revenue gains from base broadening are reduced at lower rates and losses from rate reduction are increased as the base is broadened.

and followed by congressional plans, notably those of Bradley-Gebhardt (1983) and Kemp-Kasten (1983). The ambitious reform proposal of Treasury I (1984) came next, and the Administration's Treasury II plan (1985) with much lower aspirations set the stage for congressional action. All these plans strive to broaden the income base on which the tax is assessed. They bypass and indeed run counter to a different direction of reform which has gained much academic support over the last decade. This type of reform would have substituted a consumption tax, be it a progressive expenditure tax or a flat rate value added tax with an exemption on wage income (Hall and Rabushka, 1983). True to the spirit of income tax reform, the Reform Act of 1986 moves in the opposite direction by curtailing savings incentives and by reaching capital income more fully. Focus on the familiar task of income tax reform was wise, as transition to a truly comprehensive expenditure tax would have called for lengthy analysis and debate, especially regarding the inclusion of gifts and bequests in the base, an extension which seems essential to render this alternative acceptable (Musgrave and Musgrave, 1984; Aaron and Galper, 1985).

Raising the Floor

The income tax reform substantially increased the floor above which income becomes subject to tax. The personal exemptions rose from $1,080 to $2,000 and (for the case of joint returns) the standard deduction from $3,670 to $5,000. (Here as throughout the reference is to the final reform, bypassing a mass of complex transition rules.) For a family of three, the tax-free limit is thus raised from $6,910 to $11,000. As a result, some six million taxpayers (about 5 percent of the total) are dropped from the tax rolls. This achievement is major, but as noted before, not revolutionary. The adjustment only corrects for how personal exemptions and standard deductions had been eroded by inflation. In 1979, the tax-free limit about equaled poverty income; by 1986, it covered only about two-thirds of poverty income.

Additional low-end tax relief is provided by an increase in the earned income tax credit and by rendering it available to single taxpayers with dependents. At the same time, the two-earner credit is repealed, evidently held unnecessary by the flattening of rates. Nevertheless, its repeal will reinstate some degree of marriage penalty. Increasing the value of exemptions relative to the standard deduction will improve the relative position of large families. Except for extension of the earned income credit, these changes are not major. A future reform will still need to come to terms with the ongoing changes in the American family structure.

Broadening the Base

Broadening the tax base produces revenue and thus is essential to its counterpart of rate reduction. Also, it meets the traditional goal of tax reformers. Dating back to the agendas of Schanz (1896), Haig (1921), and Simons (1938), the goal has been to move towards an accretion concept of income or, to put it differently, a base which would cover all sources of income, whether imputed, accrued, or realized in money terms. All uses of income would be included, be they consumption or saving. Given this comprehensive definition of the base, taxpayers with equal levels of income or accretion would be taxed alike, meeting the stricture of horizontal equity. In moving from theory to practice, this global goal had to be reduced to focus on the more measurable and obvious omissions from the tax base (Goode, 1964; Musgrave, 1967, 1968; Surrey, 1973; Pechman, 1984). In 1975, Congress gave these omissions official status as "tax expenditures" and required annual estimates of how much revenue was lost by each.

How far does the reform move towards a complete base and which omissions are corrected? Under the pre-reform law, the 1988 loss from tax expenditures has been estimated at about $400 billion (Joint Committee on Taxation, 1983; Congressional Budget Office, 1983). This loss nearly matches the estimated income tax revenue for that year, so that broadening the base completely would permit a potential tax rate cut of nearly 50 percent. In the reform, the 1988 revenue gain from base broadening is estimated at less than $50 billion. It thus accounts for only 12 percent of the potential recoupment.

The reason for this disappointing result is that major items in the traditional list of base omissions have remained largely untouched, including social security benefits and employer contributions to pensions and health insurance. These and similar employment-related items, which benefit low and middle as well as high incomes, account for one-third of the total revenue loss from tax expenditures. Other bypassed items, mainly benefiting the middle range, include homeowner preferences via deductions of mortgage interest and property tax and the deduction of itemized charitable contributions and state income taxes. The reform also leaves untouched the high income benefit provided by exclusion of interest on state–local revenue bonds. Together these items account for another third of the revenue loss.

Having bypassed these large items, the reform then deals with a substantial part of the remainder. In particular, it severely limits provisions which have led to the expansion of high income tax shelters in recent years. These include the interest deduction on debt used to finance tax-free or postponed investment, the carryover of losses from passive partnership investments against other income, and the transfer of income to minor children. Deduction of business interest will now be limited to investment income, deduction of passive losses will be restricted to income from such investments, and the income of children will be taxed at the marginal rate of the parents. Preferential pension arrangements for executives are limited, and so forth. In what may be the most striking achievement of the reform, it provides for full taxation of realized capital gains. Although this change was facilitated by the reduction of bracket rates, removing the 60 percent exclusion on capital gains will still raise the top rate on such gains from 20 to 28 or 33 percent. Taxation of realized gains as ordinary income meets a goal long sought by tax reformers, although it still falls short of the more ambitious task to tax gains on an accrual basis. These changes are of primary importance for high incomes. Reaching into the middle income range, the reform severely restricts deductible contributions to IRAs and other private pension plans. Reaching further down the income scale, the reform disallows the interest deduction on consumer debt and repeals the state and local sales tax deduction, but not that for state and local income tax. Of course, these changes are relevant only for incomes sufficiently high or unusual to make use of itemized deductions.

The base broadening is thus aimed primarily at correcting practices that serve directly as tax shelters and at high income shelters in particular. Less attention is given to base omissions such as the deduction of charitable contributions which may be considered as matching grants given to induce certain uses of income. Such relief may be viewed as given in lieu of direct subsidy to charity and more nearly deserving the tax expenditure label than outright shelters do. Nevertheless, a strong presumption remains against the use of tax relief in lieu of expenditure measures. Expenditure objectives, to be judged properly, should be evaluated before appropriation, not tax, committees. The homeowner preferences (deduction of property tax and mortgage interest), for instance, would hardly pass as a $45 billion expenditure item. Moreover, using tax devices, especially deductions, creates inequities which may be avoided by using direct outlays. Unfortunately, the reform has failed to confront the validity (or lack thereof) of such items as the deductibility of mortgage interest which has been retained even for second homes, or the exclusion of interest on state and local securities which has been limited only for non-revenue bonds.

But what has been accomplished is enough for gratitude. Removing shelters improves horizontal equity over the high income ranges and yields substantial efficiency gains. Widespread use of high income shelters has distorted the form in which business is done and diverted investment into favored uses like real estate. The reform should thus improve the efficiency of capital flows. Limiting tax postponement under IRA and pension plans should also free the flow of savings. At the same time, the level of saving may be affected adversely. In view of past experience, this factor is not likely to be major, but it does run counter to the savings neutrality offered by an expenditure tax approach, as it had to by the nature of income tax reform. Finally, the reduction in marginal rates should raise work effort at the upper end of the scale where the cut in marginal rates is sharpest. Note, however, that the marginal dollar of high income executives and professionals may be earned for purposes of investment rather than consumption, so that the fuller taxation of investment income may offset the lower rates. Reducing top rates, moreover, carries the opportunity cost of maintaining higher rates on lower incomes. Therefore, the reform may or may not raise work effort on balance.

Before leaving this appraisal of base reform, one major failing should be noted: the reform fails to index the tax treatment of capital income. The reform does complete the indexing of exemptions, standard deductions, credits and bracket limits introduced in 1981, but it does not come to grips (except for inventory gains) with indexing the capital base. The accretion concept not only requires that all accretion be included in the base, but also that the accretion be defined in real terms. Inflation generates nominal gains which are not real, and real losses which are not nominal. Treasury I made a brave attempt to deal with this problem by proposing to index real assets in measuring capital gains and to index interest payments and receipts in dealing with debt. However, Treasury II and the reform legislation dropped these proposals. The problem may be minor at the present low rate of inflation but the tax system should not gamble on inflation always remaining low.

Indexing capital income is not a simple task, but the alternatives are worse. For one thing, full taxation of capital income (even in a world of only moderate inflation) is difficult to accomplish unless indexation is faced (Helperin and Steuerle, 1986). Full taxation of realized gains, if it is to survive, should thus have been combined with indexing of the base. Indexing is needed to protect the Treasury, too. To close inflation-based loopholes, the reform had to introduce complex counter-provisions, such as the limitations based on interest and loss deductions. The resulting linkage of particular sources and uses of income recalls the earlier practices of schedular taxation and greatly complicates the tax code.

Since the closing of loopholes remains incomplete, the reform moves to a substantially strengthened minimum tax, a step which the more severe approach of Treasury I (including indexing) had avoided. The previous add-on tax is replaced by an outright minimum tax, the rate is raised to 21 percent, and remaining preference items are severely limited, including the deduction of untaxed appreciation on charitable contributions. Given the potential loopholes remaining, the minimum tax avoids compounding and is a helpful safeguard, but correcting the questionable provisions would have been the better approach.

Cutting Rates

In the final part of the reform triad, the fourteen-rate structure ranging from 11 to 50 percent collapses into what is basically a two-bracket system with rates of 15 and 28 percent. The higher rate which begins at $17,800 for single and at $29,750 for joint returns may be expected to reach about one-quarter of all returns and to cover as much as two-thirds of taxable income. But the story is more complex. The reform also provides for a phaseout of the benefit derived from personal exemptions (not a new idea) and from the lower bracket rate, which is accomplished by imposing a 5 percent surcharge over a specified income range. For a joint return, the tax thus equals 15 percent on the first $29,749, and 28 percent on the next $29,750 to $71,900, as follows from the basic rates. But the tax equals 28 plus 5 or 33 percent on $71,900 to $192,930, before falling again to 28 percent on income above that level. As a result, the 15 percent rate vanishes and the tax on income above $192,930 comes to be imposed at a flat rate of 28 percent. To accomplish this result, the roller coaster pattern of bracket rates had to be accepted, but what was gained? The purpose, it appears, was to abolish progressive rates and to set a 28 percent ceiling at the top of the income scale. Having done so, additional revenue had to be obtained by raising the marginal rate for more taxpayers in the middle to upper range.

While this anomaly is unlikely to survive, the collapse of the rate structure takes a giant step towards the principle of a flat rate tax; that is, a tax that applies a single rate on income above a personal exemption. A rising effective rate is maintained over lower incomes, but progression ceases over the upper range, thus approaching a long-sought goal of conservative critics of progressive taxation. This result is the crucial significance of reducing the number of bracket rates and not, as the public has been led to believe, its contribution to tax simplification. Reducing the number of bracket rates has little if anything to do with simplification, because taxpayers will use rate tables in determining their liabilities with fourteen rates, or two, or only one. The claims for greater simplification are thus disturbing and lack candor, especially since the 5 percent surcharge adds greatly to the complexity of the system.

How have these changes affected the distribution of the income tax burden? Taking the entire income range as a whole, progressivity may be said to have increased (Kiefer, 1986), but the picture differs at various places on the income scale. At the low end, progressivity or the slope of the effective rate schedule is dominated by the level of tax-free income as set by the personal exemption and standard deduction. Thus, the reform raises progressivity here. Higher up, progression depends increasingly on the pattern of bracket rates, as the level of tax-free income becomes relatively less important. Reducing the number of basic brackets to only two thus severely limits the possibility of continued progression. Without base broadening for higher incomes, the reform would have greatly flattened the effective rate curve. But given the combination of reduced bracket rates and base broadening, the net effect (after allowing for a slight decline in the overall level of rates) has been to leave the pattern of effective rates over a broad middle range largely unchanged. Columns 1 and 2 of Table 2 demonstrate this conclusion by showing pre- and post-reform tax rates. As also shown in Table 2, the tax reduction has been more substantial above $100,000 but the change is still small over a wide range.

Given this neutrality, it would be easy to conclude that the base broadening plus rate cut package is beyond criticism. Yet, the outcome is very different from what would have resulted had base broadening been undertaken without changing the general pattern of bracket rates. By patterning rate reduction to offset the closing of loopholes over the higher income range, the reform in effect legitimizes the pre-reform role of such loopholes in voiding progressive bracket rates. This policy choice was not a necessary consequence of base broadening. The goals of revenue neutrality and of base broadening (with resulting horizontal equity and efficiency gains) might also have been achieved in the progressive spirit of pre-reform bracket rates. To illustrate, column 4 of Table 2 shows the result of first applying the old bracket rates to the broadened base (as shown in column 3) and then reducing all tax liabilities by a flat 9 percent to maintain revenue neutrality. The resulting top rate is 42.6 percent, not 28 percent. Upper bracket liabilities would have been raised substantially while those over the middle range would have been reduced somewhat. The principle of upper end progression reflected in the old bracket rates would have been retained and strengthened. Other solutions, falling between this illustration and the reform formula, might also have been chosen.

Table 2   Effective Rates for 1988 (Joint Return, One Dependent)

AGI (Pre-Reform Law)	Pre-Reform Law[a] 1	Reform Law 2	Pre-Reform Rates, Reform Base[b] 3	Alternative Patterns[c] 4
0–10,000	0%	0%	0%	0%
10,000–20,000	5.2	4.3	1.7	1.6
20,000–30,000	8.8	8.3	6.0	5.6
30,000–50,000	12.3	11.0	10.5	9.6
50,000–100,000	16.5	16.0	16.9	15.5
100,000–200,000	23.8	21.8	28.6	26.2
200,000–500,000	29.6	25.0	38.0	34.8
500,000–1,000,000	29.8	26.8	43.2	37.6
1,000,000 +	27.9	26.6	45.3	41.6
Total	14.5	13.4	14.7	13.4

Source: Brookings Tax Simulation File. Effective rates are tax liability divided by the appropriate definition of AGI. I am indebted to Chuck Byce for providing the calculation.
[a]1986 law applicable to 1988 levels of income. Bracket limits and exemptions are applied as estimated for 1988 levels.
[b]1986 rates (including zero bracket amount) are applied to broadened base, increased exemptions, and standard deductions under the reform. To avoid double counting, the reform standard deduction is reduced by zero bracket amount.
[c]Effective rates in column 3 are reduced by 9.0 percent so as to equalize total revenue with that of column 2.

The way in which tax reform was formulated from the outset excluded such alternative patterns. From *Blueprints* on, the goal was to broaden the base while leaving effective rates (except for the inflation correction at the bottom) essentially unchanged. This approach may have offered the key compromise which permitted the reform (including its full inclusion of realized capital gains) to succeed in the political arena, but it also permitted the Congress to bypass the important question of vertical equity. Had Congress never meant the old bracket rates to apply against a broadened base, or has there been a major change in what is an equitable pattern of effective rates? This central issue deserved an explicit review, rather than just emerging as the by-product of a formula calling for base broadening and revenue neutrality. Yet the drastic reduction of the rate ceiling from 50 to 28 percent (following the 1981 cut from 70 to 50 percent) may well prove the key feature of the reform, one which (for better or for worse) is likely to set the pattern for the western world. As noted below, the increase in the corporation tax will offset this change somewhat, but that form of correction is hardly the most appropriate.

Focus on horizontal rather than vertical equity avoids controversy and appeals to practical judgment. The case for horizontal equity (that people in the same situation should pay the same amount) seems intuitively obvious and is generally accepted, while that of vertical equity (that people in dissimilar situations should pay the appropriate differing amounts) seems nebulous and unmanageable. At closer consideration, however, the two concepts are linked. The one makes little sense without the other. Equality or inequality must be measured by a meaningful index, such as income, and this index must be the same in both the horizontal and the vertical context. The propositions that A and B should pay the same since they have the same income and that A and C should pay differently because their incomes differ derive from the same prior principle; that is, each should pay in line with ability as measured by the accepted index.

Comparison of unequals, to be sure, requires specifying a social welfare function to assign weights to successive units of income. The shape of this function is not given by scripture or the laws of nature, nor by mathematical convenience. Rather, it has to be determined by a political process. This task is troublesome, but it is nevertheless an essential part of designing a tax structure. It cannot be replaced by efficiency considerations. Other things equal, of course, the less costly tax dollar is superior. But equity and efficiency are supplements, not alternatives, for good tax policy. When determining an equitable distribution of the tax burden, the latter should be defined so as to include deadweight loss, not only tax dollars paid; when measuring efficiency cost, allowance should be made for the social valuation of the tax burden and not (as is typically done) for dollar amounts only. Convenient or not, the problem of vertical equity remains important.

A further word regarding the role of progressivity and the structure of the income tax should be added. Effective rate progression over the lower and middle income range is dominated by the exemption and standard deduction (in effect a zero rate bracket) with rising bracket rates contributing substantially to progressivity only above $50,000 or more. If the recent move toward reducing or abandoning effective rate progression over the middle to upper range were to continue, this trend might carry important implications for tax structure design. The cumbersome aggregation of all incomes derived by any one individual is essential for a system of personal taxation and progressive bracket rates, but it might no longer be needed in a flat rate setting. Indirect taxation of income at the source might then take the place of a direct personal tax, either via a schedular system with a uniform rate or an income type value added tax. The role of the exemption in securing effective rate progression over the lower and middle income range might then be met by a per capita transfer. The same reasoning applies to a consumption base, where a personal expenditure tax might be replaced by a value added tax with exemptions for low income items. These considerations are added here not to advocate such indirect taxation, as I favor an effective application of bracket rates rising up to, say, 50 percent, but to note the implications of flattened bracket rates for tax design. The direction of the current reform, therefore, not only contributes to traditional reform goals pertinent to the role of the income tax as the progressive component of the tax system, but may also foreshadow a quite different setting for income taxation.

Reforming the Corporation Tax

Given the individual income tax reform losing about 10 percent of revenue or $40 billion (1988 level), strict revenue neutrality would have called for an offsetting 40 percent increase in the corporation tax. Instead, corporation tax revenue is increased by only about 25 percent. Nevertheless, this boost reverses the sharp drop in corporation relative to income tax revenue which began in the 1950s, a trend that was pushed further by the "supply-side" reform of 1981. Corporation tax revenue had fallen from 50 percent of individual income tax yield in the mid-1960s to only 20 percent in 1986. The recent reform will increase the corporation tax take to about 30 percent (1988) of individual income tax revenue.

As in the case of the individual income tax, the thrust of the corporate reform is to trade base broadening for rate reduction. Rate reduction from 46 to 34 percent loses $20 billion in revenue (1988 levels) and is offset by an equal gain from repeal of the investment tax credit, leaving a net gain of $25 billion from other provisions. These range from the relatively trivial but popular case of deductions for meals and travel (largely disallowed by Treasury I but left at 80 percent by the reform) to the major issue of how to set the rates at which capital costs may be recovered. The correct approach, that is, "economic depreciation," sets depreciation rates to match asset lives, thereby rendering the effective tax rate independent of the life of an asset. The tax becomes neutral across industries with short- and long-lived assets and with different capital/labor ratios. Reaching such a goal has been complicated by the practice of providing investment incentives through accelerated depreciation. By 1981, a drastic shortening of depreciation patterns, combined with the investment credit, not only protected corporations against inflation but greatly reduced the effective rate of corporation tax. Moreover, it resulted in widely differing effective rates across industries, varying from negative rates to rates over 40 percent. Though modified in 1982, such differentials continued to prevail and have become more pronounced with abating inflation.

The current reform largely corrects these differentials. The investment tax credit is repealed and depreciation schedules are lengthened somewhat. While schedules remain on the short side of economic depreciation, they are set more nearly in line with actual asset lives. The revenue gain from these changes is then used in large part for lower rates. Some traditional preferences are retained, especially in the case of oil and gas, but the general effect is to neutralize the impact of the tax substantially. As a consequence, previously disadvantaged industries such as services and some consumer goods are helped by the reform while equipment intensive industries will lose. Real estate will be hit especially hard, not only by slower depreciation but also by the closing of income tax shelters. In general, this equalization will reduce tax-induced distortions and expedite structural shifts in industry which are already occurring. Competitive forces will operate more freely, but adjustment costs and hardships for already troubled sectors cannot be disregarded.

While revising the prevailing incentive structure was urgently needed, relying exclusively on accelerated depreciation as an investment incentive may be questioned. When a group of advisers headed by Stanley Surrey proposed the investment tax credit to candidate John F. Kennedy over twenty years ago, we argued that it would permit depreciation schedules to be set in line with economic depreciation, while offering the credit as a distinct and visible tool for providing an incentive to new capital investment. This argument still holds, and retention of a restructured (and neutralized) investment credit combined with economic depreciation might well have been the better solution. But investors, like everyone else, prefer their preferences hidden, an objective acceleration conveniently serves. To be sure, rate reduction also increases net returns, but it cannot be as effective (per dollar of revenue cost) as the investment credit since old as well as new capital stands to gain from lower rates.

As with the individual income tax, the reform again fails to address inflation. The Treasury I recommendation that the depreciation base be indexed was not accepted. Once more the reform resorts to a much toughened minimum tax set at 20 percent. This minimum tax is applied to a base which disallows or limits many of the remaining preferences, including accelerated depreciation and intangible drilling costs. The reform also introduces accounting income as an alternative tax base, a major innovation which may be difficult to interpret and raise compliance costs. As noted previously, the minimum tax is no substitute for a truly comprehensive tax, but it does limit the effect of remaining omissions from a comprehensive tax base.

The reform does secure a fuller inclusion of corporate source income into the tax base, but it bypasses a further concern of traditional tax reform: integrating the individual and corporation tax. While the corporation has a separate legal existence, its income eventually accrues to the shareholders and should be taxed, along with their other income, under the individual income tax. But if such income is taxed under the individual income tax, imposing an extra tax on corporate income (except for income flowing abroad) discriminates against the income source and offends the principle that all income should be treated alike. Integration may be approached in various ways; for example, Treasury I proposed that 50 percent of dividend distribution be deducted from the corporate tax base, but the reform did not adopt this step. Of course, integration would have involved a revenue loss, thus requiring higher income tax rates. But that correction would have been shared by all incomes, thus avoiding discrimination against income from corporate sources. Although the revenue gain from base broadening is largely offset by rate reduction, the reform increases the corporation tax somewhat.

This increase will add to the progressivity of the tax system since corporate source income weighs more heavily when moving up the income scale. But as noted before, an increase in corporate taxes is hardly the correct way to offset an excessive cut in high-bracket rates.

Epilogue

The reform of the individual income tax offers low income relief and closes upper income loopholes. Capital income, which had been the primary beneficiary of loopholes, will pay more while other sources will pay less, thus improving horizontal equity. But the reform does little to broaden the base over the lower and middle income range and leaves major tax expenditures intact. Realized capital gains are included fully in the expanded tax base, but failure to index capital income will prove a serious defect. Bracket rates are collapsed and progression over the high income range is largely discarded. With a 70 percent rate still in effect over a decade ago, dropping the rate ceiling to only 28 percent takes a giant and, as this observer sees it, excessive step towards a flat rate tax. Such is the case especially at a time when inequality is tending to widen (Bureau of the Census, 1986) and when the importance of the income tax in the overall tax structure is declining. The reform thus strengthens the income tax by broadening its base and also signals a departure from its traditional role as an instrument of progressive taxation.

The reform of the corporation tax also closes loopholes and broadens the tax base. Repeal of the investment credit, combined with depreciation reform and rate reduction, equalizes treatment across industries, but the failure to index the depreciable base again leaves a serious problem. The reform is no supply-side panacea. Economic efficiency will increase as shelters are removed and differentials in the treatment of corporate investment are flattened. Reducing the marginal rates applicable to high executive and professional incomes may stimulate greater effort as may the effect on low income recipients who are now dropped from the income tax roll. But the first bracket rate is increased and work effort will hardly be raised substantially. The effect of lower corporate tax rates on new investment is not likely to counterbalance the repeal of the investment tax credit. Savings incentives are reduced, which may have little negative effect but will surely not help in meeting the prerequisite for faster growth, an increase in the savings rate.

The importance of economic growth raises a final point. Whatever the potential effects of tax reform on the private savings rate, including even transition to an expenditure tax, such efforts dwindle when compared to the contribution that should be made by reducing the budgetary dissaving of the federal deficit. Here the tax reform has made no contribution. On the contrary, preoccupation with a reform yielding income tax reductions for 80 percent of taxpayers has made it difficult to focus on the revenue increases needed to correct a lopsided macroeconomic policy mix, to reduce public dissaving, and to relieve undue pressure on expenditure programs. More-over, the reform is now followed by a tacit agreement to leave the income tax alone for some time. This agreement will further block the needed revenue increase, a need which can hardly be met adequately while bypassing the core of the federal tax system. As noted at the outset, the reform brings substantial improvements, but they have come at a price.

REFERENCES

Aaron, Henry and Harvey Galper, *Assessing Tax Reform*. Washington, D.C.: The Brookings Institution, 1985, p. 29.

Bradford, David, *Blueprints for Basic Tax Reform*. 2nd ed. rev. Arlington, Va.: Tax Analysts, 1984.

Bradley, Bill, *The Fair Tax*. New York: Pocket Books, 1986.

Break, George F. and Joseph Pechman, *Federal Tax Reform, The Impossible Dream?* Washington, D.C.: The Brookings Institution, 1979.

Bureau of the Census, *After Tax Income Estimates of Households: 1984*, August 6, 1986.

Congressional Budget Office, *Tax Expenditure: Current Issues and Projections for Fiscal Years 1984–1988*. Washington, D.C., 1983.

Goode, Richard, *The Individual Income Tax*. Washington, D.C.: The Brookings Institution, 1964.

Haig, R. M., "The Concept of Income." In Haig, R. M., ed., *The Federal Income Tax*. New York: 1921.

Hall, Robert E. and A. Rabushka, *Low Tax, Simple Tax, Flat Tax*. New York: McGraw-Hill, 1983.

Helperin, D. and G. Steuerle, *Indexing the Tax System for Inflation*, Paper prepared for Brookings Tax Conference, October 30, 1986.

Joint Committee on Taxation, *Estimation of Federal Tax Expenditures for Fiscal Years 1983–1988*. Washington, D.C.: U.S. Government Printing Office, 1983, p. 18.

Kiefer, Donald W., *The Progressivity Effects of the Individual Income Tax Revisions in the Tax Reform Act of 1986*. Congressional Research Service, The Library of Congress, Report No. 86-892E, 1986.

Minarik, S. J., *Making Tax Choices*. Washington, D.C.: Urban Institute Press, 1985.

Musgrave, Richard, "In Defense of an Income Concept," 1967, *Harvard Law Review,* 81.

Musgrave, Richard, *The Theory of Public Finance*. New York: McGraw-Hill, 1957, Ch. 1.

Musgrave, Richard. In Bittker, Boris I., ed., *A Comprehensive Income Tax? A Debate*. Branford, Conn.: Federal Tax Press, 1968.

Musgrave, Richard, and Peggy Musgrave, *Public Finance in Theory and Practice*. New York: McGraw-Hill, 1984, p. 237.

Musgrave, Richard and Alan Peacock, *Classics in the Theory of Public Finance*. London: MacMillan, 1958, p. 108.

Pechman, Joseph, *Federal Tax Policy*. Washington, D.C.: The Brookings Institution, 1984.

Schanz, G. "Der Einkommensbegriff und die Einkommensteuergesetze," *Finanz Archiv,* 1896, *xiii.*

Simons, Henry C., *Federal Tax Reform*. Chicago: The University of Chicago, Press, 1950. First circulated in 1943.

Simons, Henry C., *Personal Income Taxation*. Chicago: University of Chicago Press, 1938.

Surrey, Stanley, *Pathways to Tax Reform*. Cambridge, MA: Harvard University Press, 1973.

U.S. Department of the Treasury, The President's Tax Proposal to the Congress for Fairness, Growth, and Simplicity, May 1985.

U.S. Department of the Treasury, *Tax Reform for Fairness, Simplicity, and Economic Growth: The Treasury Department's Report to the President*. Washington, D.C., 1984.

Economics of Fiscal Federalism

Fiscal federalism refers to the partition of taxation and expenditure functions among levels of government. Thus, the United States is said to have a federal form of government because it is composed of a central government, state governments, and local governments. A multilevel governing system gives rise to some interesting and important questions. What functions of government can best be performed by each level? What are the benefits and costs of a system in which households and businesses can choose among subnational governments with different tax and expenditure policies? How does national tax reform affect state and local governments?

SELECTION 41

WALLACE E. OATES

An Economic Approach
to Federalism

What form of government best performs the economic functions of
the public sector? Some believe that local governments perform
these functions most efficiently, while others assert that state or
national governments have the advantage. In reality, it is more
likely that each level of government has a comparative advantage
in performing certain governmental functions. This issue is
explored by Wallace Oates, as he compares the centralized,
decentralized, and federal forms of government.

QUESTIONS TO GUIDE THE READING

1. Why is a centralized government better suited to perform the
   function of economic stabilization?
2. What limits the effectiveness of local redistribution programs?
3. Why will communities tend to produce a less than efficient
   amount of a pure public good?
4. What are the advantages of a decentralized government?
5. What does the author believe is the central problem of
   federalism?

*The federal system was created with the intention of combining
the different advantages which result from the magnitude and the
littleness of nations.*

   ALEXIS DE TOCQUEVILLE, DEMOCRACY IN AMERICA

The functions of the public sector are to ensure an efficient use of resources,
to establish an equitable distribution of income, and to maintain the economy at high levels of employment with reasonable price stability. The concern in this chapter is the organization of the public sector that will best
allow the government to perform these tasks. In short, the question is, What
form of government promises the greatest success in resolving the allocation, distribution, and stabilization problems? To get at this issue, it is useful

Wallace E. Oates, "An Economic Approach to Federalism," in *Fiscal Federalism*, Harcourt
   Brace Jovanovich, 1972, 3–20. Reprinted by permission of the author.

Wallace E. Oates is Professor of Economics at University of Maryland.

to consider at a conceptual level two polar or nearly polar forms of government. At one end of the spectrum is complete centralization: a unitary form of government. In this case, the central government, in the absence of other levels of government, assumes full responsibility for the three economic functions of the public sector. As we move in the opposite direction on this spectrum of governmental forms, we approach total decentralization of government. For my purposes, it is useful to stop a bit short of total decentralization, which would presumably represent a state of anarchy. Rather, let us consider as our opposite extreme a highly decentralized system in which the central government is almost completely devoid of economic responsibility. In this instance, a system of small local governments performs virtually all the economic tasks of the public sector. In both cases, however, the society under consideration is understood to be a nation with a single currency and with an absence of restrictions on the movements of goods and services within the system. The sole difference in the two cases is the extent of decentralization of the public sector.

While these cases, especially the latter, are admittedly highly unrealistic (and this in a way is the point), it is instructive to consider briefly the relative economic advantages of the two alternatives. From such an examination, a powerful economic case for federalism emerges.

The Economic Case for Centralized Government

An examination of the stabilization problem suggests that a centralized, or unitary, form of government would possess a far greater capability to maintain high levels of employment with stable prices than would a public sector characterized by extreme decentralization. At the outset, it is obvious that there must exist a central agency to control the size of the money supply. If, in contrast, each level of government was able to create and destroy money, there would exist an irresistible incentive to rapid monetary expansion. By simply using a printing press, any local government could create paper with which to purchase real goods and services from neighboring communities. It would clearly be in the interest of each municipality to finance its expenditures by creating money rather than by burdening its own constituents with taxation. The likely outcome would be rampant price inflation; for this reason, some form of centralized monetary control is imperative.

Without access to monetary policy, local governments would have to rely on fiscal policy—that is, expenditure and revenue programs—to stabilize their respective economies. The scope, however, for an efficacious fiscal policy is severely limited. First, small local economies are, in general, highly open economies, as their constituents typically purchase a large portion of the goods and services they consume from other localities. This implies that the leakages from a marginal dollar of private spending are likely to be quite large. As a result, in a simple Keynesian system, the expenditure multiplier (that is, the reciprocal of the sum of the marginal propensity to save and the marginal propensity to import out of income) will tend to be quite small.

Much of the expansionary impact of a local tax cut, for example, will be dissipated, since only a relatively small proportion of the new income generated will be spent on locally produced goods and services. . . .

Second, the use of Keynesian deficit-finance policies to stimulate the local economy carries with it a cost to local residents, a cost that is largely absent for such policies at the national level. The cost stems from the nature of local government debt. Within a national economy, there normally exists a high degree of mobility of financial capital; debt issued in one community is generally held to a large extent by residents of other communities. This means, as Alvin Hansen and Harvey Perloff have pointed out, that the use of debt finance by a local government will tend to saddle the community with an external debt.[1] In later years, repayment of principal and interest will necessitate a transfer of real income from the residents of the community to outsiders. In contrast, since the international mobility of capital is normally far less than that which exists within a nation, interest-bearing debt issued by the central government will take the form primarily of an internal debt. The central government is thus in a position to stimulate the economy without burdening society with the prospect of future income transfers to outsiders.

The logic therefore suggests that, as regards the stabilization problem, a unitary form of government is distinctly superior to a government organization exhibiting an extreme degree of decentralization. A central government is in a position to make good use both of monetary and of fiscal policy in maintaining the economy at high levels of output without excessive inflation. Local governments, in contrast, are seriously constrained in their capacity to regulate the aggregate level of economic activity in their jurisdictions. Moreover, it should be stressed that, among a highly interdependent group of local economies, movements in levels of business activity tend to parallel one another. Contractions or booms in some areas are rapidly communicated to neighboring areas through a contracted or increased demand for exports. This means that cyclical movements in aggregate economic activity are largely national in scope and as such can best be treated by countercyclical policies operating on a nationwide scale.

As in the case of the stabilization problem, the resolution of the distribution problem is a difficult matter in a system characterized by a high degree of decentralization of the public sector. Suppose that the members of society desire a more egalitarian distribution of income than that which emerges from the unfettered operation of the market system. Assume, moreover, that the socially desired distribution of income is one in which the disposable income of each individual or family depends only on the unit's level of income before any redistributive taxes and transfers. The idea here is simply that the desired distribution of income requires the transfer of certain amounts of income from the wealthy to the poor, and the tax paid, or, alternatively, the subsidy received, by a particular individual depends solely on his level of income. In this case, the program required to achieve society's desired pattern of income distribution is clearly a negative income tax. The existing distribution of income can be translated into the desired one by adopting a certain tax-subsidy schedule by which higher-income units pay taxes that are distributed in the prescribed pattern to lower-income units.

The difficulty is that within the highly decentralized fiscal system, local governments working independently to achieve differing redistributional objectives are likely to run into real trouble. Consider, for example, a community that adopts a strong negative income-tax program designed to achieve a significantly more equalitarian distribution of income than exists in the rest of the nation. Such a program, in view of the relatively high degree of individual mobility that characterizes a national economy, would create strong incentives for the wealthy to move out to neighboring municipalities and for the poor to migrate into the community. A more nearly equal distribution of income might well result, but it would be caused largely by an outflow of the rich and an influx of the poor, with a consequent fall in the level of per-capita income in the community under consideration.

The curious part is that this could happen even if all the members of the community, including the wealthy, genuinely desired to eliminate poverty through an explicitly redistributive policy. Every individual might stand willing to vote for a negative income tax program, and yet, if any one person perceived an avenue through which he could avoid his own contribution to the program, it might well be in his interest to do so. The point is that the contribution of any single person or family to the general elimination of poverty in a society is likely to be negligible. There is, therefore, a real incentive for so-called free-rider behavior by which an individual would leave to others the burden of financing redistributive programs. For this reason, the migration of relatively wealthy individuals from a locality that adopts an aggressive redistributive program may be perfectly consistent with a general commitment on the part of that society to a policy aimed at reducing or eliminating poverty.

The scope for redistributive programs is thus limited to some extent by the potential mobility of residents, which tends to be greater the smaller the jurisdiction under consideration. This suggests that, since mobility across national boundaries is generally much less than that within a nation, a policy of income redistribution has a much greater promise of success if carried out on the national level. A unitary form of government is therefore likely to be far more effective in achieving the redistributional objectives of the society than is a governmental organization at the opposite end of the spectrum.

Turning last to the allocation problem, one finds again that, for a certain class of goods and services, a highly centralized government is likely to be far more successful in providing appropriate levels of output than is a system of local governments. It is the responsibility of the public sector as a whole either to institute incentives for private production or, alternatively, to provide directly appropriate levels of output of those goods and services not forthcoming in efficient quantities through the operation of free markets. Some of these goods and services may be of such a character that they confer, or could confer, significant benefits on everyone in the nation. Consider, for example, a pure public good whose benefits extend to the individuals in all communities. The production of X units of the commodity in one community implies that X units are consumed by the residents of all municipalities. A rough approximation to such a commodity might be a missile system established by one community that is bound by an alliance to other communities to regard an attack on one as an attack on all. Under these circumstances, a missile system in any single community would serve as a deterrent to a potential aggressor against any of the others, for the enemy would have to expect missile retaliation should he invade any of the localities. In this case, then, a missile system in one community serves as a substitute for a similar system in a neighboring jurisdiction.

For such a public good, is a system of decentralized decision-making likely to result in the efficient level of output of the commodity? Will the individual communities, each seeking to maximize the welfare of its own constituents, end up providing a missile system such that the cost of a marginal missile is equal to the sum of the values placed on that missile by the residents of all the communities? The answer, as Mancur Olson and Richard Zeckhauser has shown, is generally no.[2] The reason is that each community in determining whether it will or will not produce an additional unit of the good (that is, another missile implacement) considers only the benefits its own residents will receive from the marginal unit. As a result, the full social value of an additional unit of the good is not taken into consideration. As Olson and Zeckhauser explain it, a subefficient output results

> because each ally gets only a fraction of the benefits of any collective good that is provided, but each pays the full cost of any additional amounts of the collective good. This means that individual members of an alliance or international organization have an incentive to stop providing the collective good long before the Pareto optimal [that is, economically efficient] output for the group has been provided. This is particularly true of the smaller members who get smaller shares of the total benefits accruing from the good, and who find that they have little or no incentive to provide additional amounts of the collective good once the larger members have provided the amounts they want for themselves, with the result that the burdens are shared in a disproportionate way.[3]

The one special case in which an efficient output may be attained is where the various communities have an agreement to share the cost of an additional unit of the good in the same proportion as they share the benefits. In this case, all communities would be willing to support the production of an additional missile site if the value of the marginal missile exceeded its cost. However, in general, one would expect such public goods to be underproduced in a system of decentralized decision-making. In contrast, under a unitary form of government, assuming that public decision-makers seek to maximize the welfare of the entire citizenry, the value of a marginal unit of the public good to members of all the communities would presumably be taken into account. One would therefore expect a central government to provide a better approximation to the efficient level of output of those public goods that benefit the members of all communities than would a system of decentralized decision-making.

The preceding discussion suggests that a unitary form of government has several important advantages over its counterpart at the opposite end of the spectrum. In a system comprising only local governments, the public sector would be seriously handicapped in its capacity to meet its economic responsibilities. Local governments, I have argued, would find it extremely difficult to stabilize their respective economies, to realize the most equitable distribution of income, and to provide efficient levels of output of those public goods that confer benefits on the members of all or several communities. A central government, in contrast, is much more capable of performing these tasks satisfactorily. Nonetheless, a system of local governments does possess attractive economic attributes to which we turn next.

The Economic Case for Decentralized Government

A basic shortcoming of a unitary form of government is its probable insensitivity to varying preferences among the residents of the different communities. If all public goods are supplied by a central government, one should expect a tendency toward uniformity in public programs across all communities. The problem here is that the level of consumption of a public good almost always involves compromise. Some individuals may prefer an expanded and high-quality program of public services, while others may want less public output and the accompanying reduced level of taxes. For truly national public goods (that is, those goods all individuals consume in identical quantities regardless of their community of residence), such compromise is inevitable. However, for other public goods whose benefits are limited to a specific subset of the population (for example, the members of a single community), there is at least a partial solution in greater decentralization of the public sector.

Consider, for example, a public good whose consumption is limited to the residents of the community in which it is provided. If provided by the central government, the most likely outcome would be similar levels of consumption of the good in all communities. However, such uniform levels of consumption may not be efficient, because they do not take into consideration possible variations in the tastes of residents of differing communities. If, in contrast, each community had its own local government, one might expect variations in the level of provision of this public good across the different localities, variations that would, to some extent at least, reflect the differences in tastes of the constituencies of the communities. The point here is that economic efficiency is attained by providing the mix of output that best reflects the preferences of the individuals who make up society, and if all individuals are compelled to consume the same level of output of a good when variations in individual consumption—or, in this case, variations in consumption among different subsets of the population—are possible, an inefficient allocation of resources is the likely result. A decentralized form of government therefore offers the promise of increasing economic efficiency by providing a range of outputs of certain public goods that corresponds more closely to the differing tastes of groups of consumers.

The possibilities for welfare gains through decentralization are further enhanced by the phenomenon of consumer mobility. As Charles Tiebout has argued, in a system of local government, a consumer can to some extent select as his place of residence a community that provides a fiscal package well suited to his preferences.[4] One can envision a system of local governments where, for example, each community provides a different level of consumption of a local public good and in which the consumer by "voting on foot" selects the community that provides the level of public output that best satisfies his tastes. Through this mechanism, one can get a sort of market solution to the problem of producing efficient levels of output of some public goods. A decentralized form of government thus possesses the advantage of allowing various levels of output of certain public goods, by means of which resources can be employed more efficiently in satisfying the preferences of consumers.

Decentralization may, moreover, result in greater experimentation and innovation in the production of public goods. With a large number of independent producers of a good, one might expect a variety of approaches (for example, varying techniques of instruction in local public schools) that, in the long run, promises greater technical progress in modes of providing these goods and services. Closely connected to this point are the competitive pressures that result from an enlarged number of producers; such pressures will tend to compel the adoption of the most efficient techniques of production. If, for example, public officials in one community have discovered a particularly effective way of providing a certain service, the governments of neighboring jurisdictions will, in all probability, be compelled to adopt similar techniques of production in order to avoid serious criticism from local residents. In contrast, if a single central government provides all public goods with no competitors, one might well expect the forces inducing innovation and efficiency to be less strong. A system of local government may thus promote both static and dynamic efficiency in the provision of public goods and services.

Finally, there is some reason to believe that decentralization may lead to more efficient levels of public output, because expenditure decisions are tied more closely to real resource costs. If a community is required to finance its own public program through local taxation, residents are more likely to weigh the benefits of the program against its actual costs. In the United States, for instance, proposals to improve local school systems are frequently submitted to the local electorate along with a proposed increase in property tax rates to fund the program. In contrast, if funds for local public projects come wholly from a central government, residents of a given community have an incentive to expand levels of local public services as far as possible, since they may bear only a negligible part of the costs of the program. To discourage this tendency, the central government could adopt other fiscal measures; it could, for example, require a community to bear the cost of many of its own programs by varying tax rates among communities or, where possible, by employing user charges. Often, however, this is not an easy matter; the federal government in the United States, for example, is prohibited by the Constitution from levying direct taxes with rates that vary on a geographical basis.

In summary, a decentralized public sector possesses several economically desirable characteristics. First, it provides a means by which the levels of consumption of some public goods can be tailored to the preferences of subsets of the society. In this way, economic efficiency is enhanced by providing an allocation of resources that is more responsive to the tastes of consumers. Second, by promoting increased innovation over time and by providing competitive pressures to induce local governments to adopt the most efficient techniques of production, decentralization may increase both static and dynamic efficiency in the production of public goods. Third, a system of local government may provide an institutional setting that promotes better public decision-making by compelling a more explicit recognition of the costs of public programs.

The Optimal Form of Government: A Federal System

The preceding discussion suggests that both a unitary form of government and one characterized by extreme decentralization possess distinct advantages and serious shortcomings in performing the three fundamental economic tasks of the public sector. A central government can best resolve the stabilization and distribution problems, but in the absence of what I have called local governments, serious welfare losses from uniformity in the consumption of public goods and technical waste in their production are quite likely. What is clearly desirable is a form of government that combines the advantages of these two polar forms and avoids the most serious shortcomings of each; a federal organization of government meets this need.

Federalism represents, in one sense, a compromise between unitary government and extreme decentralization. In a federal system there exist both a central government and subcentral government units, each making decisions concerning the provision of certain public services in its respective geographical jurisdiction. From an economic standpoint, the obvious attraction of the federal form of government is that it combines the strengths of unitary government with those of decentralization. Each level of government, rather than attempting to perform all the functions of the public sector, does what it can do best. The central government presumably accepts primary responsibility for stabilizing the economy, for achieving the most equitable distribution of income, and for providing certain public goods that influence significantly the welfare of all members of society. Complementing these operations, subcentral governments can supply those public goods and services that are of primary interest only to the residents of their respective jurisdiction. In this way, a federal form of government offers the best promise of a successful resolution of the problems that constitute the economic *raison d'être* of the public sector. It is in this sense that federalism may, in economic terms, be described as the optimal form of government. . . .

The argument presented thus far suggests that a federal structure of the public sector has, at least in economic terms, compelling advantages over alternative forms. If this is true, one would expect to find the federal structure the typical form of government. And yet, political scientist Daniel Elazar's list of federal countries numbers only sixteen nations.[5] Even this list would be considered by some to be overly inclusive; as I have mentioned in the Introduction, Kenneth C. Wheare, writing in the 1940s, was willing to grant federal status to only four nations. This suggests that the economic meaning of federalism differs in some fundamental way from its meaning to most political scientists, which is in fact the case. Therefore, in order to place the analysis in a clearer perspective, it will prove useful to examine more closely what an economist means by a federal system.

The Economic Meaning of Federalism

In his pioneering study of federalism, which has provided the basis for much of the later work on federal political institutions, Kenneth C. Wheare defined federalism as ". . . the method of dividing powers so that the general and regional governments are each, within a sphere, co-ordinate and independent."[6] From this definition and from his observations of actual governments (largely that of the United States), Wheare was able to set forth a number of characteristics that a political system must possess in order to qualify as federal; these were primarily constitutional provisions that protected the autonomy of different levels of government. I think it is fair to say that this largely legalistic approach, though not employed in nearly so restrictive a fashion as by Wheare, has characterized much of the later work in political science on this subject.

Such an approach makes a good deal of sense for a political study of federalism. Since a political scientist is interested in the division and use of power, there is real reason to exclude from the federal category a system in which, for example, the power of subcentral governments is exercised solely at the convenience of the central government. A system in which a central government merely delegates certain decision-making functions to regional or local governments will typically have a quite different power structure from one in which the scope of responsibility and independence of each level of government is carefully defined and protected by a written constitution. Related to this, Poul Meyer, among others, has been careful to distinguish between "decentralization," which represents a genuine possession of independent decision-making power by decentralized units, and "deconcentration," which implies only a delegation of administrative control to lower levels in the administrative hierarchy.[7] On the basis of such distinctions, political scientists have naturally been willing to recognize as federal countries only the limited number of nations in which, to a significant extent at least, different levels of government each possess an explicitly independent scope of responsibility and authority.

The problem of federalism is, however, quite different for an economist. In particular, the economist's central concerns are the allocation of resources and the distribution of income within an economic system. The structure of government is, for this reason, of interest to him only to the extent that it carries with it implications for patterns of resource use and income distribution. From this perspective, decentralization of the public sector is of importance primarily because it provides a mechanism through which the levels of provision of certain public goods and services can be fashioned according to the preferences of geographical subsets of the population. Therefore, I suggest the following *economic* definition of federalism:

> *Federal Government:* A public sector with both centralized and decentralized levels of decision-making in which choices made at each level concerning the provision of public services are determined largely by the demands for these services of the residents of (and perhaps others who carry on activities in) the respective jurisdiction.

One element of this definition requires special comment. In contrast to the conception of federalism in political science, it makes little difference to the economist whether or not decision-making at a particular level of government is based on delegated or constitutionally guaranteed authority. What matters is simply that decisions regarding levels of provision of specified public services for a particular jurisdiction (be they made by appointed or elected officials, or directly by the people themselves through some form of voting mechanism) reflect to a substantial extent the interests of the constituency of that jurisdiction.

This is not to say, however, that constitutional provisions are wholly irrelevant to the economics of federalism. On the contrary, constitutional constraints may make it quite difficult or costly in some instances for central government agencies to interfere with local government decisions. To this extent, a formally federal constitutional structure may typically result in a process of public decision-making in which local interests have a relatively major impact on choices affecting primarily the welfare of local residents. Legalistic factors may thus have a real influence on decision-making procedures. . . . However, it is to be emphasized that it is the extent to which the decisions themselves reflect local interests that matters for the economist, and constitutional structure assumes importance only to the degree that it affects the responsiveness of the provision of local services to local preferences.

This is obviously a far broader view of federalism than that typically employed in political science. In fact, the most useful way for an economist to approach this issue is to treat federalism not in absolute but in relative terms.[8] As suggested earlier, we can envision a spectrum of structures of the public sector along which the difference is essentially one of degree rather than kind. At one end of the spectrum is a unitary form of government with all decisions made by the central authority, and at the opposite pole is a state of anarchy. Aside from the two polar points themselves, the other positions on the spectrum represent federal organizations of the public sector moving from a greater to a lesser degree of centralization of decision-making.

This would imply, however, that *in economic terms* most if not all systems are federal. Aside from an absolute degree of centralization of decision-making—which in practice is almost impossible to imagine—the public sectors of all countries would be federal, with distinctions being made in terms of differing degrees of centralization. I think this is the most useful way to see the issue; and it explains the ease with which I was able to reach the conclusion that, from an economic perspective, a federal system is the optimal form of organization of the public sector.

Of course, the problem is that within this framework such a conclusion is a vacuous one. If all public sectors are more or less federal in structure, it is obviously tautological to say that federalism is the optimal form of government. The real issue becomes the determination of the appropriate degree of decentralization for a particular government sector. Where along this centralization spectrum should a particular public sector be?

To answer this question requires matching public functions, including the provision of each public service, with appropriate levels of decision-making. This, as I see it, is the central theoretical problem of the subject of fiscal federalism: the determination of the optimal structure of the public sector in terms of the assignment of decision-making responsibility for specified functions to representatives of the interests of the proper geographical subsets of society. This suggests, moreover, that the arguments developed in this chapter, although they may have led initially to a conclusion without great substance, do take us some way into the analysis of the real problem; they indicate, in rough terms at least, a general outline for the appropriate division of fiscal functions between the central and decentralized levels of government. A more careful examination of this issue reveals, however, that the selection of the proper level of government to provide a particular public good or service is not an easy problem; there are typically a number of variables that figure in this decision, and in most instances, some form of trade-off between welfare gains and losses is involved. It is the exploration of this problem that we proceed next.

NOTES

1. *State and Local Finance in the National Economy* (New York: W. W. Norton, 1944), pp. 194–200. For an alternative view of the relative burden of internal and external debt on later generations, see James Buchanan, *Public Principles of Public Debt: A Defense and Restatement* (Homewood, Ill.: Richard D. Irwin, 1958).

2. "An Economic Theory of Alliances," *Review of Economics and Statistics*, vol. 48 (Aug., 1966), pp. 266–75.

3. *Ibid.*, p. 278.

4. "A Pure Theory of Local Expenditures," *Journal of Political Economy*, vol. 64 (Oct., 1956), pp. 416–24.

5. "Federalism," in David L. Sills, ed., *International Encyclopedia of the Social Sciences*, vol. 5 (New York: Macmillan, 1968), p. 365.

6. Wheare, *Federal Government*, p. 10.

7. *Administrative Organization* (Copenhagen: Nyt Nordisk Forlag Arnold Busck, 1957), pp. 56–61.

8. This is the approach suggested by Livingston, "A Note on the Nature of Federalism."

SELECTION 42

CHARLES M. TIEBOUT

A Pure Theory of
Local Expenditures

Charles Tiebout develops a model in which a household chooses to
live in a locality that has the mix of taxes and expenditures most
closely matching its preferences. With many local governments
present in an area, a household can choose the one that best meets
its desires. People who do not like the government where they live
can "vote with their feet" by moving to another jurisdiction. Such
mobility establishes a pattern of public sector demands resulting in
a variety of output from different governments.

QUESTIONS TO GUIDE THE READING

1. Under what circumstances is it most likely that Tiebout's
   assumption of household mobility will be met?
2. What policy implications concerning the consolidation of
   localities can be drawn from Tiebout's paper?
3. What policies does Tiebout recommend to improve local
   government services?

One of the most important recent developments in the area of "applied economic theory" has been the work of Musgrave and Samuelson in public
finance theory.[1] The two writers agree on what is probably the major point
under investigation, namely, that no "market type" solution exists to determine the level of expenditures on public goods. Seemingly, we are faced with
the problem of having a rather large portion of our national income allocated
in a "non-optimal" way when compared with the private sector.

This discussion will show that the Musgrave-Samuelson analysis, which
is valid for federal expenditures, need not apply to local expenditures. The
plan of the discussion is first to restate the assumptions made by Musgrave
and Samuelson and the central problems with which they deal. After looking
at a key difference between the federal versus local cases, I shall present a

Charles M. Tiebout, "A Pure Theory of Local Expenditures," *Journal of Political Economy* 64
(February 1956), 416–24. Reprinted by permission of the author and The University of Chicago.

Charles M. Tiebout, former Professor of Economics at the University of Washington, died in
1968.

simple model. This model yields a solution for the level of expenditures for local public goods which reflects the preferences of the population more adequately than they can be reflected at the national level. The assumptions of the model will then be relaxed to see what implications are involved. Finally, policy considerations will be discussed.

The Theoretical Issue

Samuelson has defined public goods as *"collective consumption goods* $(X_n + 1, \ldots, X_n + n)$ which all enjoy in common in the sense that each individual's consumption of such a good leads to no subtraction from any other individual's consumption of that good, so that $X_n + j = X_n^i + j$ simultaneously for each and every ith individual and each collective good."[2] While definitions are a matter of choice, it is worth noting that "consumption" has a much broader meaning here than in the usual sense of the term. Not only does it imply that the act of consumption by one person does not diminish the opportunities for consumption by another but it also allows this consumption to be in another form. For example, while the residents of a new government housing project are made better off, benefits also accrue to other residents of the community in the form of the external economies of slum clearance. Thus many goods that appear to lack the attributes of public goods may properly be considered public if consumption is defined to include these external economies.

A definition alternative to Samuelson's might be simply that a public good is one which should be produced, but for which there is no feasible method of charging the consumers. This is less elegant, but has the advantage that it allows for the objections of Enke and Margolis.[3] This definition, unfortunately, does not remove any of the problems faced by Musgrave and Samuelson.

The core problem with which both Musgrave and Samuelson deal concerns the mechanism by which consumer-voters register their preferences for public goods. The consumer is, in a sense, surrounded by a government whose objective it is to ascertain his wants for public goods and tax him accordingly. To use Alchian's term, the government's revenue-expenditure pattern for goods and services is expected to "adapt to" consumers' preferences.[4] Both Musgrave and Samuelson have shown that, in the vertically additive nature of voluntary demand curves, this problem has only a conceptual solution. If all consumer-voters could somehow be forced to reveal their true preferences for public goods, then the amount of such goods to be produced and the appropriate benefits tax could be determined. As things now stand, there is no mechanism to force the consumer-voter to state his true preferences;* in fact, the "rational" consumer will understate his preferences and hope to enjoy the goods while avoiding the tax.

Editors' note: See the 1976 paper by Tideman and Tullock, selection 15, this volume.

The current method of solving this problem operates, unsatisfactorily, through the political mechanism. The expenditure wants of a "typical voter" are somehow pictured. This objective on the expenditure side is then combined with an ability-to-pay principle on the revenue side, giving us our current budget. Yet in terms of a satisfactory theory of public finance, it would be desirable (1) to force the voter to reveal his preferences; (2) to be able to satisfy them in the same sense that a private goods market does; and (3) to tax him accordingly. The question arises whether there is any set of social institutions by which this goal can be approximated.

Local Expenditures

Musgrave and Samuelson implicitly assume that expenditures are handled at the central government level. However, the provision of such governmental services as police and fire protection, education, hospitals, and courts does not necessarily involve federal activity. Many of these goods are provided by local governments. It is worthwhile to look briefly at the magnitude of these expenditures.

Historically, local expenditures have exceeded those of the federal government. The thirties were the first peacetime years in which federal expenditures began to pull away from local expenditures. Even during the fiscal year 1954, federal expenditures on *goods and services exclusive of defense* amounted only to some 15 billions of dollars, while local expenditures during this same period amounted to some 17 billions of dollars. There is no need to quibble over which comparisons are relevant. The important point is that the often-neglected local expenditures are significant and, when viewed in terms of expenditures on goods and services only, take on even more significance. Hence an important question arises whether at this level of government any mechanism operates to insure that expenditures on these public goods approximate the proper level.

Consider for a moment the case of the city resident about to move to the suburbs. What variables will influence his choice of a municipality? If he has children, a high level of expenditures on schools may be important. Another person may prefer a community with a municipal golf course. The availability and quality of such facilities and services as beaches, parks, police protection, roads, and parking facilities will enter into the decision-making process. Of course, non-economic variables will also be considered, but this is of no concern at this point.

The consumer-voter may be viewed as picking that community which best satisfies his preference pattern for public goods. This is a major difference between central and local provision of public goods. At the central level the preferences of the consumer-voter are given, and the government tries to adjust to the pattern of these preferences, whereas at the local level various governments have their revenue and expenditure patterns more or less set. Given these revenue and expenditure patterns, the consumer-voter moves to that community whose local government best satisfies his set of preferences. The greater the number of communities and the greater the variance among them, the closer the consumer will come to fully realizing his preference position.

A Local Government Model

The implications of the preceding argument may be shown by postulating an extreme model. Here the following assumptions are made:

1. Consumer-voters are fully mobile and will move to that community where their preference patterns, which are set, are best satisfied.

2. Consumer-voters are assumed to have full knowledge of differences among revenue and expenditure patterns and to react to these differences.

3. There are a large number of communities in which the consumer-voters may choose to live.

4. Restrictions due to employment opportunities are not considered. It may be assumed that all persons are living on dividend income.

5. The public services supplied exhibit no external economies or diseconomies between communities.

Assumptions 6 and 7 to follow are less familiar and require brief explanations:

6. For every pattern of community services set by, say, a city manager who follows the preferences of the older residents of the community, there is an optimal community size. This optimum is defined in terms of the number of residents for which this bundle of services can be produced at the lowest average cost. This, of course, is closely analogous to the low point of a firm's average cost curve. Such a cost function implies that some factor or resource is fixed. If this were not so, there would be no logical reason to limit community size, given the preference patterns. In the same sense that the average cost curve has a minimum for one firm but can be reproduced by another there is seemingly no reason why a duplicate community cannot exist. The assumption that some factor is fixed explains why it is not possible for the community in question to double its size by growth. The factor may be the limited land area of a suburban community, combined with a set of zoning laws against apartment buildings. It may be the local beach, whose capacity is limited. Anything of this nature will provide a restraint.

In order to see how this restraint works, let us consider the beach problem. Suppose the preference patterns of the community are such that the optimum size population is 13,000. Within this set of preferences there is a certain demand per family for beach space. This demand is such that at 13,000 population a 500-yard beach is required. If the actual length of the beach is, say, 600 yards, then it is not possible to realize this preference pattern with twice the optimum population, since there would be too little beach space by 400 yards.

The assumption of a fixed factor is necessary, as will be shown later, in order to get a determinate number of communities. It also has the advantage of introducing a realistic restraint into the model.

7. The last assumption is that communities below the optimum size seek to attract new residents to lower average costs. Those above optimum size do just the opposite. Those at an optimum try to keep their populations constant.

This assumption needs to be amplified. Clearly, communities below the optimum size, through chambers of commerce or other agencies, seek to attract new residents. This is best exemplified by the housing developments in some suburban areas, such as Park Forest in the Chicago area and Levittown in the New York area, which need to reach an optimum size. The same is true of communities that try to attract manufacturing industries by setting up certain facilities and getting an optimum number of firms to move into the industrially zoned area.

The case of the city that is too large and tries to get rid of residents is more difficult to imagine. No alderman in his right political mind would ever admit that the city is too big. Nevertheless, economic forces are at work to push people out of it. Every resident who moves to the suburbs to find better schools, more parks, and so forth, is reacting, in part, against the pattern the city has to offer.

The case of the community which is at the optimum size and tries to remain so is not hard to visualize. Again proper zoning laws, implicit agreements among realtors, and the like are sufficient to keep the population stable.

Except when this system is in equilibrium, there will be a subset of consumer-voters who are discontented with the patterns of their community. Another set will be satisfied. Given the assumption about mobility and the other assumptions listed previously, movement will take place out of the communities of greater than optimal size into the communities of less than optimal size. The consumer-voter moves to the community that satisfies his preference pattern.

The act of moving or failing to move is crucial. Moving or failing to move replaces the usual market test of willingness to buy a good and reveals the consumer-voter's demand for public goods. Thus each locality has a revenue and expenditure pattern that reflects the desires of its residents. The next step is to see what this implies for the allocation of public goods at the local level.

Each city manager now has a certain demand for n local public goods. In supplying these goods, he and $m - 1$ other city managers may be considered as going to a national market and bidding for the appropriate units of service of each kind: so many units of police for the ith community; twice that number for the jth community; and so on. The demand on the public goods market for each of the n commodities will be the sum of the demands of the m communities. In the limit, as shown in a less realistic model to be developed later, this total demand will approximate the demand that represents the true preferences of the consumer-voters—that is, the demand they would reveal, if they were forced, somehow, to state their true preferences.

In this model there is no attempt on the part of local governments to "adapt to" the preferences of consumer-voters. Instead, those local governments that attract the optimum number of residents may be viewed as being "adopted by" the economic system.[5]

A Comparison Model

It is interesting to contrast the results of the preceding model with those of an even more severe model in order to see how these results differ from the normal market result. It is convenient to look at this severe model by developing its private-market counterpart. First assume that there are no public goods, only private ones. The preferences for these goods can be expressed as one of n patterns. Let a law be passed that all persons living in any one of the communities shall spend their money in the particular pattern described for that community by law. Given our earlier assumptions 1 through 5, it follows that, if the consumers move to the community whose law happens to fit their preference pattern, they will be at their optimum. The n communities, in turn, will then send their buyers to market to purchase the goods for the consumer-voters in their community. Since this is simply a lumping together of all similar tastes for the purpose of making joint purchases, the allocation of resources will be the same as it would be if normal market forces operated. This conceptual experiment is the equivalent of substituting the city manager for the broker or middleman.

Now turn the argument around and consider only public goods. Assume with Musgrave that the costs of additional services are constant.[6] Further, assume that a doubling of the population means doubling the amount of services required. Let the number of communities be infinite and let each announce a different pattern of expenditures on public goods. Define an empty community as one that fails to satisfy anybody's preference pattern. Given these assumptions, including the earlier assumptions 1 through 5, the consumer-voters will move to that community which *exactly* satisfies their preferences. This must be true, since a one-person community is allowed. The sum of the demands of the n communities reflects the demand for local public services. In this model the demand is exactly the same as it would be if it were determined by normal market forces.

However, this severe model does not make much sense. The number of communities is indeterminate. There is no reason why the number of communities will not be equal to the population, since each voter can find the one that exactly fits his preferences. Unless some sociological variable is introduced, this may reduce the solution of the problem of allocating public goods to the trite one of making each person his own municipal government. Hence this model is not even a first approximation of reality. It is presented to show the assumptions needed in a model of local government expenditures, which yields the same optimal allocation that a private market would.

The Local Government Model Re-examined

The first model, described by the first five assumptions together with assumptions 6 and 7, falls short of this optimum. An example will serve to show why this is the case.

Let us return to the community with the 500-yard beach. By assumption, its optimum population was set at 13,000, given its preference patterns. Suppose that some people in addition to the optimal 13,000 would choose this community if it were available. Since they cannot move into this area, they must accept the next best substitute. If a perfect substitute is found, no problem exists. If one is not found, then the failure to reach the optimal preference position and the substitution of a lower position becomes a matter of degree. In so far as there are a number of communities with similar revenue and expenditure patterns, the solution will approximate the ideal "market" solution.

Two related points need to be mentioned to show the allocative results of this model: (1) changes in the costs of one of the public services will cause changes in the quantity produced; (2) the costs of moving from community to community should be recognized. Both points can be illustrated in one example.

Suppose lifeguards throughout the country organize and succeed in raising their wages. Total taxes in communities with beaches will rise. Now residents who are largely indifferent to beaches will be forced to make a decision. Is the saving of this added tax worth the cost of moving to a community with little or no beach? Obviously, this decision depends on many factors, among which the availability of and proximity to a suitable substitute community is important. If enough people leave communities with beaches and move to communities without beaches, the total amount of lifeguard services used will fall. These models then, unlike their private-market counterpart, have mobility as a cost of registering demand. The higher this cost, *ceteris paribus,* the less optimal the allocation of resources.

This distinction should not be blown out of proportion. Actually, the cost of registering demand comes through the introduction of space into the economy. Yet space affects the allocation not only of resources supplied by local governments but of those supplied by the private market as well. Every time available resources or production techniques change, a new location becomes optimal for the firm. Indeed, the very concept of the shopping trip shows that the consumer does pay a cost to register his demand for private goods. In fact, Koopmans has stated that the nature of the assignment problem is such that in a space economy with transport costs there is *no* general equilibrium solution as set by market forces.[7]

Thus the problems stated by this model are not unique; they have their counterpart in the private market. We are maximizing within the framework of the resources available. If production functions show constant returns to scale with generally diminishing factor returns, and if indifference curves are regularly convex, an optimal solution is possible. On the production side it is assumed that communities are forced to keep production costs at a minimum either through the efficiency of city managers or through competition from other communities. Given this, on the demand side we may note with Samuelson that "each individual, in seeking as a competitive buyer to get to the highest level of indifference subject to given prices and *tax,* would be led as if by an Invisible Hand to the grand solution of the social maximum position."[8] Just as the consumer may be visualized as walking to a private market place to buy his goods, the prices of which are set, we place him in the position of walking to a community where the prices (taxes) of community services are set. Both trips take the consumer to market. There is no way in which the consumer can avoid revealing his preferences in a spatial economy. Spatial mobility provides the local public-goods counterpart to the private market's shopping trip.

External Economies and Mobility

Relaxing assumption 5 has some interesting implications. There are obvious external economies and diseconomies between communities. My community is better off if its neighbor sprays trees to prevent Dutch elm disease. On the other hand, my community is worse off if the neighboring community has inadequate law enforcement.

In cases in which the external economies and diseconomies are of sufficient importance, some form of integration may be indicated.[9] Not all aspects of law enforcement are adequately handled at the local level. The function of the sheriff, state police, and the FBI—as contrasted with the local police—may be cited as resulting from a need for integration. In real life the diseconomies are minimized in so far as communities reflecting the same socioeconomic preferences are contiguous. Suburban agglomerations such as Westchester, the North Shore, and the Main Line are, in part, evidence of these external economies and diseconomies.

Assumptions 1 and 2 should be checked against reality. Consumer-voters do not have perfect knowledge and set preferences, nor are they perfectly mobile. The question is how do people actually react in choosing a community. There has been very little empirical study of the motivations of people in choosing a community. Such studies as have been undertaken seem to indicate a surprising awareness of differing revenue and expenditure patterns. The general disdain with which proposals to integrate municipalities are met seems to reflect, in part, the fear that local revenue-expenditure patterns will be lost as communities are merged into a metropolitan area.

Policy Implications

The preceding analysis has policy implications for municipal integration, provision for mobility, and set local revenue and expenditure patterns. These implications are worth brief consideration.

On the usual economic welfare grounds, municipal integration is justified only if more of any service is forthcoming at the same total cost and
without reduction of any other service. A general reduction of costs along
with a reduction in one or more of the services provided cannot be justified
on economic grounds unless the social welfare function is known. For example, those who argue for a metropolitan police force instead of local police
cannot prove their case on purely economic grounds. If one of the communities were to receive less police protection after integration than it received
before, integration could be objected to as a violation of consumers' choice.

Policies that promote residential mobility and increase the knowledge of
the consumer-voter will improve the allocation of government expenditures
in the same sense that mobility among jobs and knowledge relevant to the
location of industry and labor improve the allocation of private resources.

Finally, we may raise the normative question whether local governments *should,* to the extent possible, have a fixed revenue-expenditure pattern. In a large, dynamic metropolis this may be impossible. Perhaps it could
more appropriately be considered by rural and suburban communities.

Conclusion

It is useful in closing to restate the problem as Samuelson sees it:

> However, no decentralized pricing system can serve to determine
> optimally these levels of collective consumption. Other kinds of
> "voting" or "signaling" would have to be tried. . . . Of course uto-
> pian voting and signaling schemes can be imagined. . . . The failure
> of market catallactics in no way denies the following truth: given
> sufficient knowledge the optimal decisions can always be found by
> scanning over all the attainable states of the world and selecting the
> one which according to the postulated ethical welfare function is
> best. The solution "exists"; the problem is how to "find" it.[10]

It is the contention of this article that, for a substantial portion of collective
or public goods, this problem *does have* a conceptual solution. If consumer-
voters are fully mobile, the appropriate local governments, whose revenue-
expenditure patterns are set, are adopted by the consumer-voters. While the
solution may not be perfect because of institutional rigidities, this does not
invalidate its importance. The solution, like a general equilibrium solution
for a private spatial economy, is the best that can be obtained given preferences and resource endowments.

Those who are tempted to compare this model with the competitive private model may be disappointed. Those who compare the reality described
by this model with the reality of the competitive model—given the degree of
monopoly, friction, and so forth—*may* find that local government represents
a sector where the allocation of public goods (as a reflection of the preferences of the population) need not take a back seat to the private sector.

NOTES

Note: I am grateful for the comments of my colleagues Karl de Schweinitz, Robert Eisner, and Robert Strotz, and those of Martin Bailey, of the University of Chicago.

1. Richard A. Musgrave, "The Voluntary Exchange Theory of Public Economy," *Quarterly Journal of Economics,* LII (February, 1939), 213–17; "A Multiple Theory of the Budget," paper read at the Econometric Society annual meeting (December, 1955); and his forthcoming book, *The Theory of Public Economy;* Paul A. Samuelson, "The Pure Theory of Public Expenditures," *Review of Economics and Statistics,* XXXVI, No. 4 (November, 1954), 387–89, and "Diagrammatic Exposition of a Pure Theory of Public Expenditures," *ibid.,* XXXVII, No. 4 (November, 1955), 350–56.

2. "The Pure Theory . . . ," *op. cit.,* p. 387.

3. They argue that, for most of the goods supplied by governments, increased use by some consumer-voters leaves less available for other consumer-voters. Crowded highways and schools, as contrasted with national defense, may be cited as examples (see Stephen Enke, "More on the Misuse of Mathematics in Economics: A Rejoinder," *Review of Economics and Statistics,* XXXVII [May, 1955], 131–33; and Julius Margolis, "A Comment on the Pure Theory of Public Expenditure," *Review of Economics and Statistics,* XXXVII [November, 1955], 247–49).

4. Armen A. Alchian, "Uncertainty, Evolution and Economic Theory," *Journal of Political Economy,* LVIII (June, 1950), 211–21.

5. See Alchian, *op. cit.*

6. Musgrave, "Voluntary Exchange . . . ," *op. cit.*

7. Tjalling Koopmans, "Mathematical Groundwork of Economic Optimization Theories," paper read at the annual meeting of the Econometric Society (December, 1954).

8. "The Pure Theory . . . ," *op. cit.,* p. 388. (Italics mine.)

9. I am grateful to Stanley Long and Donald Markwalder for suggesting this point.

10. "The Pure Theory . . . ," *op. cit.,* pp. 388–89.

SELECTION 43

CHARLES E. MCLURE

Tax Competition: Is What's Good for the Private Goose Also Good for the Public Gander?

Following Tiebout, subnational (state or local) governments are often cast as competitors, providing government services in exchange for taxes. Just as competition among private firms benefits consumers, competition among subnational governments benefits taxpayers, leading to a mix of public services better in line with preferences. However, state and local government officials often complain that tax competition can lead to inefficiently low levels of public services as subnational governments compete for taxpayers by holding taxes low.

QUESTIONS TO GUIDE THE READING

1. How does the author argue that proposals to prevent tax competition are misguided second-best policies?
2. Why might it be difficult to defend the deductibility of state and local taxes with the benefit spillover argument?
3. According to McLure, what relevance does the behavior of bureaucrats and politicians have in an appraisal of the benefits and costs of tax competition?
4. Do you agree with McLure's conclusion that the costs of tax competition are slight and its benefits are large?
5. Under what circumstances do you think tax competition would have more costs than benefits?
6. "Arguments against tax competition often ignore the expenditure side of the budget." Discuss.

Charles E. McLure, "Tax Competition: Is What's Good for the Private Goose also Good for the Public Gander?" *National Tax Journal* 39 (September 1986). Reprinted by permission of the author.

Charles E. McLure is Economist at the Hoover Institution, Stanford University.

I. Introduction

During the debate on the Treasury Department's proposals to President Reagan for tax reform (1984), and later in the discussion of the President's Proposal (1985), opponents of the elimination of the itemized deduction for state and local taxes often pointed out that eliminating the deduction would cause increased tax competition between states and localities. I did not agree that this self-evident statement provided dispositive proof that deductibility should be maintained; rather, I said "good," and pointed out that competition among governments should produce the same kinds of benefits in the public sector that we commonly associate with competition among private firms. Of course, the issue is somewhat more complicated than that, and in this paper I examine the pros and cons of the tax competition argument somewhat more systematically, if not dispositively.

At least four lines of reasoning suggest that tax and spending decisions by subnational governments may not be optimal. First, spending may be less than would be required for welfare maximization (as indicated by the failure to achieve a Pareto optimal solution) because of spillovers of benefits between jurisdictions. Second, even if there are no spillovers, if (a) property taxes and other taxes on capital are employed to finance government spending that does not benefit production and (b) capital is mobile between jurisdictions, tax competition may result in suboptimal levels of expenditures. Third, in the absence of competition between jurisdictions, politicians and bureaucrats may act against the best interests of their constituents, as predicted by the Leviathan model.[1] Finally, interstate migration based on fiscal considerations may be excessive, because of the congestion migration creates.

In my remarks today I want to discuss briefly the implications of the first three of these theories for the costs and benefits of tax competition and/ or the deductibility of state and local taxes. In addition, I will direct some concluding remarks to the treatment of the deductibility issue in the tax reform package that was recently endorsed unanimously by the Senate Finance Committee.

II. Taxation of Mobile Capital

I have been quite surprised—not to say flabbergasted—by much of the formal literature that presumes to examine the supposed adverse effects of tax competition. At the risk of substantial oversimplification, I would describe the problem addressed in much of that literature in the following terms. Suppose that the spending of subnational governments benefits primarily residents of the various jurisdictions, but is financed by a tax on capital that is geographically mobile, presumably via the local property tax or state corporation income tax. In such a situation the mobility of capital between jurisdictions results in tax competition, as the various jurisdictions attempt to avoid driving out business, which would reduce the productivity of labor or employment in the jurisdiction (or both). Tax competition, in turn, results in suboptimal expenditure by the subnational jurisdictions.

The implication that is commonly drawn from this conclusion, either explicitly or implicitly, is that tax competition is undesirable and should be avoided. Wildasin (1986) likens the effects of tax competition to those of benefit spillovers, suggests that a federal subsidy of as much as 40 percent might be appropriate to compensate for the externality, and thereby prevent tax competition and suboptimal public expenditures. He notes (p. 19), however, that the subsidy provided by existing intergovernmental grants is large enough that "there is only a weak case for further subsidies on fiscal externality grounds." An alternative way to reduce tax competition would be a federal credit for some portion of state and local taxes. This line of reasoning has also been seized upon by advocates of the deduction for state and local taxes to justify their position.

I suspect that virtually all serious economists who write on this topic realize that there is a fundamental objection to this line of reasoning. Surprisingly, they seldom give it prominence, though Oates and Schwab (1985) do so quite clearly and Wildasin has done so in his latest paper (1986). Recall that the issue being examined is whether or not tax competition causes suboptimal spending on public services by subnational governments *if* benefits for residents of the taxing jurisdiction must be financed by taxes on capital that is mobile between jurisdictions. That spending should be suboptimal under these circumstances is hardly surprising. In the extreme case this amounts to asking whether spending on school lunches in Gloucester, Massachusetts would be optimal if financed entirely by a property tax on the fishing fleet docked there. I suspect that most of us would agree that competition from neighboring harbors (in the markets for both fish and dock facilities) would prevent the cost of school lunches in Gloucester from being borne by either consumers of fish or (except in the very short run) owners of boats. Rather, one would expect that boats would be docked elsewhere, little revenue would be collected by Gloucester, the burden of the tax would be borne by owners of the least mobile factors in Gloucester, and school lunches would be supplied at suboptimal levels in Gloucester. If we further constrained all competing harbors to finance school lunches only in this way, without collusion, tax competition would induce underspending in all the fishing centers.

Most of us would not, however, conclude from this simple example that tax competition was the basic cause of suboptimal spending or that such competition should be dampened by providing a federal subsidy to offset the local taxes on fishing fleets. Rather, we would conclude that policies such as this would, at best, be second-best responses forced on us by the adoption of a patently idiotic scheme for the finance of school lunches.

The first-best solution from an allocative point of view would be to charge market prices for the lunches, rather than trying to cover their cost through the taxation of an entirely different and mobile activity. Standard microeconomic analysis would suggest that in the absence of external costs and benefits, and subject to the usual assumptions underlying such analysis, charging those who eat the lunches (or their parents) for the cost of providing them would cause an optimal quantity of lunches to be provided. If, contrary to the basic assumption of much of the literature of tax competition, the financing of state and local public services reflected more accurately the benefits of such services, the case for reducing tax competition via federal subsidies would be weak and perhaps vanish. Indeed, in a world of user charges and benefit taxes the existence of such subsidies would worsen the allocation of resources, rather than improving it, by reducing the cost of such services to state and local beneficiaries/taxpayers and causing over-production of the subsidized activity.

The natural question to ask at this point is whether it is realistic to suggest that user charges and benefit taxation could be used much more in the finance of the services provided by state and local governments. Even if one agrees that beneficiaries of public services should be charged for benefits received to the extent possible, it is clear that a great proportion of the expenditures of state and local governments must be financed through taxes, rather than through fees and charges. But this does not imply that the case for reducing tax competition has been proven.

Taxes levied by state and local governments could—and should—reflect more closely benefits received by taxpayers. Property taxes levied on home-owners almost certainly reflect the benefits of public education more closely than do those levied on commercial and industrial property. Similarly, individual income taxes and sales taxes probably correspond more closely to benefits of public services than do state corporation income taxes. I submit that greater reliance on these broad-based taxes paid by individuals, and less on taxes imposed on business that do not reflect benefits, would be both feasible and appropriate. If that first-best approach were taken, the second-best question of whether tax competition is good or bad would have substantially less urgency.

Even if there were a shift to greater reliance on taxes that better reflect benefits provided to individuals, on average, the question of tax competition would still arise. Tax competition might, for example, cause migration from jurisdictions whose taxes on families with high incomes and/or no children exceed the value of public services provided to such families. Again, attempting to prevent tax competition in such a case would be a misguided second-best policy. As in the case of non-benefit taxes levied on mobile capital, the more appropriate response would be to adopt financing techniques that reflected even more closely the benefits of public services.

More problematical is the case in which pure public goods (in the Samuelsonian sense) are provided to business. Since the quantity of such services received by a particular business would be largely independent of its own tax payments, tax competition can be expected to result in under-provision of such services. I do not believe, however, that this is the basic problem of tax competition that has motivated much of the recent furor over ending deductibility; in any event, such competition would be reduced by deductibility of taxes on business. Even if a conscious effort were made to shift to taxes reflecting benefits received, including appropriable benefits to business, taxes would be levied on business capital or income. In such cases deductibility would be appropriate—but because all business costs should be deductible, not to reduce tax competition, per se.

III. Benefit Spillovers

Spillovers of benefits between jurisdictions that do not cooperate in the financing of public services will ordinarily be underprovided. For example, no single city has a substantial incentive to finance research on cancer if it believes that its citizens will benefit from the results of research financed elsewhere. The usual prescription for activities such as this is to have them conducted—or at least financed—by a higher level of government that can internalize the benefits that may be largely external to any given smaller jurisdiction. An alternative is to provide categorical matching grants that reflect the ratio of expected external benefits to total benefits from the activity in question.

Though this particular source of suboptimal spending is not ordinarily identified as resulting from tax competition, two alternative approaches that would reduce tax competition could, at least in theory, move independent subnational decisions closer to the optimal level. First, the federal government could provide credit for a fraction of subnational taxes devoted to the finance of the activity generating inter-jurisdictional spillovers. This is, of course, tantamount to providing a categorical matching grant for such expenditures. Alternatively, all jurisdictions could agree to levy a certain minimal level of taxes for the support of the activity generating spillovers. This would be nearly equivalent to federal imposition of such a tax, with funds earmarked for expenditure on the activity in various jurisdictions. This approach suffers from the practical disadvantage that an agreement between jurisdictions not to compete lacks the enforcement features of either federal taxation and expenditure or a federal matching grant or credit for state taxes.

Deductibility of state and local taxes is often defended as a means of compensating for inter-jurisdictional spillovers between state and local governments. That is, it is portrayed as a kind of matching grant that stimulates state and local government to engage in expenditures characterized by spillovers.

While there is obviously some truth in this description of deductibility, the inaccuracy of the description may be more important than the accuracy. First, the availability of the tax deduction does not depend on the degree of spillovers between jurisdictions. It is equally available for taxes that finance expenditures with virtually no inter-jurisdictional spillovers, such as street lighting, as for expenditures with benefits that flow across jurisdictional boundaries; indeed, deduction available for state and local taxes that finance activities generating negative externalities for neighboring jurisdictions, such as construction of thoroughfares that increase congestion, noise, and automobile accidents in surrounding jurisdictions. In short, the subsidies inherent in deductibility are not targeted toward expenditures yielding positive spillovers, as would be appropriate to compensate for such spillovers.

Second, it is difficult to rationalize a system of implicit subsidies that increase with the marginal tax rate, and therefore the income level, of the residents of the jurisdiction, as do the benefits of deductibility. Let me use an extreme example to make this concrete. It is difficult to understand why, in general, almost half the benefits of public spending in Beverly Hills or Scarsdale should be argued (at least implicitly) to accrue to non-residents, while virtually none of the benefits of spending in Watts or Harlem do so; I would have expected the pattern to be reversed.

In short, while inter-jurisdictional spillover of benefits may result in sub-optimal spending by state and local government, it is unlikely that using the itemized deduction for state and local taxes is the proper policy response to the problem.

IV. The Leviathan Problem

The discussion to this point has contained no description of the decision-making process of governments or the activities of politicians and bureaucrats. So far, suboptimal behavior by state and local governments occurs simply because governments interested in maximizing the welfare of their constituents act in a way that is inconsistent with welfare maximization for the entire nation, either because of benefit spillovers or tax competition resulting from reliance on taxes not related to benefits of public services. I do not intend to venture into discussion of the propriety of majority voting models or a discussion of the likelihood that decisions of state and local governments determined through majority voting will be optimal from the national point of view. I must, however, comment on the relevance of the likely behavior of politicians and bureaucrats for the appraisal of the costs and benefits of tax competition. I will not attempt a systematic discussion of literature on what might be called the Leviathan problem; rather, I will rely primarily on common sense arguments that suggest that tax competition between subnational jurisdictions may have a salutary effect quite analogous to that of competition between firms in the private sector.

The traditional case for competition among private firms suggests that the combination of profit maximization and perfect competition creates substantial benefits for society. In particular, it induces producers to provide the goods and services that consumers want and to produce them in the most efficient way, in order to minimize costs. If competition is restrained, whether by outright monopolization, collusion between oligopolistic firms, regulation that prohibits competition, tariff protection, or whatever, it can generally be expected that economic welfare will suffer. In the absence of competition there is less incentive to be responsive to the desires of consumers and less pressure to minimize costs. In such a situation it is not uncommon to find powerful labor unions that appropriate for their members part of the surplus resulting from the failure to compete. For reasons such as this, employees of non-competitive sectors, as well as managers, resist attempts to increase competition, for example, through deregulation or elimination of protection.

I see little reason that the analysis just presented is not applicable, in general terms, to the appraisal of the costs and benefits of tax competition. After all, state and local governments are not simply mechanistic black boxes in which the wishes of voters are efficiently converted into the implied public policies. Rather, governments consist of collections of politicians and bureaucrats whose motivations are probably not totally dissimilar from those of managers and employees in the private sector. (We return to discuss this proposition below.) It is reasonable to expect that governments so constituted will not behave in such a way as to maximize the welfare of their constituents, in the absence of the pressures of competition from other governments. Rather, politicians and bureaucrats can be expected to want to further their own agendas through influence over public policy, regardless of whether such policy furthers the objectives of their constituents. Maintenance of employment, salary, and "perks" and freedom from the rigors of cost-minimizing efficiency may be a large part of the agenda, as in the case of employees in non-competitive parts of the private sector.

If jurisdictions compete with each other and taxpayer/consumers are able to vote with their feet, there may be fairly strong pressures for subnational governments to respond to the wishes of the electorate, as expressed in willingness to pay taxes to finance public services (though presumably less pressure than in the private sector to respond to the desires of the consumers, as expressed in the market place). Moreover, competition between jurisdictions would create pressures to increase productivity and reduce costs, in order to avoid becoming uncompetitive, relative to other jurisdictions.

While the brief description of governmental behavior above may sound quite compelling to most Americans, academic critics can almost certainly note points at which it is less than fully rigorous. Moreover, they might ask whether there is any empirical evidence for the proposition that the real world corresponds to the stylized description of political and bureaucratic behavior just presented. Rather than addressing either of these issues in a comprehensive and fully satisfactory way, I would like to offer a bit of anecdotal evidence from my experience during the debate on tax reform that suggests that the description is not too far-fetched.

First, virtually the only organized opposition to the elimination of the deduction for state and local taxes based on a tax competition argument came from governors, mayors, and public employees; I recall no one not in the public employ raising the possibility that tax competition might be harmful. It is interesting that such objections were expressed even by governors of low-tax states whose residents would benefit, on balance, from the combination of elimination of the state and local deduction and the reduction of marginal tax rates. Now I recognize that such a stance could be motivated by an honest concern that tax competition would be undesirable, or that the deduction should be retained for some other reason. But again it is interesting that little objection to ending deductibility was heard from representatives of low-tax states who were not politicians or bureaucrats.

Second, I would note that the American Federation of State, County, and Municipal Employees strongly opposed elimination of the deduction for state and local taxes. I presume that the analogy to opposition to deregulation of the airline industry by airline employees is sufficiently clear that it need not be pressed. As in the case of deregulation, avoidance of tax competition would help keep secure the protected position of the public employees who are members of that union and allow them greater latitude in furthering their own agendas.

Certain means of combatting tax competition are quite closely analogous to measures that commonly reduce competition in the private sector. Thus, having the federal government undertake a particular activity is similar to monopolization. An agreement among states not to compete in taxation would be similar to a cartel. Given the notorious difficulty of maintaining cartel arrangements, it is hardly surprising that those who are most likely to be hurt by competition between jurisdictions support federal policies that would reduce competition. State and local governments have one advantage not shared by private-sector firms who would seek to reduce competition; the federal government currently softens the impact of competition through the deduction for state and local taxes.

V. Concluding Assessment

My consideration of the issues discussed above suggests that the likely benefits of reducing tax competition are relatively slight, particularly if more appropriate means of avoiding suboptimal decisions could be utilized more fully. On the other hand, the benefits of tax competition are potentially quite important. This leads me to conclude that tax competition is, on balance, good and that the case for continued deductibility of state and local nonbusiness taxes is quite weak.

Inherent in this argument is, of course, the view that it might be desirable to expand reliance on matching categorical grants designed explicitly to compensate for spillover of benefits of services provided by state and local governments. Moreover, it would be desirable to rely more heavily on user charges and benefit-related taxes, including broad-based taxes on individuals, and less on taxation of business not related to benefits received, such as state corporation income taxes and property taxes on commercial and industrial property.

Some may object to this conclusion on distributional grounds emphasizing that it would be unfair not to tax business, as well as individuals. To such objections I would offer the following standard replies: first, state and local governments should confine themselves primarily to benefit taxes, leaving income distribution policies to the federal governments. Second, state and local governments cannot expect to be very successful in efforts to engage in progressive taxation, even if they are inclined to neglect the above prescription to eschew efforts to engage in redistributive taxation. Taxes levied on mobile capital by geographically limited jurisdictions are likely to be borne by whatever is substantially less mobile—land and perhaps workers and consumers.

Despite the above assessment, I have some misgivings about the Senate Finance Committee's proposal to repeal the itemized deduction for only state sales taxes. I believe sales taxes to be the most appropriate form of tax for state and local governments to use. Repeal of only the sales tax deduction would artificially encourage a shift from sales taxation to income and property taxation. All of the broad-based taxes on individuals (income, sales, or property) should be treated the same way, in order to avoid this type of distortion. Based on the arguments presented above, I believe that none of these taxes should be deductible. All should be made non-deductible, and marginal tax rates should be dropped even further than in the Senate Finance Committee bill. Alternatively, all should be made only partially deductible, or the deduction should be converted to a credit.

NOTES

Note: The author thanks George Zodrow for helpful comments on an earlier draft of this paper.

1. The Leviathan model is commonly associated with Brennan and Buchanan; see, for example, (1980).

REFERENCES

Brennan, G., and J. Buchanan, *The Power to Tax: Analytic Foundations of a Fiscal Constitution,* (New York: Cambridge University Press, 1980).

Oates, Wallace E. and Schwab, Robert M. "Economic Competition Among Jurisdictions: Efficiency Enhancing or Distortion Inducing?" July 1985.

The President's Tax Proposals to the Congress for Fairness, Growth, and Simplicity (Washington: U.S. Government Printing Office, 1985).

U.S. Department of the Treasury, *Tax Reform for Fairness, Simplicity, and Economic Growth* (Washington: U.S. Government Printing Office, 1984).

Wildasin, David E., "Interjurisdictional Capital Mobility: Fiscal Externality and a Corrective Subsidy." Department of Economics, Indiana University, March 1986.

Wildasin, David E., *Urban Public Finance* (New York: Harwood Academic Press, forthcoming).

SELECTION 44

PAUL N. COURANT AND DANIEL L. RUBINFELD

Tax Reform: Implications for the State-Local Public Sector

In a federal system of government, decisions at one level of government often affect government at other levels. The 1986 Tax Reform Act made sweeping changes in U.S. national tax policy. The authors examine some of the effects of this act on expenditures and revenues of state and local governments.

QUESTIONS TO GUIDE THE READING

1. What is the "decisive voter model"?
2. What effects is the act predicted to have on average state and local spending?
3. What effect might the act have on location decisions by households and businesses?
4. What will be the short-run and long-run effects on the governments' revenue mix?
5. Why do the authors believe the act will enhance efficiency?

The Tax Reform Act of 1986 should provide valuable information which will allow economists to distinguish among competing models of the determinants of state and local spending and taxes. This paper outlines the implications of current public finance theory and empirical work for the direction and (where possible) likely magnitudes of the effects of the tax bill after it is fully in effect in 1988. We analyze separately the effects of the bill on the level and distribution of state and local spending, and on the mix of revenue sources employed by state and local governments.

The effects of the tax reform in this area will be fairly small; we expect state and local spending to fall by between 0.9 percent and 1.9 percent, with the lower end of the range the more plausible. A reduction in the number of itemizers—taxpayers who will be unable to deduct their state and local in-

Paul N. Courant and Daniel L. Rubinfeld, "Tax Reform: Implications for the State-Local Public Sector," *Journal of Economic Perspectives* 1 (Summer 1987), 87–100. Reprinted by permission of the authors and the publisher.

Paul N. Courant is Professor of Economics and Public Policy at the University of Michigan. **Daniel L. Rubinfeld** is Professor of Law and Economics at the University of California, Berkeley.

come and property taxes—will account for about half of this change. The elimination of sales tax deductibility, which also makes citizens pay more for state and local government, accounts for slightly more than a third of the decrease in spending. Finally, reductions in marginal tax rates, which make the deductions for income and property taxes worth less to taxpayers who continue to itemize, accounts for the rest. Moreover, states will probably shift away from sales taxes toward deductible sources of revenue, thereby making the effect of the tax reform on state spending smaller still.

The conclusion that aggregate spending is unlikely to change very much does not imply that the Tax Reform Act is unimportant to the state and local public sector. The fiscal and economic circumstances of state and local governments vary enormously, and the federal tax reform will therefore affect them very differently. Local governments with relatively large numbers of high income homeowners can be expected to reduce their expenditures substantially and to expand their reliance on user charges. The relative fiscal attractiveness of localities within metropolitan areas will be altered, leading to changes in population distribution and house values, and increasing the incentives for higher income households to segregate themselves from lower income households. From both an efficiency and an equity perspective, these effects on local governments are likely to be much more important than the aggregate effect on either state or local spending.

The Tax Reform Act has the immediate effect of changing state revenues; most states will enjoy an increase at current rates, while some will lose revenue. Over the longer run, apart from the obvious incentive to move away from the non-deductible sales tax to other deductible taxes, the effect of tax reform on the mix of revenue instruments is difficult to predict. The new tax bill also has major implications for bond financing: it limits the use of the tax-exempt bond instrument (since industrial development bonds have been cut back and regulations regarding the use of tax-exempt bonds generally have been tightened), and may also change the relative attractiveness of the instrument in financial markets.

The Effect of Tax Reform on Aggregate State and Local Expenditures

Voters' demands for state or local government spending can be modeled the way economists model demands for private goods—as functions of income, prices, and social, economic, and demographic variables that are proxies for voters' tastes. Based on the preferred spending levels of each voter, political processes determine the level and content of public spending. Unfortunately, viewing the problem in this way is not very helpful, since the data required to calculate the distribution of demands for public spending and to specify the political algorithm that determines spending would be expensive to obtain even if it were conceptually clear how to do so. An alternative that has been widely employed is to model the level of expenditure in a given jurisdiction as depending on the preferences of the "decisive voter"—a hypothetical individual whose voting behavior best explains the choices made by the electorate of the jurisdiction as a whole.

Decisive voter models pose both theoretical and empirical pitfalls; one must be especially wary of drawing welfare implications from demand functions for public spending that are estimated in this way. Yet, such models have done well in predicting the behavior of local governments, the area in which they have been used most. No one would claim that there is an identifiable "decisive voter," and even if there were, the identity of such a person would change in response to a change in the environment. But here, as in many other cases, it has proven useful to model as if such a person existed.

Models of Expenditure Determination

In one form of the model, the decisive voter is taken to be the "median voter," the voter with the median demand who, given prices and incomes, separates into equal-sized groups voters who want more and less spending. In most empirical work that employs the median voter model, the median voter is identified as the individual or household with the median income, although the conditions under which this assumption is warranted are quite restrictive. The median voter construct is an appealing one because the desired spending level of the median voter will defeat any other spending level in a majority rule referendum.[1] Richer forms of the decisive voter model take into account the fact that intensity of preferences and the structure of political institutions, rather than just a desire for "more" or "less" spending, generally affect spending outcomes. The "mean voter" model is perhaps the simplest of this class.

In the "mean voter" model it is assumed that voters are able to organize matters (presumably through political institutions) so that the intensity of preferences matters. Indeed, under the mean voter model it is assumed implicitly that all potential gains from trading income for votes are realized. (This assumption is not so farfetched when one considers the practice of "logrolling," in which proponents of one element of public spending form coalitions with those who favor another and vote to have both, and the fact that voter turnout is positively correlated with intensity of preference.) In the mean voter model, the entire distribution of tastes for public spending affects the outcome. It is conceptually difficult to choose a single measure of income and tax price that reflects the entire population distribution. In this paper, we choose the easy way out by using measures of mean income and mean price for the jurisdiction. A more sophisticated analysis would look for the characteristics of the mean voter, which may well differ from the mean characteristics of the jurisdiction.

Clearly, the difference between the median and mean voter models will be greatest when the distribution of preferred spending levels is most skewed. For example, where many voters prefer a small amount of spending and a few prefer a much larger amount, the median voter model will predict a lower level of spending than will the mean voter model.

In using either form of the decisive voter model to predict responses to the Tax Reform Act, we look at the effects of the Act on the income and tax price faced by the decisive voter. The Tax price P can be interpreted as the cost to the taxpayer of a one dollar increase in tax-financed per capita public spending. This concept can be expressed by the formula

$$P = ns(1 - gt)$$

where n is the population of the jurisdiction, s is the share of total taxes in the jurisdiction that the individual pays (it would equal the individual's taxable income divided by aggregate taxable income if all public spending in the jurisdiction were financed by a proportional income tax), t is the individual's federal marginal tax rate, and g is the proportion of state and local taxes that the individual may deduct from federal taxable income. The ns term weights individuals by how much tax they pay relative to the mean in their jurisdiction; ns will equal 1 if the individual pays an average amount of tax, 2 if he pays twice the average, and so on. The term in parenthesis adjusts for what share of the individual's state and local tax payments are deductible. If the individual does not itemize, gt falls to zero and the tax price reduces to ns.

Of course, the same taxpayer will face different tax prices for state government and local government expenditures, provided that the individual accounts for different shares of the taxes paid in the two cases. Thus, any discussion that combines the tax price of state and local government, like the one that follows, involves a degree on averaging that masks much variation in the population.

Effects on State and Local Spending

The major effects of the Tax Reform Act on the tax price facing voters in states and localities are through a lower federal marginal tax rate t and the reduction in the deductibility of state and local taxes g, which falls both because sales taxes are no longer deductible and because many taxpayers who currently itemize will no longer do so. To estimate the effect of the tax reform, then, first we estimate how the tax reform will affect the federal marginal tax rate of the decisive voter and the percentage of state and local taxes g that voter can deduct; then we calculate the percentage change in the tax price P of state and local spending; and finally use estimates of the price elasticity of demand for tax-financed state and local expenditure to calculate the change in expenditure demand. Fortunately, we can and do assume that the populations within jurisdictions (n) and each individual's share of state and local taxes paid (s) do not change.

In 1982, 40.8 percent of all taxpayers itemized deductions, and 81.8 percent of state and local taxes were deductible. The average marginal tax rate of itemizers was .284, ranging from .307 in the District of Columbia to .210 in Mississippi (Kenyon, 1985, p. 37). Those figures imply that the average level of P for tax-financed state and local spending was .905 in 1982. In fiscal year 1984 general sales taxes accounted for 23.5 percent of state and local tax revenue (U.S. Bureau of the Census, 1985, p. 4). Assuming that this ratio still holds, making sales taxes non-deductible will reduce the deductible share g of state and local taxes paid by itemizers to .583. The federal tax rate facing the average itemizer will fall to about 25 percent under the Tax Reform Act, and the fraction of taxpayers itemizing will fall to about .26. Thus, the average level of P will rise in 1988 to .962 (that is, $1 - .26 \times .583 \times .25$), an increase of 6.3 percent over its 1982 levels.

Our reading of the current literature places the price elasticity of demand for state and local spending between $- .50$ and $- .25$, implying that increasing P by 6.3 percent will reduce tax-financed state and local spending by from 3.2 percent to 1.6 percent. The Tax Reform Act does not alter the taxpayer's cost of (and thus demand for) expenditure financed by user charges and federal grants. These latter two categories accounted for 41 percent of state and local general revenue in 1983–84, leaving 59 percent of state and local spending that was tax-financed.[2] Assuming that marginal changes in public spending are tax financed, our best estimate from the mean voter model is that total spending will fall by from 1.9 percent to 0.9 percent relative to what it would have been.[3]

The median voter model cannot be applied meaningfully to national averages. Since the median voter is not an itemizer, such a model would imply that changes in g and t for itemizers should have no effect on state and local spending. Some estimates of the effect of the Tax Reform Act on state and local spending have been made assuming that the median voter is the median itemizer. Such estimates imply reductions in spending that are many times larger than the ones we present here, but we do not believe the underlying assumption. We present mean voter estimates here because we believe that the appropriate version of the decisive voter model should represent an amalgam of the preferences of all influential interest groups in the jurisdiction. This view implies that expenditures will fall in jurisdictions with a substantial number of itemizers, whether or not the median voter is an itemizer, but they will not fall by as much as is predicted by models in which only itemizers matter.

The Effect of Tax Reform on Individual Communities

That the average effects on state and local spending will be fairly modest does not imply that they will be small in all cases. High income communities in which the median voter is an itemizer whose tax rate falls from 50 percent to 28 or 33 percent will experience large increases in the tax price facing the decisive voter. In the extreme case of a change from 50 percent to 28 percent (a very high income suburb) the tax price for local public services would rise by 44 percent, or enough to reduce expenditures on public schools by over 10 percent. Of course, this increase in tax price is an increase in the relative price of public education, and built into the elasticity estimates is some shift towards private education. Such substitution towards private spending is implicit in all of our estimated responses to increases in tax prices. Similarly, states that rely heavily on sales taxes will have much greater than average increases in the tax price of state expenditures, although not as high as 44 percent. On the other hand, local jurisdictions in which almost no one currently itemizes will experience smaller than average effects on spending.

Because the effects on tax-price will vary greatly among jurisdictions, the change in federal rules should provide a natural experiment for distinguishing among models of expenditure determination. By examining household microdata within communities, it should be possible to discover which form of the decisive voter model predicts best. Ideally, such new studies of the determinants of state and local expenditure will also characterize the effects of the different types of rules (referendum, elected city council, and so on) under which public choices are made.

Mobility Effects and Capitalization

The preceding analysis implicitly assumes that voters will not relocate in response to changes in their state and local tax burdens. But in some cases the relative fiscal attractiveness of different locations will change appreciably, especially for high income residents of relatively high tax jurisdictions with lower tax jurisdictions nearby. What matters here is not so much relative changes in tax-price as changes in the total tax bill paid; for high income itemizers, these can be quite large. The most important consequence of this change is that reductions in federal marginal tax rates may increase the pressures for economic segregation.

Deductibility tends to reduce the differences in tax-prices and tax bills between locations that have different tax rates, since it reduces big tax bills in localities that generally pay high federal marginal rates more than it will reduce smaller tax bills in localities that pay lower federal marginal rates. This increased differential by itself is probably not sufficient incentive to move, given the transaction costs involved, but it surely is enough to alter the location choices of some households that are new to the area or that were planning to move within the area for other reasons. Thus, reducing the deductibility of local taxes will: (1) lead to some shift in population towards low-tax, low-spending jurisdictions; (2) lead to a reduction in the price of high income housing in high-tax, high-spending jurisdictions relative to the price of similar housing in low-tax jurisdictions, to compensate for the fact that less of a local property tax bill can be deducted; and (3) reduce spending more in high-tax jurisdictions than in low-tax ones (where spending may even rise) because of the effects that (1) and (2) will have on the property tax base.

Edward Gramlich (1985) points out that deductibility of local taxes currently serves as a bribe to higher-income households to live in high-tax, lower income communities, because much of their increased tax share is returned through the federal income tax. Gramlich thus argues that one unfortunate consequence of reducing federal marginal tax rates (indeed, in this view, the only unfortunate consequence) is that the reduction will tend to enhance the already powerful fiscal incentives for higher income households to segregate themselves from lower income households by living in high income, lower-tax jurisdictions. Gramlich argues that reductions in federal tax rates will tend to widen income differentials between Detroit and its suburbs. Similar incentives will exist between New York City and its suburbs, some of which are in low-tax states, making the fiscal differentials larger to begin with and more affected by the new federal tax rates. The same analysis should apply to large metropolitan areas throughout the country.

For these same reasons, tax reform will tend to increase business tax differentials across communities, too. Corporations will still be allowed to deduct all state and local taxes paid, but will face a marginal rate of 34 percent rather than 46 percent. If state and local fiscal policy is unchanged, the net differential between tax rates in different locations will increase by .12 (the change in the federal marginal rate) times the statutory differential; similarly, the differential in tax payments will rise by 12 percent of its previous value. The incentive for businesses to locate in lower-tax jurisdictions will be increased, and recent evidence indicates that business is somewhat responsive to such differentials.[4] Again, the implication is that tax reform will tend to reduce tax bases and expenditures in high-tax communities relative to low ones.

Public finance economists have long argued that redistributive activity is best undertaken at the federal level because if state and local governments engage in such behavior, lower income households will tend to migrate towards the "generous" jurisdiction and higher income households tend to migrate away. By making low-tax jurisdictions relatively more attractive to both households and businesses, the Tax Reform Act further reduces the ability of state and local governments to engage in redistributive activities. Were the federal government to establish a national system of income maintenance, this effect would not be a problem. Reducing the implicit federal subsidy to state and local spending would only enhance economic efficiency, partly because it would bring the relative prices of privately and publicly provided goods closer together. In the world we live in, where many of the largest (and highest tax) states and localities engage in greater than average levels of income redistribution, and where federal programs are very limited in their coverage, this poses a genuine problem. The incentives to migration set up by the Tax Reform Act will increase economic efficiency in the allocation of resources, but absent a nationwide program of income redistribution, they will also reduce the ability of more generous localities to implement their preferences for redistribution.

Effects on the Property Tax Base

The conclusion that the aggregate spending effects of the new tax bill are small, although the effects on some individual jurisdictions will be larger, must be tempered by the possibility that the value of the local property tax base may change. It is impossible to predict with any accuracy how important this possibility may be, but we can list some important considerations.

First, the cost of capital net of tax used for owner-occupied housing will tend to rise (especially so for the most expensive housing), because fewer individuals will be itemizing and those individuals who do will generally face lower marginal tax rates (so that the mortgage interest deduction and property tax deduction are worth less). Additionally, rental housing will receive much less favorable tax treatment, as the new law severely limits the extent to which "passive losses" in real estate (and other activities) can be used to offset other income, and also reduces the value of depreciation allowances for rental real estate. All other things equal, then, the value of the residential tax base should fall.

But all other things are not equal. From the perspective of the overall portfolio effects of the tax bill, owner-occupied housing continues to do well because other forms of capital investment are treated even less generously. (Under the Tax Reform Act, mortgage interest is the only kind of personal interest that remains deductible.) Commercial and industrial capital are also in the local property tax base. Since the effect of the tax bill will be to reduce the attractiveness of essentially all forms of domestic investment relative to investment abroad, the local property tax base may fall further still. On the other hand, if the decreased demand for capital lowers interest rates, the present discounted value of the net income stream that remains will go up, raising property values. And in any case, macroeconomic policy can be used to influence both the real interest rate and the fraction of wealth that is held in the form of government debt and not subject to property taxation, thus indirectly affecting the value of the property tax base in ways that may overwhelm the effects of the Tax Reform Act.

The overall effect of the tax reform act on the local property tax base is impossible to predict, but it is potentially important. Given the long-standing reliance of the local public sector on property taxes, major changes in the property tax base would cause major shifts in the mix of revenue instruments used by local government.

The Effect of Tax Reform on the Mix of Revenue Instruments

The income tax statutes in most states define state income liability as some function of federal taxable income or federal tax liability. Thus, unless and until offsetting actions are undertaken, the Tax Reform Act has the immediate effect of changing state (and in some cases local) income tax revenue. These effects will differ among states. The eight states that use federal taxable income—adjusted gross income less deductions and exemptions—as their income tax base will enjoy increased revenues at current tax rates because of the broadening of the federal tax base. Similarly, the seventeen states that use federal adjusted gross income and some but not all deductions and exemptions in defining taxable income all get substantial revenue increases at current rates, because federal adjusted gross income will rise and deductions will fall. The seven states that use federal adjusted gross income have smaller increases.[5] The effect will be similar but smaller in those states that have tied their corporate income taxes to the federal corporate income tax. However, the four states that piggy-back their income taxes directly on federal personal income tax collections will lose revenue, because they collect fixed shares of federal income tax revenue, which will fall as federal corporate taxes increase.

The response of states to these windfall revenue changes (mostly windfall gains) will be of some interest to political economists. The classic static equilibrium models of budget determination suggest an immediate adjustment of tax rates to offset the federal changes (except insofar as they affect the demand for state and local public services, as discussed above) while dynamic political and economic models predict a more gradual response; that is, states with positive windfalls will be able to improve their fiscal positions because of the tax reform while those with negative windfalls will have to "eat" some of their losses. In almost all states, however, these direct effects on state income tax receipts should be large enough to prompt a major political examination of state tax structures.

The dynamic responses of state and local governments to budgetary windfalls has been a subject of substantial recent debate. The empirical literature provides some evidence for a "flypaper effect," in which windfalls are spent publicly rather than returned to the citizenry as tax reduction ("money sticks where it hits") and theoretical treatments have approached the issue as well (for example, Courant, Gramlich and Rubinfeld, 1979). The Tax Reform Act of 1986 should provide a natural experiment to help resolve the question of the size and existence of the "flypaper effect."

Long-Run Effects on Revenue Sources

Tax reform will have a number of effects of the way that state and local governments raise revenue. First, state and local governments will almost surely move away from the sales tax and toward deductible taxes. In considering a repeal of all personal deductions for state and local taxes, Feldstein and Metcalf (1985) argued that state and local governments would shift toward business taxes, which would remain deductible. But given that income and property taxes remain deductible for households under the new tax bill, and given the tremendous competition among states and localities to foster a favorable "business climate," it seems likely that the shift will be toward income taxes at the state level and property taxes at the local level, but not toward business taxes at either level. States that currently rely most heavily on sales taxes may encounter pressure to shift to a value-added tax, which would act much like a sales tax but also be deductible by business. Since federal tax reform will result in a windfall increase in personal income taxes in most states, one obvious response would be let at least some of that windfall stand and use the proceeds to reduce sales taxes.[6]

Second, the higher tax-price associated with the use of deductible taxes encourages the recent trend towards an increased reliance on user charges, especially at the local level. This change appeals to those who view goods provided by the local public sector as essentially private in character, since user charges generally resemble prices more than property taxes do. In fact, one of the efficiency arguments against the deductibility of state and local taxes is that it leads to a bias against user charges even when the latter would be more efficient. Reducing federal tax rates reduces this bias.

Third, the Tax Reform Act has major implications for bond financing. It curtails severely the ability of local governments to issue industrial development bonds by limiting the volume of such issues to $50 per person (or $150 million per state, whichever is less), compared to $100 per person under previous law. It also makes interest on industrial development bonds subject to the alternative minimum tax in the personal income tax, reducing the value of such bonds as a tax shelter. These changes, in combination with an extremely complicated set of new regulations designed to prevent localities from using tax-exempt issues to invest in private financial instruments, will clearly reduce the incentives to issue tax-exempt bonds.

However, if the spread between tax exempt and taxable bonds rises, there may be a (partially) offsetting increase in the incentive to use tax-exempt bonds. On the face of it, the spread should fall because federal tax rates will fall, and being exempt from a lower tax rate has less value. However, the sharp curtailment of other kinds of tax shelters under the personal income tax—notably the curtailment of deductions for investing in IRAs and other supplemental retirement programs and the treatment of capital gains as ordinary income—makes municipal bonds more attractive to investors seeking tax-exempt financial instruments. Whether the portfolio effect (making bonds more attractive) outweighs the effect operating through changed tax rates is unclear. Given that the spread between tax-exempt and taxable issues has been low by historical standards in recent years, and this phenomenon is widely alleged to be due to the many other methods of tax-preferred saving available, we believe that municipals will become relatively more attractive and the yield spread will rise.

In any event, the municipal bond market aspects of tax reform should not have much effect on municipal spending in the aggregate. The new tax law sharply increases the restrictions on direct arbitrage, whereby governments issue tax-exempt debt and invest in private-sector financial instruments with the proceeds. But nothing in the new law prevents indirect arbitrage, issuing tax-exempt debt as a substitute for taxation.

This indirect arbitrage mechanism is especially attractive to low income communities with few itemizers and low personal tax rates, as it enables residents of such communities to "borrow" (by substituting the issuance of debt for tax levies) at the municipal bond rate and invest, privately, at the after-tax rate on private financial instruments. Even for the lowest income communities, however, the tax savings for residents is very small, suggesting that the effect on municipal spending would not be noticeable. This finding is controversial: the traditional view is that exempting municipal bonds from taxation stimulates capital spending. Again, the Tax Reform Act provides a natural experiment. If the yield spread (controlling for the portfolio effects) changes as a result of the tax bill, will the proportion of the public budget spent on physical capital improvements change? (If it does not, the implication is that the requirement that bond funds be used for "capital spending" does not bind.) Will the debt-financed proportion of the budget change? Will these changes be correlated with the income of the jurisdictions involved? The answers to these questions should help us to evaluate the role of tax-exempt bonds in financing the local public sector.

Evaluating the Tax Reform Act of 1986

By all accounts the broadening of the federal income tax base is a good idea, as is the limitation on the use of industrial development bonds. The other limitations on bonds are probably also warranted, although anything that requires as many detailed regulations to implement as the "anti-arbitrage" provisions of the new bill is not likely to be very effective.

Evaluation of the elimination of sales tax deductibility must begin with an evaluation of deductibility in general. According to one popular view of state and local public economics, most state and local public expenditures (especially local) are essentially private in character, even if the goods are publicly provided. From this perspective, competition among communities allows citizens to "vote with their feet" for desired spending and tax packages, and mobility assures an efficient allocation of resources. Local taxes can be considered benefit taxes. In this view, deductibility creates inefficiencies by distorting spending choices and weakening the link between benefits received and taxes paid.

An alternative theoretical view holds that state and local governments provide purely public goods. Tax payments for these goods are real reductions in disposable income, not tied to any particular benefits received, and should therefore be deducted from the federal tax base. In this view, full or partial deductibility of state and local taxes makes sense for reasons of equity. A more pragmatic "rough efficiency" argument that yields the same result in that deductibility encourages state and local spending, thus repaying state and local governments for positive spillovers that arise when public spending undertaken in one jurisdiction benefits residents of other jurisdictions. A weakness in this argument is that the value of deductibility depends on the federal marginal tax rates of the citizens of jurisdictions. It is hard to make an efficiency case, and probably impossible to make an equity case, for a program that subsidizes (say) education more in high income suburbs than in lower income central cities, but that regressive pattern of subsidy is exactly what deductibility generates.

In general, we believe that state and local taxes should not be deductible; that is, the goods that they finance have a substantial private component. Where spillovers exist, direct matching grants from the federal government would be a better way of internalizing the externalities, because the matching rates could (in principle) be varied with magnitude of the spillover. In addition, deductibility imposes efficiency costs by making user charges less attractive. But this general argument against deductibility is much weaker as an argument against eliminating deductibility of only one tax, such as the sales tax. Governments will tend to substitute other sources of deductible revenue for the sales tax in the long run. To the extent that the sales tax belongs in the optimal tax mix, the result will be a distortion in the mix of state and local tax instruments, and official estimates of the federal revenue gain from eliminating deductibility of the sales tax will be too high.

Given the conclusion that deductibility in general is not good policy, it follows that lower marginal tax rates will enhance efficiency by reducing the federal subsidy to local and state spending. Those states that use federal taxable income (in whole or in part) as their tax base should also receive an efficiency gain because the same revenue can be collected at lower marginal rates. (Of course, such jurisdictions could have reformed their tax bases at any time, but the fact the federal government has done so greatly simplifies the task.) However, if local property tax bases do fall, then higher marginal tax rates would be required to maintain a given level of local government revenue.

While the efficiency aspects of the tax bill are somewhat appealing, the increased burden on high tax states and localities remains troubling. The biggest decreases in state and local public spending should occur in high tax states and localities, many of which allocate a relatively large share of their budgets towards redistributive programs. At the local level, the pattern will be mixed, with the richer communities losing more than the poorer communities initially, but with the real possibility that the fiscal incentive for the rich to leave higher-tax, lower income jurisdictions will impair the fiscal position of large central cities over time. Still, increasing federal tax rates with the goal of restoring the importance of deductibility is hardly the optimal policy response to this problem. We hope (without much confidence) that these effects of reducing deductibility may lead to reform of the intergovernmental grant and national income maintenance systems. If that were to happen, we could unambiguously favor the Tax Reform Act from the perspective of its effects on the state and local sectors.

NOTES

Note: We are grateful to Henry Aaron, Edward M. Gramlich, Daphne R. Kenyon, Carl Shapiro, Joseph Stiglitz, and Timothy Taylor for helpful comments and discussions.

1. This conclusion requires the additional assumption that if a voter prefers spending level x to level y, the voter also (weakly) prefers y to any level farther from x than y, for all x and y. Preferences of this form are termed "single-peaked."
2. U.S. Bureau of the Census, table 3, p. 4. We exclude utility, liquor store, and insurance trust revenue from general revenue.
3. These calculations ignore the increase in household disposable income arising from the Tax Reform Act.
4. See Wasylenko and McGuire (1985) for a review of the recent evidence.
5. The source of the data in this paragraph is "Governor's Weekly Bulletin," May 16, 1986, pp. 1–3.
6. We do not expect the shift away from sales taxes to take place rapidly. In many

states specific portions of the sales tax revenues are earmarked to go to localities, school districts and the like. To obtain political agreement to shift away from sales taxes, it may be necessary to prevent harm to many of the beneficiaries of such existing rules, and that, in turn should require some revenue increase.

REFERENCES

Bergstrom, Theodore C., Daniel L. Rubinfeld, and Perry Shapiro, "Micro Based Estimates of Demand Functions for Local School Expenditures," *Econometrica,* September 1982, *50,* 1183–1205.

Chernick, Howard, and Andrew Reschovsky, "Federal Tax Reform and the Financing of State and Local Governments," *Journal of Policy Analysis and Management,* Summer 1986, *5,* 683–706.

Courant, Paul N., Edward M. Gramlich, and Daniel L. Rubinfeld, "The Stimulative Effects of Intergovernmental Grants: or Why Money Sticks Where it Hits." In Mieszkowski, P., and W. Oakland, eds., *Fiscal Federalism and Grants-in-Aid.* The Urban Institute, 1979.

Feldstein, Martin, and Gilbert Metcalf, "The Effect of Federal Tax Deductibility on State and Local Taxes and Spending." NBER Working Paper No. 1791, January 1986.

Gordon, Roger H., and Joel Slemrod, "An Empirical Examination of Municipal Financial Policy." In Rosen, Harvey S., ed., *Studies in State and Local Public Finance.* Chicago: University of Chicago Press, 1986, pp. 53–78.

Gramlich, Edward M., "The Deductibility of State and Local Taxes," *National Tax Journal,* December 1985, *38,* 447–466.

Gramlich, Edward M., and Daniel L. Rubinfeld, "Micro Estimates of Public Spending Demand Functions and Tests of the Tiebout and Median Voter Hypotheses," *Journal of Political Economy,* June 1982, 536–560.

Inman, Robert, "Markets, Government, and the 'New' Political Economy." In Auerbach, A. J. and M. Feldstein, eds., *Handbook of Public Economics,* vol. 2. North-Holland, 1987.

Kenyon, Daphne A., "Federal Income Tax Deductibility of State and Local Taxes." To be published in U.S. Treasury, Office of State and Local Finance, *Federal-State-Local Fiscal Relations: Report to the President and the Congress.* Draft dated June 1985.

Netzer, Dick, "The Effect of Tax Simplification on State and Local Governments." In Aaron, Henry *et al., Economic Consequences of Tax Simplification.* Boston: Federal Reserve Bank of Boston, 1985, pp. 222–251.

Tiebout, Charles, "A Pure Theory of Local Expenditures," *Journal of Political Economy,* 1956, *64,* 416–424.

U.S. Bureau of the Census, *Government Finances in 1983–1984.* Washington, D.C.: GPO, October 1985.

Wasylenko, Michael, and Therese McGuire, "Jobs and Taxes: The Effect of Business Climate on States' Employment Growth Rates," *National Tax Journal, XXXVIII, 4,* 497–512.

Further Readings on Economics of the Public Sector

The *Journal of Economic Literature* is an excellent source of current books and articles in this field.

SECTION I: Perspectives on Economics and the Public Sector

Arrow, Kenneth J. "The Organization of Economic Activity: Issues Pertinent to the Choice of Market vs Non-Market Allocation." In *Public Expenditures and Policy Analysis*, ed. R. H. Haveman and J. Margolis. Chicago: Markham, 1970.

————. "Values and Collective Decision Making." In *Philosophy, Politics, and Society*, ed. P. Luslett and W. Runcman. New York: Barnes Noble, 1967, 215–232.

Bator, Francis. "The Anatomy of Market Failure." *Quarterly Journal of Economics* (August 1958): 351–379.

————. "The Simple Analytics of Welfare Maximization." *American Economic Review* (March 1957): 22–59.

Buchanan, James M. "The Constitution of Economic Policy." *American Economic Review* (June 1987): 243–250.

Heller, Walter W. "What Is Right with Economics." *American Economic Review* (March 1975): 1–26.

Larkey, Patrick D., Chandler Stolp, and Mark Winer. "Explanations of Public Sector Growth: A Review." In *Proceedings of the Seventy-Sixth Annual Conference on Taxation of the National Tax Association–Tax Institute of America*, ed. Stanley J. Bowers. Columbus, Ohio, 1983, 16–26.

Schultz, Charles L. "The Role and Responsibilities of the Economist in Government." *American Economic Review* (May 1982): 62–66.

Schultz, George. "Reflections on Political Economy." *Challenge* (March/April 1974): 6–11.

Stigler, George F. *The Citizen and the State*. Chicago: University of Chicago Press, 1975, ch. 1, 2, 5.

SECTION II: Economics of Externalities

Baumol, William J. "On Taxation and the Control of Externalities." *American Economic Review* (June 1972): 307–322.

Baumol, William J., and Wallace E. Oates. *Economics, Environmental Policy, and the Quality of Life*. Englewood Cliffs, N.J.: Prentice-Hall, 1979.

Dahlman, Carl J. "The Problem of Externality." *Journal of Law and Economics* (April 1979): 141–162.

Davis, Otto A., and M. I. Kamien. "Externalities Information and Alternative Collective Action." In *Public Expenditures and Policy Analysis,* ed. R. H. Haveman and J. Margolis. Chicago: Markham, 1970.

Demsetz, Harold. "Towards a Theory of Property Rights." *American Economic Review* (May 1967): 347–359.

Furubotn, Eirik, and Svetozar Pejovich. "Property Rights and Economic Theory: A Survey of the Recent Literature." *Journal of Economic Literature* (December 1972): 1137–1162.

Head, John G. "Externality and Public Policy." Reprinted in *Public Goods and Public Welfare,* ed. J. G. Head. Durham, N.C.: Duke University Press, 1974, 184–213.

Johnson, David B. "Meade, Bees, and Externalities." *Journal of Law and Economics* (April 1973): 35–52.

Lave, Lester B., and Gilbert S. Omenn. *Clearing the Air: Reforming the Clean Air Act.* Washington, D.C.: Brookings Institution, 1981.

Meade, J. E. "External Economics and Diseconomies in a Competitive Situation." *Economic Journal* (March 1952): 54–67.

Mishan, Edward J. "The Relationship Between Joint Products, Collective Goods, and External Effects." *Journal of Political Economy* (May/June 1969): 329–348.

Veljanovski, C. G. "The Coase Theorems and the Economic Theory of Markets and Law." *Kyklos* (1982, fasc.1): 53–74.

White, Lawrence J. "Effluent Charges as a Faster Means of Achieving Pollution Abatement." *Public Policy* (1976): 111–125.

Zerbe, Richard O., Jr. "The Problem of Social Cost in Retrospect." *Research in Law and Economics* (1980): 83–102.

SECTION III: Economics of Public Goods

Blinder, Alan S. "The Level and Distribution of Economic Well Being." In *The American Economy in Transition,* ed. Martin Feldstein. Chicago: University of Chicago Press, 1980, 415–479.

Borcherding, Thomas E. "Competition, Exclusion, and the Optimal Supply of Public Goods." *Journal of Law and Economics* (April 1978): 111–132.

Brubaker, Earl R. "Free Rider, Free Revelation, or Golden Rule?" *Journal of Law and Economics* (April 1975): 147–161.

Buchanan, James M. *The Demand and Supply of Public Goods.* Chicago: Rand McNally, 1968.

————. "An Economic Theory of Clubs." *Economica* (February 1965): 1–14.

Clarke, Edward H. *Demand Revelation and the Provision of Public Goods.* Cambridge, Mass.: Ballinger, 1980.

Goldin, Kenneth D. "Equal Access vs Selective Access: A Critique of Public Goods Theory." *Public Choice* (Spring 1977): 53–71.

Holtermann, S. E. "Externalities and Public Goods." *Economica* (February 1972): 78–87.

Kormendi, Roger C. "Further Thoughts on the Free Rider Problem and Demand Revealing Processes." *Research in Law and Economics* (1980): 219–225.

Marwell, Gerald, and Ruth E. Ames. "Economists Free Ride, Does Anyone Else? Experiments on the Provision of Public Goods. IV." *Journal of Public Economics* (June 1981): 295–310.

Mueller, Dennis C. "Achieving the Just Policy." *American Economic Review (May 1974): 147–152.*

———. "Public Choice: A Survey." *Journal of Economic Literature* (June 1976): 395–433.

Okun, Arthur. *Equality and Efficiency: The Big Trade-Off.* Washington, D.C.: Brookings Institution, 1975.

Samuelson, Paul A. "Diagrammatic Exposition of a Theory of Public Expenditures." *Review of Economics and Statistics* (November 1955): 360–366.

Stiglitz, Joseph E. "The Demand for Education in Public and Private School Systems." *Journal of Public Economics* (November 1974): 349–385.

Thurow, Lester C. "A Surge in Inequality." *Scientific American* (May 1987): 30–37.

Tideman, T. Nicolaus. "Ethical Foundations of the Demand-Revealing Process." *Public Choice* (Spring 1977, Supplement): 71–77.

Wicksell, Knut, and Erik Lindahl. Excerpts of writings in *Classics in the Theory of Public Finance,* ed. R. A. Musgrave and A. Peacock. New York: Macmillan, 1958.

SECTION IV: Economics of the Political Process

Anderson, Lee G., and Russell F. Settle. *Benefit-Cost Analysis: A Practical Guide.* Lexington, Mass.: D.C. Heath, 1977.

Arrow, Kenneth J. *Social Choice and Individual Values,* 2d ed. New York: Wiley, 1963.

Baumol, William J., and David F. Bradford. "Optimal Departures from Marginal Pricing." *American Economic Review* (June 1970): 265–283.

Baumol, William J., and A. K. Klevorick. "Input Choices and the Rate of Return Regulation: An Overview of the Discussion." *Bell Journal of Economics and Management Science* (Autumn 1970): 162–190.

Bennett, James T., and Manuel H. Johnson. "Tax Reductions Without Sacrifice: Private-Sector Production of Public Services." *Public Finance Quarterly* (October 1980): 363–396.

Black, Duncan. *The Theory of Committees and Elections.* Cambridge: Cambridge University Press, 1958.

Bridge, Gary. "Citizen Choice in Public Services: Voucher Systems." In *Alternatives for Delivery Public Services: Toward Improved Performance,* ed. E. S. Savas. Boulder, Colo.: Westview Press, 1977, 51–109.

Buchanan, James M. *Fiscal Theory and Political Economy: Selected Essays.* Chapel Hill: University of North Carolina Press, 1960.

Buchanan, James M., and Gordon Tullock. *The Calculus of Consent.* Ann Arbor: University of Michigan Press, 1962.

Downs, Anthony. *An Economic Theory of Democracy.* New York: Harper & Row, 1957.

Feldstein, Martin S. "Unemployment Insurance: Time for Reform." *Harvard Business Review* (March-April 1975): 51–61.

Green, Jerry, and Jean-Jacques Laffont. *Individual Incentives in Public Decision-Making.* Amsterdam: North Holland, 1979.

Mishan, Edward J. *Cost-Benefit Analysis*. New York: Praeger, 1976.

Niskanen, William A., Jr. *Bureaucracy and Representative Government*. Chicago: Aldine-Atherton, 1971.

Ramsey, Frank P. "A Contribution to the Theory of Taxation." *Economic Journal* (March 1927): 47–61.

Riker, William H. "Arrow's Theorem and Some Examples of the Paradox of Voting." In *Mathematical Applications in Political Science,* ed. John M. Claunch. Dallas, Tex.: Arnold Foundation, 1965, 41–60.

Ruttan, Vernon W. "Bureaucratic Productivity: The Case of Agricultural Research." *Public Choice* (Fall 1980): 529–547.

Thompson, Lawrence H. "The Social Security Reform Debate." *Journal of Economic Literature* (December 1983): 1425–1467.

Tullock, Gordon. *Private Wants, Public Means*. New York: Basic Books, 1970.

Tullock, Gordon, and Colin D. Campbell. "Computer Simulation of a Small Voting System." *Economic Journal* (March 1970): 97–104.

SECTION V: Economics of Taxation

Atkinson, A. B. "Optimal Taxation and the Direct Versus Indirect Tax Controversy," *Canadian Journal of Economics* (November 1977), 590–606.

Bartlett, Bruce, and Timothy P. Roth. *The Supply-Side Solution*. Chatham, N.J.: Chatham House, 1983.

Boskin, Michael J. "Efficiency Aspects of the Differential Tax Treatment of Market and Household Economic Activity." *Journal of Public Economics* (February 1975): 1–25.

Bradford, David F., and Harvey S. Rosen. "The Optimal Taxation of Commodities and Income." *American Economic Review* (May 1976): 94–101.

Burtless, Gary T., and Jerry A. Hausman. "The Effect of Taxation on Labour Supply—Evaluating the Gary Negative Income Tax Experiment." *Journal of Political Economy* (December 1978): 1103–1130.

Devaragar, S., D. Fullerton, and R. Musgrave. "Estimating the Distribution of Tax Burdens: A Comparison of Alternative Approaches," *Journal of Public Economics* (April 1980): 155–182.

Friedman, Benjamin M. "New Directions in the Relation Between Public and Private Debt." *Science* (April 1987): 397–403.

Hall, Robert E., and Alvin Rabushka. *Low Tax, Simple Tax, Flat Tax*. New York: McGraw-Hill, 1983.

Harberger, Arnold C. *Taxation and Welfare*. Boston: Little, Brown, 1974.

Haveman, Richard H., and Harold W. Watts. "Social Experimentation as Policy Research: A Review of Negative Income Tax Experiments." In *Public Economics and Human Resources,* ed. V. Halberstadt and A. J. Culyer. Cujas, 1977.

Kotlikoff, Laurence J. "Taxation and Savings: A Neoclassical Perspective." *Journal of Economic Literature* (December 1984): 1576–1624.

Krauss, Melvin B., and Harry J. Johnson. "The Theory of Tax Incidence: A Diagrammatic Analysis." *Economica* (November 1972): 357–382.

Mieszkowski, Peter M. "The Property Tax: An Excise Tax or a Profits Tax?" *Journal of Public Economics* (April 1972): 73–96.

————. "Tax Incidence Theory: The Effects of Taxes on the Distribution of Income." *Journal of Economic Literature* (December 1969): 1103–1124.

Sandmo, Agnar. "The Effects of Taxation on Savings and Risk Taking." In *Handbook of Public Economics,* ed. A. J. Auerbach and M. Feldstein. Amsterdam: North Holland, 1985.

Simon, Carl P., and Ann D. Witte. "The Underground Economy: Estimates of Size, Structure, and Trends." In *Special Study on Economic Change.* Vol. 5. *Government Regulation: Achieving Social and Economic Balance.* Washington, D.C.: U.S. Government Printing Office, 1980, 70–120.

Stiglitz, Joseph E. "Pareto Efficient and Optimal Taxation and the New Welfare Economics." In *Handbook of Public Economics,* ed. A. J. Auerbach and M. Feldstein. Amsterdam: North Holland, 1985.

Thurow, Lester C. "The Economics of Public Finance." *National Tax Journal* (June 1975): 185–194.

SECTION VI: Economics of Fiscal Federalism

Bradford, David F., and Wallace E. Oates. "Suburban Exploitation of Central Cities and Governmental Structure." In *Redistribution Through Public Choice,* ed. Harold M. Hochman and George E. Peterson. New York: Columbia University Press, 1974, 43–90.

Break, George F. *Financing Government in a Federal System.* Washington, D.C.: The Brookings Institution, 1980.

Buchanan, James M. "Federalism and Fiscal Equity." *American Economic Review* (September 1950): 583–599.

Filer, John E., and Lawrence W. Kenny. "Voter Reaction to City-County Consolidation Referenda." *Journal of Law and Economics* (April 1980): 179–190.

Gold, Steven D. *State and Local Fiscal Relations in the Early 1980s.* Washington, D.C.: Urban Institute Press, 1983.

Gramlich, Edward M., and Harvey Galper. "State and Local Fiscal Behavior and Federal Grant Policy." In *Brookings Papers on Economic Activity,* no. 1 (1973): 15–58.

Grewal, Bhajan S., Geoffrey Brennan, and Russell L. Mathews. *The Economics of Federalism.* Canberra: Australia National University Press, 1980.

Inmar, Robert P., and Daniel L. Rubinfeld. "The Judicial Pursuit of Local Fiscal Equity." *Harvard Law Review* (1979): 1662–1750.

Linneman, Peter D. "The Capitalization of Local Taxes: A Note on Specification." *Journal of Political Economy* (December 1981): 1251–1260.

Maxwell, James A., and J. Richard Aronson. *Financing State and Local Governments.* Washington, D.C.: Brookings Institution, 1977.

Neenan, William B. "Suburban-Central City Exploitation Thesis: One City's Tale." *National Tax Journal* (June 1979): 117–139.

Pomerehne, Werner W. "Quantitative Aspects of Federalism: A Study of Six Counties." In *The Political Economy of Fiscal Federalism,* ed. Wallace E. Oates. Lexington, Mass.: D.C. Heath, 1977, 275–355.

Reinhard, Richard M. "Estimating Property Tax Capitalization: A Further Comment." *Journal of Political Economy* (December 1981): 1251–1260.

Sonstelie, Jon C., and Paul R. Portney. "Profit Maximizing Communities and the Theory of Local Public Expenditure." *Journal of Urban Economics* (April 1978): 263–277.

Weicher, John C. "The Effect of Metropolitan Fragmentation on Central City Budgets." In *Models of Urban Structure,* ed. David C. Sweet. Lexington, Mass.: D.C. Heath, 1972, 177–203.

Zodrow, George R. *Local Provision of Public Services: The Tiebout Model after Twenty-Five Years.* New York: Academic Press, 1983.